Robert A. Lipinski
and
Kathleen A. Lipinski

THE
COMPLETE
BEVERAGE DICTIONARY

VNR VAN NOSTRAND REINHOLD
NEW YORK

To our sons Johnnie and Matthew:
We are twice blessed.

Copyright © 1992 by Van Nostrand Reinhold

Library of Congress Catalog Card Number 91–41315
ISBN 0–442–23987–4

Manufactured in the United States of America.

Van Nostrand Reinhold
115 Fifth Avenue
New York, New York 10003

Chapman and Hall
2-6 Boundary Row
London, SE 1 8HN, England

Thomas Nelson Australia
102 Dodds Street
South Melbourne 3205
Victoria, Australia

Nelson Canada
1120 Birchmount Road
Scarborough, Ontario MIK 5G4, Canada

16 15 14 13 12 11 10 9 8 7 6 5 4 3 2 1

Library of Congress Cataloging-in-Publication Data

Lipinski, Robert A.
    The complete beverage dictionary / by Robert Lipinski.
        p.   cm.
    ISBN 0-442-23987-4
    1. Beverages—Dictionaries. 2. Alcoholic beverages—Dictionaries.
I. Title.
TP503.L56   1992
663'.03—dc20   91–41315
                                                            CIP

FOREWORD

A dictionary is such a basic thing that I was astonished to realize that there was no single lexicon for an industry that has served—literally—so many, so well, for so long. The beverage industry, both alcoholic and nonalcoholic, is ages old and international in scope. As with every speciality, it has developed a language of its own—complete with idiom, acronyms, and, of course, slang. Fluency in that language is vital for success in the industry and in the related fields of hospitality and food service. It becomes more important every day, as the marketplace we share is increasingly international rather than national, regional, or local. Since I always try to use words familiar to my audience and hope to be shown the same courtesy, it was with pleasure that I accepted the invitation to write the foreword to this book, which can help all of us communicate more easily with one another.

I'm told that this volume is the product of more than 20 years' work, begun as a teacher's labor of love for his students, who were asking him questions he could not answer without referring to countless books. The teacher was Robert A. Lipinski, then at the School of Hotel Administration and Culinary Arts at the New York Institute of Technology. I am pleased to say that Bob and his wife Kathleen, a medical educator whose knowledge and skill resulted in her co-authorship of this book, moved to Louisville in 1990 so that Bob could become the national director of our wine development program. I mention this only to emphasize that Brown-Forman Beverage Company, though proud of its association with the authors, cannot claim credit for having been involved in the production of the book.

This dictionary is the first to cover wines, spirits, beer and nonalcoholic beverages. It is not brand-specific, which is as it should be, since it is a work of scholarship, not sponsorship. The Lipinskis set out to fill a need and they have succeeded. We owe them our thanks and our admiration. Certainly, they have mine.

Owsley Brown II
Chairman and Chief Executive Officer
Brown-Forman Beverage Company
Louisville, Kentucky

August 1991

PREFACE

This book is a dictionary of terminology used in the beverage industry—both alcoholic (wines, beers, and distilled spirits) and nonalcoholic. It encompasses international words and terms, label terminology, terms relating to the production, sale, and service of beverages, slang, and geography, as well as origins of historical significance.

The dictionary is quite comprehensive in nature (containing more than 6,100 terms), serving as a quick resource, as well as providing much needed research and reference material, with in-depth coverage. It defines everyday and technical terms, making it a necessity for everyone's library or bookcase.

This dictionary is written for the hospitality industry, which is made up of foodservice operators, restaurateurs, colleges, bartenders, and food and beverage directors, as well as interested consumers. It is needed to fill a vacuum that exists in the beverage industry relative to correct terminology usage and accurate definitions. Currently, there are two foodservice dictionaries: Knight's Foodservice Dictionary and The Chef's Companion, both published by Van Nostrand Reinhold. This beverage dictionary will complement both food dictionaries.

ABAFADO (PORT)   *See* Vinho Abafado.

ABBADIA (ITAL)   Abbey.

ABBEY ALE   Ales made for centuries by Cistercian monks in Belgium, who brewed them for personal consumption and enjoyment with guests. Typically, they are deep golden to coffee in color, with a heavy, pronounced malty bouquet.

ABBOCCATO (ITAL)   *See* Semidry. Also known as *amabile*.

ABC LAWS   Alcoholic Beverage Control Laws.

ABFÜLLER (GERM)   Bottling or bottler—must be listed on all quality wines.

ABFÜLLREIF (GERM)   A wine that is ready for bottling.

ABGANG (GERM)   *See* Aftertaste.

ABGEBAUT (GERM)   A wine that has declined.

ABGEFÜLLT FÜR (GERM)   Bottled for; the firm that bottled the wine.

A BLEND OF STRAIGHT WHISKIES   A mixture of straight whiskies. A blend of straight whiskies consisting entirely of one of the types of straight whiskey and not conforming to the standard for "straight whiskey" shall be further designated by that specific type of straight whiskey; for example, "a blend of straight rye whiskies" (blended straight rye whiskies).

ABOCADO (SP)   *See* Semidry.

A BOIRE (FR)   Ready to drink.

ABRUZZI (ITAL)   *See* Abruzzo.

ABRUZZO (ITAL)   A mountainous region located just south of Latium in the south-central part of Italy off the Adriatic Sea. Known as *Abruzzi* in Italy.

ABSCISSION   The normal separation or "dropping off" of leaves or fruits from plants as a result of a breakdown of a thin layer of pithy cells at the base of their stems.

ABSINTHE   An aromatic, yellow-green distilled spirit, flavored with oil of wormwood. This anise-based distilled spirit was officially banned throughout most of the world on March 16, 1915. The technical name of the main ingredient was *Artemisia absinthium* (wormwood), an Old World plant or herb that grows about three feet high and is botanically related to our southwestern sagebrush. The oil from the leaves, called *absinthol*, contains a rather strong narcotic, *thujone* ($C_{10}H_{16}O$), which is poisonous in large doses.

Some of the problems associated with absinthe ingestion were convulsions, mania, gastrointestinal irritation, extreme nervousness, drugged stupor, hallucination, and loss of hearing and sight. In large doses, absinthe induced a coma or even death. In 1905, a drunken and crazed man killed his wife and two daughters but failed to kill himself. His daily alcoholic consumption was six quarts of wine, six brandies, and a couple of absinthes; he was said to be in an absinthe-induced delirium. Stories of the outrage spread throughout the world, fired by temperance groups, causing the courts to ban the production of absinthe first in Switzerland, then in France. The French government, on the pretext that alcohol was needed for the manufacture of gunpowder for the war, waited until 1915 to finally prohibit the manufacture and sale of absinthe, putting an end to a century of popularity. Its sale is prohibited in most countries.

ABSOLUTE ALCOHOL   Clinically pure or 200 proof (100 percent) ethyl alcohol. Pure ethyl alcohol does not really exist because alcohol and water form an azeotropic mixture—one with a boiling point lower than either pure alcohol or water—that does not separate during simple distilling. The final portion of water can be removed by distilling in a system under vacuum, by adding a solvent such as benzene that "breaks" the azeotrope, or by passing through an absorbent column.

Measurements in absolute alcohol provide a meaningful way of describing alcohol consumption in a population or relating the alcohol content of different beverages. Also known as *anhydrous alcohol*.

ABSOLUTE THRESHOLD   The sensory threshold of a given compound or substance, which is the minimum concentration in an aqueous (containing water) solution that a person is able to correctly identify.

ABSORPTION   The taking in of nutrients and other minerals by feeder roots or through the cuticle of the foliage.

ABSTICH (GERM)   *See* Racking.

ABSTICHREIF (GERM)   A wine that is ready for racking.

ACACIA   A chemical used to clarify and to stabilize wine.

ACADÉMIE DU VIN DE BORDEAUX (FR)   Bordeaux Wine Academy. Created in 1948 to spread the word about Bordeaux wines, with 40 members, including shippers, brokers, and producers.

ACCIAIO INOSSIDABILE (ITAL)   *See* Stainless Steel.

ACCLIMATIZATION   Involves the greenhouse transfer of plants cultivated *in vitro* to a horticultural substract, and the gradual readjustment of these plants to open air and to the usual level of humidity around.

ACCOUNTS PAYABLE   Debts to suppliers of goods or services.

ACCOUNTS RECEIVABLE   Amounts due from customers.

ACERBE (FR)   *See* Acerbic.

ACERBIC   An unpleasant, bitter, tart, astringent, coarse, or disagreeable taste that comes from unripe grapes. Also known as *acerbe* and *acerbo*.

ACERBO (ITAL)   *See* Acerbic.

ACESCENCE   A name given to the vinegar smell and taste of a wine that has undergone aerobic bacterial spoilage. Equivalent to volatile acidity (VA). In some wines, notably port and well wood-aged red table wines, a small amount of acescence is considered a desirable part of the wine's nose. However, when excessive, acescence will completely destroy the acceptability of any wine. When a wine contains an excessive amount of acetic acid and ethyl acetate, a translucent gray film often forms on the surface and acescency occurs; then the wine acquires a stinging, sharp, vinegary taste. *See* Acetic Acid, Acetobacter, and Volatile Acidity.

ACETALDEHYDE   A colorless, soluble, volatile liquid (CH_3CHO), formed when the enzyme carboxylase forms acetaldehyde and carbon dioxide from pyruvic acid. It is at this next and final stage of a complete fermentation that acetaldehyde is reduced to ethyl alcohol, but a minute quantity remains and adds to the flavor of the wine. In large amounts, acetaldeyhde has a sharp, vinegary odor. *See* Volatile Acidity.

ACETATE   An ester of acetic acid.

ACETIC   A wine that has gone irredeemably sour through prolonged exposure to oxygen. Acetic acid combines with ethyl acetate to give the vinegary smell and taste that a spoiled wine emits. Also known as *acide acétique* and *sour*. *See* Acetic Acid and Volatile Acidity.

ACETIC ACID   (CH_3CO_2H) A colorless, volatile acid found in all wines. It is usually present in tiny quantities, and, if there is excessive development of it, the wine turns to vinegar. A pun gent substance that is the chief ingredient of vinegar. Also known as acetic. *See* Acetobacter and Volatile Acidity.

ACETIC ACID   Used to correct natural deficiencies in grape wine.

ACETO (ITAL)   *See* Vinegar.

ACETOBACTER   Airborne, aerobic microorganisms (bacteria) that cause the oxidation of alcohol (wine) primarily to ace taldehyde by prolonged exposure of oxygen. Oxygen is essential for its formation; therefore, barrels should be kept "topped" and air spaces in bottles kept to a minimum. Also known as *Mycoderma aceti*. *See* Acetic Acid and Volatile Acidity.

ACID A substance having a sharp and biting taste. Acid is a compound present in all grapes.

ACID BLEND A mixture of organic acids—citric, malic, and tartaric—generally added to the *must*, prior to fermentation, for correcting acid deficiencies.

ACIDE ACÉTIQUE (FR) *See* Acetic.

ACIDE TARTRIQUE (FR) *See* Tartaric Acid.

ACIDEZ (PORT OR SP) *See* Acidity.

ACIDIC A term that describes wines (often very young or very old) that are improperly balanced because of an abnormally high acid content. The total acid in this case is so high that it tastes sour and has a sharp feel in the mouth.

ACIDITÀ (ITAL) *See* Acidity.

ACIDITÀ FISSE (ITAL) Fixed acids—citric, lactic, malic, and tartaric.

ACIDITÄT (GERM) *See* Acidity.

ACIDITÀ TOTALE (ITAL) *See* Total Acidity.

ACIDITÀ VOLATILE (ITAL) *See* Volatile Acidity.

ACIDITÉ (FR) *See* Acidity.

4

ACIDITY Indicates the quality of tartness or sharpness to the taste due to the presence of agreeable fruit acids. An important constituent that contributes flavor and freshness to wine when it is in proper balance, and contributes to its aging. Not to be confused with sourness, dryness, or astringency. The principle acids found in wine are tartaric, citric, malic, and lactic. Also known as *acidità, acidität, acidez, acidité, acido,* and *saüre.*

ACIDO (ITAL) *See* Acidity.

ACIDO CARBONICO (ITAL) CO_2, produced by fermentation.

ACID SOIL Soil with a pH measurement of 6.9 or less.

ACIDULÉ (FR) *See* Acidulous.

ACIDULO (ITAL) *See* Acidulous.

ACIDULOUS A wine that displays an unpleasantly sour taste due to high acidity, often more than 1 percent of total acid. Also known as *acidulé, acidulo, agrillo,* and *säuerlich.*

ACKER (GERM) *See* Acre.

ACQUA (ITAL) Water.

ACQUA MINERALE (ITAL) *See* Mineral Water.

ACQUAVITE (ITAL) Brandy.

ACQUIT (FR) A key document controlling all transportation of wines or distilled spirits on which government taxes have not been paid. Its color depends upon the category of wine designated; it is green for AOC, yellow-gold for cognac and Armagnac, orange for appellation contrôlée dessert wines, and manila for ordinary wines.

ACRE American and English surfaced measurement equivalent to 4,047 square meters (0.4047 hectares), or 43,569 square feet. Also known as *acker* and *morgen*.

ACRE (ITAL) *See* âcre.

ÂCRE (FR) Harsh, acrid, a wine with an excess of acidity. Also known as acre.

ACRID Harsh or bitter in taste or smell.

ACTIFERM (ROVIFERM) A fermentation adjunct.

ACTIVATED CHARCOAL A substance used to assist precipitation during fermentation, to clarify and purify wine, or to remove excess color in white wine.

ACTUAL BEVERAGE COST The cost of beverages sold, as determined by a factual weekly or monthly record.

ACTUAL BEVERAGE COST PERCENTAGE The actual cost divided by sales and multiplied by 100.

ACTUAL COST PRICING Pricing based on what the actual costs for the item are, including purchase, labor, and operating costs.

ACUTE Term meaning strong or sharply defined.

ADAMADO (PORT) *See* Doce.

ADDED BRANDY Brandy or wine spirits for use in fortification of wine as permitted by internal revenue law.

ADDITIVES A collective name for a group of materials added to beverages, such as preservatives, to improve or strengthen it. Some additives are colors, flavors, acids, vitamins, minerals, yeast, and bacterial inhibitors. While these might not be essential to the product, they could be added to improve or ease production.

ADEGA (PORT) *See* Wine Cellar.

ADJUNCT Unmalted grains used in the production of American-made beer, which include corn, corn grits, and brewer's rice. Refined corn grits tend to produce the milder, lighter bodied beer preferred by the American consumer. Like malt, corn is a source of starch that is converted to sugar in the brewing process.

AD REPRINT Copy of an ad published in an identified print medium. To be used as a selling tool.

AD SLICK Sheet of paper with various illustrations of brands of alcoholic beverages. Illustrations can be cut out and used by a retailer in an ad.

ADSTRINGENTE (PORT) *See* Astringency.

ADSTRINGEREND (GERM) *See* Astringency.

ADULTERATED WINE A wine that has been treated with, exposed to, or had unauthorized or prohibitive ingredients or materials added to, or that possesses excessive levels of a permitted substance. Also known as *adulterato*.

ADULTERATO (ITAL) *See* Adulterated Wine.

AD VALOREM A phrase applied to certain duties levied on imported alcoholic beverages according to their invoiced value.

ADVOCAAT *See* Advokatt.

ADVOKATT A 30-proof, creamy yellow, eggnog liqueur made in Holland and Germany from egg yolks, brandy, cream, and sugar. Also spelled *advocaat*. *See* Eggnog.

ADZ an ancient long-handled, axe-like tool used to cut and shape the staves or sides of wooden barrels.

AERATE *See* Aeration.

AÉRATION (FR) *See* Aeration.

AERATION Letting a wine "breathe" in the open air, or swirling wine already present in a glass. Also known as *aerate* and *aération*. *See* Breathing and Decanting.

AEROBIC FERMENTATION A fermentation conducted in the presence of oxygen.

AFERRIN A substance used to reduce trace metals from wine.

AFFINÉ (FR) *See* Fining.

AFSTIRÓS (GREECE) *See* Austere.

AFTER-DINNER WINES Sweet fortified and nonfortified wines.

AFTERTASTE What lingers or remains in the throat or on the tongue after a wine is swallowed. Both the character and the length of the aftertaste may be described collectively as "finish." Also known as *abgang, arrière goût, length, lingering, long, nach geschmack, ressaibo, retrogusto, schwanz,* and *schweif. See* Finish.

AGAR A gelatinous polysaccharide material extracted from certain saltwater algae and used in bacterial cultures to grow yeast and for thickening foods. *See* Alginate and Yeast.

AGAVE A large plant indigenous to Mexico with large leaves and prickly, needle-like thorns, resembling cactus. The agave, which belongs to the botanical family *Amaryllidaceae*, is used in the making of tequila and mezcal.

AGE Period of storage in oak containers, after distillation and before bottling of distilled spirits, to develop character and palatability.

For most American whiskeys, it means storage in charred, new oak barrels. the exceptions are corn and light whiskeys, which may be aged in uncharred, new or charred, reused oak barrels. Rum, brandy, and scotch are aged in used oak containers. Age may not be designated for gin.

According to the United States government standards of identity, the time a whiskey spends outside of an oak container does not add to its age.

AGGLOMERATED CORK This unusual cork, developed in 1925, consists of scraps of cork glued together and then reformed into the shape of a cork. Also known as *composition cork* or *particle cork.*

AGGLOMERATION   *See* Flocculation.

AGGRESSIVO (ITAL)   Aggressive; raw; unripe; unharmonious.

AGING   The process wherein wine, whiskey, or brandy is stored in oak barrels, stainless steel tanks, or glass so that complex changes, that only time can implement take place. Aging smooths a rough, new wine, whiskey, or brandy and adds bouquet and character. *See* Barrel Aging, Bottle Aging, Mature, Ripe, and Ripe For Bottling.

AGITADOR (SP)   A tool often made of iron, used to incorporate or stir fining agents after they have been added to wine.

AGLIANICO (ITAL)   A very dark red grape variety, producing full-bodied wines. According to legend, the Aglianico grape was brought to Italy by ancient Greek settlers around 800 b.c. Its name is a corruption of the ancient Greek grapevine *Ellenico* or *Hellenica.* Today, the Aglianico grape is widely cultivated throughout much of southern Italy, especially in Basilicata and Campania.

AGOSTADO (SP)   A deep ploughing of the suitable soil for vineyards carried out during the month of August as a first step for planting the new grapevines. Because of this labor, the soil is completely freed from the deepest weeds and roots.

AGRAFE   A metal clip that holds the champagne cork in place during the secondary fermentation. Also spelled *agraffe.* Also known as *grapa.*

AGRÉABLE (FR)   *See* Agreeable.

AGREEABLE   Referring to taste; it is used for a wine that is well-defined in taste and satisfies the palate. Also known as *agréable.*

AGRESSIF (FR)   Aggressive; a young wine or brandy whose fiery taste has not yet mellowed.

AGRICULTURAL WINE   Wine made from suitable agricultural products other than the juice of grapes, berries, or other fruits.

AGRILLO (SP)   *See* Acidulous.

AGRIO (SP)   Sour.

AGUA (SP)   Water.

ÁGUA (PORT)   Water.

AGUAMIEL (SP)   The sticky sap (or *honey water*) released from the agave plant, which is used in the production of tequila or mezcal.

AGUARDENTE (PORT)   Brandy used to fortify port wines.

AGUARDIENTE (SP)   *See* Grappa.

AHR (GERM)   One of 11 qualitätswein (quality) regions.

AIGRE (FR)   Sour, vinegary, acetic acid taste. Also known as *vappa.*

AIMABLE (FR) Pleasant, agreeable, easy-to-drink.

AÎNÉ (FR) Elder.

AIRLINE BOTTLES *See* Miniature Bottles.

AJEÑJO (SP) Wormwood. *See* Vermouth.

AKTIEN GESELLSCHAFT (AUS) The "A.G." after the name of a firm on a wine label, equivalent to *incorporated*.

AKVAVIT It is a high-proof distilled spirit made from a distillate of grain or potatoes, and redistilled in the presence of caraway seeds; because of its potency, it was nicknamed "Black Death." It is quite popular in the Scandinavian countries, where it is also spelled *aquavit*, and also known as *brännvin*.

ALAAI An ancient Chinese spirit distilled from rice in about 800 b.c. Also known as *Santchoo*.

ALAMBIC A large, onion-shaped copper pot still used for the double distillation of cognac and other brandies. It was originally used by the Moors, who had used it to distill the nectar of flowers for perfume. (Later, it was used by medieval alchemists in attempts to turn nonprecious metals into gold.) Also spelled *Alembic*. Also known as *alambique*. *See* Pot Still.

ALAMBIC BRANDY Grape brandy made in accordance with the methods utilized in France's Cognac and Armagnac regions, which rely solely on the *alambic pot still*.

ALAMBIQUE (SP) *See* Alambic.

ALAMBRADO (SP) The golden wire net often found on bottles of red wine.

ALAMEDA A grape growing county in northern California, east of San Francisco Bay. The principal growing area is Livermore.

ALAR The trade name for daminozide, a pesticide. Its use is now prohibited by the Food and Drug Administration.

ALBA (ITAL) An important red wine–producing province in the northwest region of Piedmont. Alba is also the location of one of Italy's important viticultural and enological schools, which was founded in 1881.

ALBALONGA (GERM) A white grape variety, developed in Würzburg from a cross of Sylvaner and Rieslaner.

ALBAN (SP) *See* Palomino.

ALBAN An ancient Roman wine.

ALBANA (ITAL) A white grape variety of average size, easily separable, with persistent stems, and skin of golden-yellow color tending toward amber. It is also known as *Greco*, *Greco di Ancona*, and *Biancame*. Albana is grown primarily in the Emilia-Romagna region, where it produces Albana di Romagna.

ALBANA DI ROMAGNA (ITAL) A dry white wine produced from the Albana grape variety in the eastern region of Emilia-Romagna. On April 13, 1987, it became the first white wine to receive the DOCG designation.

ALBANO (ITAL)   *See* Trebbiano.

ALBARIZA   A chalky type of soil, considered by many to produce the very best sherry. Its texture is a spongy clay that soaks up and traps the winter rains and stores them, which is a plus because irrigation is not permitted. This texture also provides a perfect aeration of the soil and allows deep penetration by the grapevine roots. The soil contains approximately 40 percent white chalk, so the grapevines are nourished by its lime content. Approximately 85 percent of the soil in Jerez, Spain is made up of albariza. However, the yield per acre from albariza is the lowest of any soil type. *See* Barro and Arena.

ALBEISA (ITAL)   A type, style, or shape of a bottle used in Alba, Piedmont for Barbera, Barolo, Dolcetto, Barbaresco, or other Nebbiolo-based wines.

ALBERELLO (ITAL)   A system of head pruning "little trees," created by training the taller grapevine shoots back on themselves and tying them in looped supports for the fruit. While this can be accomplished by individual grapevine dressers working on one plant at a time, it also limits the exposure of the leaves and the graftable limbs on which additional grape clusters can be encouraged to grow. A major drawback of this method is that the grapevines are grown close to the ground so that they are able to derive reflected heat from the ground onto the leaves. This method of training is seldom employed in Italy nowadays.

ALBUMEN   Egg whites, either in a fresh or dried state that are used as a fining agent, mostly in winemaking. Albumen carries a positive charge and could cause a protein haze if excessive amounts are used. *See* Fining.

ALCOHOL   The unqualified term for a colorless, volatile, flammable liquid that is the intoxicating agent in all beverages, which are fermented and/or distilled. Alcohol is an important by-product of the fermentation process. Yeasts working upon the sugar contained in a liquid transforms it into carbon dioxide and alcohol. The potable beverage known as alcohol is technically *ethyl alcohol* (ethanol) C_2H_5OH—the preservative and intoxicating constituent of wine, beer, and distilled spirits. *See* Aqua Ardents, Ardent Spirits, and Ethyl Alcohol.

ALCOHOL-BY-VOLUME   The alcoholic content of a liquid, usually expressed as a numerical percentage of the volume. *See* Alcohol Content.

ALCOHOL CONTENT   A statement of alcohol content in percentage by volume appears on most labels. As an alternative, some bottlers prefer to label wine with an alcohol content between 7 and 14 percent as "table wine." For table wines, the law allows a 1.5-percent variation in either direction from the stated percentage as long as the alcohol does not exceed 14 percent.

In order to provide the consumer with clearer and more useful information on labels for distilled spirits, the BATF also issued regulations (November 10, 1986) for labeling: Alcohol content must be indicated by percentage—not just in proof. This is a more readily understood way to convey alcohol content to the purchaser.

Since the repeal of Prohibition, the requirement that labels state alcohol content (formerly expressed in degrees of proof) has remained unchanged. Proof is a traditional term for alcohol content (equal to twice the percentage by volume). Thus, 80 proof means 40-percent alcohol by volume; 100 proof means 50-percent alcohol by volume, and so on.

According to the regulations, labels *must* show percentage by volume of alcohol, but both forms (proof and percentage) may be used. If a proof statement is used, it must be shown in direct conjunction with the percent by volume, emphasizing the fact that both expressions mean the same thing. *See* Alcohol-By-Volume.

ALCOHOLERIA (SP)   A distillery where the stems, skins, and seeds are sent to be made into *aguardiente*.

ALCOHOL FERMENTATION   *See* Primary Fermentation.

ALCOHOLIC   A person who suffers from alcoholism. *See* Alcoholism.

ALCOHOLIC   A term used to describe a wine or distilled spirit that has too much alcohol for its body and weight, making it unbalanced. This can be discerned either in the bouquet or mouth.

ALCOHOLIC BEVERAGE   As defined by law, includes any beverage in liquid form that contains not less than one-half of 1 percent (0.5 percent) of ethyl alcohol (ethanol) by volume and is intended for human consumption.

These beverages are classified by their method of production:

1.   Fermented beverages. Produced through fermentation alone, these beverages are of two kinds: malted beverages, brewed principally from cereal grains and malted barley, flavored with hops; and wine, the result of fermentation of grape or other fruit juices.

2.   Distilled spirits. Produced by distillation of any alcohol-containing mixture—wine or the distiller's beer from a fermentation process. Whiskey, vodka, rum, brandy, gin, and tequila comprise the principal classes of distilled spirits. Another class—liqueurs or cordials—is not directly distilled but consists of beverage spirits treated with flavoring materials.

These versatile beverages have played a continuing role in human history as sacred symbol, medicine, social lubricant, adjunct to gracious living, and thirst quencher.

ALCOHOLISM   The chronic or habitual use of alcohol to the extent that its use contributes to sickness, accidents, or dependency on it to avoid withdrawal symptoms. *See* Alcoholic.

ALCOHOLIZED   A slang term for an individual significantly under the influence of beer, wine, or distilled spirits.

ALCOHOLOMETER   An instrument utilized for determining the quantity of pure alcohol in a liquid. *See* Ebulliometer.

ALCOL COMPLESSIVO (ITAL)   The actual alcohol in the finished wine plus the potential alcohol in the residual sugar.

ALCOL DA SVOLGERE (ITAL)   The potential alcohol that can be produced from the *must*.

ALCOLISADO (PORT)   *See* Vinho Alcolisado.

ALCOOL (ITAL)   Alcohol, usually stated percentage by volume.

ALCOOL ÉTHYLIQUE (FR)   *See* Ethyl Alcohol.

ALCOOLS BLANCS (FR)   White or clear distilled spirits. Generally refers to brandies distilled from fruits other than grapes; cherries, pears, raspberries, and others. They are clear because they are not aged in wooden barrels. Also known as *virgin brandy*. *See* Grappa and Eau-de-Vie.

ALDEHYDE   A colorless, volatile fluid with a distinct odor that is a natural by-product of fermentation and increases in concentration as a wine or distilled spirit ages. One of the organic chemical ingredients of wine and distilled spirits formed by the partial oxidation of alcohol. It adds to the beverage's aroma, but may be unpleasant if in large quantities.

ALDEN   A red grape variety developed from a cross of Ontario and Gros Guillaume at New York State Experimental Station, in 1952.

ALE   A top-fermented beer with a slightly darker color than lager beer. It usually has more hops in its aroma and taste and is often lower in carbonation than lager-type beers. Ale is usually bitter to the taste, with a slight tanginess, although some ales can be sweet. Ales are usually fermented at warmer temperatures than lager-type beers (60 degrees to 70 degrees Fahrenheit) for three to five days, and generally mature faster. Ales should ideally be served at 38 degrees to 45 degrees Fahrenheit.

ALEATICO   A dark red grape variety of the Muscat family, grown predominantly in Italy. Aleatico generally produces sweet dessert wines, although some table wines can be found. Some is also cultivated in California, but its acreage is dwindling.

ALECONNERS   An old title for an English town official or officer in London, whose business was to inspect public houses or ale houses for fraud. He was also in charge of the testing and tasting of ale, to determine its authenticity.

ALEHOUSE   A store where ale is retailed.

ALEMBIC   *See* Alambic.

ALE POSSET   A mildly intoxicating English drink made from a mixture of heated ale and curdled milk, with spices added. Also the name of an English beer, lightly hopped and slightly bitter.

ALEXANDER   A cocktail made with brandy or gin, white crème de cacao, and heavy cream.

ALEXANDER   A red native American *Vitis labrusca* grape variety first discovered between 1732 and 1741. It was miscalled Black Madeira, Cape, Cape Constantia, Clifton's Constantia, Constantia, Schuylkill Muscadelle, and Vevay. James Alexander, a gardener to Thomas Penn (son of Governor William Penn), found it growing near the Schuylkill River in Philadelphia, Pennsylvania.

In 1809, President Thomas Jefferson wrote about the Alexander grape stating, "I think it will be worth well to push the culture of this grape without losing time and efforts in the search of foreign grapevines, which it will take centuries to adapt to our soil and climate."

ALEXANDER VALLEY   A grape-growing area, located in northern Sonoma County, California.

ALGINATE   Compound extracted from certain seaweeds from which it is easy to obtain gel. Common in the food industry as a thickener, stabilizer, and gellifier. *See* Agar, Encapsulated Yeast, and Yeast.

ALICANTE BOUSCHET   A red-juice grape variety, developed in France in 1865 by Henri Bouschet, a viticulturist, which is a cross of Petit Bouschet and Grenache. Alicante Bouschet is used for blending because of its deep, dark color and abundance of juice; however, it is rarely bottled as a separate variety. It is grown extensively in California, southern France, and Algeria.

ALIGOTÉ   A white grape variety grown predominantly in France and California. It produces a highly acidic white wine that has been used for years in Burgundy, France as a base for the popular drink, Kir. Also known as *Plant Gris*.

ALIOTIQUE (FR)   A type of sandstone peculiar to the southwest of France.

ALKALINE SOIL   Soil with a pH in excess of 7.0.

ALKOHOLREICH (GERM)   A wine that is high in alcohol. Also known as *brandig* and *spritig*.

ALKY   Slang term for a person who is addicted to alcoholic beverages.

ALLAPPANTE (ITAL)   *See* Astringency.

ALLEGRO (ITAL)   Lively, bright, joyous.

ALLIED PRODUCTS   Commercial fruit products and by-products (including volatile fruit-flavor concentrate) not taxable as wine.

ALLIER OAK (FR)   A small forest centered around the city of Moulins, noted for its production of wooden barrels, which are in between Troncais and Nevers in terms of hardness, Allier oak has a medium-tight grain, with moderate oak flavor and tannin extractions, displaying an intense, earthy component, and a floral perfumed character.

ALL-IN-BOND   *See* In Bond.

ALLUVIAL SOIL   A type of soil made of predominantly sand and clay, which was formed by gradual deposits in the bottomlands along rivers by moving water, as along a river bed or the shore of a lake. Also known as *alluvions*.

ALLUVIONS (FR)   *See* Alluvial Soil.

ALMACENISTA (SP)   Shopkeepers who purchase sherry wine, then carefully mature it in their cellars.

ALMIBAR (SP)   A solution of invert sugar that, when mixed, is occasionally used to sweeten pale sherries.

ALMIJAR (SP)   An outside location or open house where grapes are left to dry prior to being pressed.

ALMOND-SCENTED   Referring to taste and smell; it is said of a wine recalling the scent of almonds.

A "LOT" OF BOTTLED WINE   Wine of the same type bottled on the same bottling date into bottles or consumer units of the same measure on the same bottling line.

ALOXE-CORTON (FR)   A red wine-producing village in Côte de Beaune in the region of Burgundy. Aloxe-Corton was the favorite wine of French satirist, philosopher, and historian Voltaire (1694–1778).

A

ALSACE   One of France's six major wine-producing regions, located in the northeast. This region, which is dotted with picturesque villages, occupies a narrow strip of land between Strasbourg and Mulhouse. It is not more than a mile or two wide and about sixty miles long, with an area of approximately 30,000 acres. It is nestled between the Vosges Mountains and the Rhine River, just east of Champagne and Burgundy.

Alsace produces one-fifth of all of France's white wines entitled to the AOC designation. Because it is located so far north, there is generally insufficient sunshine to fully ripen the red grapes. Therefore, better than 90 percent of all wines are white.

ALSTERWASSER (GERM)   *See* Shandy.

ALT (GERM)   Old; used when referring to beer.

ALTAR WINE   *See* Sacramental Wines.

ALTBIER (GERM)   A top-fermented beer (ale) with a high barley and hops content; quite bitter.

ALTERATO (ITAL)   A wine that has been either adulterated or badly handled.

ALUS   Lithuanian and Latvian term for beer.

ALWOOD   A red grape variety developed from a cross of Fredonia and Athens at the New York State Experimental Station in 1967.

AMA SPECIAL GELATIN   A chemical substance approved for the clarification of wine.

AMABILE (ITAL)   *See* Abboccato.

AMADURECIDO (PORT)   A mellow wine.

AMANGO (PORT)   *See* Bitter.

AMARETTO   A generic almond-apricot liqueur, russet in color, flavored with bitter sweet almond oils from the coasts of the Mediterranean. It is produced in Italy and the United States.

AMARGO (SP)   *See* Bitter.

AMARO (ITAL)   *See* Bitter.

AMAROGNOLO (ITAL)   Slightly bitter.

AMARONE (ITAL)   Amarone is produced on hilly portions of the Valpolicella Classico Zone in the northeastern part of Veneto, bordered on the west by the Adige River.

The word *Amarone* comes from the Veronese dialect, meaning bone dry almost to the point of bitterness. The grapes used are the same as those in Valpolicella: Corvina Veronese, Rondinella, Molinara, Rossignola, Negrara, Sangiovese, and Barbera. Amarone, however, unlike Valpolicella, is made exclusively from the best grapes, which are located at the top and outside perimeter of the clusters. The grapes used for Amarone are grown on three-foot-high trellises in the hills of Valpolicella that rise one to two thousand feet above sea level.

In the picking process, 50 percent of the grapes are immediately rejected because they are not ripe enough. In addition, the bunches that are selected are those whose grapes are sufficiently spaced to allow air to circulate between them in the eventual drying process (this limits the formation of gray mold). These grapes, whose sugar levels are the highest because of the amount of sunlight they receive, are picked and then arranged on flat drawers that easily fit into racks, which allow a good circulation of air. It is very important that they be kept in a dry, cool, well-ventilated room. In years past, bamboo, wicker mats, or trellises were used to dry the grapes. Each mat is clearly marked with the day the grapes were picked and the part of the vineyard from which they originate. The grapes are cleaned and turned about every 20 days and are constantly inspected during the two-and-one-half- to three-month drying period. This drying period causes a 40-percent loss of juice, resulting in grapes low in juice but extremely high in sugar and varietal character. The dried grapes, which resemble shriveled raisins, are pressed just after Christmas and fermented slowly for approximately 45 days with the skins and stems intact. The wine is aged for a minimum of one year in wood, but it is not uncommon for Amarone to be aged for five years or more in barrels prior to bottling and further bottle aging.

The resultant wine is, not surprisingly, highly alcoholic—a minimum of 14 percent under DOC law. However, most Amarones are higher in alcohol, sometimes even 17-percent alcohol. When produced in the heart of the DOC

14

production zone, the wine may be labeled *classico*. Amarone received its DOC status on August 21, 1968.

Amarone can be described as having a remarkably beautiful, darkish ruby red color, with a lush persistent bouquet—a moderately heavy, strong, concentrated, complex flavor of fruit, reminiscent of raisins, with considerable finesse; velvety rich, with a dry, spicy taste, and slightly bitter. The aftertaste is warming and quite dry, with sensations of rich spicy fruit. It is suitable for long aging, often decades. Formerly known as Recioto della Valpolicella "Amarone." *See* Recioto.

AMBER As a white wine ages, it takes on golden tints reminiscent of the color *amber*. This color change results from oxidation of the anthocyanins (coloring matter). It can also be used to describe the color of some sherries. Also known as *ambrato* and *ambre*.

AMBER FLUID (AUSTRAL) Beer.

AMBRATO (ITAL) *See* Amber.

AMBER (FR) *See* Amber.

AMELIORATION The addition to juice or natural wine before, during, or after fermentation, of either water or pure dry sugar, or a combination of water and pure dry sugar, or liquid sugar or invert sugar syrup, to adjust the acid level. Also known as *amélioré*. *See* Calcium Carbonate and Gallization.

AMÉLIORÉ (FR) *See* Amelioration.

AMER (FR) Bitter; possibly from prolonged contact with the skins, stems, seeds, or wood.

AMÉRICAIN GOÛT (FR) Fairly sweet (in relation to champagne). More vulgarly, implies a sugared-up blend of wine for the American market.

AMERICAN-MADE WHISKEY Whiskey that was defined when the Federal Alcohol Administration Regulations were formulated in 1936. American whiskey can only be made from grains specified for each category; potatoes and beets, used in vodka production, cannot be used to make whiskey. *See* Whiskey.

AMERICAN OAK Commonly considered higher than European oak in odorous components, including vanillin and related compounds and especially "oak lactone." European oak, on the other hand, has about one and one-half times the total extractables, double the extractable phenols including tannins, and considerable colored components compared to American oak.

AMERICAN WINE Any wine (table, sparkling, fortified) produced in the United States that meets the requirements of the BATF, as well as conforming to the requirements of a particular state in which the wine is made.

AMERTUME (FR) Bitterness; usually a sign that a wine was kept too long on the skins or in the barrel.

AMINO ACIDS An essential component of protein present in grape juice that play an important role in the production of aroma in wine. Because of their nitrogenous organic compounds, they are indispensable to yeasts for the fermentation process.

AMMACCATO (ITAL)   Disagreeable taste; musty.

AMMONIUM CARBONATE   A yeast nutrient used to facilitate fermentation in wine.

AMMONIUM PHOSPHATE   An available nitrogen and nutrient source, sometimes added to fermentations where there is doubt as to the level of available nitrogen. Nitrogen is needed for healthy yeast growth and fermentation. *Ammonium sulfate* can be substituted, but ammonium phosphate is preferable. *See* Energizer.

AMMONIUM SULFATE   *See* Ammonium Phosphate.

AMMOSTATE (ITAL)   Grapes that are "partially pressed."

AMONTILLADO (SP)   A style of sherry that has more color and body than *finos*, with a medium dry taste and nutty flavor. True *amontillado* sherries are the best to use for cooking, for they impart a nutty-tangy flavor to food. *Fino* sherry is too dry for cooking and seems to lack the *amontillado* sherries' charm and depth, while *oloroso* and cream sherries are simply too sweet. Also known as *cocktail sherry* or *dry sherry*.

AMOROSO (SP)   A seldom-used term that refers to a sweet oloroso sherry.

AMPELOGRAPHY   The descriptive study and identification of grapevines; grapevine botany. The science, the study, and the knowledge of *Ampelidacedes*—in Greek, ampelos means vine—teaches us that there exist almost unlimited varieties of grapevines, resulting from different modes of cultivation, or the innumerable mutations and crossings, which have taken place over the centuries. Also known as *ampélographie*.

AMPÉLOGRAPHIE (FR)   *See* Ampelography.

AMPELOS AMPELOS (GREECE)   *See* Grapevine.

AMPHORA   An ancient vessel often made of ceramic or earthenware, usually with two handles, which was used as a container for wine.

AMPIO (ITAL)   *See* Ample.

AMPLE   Full, harmonious, rounded, substantial. Also known as *ampio*.

AMPLEUR (FR)   *See* Well-balanced.

AMPUL, AMPULE   A small, glass container that can be sealed and its contents sterilized, intended for hypodermic injections.

AMTLICHE PRÜFSTELLE (GERM)   State Institute for Quality Control.

AMTLICHE PRÜFUNGSNUMMER (GERM)   The "A.P." number that appears on the bottom of some wine labels. It certifies that the wine met all legal requirements and has passed a rigid battery of laboratory and sensory tests. Also known as *prüfungsnummer*.

AMYLASE   Any of various enzymes that convert starch to sugar. *See* Dextrin and Diastase.

AÑADA (SP)   Year of harvest. *See* Vendimia.

ANAEROBIC FERMENTATION   A fermentation during which the atmosphere is oxygen-free.

ANCIENNE (FR)   Ancient.

AÑEJO OR AÑEJADO POR (SP)   Aged by.

AÑEJO (SP)   Aged; in reference to rum and tequila.

ANESONE (ITAL)   A high-proof, dry, generic anise-licorice-flavored liqueur, clear in color. *See* Anise-Based Spirits.

ANGEGOREN (GERM)   *See* Fermentation.

ANGELICA   A sweet fortified wine, generally produced in California, which is seldom made today.

ANGEL'S SHARE   *See* Evaporation.

ANGLAIS GOÛT (FR)   This depends on the district and context of its usage. In Champagne, dry; in Burgundy, big and smooth.

ANGOSTURA BITTERS   Concentrated bitter flavoring from Trinidad, used in cocktails.

ANGULAR   Wines without charm or grace, often referred to as being "stiff" or hard, often with bitter or tart flavors. Angular wines are the opposite of soft, yielding, and supple.

ANHYDROUS ALCOHOL   *See* Absolute Alcohol.

ANIDRIDE SOLFORSO (ITAL)   *See* Sulfur Dioxide.

ANÍS (SP)   *See* Anisette.

ANISE   It is the dried ripe fruit (incorrectly called seeds) of an annual Umbelliferous plant (*Pimpinella anisum*), which is native to Egypt and the Mediterranean region. It has a definitive licorice-like taste and is used globally as a flavoring base of many liqueurs, candy, bread, and pastry.

ANISE-BASED SPIRITS   They are distilled spirits produced by either infusion or the addition of flavoring (usually licorice and aniseed), have a high alcoholic content, and contain a minimum of 2.5 percent sugar. These beverages, which are produced globally, include Anesone, Chinchon, Masticha, Ojen, ouzo, Pernod, Ricard, and others.

ANISETTE   A generic anise licorice–flavored liqueur, clear in color, which is mostly produced in Italy, although anisette is produced globally. Also known as *anís*.

ANJOU (FR)   A grape growing district in the central Loire Valley famous for its Rosé d'Anjou (made from mostly Cabernet Franc grapes) wine.

ANNATA (ITAL)   Year of harvest. *See* Vendemmia.

ANNÉE (FR) A term that implies the year of the harvest, crop or vintage, not the wine of a particular vintage. Also known interchangeably as *millésime*, *récolte*, and *vendange*. *See* Millésimé and Vintage.

ANO (PORT) Year of harvest. *See* Vindima.

AÑO (SP) Year of harvest. *See* Vendimia.

ANO DE COLHEITA (PORT) *See* Vindima.

ANON BRAICH A Gaelic term that means *single malt*, which appears on certain Scotch whisky label.

ANREICHERN (GERM) *See* Chaptalization and Verbessern.

ANSPRECHEND (GERM) Appealing, attractive.

ANSTELLEN The addition of yeast to wort in order to start a fermentation.

ANTHOCYANIN One of the phenolic compounds of wine that gives it its red color. The purpley-red color of young wine is almost exclusively caused by fairly unstable anthocyanin molecules that, in the course of aging, join up with tannins (also phenolic elements) to give the wine its ruby-red color. This polymerization of tannin and anthocyanin is helped by the dissolution of oxygen in the wine. Also known as *pigment*.

ANTHOSIMÍA (GREECE) *See* Bouquet.

ANTIOXIDANT Tablets or crystals (oftentimes *ascorbic acid*) added to wine or beer at the time of bottling to prevent excess oxidation, browning, or deterioration of flavor. *See* Campden Tablets.

ANTITRUST LAWS Laws designed to control monopoly power and practices.

AOC (FR) *See* Appellation d'origine Contrôlée.

AOUTEMENT (FR) The moment when the soft, green tendrils on a grapevine become hard and woody.

AP *See* Amtliche Prüfungsnummer.

AP *See* As Purchased.

APALEADOR (SP) A wooden stick used to stir the wine while it is being fined.

APÉRITIF (FR) An alcoholic beverage taken before meals to stimulate the appetite. Also known as *aperitivo*.

APÉRITIF WINE A wine having an alcoholic content of not less than 15 percent by volume, compounded from grape wine containing added brandy or other distilled spirits. It is flavored with herbs and other natural aromatic flavoring materials, with or without the addition of caramel for coloring purposes, and possessing the aroma and characteristics generally attributed to an apéritif wine and shall be so designated unless designated as "vermouth."

There are many factors that must be considered when determining which wines are apéritifs. The beverage should be dry, light, chillable, and refreshing; it should be relatively acidic, to cleanse the palate; it should perhaps also be slightly bitter. Also referred to as *flavored wines* and *vinho aperitive*. *See* Aperire.

APERIRE Latin for *to open*, which is the origin of our word *apéritif*; a wine that usually "opens" lunch or dinner as a stimulant to the appetite. Most apéritifs have an initial sweet taste with a somewhat bitter aftertaste because of the use of quinine as one of the ingredients. This slight bitterness tends to whet the appetite and cleanse the palate. The French government mandates that apéritifs be produced at least 80 percent from wine with an alcoholic strength of at least 10 percent before alcohol is added to raise the strength to between 16 and 19 percent. *See* Apéritif.

APERITIVO (ITAL) *See* Apéritif.

APIANA (ITAL) The name of an ancient Roman wine made from the Muscat grape and named after the Latin word *apis*, for bee, because the bees would be alerted to the sweet taste.

APFELSCHNAPPS (GERM) *See* Applejack.

APPARENT CONSUMPTION Estimate of the gallons of distilled spirits sold at retail—based on state excise tax receipts, sales by state stores, shipments by producers to wholesalers, or shipments by wholesalers to retailers.

APPASSIMENTO (ITAL) The drying of the best clusters of grapes. *See* Amarone.

APPEARANCE Refers to clarity, not color. Wines should be free of cloud and suspended particles when evaluated in a glass.

APPELLATION OF ORIGIN Place name of geographic origin, that is, from which the wine came. Also known as *denomination of origin*.

APPELLATION D'ORIGINE CONTRÔLÉE (AOC) (FR) The *appellation d'origines contrôlées* were created by the French authorities in 1935 to establish areas of production, grape varieties, minimum levels of sugar in the *must*, and of alcohol in the wine, maximum yield per hectare, pruning of the grapevine, and cultivation and vinification methods. *See* Appellation d'origine Contrôlée.

APPETIZER WINES An incorrectly used term to denote wines taken before dinner. The correct term is apéritif. Appetizers are foods. Beverages, especially wine-based, are apéritifs.

APPLE An odor (hexyl acetate) occasionally detected in certain wines, like Chardonnay and Johannisberg Riesling. Also a taste detected in some wines due to high levels of malic acid.

APPLE BRANDY *See* Applejack.

APPLEJACK American brandy distilled from apples. Also known as *apple brandy, apfelschnapps,* and *batzi*. *See* Blended Applejack and Calvados.

APPLE JUICE The natural, unsweetened juice from apples, which has been pasteurized, and may be partially or completely filtered. *See* Cider, Hard Cider, and Sweet Cider.

APPLES   A fruit smell present in some wines (Johannisberg Riesling), associated with the presence of malic acid. An odor characteristic of *manzanilla* sherries.

APPLE WINE   Sweet cider is chaptalized and allowed to ferment, as would white grapes. The final product, also like wine, has a fairly long shelf life. *See* Cider, Hard Cider, and Sweet Cider.

APPLIED CARBON DIOXIDE PRESSURE   Carbon dioxide gives a beverage its "carbonization" and is used as a liquid gas under pressure. As the gas leaves the cylinder, a regulator is used to reduce the pressure to a desired level for service. This type system is often used for soft drinks or beer dispensing.

APPROVED VITICULTURAL AREA (AVA)   A delimited, geographical grape-growing area that has officially been given appellation status by the BATF. Two examples are Napa Valley and Sonoma Valley.

APRE (FR)   *See* Rough.

ÂPRETÉ (FR)   *See* Hard.

APRICOTS   An odor present in wines affected by *Botrytis cinerea* (the noble rot) that totally masks the varietal character and substitutes an odor reminiscent of apricots. Some of the grapes affected are Sauvignon Blanc, Sémillon, Muscat, and Johannisberg Riesling.

APRICOT-FLAVORED BRANDY   A mixture of brandy, with a minimum of 2.5-percent sugar, and flavored and colored with apricots. By federal law it cannot be bottled at less than 70 proof (35-per cent alcohol by volume).

APRICOT LIQUEUR   A sweetened alcoholic beverage consisting of a base of alcohol, minimum 2.5-percent sugar, and flavored and colored with apricots. It is sweeter and lower in proof than apricot-flavored brandy.

ÁPSITOS (GREECE)   *See* Immature.

APULIA (ITAL)   One of 20 wine-producing regions that stretches from the "spur" to the "heel" of the boot-shaped Italian peninsula. The southwestern shore of the region lies along the Ionian Sea, while its entire eastern shore lies along the Adriatic. Apulia is bordered by Molise to the north and Campania and Basilicata to the west. The region's climate is temperate and the country is mainly flat.

For years this region was considered by many to be incapable of producing quality table wines because of its intense heat and arid climate. The wines that were produced (mostly reds) were heavy, dark in color, highly alcoholic, and flat tasting (lacking acidity). Therefore, a good percentage of the wines were shipped north to Piedmont where they were blended with other varieties and used in the production of vermouth.

Within the last few years, however, modern technology has overtaken the region's vineyards, drastically lowering its total wine production. In place of the heavy alcoholic wines, today's vineyards produce lighter, fresher wines with surprisingly good acidity levels. Known as *Puglia*, in Italy.

AQUAVIT *See* Akvavit.

AQUA ARDENS The Latin term for alcohol, frequently used by writers of early treatises. *See* Alcohol.

AQUA VITAE From Latin, which literally means water of *life*, used by the French to refer to clear distillates or brandies. Also known as *okowita, usquebaugh*, and *uisgebeatha*.

AQUEOUS Containing water, or watery.

AQUIFER Moderately to highly permeable rocks through which water readily moves.

AQUITAINE The ancient name given to the region of Bordeaux, France.

ARANCIATO (ITAL) Orangish.

ARATURA (ITAL) Ploughing.

ARANZADA (SP) A land measurement equal to 0.475 hectares or 1.1737 acres.

ARCHES *See* Legs.

ARDENT Intense, strong-flavored, fruity, lively.

ARDENT SPIRITS An old name for distilled spirits. *See* Alcohol.

ARDENTE (ITAL) A wine with a high alcoholic content.

ARENA A type of soil found in approximately 17 percent of the sherry region of Spain. It consists of about 80-percent sand, red-yellow in color, with alumina, silica, and clay. The soil is very tillable, but produces coarser wines than either albariza or barro soils. *See* Albariza and Barro.

ARGILE (FR) *See* Clay.

ARISTOCRATICO (ITAL) Aristocratic; wine of fine pedigree; good soil, grapevines, vinification, and vintage year.

ARJAN *See* Kumiss or Koumiss.

ARJOADO (PORT) A system of training grapevines onto wires in between posts.

ARM (GERM) A wine that is thin, lacking body, or said to be poor.

ARMAGNAC (FR) A brandy made in the demarcated region of Armagnac, which comprises approximately 52,000 acres of quite sandy soil, mixed with some limestone, clay, and chalk. It is bounded roughly by the Garonne Valley to the north, Toulouse to the east, Bayonne and Bordeaux to the west, and the Pyrenees to the south. Its average annual production of wine is under 79 million gallons. About one-quarter of this wine is distilled into brandy; the remainder is consumed as table wine.

The Armagnac region is divided into three zones: Upper Armagnac (Haut-

Armagnac), the smallest area (3 percent of the total brandy production comes from this zone), which is often called "White Armagnac" because of its chalky, limestone-containing calcareous soil; Lower Armagnac (Bas-Armagnac), which is by far the largest zone (57 percent of production), and is often called "Black Armagnac," because of its forests; and Tenareze (40 percent of production). The quality, style, and taste of Armagnac varies from zone to zone, and it is generally agreed that the finest Armagnacs come from the Bas-Armagnac zone, whose name appears on bottle labels.

Arôme (fr) *See* Bouquet.

Armonico (ital) *See* Balance.

Armazém (port) Warehouse.

Arms The major branches of the trunk of a grapevine on which canes and renewal spurs are borne. These are the branches of older wood extending from the trunk. In a well-pruned vineyard they should not be more than one to two feet in length. Several ages of wood may make up an arm; all more than one year of age. The best arms, however, are of wood, which is two or three years old.

Ároma (greece) *See* Aroma.

Aroma The particular smell, odor, or fragrance of a specific grape used to produce the wine. White wines that are usually produced by a single grape variety are associated with aroma, and are said to have *varietal character*. Also known as *ároma* and *arôme*. *See* Bouquet and Nose.

Aromatic A term for wines that have intense aromas—fruits, herbs, or other odors either directly from the grape, or developed by the winemaking process.

Aromatico (ital) Amply scented, aromatic.

Aromatic Rum The combination of the special quality of the river water on the island of Java in Indonesia and the addition of dried red Javanese rice cakes, which are added to the mash during fermentation, results in a highly aromatic nature and dry taste of this rum. Aromatic rums are generally aged for three to four years in Java, then shipped to the Netherlands where additional aging takes place prior to blending and bottling. One brand available in the United States is Batavia Arak. (According to legend, ancient Arabian seafarers voyaging to the Caribbean islands gave this most unusual product its name.)

aromatic Wine *See* Aromatized Wine.

Aromatized Wine A fortified wine that has any number of related aromatic plants (*Artemisia absinthium*) or bitter herbs, roots, bark, or other plant parts, infused into its bouquet. An example of an aromatic wine is vermouth. Also known as *aromatic wine* and *aromatizzato*.

Aromatizzato (ital) *See* Aromatized Wine.

Arôme (FR) *See* Aroma.

Arneis (ITAL) A local white grape variety grown exclusively in the Piedmont region. The origins of Arneis are not known, but it has been traditionally cultivated in the area around Alba—but always in a secondary role. Also known as *Bianchetto, Bianchetta,* and *Nebbiolo Bianco.*

Aromatico (ITAL) Amply scented, aromatic.

Arpent During the eighteenth century in France, one *arpent* was translated to mean one and one-quarter acres of land.

Arrack An alcoholic beverage distilled from the "juice" or sap of palm trees, as well as different ingredients in different parts of the world. Arrack is produced mainly in the Middle East and Egypt and is referred to by many names: Arack, Arak, Arrac, Arrak, Arraki, or Raki. *See* Batavia Arrack.

Arrière-goût (FR) *See* Aftertaste.

Arroba (SP) A measurement of approximately 16 to 16.5 liters or slightly more than four U.S. gallons.

Arrope (SP) Concentration unfermented grape juice formerly used to color and sweeten some sherries.

Arrumbador (SP) A vineyard or bodega worker.

Art (GERM) A wine that is characteristic of its origin.

Artificial Carbonation Probably the quickest and cheapest method of making wines sparkle is similar to the way sodas are made to "fizz"—that is, by pumping them full of carbon dioxide. With this method the bubbles are not an integral part of the wine and do not last long after it is poured. Sparkling wines made via this method are easy to spot; their bubbles are very large and the wine froths up very quickly for a few moments and then appear to go flat. *See* Artificially Carbonated Wine, Carbonated Beverages, and Carbonated Water.

Artificially Carbonated Wine It is grape wine made effervescent with carbon dioxide other than that resulting solely from the secondary fermentation of the wine within a closed container, tank, or bottle. Effervescent wine is artificially charged with carbon dioxide and contains more than 0.392 grams of carbon dioxide per 100 milliliters. *See* Artificial Carbonation and Perlwein.

Art (GERM) Big and full-bodied.

Artig (GERM) Smooth, rounded.

Artisan Distillers of California An organization formed in September 1990, designed to develop marketing strategies and promotion of what they consider to be traditional European distilling methods, requiring more time to make smaller, higher-quality batches, and using equipment originally developed in Europe.

Asali The name of a fermented beverage that is made from honey in East Africa.

ASCIUTTO (ITAL)   A wine that is extremely dry.

ASCORBIC ACID (VITAMIN C)   *See* Antioxidant and Campden Tablets.

ASPARTAME   An artificial, low-calorie sweetener ($C_{14}H_{18}N_2O_5$), made from a compound of phenylalanine and aspartic acid, which is about 200 times sweeter than sucrose, used in the manufacture of soft drinks. Its trade name is Nutra-Sweet.

ASPILLA (SP)   A wooden dipstick used for gauging the capacity of the butts containing sherry wine.

ASPRETTO (ITAL)   A wine that is "sharp," yet pleasing.

ASPRIGNO (ITAL)   A wine that is "sharp," but not pleasing because of too much acidity.

ASPRO (ITAL)   *See* Rough.

AS PURCHASED (AP)   As the item is purchased or received from the supplier.

ASSAGGIO (ITAL)   *See* Degustazione.

ASSEMBLAGE (FR)   Blending of various cuvées in the making of champagne.

ASSET   Something that is owned.

ASSOCIADO (PORT)   An associate or partner in a cooperative winery.

ASTE (FR)   Fruit-bearing branch roughly 50 centimeters long, from which the end buds are cut off to leave only four live buds.

ASTESANA   An ancient wine bottle of Piedmont, Italy.

ASTI (ITAL)   A town in southern Piedmont, famous for production of its sparkling wine, Asti Spumante, as well as some DOC red wines (Barbera, Dolcetto, Grignolino, and Freisa) and one DOC white wine, Moscato.

ASTI SPUMANTE (ITAL)   A white, sweet sparkling wine produced in the town of Asti, in southern Piedmont. The wine displays a full, rich, and aromatic spicy odor, characteristic of the Moscato grapes it is made from. For Asti Spumante, the minimum residual sugar after the secondary fermentation must be 75 to 90 grams per liter (or 7.5 to 9.0 grams per 100 milliliters), under the DOC regulations.

Most of the Asti Spumante is made today in a modified Charmat method, which is favored over the *méthode champenoise.*

ASTRINGENCY   A tactile (touch), bitter sensation that makes the mouth pucker. Wines with high levels of astringency can be described as coarse, harsh, and rough. Also denotes too much tannin, which is derived from the stems, skins, and seeds, and is generally found in red wines. Also known as *adstringente, adstringerend, allappante, astringent, astringente, harsh, puckery, rude,* and *stryfnós. See* Astringent. *See* Phenols, Phenolics, and Tannin.

ASTRINGENTE (ITAL OR SP)   *See* Astringency.

ASTRINGENT   *See* Astringency.

ASZTALI BOR (HUN)   Table wine.

ASZÚ (HUN)   Overripe, dried-out grapes used in the making of Tokay wine.

ATESINO (ITAL)   A term occasionally encountered on wine labels that describes wines produced along the Adige River, in the region of Trentino-Alto Adige.

ATF   *See* Bureau of Alcohol, Tobacco, and Firearms.

ATM   *See* Atmosphere.

ATMOSPHERE (ATM)   In physics, a unit of pressure equal to 14.69 pounds per square inch (equivalent to one atmosphere), or the pressure exerted upon the human body at 30 feet under water. In bottles of sparkling wines, there is usually five to six atospheres of pressure, or about 110 pounds per square inch of CO_2 is formed.

ATTITUDE ADJUSTMENT HOUR   *See* Happy Hour.

AUBAINE (FR)   The local name for the chardonnay grape in the Chablis district of Burgundy.

AUFZIEHEN (GERM)   The agitation or aeration of yeast during the fermentation process of beer.

AU LAIT (FR)   Served with added milk.

AUM (GERM)   A barrel with a capacity of 30 U.S. gallons. *See* Barrel.

AUME (FR)   A large barrel for storage purposes used in Alsace, usually contains as much as 1,000 liters (260 U.S. gallons). *See* Barrel.

AURORA   *See* Aurore.

AURORA BLANC   *See* Aurore.

AURORE   A white French-American hybrid, developed by Louis Seibel in the late 1880s near the Burgundy region of France. Aurore was introduced into the Finger Lakes region of New York in the early 1940s, and used for white table wines and sparkling wines.

An early maturing, white-pinkish grape variety with large, thick-skinned, medium-loose to compact clusters. Aurore produces soft, fragrant white wines with leafy-green overtones. Formerly known as *Seibel 5279*. Aurore is also incorrectly known as *Aurora* or *Aurora Blanc*.

AUSDRUCK (GERM)   A wine with character.

AUSEIGENEM LESEGUT (GERM)   Estate bottled.

AUSGEBAUT (GERM)   Mature; a wine ready to consume.

AUSGEGLICHEN (GERM)   *See* Balance.

AUSLESE (GERM)   A prädikat wine made from particularly ripe, selected late harvested bunches of grapes; all unripe grapes, as well as bunches are discarded. Auslese wines are especially full, rich, and somewhat sweet. They may not be *sugared* and must attain a minimum must weight of 95 degrees

Öechsle. Auslese wines are generally sweeter and more expensive than spätlese wines. Also known as *szemelt*.

AUSTERE   Term used to describe wines, generally dry, high in acidity, and bitter from excessive tannins. It implies a tactile sensation of relative hardness and a uncomplex, possible undeveloped character in a wine that may be caused by grapes grown in cool climates or harvested earlier than usual. Also known as *afstirós, austère, austero,* and *severe*.

AUSTÈRE (FR)   *See* Austere.

AUSTERO (ITAL)   *See* Austere.

AUTOCLAVE (ITAL)   *See* Charmat Method.

AUTOLYSIS   Self-destruction of yeast cells, which release their different cell compounds into the surrounding medium. Often gives wine a toasty or "bad" aroma and flavor.

In sparkling winemaking, it is the breakdown of yeast cells inside the sparkling wine bottle after the secondary fermentation is completed. This process contributes to the complexity and elegance of the wine. *See* Sur Lie.

AUTOMATIC BAR   A type of self-service bar that, at the push of a finger, dispenses a predetermined portion-controlled quantity of distilled spirit.

AUXERROIS (FR)   *See* Malbec.

AUXERROIS BLANC (FR)   A white grape variety that is cultivated in the Alsace region, selected for its improved sugar to acid ratio at maturity. The grape was named in honor of the Earldom of Auxerrois in Northern Burgundy. Also known as *Pinot Auxerrois*.

AUXERROIS GRIS (FR)   *See* Pinot Gris.

AUXEY-DURESSES (FR)   A small red wine–producing village in Côte de Beaune in the Burgundy region. In the ninth century, Auxey was known as *Aulessiacum*.

AVA   *See* Approved Viticultural Area.

AV ALARM   A system that broadcasts irritating sounds to harass birds; commonly used during harvest.

AVELUDADO (PORT)   A luscious wine.

AVIGNON (FR)   A small, but historic city located in the Côtes du Rhône region, which from 1309 to 1377 was the papacy stronghold. *See* Châteauneuf-du-Pape.

AVILLO (SP)   *See* Folle Blanche.

AWAMORI (JAPAN)   A high-proof spirit distilled from rice, made in Okinawa.

AWARE   American Wine Alliance for Research and Evaluation.

AWKWARD   Describes a wine that has poor structure or is out of balance.

AY (FR) A village in the Champagne region that predominantly grows Pinot Noir grapes for champagne making.

AZIENDA AGRARIA (ITAL) *See* Azienda Agricola.

AZIENDA AGRICOLA (ITAL) Only companies that can prove that their wines have been made solely from grapes gathered in their own vineyards, and vinified in their own cellars, have the right to describe themselves as an *azienda agricola* or winery. Also known as *Azienda Agraria*.

AZIENDA VINICOLA (ITAL) Winery; agricultural concern.

AZIENDA VITIVINICOLA (ITAL) Vintners; a grape-growing and winemaking company. Generally means the same as *azienda vinicola*.

BAC   *See* Blood Alcohol Level.

BAC À GLÂCE (FR)   A shallow brine bath used to freeze the necks of champagne bottles prior to dégorgement.

BACARDI   A cocktail containing Bacardi rum, grenadine syrup, sugar, and lime juice. Also the brand name of a rum, originally produced in Cuba, but now in Puerto Rico.

BACH (GERM)   Stream.

BACCHAE (FR)   The female brotherhood or companions of Bacchus.

BACCHUS   The Roman God of wine; also known as *Dionysus*, the Greek God of wine. Also known as *Bacco*.

BACCHUS (GERM)   A white grape variety, developed from a cross of (Sylvaner and Johannisberg Riesling) and Müller-Thurgau, developed at the Geilweilerhof Grape Research Institute, located in the Rheingau.

BACCO (ITAL)   *See* Bacchus.

BACK BAR   The cabinet or display area behind the bar usually used for merchandise, placement of the register, supplies, and storage.

BACK BONE   A term used to denote those wines that are often full-bodied, well-structured, and balanced by a desirable level of acidity. Also known as *rückgrat*.

BACKINGS   *See* Tails.

BACK-OF-THE-HOUSE   Those areas of a hotel, restaurant, tavern, or any facility that is not in "the public eye." It is considered the work area where guests and customers are not permitted. The kitchen, storeroom, and food preparation area are such examples.

BACKWARD   A term used to describe a young wine that is less developed than others of its type and class from the same vintage. When referring to red wines, it means they are still somewhat harsh from youthful tannins and closed in.

BACO BLANC A white French-American grape variety developed in 1898, from a cross of Folle Blanche and Noah, by Maurice Baco. It is the only French-American hybrid grape variety permitted in France in an AOC region (Armagnac), which is used for blending. Formerly known as *Baco 22A*.

BACO NOIR (Also called Baco #1) A red hybrid grape variety named after Francois Baco (1865–1947), the French hybridizer (who is often confused with his son Maurice, for whom Baco #1 is named) who developed this grape variety in the late 1800s, near the Burgundy region. Baco is a cross of Folle Blanche and a wild *Vitis riparia* variety from the United States. It is believed to be the first commercially planted French hybrid (1949) in the United States. Baco Noir is mostly cultivated in the northeast of the United States. The wines tend to be sturdy and full-bodied, with pronounced flavor and high acidity.

BACTERIAL SPOILAGE A general name for most types of spoilage bacteria that attacks *must*, wine, or beer, during and after fermentation. Often due to formation of mold from improperly cleaned equipment, sloppy winemaking or brewing practices, lack of sterile conditions, or faulty sanitation procedures. In these instances where bacterial infestation is present, the wine or beer often turns to vinegar or becomes spoiled, and is unfit for consumption. *See* Sick and Spoiled.

BADD Bartenders Against Drunk Driving.

BADEN (GERM) A large grape-growing region in southwestern Germany, which lies along the Rhine River, known for its full-flavored wines.

BAGA (PORT) Elderberry juice, used in ancient times to add color to some port wines.

BAGACEIRA (PORT) *See* Grappa.

BAGASSE The sugar-laden center of the sugar cane.

BAGUE CARÉE (FR) The rounded lip or edge on a sparkling wine bottle, similar to that on a bottle of still wine.

BAGUE COURONNE (FR) The rounded lip or edge on a sparkling wine bottle, similar to that on a beer bottle.

BAKED The flavor that results from extremely ripe grapes grown in hot climates; a warm, cooked, or roasted smell and flavor.

BAKING A process used on the island of Madeira to give this unique fortified wine its distinctive character.

BALANCE Pleasant harmony of the elements and components of a beverage, used especially with wine. A balanced wine is one whose components, sugar, fruit, tannin, acid, alcohol, wood, extract, and so forth, are evident, but do not mask or dominate one another. Acid is balanced by sweetness; fruit by oak and tannin; alcohol by acidity and flavor. The olfactory and tactile elements are cohesive, proportioned, and seem to blend or meld together. Also known as *armonico, ausgeglichen, equilibrado, équilibré, harmonious, harmonisch,* and *proportioned.*

BALANCED PRUNING   The pruner adjusts the potential crop left at pruning time so that it is in balance in relation to the grapevine's potential to produce a crop in the subsequent growing season. Balanced pruning also regulates cane and shoot growth. *See* Pruning.

BALLING   Name of a system (after Karl J.N. Balling, 1868, German chemist). *See* Brix.

BALLOON GLASS   An oversized wine glass with the bowl, which is in the shape of a balloon, having a capacity of between 10 and 26 fluid ounces.

BALSAM   A banana-flavored liqueur produced in the West Indies.

BALSEIRO (PORT)   A large wooden barrel on legs often used to transport or hold wine. *See* Barrel.

BALTHAZAR   An oversized champagne bottle, equal to 16 750-milliliter bottles or 12 liters. Balthazar was the name given to one of the three Wise Men, known as the "Lord of the Treasury." He was a sixth century B.C. king of Babylon and a grandson of Nebuchadnezzar, the first king of Babylon.

BAMBOO JUICE   The name given to alcoholic beverages by members of the U.S. Air Force who were stationed in the South Pacific during the Korean War.

BANANA LIQUEUR   *See* Crème de Banana.

BANANAS   With some very young white wines (tank samples as well as freshly bottled), there is either a faint smell or noticeable odor of bananas, which is a by-product of fermentation. The odor responsible for this is amyl or isoamyl acetate, which diminishes with age.

BAN DE VENDANGE (FR)   The official ceremony announcing the beginning of the harvest.

BANDOL (FR)   A province located just to the west of Toulon, in Provence along the Mediterranean coast. In the vineyards of Bandol, the grapevines are planted in terraces made of chalky, silicate soil, which is also very arid. To be entitled to the appellation for its red and rosé wines, a high percentage of Mourvèdre and Grenache must be used; for its whites, Clairette and Ugni Blanc are utilized.

BANG   A wine made in India from hemp leaves and twigs infused in water. Also spelled *bhang.*

BANYULS (FR)   A sweet, fortified wine made predominantly from the black Grenache grape variety. Banyuls is produced in the Languedoc Roussillon region on the Mediterranean coast, near Spain.

BAPTISM   A formerly used French process of collecting bad wine and improving it by the use of chemicals.

BAR   A place of business that sells and serves alcoholic beverages by the drink to customers. There are three parts of a bar: the front bar or counter top where alcoholic beverages are served to customers; the underbar or work station where bartenders assemble drinks; and the back bar, usually with a cabinet or display area behind the bar, used for merchandise, placement of register, supply, and storage. Also known as *bar and grill. See* Barroom, Cocktail Lounge, Inn, Pub, Saloon, Tavern, and Watering Hole.

BARACK PÁLINKA   An apricot brandy produced in Austria and Hungary.

BAR AND GRILL   *See* Bar.

BAR BACK   A bartender's helper or an apprentice bartender. A bar back replenishes ice, nonalcoholic beverages, and mixes; cuts up garnishes; cleans the bar area; and generally assists in all but the final presentation of drinks and collection of monies.

BARBADOS BRANDY   *See* Rum.

BARBADOS WATER   *See* Rum.

BARBARESCO (ITAL)   A dry, red wine produced from 100-percent Nebbiolo grapes (or its subvarieties Lampia and Michet) grown in vineyards located in the towns of Barbaresco, Neive, Treiso, and Alba, all in the southern province of Cuneo, in the northwest region of Piedmont. Barbaresco is garnet red with characteristics orange highlights, and has an intense bouquet reminiscent of violets; dry and full-bodied, it nevertheless exhibits a surprising gentleness. Barbaresco must have a minimum of 12.5 percent alcohol and be aged a minimum of two years; if aged four years, may be labeled *riserva.*

Barbaresco received its DOCG status on October 3, 1980. The Barbaresco *consorzio* features on its neck label the ancient tower of Barbaresco, in gold, on a blue background.

BARBERA   A red grape variety grown predominantly in Piedmont, Italy, and in small quantities in the United States. It produces wines that are generally full-bodied and slightly tannic, with a high natural amount of acidity, and a vinous, tart, fruity taste.

Although its exact origins are uncertain, it is believed to have originated there from a spontaneous crossing of seeds from ancient grapevines growing in the hilly area known as "Monferrato" in southern Piedmont; in fact, its ampelographical name is *Vitis vinifera Montisferratensis.*

BARBERONE   A made-up California name for inexpensive, heavy, full-bodied red wines that are likely to be slightly sweet. Popular during the 1950s to 1960s, it is of little consequence today.

BAR BRANDS   *See* Well Brands.

BARDO (SP)   A system of training grapevines onto wires in between posts.

BARDOLINO (ITAL)   Light-bodied, dry red wine made from a blend of Corvina Veronese, Rondinella, and other grapes. It is produced in the northeastern region of Veneto.

BARENTRANK (GERM) The name of a spirit distilled from potatoes and flavored with honey.

BAR FLY A term used from the 1940s to 1960s to describe someone (usually female) who spends time hanging out and drinking alcoholic beverages at bars.

BARK The outermost layer of a woody stem or plant.

BARKEEPER Literally the "keeper of the bar." A bartender or owner who is charge of the establishment and responsible for serving and selling alcoholic beverages. Also known as *bartender*.

BARLEY A widely-cultivated cereal plant. Its seed or grain are extracted, then converted into malt for beer or whiskey making.

BARLEY BEER A drink of the ancient Greeks.

BARLEY MALT *See* Malt.

BARLEY WATER A nonalcoholic grain beverage made by boiling the grain in water and cooling it to room temperature. Popular in Victoria England, the drink commonly is served with meals in present-day Korea.

BARLEY WINE Not actually a wine, but an English term for an extra strong dark ale.

BARMAID A cocktail waitress or female worker who works behind the bar, mixing, serving, and selling alcoholic drinks.

BAR MANAGER A person who forecasts, directs, organizes, and controls every phase of a beverage department or bar.

BARNYARD An unpleasant odor occasionally found in some wines due to unsanitary winemaking techniques or facilities.

BAROLISTA (ITAL) Someone who makes Barolo wine.

BAROLO (ITAL) Renowned, full-bodied, dry red wine produced in the area centering around the town of Barolo in the Langhe Hills just southeast of Alba, in the northwest region of Piedmont. Barolo, which must be produced from 100 Nebbiolo grapes, is garnet red in color with orange highlights and an intense but delicate bouquet. Very dry and full-bodied, it has an austere taste that becomes velvety and harmonious with age. Barolo must have a minimum of 13 percent alcohol and be aged a minimum of three years; if aged five years, may be labeled *riserva*.

Barolo received its DOCG status on July 1, 1980. The Barolo *consorzio* features on its neck label a golden lion or a helmeted head on a blue background, according to the particular district it comes from.

BAR PARS *See* Par Stock.

BARREL A container of any size, in which wine, beer, or distilled spirits are stored, aged, and sometimes shipped. The barrel can be made of any material, such as wood, stainless steel, or glass. A finished 50-gallon wooden barrel typically weighs 110 pounds empty and about 525 pounds when full. The head diameter is 20 to 21 inches, stave length 33 to 35 inches. The individual staves vary in width from two to four inches. Barrels, depending on capacity, country of origin, and what type of alcoholic beverage they contain are referred to by many names. Among them are Aum, Aume, Balseiro, Barrica, Barrique, Barriquot, Bocoy, Bordelesas, Bota, Bota Chica, Bota Bodeguera, Bota De Embarque, Bota De Recibo, Bota Gorda, Botte, Butt, Caratello, Casco, Cask, Corredor, Cuva, Demi-Muid, Déposito, Doppleohm, Dopplestück, Double Aum, Fass, Feuillette, Firkin, Foudre, Fuder, Fusto, Fût, Gönci, Halbfuder, Halbstück, Hogshead, Keg, Kilder kin, Media, Octave, Pièce, Pin, Pipe, Puncheon, Quartaut, Queue, Scantling Pipe, Stück, Tank, Tercero, Terzo, Tierce, Tina, Tonel, Tonne, Tonneau, Tun, Viertelstück, and Vat.

BARREL AGING   The process of mellowing an alcoholic product through extraction, as the alcohol dissolves flavor-affecting chemicals present in the wooden barrels. The wine extracts certain elements present in the wood. Flavor components, aromatic substances, and wood tannins all contribute to the body, character, and complexity of the wine. The pine-type trees (Douglas fir, pine, and spruce) have resinous flavors that are undesirable to wine, while acacia imparts a yellow pigment to wine.

During aging, the liquid nearest the barrel wall becomes more dense from taking on the added weight of the extractables; this heavier liquid then falls away, causing circulation, which brings the lighter liquid from the center of the barrel to the walls to pick up added extractable elements. The smaller the barrel, the more rapid the circulation and the extraction, and hence the more rapid the aging process. Also known as *wood aging*. *See* Aging, Bottle Aging, Mature, Ripe, and Ripe For Bottling.

BARREL DOGGING   A seldom-used moonshining operation where wooden barrels (formerly utilized by legal distilleries) are disassembled, steamed, or sweated out in order to capture any residual alcohol that soaked into the wood during aging.

BARREL FERMENTATION   A technique utilized in Burgundy, France for centuries, and now in wine regions around the world, for the production of certain white wines (primarily Sauvignon Blanc and Chardonnay). The *must*, after being separated from its stems, skins, and seeds, is fermented in wooden barrels (usually 55 gallons) rather than temperature controlled stainless steel containers. During this process, extractables, such as tannin, color, various odors, and flavors are leached into the wine, creating more complexity and depth. Certain flavor extractables are available to a wine only at certain levels of alcohol. In other words, some flavor compounds found in oak might be available to a wine from the barrel only at an alcohol level of 2 percent, while other flavors might be available only at 10 percent, and so forth. Therefore, if the wine is not in wood at these times, the extractives will not be in the wine.

Some winemakers believe that certain white wines benefit from barrel fermentation for harmony of taste, while increasing body. The cost and risk of spoilage often outweigh the benefits obtained. Also referred to as Barrel-Fermented on certain wine labels.

BARREL HOUSE   An English term for an establishment that primarily serves lager and ale.

BARREL LEAK   *See* Leakage.

BARREL OF BEER   A stainless steel barrel containing 31 U.S. gallons (13.8 cases of 12-ounce cans or bottles of beer).

BARREL-STORE   Large storeroom where the young wine, beer, or distilled spirits are kept in oak casks before bottling.

BARREL THIEF   *See* Wine Thief.

BARRICA (SP)   *See* Barrel and Barrique.

BARRIQUE (FR)   A small barrel. A law that appeared in the "Moniteur" on June 13, 1866 ratified a meeting of the Bordeaux Chamber of Commerce, held on May 12, 1858, which established that barrels' dimensions should be uniformly expressed in metric terms. It stipulated that the Bordeaux barrique should contain precisely 225 liters (59.4 U.S. gallons) of wine; length 91 cm (35.8 inches); external circumference at the bilge 218 cm (7 feet 1.8 inches); an extrusion of 7 cm (2.8 inches) from the closed head of the barrel to the end of the staves; thickness of head 16 to 18 mm (6/10 to 7/10 of an inch); thickness of the staves at the bilge 12 to 14 mm (8/16 to 9/16 of an inch); and so forth. Also known as *barrica*. *See* Barrel.

BARRIQUOT (FR)   An old term for a small barrel. *See* Barrel.

BARRO   A heavy, dark soil (because of the high iron oxide content), with some chalk, but mostly made of clay and sand. Barro is often found in valleys between hills of albariza. It is more fertile and yields about 20 percent more grapes per ton than albariza. Barro soil is important in the sherry producing vineyards of Jerez de la Frontera, Spain. *See* Albariza and Arena.

BARROOM   A room with a bar or counter at which alcoholic drinks are sold. Also known as *taproom*. *See* Bar, Cocktail Lounge, Inn, Pub, Saloon, and Tavern.

BARSAC (FR)   Sweet, white wine made from a blend of Sauvignon Blanc, Sémillon, and Muscadelle grape varieties. It is also one of the five communes within Bordeaux's Sauternes district entitled to be called "Sauternes." Only wines from the commune of Barsac are entitled to the Barsac *appellation contrôlée*; however, a decree of 1936 gave this commune the right to the illustrious Sauternes appellation as well. On September 11, 1936, Barsac was officially given its *appellation contrôlée* designation.

BAR SPOON   An elongated stainless steel spoon used behind the bar for stirring cocktails, especially those containing carbonated beverages.

BAR STRAINER   *See* Cocktail Strainer.

BAR SUGAR   Superfine sugar that dissolves quickly in cocktails.

BARTENDER   An employee responsible for the operation of a bar, which includes the mixing, serving, and selling of alcoholic beverages. They are also referred to as a "tapman" when the operation does a large volume of beer. Also known as *barkeeper* and *mixologist*.

BARTZCH   A local Asian distilled beverage made from fermented hogweed, which is a general name for any coarse plants, such as ragweed or sow thistle.

BAR WHISKEY   *See* Well Brands.

BAR WORKBOARD   Equipment below the top of a bar containing sinks, drainboards, glass washers, glass chillers, beverage coolers, ice storage compartments, cocktail mix stations, beer system, and so on. Also known as *sink workboard*.

BASAL   A shoot originating on the trunk area of a grapevine.

BAS ARMAGNAC (FR)   A zone in the Armagnac region that produces the finest quality Armagnacs.

BASE   The flat bottom of a tumbler or stem glass. Also known as *foot*.

BASI   The name of a spirit distilled from sugar cane, which is produced in the Philippines.

BASIC PERMIT   Formal document issued under the Federal Alcohol Administration Act authorizing the person named (individual or firm) to engage in specified activities at the stated location.

   Such permits are required for importers, domestic producers, blenders, and wholesalers.

BASILICATA (ITAL)   A relatively small and unknown wine-producing region best known for its steep, rugged mountains, hot weather, and full-bodied red wines. Its most famous wine is Aglianico del Vulture, a dry and full-flavored red wine.

BASKET   *See* Wine Cradle.

BASKET PRESS   A type of press wherein grapes are put in a wooden tub with slotted sides. Pressure is applied by means of a large screw, which presses the grapes and allows the juice to run out through the slots.

BASQUAISE (FR)   An oval-shaped bottle, traditionally used for Armagnac brandy.

BASTER   *See* Wine Thief.

BASTO (SP)   A term meaning coarse, common, or rough-textured; usually refers to a sherry wine lacking breed.

BAT AND A BALL   Slang term for a shot of whiskey accompanied by a glass of beer. Also known as a *beer and a ball*.

BATAVIA ARRACK   A highly aromatic rum distilled in Java from dried red Javanese rice cakes. *See* Arrack.

BATF   *See* Bureau of Alcohol, Tobacco, and Firearms.

BATHTUB GIN   An illicit alcoholic beverage made during prohibition by mixing together neutral spirits, glycerin, and extracts or oils of juniper berries inside a bathtub. after being stirred with an "oar," it was bottled and either sold or consumed.

BATZI (SWISS)   Apple brandy. *See* Applejack.

BAUM (GERM)   Tree.

BAUMÉ (FR)   Name of a system (after Antoine Baumé). A term used to measure the level of unfermented sugar present in the *must*. If degrees Baumé are multiplied by 1.8, the result will be degrees Brix. To determine Baumé, take degrees Brix and divide by 1.8. *See* Brix.

BAYLETON   The trade name of a systemic fungicide called Triadimefon (common name), which is effective against powdery mildew and black rot.

BEADS   Term often used to describe the chains of pin-point bubbles found in sparkling wines, beers, and carbonated soft drinks, formed by the presence of carbon dioxide. Also the bubbles that form on the surface of a distilled spirit when shaken. *See* Pin-Point Bubbles.

BEAUJOLAIS (FR)   Fruity, light-bodied red and white wines made from the Gamay grape variety. A small amount of white Beaujolais from the chardonnay grape is also produced. Beaujolais is produced in the southern tip of Burgundy. Most Beaujolais wines are made by carbonic maceration.

BEAUJOLAIS DE L' ANNÉE (FR)   *See* Beaujolais Nouveau.

BEAUJOLAIS NOUVEAU (FR)   The "new" Beaujolais that is rushed through fermentation, then sold only a matter of weeks after harvest. Nouveau is at its best when it first appears on the market. After one year it is tired, and with few exceptions should be forgotten.

Beginning in 1967, the official date of first release or sale of the nouveaus was November 15. However, since 1985, the official date is the third Thursday in the month of November, regardless of the specific date. Also known as *Beaujolais de l'année* and *beaujolais primeur*. *See* Carbonic Maceration and Nouveau.

BEAUJOLAIS PRIMEUR (FR)   *See* Beaujolais Nouveau.

BEAUJOLAIS-SUPÉRIEUR (FR)   A designation of wine containing one degree more alcohol than simple Beaujolais and is probably from one of the 59 communes in the Bas-Beaujolais area. It rarely is exported to the United States.

BEAUJOLAIS-VILLAGES (FR)   Wines produced in 35 communes located in the northernmost section of the Haut-Beaujolais area. These wines contain more body and flavor than ordinary Beaujolais wines.

BEAUNE (FR)   A principal town in the southern half of Burgundy's Côte d'Or, noted for its exceptional white and red wines.

BEAUNOIS (FR)   A local name for the Chardonnay grape in the Chablis district of Burgundy.

BEECHWOOD AGING   As practiced by Anheuser-Busch, beechwood aging is quite different from aging wine in barrels at a winery. In beechwood aging, either beechwood chips, or a number of short slats of beechwood are tied together and then immersed into a tank where the beer is undergoing a process known as *kräusening*. The beechwood doesn't impart any particular flavor to the beer, but rather it attracts impurities and promotes clarification of the yeast. It accomplishes this by increasing the surface area for encouraged fermentation. After use, these slats are washed off and used over and over again.

BEER   Generic term for all alcoholic beverages that are fermented and brewed from malted barley, hops, water, and yeast. Other starchy cereals may also be used where legal.

BEER AND A BALL   *See* Bat and a Ball.

BEER AND SKITTLES (ENG)   Slang term for drinks and enjoyment, or pleasure.

38

BEER BALL   A nonreturnable, plastic, oversized ball containing one or more U.S. gallons (128 fluid ounces) of beer. It is generally fitted with a type of spigot for dispensing.

BEER BASH   Campus, college fraternity, or teen term for a party at which the primary beverage is beer, often served from a keg. Also known as *keg party*.

BEER BOTTLE   A glass container for the storage and service of beer. In 1953, the nonreturnable beer bottle made its debut.

BEER BOX   A specially constructed refrigerated compartment or cooler used for the storage of draft beer and its corresponding system. Also known as *tap box*. *See* Beer Cooler.

BEER CAN   An aluminum container for the storage and service of beer. First introduced in 1935 by the Kreuger Brewery of Richmond, Virginia.

BEER CLEAN GLASS   A glass that is free of grease (petroleum and its products), lint, soap, and odor, which is necessary for the proper service of beer.

BEER COOLER   An enclosed refrigerated cooler (includes walk-in) used for the storage of kegs, cans, and bottles of beer. *See* Beer Box.

BEER DISPENSER   *See* Beer Standard.

BEERENAUSLESE (GERM)   "Berry selection" wines made from overripe grapes, picked individually and produced in very small quantities only in best vintages. These grapes may be affected by *Botrytis cinerea*. The resultant wine is intensely sweet and can generally age for several decades.

BEERENTON (GERM)   The taste of fully ripened or mature grapes.

BEER FLIP   *See* Flip.

BEER GARDEN   Slang term for a pub.

BEER HALLS   Seldom-used term for social gathering centers (usually for the lower and middle classes, and senior citizens) that serve primarily beer. Also known as *beer houses*.

BEER HOUSES   *See* Beer Halls.

BEER PACKS   Containers, such as bottles, cans, or barrels with various capacities used for the storage and service of brewed beverages.

BEER STANDARD   That portion of a draft beer system that is above the counter and visible to the eye. It includes the tap, faucet, drain, and stainless steel housing. Also known as *beer dispenser* or *tapping cabinet*.

BEER SYSTEM   A draft-beer system that consists of a keg of beer, CO_2 tank, regulator, beer box, beer lines, and beer standard.

BEESWAX   Soft, pliable wax generally used to fill in or seal minute leaks in a barrel.

BEERY   An odor or taste that is typical of beer or other malt beverages with a pronounced odor of hops.

BEESWING (PORT)   The name of the light thin crust that resembles the transparent wing of a bee and often forms in some bottles of port. *See* Sediment.

BEET SUGAR   A sugar used in Europe for Chaptalization.

BELIMNITA QUADRATA (FR)   The name of the chalky soil that composes the hills of the Champagne region.

BELLINI   A cocktail consisting of peaches, lemon juice, dry Italian spumante, and grenadine syrup. This drink was created by Giuseppe Cipriani at Harry's Bar in Venice, Italy.

BELL PEPPER   An odor characteristic of "bell peppers" occasionally detected in Cabernets (Franc and Sauvignon), Sauvignon Blanc, and certain other grape varieties. This odor has been identified as being a pyrazine compound, 2-methoxy-3-isobutyl pyrazine (MIP). It is most noticeable in the above wines when grown in certain counties of California, such as Monterey County.

BELOE (RUSS)   *See* White.

BENCH GRAFTS   A common propagation method of producing grafted grapevines of a desired fruiting species on rootstocks resistant to phylloxera or nematodes. Also referred to indoor grafting, because the grafting usually takes place during the winter in appropriate warm environments, like greenhouses.

BENCHGRAFTING   Indoor grafts done during late winter or early spring during the dormant season, calloused-in in a warm environment, rooted and grown for one year in the nursery, then vineyard planted in the second spring. Normal take for benchgrafts is well above 90 percent, making for uniform stands (vineyards with grapevines of similar maturity). (The term came about since these grafts were accomplished during the winter while sitting comfortably at a warm bench, rather than stooping in a cold field.) Also referred to as *field budding* and *chip budding*.

BENCH TESTING   Also referred to as *laboratory testing.*

BENDING AN ELBOW   A slang term for drinking beer or whiskey at a bar.

BENEUA (FR)   A grape harvest holder, made either of wood or plastic.

BENIN WINE   A distilled product made from fermented palm sap that is produced in Nigeria.

BENTONITE   An excellent fining agent first used in 1931 by Lothrop and Paine for fining honey. It is basically clay (resembles gray crystalline powder) originating from the state of Wyoming and consists of "montmorillonite," produced from decomposition under water of volcanic glass. Chemically bentonite is hydrated aluminum silicate and carries a negative charge. *See* Fining and Fining Agents.

BEOR   An old English term for beer.

BERE (RUM)   Beer.

BEREICH (GERM)   A subregion within a Gebiet (region).

BEREITUNG (GERM)   The preparation, manufacture, or making of alcoholic beverages.

BERG (GERM)   Mountain or hill.

BERGERON, VICTOR   The originator of "Trader Vics."

BERLINER WEISSE (GERM)   Berlin's classic wheat beer. *See* Weisse Beer.

BERM   A ledge or ridge of soil in between grapevine rows.

BERNKASTEL (GERM)   The principle vineyard town of the Middle Mosel.

BERRIES   Berry-like quality is a nebulous, fruity characteristic often associated with young red wines such as Zinfandel, Gamay-Beaujolais, and others.

BERRY   An individual grape, which varies in color, size, and the number of seeds it contains.

BERRY DESSERT WINE   *See* Fruit Dessert Wine.

BERRYLIKE   Term equated with the fruity olfactory qualities associated with such berries as blackberry, cherry, cranberry, raspberry, strawberry, and others. Berry-like can be used to describe young red wines, such as Zinfandel, Gamay-Beaujolais, Beaujolais, and so on.

BERRY SET   The successful pollination of grape flowers. The pollinated grape blossoms start to develop, with each flower in the floral cluster transformed into a miniature grape berry about the size of a small BB. Also known as *set*. *See* Shatter and Shot Berries.

BERRY TABLE WINE   *See* Fruit Table Wine.

BERRY WINE   Fruit wine produced from berries.

BESTE (GERM)   Best.

BESTES FASS (GERM)   The best barrel or the producer's best wine.

BEVA (ITAL)   A wine term denoting a pleasurable dry taste and drinkability.

BEVANDA (ITAL)   *See* Beverage.

BEVERAGE   Any liquid for drinking, whether it is alcoholic or nonalcoholic. Also known as *bevanda*.

BEVERAGE COST   The total costs for all ingredients necessary to make the drink served in a beverage facility. It includes alcoholic as well as nonalcoholic beverages. Factors such as pilferage, waste, overproduction, and so on must also be included because they tend to raise the cost. Also known as *standard beverage cost* or *standard cost*.

BEVERAGE COST PERCENTAGE   The costs incurred for each one dollar of sales. Beverage cost is expressed as a percent of sales. Costs divided by sales equals cost percentage (C/S = C%). Also known as *cost percentage* and *standard cost percentage*.

BEVERAGE INVENTORY TURNOVER   The number of times the dollar value of your beverage inventory turned over.

BEVERAGE MANAGER   A person who is in charge of all phases of running a beverage operation.

B

BEVERAGE MULTIPLIER   Beverage costs divided into 100 will yield a number called a multiplier. Take this multiplier and times it by the beverage costs. This will determine the selling price.

BEVERAGE SALES   Total revenue for a given or projected period of time that can include all beverages (alcoholic and nonalcoholic). Can also be segmented by specific type: wine, beer, distilled spirits, and nonalcoholic beverages.

BEVERAGE TRANSFERS   The wholesale cost of beverages, both alcoholic and nonalcoholic that are used in departments other than bar operations.

BEVO   The name of a nonalcoholic malt beverage produced by the Anheuser-Busch brewing company during Prohibition. *See* Near Beer and Nonalcoholic Malt Beverage.

BEYAZ (TURKEY)   *See* White.

BHANG   *See* Bang.

BIANCAME (ITAL)   *See* Albana.

BIANCHETTO (ITAL)   *See* Arneis.

BIANCHETTA (ITAL)   *See* Arneis.

BIANCO (ITAL)   *See* White.

BIANCO ACQUA (ITAL)   Water white.

BIANCO CARTA (ITAL)   A white wine so light in color that it is said to be "paper-white."

BIBIERE   The ancient Latin term for beer.

BIBLINO (ITAL)   An ancient white wine from Sicily.

BICCHIÉRE (ITAL)   A drinking glass.

BIDULE   A small, circular plastic cap or plug that fits securely inside the neck of a sparkling wine bottle, to form a tight seal. During secondary fermentation and during remuage, the bidule will capture some of the decomposed yeast before it is expelled prior to the final dosage.

BIEN EQUILIBRÉ (FR)   *See* Well-Balanced.

BIENTEVEO (SP)   A kind of rustic observatory built of wooden trunks, covered with straw or straw mats, above the level of the grapevines, from which the vineyard keeper dominates the widest view of the property unobserved and protected from the hot sun.

BIER (GERM OR DUTCH)   Beer.

BIÈRE (FR AND BELGIUM)   Beer.

BIERHALLE (GERM)   Beer hall. Also known as *bierstube*.

BIERSTUBE (GERM)   *See* Bierhalle.

BIG   A rich powerful, full-bodied and intensely-flavored wine. Big wines generally are high in alcohol, tannin, and/or extract. Both dry and sweet wines can be full-bodied or light-bodied. Beers that have high levels of malt and hops are also referred to as big. *See* Robust.

BIGOT (FR)   A special hoe occasionally used in parts of northern Rhône Valley vineyards.

BIJELO (YUG)   *See* White.

BILBERRY   A species of North American blueberry occasionally used in the production of fruit-flavored liqueurs or brandies.

BILGE   The greatest diameter or widest part, which is at the center of the staves on a wooden barrel.

BILLY (AUSTRAL)   A term for a tin container used for boiling water to make tea.

BINA (SP)   A yearly carried-out labor consisting of lightly dug earth, which is then "flattened" to make the surface more compact, thus avoiding evaporation of moisture during the dry season.

BIN CARD   A small storeroom card, usually attached to shelves for each beverage item that shows the bin number and stock on hand. It is a form of a perpetual inventory.

BINNING   Putting away or storing bottles of wine in the cellar for further aging.

BIOR   Israeli term for beer.

BIR   Indonesian term for beer.

BIRA   Bulgarian or Turkish term for beer.

BIRCH BEER   A sweetened, carbonated soft drink flavored with sap from the black birch tree.

BIRD-BATH GLASS   *See* Saucer-Shaped Glass.

BIRRA (ITAL)   Beer.

BIRRE   Albanian term for beer.

BIRU   Japanese term for beer.

BISCHOF (GERM)   Bishop.

BISER (YUG)   *See* Sparkling Wine.

BISHOP   One of the many versions of a mulled wine. It is made from port wine, sugar, spices, and an orange stuck with cloves. The drink is then heated and served warm.

BISON VODKA   *See* Zubrówka.

BISTRO (FR)   A small outdoor cafe or restaurant where wine is served.

BITARTRATES   *See* Tartrates.

BITE   Infers a substantial degree of acidity and/or tannin and alcohol, generally from excessive levels of any of these.

BITTER (GERM)   *See* Bitter.

BITTER   A term related to amber-colored, well-hopped beers that display a rather strong alcohol content. A strong ale with certain levels of hops or barley will also exhibit levels of bitterness. Also an English term for dark, bitter beers. If measured by utilizing European Bitterness Units, it refers to the degree of bitterness in the hops.

BITTER   A sharp, often unpleasant taste sensation found in wine due to excessive levels of tannin; acrid as quinine or peach stones. Excessive tannin is extracted during crushing, fermentation, or excessive pressing of the stems, skins, or seeds. Also known as *amango, amargo, amaro, amer*, and *pikrós*.

BITTER   One of the four basic sensations recognized by the taste buds, the others being salt, acid, and sweetness. Bitterness is detected on the palate on the rear, flat part of the tongue.

BITTERNESS   The taste in wine caused by excessive levels of bitters.

BITTER ROT   Recognized as a disease of grapes since 1887. The name was derived from the bitter taste that develops in infected berries. Bitter rot is caused by the fungus *Melanconium fuligi neaum*.

BITTERS   Distilled spirits containing an infusion of bittering compounds such as herbs, roots, or barks. The basic elements are certain aromatic herbs, such as gentian, rhubarb, quinquina or quinine, saffron, calamus or sweet rush, and centaury, among others. Bitters usually contain alcohol and were originally produced to soothe and relax the stomach after meals, and therefore are often referred to as "digestives." They are also used as a medicine or tonic and as an ingredient in some cocktails. Also served as apéritifs or digestives. *See* Digestive.

BITTER STOUT   *See* Stout.

BITTERSWEET   A characteristic generally attached to bitters or some beers that display an underlying bitterness while at the same time are also sweet.

BIYAR (IND)   Beer.

BJALO (BUL)   *See* White.

BLACK   Opaque-colored, sometimes used when describing stout or porter-type beers.

BLACK   Coffee served minus milk, cream, or other products used to "lighten" its color.

BLACK AND TAN   Equal parts of stout and british ale.

BLACKBERRY-FLAVORED BRANDY   A mixture of brandy, with a minimum of 2.5 percent sugar, and flavored and colored with blackberries. By federal law it cannot be bottled at less than 70 proof (35 percent alcohol by volume).

BLACKBERRY LIQUEUR   A sweetened alcoholic beverage consisting of a base of alcohol, minimum 2.5 percent sugar, and flavored and colored with blackberries. It is sweeter and lower in proof than blackberry-flavored brandy.

BLACK COFFEE   Often-used term when referring to or ordering espresso coffee.

BLACK CURRANT   A smell characteristic of some red wines, especially Cabernet Sauvignon.

BLACK CURRANT LIQUEUR   *See* Cassis.

BLACK DEATH   *See* Akvavit.

BLACK HAMBURG   *See* Schiava Grossa.

BLACKISH   An extremely young red wine, usually very tannic, which often takes a long time to mature.

BLACK MUSCAT   *See* Muscat Hamburg.

BLACK OLIVES   An odor often found in wines made from Cabernet Sauvignon or Cabernet Franc grapes.

BLACK PATENT   Malted barley that has been roasted for a prolonged period of time at a high temperature until it is black in color and displays a bitter-sweet taste.

BLACK ROT   A fungus rot of the grapevine caused by the fungus *Guignardia bidwellii*, usually occurring in moist areas with relatively high humidity. This disease appears as black spots on the leaves of the grapevine and shrivels the fruit.

BLACK SPANISH   *See* Lenoir.

BLACKSTRAP MOLASSES   *See* Molasses.

BLACK ST. PETER   *See* Zinfandel.

BLACK TEA   A rolled, dried leaf of the tea plant, fully fermented (or "finished") and fired through drying ovens to stop further oxidation. It accounts for more than 90 percent of the tea consumed in the United States.

BLACK VELVET   A mixture of stout and champagne popular in England during the Edwardian days (nineteenth century). It was created when Prince Albert died, which sent Queen Victoria (mother of Edward VII, King of England 1901–1910), along with the entire country into shock. They shrouded everything in black, including champagne, which was mixed with stout.

The Black Velvet has had a resurgence in popularity; today, ginger ale is usually substituted because of the high cost of champagne.

BLACK ZINFANDEL   *See* Zinfandel.

BLADE   The flat, expanded portion of a leaf on a grapevine.

BLANC (FR)   *See* White.

BLANC D'ANJOU (FR)   *See* Chenin Blanc.

BLANC DE BLANCS (FR)   White wine made entirely from white grapes. Champagnes or sparkling wines so labeled are usually "lighter" in body. Also known as *weisswein*.

BLANC DE NOIRS (FR)   White wine made entirely from black grapes. Champagnes or sparkling wines so labeled are usually "fuller" in body.

BLANC DOUX (FR)   *See* Sémillon.

BLANC FUMÉ (FR)   The local name for the Sauvignon Blanc grape variety around the town of Pouilly-sur-Loire, in the Loire Valley. *See* Sauvignon Blanc.

BLANCO (SP)   *See* White.

BLAND   A mild, neutral wine, with modest discernible odor or taste.

BLANK (GERM)   A wine that is said to be bright.

BLASS (GERM)   Pale; lacking in color.

BLAU (GERM)   Blue; a term used to describe the "red" or "black" color grapes.

BLAUBURGUNDER (GERM)   *See* Pinot Noir.

BLAUER PORTUGIESER (GERM)   A red grape variety that produces wines that are mild, with a delicate spicy flavor, and characterized by a deep red color. The grape variety was brought to the Rheinpfalz in the middle of the nineteenth century. Its country of origin is Hungary/Austria, where it has been cultivated for centuries past. The origin does not indicate Portuguese origin. Also known as *Portugieser*.

BLAUER SPÄTBURGUNDER (AUS)   *See* Pinot Noir.

BLEICHERT (GERM)   *See* Rosé Wine.

BLENDED AMERICAN WHISKEY   A mixture that contains at least 20 percent of straight whiskey on a proof basis and, separately or in combination, whiskey or neutral distilled spirits. A blended whiskey containing not less than 51 percent, on a proof gallon basis, of one of the types of straight whiskey shall be further designated by that specific type of straight whiskey; for example, "blended rye whiskey" (rye whiskey—a blend). The blending usually takes place after the whiskies reach full maturity; they are then allowed to rest for further aging. Caramel coloring is usually added prior to bottling.

Blended whiskies made with distilled neutral spirits will carry a label on the back of the bottle showing the percentages of distilled neutral spirits and straight whiskies contained.

BLENDED AND BOTTLED BY   The bottler/packer must have produced the final wine by the simple mixing of two or more wines without changing the class or type of the wines used.

BLENDED APPLEJACK   A mixture that contains at least 20-percent apple brandy (applejack) on a proof gallon basis, stored in oak containers for not less than two years, and not more than 80 percent of distilled neutral spirits, on a proof gallon basis, if such mixture at the time of bottling is not less than 80 proof. *See* Applejack.

BLENDED SCOTCH WHISKY   A blend of pot-stilled malt whiskies with whiskies produced in Scotland by the column still method from a cereal mix that may contain unmalted as well as malted barley and other grains.

The blended Scotches, as we know them today, did not really come into existence until about 1860. Prior to that, Scotches were distilled in old-fashioned pot stills at lower proof levels, which produced Scotches with a full body and heavy taste. In 1832, the continuous still was perfected by Aeneas Coffey, for use in the distillation of Scotch whisky. This enabled distillers to produce a lighter-bodied and flavored Scotch whisky, which were then blended with the heavier malted Scotches. In 1853, in Edinburgh, Andrew Usher produced the first blended Scotch whisky.

BLENDING   One of three methods of incorporating ingredients into a cocktail by use of an electric blender.

BLENDING   Wines are blended for several reasons. In a given growing season, for instance, two red grapes might ripen completely, but one of the grapes may be deficient in natural acidity and the second grape have an excess of it. By blending together these two wines, the acid level will even out somewhat, producing a relatively smooth wine. Other factors, among which are the amount of sugar, the pH, flavonoids, anthocyanins (red pigmentation), and total phenolics (tannin), must be considered prior to the blending. Blending two or more wines together either from the same or different years, creates a synergistic effect; the total is greater than the sum of its parts. In addition, with blending, a consistent product can be produced year after year that some winemakers often call the "house style." The same concept is also applied to beers and distilled spirits. Also known as *coupage, cutting wine, marrying wines, taglio, verschneiden,* and *vino da taglio. See* Nonvintage and Reserve Wine.

BLIND   Slang term for being drunk.

BLIND RECEIVING   Receiving goods either without an accompanying invoice, or with an invoice that contains no more than the names of the items delivered. Information relative to quantity, quality, weight, and price are omitted from the invoice. The receiver is then forced to count, weigh, and record each item individually.

BLIND TASTING   An evaluative tasting of alcoholic beverages without knowledge of the name of the product, the brand name, the country of origin, the vintage year, and so on. It forces the taster to concentrate on quality and other sensory perceptions rather than predisposed decisions based on bias.

BLIND TIGER   A place of concealment where illicitly made distilled spirits can be purchased.

BLISTERS   Blemishes that occur inside the glass during the glass-making process. These blemishes resemble air bubbles.

BLOCKADER   Slang term for one engaged in the transportation or possible sale of untax-paid distilled spirits.

BLOND   Beer that is deep yellow-golden in color.

BLONDE & RED HEAD   A cocktail consisting of equal parts of white (dry or sweet) and red vermouth.

BLOOD ALCOHOL LEVEL (BAC)   Blood alcohol concentration is a measurable level of the amount of alcohol found in the human body at a given time. It reflects the amount of alcohol a person has consumed and is expressed in a percentage.

BLOODY MARY   A cocktail created by Ferdinand Petiot, a bartender at Harry's Bar in Paris in the 1920s. It was named after Queen Mary I of England who, because of her persecution of Protestants, attained the nickname Bloody Mary. It was later called a "Bucket of Blood," then "Red Snapper," and "Morning Glory." It was introduced into the United States in the 1930s. It consists of vodka, tabasco sauce, worcestershire sauce, tomato juice, lemon juice, salt, and pepper.

BLOOM   In the vineyard, it is the time when the young flowers open and caps (calyptras) fall from the flowers.

BLOOM   The visible white, powdery coating of the grape berry. It is a waxy material produced by the fruit (not yeast cells), even though a considerable yeast population may stick to it. It is more noticeable on dark-colored grapes.

BLUE ANCHOR   The first American tavern is said to have been the "Blue Anchor," a safe haven for seafaring men. It opened its doors early in the 1600s in Philadelphia.

BLUE IMPERIAL (AUSTRAL)   *See* Cinsaut.

BLUE LAWS   State and local laws that regulate or prohibit certain business operations on Sunday.

BLUME (GERM)   Aroma or bouquet.

BLUMIG (GERM)   Flower.

BLUSH WINE   Basically a white wine made by limited skin contact (several hours) with black grapes, extracting a hint of color.

BNIA (FR)   *See* Bureau National Interprofessionel de l'Armagnac.

BNIC (FR)   *See* Bureau National Interprofessionel du Cognac.

BOAL (PORT)   Semisweet Madeira wine. Also spelled *bual*.

BOCK BEER   It is produced from grain that is considerably higher in extracts than the usual grains destined for use in lager beers. Bock, in German, means a male goat. Bock beer was originally produced around 1200 a.d. in the town of Einbeck, Germany. Today it is produced in virtually every country, in one form or another, on a seasonal basis, mostly during the winter so that it can be consumed in the early spring. Bock beers are usually quite dark in color with an intense, sharp, sweet aroma. They have a full-bodied flavor, followed by a slightly sweet, malty taste. A stronger version produced in very limited quantities in Germany is called Doppelbock. Bock beer is ideally served at 45 degrees to 50 degrees Fahrenheit. Also spelled *bockbier*. *See* Maibock.

BOCKBIER (GERM)   *See* Bock Beer.

BOCKSBEUTEL   An unusual, short, flat-sided, "flask-shaped" bottle used in Franconia, Germany, parts of Chile, and Portugal. Also spelled *boxbeutel*.

BÖCKSER (GERM)   The smell of rotten eggs. *See* Hydrogen Sulfide.

BOCOY (SP)   A large barrel with a capacity of approximately 160 U.S. gallons. *See* Barrel.

BODEGA (PORT, SO. AMERICA, SP)   Literally, a wine storage and aging cellar, but the term is also used to designate the producer and shipper.

BODEGUERO (SP)   *See* Winemaker.

BODENGESCHMACK IM WEIN (GERM)   *See* Earthy.

BODY   The tactile sensation of weight or fullness (roundness) on the palate usually from a combination of alcohol, extracts, glycerin, possibly residual sugar, tannin, and other physical components. Light-bodied wines tend to be low in alcohol, tannin, and extract. Full-bodied wines tend to be alcoholic, tannic, and, if white, occasionally sweet. Also known as *corpo, corps*, and *cuerpo*.

BOILER   Any container, such as a still, evaporator, kettle, or cooker, where clarified wort or cooked mash are added for boiling in either brewing or distillation. Also known as a *brew kettle*.

BOILERMAKER   A shot of whiskey drunk straight and immediately followed by a glass of beer.

BOIRE (FR)   To drink.

BOISÉ (FR)   Woody; an odor or flavor obtained after long maturing in wood.

Bolo (ital)   The blob of molten glass that is gathered on the end of a metal tube prior to being "blown" and shaped by a glass blower.

Bomba (sp)   A pump or siphon necessary for moving wine from tank to tank.

Bombed   Slang for intoxicated.

Bombona (sp)   A large glass jar or bottle occasionally used to age certain wines outdoors.

Bommes (fr)   Sweet, white wine made from a blend of Sauvignon Blanc, Sémillon, and Muscadelle grape varieties. It is also one of the five communes within Bordeaux's Sauternes district entitled to be called "Sauternes."

Bonde (fr)   *See* Spile.

Bonded Wine Cellar   A wine premises designated a bonded winery is also a bonded wine cellar. *See* Bonded Wine Premises and Bottled-In-Bond.

Bonded Wine Premises   Operations in untax-paid wine are authorized to be conducted. *See* Bonded Wine Cellar, Bonded Wine Ware house, Bonded Winery, Bottled-In-Bond, and In Bond.

Bonded Wine Warehouse   Bonded warehouse facilities on wine premises by a warehouse company or other person for the storage of wine and allied products for credit purposes. *See* Bonded Wine Premises and Bottled-In-Bond.

B
49

Bonded Winery   Wine production operations are conducted and other authorized operations may be conducted. *See* Bonded Wine Premises and Bottled-In-Bond.

Bone Charcoal   Ground charcoal used to clarify wine.

Bone Dry   A meaningless term that usually denotes wines with no residual sugar that often display a certain austerity.

Bonne-Chauffe (fr)   The second distillation in the cognac process.

Bon goût (fr)   A good or pleasing taste.

Bontemps (fr)   A small, shallow, wooden or ceramic bowl, traditionally used in the Bordeaux region for mixing of egg whites for fining purposes.

Bonus Case   Any case where the number of bottles included in the case varies from the standard configuration (i.e., 15 bottles of 750 ml instead of 12). These cases are usually used in introducing a product or in special promotions.

Bootlegger   It was a practice of stagecoach travelers to conceal a pint-sized, thick-glass, flat bottle in their boot, to have refilled at taverns along their way. It was also a practice of secreting bottles of distilled spirits for later illegal sale to the Indians.

Booze   From E. G. Booz, a grocer in Philadelphia around 1840. He used to bottle and sell bourbon whiskey, which he bought in barrels.

Bor (hun)   *See* Wine.

BORACHO (PORT)   A goatskin, which in ancient times was utilized to transport wine.

BORDEAUX (FR)   One of France's six major wine-producing regions famous for its red and white wines. Major districts include Médoc, Saint-Emilion, Pomerol, Graves, and Sauternes.

In May of 1152, Eleanor of Aquitaine, age 30, heiress to William X, Duke of Aquitaine, divorced Louis VII, King of France (1137–1180), and married Henri Plantagenet (Henry II), age 19, King of England. As her dowry, she gave him all of the land that was then called "Aquitaine," now known as Bordeaux.

BORDEAUX-BOTTLE   A bottle shape originating in Bordeaux, France. It can easily be recognized by its regular cylindrical form, characterized by a short neck and high shoulders. The 750-ml bottle traditionally used in the Bordeaux region.

BORDEAUX BLANC (FR)   French white table wine, from the Bordeaux region, which can be dry or sweet.

BORDEAUX MIXTURE   A blend of copper sulfate and slaked lime, used as a fungicide spray in the vineyards against oïdium, mildew, and other disorders. First introduced into Europe from the United States in 1878. Also known as *bouillie Bordelaise*. *See* Fixed Copper and Lime.

BORDEAUX ROUGE (FR)   French dry, red table wine.

BORDEAUX SHIPPER   Red and white table wines sold in barrels from vineyards to shippers who bottle and then sell the wine.

BORDEAUX WINE ACADEMY   Modeled after the French Academy and resembling it in its statues, constitution, and aims, the Bordeaux Wine Academy was created in February 1948. It is intended to defend, protect, and maintain the purity and quality of Bordeaux wines. There are 40 academicians, who make up a forum of connoisseurs and counselors of unequaled competence.

BORDELAISE (FR)   The name of the inhabitants of Bordeaux.

BORDELAISE BOTTLE (FR)   The traditional, narrow, high-shouldered bottle, which now contains 750 milliliters.

BORDELESAS (SP)   A barrel with a capacity of 225 liters (59 U.S. gallons). *See* Barrel.

BORE   *See* Worm.

BORRACHO (SP)   Drunk.

BORGOGNA BIANCO (ITAL)   *See* Pinot Blanc.

BORGOGNO NERO (ITAL)   *See* Pinot Noir.

BOSADOR (SP)   *See* Fermentation Lock.

BOTA (SP)   A bag, usually made of goatskin from which some Spaniards and Portuguese like to squirt wine into the mouth. Also a sherry butt or barrel with a capacity of approximately 130 U.S. gallons. *See* Barrel.

BOTA CHICA (SP)   *See* Barrel.

BOTA BODEGUERA (SP)   *See* Barrel.

BOTA DE EMBARQUE (SP)   *See* Barrel.

BOTA DE RECIBO (SP)   *See* Barrel.

BOTA GORDA (SP)   *See* Barrel.

BOTANICALS   Those parts of a plant suitably used for the production of various alcoholic beverages. They include roots, stems, barks, leaves, flowers, berries, fruit, beans, seeds, pits, stems, skins, and so on.

BOTELLA (SP)   *See* Bottle.

BOTRYTICIN   An antibiotic substance produced during fermentation that inhibits total fermentation of sugars in the *must*.

BOTRYTIS CINEREA   (From the Greek *botrus*, grape, and the Latin *cineris*, ashes or cinders). Botrytis is an ugly, hairy mold, gray or even pinkish-brown in color. This mold is present as spores at all times in most vineyards. Depending on the grape variety, the time of year, and climatic conditions, it can greatly enhance or severely damage the grapes in a vineyard. Johannisberg Riesling, Sauvignon Blanc, and Sémillon are the grape varieties most susceptible to Botrytis attack.

Affected berries may resemble dessicated, cracked raisins, but do not have the caramelized taste of a raisin. Long threads resembling spikes penetrate the skins, allowing the spores to grow safely inside, protected by the biological barrier. There is no exposure of the pulp or juice to air.

The action of the *micellae* of the mold causes dehydration. Water is evaporated as sugar concentration increases some 30 percent to 40 percent. Flavor, grape acids, grape essence, and aromatic compounds in the remaining juice are greatly magnified. Glycerin is produced in high levels, giving the wine a soft, almost oily tinge on the tongue and palate.

For the production of sweet wines, high humidity from an early rainfall or fog just before harvest time allows moisture to form on the surface of the fruit. If this is followed by dry, warm (60 degrees to 70 degrees Fahrenheit) air, the desired Botrytis growth can form in as little as 18 hours. If, on the other hand, the high humidity is followed by cold weather and the skins crack, a deleterious infection will occur. The fungus that forms on the moist grape skins is quite uneven in any given grape cluster and will often require multiple pickings, berry by berry, to obtain the maximum amount of berries.

The grapes that have been attacked by the "noble rot" are extremely overripe and may be handpicked individually after the ripeness has been determined. From each bunch of grapes the pickers might select one or two berries for use. The same vineyard might have to be picked over several times in order to obtain all the affected grapes. It is said that it takes one picker one full day to pick enough grapes to produce one bottle of this sweet wine. Obviously, the result is an extremely high cost of production.

Wines made from these grapes are yellow to gold-amber in color with a distinctive honeylike, raisiny character. They are extremely sweet and have an unusually long bottle life, lasting easily five to ten years, and if from an excellent vintage, as long as 50 years or more.

Botrytis is also known as *Botrytis bunch rot* (or simply *bunch rot*), *edelfäule*, *muffa nobile*, *noble rot*, and *pourriture noble*. *See* Dessicated Grapes.

BOTRYTIZED   Wines made from grapes affected by the noble rot (Botrytis cinerea).

BOTTE (ITAL)   *See* Barrel.

BOTTE MADRE (SP)   "Mother-Barrel," the solera system as used in the production of sherry wines.

BOTTIGLIA (ITAL)   *See* Bottle.

BOTTLE   A container four liters or less in capacity, regardless of the material from which it is made, used to store wine or to remove wine from the wine premises.

BOTTLE   A glass container that typically holds 750 milliliters (25.4 fluid ounces). Derived from the French *bouteille*, which in turn was probably from *bautille*, the familiar wine flask. While early bottles had many names, such as flask, flagon, and carafe, only a vessel containing wine could correctly be called a bouteille. Also known as *botella, bottiglia, flasche*, and *garrafa*.

BOTTLE AGING   Term that refers to the aging process, which takes place in the bottle at the winery and/or in private cellars.

As used in sparkling wines, it allows the sparkling wine to acquire complexity, depth, and fine texture in the bottle. Also known as aging *on-the-yeast, sur lies*, or *en tirage. See* Aging, Barrel Aging, Mature, Ripe, and Ripe for Bottling.

BOTTLE-BREAKER   A motor-driven machine utilized for the destruction of empty bottles by means of steel bars. Also known as *bottle crusher* or *bottle disposer*.

BOTTLE CHUTE   A flexible cylindrical tube where empty bottles are conveyed to the bottle-breaker for eventual destruction.

BOTTLE CLUB   Slang for a bar.

BOTTLE CODING   A special code put onto each bottle as it leaves the storeroom to the bar as a means of controlling inventory.

BOTTLE CRUSHER   *See* Bottle-Breaker.

BOTTLED-IN-BOND   Whiskey that is bottled-in-bond is mandated by federal regulations to be produced by one distillery in one distilling season, aged a minimum of four years in new charred oak barrels, and bottled at 100 proof. Whiskey that is bottled-in-bond has also been stored and bottled in a Treasury

Department bonded warehouse; no excise tax is paid on the whiskey until the beverage is withdrawn or shipped from the warehouse. The term bonded on the label, therefore, does not refer to quality; it means nothing more than that the treasury agent was present to collect the taxes. *See* Bonded Wine Premises and In Bond.

BOTTLE DISPOSER *See* Bottle-Breaker.

BOTTLED SUNSHINE Slang term used by the British during World War II for a bottle or can of beer.

BOTTLED WATER Water that is sealed in bottles or other containers and intended for human consumption.

BOTTLE FERMENTED On a sparkling wine label, the term means that the secondary fermentation took place in the bottle or that the transfer method was used. It could also apply to all méthode champenoise–produced sparkling wines.

BOTTLE-FOR-BOTTLE The practice of turning in an empty bottle for a full one as a means of inventory checks and balances. Also known as *empty-bottle return*.

BOTTLE LABEL A paper label suitably glued onto the front and sometimes rear flat part of a glass bottle that depicts certain mandatory information.

BOTTLE MAKING MACHINES In 1903, the routine use of paper labels closely followed the invention of the fully automatic bottle making machines by Michael J. Owen, plant manager of Libbey Glass Company of Toledo, Ohio.

BOTTLE MARKING The practice of marking bottles of alcoholic beverages by means of stickers, adhesive labels, magic markers, and so on, in order to identify them as house property. The marked bottles are then recorded in a ledger and placed into use.

BOTTLE NECKER Coupon, rebate, or other attention-getting promotion vehicle that fits around the neck of a bottle.

BOTTLER A proprietor of wine premises who fills wine into a bottle.

BOTTLE SALES INCOME SYSTEM A method of estimating the sales potential and income expected to be generated by the sale of each bottle of alcoholic beverage.

BOTTLES & BINS It is the oldest winery newsletter (since July 1949) in California. It is published by the Charles Krug Winery of Napa Valley.

BOTTLESCREW The original name for a corkscrew used around 1750. *See* Corkscrew.

BOTTLE SHOCK *See* Bottle Sickness.

BOTTLE SICKNESS A stage that may affect a wine just after bottling. During it, the aroma, flavor, and/or balance of a wine may be temporarily diminished. It affects some wines and is characterized by a flat, lifeless taste. Also known as *bottle shock*.

BOTTLE SIZES The BATF has authorized only certain metric sizes for wines and distilled spirits sold in the United States.

WINES (ALL TYPES)

BOTTLE SIZE	CAPACITY IN OUNCES	(OTHER NAMES)
15 liters	507	Nebuchadnezzar
9 liters	304.2	Salmanazar
6 liters	202.8	Imperial
4 liters	135.2	
3 liters	101.4	Double Magnum or Jeroboam
1.5 liters	50.8	Magnum
1 liter	33.8	
750 milliters	25.4	Standard-size bottle
500 milliters	16.9	
375 milliters	12.7	Half-bottle
187 milliters	6.3	Split
100 milliters	3.4	

DISTILLED SPIRITS (ALL TYPES)

BOTTLE SIZE	CAPACITY IN OUNCES
1.75 liters	59.2
1 liter	33.8
750 milliters	25.4
500 milliters	16.9
200 milliters	6.8
50 milliters	1.7

BOTTLES SUR LATTE (FR) Bottles laid horizontally during the "prise de mousse" (secondary fermentation of sparkling wine) and aging processes. They formerly used wooden slats in order to make the piles of bottles more stable.

BOTTLES SIR POINTE (FR) Bottles placed neck downwards, awaiting "dégorgement" (expulsion of the sediment) in sparkling wine production.

BOTTLE STINK An odor occasionally found in some wines that may be an indication of bacterial spoilage or winemaking flaw. The odor may dissipate with aeration. *See* Moldy, Mousy, and Musty.

BOTTLE TROUGH *See* Speed Rack.

BOTTLING The procedure of packaging all types of alcoholic beverages, usually in glass containers.

BOTTOM-FERMENTED   A process that refers to beers produced by the use of a type of yeast (lager yeast), which will generally convert sugars to alcohol and CO_2 at lower temperatures, at the tank's bottom. The most common type of bottom-fermented beer is lager, which ferments at cooler temperatures for a longer period of time than ales (which are top-fermented beers).

BOTTOMS   *See* Lees.

BOUCHÉ (FR)   *See* Corked.

BOUCHET (FR)   The local name in Saint-Emilion and Pomerol for the Cabernet Franc grape variety. *See* Cabernet Franc.

BOUCHON (FR)   *See* Cork.

BOUCHON DE TIRAGE (FR)   The temporary cork sometimes used to close the bottle during secondary fermentation of sparkling wines.

BOUCHON D'EXPÉDITION (FR)   The final cork used in a finished bottle of sparkling wine.

BOUCHONNÉ (FR)   *See* Corked.

BOUILLAGE (FR)   In the production of champagne, the fermentation.

BOUILLEURS DE PROFESSION (FR)   Professional distillers.

BOUILLIE BORDELAISE (FR)   *See* Bordeaux Mixture.

BOUQUET   The various fragrances noted by smell, created by a wine's development, and imparted to the wine from the fermentation and aging process, whether in barrel or bottle. The many acids present and the combination of organic acids with alcohol are vital contributions to the wine's bouquet. Also known as *anthosimía, arôme, bouqueté* and *bukett. See* Aroma and Nose.

BOUQUETÉ (FR)   *See* Bouquet.

BOURBEUX (FR)   Bright. *See* Falling Bright.

BOURBON AND BRANCH   *See* Branch Water.

BOURBON LIQUEUR   A liqueur bottled at not less than 60 proof, in which not less than 51 percent, on a proof gallon basis, of the distilled spirits used is bourbon whiskey, which possess a predominant characteristic bourbon flavor derived from such whiskey.

BOURBON WHISKEY   Bourbon whiskey is a distinctive whiskey of Kentucky, made predominantly from corn. Federal regulations require that bourbon whiskey be made from a minimum of 51 percent corn; generally, 65 to 75 percent is used. When the corn in the mash reaches 80 percent, the product by government definition, becomes corn whiskey—not bourbon. The higher the corn content and the lower the percentage of other grains, the lighter the whiskey. The blend of the other grains is dictated by the distiller's own private formula; rye, wheat, or barley malt can be used in the grain mix.

The bourbon must be barreled at not less than 80 proof and not more than 125 proof. The raw bourbon is then put into new, large charred white oak barrels ranging in capacity from 50 to 66 gallons.

Bourbon whiskey, by law, must be aged for a minimum of two years. Most distillers age their bourbon anywhere from four to ten years.

BOURGEOIS GROWTHS (FR)   *See* Cru Bourgeois.

BOURGOGNE (FR)   *See* Burgundy.

BOURGOGNE OAK (FR)   A forest in the hills behind and on the plains in front of the Côte d'Or, in Burgundy, noted for its production of wooden barrels, similar to Allier in terms of hardness. Bourgogne oak has a medium-open grain, with moderate flavor and tannin extraction. It displays some of the buttery flavors of Nevers, with a bitter, slightly weedy component. Bourgogne oak helps soften wine's acidity and gives a slightly richer feel to the wine. Bourgogne is traditionally used for Pinot Noir, Gamay, Sauvignon Blanc, Sémillon, and barrel-fermenting of Chardonnay. It gives a very rich vanilla character that mingles beautifully with the fruit in the wine.

BOURGUEIL (FR)   Red wine commune in Touraine, in the Loire Valley.

BOURGUIGNON NOIR (FR)   *See* Gamay.

BOURRET (FR)   The new wine in Gascony, Armagnac, destined for distillation.

BOURRU (FR)   Meaning surly or rude; used for a wine still resting on the lees that has not yet deposited its yeasts and impurities. With white wines, it applies to the fresh still-fermenting grape *must* of characteristically cloudy appearance.

BOUTIQUE WINERY   The name applied to small wineries of modest size and production, usually in reference to California wineries.

BOUTIQUE WINES   Wines made in very limited quantity by boutique wineries.

BOUTEILLE (FR)   *See* Bottle.

BOUTON (FR)   *See* Bud.

BOUTS (FR)   Hand-shaping of the soil at the ends of the rows of grapevines to facilitate drainage of the water.

BOUZY (FR)   The name of a *still* red wine produced in the village of Bouzy in the Champagne region.

BOWL   That part of a goblet or glass that contains the wine.

BOWLE (GERM)   A goblet that is filled with wine, fresh fruit, herbs, and occasionally liqueurs.

BOXBEUTEL   *See* Bocksbeutel.

BOXES   *See* Case.

BRACHETTO (ITAL)   A red grape variety grown in the Piedmont region where, according to DOC law, it produces a dry wine or slightly sweet spumante wine.

BRACKISH   A term sometimes applied to beers that display a salty taste.

BRAMBLE   A term used to describe the zesty, fruity, berrylike characteristic of wines made from the Zinfandel grape. Also known as *briary*.

BRANCH WATER   A Southern term for cold water, specifically from a small stream, creek, or brook, that is added to distilled spirits. One such drink is known as *Bourbon and Branch*.

BRANCO (PORT)   *See* White.

BRANDIG (GERM)   *See* Alkoholreich.

BRAND LABEL   The label carrying, in the usual distinctive design, the brand name of the wine.

BRAND NAME   Usually, the bottling or producing winery, brewery, or distillery owns the name so that competitors are barred from its use. Also known as *proprietary brand name, proprietary name*, or *proprietary wine*.

BRANDY   A spirit made by distilling (less than 190 proof) wines or the fermented mash of fruit, which then may or may not be aged in oak barrels. The varying characteristics of different brandies are the result of differences in fruit and grape varieties, climate, soil, and production methods, which vary from district to district and country to country. If a brandy is produced from fruits other than grapes, then the name of the fruit must be stated on the label.

The name brandy originates with the Dutch, who are believed to have been the first great connoisseurs of this drink; they called it *brandewijn*, meaning burnt wine. This referred to the process by which brandy was made: wine was heated and the resulting vapor distilled. This term was carried over into Germany as branntwein (weinbrand) and into France as brandevin. The English adopted the word as brandywine, which was later shortened to brandy. Also known as *gnôle*.

BRANDY GLASS   *See* Snifter.

BRANDY HEATER   A popular item, often sold in specialty stores or catalogues, which features a brandy snifter, perched at a 45-degree angle on a metal holder, above a short candle. According to the directions, pour some brandy into the glass, light the candle below the bowl of the glass, and allow the candle to gently warm the liquid. In reality, if one follows these directions, one will burn one's hands on the glass. And, subjected to an intensified heat, the brandy's vapors, which are an intrinsic part of its enjoyment, will "burn off." Also known as a *heater*.

BRANDY SNIFTER   *See* Snifter.

BRÄNNVIN   *See* Akvavit.

BRASSERIE (FR)   A brewery or small restaurant.

BRAWNY   A term loosely defined to mean a muscular red wine with high levels of tannin and alcohol. It usually refers to young red wines that are low in elegance, breed, and suppleness. *See* Powerful and Muscular.

Breakage   Losses in shipment.

Break-Even Point   The output at which costs just equal revenues, making the profits equal zero.

Breathing   The practice of allowing air to reach wine by uncorking and pouring it. Wine breathes to shed any unpleasant odors and bring out its aroma or bouquet. *See* Aeration and Decanting.

Breed   A wine of distinguished character and distinctive quality. A balance of qualities in good wine due to a combination of grapes, soil, and skill of the producer. Also known as *razza*.

Bref (Fr)   Brief or short. A wine that leaves no distinctive, pleasant, or lingering aftertaste.

Breit (Germ)   Uninteresting, dull.

Brenta (Ital)   A small tank with shoulder straps, carried on the back, that is filled with wine or *must* and then carried and dumped into another barrel. It is seldom used in today's winery. Also, small straw baskets used by grape pickers in which grapes are carried onto waiting trucks, in various parts of the world. Also known as *cunacho, portador,* and *tineta. See* Hotte de Vendange and Panier à Vendange.

Brepon (Ital)   *See* Molinara.

Breton (Fr)   The local name in the Loire Valley for the Cabernet Franc grape variety. *See* Cabernet Franc.

Brew   A slang term or name for a beer, especially draught.

Brew   To make coffee or tea by steeping or boiling in a liquid.

Brewage   Anything brewed, especially beer.

Brewer   One who brews beer. *See* Brewmaster.

Brewer's Yeast   *Saccharomyces cerevisiae,* a yeast that is specifically cultured and used in brewing beer.

Brewery   An establishment where beer is brewed.

Brewhouse   An archaic term for a brewery.

Brewing   The stage during the making of beer when wort is boiled in the presence of the hops.

Brewing Salt   Mixture of Epson salt, gypsum, noniodized salt, or other minerals, occasionally added to water, which is considered "too soft" for the fermentation of beer.

Brew Kettle   *See* Boiler.

Brewmaster   The master blender who oversees the entire brewing process. *See* Brewer.

Brewpub   A tavern that brews its own beer for on-premise consumption as well as off-premise sales. *See* Microbrewery.

BREWSTERS During the middle ages, name given to the female member of the family who was in charge of brewing in the home.

BRIARY *See* Bramble.

BRICCO (ITAL) A prime hilltop vineyard site.

BRICK A shade of red-brown often found in well-aged, mature red wines or slightly old red wines.

BRIGHT Often referred to as "falling bright." When a wine begins to naturally clarify shortly after fermentation has ceased. Also a wine crystal clear, free from suspended material, that affects the clarity of a wine. *See* Falling Bright.

BRILHANTE (PORT) *See* Brilliant.

BRILLANTE (ITAL OR SP) *See* Brilliant.

BRILLIANT The quality of a wine or beer when it is free from any visible, suspended solids or haziness, and has a sparkling clarity. Also known as *brilhante, brillante*, and *glanzhell.*

BRIOSO (ITAL) Lively, sprightly.

BRISK A wine that displays a high level of acidity, making it crisp and refreshing.

BRISTOL CREAM Specially blended sherries coming from Bristol, England. They are made by a secret blending of mostly amontillado and oloroso sherries, and additionally sweetened with P.X. grapes.

BRITISH GALLON *See* Imperial Gallon and Gallon.

BRITISH PROOF GALLON It is an Imperial gallon of 277.4 cubic inches containing 57.1 percent by volume of ethyl alcohol (50 percent of alcohol by weight). Same as Canadian Proof Gallon.

BRIX Name of a system (after Adolf F. Brix, 1870, a German scientist) used by American winemakers to measure the sugar content of grapes, *must*, and occasionally wine. A measure of total soluble solids in grape juice, more than 90 percent of which are fermentable sugars. Hence, degrees Brix essentially indicates sugar content. Brix is expressed as grams of sucrose in 100 grams of solution at 68 degrees Fahrenheit (20 degrees Celsius). For every gram per hundred grams of solution, the hydrometer reads "one degree brix." For most table wines, the usual range at the harvest is 20 to 25 degrees Brix. By multiplying the stated Brix at harvest by roughly 0.55, the potential alcohol by volume (if the wine were fermented to dryness) may be obtained. Also known as *Balling* in the United States; *Baumé* in France; *Essenz* in Hungary; *Klosterneuburg* in Austria; and *öechsle* in Germany. Also known as *degrees balling* or *degrees brix. See* Plato.

BROKEN CASE A case of bottles made up of several brands or types of wine or distilled spirits when purchased from a wholesale distributor. Same as a Split Case.

Broken Case Room   A locked storage room where opened cases of alcoholic beverages are stored.

Broken Orange Pekoe   *See* Orange Pekoe and Pekoe.

Broker   A middleman who could be an individual or firm that buys from the grower and sells to the shipper or is the shipper. An important player in distribution channels, the broker brings good, marketable wine to the trade. Also known as *commerciante, commissionaire, courtier, dealer, éleveur, négociant, négociant-eleveur, partidista, trader,* and *wine broker.*

Broker Commissions   Payments made to brokers for handling alcoholic beverages.

Bronze   The amber hue apparent around the rim of a glass of aged red or white wine.

Brou (Fr)   A sweet liqueur made from walnut shells.

Brouillis (Fr)   The heart of the first distillate in the making of cognac.

Brouilly (Fr)   The largest cru commune in Beaujolais.

Brown Ale   A dark brown or cocoa-colored ale that has a malty bouquet and bittersweet taste. It is light to medium in body, usually rather low in alcohol, and traditionally produced in Great Britain, Belgium, and occasionally Canada.

Brown Bagging   A practice of allowing customers in an on-premise unlicensed or occasionally licensed facility to bring in their own bottles of alcoholic beverages for consumption on the premise. Many facilities often charge a "corkage fee."

Brown Brandy   During the second half of the last century, there was a beverage made in France that consisted of brandy mixed with molasses.

Brown Goods   A term often used to describe those distilled spirits (gererally whiskey) that possess a *brown* color. Examples are blended, bourbon, Canadian, Irish, light, rye, Scotch, and Tennessee. *See* White Goods.

Brownian Movement   Irregular, random, and continuous erratic zigzag movement of minute microscopic solid particle (called colloidal) dispersions in a liquid medium, caused by collision with other molecules in the liquid. The small particles remain in suspension because they are kept agitated and vibrate by the normal movement of molecules in the liquid. This movement is unrelated to outside disturbances; however, variation in external temperature could influence this. This phenomena was first studied in 1827 by the Scottish Botanist Robert Brown.

Brown Sherry   An old British term for a particular type of dark sweet sherry wine from Spain.

Browning   The oxidative effect on the color, odor, and taste of a wine, which is past its prime or has been carelessly exposed to a prolonged period of aeration.

BRUGH-FER   An ancient Gaelic term for a brewer.

BRUISED BEER   Beer that has been cooled, allowed to return to room temperature, and then cooled again. A loss of carbonation and quality results.

BRÛLANT (FR)   Burning sensation given by an excess of alcohol in the wine; a warm sensation.

BRUNELLO (ITAL)   *See* Brunello di Montalcino and Sangiovese Grosso.

BRUNELLO DI MONTALCINO (ITAL)   An extremely full-bodied, dry red wine made 100-percent Sangiovese Grosso (also known as *Brunello*) in the Tuscany region. It is one of Italy's finest and longest-lived wines, and received its DOCG status on July 1, 1980.

The first documented use of the name Brunello was in 1842 when Canon Vincenzo Chiarini of Montalcino praised the wine produced from the Brunello grape. In 1862, Clemente Santi (of the Biondi-Santi family) first made a wine called "Brunello di Montalcino," which won several citations for its excellence at Expositions in London and Paris. However, it wasn't until 1880 that Ferruccio Biondi-Santi, grandson of Clemente Santi and son of Caterina (Clemente's daughter) and Jacopo Biondi, first discovered the clonal selection (subvariety) of the Sangiovese grape in his family vineyards called "Il Greppo."

In 1967, the producers of Brunello voluntarily formed a consorzio to establish a uniform price structure and quality control system. The seal of the consorzio is a south European evergreen oak with holly-like leaves on a green background. *See* Montalcino, Rosso di Montalcino, and Sangiovese Grosso.

BRUNNEN (GERM)   Fountain or stream.

BRUT   Very dry. Among the driest French champagnes. According to the European Common Market, brut champagnes contain less than 15 grams of sugar per liter (most brut champagnes have 8 to 10 grams per liter). When the term is used elsewhere, there is an absence of a legal definition as to the relative dryness or sweetness of the sparkling wine. Brut champagne was first produced in 1874 by Madame Pommery of the Pommery Champagne house. Also known as *bruto* and *strencherb*.

BRUT DE BRUT   *See* Extra Brut.

BRUTO (PORT OR SP)   *See* Brut.

BRUT SAUVAGE   *See* Extra Brut.

BRUT ZERO   *See* Extra Brut.

BUAL   The English spelling of Boal.

BUBBLY   A slang term for any wine that sparkles.

BUCK   A type of cocktail.

BUCKET   Slang term for an oversized (double) "rocks" glass.

BUCKET OF BLOOD   *See* Bloody Mary.

Bucket of Suds   A slang term for beer. *See* Suds.

Buckman's Tavern   When Paul Revere made his historic ride early April 19, 1775, notifying that the British were marching on Lexington, Massachusetts, he stopped at this tavern and relayed the message.

Bud   A compressed shoot located at the node of a cane. The bud of the grape is a compound bud, usually made up of three buds. The center bud at a node is the one that usually starts growth in the spring and produces the fruit. Often, one of the smaller buds will make a short growth but not produce any fruit. If a late frost kills the main shoot, another shoot will grow that will usually produce a half crop. Also known as *bouton* and *gemma*.

Bud break   As sap rises in a grapevine, its pressure increases, forcing the buds to swell until their protective cover, called corolla or calyptra, splits and the first tiny leaf, new shoots, and floral cluster emerges. This usually occurs about 45 days after the buds form.

Budding   Asexual form of reproduction occurring in yeasts.

Budding   *See* Field Grafting.

Budget   An operational plan for the income and expenditure of money for a given period.

Buffalo   A red grape variety developed from a cross of Herbert and Watkins, in 1938, at the New York State Experimental Station. Clusters and berries are large, loosely formed, and covered with a delicate blue bloom.

Buffalo Vodka   *See* Zubrówka.

Bukett (germ)   *See* Bouquet.

Bukettreich (germ)   A wine with a rich bouquet.

Bulk   Any container that has a capacity in excess of one wine gallon. In practice, shipments in bulk involve much larger containers.

Bulk Buying   Purchasing beverages in quantity, usually at a lower "as purchased" price per unit cost. Also called Discount Purchasing or Quantity Purchasing.

Bulk Container   Any container larger than 60 liters. *See* Container.

Bulk-Fermented   *See* Charmat Method.

Bulk Gallon   *See* Gallon.

Bulk Wine   *See* Jug Wine.

Bukettreich (germ)   Rich bouquet.

Bumper   A cup or glass filled to the brim with an alcoholic drink. An old English toast, "To Drink a Bumper."

Bunch Rot   Same as Botrytis Bunch Rot. *See* Botrytis Cinerea.

Bundessortenamt (germ)   Federal Bureau for Grape Cultivars.

Bung   A plug (usually cork, wood, or silicon) that fits into the opening at the top of a barrel for a tight seal. Bungs should be made of a fairly soft wood and definitely softer than the type of wood used for the barrel. It will swell faster and what's more, a hard wood bung could crack the wooden barrel's opening.

BUNG HOLE   The opening at the top of the barrel where liquids are added to and emptied from.

BUNGING   The process of "hammering" a bung into the bunghole of a barrel.

BUNGSTARTER   A rubber mallet used to either "tap" open or closed, a bung on a barrel. *See* Zwickle.

BURDIGALA (FR)   The name that the region of Bordeaux was known as when the Romans took it in 55 b.c. from the Celtic Gauls.

BUREAU OF ALCOHOL, TOBACCO, AND FIREARMS (BATF)   This bureau of the U.S. Department of the Treasury regulates the production, transportation, and sale of alcoholic beverages; enforces legal sale; and insures the collection of federal excise taxes that are sent to the Internal Revenue Service. Also known as *ATF*.

BUREAU NATIONAL INTERPROFESSIONEL DE L'ARMAGNAC (BNIA)   The professional body in Armagnac controlling and safeguarding the production and quality of Armagnac.

BUREAU NATIONAL INTERPROFESSIONEL DU COGNAC (BNIC)   A governing agency that oversees production, quality, labeling designations, and exportation for the cognac industry of France.

BURGER   A white grape variety grown in many parts of the world, producing mostly neutral tasting wines, with a pronounced aroma, suitable for sparkling wine production. Also known as *Elbling, Kleinberger,* and *Monbadon.*

BURGUNDY (FR)   One of France's six major wine-producing regions. It produces both red and white dry wines. Approximately 80 percent of the Burgundy wine produced is red; most of it is from the Côte de Nuits. The other 20 percent is white, mostly from the Côte de Beaune. Burgundy's four wine-producing districts (Sâone-et-Loire, Côte d'Or, Rhône, and Yonne), are known around the world. Burgundy is the northernmost great red wine-producing region in the world. Also known as *Bourgogne.*

BURGUNDY   Term used in the United States and Australia for generic red wines. They have little or no resemblance to the French product.

BURGUNDY-BOTTLE   A bottle of conical shape, although not regular in form and rather fat-bellied, used to house both red and white wines of Burgundy, France.

BURNED DRINKS   A standard drink served in a small glass so that there is only a small amount of mixer. *See* Overpouring and Short Drink.

BURNT   A wine having cooked or baked characteristics. Often descriptive of wines from Madeira, Portugal.

BURNT ALE *See* Pot Ale.

BUSCHENSCHANK (AUS) Seasonal wine taverns.

BUTT A barrel used to store or ship ale, sherry wine, or other wines. It varies in proportion to the area in which it is used. *See* Barrel.

BUTTAGE (FR) A ploughing method identical to the *chaussage* but deeper.

BUTTERMILK A cultured milk, minus the butterfat that has been treated with certain bacteria.

BUTTERY Term often used to indicate the characteristic odor and sometimes taste of creamy butter, usually associated with chardonnay wines. It is often encountered with chardonnay wines that undergo partial or complete malolactic fermentation prior to bottling.

BUTTONS UP An old Scandinavian custom at formal gatherings to drink as many toasts, often with aquavit or akvavit, as there were buttons on a man's dress coat.

BUTYRIC ACID A "spoiling" acid caused by micro-infection (bacteria) that gives a rancid odor (reminiscent of perspiration or rancid butter) and bitter, disagreeably acid taste to the wine or beer. Fortunately, its occurrence is now rare. Also known as *goût de rance*.

BUVETTE (FR) Slang for beer.

BUY BACKS A customary method of showing customer appreciation by management with a "free drink" offered for every three or four purchased. Not a legal term, nor widely practiced.

BUZA The name of an alcoholic beverage distilled from dates in Egypt.

BUZZING The now defunct custom of "buzzing" a bottle of port consisted of placing a wager on your ability to determine if the remaining port in a specified decanter could fit into your glass, without spilling a drop of the precious liquid. If you were correct and all fit, you were then "buzzed" (bought) a bottle by all of those who lost the wager. However, if you lost the wager, you would then have to "buzz" (buy) the winner a bottle. The bottles won would then have to be consumed during the setting! This is the origin of the expression "I feel quite a buzz on," or "I have a little bit of a buzz on," when referring to the inebriating effect that alcohol has on the body.

BYBLINE (GREECE) An ancient wine.

CABACEO (SP)   A wine blend or the blending of wine.

CABARET   A restaurant or nightclub providing live entertainment.

CABERNET FRANC   A red grape variety grown extensively in Bordeaux, France, where it is used in small amounts as a blending grape in the Médoc, as well as Pomerol and Saint-Emilion. Cabernet Franc also grows in other parts of France, including the Loire Valley. Some Cabernet Franc is also cultivated in California, Australia, Chile, throughout eastern Europe, and some northern regions of Italy. Cabernet Franc produces wines with a distinct aroma and taste of green olives, herbaceous, minty, and weedy. Also known as *Bouchet, Breton,* and *Carmenet.*

CABERNET SAUVIGNON   A major red grape variety predominant in the Médoc district of France, sometimes accounting for as much as 90 percent of blend; known locally in Graves as *Vidure.* The grape also flourishes in many countries of the world, including California, Chile, Italy, and Australia. Cabernet Sauvignon produces wines with a distinct aroma and taste of black tea, herbs, black or green olives, cedar, bell pepper, blackberry, and black currants. It is often referred to as the noblest of all red grape varieties.

CABINET (GERM)   Term used until July 1971 to denote a quality wine.

CAECUBAN   An ancient Roman wine.

CAFE   A coffeehouse or small restaurant serving alcoholic beverages.

CAFÉ (FR, PORT, OR SP)   *See* Coffee.

CAFÉ AU LAIT (FR)   Strong coffee with equal parts of scalded or hot milk added. Known as *caffèlatte* in Italian.

CAFÉ FILTRE (FR)   Coffee made by pouring hot water through ground coffee beans in a filtering device that fits over a cup or pot.

CAFÉ NOIR (FR)   Black coffee.

CAFFÈ (ITAL)   *See* Coffee.

Caffè Corretto (Ital)   An espresso coffee that has been "corrected" by the addition of grappa or other types of distilled spirits or bitters.

Caffeina (Ital)   Caffeine.

Caffeine   A crystalline, bitter-tasting, but odorless alkaloid present in coffee, tea, and certain soft drinks. It acts as a stimulant to the heart and central nervous system.

Caffèlatte (Ital)   *See* Café au Lait.

Caffè Ristretto (Ital)   A thicker, more concentrated version of espresso, usually one ounce or less. It is made by turning off the pump a few seconds sooner than normal.

Caffeol   The natural oil responsible for the characteristic odor and taste of coffee.

Cage   *See* Wire Hood.

Cajuada   A West African beverage made from fermented cashew nuts.

Cake   *See* Pomace.

Calabria (Ital)   One of 20 wine-producing regions. Calabria traces its history back more than 2,500 years when it was called *Magna Grecia* by the ancient Greeks who occupied this barren, dry region located at the "toe" of boot-shaped southern Italy.

Calcaire (Fr)   Limestone soil.

Calcium Alginate Beads   *See* Encapsulated Yeast.

Calcium Carbonate   Used to reduce the excess natural acids in high acid wines. Precipitated *chalk* is sometimes used for amelioration of the acidity. *See* Amelioration.

Calcium Sulfate (Gypsum)   Often used in the production of Spanish-type or *flor* sherry wine to lower the pH. *See* Plastering.

Caldo (Ital)   *See* Warmth.

Caler (Fr)   The attaching of each grapevine stem to a stake by means of tying.

California Brandy   All California brandy must be made, by law, from grapes grown and distilled in California. It must be aged a minimum of two years in oak barrels, and if aged for less time, it must be labeled an "immature brandy." For brandies that are aged more than two years, the age may be stated on the label.

There is no required grape variety for use in brandy production in California; many different varieties are used. Most distillers use the Thompson Seedless or Flame Tokay grapes, as they are inexpensive, nondescript, and produce a fairly good product.

California Grape Grower   The original name of Wines & Vines, a California alcoholic beverage industry magazine.

CALISAY (SP) A very bitter quinine-based liqueur that derives its taste from "cinchona bark," and other parts of a tree.

CALL BRAND *See* Call Liquor.

CALL LIQUOR Those brands of alcoholic beverages that have brand recognition for which the customer will "call" for by name. Also known as *call brand* or *name brand*.

CALORIC VALUE The number varies with the percent alcohol by volume and weight of sugar present in the finished product. To determine the calories of a dry wine, beer, or distilled spirit: 0.8 × proof × ounces = calories per drink size, but only the alcohol, not any added mixers, water, and so on.

CALVADOS An apple brandy, made from different varieties of apples that grow in the Normandy, Brittany, and Maine regions of northwest France. Calvados is actually an *eau-de-vie* of cider, or a brandy distilled from either cider or the juice of fresh apples. *See* Applejack.

CALYPTRA The fused petals of the grape that fall off the flower at anthesis. *See* Bud Break.

CALZIN A red grape variety introduced in 1958 by the University of California at Davis. It is a cross of Zinfandel and Refosco (Mondeuse).

CAMBIUM LAYER It is a thin, green layer just under the outer bark of grapevines that gives rise to new cells and promotes secondary growth. It is the artery of life for the grapevine.

CAMERA (SP) *See* Candling.

CAMPANIA (ITAL) One of 20 wine-producing regions, it is on the coast of the country south of Rome. Famous for its Lacryma Christi, Fiano di Avellino, and Taurasi wines.

CAMPBELL EARLY A red, French-American hybrid grape variety that was developed in the mid-1930s by George W. Campbell on Stretch Island in Washington State. Formerly known as *Island Belle*.

CAMPDEN TABLET A seven-grain tablet of potassium metabisulfite that dissolves in the *must* or wine and releases sulfur dioxide, which acts as a sterilant and antioxidant. *See* Antioxidant, Potassium Metabisulfite, and Sulfur Dioxide.

CAN A form of packaging for beer and some wines.

CANADA (PORT) An old Portuguese measure equal to 1.7 liters or approximately 59 U.S. fluid ounces.

CANADIAN PROOF GALLON *See* British Proof Gallon.

CANADIAN WHISKY (In Canada, it is spelled *whisky*.) Although Canadian whisky is a distinctive product of Canada, the Canadian government doesn't set regulations relative to the mixture of the grain blend, the proof level at which it is distilled, or the type of barrel used. Each distiller is allowed to make his or her own whisky as he or she sees fit. Canadian whisky is matured in white oak barrels (mostly used) and, for the American market, is bottled at a minimum of 80 proof. Canadian whisky is made only from grains (corn, rye, and barley malt) and may be bottled after three years of age. Canadian whisky sold in the United States is generally four to six years old. Canadian whisky cannot be designated as a "straight" whisky.

In 1891, a U.S. law required the country of origin to appear predominantly on a product's label. It was at this time that Canadian Club whisky started using the word, "Canadian" on its label.

CANADICE A red seedless grape variety developed from a cross of Bath and Himrod, at the New York State Experimental Station in 1977.

CANAIOLO NERO (ITAL) A red grape variety used in small proportions in the making of Chianti, Torgiano, and Vino Nobile di Montepulciano wines. The Canaiolo grape variety was already being cultivated in Tuscany during the thirteenth century.

CANARY SACK *See* Sack.

CANARY WINES Red and white wines from the Canary Islands of Spain, where only small quantities of wine are produced.

CAÑAS (SP) A small, stumpy, and cylindrical glass in which Manzanilla sherry is traditionally drunk.

CANCELLATION SYSTEM A system whereby the bartender or other service personnel tears, punches a hole through, or draws a red mark across the stub, indicating that drinks, which have been recorded on a guest's check, have in fact been served.

CANDIDA MYCODERMA *See* Flowers of Wine.

CANDLES Used as a substitute for paraffin on leaking wooden barrels. Candles are a necessary piece of equipment for decanting wines. Also necessary for *candling* (testing the clarity of) wine. *See* Candling.

CANDLING A process that determines the clarity and amount of sediment, if any, which has formed in the bottle. To candle the bottle, carefully hold it, horizontally, in front of an exposed light bulb (60 to 100 watts) so that light penetrates the glass, displaying any sediment on the bottom side of the bottle. Knowing which wines have started to "throw" sediment aids in serving wines. Also known as *camera* or *obscura*.

CANDYLIKE Attributes often associated with very young, fruity red wines vinified for early consumption. These wines display extremely fruity, berry-like aromas, likened to candy.

CANE The stem or woody structure of a grapevine on which leaves, flowers, and fruit grow. In autumn, after the leaves fall off, canes darken and harden. *See* Shoots.

CANE PRUNING With this method, each year at pruning time all of the extraneous growth is pruned from the grapevine, retaining only the strongest canes that will bear fruit the following fall. These canes, usually four, are tied to a two-tiered trellis for support. With cane pruning, the grapevine is vertical in its growth (except for the fruit-bearing canes), whereas with cordon pruning the grapevine is rather "T" shaped. The obvious advantage with the cane system over the head-trained system where the grapevine is shaped rather like a bush is that the grapevine is stretched out on a lateral plane and is considerably more open to sunlight and air. The one disadvantage of the cane system is that sometimes crop levels are hard to control. *See* Pruning and Spur Pruning.

CANE SUGAR   Sucrose, obtained from sugar cane, sometimes used in fermentation.

CANE WEIGHT   Related to potential crop by multiplying the weight by a factor in order to determine the number of buds (potential crop) that the grapevine could bear. Also known as *vine size*. *See* Vine Capacity.

CANNICI (ITAL)   Wicker or straw mats utilized for the drying of grapes that will be used in the *governo toscano* method of producing very young Chianti wine. Also known as *castelli*. *See* Governo.

CANOA (SP)   A wedge-shaped metal or wooden funnel used to fill wooden barrel with wine.

CANTINA   An establishment, generally found in Europe, which serves primarily wine and beer.

CANTINA (ITAL)   A winery or wine producer.

CANTINA SOCIALE (ITAL)   A cooperative winery.

CANTINE (ITAL)   Winery or wine cellar.

CANTINIERE (ITAL)   *See* Cellarmaster.

CANUTO (SP)   *See* Wine Thief.

CAP   during fermentation of red wine, the grape skins, stems, seeds, and so forth, rise to the surface of the tank or barrel due to the fact that pigments, flavonoids, tannins, and other compounds are being extracted, making the skins lighter than the *must*. When the skins reach the surface, they harden, forming what is known as the "cap" or "hat." Several times a day this cap must be broken up to allow the carbon dioxide gas to escape. It is also important for the skins to stay in contact with the fermenting juice, to aid extraction. To accomplish this, the wine is pumped from the bottom of the tank over the cap of floating skins and seeds at the top of the tank three times a day. Some wineries, with the aid of long paddles or oars, break up the cap and stir the skins back into the juice. Also known as *cappo, chapeau, hat*, and *manta*.

CAPATAZ (SP)   A cellarmaster as used in Jerez de la Frontera.

CAPE   *See* Alexander.

CAPITEUX (FR)   Heady; warmly rich or high in alcohol.

Capping Machine   A hand-operated device (it is seldom employed today) utilized for putting crown caps on soft-drink and beer bottles.

Cappo (Ital)   *See* Cap.

Cappuccino (Ital)   Espresso coffee served with a creamy head made from steamed or scalded milk or cream.

Cap Stem   The stem of individual flowers or grape berries.

Capsula (Ital)   *See* Capsule.

Capsule   A plastic, lead, or aluminum cover placed over the cork of a wine bottle to give a more secure closure and to improve the appearance of the package. Also known as *capsula*.

Caque (Fr)   *See* Hotte de Vendange.

Carafe (Fr)   A decanter or glass bottle used in restaurants for serving house wines. *See* Decanter.

Caramel   Burnt sugar or roasted barley, slightly bitter but otherwise tasteless, used for coloring whiskey, rum, brandy, beer, and so forth.

Caramel Coloring   Caramel added to brown whiskey or brandy prior to bottling for color adjustment.

Caramelization   A condition often associated with wines that have been exposed to high temperatures for prolonged periods of time causing an odor and taste of caramel.

Caramelize   To heat sugar to the point of browning.

Caramel Malt   (Also known as crystal malt or specialty malt.) It is made from "green malt," which is malted barley that has had its sugars crystallized while still in the form of grain. It has not yet been kiln dried and is produced by drying the wet germinated barley at controlled temperatures. It enriches the color, giving a reddish-golden color and a caramel, almost sweetness to the beer. Caramel malt also increases the body and aids in the head retention.

Carasson (Fr)   Acacia (ornamental tree) stake used to support each grapevine stem.

Caratello (Ital)   A 50-liter (13 U.S. gallons) barrel used for making Vin Santo.

Carattere (Ital)   A wine with character and typical traits of its type.

Caratteristico (Ital)   A wine with characteristic and individual traits.

Carbon   A black powdery substance used to clarify and purify wine.

Carbonated Beverages   Those beverages, both alcoholic and nonalcoholic, that obtain their carbonation from CO_2, which has been added or obtained naturally from fermentation. *See* Artificial Carbonation, Carbonated Water, and Artificially Carbonated Wine.

Carbonated Beverage System   *See* Postmix, Soda System, and Premix Soda System.

CARBONATED WATER   Ordinary water to which carbon dioxide gas has been injected under pressure. *See* Artificial Carbonation, Carbonated Beverages, and Artificially Carbonated Wine.

CARBONATION   The amount of carbon dioxide in a given amount of water or other liquid. The ideal condition for carbonating water is for relatively low water temperature (35 degrees Fahrenheit) and a high level of carbon dioxide pressure.

CARBONATION "BURN OFF"   The escape of carbon dioxide from a beverage (alcoholic or nonalcoholic) that has not been previously chilled when poured over ice, resulting in a diminished level of carbonation.

CARBONATOR   A mechanical device that mixes (at point of delivery) water, carbon dioxide, and syrup, to produce soft-drinks.

CARBONATOR TANK   A tank where the water and carbon dioxide are exposed to each other, preferably at a low temperature, above freezing. The carbonator includes a pump that injects water into the tank at a fixed ratio of water pressure to carbon dioxide.

CARBON DIOXIDE   A naturally occurring odorless, colorless, inert gas, which is a by-product of fermentation. During fermentation, roughly half the weight of sugar is converted into CO_2, the other into ethyl alcohol. Carbon dioxide is allowed to dissipate into the atmosphere when making still wines. However, during the production of sparkling wines and beers, the carbon dioxide gasses are trapped to retain the "effervescence" in the product. Carbon dioxide will increase the perceived impression of acidity on the palate when converted to carbonic acid in the wine.

CARBONIC ACID   A weak, colorless acid (H_2CO_3), formed by the solution of carbon dioxide in water and existing only in solution. It is produced in fermentation and remains in the wine for varying periods of time.

CARBONIC MACERATION   A very technical and complex procedure in which whole, uncrushed clusters of grapes are placed into a stainless steel fermenter. Care is taken to maintain the anatomical integrity of the berries without cuts, scrapes, or bruises. The tank is then pumped full with carbon dioxide and sealed. The sheer weight of the grapes is sufficient to break the skins, beginning an intracellular fermentation. These grapes are held under carbon dioxide pressure, causing the malic acid to break down while a complex fermentation takes place within the berries themselves. Because of the lack of oxygen, the skin cells asphyxiate and die, permitting color pigments to diffuse into the pulp. As a result of this, both tannin and the development of volatile acidity is kept to a minimum.

The juice is pressed and conventionally fermented, producing light-bodied, less alcoholic, young, and fruity wines meant for consumption several weeks after fermentation. In the United States, this process is often referred to as "whole berry fermentation." Carbonic maceration is used to make the Beaujolais *nouveau* wines of France. Also known as *macération carbonique, macerazione carbonica*, and *méthode carbonique*. *See* Beaujolais Nouveau, Flanzy, Morel, and Nouveau.

CARBOY   *See* Demijohn.

CARDBOARD   An odor or taste found in some beers or wines that is reminiscent of wet cardboard or newspaper. Usually as a result of the formation of mold or other types of bacterial growth.

CAREZZEVOLE (ITAL)   Caressing; rich; flowing.

CARICO (ITAL)   Deep.

CARIGNAN   A red grape variety, grown predominantly in the south of France's Midi region and Africa, where it is used for blending purposes. Some Carignan is also grown in Spain and California (where it is spelled Carignane). Also known as *Mazuelo*.

CARMENET (FR)   The local name in the Médoc for the Cabernet Franc grape variety. *See* Cabernet Franc.

CARMINE   A red grape variety, developed in 1975, from a cross of (Cabernet Sauvignon and Carignan) and Merlot, by Dr. Harold P. Olmo of University of California, Davis.

CARNELIAN   A red grape variety, developed in 1973, from a cross of (Cabernet Sauvignon and Carignan) and Grenache, developed by Dr. Harold P. Olmo of University of California, Davis.

CARNEROS (SP)   Ram.

CARRIER   A railroad car, motor truck, ship, airplane, or other vehicle used for transporting beverages and supplies. Sometimes used to denote an entire rail, trucking, shipping, or air transport system. Also known as *common carrier*.

CARTON   *See* Case.

CARTONS   Short for Gift Cartons.

CASA ESTABLECIDA (SP)   Estate bottled.

CASA FONDATA (ITAL)   Winery founded...followed by a date.

CASA VINICOLA (ITAL)   A winery.

CASCADE   A red French-American hybrid grape variety, developed from a cross of Seibel 7042 and Seibel 5409. It is mainly used in the production of rosé wines because of its rather neutral flavor. Formerly known as *Seibel 13053*. Incorrectly referred to as *Cascade Noir*.

CASCADE NOIR   *See* Cascade.

CASCINA (ITAL)   An estate or farm.

CASCO (SP)   An oak barrel with varying capacities, utilized for aging and/or shipping wines. *See* Barrel.

CASE   Two or more bottles, or one or more containers larger than four liters, enclosed in a box or fastened together by some other method.

CASE A container that houses bottles or cans of wine, beer, or distilled spirits. A case of 3- or 4-liters contains 4 individual units; a case of 1.5- or 1.75-liters contains 6 individual units; a case of 750-ml or 1-liters contains twelve individual units; a case of 375 ml contains 24 individual units; a case of beer contains 24 individual units. Also known as *cartons* or *boxes.*

CASEIN A protein fining agent derived from cow's milk. It carries a positive charge. Also known as *caseina* and *caséine.. See* Fining and Fining Agents.

CASEINA (ITAL) *See* Casein.

CASÉINE (FR) *See* Casein.

CASE CARD *See* Cut Case Card.

CASE PRICE The wholesale price per case, rather than cost per individual unit that makes up the case. The case price is generally lower than purchasing units individually.

CASH BAR At a private function when guests pay for their individual drinks. Also known as a *no-host* bar.

CASHIER'S BANK The opening cash available at the start of a shift necessary to make appropriate change for customers.

CASK *See* Barrel.

CASKINESS A flavor imparted to wine by barrels that have not been properly cleaned or maintained.

CASSE A cloudiness present in some wines due to the formation of colloidal complexes of metals, most notably iron and copper. In some European countries, these excess metals may be removed by the addition of potassium ferrocyanide. However, this practice is not accepted in the United States. Instead, Cufex, a proprietary product is the acceptable treatment. Also known as *iron haze. See* Citric Acid.

CASSIS (FR) Black currant liqueur.

CASTA (PORT) *See* Grape Variety.

CASTELLI (ITAL) *See* Governo and Cannici.

CASTELLO (ITAL) Castle.

CATADOR (SP) A wine taster.

CATARRATTO (ITAL) A white grape variety with large clusters and firm fruit, cultivated primarily in Sicily where it is used as a blending grape.

CATAVINO (SP) A fine crystal glass for tasting and drinking sherry wine. It is like a small glass chalice with a circular pedestal, thin cylindrical stem, and elongated tulip-like receptacle.

CATAWBA A light red-colored *Vitis labrusca* grape variety, which takes its name from the Catawba River in western North Carolina. In 1847, Nicholas Longworth made the first American sparkling wine from Catawba grapes in Cincinnati, Ohio.

CATCH WIRE Any horizontal wire used for catching and training grapevine tendrils or canes. Also known as *foliage wire*.

CATECHINS Phenolic compounds related to tannin, which are extracted from the stems, skins, and seeds in the *must* during the primary alcoholic fermentation. They assist in the browning of damaged fruit and are sometimes the cause of bitterness.

CATION EXCHANGE CAPACITY The measured ability of a soil to hold nutrients to soil particles or colloids.

CATION EXCHANGE PROCESS A process where sodium chloride is used as a regenerator to help eliminate sediment from wine.

CATRAME (ITAL) The odor and taste of tar, as sensed in some red wines, most notably from Piedmont. Also known as *catramoso*.

CATRAMOSO (ITAL) *See* Catrame.

CAVA (SP) The official designation for sparkling wines made by the *méthode champenoise* technique. The sparkling wine must remain in the cellar for a minimum of nine months, and carry a "four-cornered" star on the bottom of its cork. Cava is also the name of the place where the sparkling wine is made. *See* Sparkling Wine.

CAVATAPPI (ITAL) *See* Corkscrew.

CAVE (FR) Wine cellar. A well tended wine cellar is guarded from abrupt temperature change and ideally kept at a constant temperature. *See* Cellar Temperature.

CAVEAU (FR) A tasting cellar open to the public.

CAVE COOPÉRATIVE (FR) The source of many of the well-made, regional, "non-estate" wines.

CAVES Underground cellars.

CAVISTE (FR) *See* Maître de Chais.

CAYUGA WHITE A white French-American hybrid grape variety, developed in 1945 (named in 1972), from a cross of Seyval and Schuyler.

CEDAR A characteristic smell often associated with oak-aged red wines of Bordeaux, France, and Rioja, Spain.

CELERY SODA A carbonated soft drink, first made in 1868 by the American Beverage Company, of Brooklyn, New York. This celery-flavored beverage is made of oils extracted from celery seeds and other natural flavors. The most popular brand found on the East Coast is Dr. Brown's (fictitiously named) Cel-Ray Tonic.

CELLAR An underground storage or aging facility for alcoholic beverages. Also known as *keller*. *See* Cellar Temperature.

CELLARED AND BOTTLED BY The bottler/packer must have aged the wine without changing the class and type of the wine.

CELLARMAN   A winery worker who is responsible for the movement or transferring of wines, sanitary conditions of the facility, and general maintenance.

CELLARMASTER   An individual of considerable importance to both the vineyard and winery. The success of any wine depends upon his or her experience and technical skills and is subject to his or her sole authority.

One characteristic of a European cellarmaster is his or her dress, the same for centuries, consisting of a black jacket and a leather apron. Also known as *cantiniere, chef de cave*, and *kellermeister.*

CELLAR RAT   A self-description of a winery worker. During the harvest, crush, and subsequent fermentation, he stays in the cellar, busily working, never seeing the sun.

CELLAR TEMPERATURE   The proper cellar temperature is 52 degrees to 55 degrees Fahrenheit, but a few degrees higher or lower is satisfactory, providing that the temperature is constant. Wide and frequent fluctuations in temperature should be avoided. Wines can be safely stored for years in a fairly stable temperature, ranging from 55 degrees to 70 degrees Fahrenheit. The cooler the bottle's aging conditions, the more a young wine's character is retained over a longer period of time. Temperatures are cooler at floor level and on interior walls or closets; exterior walls are affected by sunlight and daily temperature changes. Uninsulated rooms should not be used, as their wide temperature changes damage the wine and shorten its life. *See* Cellar and Cave.

CELLIER (FR)   A wine vault.

CELL WALL   Outer layer of the cell of a micro-organism directly in contact with the surrounding external medium.

CENCIBEL (SP)   The local name in LaMancha for the Tempranillo grape variety. *See* Tempranillo.

CENTIGRAM   A metric unit of weight equal to $1/100$ of a gram.

CENTILITER $1/100$ part of a liter.

CENTIMETER   A metric unit of length equal to $1/100$ of a meter.

CENTRIFUGE   A machine whose inner cylinders spin and utilize centrifugal force to separate particles of varying density, as yeast from wine. It is also used to remove solids (pulp, skin, etc.) from wine.

CENTURION   A red grape variety developed in 1975, from a cross of (Cabernet Sauvignon and Carignan) and Grenache, by Dr. Harold P. Olmo, at the University of California, Davis.

CENTURY PLANT   An incorrect name given to the agave plant by early Southwest pioneers, because it was mistakenly believed to bloom only once every 100 years.

CEP (FR)   Grapevine stock.

Cepa (port or sp)   Grape or grapevine.

Cépage (fr)   Grape variety.

Ceppo (ital)   The trunk of a grapevine.

Cerasuolo (ital)   Deep pink or cherry red–colored.

Cereals   A broad base of grains, including barley (malted and unmalted), wheat, oats, rye, corn, dried corn maize, rice, and many others. All of these grains contain starch that must be converted into a readily fermentable sugar before fermentation can take place. Cereals are necessary for the production of beer, whiskey, and some other alcoholic products.

Certified Stock   A grapevine stock that is certified free from known virus diseases and has been heat treated under a government certification program.

Cerveja (port)   Beer.

Cerveza (sp)   Beer.

Ceylon   Rich and pungent tea from the island of Sri Lanka. It has an intense flavor, pleasant aroma, and bright color.

Chablis (fr)   This grape-growing area takes its name from the village of Chablis, which is nestled by the side of the Serein River, in the northern part of Burgundy. The chalky soil gives the wines of Chablis their clean taste, while fruitiness and a bouquet are contributed by the Chardonnay grape. It is an extremely dry, crisp white wine with a refreshing acidity. By law there are four Chablis: grand cru, premier cru, chablis, and petit chablis. Chablis is also a generic name for mostly nondescript white wines produced in California.

Chah (ind)   Tea.

Chai (fr)   An above-ground facility for the storage and aging of wines.

Chalk   *See* Calcium Carbonate.

Chalybon (greece)   An ancient wine.

Chambertin (fr)   A famous grand cru vineyard located in the Côte de Nuits area of Burgundy, noted for its exceptional red wines.

Chambolle-Musigny (fr)   A red wine commune in the Côte de Nuits area of Burgundy, noted for its exceptional red wines.

Chambré (fr)   Room temperature. Cellars are always cool, and red wines, when they are taken out of the cellar, have to be brought to the temperature of the room in which they are to be drunk for proper enjoyment.

Chamomile   A plant (*Anthemis nobilis*) whose dried, daisy-like white flower heads are brewed and used in a medicinal tea. Chamomile has a very powerful, fragrant scent, and a calming, antispasmodic effect on the stomach. Also spelled Camomile.

Champagne (fr)   A sparkling wine produced only in the Champagne region and by the *méthode champenoise*, from which it derives its characteristic sparkle from a secondary fermentation in a stoppered bottle. The word "champagne" must be stamped on every cork that is used for a bottle of French champagne. French champagne corks must also contain three layers, usually two solid and one "particle-type."

The Champagne region is 90 miles northeast of Paris. A law passed on July 22, 1927, demarcated a zone of that region that, by virtue of its natural characteristics, is capable of supporting the vineyards whose product has the exclusive right to be called champagne. In the United States, the name "champagne" is often used as a generic name for a sparkling wine.

CHAMPAGNE (RUSS)   *See* Sparkling Wine.

CHAMPAGNE BOTTLE   The typical bottle of the Champagne region used for its sparkling wines. In shape, it greatly resembles the Burgundy bottle but is slightly puffed out in the middle and has an inverted bottom often called a *punt* or *kick*. The specifications for the classic champagne bottle were first layed down by order of King Louis XV on March 9, 1735.

CHAMPAGNE GLASSES   *See* Flute-Shaped Glass, Saucer-Shaped Glass, and Tulip-Shaped Glass.

CHAMPAGNE METHOD   *See* Méthode Champenoise.

CHAMPANSKI (BUL)   *See* Sparkling Wine.

CHANCELLOR   A blue-black French-American hybrid grape variety, developed by Louis Seibel, near the Burgundy region of France. The grape, although originally developed in the Rhône Valley of France, flourishes in the eastern United States. It produces medium–full bodied wines with good color and acidity. Formerly known as *Seibel 7053*.

CHANNELS OF DISTRIBUTION   Vehicles through which products or services may be marketed by suppliers and/or purchased by consumers.

CHANTEPLEURE (FR)   *See* Wine Thief.

CHAPEAU (FR)   *See* Cap.

CHAPTALIZATION (FR)   In certain wine-producing countries of the world there is sometimes an insufficient amount of sugar present in the grapes at harvest to produce a stable wine. The finished wine would contain a very low alcohol level and would thus be unstable for travel and subject to bacterial infestation.

A limited amount of sugar, set by law, can be added to the must prior to or during fermentation when a lack of natural sugar exists. The term chaptalization is derived from the name of Dr. Jean-Antoine Chaptal de Chanteloup (1756–1832), the Minister of the Interior and Agriculture, and President of the Academy of Science under Napoleon I in 1800. This addition increases the sugar content of the *must*, producing a higher degree of alcohol. When the fermentation is complete, the wine is dry. The purpose of sugaring the *must* is only to raise the alcoholic content of the finished wine and has nothing at all to do with producing a wine with noticeable residual sugar. In France, for example, a maximum of three kilos of sugar per hectoliter of grape juice is allowed.

Adding sugar to the *must* is permitted in most grape-growing countries north of the Alps (Austria, Germany, Luxembourg, and Switzerland) and in many northern regions of France, including Alsace, Bordeaux, Burgundy, Champagne, and Loire Valley. It is also practiced in New York and Oregon, but not in California or in Italy. Also known as *anreichern, sugaring of wine, sun in sacks*, and *zuccheraggio*. *See* Verbessern.

CHARRING The burning of the inside of a wooden barrel to be used for wine, whiskey, brandy, or other distilled spirits. The char helps to mellow or age the wine or distilled spirit, while at the same time adding coloring matter. The use of charred oak barrels for the aging of whiskey first began in the United States in 1850. Also known as *toasted barrels* and *tostatura*.

CHARACTER Attributes of a wine typical to vintage, soil, climate, and treatment (aging in wood, steel, etc.). Also known as *charaktervoll* and *kharaktír*.

That combination of a whiskey's sensory qualities, which distinguishes it from another whiskey.

CHARAKTERVOLL (GERM) *See* Character.

CHARBONO A red-skinned grape of uncertain origin, but believed to have originated in the Iseré Valley near the foothills of the Alps, between the Italian, French, and Swiss borders. Some ampelographers believe Charbono is possibly Italian or French, related to the Corbeau, Charbonneau, or Douce Noir grape variety. Charbono displays sensory characteristics similar to that of the Barbera grape variety.

CHARCOAL A fining agent often used for decolorizing and/or deodorizing wines. *See* Fining and Fining Agents.

CHARCOAL MELLOWED A term used on whiskey labels to indicate that the distilled spirit has been filtered through charcoal for a smoother taste. It is now seldom used.

CHARDONNAY A major white grape variety grown in Burgundy and Champagne, France, as well as in most other wine-producing countries. Chardonnay displays the following odor and taste characteristics: Apples, figs, pineapples, green apple, peaches, or somewhat melonlike. If aged in wood, a certain butteryness.

The small village of Chardonnay is nestled among the vineyards, just three miles from the celebrated Romanesque church of Tournus in Burgundy, France; this, supposedly, is where the grape got its name. Formerly known as *Pinot Chardonnay*.

Beaunois is the local name for the Chardonnay grape in the Chablis district of Burgundy, France.

CHARENTE (FR) The valley in southwest France that lies in the Cognac region.

CHARGE Distiller's term meaning a single filling of a pot still prior to heating and distilling.

CHARGE (FR) The number of buds left on grapevine shoots after pruning (generally from 4 to 12).

CHARM Wines and beers with pleasant, appealing character, and without defects.

CHARMAT METHOD Named after its inventor, Eugene Charmat, a French wine scientist who developed the process in 1910 to save both the time and money involved in the classic method of producing sparkling wines. The original Charmat process (which is still, with some modifications, used today) requires three tanks. "Still" wine is run into the first tank and artificially aged by being heated for 12 to 16 hours and then immediately cooled. This wine is then pumped into a second tank where yeast and sugar are added. It then ferments for 15 to 20 days. The wine is then pumped into the third tank, where it is clarified by cooling the tank to about 30 degrees Farenheit; this also aids in tartrate stabilization. Finally, the wine is filtered and then bottled under pressure. This method usually produces sparkling wines within one month, and is the least expensive of the higher quality methods. Because all of the fermentation takes place in temperature-controlled glass-lined, stainless steel pressurized tanks, bottle breakage is virtually nonexistent. Cooler fermentation allows for greater retention of fresh grapy flavors, and the fermentation can be halted at any point by simply chilling the wine. This method is also known as *autoclave, bulk-fermented, cuve close, gasificado, granvas, methodo charmat,* and *schaumwein.*

CHARNU (FR) A wine that is fleshy and rich in substance; usually full-bodied.

CHARPENTÉ (FR) A wine that is robust, rich in fruit, flavor, and extract. A wine is full-bodied and capable of lengthy aging when it is backed by a firm tannin structure.

CHARTRONS (FR) The name of the quayside in Bordeaux, derived from *Chartreuse* (a French term for the Carthusian monks who at one time occupied the location), where many négociants used to have their wine warehouses and offices.

CHASER A slang term for water, seltzer, or even a glass of beer that is drunk immediately after consuming a shot of neat or unmixed distilled spirits.

CHASSAGNE-MONTRACHET (FR) A white wine commune in the Côte de Beaune area of Burgundy. Chassagne was once known as *Cassaneas* in 886 A.D. and as *Chaissaigne* in 1321 A.D.

CHASSELAS (FR) *See* Chasselas Doré.

CHASSELAS DORÉ (SWISS) A white grape variety producing wines that are high in alcohol, while at the same time being low in aroma and varietal character. Also known as *Chasselas, Dorin, Fendant,* and *Gutedel.*

CHÂTEAU (FR)   A wine estate, particularly in the Bordeaux region.

CHÂTEAU-BOTTLED (FR)   (Mise en Bouteilles au Château) Estate bottled. Wine bottled at an estate, château, or domaine, which is made from its own grapes. *See* Estate Bottled and Domaine Bottled.

CHÂTEAUNEUF-DU-PAPE (FR)   Châteauneuf-du-Pape wines, the most popular of all Rhône Valley wines, are produced out of some 7,500 acres of vineyards. By law, their minimum alcoholic content is 12.5 percent, and, although legally they can be made from a blend of 13 grape varieties, they are usually blends of 65 percent Grenache and 35 percent Syrah grapes. A small percentage of white Châteauneuf-du-Pape is produced from a blend of Grenache Blanc, Clairette, Roussanne, and Bourboulenc grape varieties.

The village of Châteauneuf-du-Pape was the summer residence of Archbishop Bertrand de Goth, who had succeeded to the papacy as Pope Clement V (1309–1377).

CHAUCHÉ GRIS   A nondescript white grape variety that is known by different names, depending where it is propagated; *Grey Riesling* in California and *Trousseau Gris* (its proper name), grown in the Jura region of France. The grapevine is extremely large and vigorous with medium-sized clusters and large berries, which have a gray tinge to the skin when ripe.

CHAUD (FR)   *See* Warmth.

CHAUDIÈRE (FR)   The alambic boiler pot.

CHAUFFE (FR)   The first distillation in the making of cognac.

CHAUSSAGE (FR)   A ploughing method that heaps the soil onto the row of grapevines. *See* Buttage.

CHEESE BOARD   A board that fits around the screw of an old-fashioned "basket winepress" and rests directly on top of the grapes. It is shaped like boards used to press cheese.

CHEF DE CAVE (FR)   *See* Cellarmaster.

CHEF DE CULTURE (FR)   A vineyard manager.

CHEF DE TROUPE (FR)   An experienced grape picker or "foreman," generally put in charge of other less experienced pickers. Also known as *mayoral*. *See* Cuadrilla Forestera and Porteur.

CHELOIS   A red French-American hybrid grape variety, developed from a cross of Seibel 5163 and Seibel 5593, by Louis Seibel in France in the late 1880s, and brought to the United States sometime after World War II. It produces red wines of good character that improve with moderate barrel-aging. Formerly known as *Seibel 10878*.

CHEMISE   *See* Sediment.

CHEMISE (FR)   Term meaning "jacketed" or wrapped. It refers to the cloth towel servers use to gently wipe the bottle's neck after each and every pouring of wine. It also refers to the cloth placed around a bottle removed from an ice bucket, to pat dry.

CHÉNAS (FR) A cru commune of Beaujolais named after the oak trees (*chénas*), which at one time covered all of the Beaujolais area. They are among the sturdiest of the crus.

CHÊNE (FR) Oaky.

CHENIN BLANC White grape variety grown predominantly in California and the Loire Valley of France, where it is known as *Blanc d'Anjou*, or *Pineau de la Loire*. In 1954, the Charles Krug Winery of Napa Valley, California was the first winery to offer Chenin Blanc as a separate variety.

The taste of wines made from Chenin Blanc grapes can range from bone dry to semidry and even sweet. Chenin Blanc produces wines that are pleasantly fruity and melon-like, resembling a fresh fruit salad. Also known locally in South Africa as *Steen*.

CHERRY A term used to describe the aroma or taste of cherries found in some light-bodied red wines such as Zinfandel, Gamay-Beaujolais, and Pinot Noir.

CHERRY-FLAVORED BRANDY A mixture of brandy, with a minimum of 2.5 percent sugar, and flavored and colored with small, wild black cherries. By federal law it cannot be bottled at less than 70 proof (35 percent alcohol by volume).

CHERRY LIQUEUR A sweetened alcoholic beverage consisting of a base of alcohol, minimum 2.5 percent sugar, and flavored and colored with small, wild black cherries. It is sweeter and lower in proof than cherry-flavored brandy.

CHERRY SODA A soft drink usually made with carbonated water, sugar or sweetener, caramel coloring, acids, and a syrup made from small, wild black cherries.

CHERVENO (BUL) *See* Red.

CHEVRIER (FR) *See* Sémillon.

CHEWY Having a rich texture on the palate, often described as full-bodied, and slightly alcoholic, with greater than average tannin. It is usually accompanied by a strong flavor intensity, creating the impression that flavor particles can actually be sensed or "chewed." Also known as *dusty, mâche,* or *meaty.*

CHIAN WINES (GREECE) Ancient wines from the island of Chios that were purported to be extremely sweet red wines.

CHIANTI (ITAL) Geographically and historically, Chianti is an area lying between Florence and Siena, encompassing the towns of Arezzo, Pistoia, and Pisa in the region of Tuscany. In the heart of this area in the hills between Florence and Siena, lie approximately 175,000 acres of land where Chianti Classico, the largest of the seven Chianti zones, is made.

Chianti was originally known as Vermiglio in the latter part of the fourteenth century. While today's Chianti is red, documents of the fourteenth century (tracing its origin to 1260) call a local white wine Chianti.

DOCG regulations (October 20, 1984) specify that Chianti be made from four principal grapes: Sangiovese, Canaiolo Nero, Trebbiano, and Malvasia. If it is aged three years and attains an alcoholic content of 12.5 percent, it may be labeled *riserva*. These regulations, for the first time, permit winemakers to introduce up to 10 percent of nontraditional grape varieties into the Chianti blend, including Cabernet Sauvignon, Merlot, and others.

CHIANTIGIANA (ITAL)   In Chianti, it is used as a liter-and-a-half bottle.

CHIARELLO (ITAL)   *See* Chiaretto.

CHIARETTO (ITAL)   A light-colored red wine. Also known as *chiarello*.

CHIARO (ITAL)   Clear, light.

CHIAVENNASCA (ITAL)   The local name used for the Nebbiolo grape variety in the province of Sondrio in the region of Lombardy. *See* Nebbiolo.

CHICHA   A corn-based beer brewed by the ancient Incas.

CHIEW   *See* Chiu.

CHILL HAZE   Formed by the bonding of malt protein particles to polyphenols (also called tannins) in beer. When chilled, the unsightly haze will settle out during cold storage.

CHILLING A GLASS   Placing a glass in the refrigerator or glass chiller, with or without first wetting it, for the service of beer and cocktails usually served "straight up." *See* Glass Chiller and Frosting.

CHILOGRAMMO (ITAL)   *See* Kilogram.

CHIME   The rim or beveled extensions formed by the staves that overlap the heads on a wooden barrel.

CHINCHÓN (SP)   An anise-flavored distilled spirit, often diluted with water and drunk in a tall glass. *See* Anise-Based Spirits.

CHINON (FR)   A red wine commune in the Touraine district of the Loire Valley, famous for its red wine made from Cabernet Franc grapes.

CHIP BUDDING   *See* Benchgrafting.

CHIROUBLES (FR)   A cru commune in Beaujolais. Chiroubles makes robust wines of distinctive flavor. It also has a special significance as it is the home of Victor Pulliat, the first person to suggest that American root stocks be grafted to French grapevines to defeat the phylloxera plague.

CHIU   The Chinese word for wine. The original words used before Chiu were *Li* or *Chang*. Also known as *chiew*.

CHLORINE DETERGENT   A powerful bleaching and sterilizing agent utilized for cleaning bottles and equipment.

CHLOROPHYLL   The green pigment found in the chloroplasts of plant cells that absorbs light energy; it is involved in the photosynthesis process. Chlorophyll is also used as a coloring agent. *See* Photosynthesis.

CHOCOLATE MILK   It is generally made with whole pasteurized, homogenized milk containing up to 1.5 to 2 percent liquid chocolate plus a sweetener and stabilizer.

CHOCOLATY   A term that conveys the odor and taste components of chocolate, noted in some late-harvested Zinfandels and certain other red wines.

CHUG   A slang term that means to drink the contents of a glass, can, or bottle of beer or wine in large gulps. Also known as *chug-a-lug*. *See* Quaff.

CHURCH KEY   A slang term for a beer bottle opener.

CHURCH WINDOWS (GERM)   *See* Legs.

CIDER   A beverage made from freshly pressed apples or apple juice that may or may not be fermented without added sugar. It can be nonalcoholic or alcoholic, and it may contain carbon dioxide. Cider may be still or sparkling, sweet or dry. *See* Apple Juice, Apple Wine, Hard Cider, and Sweet Cider.

Most countries that produce cider, utilize their own spelling versions:

Australia	Cyder		England	Cyder
France	Sidre		Greece	Sikera
Hebrew	Shekar		Latin	Sicera
Spain	Sidra			

CIDER PRESS   A machine that presses the juice out of apples for making cider.

CIDERY   An undesirable aroma or flavor caused by bacterial infestation, occasionally found in spoiled beer. It resembles apple cider, a trait of Prohibition-style "home brew."

CINSAULT   *See* Cinsaut.

CINSAUT   A red grape variety cultivated in many parts of the world, producing deeply-colored, full-bodied wines with good acidity, and a distinctive, fruity taste. Also known as *Blue Imperial, Espagne, Hermitage,* and *Picardan Noir.* Also spelled *Cinsault.*

CISTERN   A large receptacle used for storing newly distilled spirits.

CITRIC ACID   Acid found most notably in citrus fruits in varying quantities, and also present, although in lesser quantity, in grapes. As an additive, it is controlled by regulations and may only be used in certain circumstances and in certain quantities. It has the beneficial property of combining with iron in the wine. An excess of iron causes a type of clouding called iron casse. Citric acid forms a soluble compound with iron, preventing the formation of this clouding and should only be added to the finished wine. *See* Casse and Cufex.

CITRUS   A family of fruits characterized by a high level of citric acid: Currants, elderberries, grapefruit, lemons, limes, loganberries, oranges, pineapples, raspberries, strawberries, and tangerines.

CITRUS DESSERT WINE   *See* Citrus Fruit Dessert Wine.

CITRUS FRUIT DESSERT WINE   A citrus wine having an alcoholic content in excess of 14 percent but not in excess of 24 percent by volume. Also known as *citrus dessert wine*.

CITRUS FRUIT TABLE WINE   A citrus wine having an alcoholic content not in excess of 14 percent by volume. Such wine may also be designated "light citrus wine," "light citrus fruit wine," and so forth, as the case may be. Also known as *citrus table wine*.

CITRUS FRUIT WINE   It is a wine produced by the normal alcoholic fermentation of the juice of sound, ripe citrus fruit with or without the addition, after fermentation, of pure condensed citrus *must*, and with or without added citrus brandy or alcohol, but without any other addition or abstraction. Also known as *citrus wine*.

CITRUSY   Certain white wines that display characteristics similar to citrus fruits, such as high acidity and some tartness.

CITRUS TABLE WINE   *See* Citrus Fruit Table Wine.

CITRUS WINE   *See* Citrus Fruit Wine.

CIVB   *See* Conseil Interprofessionnel du Vin de Bordeaux.

CIVC   *See* Comité Interprofessionnel du Vin de Champagne.

CIVILTÀ DEL BERE (ITAL)   The civilized influence of drink (the approximation in English); the name of Italy's premier magazine on wine and distilled spirits.

CLAIRET (FR)   A red wine fermented for a relatively short period of time and has a somewhat deeper color than rosé.

CLARET   The British name for Bordeaux red wines, derived from an old French adjective meaning a wine that was clear, light, and bright enough to be distinguished from other red wines. Claret derives from the Earl of Clare, who served under Henry II of England (1154–1189).

CLARETE (SP)   A term that applies to wines made from a mixture of either red and white grapes that experiences part of its fermentation in the presence of the skins of red grapes.

   The fermentation in contact with red grape skins generally gives the clarete a deeper color and more robust flavor than the *rosado*. Although these two wines may often have similar hue, normally *rosados* are pink to very light red, while claretes vary from light red to red. *See* Rosé Wine.

CLARIFY   *See* Clarifying.

CLARIFYING   The process of making a wine or beer clear, or free of haze by means of a fining or filtering agent. To clean up a wine by causing a settlement of the minute particles, which make it cloudy or unclear. Other clarification methods may include cold-stabilization or racking. Also known as *clarify*. *See* Filtering and Sterile Filtration.

CLARITY   The relative brilliance or absence of haze in beer or wine. In general, persistent hazes are due to very small particles in wine or beer ranging in diameter from 0.005 millimeters to 0.00005 millimeters. Larger-sized particles also cause haze, but they usually settle out rapidly.

CLARO (SP)   *See* Clear.

CLASS   Generic classification of alcoholic beverages used in the Universal Numeric Code (UNIMERC), the primary statistical code identifying brands and vendors in the alcoholic beverage industry. A class may be further divided into types. Whiskey, gin, vodka, rum, brandy, liqueurs, cocktails, and tequila are the separate classes for distilled spirits. *See* Type.

CLASSÉ (FR)   A classified wine; a wine purported to be a quality wine.

CLASSEMENT (FR)   Classification.

CLASSIC   An often-used word to describe alcoholic beverages with no legal meaning.

CLASSICO (ITAL)   A geographic term applied to DOC wines; refers to the central or original area of a production zone.

CLASSIFICATION OF 1855   The classification of 1855 applies to the wines of the Médoc (with the exception of Château Haut-Brion, in Graves) and the wines of Sauternes and Barsac.

In the Médoc, the classification divides the 62 great vineyards into five categories, known as *crus* or "growths," according to their recognized quality in 1855, based on the prices obtainable for their wine at that time (a first-growth, or *premier cru* vineyard, for instance, is of the highest quality, and a fifth-growth, one or *cinquième cru*, the lowest). The Bordeaux Wine Classification of April 18, 1855, was established under the sponsorship of Emperor Napoleon III, who wanted to showcase the classification at the 1855 Paris Exposition (World's Fair).

CLASSIFIED GROWTHS (FR)   The 62 red wines and 25 white sweet wines (from Bordeaux) that were classified in 1855 according to quality and price. A similar classification was done in 1953 in Graves and in 1954 in Saint-Emilion.

CLASSIMO (ITAL)   The official name by which all *méthode champenoise*–produced sparkling wines are known by. It became effective with the release of the 1991 vintage. *See* Metodo Classico.

CLAVELIN (FR)   A special bottle, squat in shape, used for wines of the Jura district.

CLAY   A type of soil that, because of its density and compactness, retains too much moisture due to poor drainage, especially during the early spring and just prior to harvest. There is also a problem of excessive bulk density that hampers good root penetration. Because of the problem of bulk density, roots are unable to obtain sufficient oxygen and oftentimes the roots lay in the waterlogged soil for days on end. Also known as *argile*.

CLEAN Free from bacterial and processing defects. Absence of any unpleasant odors or tastes. Also known as *net*, *nett*, *netto*, *pulito*, *reintönig*, and *sauber*.

CLEAN TASTE A clean taste that is palatable, agreeable, and refreshing; free from off aroma or taste.

CLEAR Transparent, with no suspended solids or cloudiness in the wine or beer. A brilliant wine or beer. Also known as *chiaro* and *claro*.

CLEFT GRAFTING A method of grapevine propagation that gives more strength to the grapevine and hastens the maturing of grapes. The propagation is accomplished by joining branches of a grapevine, called a scion (a short section of the stem) with a diameter of one-half inch to two inches to an understock in such a manner that the two grow together and continue development as a single plant without change in stock or scion.

CLEVNER (FR) *See* Pinot Blanc.

CLIENTELE The patrons who are served inside a beverage facility.

CLIMAT (FR) A vineyard as used in Burgundy, which defines a single field or plot in a vineyard or even a single vineyard as in a "single-vineyard" designation.

CLONAL SELECTION (CERTIFIED PLANTS) This entails *genetic clonal selection* (i.e., the search for intravarietal genetic variability in a given grapevine population), and *sanitary clonal selection* with reference to dangerous viral infections. Clonal selection is far more rigorous than selection in the mass, and it entails quantitative control over the principal parameters of quality.

CLONE A particular strain of grape variety that developed either slowly, through natural adaptation to a set of growing conditions, or asexually, propagated vegetatively from an original mother grapevine, at a viticultural research institute. A plant genetically identical to all its siblings. One mother grapevine, through careful propagation, can produce thousands of perfect replicas. A clone is selected for its special viticultural and wine merits (productivity, adaptability to particular growing conditions, and wine quality).

CLONING The process by which clones are propagated.

CLOS (FR) An enclosure or field similar to the word château and used throughout France.

CLOS DE VOUGEOT (FR) A red or white wine commune in the Côte de Nuits area of Burgundy.

CLOSED-IN A condition present in some young wines, especially reds, which have not yet come together and are still displaying youthful characteristics. Also known as *closed-up*, *tight*, and *verschlossen*. *See* Dumb and Numb.

CLOSED-UP *See* Closed-In.

CLOSURE   Corks, crown caps, screw caps, and any other devices that seal bottles of wine, beer, and distilled spirits.

CLOUDINESS   A state often characteristic of wines of low alcoholic content in which some albuminous substances refuse to settle.

CLOUDY   Wines and beers containing excess colloidal material, protein instability, yeast spoilage, refermentation in the bottle, or sediment in suspension, which impairs the clarity. The wine or beer appears hazy and dull. Also known as *hazy* and *nube*.

CLOUDY   A temporary condition of beer if exposed to temperatures below 34 degrees Fahrenheit for prolonged periods of time.

CLOYING   Applied to a sweet, often tiresome wine, which lacks acidity; unbalanced and flabby. Also known as *doucereux* and *stucchevole*.

CLUB SODA   Tap water that has been filtered, artificially carbonated, and has had mineral salts added for flavoring. *See* Seltzer.

CLUMPING   *See* Flocculation.

CLUSTER   A bunch of grapes, during maturation and prior to harvesting.

CLUSTER THINNING   *See* Thinning.

CLYDESDALES   The famous horses that pull the Budweiser Wagon. They are usually three to four years old; must be bay in color and have all four leg stockings white, with a white face. They average 2,300 pounds in weight and stand between 17 to 19 hands high. Their shoes are made from a four-and-three-quarter pound piece of steel that is almost two feet long and an inch-and-a-half-wide. The harness for the eight horse team is worth close to $30,000.00. The use of the Clydesdales was the idea of August Busch, Jr., who first used them on April 8, 1933.

CM (FR)   *See* Cooperative de Manipulant.

COAN   An ancient Greek wine.

COARSE   A rough-textured wine lacking breeding, with possibly too much alcohol or bitterness. The term also applies to beers that are overly hopped. Also known as *khondrós* and *selvatico*.

COARSE SALT   Salt used for drinks that call for their glass rims to be salted. Also known as *kosher salt*.

COASTER   A small disk or napkin placed under a glass or bottle to protect a table or other surface.

COBBLER   Tall iced drinks containing fruit juices, wines, or distilled spirits, and decorated with pieces of fruit and laden generously with ice.

COBWEBS   Often found in old wine cellars, cobwebs are really fungi that have been nurtured by alcohol fumes.

COCHINEAL   A red dye sometimes used in the nineteenth century by the French to "darken" the wines of Bordeaux.

Cochylis   A disease of grapevines.

Cocktail   A class of alcoholic beverages that is derived by mixing one or more of the other classes (whiskey, gin, vodka, rum, brandy, liqueurs, wine, or beer) with or without flavorings, eggs, nonalcoholic beverages, juices, or water. Also known as a *mixed drink.*

In 1776, Betsy Flanagan invented the American "cocktail." It was in her bar in Elmsford, New York, which was decorated with brightly-colored tail feathers of cocks, that she had the notion to add a cock's tail feather as a stirrer to each drink. Hence the name cocktail. During that time, cocktails were often referred to as "roosters."

Cocktail Glass   A squat-shaped bar glass, usually holding four to seven fluid ounces.

Cocktail Lounge   A facility that offers customers the opportunity to have an alcoholic beverage. *See* Bar, Inn, Pub, Saloon, and Tavern.

Cocktail Mix Station   A side bar equipped with ice compartments, condiment trays, and speed racks containing both distilled spirits and mixers, used for the preparation of cocktails. Also known as *stationary bar.*

Cocktail Napkin   A small square paper napkin usually served along with a cocktail. Used as an underliner or coaster.

Cocktail Strainer   A perforated stainless steel spoon, or a round metal-handled strainer often surrounded by a flexible metal coil or wire spring, with ears that fit over the rim of a shaking glass, used for straining certain cocktails that contain seeds, fruit, pulp, or ice. Also known as *bar strainer* or *strainer.*

Cocktail Sherry   An American term for a dry sherry wine from Spain, presumably an Amontillado, rather than the bone dry Fino Sherry. Also known as *dry sherry.*

Cocktail Tray   A circular or oval tray, generally 10 or 12 inches in diameter, used to serve drinks. It is usually cork-lined to prevent the glasses from slipping.

Cocoa   Powder made from cocoa seeds that have been roasted and ground, with some of the fat removed; pulverized chocolate. The process was developed in 1828 by Conrad J. van Houten, by pressing vegetable fat from the liquor paste prepared from cocoa beans.

Cocoa   A drink made by adding sugar and hot water or milk to cocoa powder.

Coconut Liqueur   A sweetened alcoholic beverage consisting of a base of alcohol, minimum 2.5 percent sugar, and flavored and colored with the juice or milk of fresh coconuts.

Coffee   A dark brown aromatic drink made by brewing in water the roasted and ground bean-like seeds of a tall tropical evergreen shrub (genus Coffea) of the Madder family. Each small tree yields about 2,000 berries a year, enough for a pound of roasted coffee beans.

In its two most widely species—the Arabica (high grown, high quality) and Robusta (hardier, lower grown, mostly in Africa) coffee comes in about 100 different varieties. The individual characteristics are determined by many factors, such as the original strain, soil conditions, climate, growing altitudes, and preparation. Also known as *café*, *caffè*, and *kaffee*.

COFFEE BREAK   A brief work stoppage or break where workers usually drink coffee or other refreshments.

COFFEE-FLAVORED BRANDY   A mixture of brandy, with a minimum of 2.5 percent sugar, and flavored and colored with coffee beans. By federal law it cannot be bottled at less than 70 proof (35 percent alcohol by volume).

COFFEE GRINDER   A machine that grinds the roasted coffee beans prior to brewing. Also called a Coffee Mill.

COFFEE HOUSE   A place where coffee and other refreshments are served and people gather to socialize.

COFFEE LIQUEUR   A sweetened alcoholic beverage consisting of a base of alcohol, minimum 2.5 percent sugar, and flavored and colored with coffee beans. It is sweeter and lower in proof than coffee-flavored brandy.

COFFEE MILL   *See* Coffee Grinder.

COFFEE POT   A container (glass, ceramic, metal, etc.) with a lid and spout used to brew and serve coffee.

COFFEE URN   A large pot, with a capacity of up to 150 gallons, in which coffee is brewed by pumping hot water over ground coffee beans.

COFFEY STILL   Named after Aeneas Coffey, Inspector-General of Irish Excise, who invented the *continuous* or *patent* still in 1832. *See* Column Still, Continuous Still, Patent Still, and Still.

COGNAC (FR)   It is located in the departments of Charente and Charente Maritime (which were established in 1791, by combining the provinces of Aunis, Saintonge, and Angoumois). The Cognac region's stony, chalk-rich soil (which is probably due to ancient oyster beds), its climate, and the specific grape varieties grown there, as well as the methods used in distilling, blending, and aging, give brandy its unique flavor. The grape varieties utilized are St-Emilion (known as *Ugni Blanc* in California and France and *Trebbiano* in Italy), Folle Blanche, and Colombard, which make for an exceedingly acidic white wine.

In 1936, the French government officially divided the delimited Cognac area into seven sections (the Bois Ordinaires and Bois a Terroir are usually grouped together; there is thus sometimes confusion over whether there are six or seven districts). The seven sections, which very roughly describe concentric circles around the town of Cognac, are Grande Champagne; Petite

Champagne; Borderies; Fin Bois; Bon Bois; and Bois Ordinaire and Bois a Terroir (also called Bois a Communs). The highest quality Cognacs are produced in Grande Champagne and Petite Champagne.

From 1946 until 1986, French law prohibited a vintage date on a bottle of Cognac. In 1987 this prohibition was lifted.

COLA   An African tree (*Cola nitida*) of a family whose seeds, or nuts, contain caffeine and yield an extract used in soft drinks. Also known as *kola*.

COLA   A soft drink usually made with carbonated water, sugar or sweetener, caffeine, caramel coloring, acids, and a cola flavoring derived from the extract of cola seeds or nuts.

COLA DE PESCADO (SP)   *See* Isinglass.

COLD BOX   A large room where champagne and sparkling wines are placed to prepare for disgorging; it is pre-chilled to 45 degrees Fahrenheit.

COLD BOX   A large walk-in "cooler room" kept at temperatures between 34 to 40 degrees Fahrenheit where beer, wine, and other beverages are often stored. Also known as *keg refrigerator* and *walk-in refrigerator*.

COLD DUCK   *Kalte Ende* means "cold ending" and is the name that identified this blend of red and white wines rumored to have been concocted by an eighteenth century German Baron. When it was introduced into the United States, the name was slightly changed to Kalte Ente, meaning "cold duck."

COLD FERMENTATION   A method usually employed for the production of white wines. The grape juice is fermented at temperatures colder than traditional (below 55 degrees Fahrenheit), which retains much of the fruit, aroma, and varietal character of the grape.

COLD FILTERED   *See* Cold Stabilization.

COLD HARDINESS   It is the ability of the grapevine to resist injury during exposure to low temperature. The survival capability of a specified tissue of a grapevine following a specified exposure to a low temperature.

COLD INJURY   It is the killing by low temperature of some portion of the grapevine. Seriousness of cold injury is the amount of decrease in fruit production or fruit quality resulting from cold injury.

COLD METHOD   *See* Maceration.

COLD ONE   A slang term for a beer.

COLD PAN   After champagne or sparkling wines are pre-chilled to 45 degrees Fahrenheit, the bottle is placed, neck down, in the *bac à glâce*, which contains a brine bath at -16 degrees Fahrenheit. This freezes the neck of the bottle to a depth of about one inch, trapping the sediment in ice.

COLD STABILIZATION   A clarification technique that involves lowering the temperature to 25 to 30 degrees Fahrenheit from one to three weeks. The cold encourages the tartrates and other insoluble solids to precipitate, rendering the wine clear. The tartrates cast by the wine are actually tasteless and harmless and are removed for appearance only. Also known as *cold filtered* and *refrigeration*. *See* Crystalline Deposits, Tartar, Tartaric Acid, and Tartrates.

COLD TENDERNESS   It is the opposite of cold hardiness.

COLHEITA (PORT)   Another name often used to denote a "port of (year)."

COLLAGE (FR)   *See* Fining.

COLLAR OF FOAM   A brewer's term for the froth or head on top of beer.

COLLER (FR)   *See* Fining.

COLLE (ITAL)   Slope or hillside where grapes grow. Also known as *collina*.

COLLI (ITAL)   Hills.

COLLINA (ITAL)   *See* Colle.

COLLINE (ITAL)   Lower hills (than *colli*).

COLLINS   Tall, cool drinks (part of the punch family) that contain gin or vodka, lemon juice, sugar, and carbonated water. Called Tom (with gin) and John (with vodka).

COLLINS GLASS   A tall, narrow glass with a capacity of 12 to 14 fluid ounces.

COLLOIDAL SILICA   *See* Fining and Fining Agents.

COLLOIDAL SUSPENSION   A state that exists in liquids when certain semi-solid and albuminous particles remain suspended. *See* Particle Matter.

COLLOIDS   A solid, gelatinous substance made up of very small, insoluble, nondiffusible particles (as single large molecules or masses of smaller molecules) that are noncrystalline and semisolid, which remain suspended or dispersed in a surrounding liquid medium of different matter. Examples are gums, pectic substances, and proteins that, as hydrocolloids, cause hazing. They carry minute electrical charges.

COLMATURA (ITAL)   *See* Topping.

COLOGNE SPIRITS   A term often used to describe distilled neutral spirits.

COLOMBARD   A white grape variety of minor importance grown predominantly in California as a blending variety, and in France for the production of both Cognac and Armagnac. Colombard produces a fairly thin wine with high fixed acidity and a lively applelike flavor, which makes it ideal for distillation. It is also known as *French Colombard* and *Pied Tendre*.

COLOMBIA   A major coffee bean–growing region of the world located in South America.

COLOMBIER (FR)   *See* Sémillon.

COLOR   Each wine has its own "right" color. Judge a wine against the color that's correct for each wine type. Golden or amber is right for many dessert wines, but not for white table wines. Rosés should be distinctly pink with only a suggestion of orange or red. Whites can be yellow, gold, or straw color, but are flawed if they're too dark or too "water white." Reds can have violet hints of young and amber tints if aged. Brown is a flaw, as is too little red color. Also known as *colore* and *couleur.*

COLORE (ITAL) *See* Color.

COLUMN STILL Two cylindrical columns fitted with a system of interconnecting steam-heated tubes. The alcoholic liquid is fed into the tubes, where it is distilled, redistilled, and taken off as highly concentrated and purified alcohol. *See* Coffey Still, Patent Still, and Still.

COME-IN Full year forecast made for the current uncompleted fiscal year.

COMITÉ INTERPROFESSIONNEL DU VIN DE CHAMPAGNE (CIVC) The interprofessional organization that consolidates relations between growers and producers, and does considerable work for the Champagne community.

COMMANDARIA (GREECE) A fortified dessert wine from Cyprus, originally known as Nama. According to the historian Hesiod (eighth century B.C.), Nama was referred to as "the sweet wine of Cyprus," made from sun-exposed grapes. Worshipers of Aphrodite, the Goddess of Love who emerged from the waves off Cyprus, celebrated with "Cyprus Nama," said to be one of the oldest known wines in history.

Commandaria is reputed to be one of the longest-lived of all wines and will often display a solera date on its label.

COMMERCIANTE (ITAL) *See* Broker.

COMMISSIONAIRE (FR) A broker; the "middleman" for the grower and *négociant. See* Broker.

COMMON A simple wine of ordinary taste; without distinction.

COMMON CARRIER *See* Carrier.

COMMUNE (FR) Town or village; a subdivision of a district.

COMPAGNONS DU BEAUJOLAIS (FR) It is the name of the Wine Brotherhood in Beaujolais, which was formed in 1947 to promote its wines.

COMPLET (FR) Balanced and harmonious.

COMPLETE Mature, well-made, balanced, and satisfying. Also known as *completo.*

COMPLETO (ITAL) *See* Complete.

COMPLEX A wine that is multi-faceted. It contains many elements—acids, alcohols, fruits, tannins, and others—that can be harmonious while each reveals its own subtle or difficult to detect character. Also known as *synthetos.*

COMPLEXITY The various elements that make up bouquet, aroma, and taste in a wine. When a wine is described as having the aroma of fresh peaches or apples, it is displaying some of its complexities.

COMPOSITION CORK *See* Agglomerated Cork.

COMPOSTO (ITAL) Composed.

COMPOUNDER   A machine that blends liqueurs and cordials.

COMPTE D'AGE (FR)   On September 1, in the year following the harvest, Cognac and Armagnac receive the designation, Zero (Compte 0); the following September 1, it receives the designation, One (Compte 1). Thus there are six registers of age for Cognac and Armagnac, from 0 to 5 years. Cognac or Armagnac that is more than 5 years old remain in the Compte "5" register.

COMPUTED COST   The adjusted cost of a product after trimming or fabrication.

CONCENTRATE   *See* Grape Concentrate.

CONCENTRATO (ITAL)   *See* Grape Concentrate.

CONCIMAZIONE (ITAL)   Fertilization.

CONCORD   A purple-black *Vitis labrusca* grape variety with a rather tough skin that separates readily from the pulpy flesh (slipskin). It produces wines that are low in sugar content, with deep color and a fruity, *foxy*, grapey aroma and taste that is slightly tangy.

   The grapevine, named after Concord, Massachusetts, was first planted in September of 1843, by Ephraim Wales Bull (1806–1895).

CONDENSED MILK   A thick, sweetened milk made by evaporating part of the water from whole milk and adding a sweetener. Also known as *condensed sweetened milk*.

CONDENSED SWEETENED MILK   *See* Condensed Milk.

CONDENSER   Also called Condenser Coil. It is that part of a distilling apparatus that converts the hot alcohol vapors into a liquid, called a distillate.

CONDENSER COIL   *See* Condenser.

CONDIMENTS   Seasonings, liquids, garnishes, or other ingredients used to *finish* or flavor a drink. Some examples are Tabasco sauce or other hot pepper sauce, worcestershire sauce, bitters (Angostura and orange), olives, onions, nutmeg, vanilla, cloves, cinnamon, cinnamon sticks, and others.

CONDIMENT TRAY   A plastic, multicompartment tray with a plastic dust cover used for storage of most garnishes used in some cocktails.

CONDITION   An assessment of a wine or beer by olfactory evaluation as well as chemical analyses to determine the relative health of the product.

CONDITIONING   A process by which new wooden barrels are thoroughly washed internally with mild alkaline solutions, such as soda ash, then rinsed with hot water. This is often done to lower or soften the tannin levels and to eliminate the "raw" taste often associated with wines aged in brand new wood.

CONDOM (FR)   A city southeast of Bordeaux that is the center of the Armagnac trade.

CONEY ISLAND HEAD   A slang term for a beer that contains all or almost all foam. Characteristic of some beers poured by unscrupulous purveyors in

Coney Island, Brooklyn, New York during the 1940s and 1950s. *See* Foam and Head.

CONFRÉRIE (FR)   A grape growers society.

CONFRÉRIE DES CHEVALIERS DU TASTEVIN (FR)   Order of Burgundian Wine Lovers, founded in 1933 by George Faiveley and Camille Rodier. This world-famous Burgundy wine brotherhood has its headquarters located at the famous Clos de Vougeot château.

CONGENERS   Trace-flavoring constituents vaporized off with the alcohol in distillation above 190 proof and developed and expanded during the aging process.

Congeners, which are produced during the fermenting process, are made up of fusel oils, esters, tannins, acids, aldehydes, and so on. In proper proportion with other elements, these components contribute to palatability and create the characteristic aroma, body, and taste of a particular distilled spirit. When the spirit is distilled at a lower proof, more congeners are present and the spirit will possess more character.

CONIFERS   Any order of evergreen trees or shrubs, such as pine, spruce, fir, and so on, occasionally used for wine barrels.

CON RETROGUSTO (ITAL)   With aftertaste.

CONSEIL INTERPROFESSIONAL DU VIN DE BORDEAUX (CIVB)   (Professional Trade Council for Bordeaux Wine) Created on August 18, 1948, it acts in cooperation with wine growers and shippers to organize and direct the wine market, control quality, and promote Bordeaux wines.

CONSEJO REGULADOR (SP)   The regulatory board (denominación de origen) of a specific region governing the production and quality control regulations and all wine produced within that region. It also helps in the promotion of its wines.

CONSOLIDATING BOTTLES   The practice of consolidating or mixing together similar types and brands of distilled spirits or wine in on-premise facilities. Federal law bars tampering with the contents of alcoholic beverages. Containers may not be refilled and contents of alcoholic beverages must remain exactly as received from the manufacturer or wholesaler. Partially emptied bottles may never be consolidated. Distilled spirits may only be kept in the licensed premises in the original containers as received from the wholesaler or manufacturer. Also known as *marrying bottles* or *refilling*.

CONSORTIA SEAL (ITAL)   Label of Growers Consortium.

CONSORZIO (ITAL)   A consortium of wine producers.

CONSORZIO TUTELA (ITAL)   Local growers association.

CONSTANTIA   *See* Alexander.

CONSUMER COUPONS   Discounts available to customers by either a mail-in rebate coupon to a central clearing house or a cash discount at time of purchase (refund coupon), offered by retailer. *See* Rebates and Refunds.

CONSUMO (PORT OR SP) An ordinary or everyday wine, generally for local consumption.

CONSUMER OFFER Premium offer available for case and/or proof of purchase. Also known as *premium*.

CONSUMPTION The intake of beverages, either alcoholic or nonalcoholic.

CONTADINO (ITAL) Peasant farmers, usually owning a few vineyards.

CONTAINER A receptacle, regardless of the material from which it is made, used to store wine or to remove wine from wine premises. *See* Bulk Container.

CONTE (ITAL) Count or earl.

CONTENUTO (ITAL) Contents.

CONTINENTAL CONGRESS The First Continental Congress met at the City Tavern in Philadelphia, Pennsylvania.

CONTINUOUS STILL There are basically two types of stills used for distilling: the pot still and the continuous still. The continuous still is often referred to as a column still, Coffey still, and even patent still. The *continuous still* provides a continuous inflow of distilling liquid, which greatly boosts volume while saving considerable time. It generally does not produce the same high quality as the pot still. *See* Coffey Still, Column Still, Patent Still, and Still.

95

CONTROLLED BY It refers to property on which the bottling winery has the legal right to perform, and does perform, all of the acts common to viticulture under the terms of a lease or similar agreement of at least three years. *See* Estate Bottled.

CONTROLLABLE COSTS *See* Variable Costs.

CONTROLS Built-in methods for measuring performance or product against standards.

CONTROL STATE A state in which all alcoholic beverages (retail off-premise) must be purchased from state-owned *liquor* stores. Currently, there are 18 control states plus Montgomery County, Maryland, that monopolize the wholesale function. Also known as a *monopoly state*. *See* License State.

CONTROL STATE PROFITS Revenue from the state sale of distilled spirits based on the state mark-up formula, but exclusive of state excise and sales taxes and less the costs of goods and operation.

CONVENTO (ITAL) Convent.

COOKED The odor and flavor exhibited by some wines made from grapes, *must*, or wine, which have been exposed to heat, as in the cooking process known as *estufa*, necessary for the production of Madeira wines. *See* Cotto, Maderized, and Oxidation.

COOKER A vessel that allows heating and boiling of the mash in the making of beer.

COOKING WINES During Prohibition, wineries choosing to remain in business either sold bulk grapes, grape juice, wine tonics, or sacramental wines, or completely circumvented the law by producing cooking wines (taking perfectly sound wines and judiciously adding salt and other seasonings, rendering them unfit for consumption). Since the repeal of Prohibition, cooking wines are still made and sold both to industry restaurants and supermarkets. Some restaurants actually made it a practice to add salt to wines designed to be used in cooking to discourage the help from consuming them. Also known as *kitchen wine*. According to the BATF, *cooking wines* must be labeled *Nonbeverage Cooking Wines* or *Not For Sale Or Consumption As Beverage Wines*.

COOLER ROOM *See* Cold Box.

COOLERS *See* Wine Coolers.

COOPER Experienced craftsman who makes wooden barrels by hand. Also known as *couper, cuper, tonelero,* and *tonnelier*.

COOPERAGE All containers, sizes, and materials, from wood to stainless steel, used for fermenting, holding, or aging beer, wine, brandy, and distilled spirits while in the cellar and prior to bottling.

COOPERATIVA (SP) *See* Cooperative.

COOPERATIVE A winery or cellar owned and operated jointly by many small producers or growers. It is a method of pooling together resources, such as labor, costs, vinification, storage, and so on. Also known as *cooperativa*.

COOPÉRATIVE DE MANIPULANT (FR) This designates champagnes produced by cooperatives. Although many co-ops sell wines to négociants, some market their own labels. This appears on some champagne labels as the initials CM.

COOPERATIVE PROMOTION A promotion involving two or more suppliers of services or products joined together in a common promotion for their mutual benefit.

COPA (SP) A long, "tulip-shaped" stem glass that contains six fluid ounces and is traditionally used for the service of sherry wine. Also known as a *Sherry glass. See* Copita.

COPITA (SP) A long, "tulip-shaped" stem glass that contains four fluid ounces and is traditionally used for the service of sherry wine. Also known as a *cordial glass* and *Sherry glass. See* Copa.

COPPER Reddish-brown color often associated with beers.

COPPER ALE (ENG) A dark, copper-colored, bitter ale with a distinctive wine-like taste and aroma.

COPPER SULFATE Clarifies and stabilizes wine; removes hydrogen sulfide and/or mercaptans from wine.

COPPERY A metallic taste owing to bad distillation.

CORDIAL Derived from the Latin word cor meaning "heart," because the earliest cordials were administered to the sick to stimulate the heart and lighten the spirit. Cordials may be designated "dry" if the sugar, dextrose, or levulose, or a combination thereof, are less than 10 percent by weight of the finished product. *See* Liqueur.

CORDIAL GLASS A small stemmed glass with a capacity of one to three fluid ounces. Also known as a *liqueur glass. See* Copa and Copita.

CORDON Extended trunk(s) and spurs of a grapevine trained along a wire, called a "cordon" wire. Also known as *cordone* and *spalliera.*

CORDON BLEU (FR) A label designation on Armagnac or Cognac bottles that indicates that the youngest brandy used in the blend is at least 5½ years old (although they contain a very high percentage of brandy that has been aged for 20, 30, or 40 years or more).

CORDONE (ITAL) *See* Cordon.

CORDON TRAINING It takes its name from the French word for rope and is used to describe the appearance of the trunk. This system involves training the grapevine into roughly the shape of a "T," which is to say the grapevine trunk with two arm-like extensions at approximately 15 inches below the top wire. The arms are distributed to the left and the right and trained to a single wire, with spurs occurring at regular intervals along the length of the arms. Since cordons are on a lateral plane, unlike, say a bush, the grapevine's growth around all parts of the grapevine and opens it up, so to speak, to the maximum amount of sunlight, yet at the same time the grapevine foliage is so situated that the grapes themselves are not exposed to direct sunlight, which can burn their delicate skins. When the grapevines are in full leaf, this system presents a somewhat "wall-like" or "hedge" appearance. This has the advantage of less complicated pruning, since all that is left for fruiting wood is a series of spurs. Finally, since growth occurs at only two locations, along the length of both of the cordons, pruning is somewhat faster than with other forms of grapevine training and considerably more precise. The grower also saves on labor costs in that no tying of canes to wires needs to be done. *See* Head Training and Training.

C

97

CORDS Blemishes that occur during the glass-making process. Discontinuities in the glass caused by a number of things, such as improper mixing of the charge. While these are not really impurities, they do produce lines in the glass that can disturb its clarity.

CORE SAMPLING The extraction of a cross-section of earth to be analyzed for nutrients or the lack of them.

CORK The spongy material used as a stopper for bottles of wine, cordials and liqueurs, distilled spirits, or even beer. Cork, with its great elasticity, expands and contracts, depending on temperature and atmospheric conditions, making it a perfect tight seal for the neck of a bottle. White wine corks are typically 1.5 to 2 inches long, and red wine corks from 2 to 2.5 inches long.

Cork is actually the bark of a special tree (*Quercus suber*) grown in Portugal and Spain. Some cork is also produced in Sardinia, Italy. Cork trees mature slowly; their outer bark, which is the cork, is harvested only when the tree reaches 25 years of age, and once every 9 years thereafter. And it is only with the third harvest, when the tree is at least 43 years old, that the cork is of a quality suitable for wine closures.

After the bark is cut from the tree, it is processed and cut into circular shapes of various lengths. There is a very strict grading system that categorizes the corks according to color, smell, texture, the age of the tree, the number of imperfections and fissures, its pliability, and so on. Also known as *bouchon, rolha, stopfen, tapon,* and *tappo. See* Agglomerated Cork.

CORKAGE   A surcharge or fee charged by a restaurant for the opening and serving of a wine that a customer brings in with him or her. Also known as *corkage fee.*

CORKAGE FEE   *see* Corkage.

CORKED   An unpleasant musty smell (mushrooms) or flavor imparted to wine by a defective (moldy, poor, soft, or disintegrating) cork or by chemicals used in the processing of corks. Also known as *bouché, bouchonné, corkiness, corky,* and *korkgeschmack.*

CORKINESS   *See* Corked.

CORKSCREW   A device used for removing the cork from a bottle. It usually consists of a knife, screw, and depending on the model, a lever. Corkscrews should have a helical worm (like wire wrapped around a pencil) instead of a bore or screw, which "drills" a hole in the cork, rather than grasping it for extraction. Formerly known as *bottlescrew.* Also known as *cavatappi* and *tire-bouchon.*

In 1895, Samuel Henshall obtained the first patent rights for a corkscrew. The waiter's lever was developed by a Mr. Dolberg in 1883. In 1978, Herbert Allen invented the "screwpull," dubbed history's easiest corkscrew.

CORKY   *See* Corked.

CORN   An integral ingredient of some alcoholic products, such as Bourbon and corn whiskey, and American-made beers. The more corn added to the mash, the lighter in body the product.

CORN SUGAR   *See* Dextrose.

CORN WHISKEY   Legally, corn whiskey is distilled at a proof not exceeding 160 from a fermented mash of at least 80-percent corn. Corn whiskey must be stored in uncharred oak barrels or used charred oak barrels at not more than 125 proof. It must be aged for a minimum of two years. Because of its dominant corn content, corn whiskey is extremely light in flavor.

COROLLA   The petals of a flower. *See* Bud Break.

CORPO (ITAL OR PORT)   *See* Body.

CORPO PIENO (ITAL)   *See* Corposo.

CORPOSO (ITAL)   Full-bodied. Also known as *corpo pieno*.

CORPS (FR)   *See* Body.

CORQUETTE (SP)   *See* Grape Knife.

CORREDOR (SP)   *See* Broker.

CORSÉ (FR)   *See* Robust.

CORTESE (ITAL)   The traditional white wine grape of Piedmont that produces wines of particular refinement. Once widely cultivated throughout southern Piedmont, its area of production is now limited to the Colli Tortonesi, Monferrato, and Novi Ligure zones of Alessandria. An extremely resilient grapevine, it thrives in vineyards that have good exposure to the sun. Wines made from the Cortese may be labeled *Cortese, Cortese di Gavi*, or *Gavi*.

CORTESE DI GAVI (ITAL)   *See* Cortese.

CORTO (ITAL)   Short, brief, wanting.

CORTON-CHARLEMAGNE (FR)   A major white wine produced entirely from Chardonnay grapes, on the steep slopes, in the commune of Corton, located in the Côte de Beaune district of Burgundy.

The vineyards of Corton-Charlemagne were named after Emperor Charlemagne (742–814 AD), who owned vineyards and reigned in the mid-770s. Henry II (1154–1189) and Charles The Bold (1467–1477), Burgundian Duke, also owned vineyards there.

CORVINA (ITAL)   A red grape variety cultivated primarily in the Veneto region, where it is used as a blending grape in the production of Bardolino, Valpolicella, and Amarone wines. Corvina, *Corvina Veronese*, or *Cruina* as locally called, was first cited in literature as early as 1818.

CORVINA VERONESE (ITAL)   *See* Corvina.

COSECHA (SP)   *See* Vendimia.

COSECHEROS (SP)   Growers with relatively small vineyard holdings.

COST   The price paid to acquire or produce an item.

COST PER PORTION   The selling price per individual unit, multiplied by the unit multiplier.

COSTING   Process of arriving at the actual cost, cost percentage, or selling price of a product by identifying the component costs of the product and then applying a percentage or formula.

COST PERCENTAGE   *See* Beverage Cost Percentage.

CO₂ TANK   Container used to hold the CO_2 gas that is used in the dispensing of beer and carbonated nonalcoholic soft drinks.

COT (FR) *See* Malbec.

COT (FR) Wood on a grapevine from the previous vintage, pruned to just two buds.

CÔTE (FR) Hill or slope in a grape-growing area.

CÔTEAU (FR) Hillside.

COTEAUX CHAMPENOIS (FR) "Still" wines produced in the region of Champagne.

CÔTE CHALONNAISE (FR) A long, low line of hills that extends southward from the Côte de Beaune in Burgundy, for about 20 miles. The grape varieties from which its classified red and white wines are made (Pinot Noir red and Chardonnay white) are the same as those grown in the Côte d'Or, but the wines of the Côte Chalonnaise are somewhat lighter and mature faster. The four most important villages in this area are Mercurey, Givry, Rully, and Montagny.

CÔTE D'OR (FR) Literally, the "golden slopes." The large area is 25 to 30 miles long and only 1 mile wide at its widest point. The greatest vineyards in Burgundy are in this district, which is traditionally divided into two wine-producing areas: Côte de Nuits in the north and Côte de Beaune in the south.

CÔTE DE BEAUNE (FR) In the southern half of the Côte D'Or of the Burgundy region lies the Côte de Beaune, which extends approximately 15 miles, from Nuits-Saint-Georges in the north to Santenay in the south. It is wider, longer, and has nearly twice the amount of land of its northern neighbor. The Côte de Beaune is known for its outstanding white wines, although there are also some very fine red wines produced.

CÔTE DE BROUILLY (FR) A cru commune in Beaujolais considered to produce finer wines than Brouilly.

CÔTE DE NUITS (FR) The northern half of the Côte D'Or in the Burgundy region famous for its red wines, all of which utilize the Pinot Noir grape variety. The Côte de Nuits stretches for about 12 miles, from the town of Fixin in the north to Nuits-Saint-Georges in the south. There are 29 *appellation contrôlée* wines produced in this region. Several white wines are entitled to the *appellation contrôlée* designation in the Côte de Nuits: Musigny Blanc; Nuits-Saint-Georges Blanc; Morey-Saint-Denis; Monts-Luisants; and Clos Blanc de Vougeot.

CÔTES DE PROVENCE (FR) A wine district in southern France situated along the Mediterranean coast, producing ordinary red and white wines, but noted for its outstanding dry rosé wines. *See* Provence.

CÔTES-DU-RHÔNE (FR) Located below Burgundy in the southeast section of France, Rhône Valley's wine production is more than 95-percent red wines. It is the second largest AOC wine-producing region (Bordeaux is the largest). The Côtes du Rhône region received its AOC status in 1937. This is the southernmost of France's six major wine regions.

The vineyards, totaling 129,675 acres, stretch along both sides of the Rhône river for about 125 miles, beginning in the south around the famous papal stronghold of Avignon, and extending north to the outskirts of the city of Lyon. In the south the grapevines work hard to survive in chalky, stone-covered soil; in the northern area they scale granite hills towering over the river.

Côtes du Rhône wines are robust and full-bodied, with plenty of bouquet and taste. They are perfect for cold winter nights. They are generally higher in alcohol (a minimum 11 percent) than red Burgundies or Bordeaux. The Rhône Valley is the most southerly fine wine-producing region in France. *See* Rhône Valley.

CÔTES-DU-RHÔNE-VILLAGES (FR)   Its appellation contrôlée was established in 1967 for 17 villages in the southern half of the Rhône area. The red, white (dry or naturally sweet), and rosé wines of this area can be marketed either under the name of the village where they were produced or under the name of Côtes du Rhône-Villages, if the wine is a blend of wines from several villages. Most wines labeled Côtes-du-Rhône-Villages are usually fruity, and a bit fuller than Beaujolais, and should be consumed relatively young.

COTTO (ITAL)   The concentrating of grape juice (*must*) by heating or boiling down. The "cooking" evaporates the water from the natural juice and enriches sugar and flavor content. During this time the must becomes thick, sweet, and caramel-like. Also known as *cuit, sancocho, vin cuit,* and *vino cotto.* *See* Cooked, Maderized, and Oxidation.

COULAGE (FR)   *See* Ullage.

COULANT (FR)   Flowing, smooth, pleasant, easy to drink. Generally used to describe light-bodied red and white wines that are low in tannin and alcohol.

COULEUR (FR)   *See* Color.

COULEUSE (FR)   Leaker; a leaking bottle.

COULURE (FR)   *See* Floral Abortion.

COUNT   The number of units or items per pound, number of units, or net pounds per container.

COUPAGE (FR)   The blending of many wines in the making of cognac or champagne. *See* Blending.

COUPÉ (FR)   A blended wine of little character.

COUPE (FR)   The often-encountered flat, saucer-shaped glass, often incorrectly used for sparkling wines.

COUPER (FR)   *See* Cooper.

COUPON   Rebate redeemable in-store.

COURMI   An ancient Gaelic term for ale.

COURT (FR)   Short, lacking balance.

COURTIER (FR)   *See* Broker.

COVER   Restaurant jargon for one paying customer, a place setting, or one seat. Refers to the practice of having a cover on each customer's plate while in transit from the kitchen. A waiter who was able to serve ten covers was therefore serving ten people. The number of covers equals the number of customers for any given meal or time period, as establishing an accurate customer count. Also known as *number of portions.*

COVER CHARGE   A basic charge or fixed fee added to the bill. It is usually for entertainment in night clubs or luxury restaurants, for some special feature that the premise offers, or for seating, independent of charges for food or drink.

COVER COUNT   Records the number of patrons using the operation for specified time periods—hourly, daily, weekly, monthly, or even quarterly.

COVER CROPS   Crops planted in between rows of vineyards late in the season in order to soak up excess moisture and prevent runoff; usually plowed into or disced into the ground for needed nutrients in the springtime. *See* Wild Mustard.

COWBOY COCKTAIL   A straight shot of whiskey.

CRABB'S BLACK BURGUNDY   The name given by Hiram W. Crabb of Napa Valley to the Mondeuse Noire grape variety when it was first planted in the United States. *See* Mondeuse Noire.

CRACHOIR (FR)   A spittoon.

CRACKLING   Slightly sparkling wines produced in any manner that results in a carbonation of less than 2.7 atmospheres of pressure. Taxed at a lower rate than champagnes and sparkling wines, crackling wines are normally low-priced. *See* Spritz.

CRADLE   *See* Wine Cradle.

CRAIE (FR)   Chalk soil.

CRANBERRY JUICE   A nonalcoholic and noncarbonated fruit juice made from the liquid constituent of cranberries. It may be sweetened or unsweetened.

CRANBERRY LIQUEUR   A sweetened and flavor liqueur consisting of a base of alcohol, minimum 2.5-percent sugar, and flavored and colored with cranberries.

CRAYÈRES (FR)   The chalk cellars in which all champagnes are produced and aged.

CREAM   A component of milk, whose butterfat content determines the form and style of the cream.

CREAM ALE   This is a blend of ale and lager beer. Cream ale is highly carbonated, which results in a rich foam and strong effervescence. Cream ale is ideally served at 38 degrees to 45 degrees Fahrenheit.

CREAM LIQUEURS   A mixture of dairy cream and whiskey (usually Irish or Scotch), generally beige in color with an alcoholic content usually between 17 and 20 percent by volume. Also known as *Irish cream liqueurs.*

CREAM OF TARTAR   A purified form of tartaric acid. *See* Tartar, Tartaric Acid, and Tartrates.

CREAM SHERRY   Rich, deep amber to a golden brown in color, cream sherries usually display an exquisite bouquet and are very sweet and "creamy" to the taste. An even sweeter cream sherry, made entirely from Pedro Ximénez (P.X.) grapes is called "brown."

Cream sherry is made by blending sweet wines made from the juice of P.X. and Moscatel grapes to a sherry base wine. The P.X. grapes are left outside in the sun for 12 to 14 hours to dry after harvesting, which concentrates their sugar levels. They are then placed on *esporto* mats (made of grass), to further dry. So intense is their sweetness that fermentation usually stops at about 14 percent alcohol, resulting in a high degree of residual sugar. Cream sherry should be served after dinner at cool room temperature.

CREAM SODA   A soft drink usually made with carbonated water, sugar or sweetener, caramel coloring, acids, and a syrup made from vanilla beans.

CREAMY   An impression conveyed by certain wines and beers.

CREMA (ITAL)   Cream.

CRÉMANT (FR)   A champagne usually produced exclusively from Chardonnay grapes. Perhaps the biggest difference between Crémant and other champagnes lies in the fact that during the secondary fermentation, less sugar is added, which in turn produces less alcohol and less carbon dioxide. In fact, Crémant champagne usually contains 2.5 to 3.5 atmospheres of pressure, compared to the normal 5 to 6 atmospheres of pressure. It is appreciated for its lightness of flavor and less gassy taste.

CRÈME   A term widely applied to liqueurs, refers to a special sweetness. These are not dairy creams. This term could in fact be used to describe most cordials/liqueurs.

CRÈME DE ALMOND   Almond-flavored liqueur.

CRÈME DE ANANAS   Pineapple-flavored liqueur.

CRÈME DE BANANA   Banana-flavored liqueur.

CRÈME DE CACAO   Cacao-flavored liqueur made from cocoa and vanilla beans.

CRÈME DE CAFE   Coffee-flavored liqueur.

CRÈME DE CASSIS   Black currant-flavored liqueur.

CRÈME DE CELERY   Celery-flavored liqueur.

CRÈME DE CHOCOLATE   Chocolate-flavored liqueur.

CRÈME DE FRAISE   Strawberry-flavored liqueur.

CRÈME DE FRAMBOISE   Raspberry-flavored liqueur.

CRÈME DE MANDARINE   Tangerine-flavored liqueur, made from the dried peel of tangerines.

CRÈME DE MENTHE   Mint-flavored liqueur made from several varieties of mint, but principally peppermint.

CRÈME DE MOKA (CRÈME DE MOCCA)   Coffee-flavored liqueur.

CRÈME DE NOGYAUX (CRÈME DE NOYA)   Almond-flavored liqueur, made from crushed apricots, cherries, peaches, and plums, with orange-peel flavor and a brandy base.

CRÈME DE PRUNELLE   Plum-flavored liqueur.

CRÈME DE ROSE   Liqueur made from essential oil of rose petals and vanilla.

CRÈME DE THÉ   Tea-flavored liqueur.

CRÈME DE VANILLA   Liqueur made from vanilla beans.

CRÈME DE VIOLETTE   Liqueur flavored with vanilla and violet petals. It is similar in color and taste to Crème Yvette and Parfait Amour.

CRÈME DE YVETTE   Lavender-colored liqueur with hints of bubblegum; made from violet petals. It was named after French actress Yvette Gilbert. It is similar in color and taste to Crème de Violette and Parfait Amour.

CRESCENT CUBE   *See* Ice Cubes.

CRESCENZ (GERM)   *See* Kreszenz.

CREUX (FR)   Hollow; lacking in body.

CRIADERA (SP)   The first or initial aging *butts* utilized in the solera system of aging sherry wine.

CRIADO POR (SP)   Produced by. Also known as *elaborado por.*

CRIADO Y EMBOTELLADO POR (SP)   Grown, produced, and bottled by.

CRIANZA (SP)   Nursery; refers to the aging process in a sherry bodega or winery. The wine (red) must be aged for not less than two years, of which at least one must be in 225-liter oak barrels. Also known as *vino de crianza.*

CRIOLLA (SP)   *See* Mission Grape.

CRISP   The term applied to wines and beers that are light, with a fairly high level of acidity making them clean and fresh tasting.

CRISTALLIN (FR)   Crystal clear; free from haze or cloudiness.

CRNO (YUG)   *See* Red.

CROP   Also known as harvest. *See* Vintage.

CROP   The quantity of fruit borne on grapevines.

CROP CONTROL   The management of the vineyard by various methods, including pruning, crop thinning, fertilization, and spraying.

CROP LOAD   The quantity of crop in relation to the grapevine's leaf and overall bearing capacity.

CROP RECOVERY The rate of crop produced from newly developed growth following an injury, usually spring frosts.

CROP THINNING *See* Thinning.

CROSSBREEDING A new grape variety created by the mating or breeding of one grape variety with another in order to obtain a more desirable offspring. Also known as *hybridization. See* Hybrid.

CROUPE (FR) A ridge or slight elevation in the ground.

CROWN *See* Head.

CROWN CAP A metal stopper whose edges are crimped over the mouth of the bottle. after used in the production of sparkling wines for secondary fermentation in a "stoppered" bottle.

CROZE The carved or cut groove that is found at both ends of a barrel to accept the "head." *See* Farine.

CROZES-HERMITAGE (FR) *See* Hermitage.

CRU (FR) Literally, growth when applied to wines, but synonymous with a special vineyard or a vineyard of high quality, whether classified or not. It reflects the particular soil, climate, and grape varieties, which gives the wine its distinctive quality. *See* Growth.

CRU BOURGEOIS (FR) A classification of Bordeaux wines (ranked just below the five classified growths), that were not classified in 1855, but were in 1966 by the Bordeaux Chamber of Commerce. The cru bourgeois classification is made up of first Grands Bourgeois (exceptionnels), second Grands Bourgeois, or third Bourgeois. Also known as *Bourgeois Growths.*

CRU CLASSÉ (FR) The classified growths. The dry red and sweet white wines of Bordeaux, which were classified or ranked in 1855, 1953, 1959, 1969, and 1985, according to potential quality and the prices the wines had been selling for prior to the classification.

CRU EXCEPTIONNEL (FR) An unofficial classification of Bordeaux wines just below *classé* and above *bourgeois*. Common Market regulations, however, do not permit use of the word *exceptionnel* on labels.

CRUINA (ITAL) *See* Corvina.

CRUSH Another term for the harvest.

CRUSHER A mechanical device utilized for breaking or cracking of the skins of grapes in order to release the juice for fermentation.

CRUSHER/DESTEMMER A mechanical device with a large hopper where grapes are dumped into, which cracks the berries, allowing the sugar-rich juice known as *free-run* to flow freely.

The second part of this simultaneous crushing/destemming operation removes the stems from the grapes by centrifugal force with the use of a large auger, which catches the stems, literally ripping off the berries. The stems exit at one side of the machine, while the berries and juice usually exit at the bottom. The stems, which are a good source of nitrogen, are loaded into trucks and dumped between the vineyard rows to decompose during the winter and be "disced" into the soil in the spring. Also known as *égrappoir, fouloir,* and *stemmer. See* Destemming.

CRUSHING   The process whereby the skins of the grapes are cracked open by a machine, liberating the juice. Also known as *pigiatura.*

CRUST   *See* Sediment.

CRUSTA   An obscure American name for an elaborate cocktail containing lemon juice, aromatic bitters, curacao, and a distilled spirit. It is often garnished with an orange slice, maraschino cherry, or lemon peel; frosted or rimmed with powdered sugar; and served in a tall wine glass, over crushed ice.

CRUSTED PORTS (PORT)   No longer produced. *See* Late-Bottled Vintage Ports.

CRUTIN (ITAL)   *See* Infernotti.

CRUZETA (SP)   A system of training grapevines onto wires in between posts.

CRYOMACERATION   Cold or freezing.

CRYOMACERATION   Meaning cold or freezing. A winemaking technique whereas the skins and juice of freshly crushed grapes are held at extremely cold temperatures prior to fermentation.

CRYPTOGAMIC DISEASES   From the Greek *kryptos* (hidden) and *gamos* (marriage). They are fungal diseases, such as *Uncinula necator* (powdery mildew), *Plasmopara viticola* (downy mildew), black rot, gray rot, and *Botrytis* bunch rot, which directly affect the grapevines, the leaves, or the grapes.

CRYPTOGAMS   Fungi.

CRYSTALLINE DEPOSITS   Crystal deposits that accumulate either at the bottom of the bottle or at the bottom of the cork. They are actually formed by potassium absorbed by grapes from the soil and tartaric acid, used during the winemaking process. They don't dissolve in the wine, but also they won't impair its quality, taste, luster, or color. Also known as *crystals. See* Cold Stabilization, Tartar, Tartaric Acid, and Tartrates.

CRYSTALS   *See* Crystalline Deposits.

CSPI   Center for Science in the Public Interest.

CUADRILLA FORESTERA (SP)   Grape pickers. *See* Chef de Troupe.

CUARTA (SP)   *See* Barrel.

CUBA (SP)   A fermenting tank.

CUBELETS   *See* Ice Cubes.

CUBIC   A dimension expressing volume.

CUERPO (SP)   *See* Body.

106

CUFEX A proprietary product used for the removal of excessive metal hazes, notably copper and iron. *See* Casse and Citric Acid.

CUIT (FR) *See* Cotto. Also known as *vin cuit*.

CULATTONE (ITAL) *See* Sediment.

CULM In brewing or distilling, barley is steeped in warm water and allowed to sprout or germinate. It is then put into a kiln where it becomes green malt that often gets roasted. The kiln dried malt is then screened or sieved to remove the dried root lets or sprouts, which are known as *culm*.

CULTIVAR A cultivated variety of grape, produced horticulturally, rather than a naturally occurring variety.

CULTIVATING The turning or loosening of the soil by mechanical means in order to control weeds and aerate the soil.

CUNACHO (SP) *See* Brenta.

CUP A U.S. volumetric equivalent to eight fluid ounces.

CUPADA (SP) *See* Cuvée.

CUPER (DUTCH) *See* Cooper.

CUP OF JAVA A slang term for a "cup of coffee."

CUP OF JOE A slang term for a "cup of coffee."

CUPPA (AUSTRAL) A "cup of tea."

CUPS Drinks containing wine, made similar to punches. They include fruits, fruit juices, and carbonated mixes.

CURACAO Light amber-colored liqueur, first produced in the sixteenth century by the Dutch from the bitter peels of Dutch West Indies oranges. When curacao was first produced (with less sugar), it was called "double curacao," then "triple sec." Curacao is usually lower in alcohol and is also available in a blue-colored version.

CUSTOMER LEVEL GOAL DEPLETION WORKSHEET Form used to allocate brand territorial depletion goals among distributors in a given territory.

CUT CASE CARD A sign used to promote a product on a small case stacking, which attaches to a displayed cut case by fitting into the back edge of a case.

CUTICULA The outer layer of the grape berry's skin.

CUTTING Before bottling, the proofage or alcohol content of distilled spirits is adjusted usually by the addition of demineralized or distilled water.

CUTTING A severed portion of the cane used for propagation.

CUTTING WINE *See* Blending.

CUVA (SP) A large barrel with a capacity of 25,000 liters (6,600 U.S. gallons), seldom used today. *See* Barrel.

CUVAISON (FR) Time spent by the wine in fermenting vats in contact with the skins.

CUVE (FR)   A barrel, or literally, the contents of a barrel of wine.

CUVE CLOSE (ITAL)   *See* Charmat Method.

CUVÉE (FR)   A blend of wines bottled as one lot. Any volume of wine produced and specially selected to be fermented a second time for sparkling wines. Also known as *cupada* and *uvaggio*.

CUVÉE DE PRESTIGE (FR)   A winery's most thoughtfully conceived, carefully crafted sparkling wine or champagne.

CUVERIE (FR)   *See* Vat Room.

CYATHI   An ancient Roman cup that held the equivalent of the modern "quartino" or quarter of a liter.

CYDER (AUSTRAL OR ENG)   *See* Cider.

CYSTER   Apple juice used with honey in place of water.

CYTRYNÓWKA (POL)   Lemon-flavored vodka.

DAILY ALCOHOLIC BEVERAGE ISSUE REPORT   A detailed report that specifies quantity of bottles, sizes of bottles, and names of beverages that were issued from storage to the bar or other departments for service.

DAILY BEVERAGE COST   The actual wholesale dollar value of all beverages used by an establishment in a given shift or day. This figure includes direct purchases as well as storeroom issues.

DAILY BEVERAGE COST PERCENTAGE   The beverage cost (for a shift or day) divided by the retail dollar amount of sales.

DAILY REPORT   A compilation of the costs and sales of the previous shift or day, for all departments in the property.

DAIQUIRI   A cocktail named after the Daiquiri Iron Mines near Santiago, Cuba, where the drink originated around the turn of the century. It consists of light rum, sugar, and lime juice.

DAISY   A very large cocktail, usually made with distilled spirits, grenadine syrup (for color), and lemon or lime juice, to which soda is added.

DAMIGIANA (ITAL)   *See* Demijohn.

DAME-JEANNE (FR)   A large glass bottle used for the transportation of wine. It holds anywhere from one to ten gallons and is usually wrapped with wicker or straw.

DAMENWEIN (GERM)   *See* Feminine.

DAMINOZIDE   *See* Alar.

DAMSON PLUMS   A variety of small, oval, bluish-black plums, used to produce Britain's damson gin.

DANDELION WINE   A fruit wine made from the fresh yellow flowers of wild dandelion plants. The other ingredients are sugar, citrus fruits (orange, lemon, and lime), yeast, and raisins.

DANK A term often applied to wines or beers that display a moldy odor, reminiscent of damp cellars.

DANUBE The great river that connects Eastern and Western Europe. It flows through classical wine regions in Lower Austria.

DANZIGWASSER (POL) *See* Goldwasser.

DÃO (PORT) A red and white wine–producing region in north-central Portugal, just south of the Douro River.

DARK Term used to describe the color of some red wines and beers.

DARK BEER Characterized by a very deep, dark color, a full-bodied flavor, and a creamy taste, with overtones of malt, bitterness, sweetness, and caramel. It is usually produced from the addition of roasted barley during the initial brewing stages. It should be served at approximately 45 degrees to 50 degrees Fahrenheit.

DARKENING The color of white wines begins to darken with age and oxidation.

DARK RUM A rum that derives its color from aging in lightly charred oak barrels for a period of five to seven years. The skimmings of sugar from the previous distillation are added to the sugarcane molasses and allowed to slowly ferment for 12 to 20 days. The mash is distilled twice in pot stills and is run off at between 140 to 160 proof. It is this special fermentation process that gives the dark rums a pungent bouquet and more pronounced flavor of butter and molasses. The rum is then aged and blended, and at bottling the proof is adjusted with distilled water. Also, considerably more caramel is added than is the case for lighter rums, to give it a deep mahogany color. *See* Rum.

DASH ⅙ teaspoon or 1/48 fluid ounce.

DE *See* Diatomaceous Earth.

DEAD A beer or wine that is old and well past its prime of drinkability. This condition could also occur due to improper handling or storage.

DEAD MARINE *See* Dead Soldier.

DEAD SOLDIER A slang term for an empty bottle of beer, which began sometime during World War I. Also known as a *dead marine*.

DEALER *See* Broker.

DEBOLE (ITAL) *See* Thin.

DEBOURBAGE (SP) Allowing the unfermented grape juice to settle, generally for 24 hours prior to fermentation. This method allows the heavier particles to settle to the bottom for later removal prior to fermentation.

DÉBOURREMENT (FR) The moment when the scales protecting the bud during the winter open up.

DECAFFEINATED The removal of caffeine from coffee beans with no significant change in natural flavor or character in coffee brewed from them. Different coffee beans have different caffeine contents, depending on their growing region and species. For example, arabica beans have one-half the caffeine content of robusta coffee beans.

Direct Contact Method The green beans are first softened by steam. Then they are flushed with methylene chloride, a solvent that soaks through all parts of the bean. The process extracts 97 percent of the caffeine in the coffee. When the softened beans are agitated in the solvent, caffeine from the beans is drawn into combination with the solvent, and a fine coffee taste is left in the bean. The beans are steamed a second time, heated, and blown dry, evaporating all traces of solvent.

Indirect Contact Method #1 Unroasted coffee beans are soaked in hot water for a long period of time. Gradually, the water, acting as a mild solvent, draws out the caffeine, along with important flavor elements and oils in the coffee. The water, which contains the caffeine as well as the vital coffee oils, is separated from the beans and treated with the solvent methylene chloride. In this process, the solvent never touches the actual bean. The solvent absorbs the caffeine, which is removed with heat by a process of evaporation. The water, containing only the flavor components found in coffee, is reunited with the coffee beans, which absorb their original oils.

Indirect Contact Method #2 The green coffee beans are steeped in hot water, which gradually removes the caffeine. The water is separated from the beans and treated with ethyl acetate. The ethyl acetate absorbs the caffeine and is removed from the water by a steaming process. The vital coffee oils in the remaining water are added to the beans. The entire process is very similar to the methylene chloride-water extraction method; however, ethyl acetate, a natural derivative of coffee and other fruits, requires more time to absorb caffeine.

Water Process (Swiss Water Process) Here the beans are immersed in water—without chemical additives—for several hours, until at least 97 percent of the caffeine is removed. The resulting solution, which contains caffeine as well as the other essential coffee elements, is passed through activated charcoal or carbon filters to remove the caffeine. Then, as in other methods, the coffee elements are added to the coffee beans. This process is sometimes called the "Swiss Water Process," a method originally developed by a Swiss Company.

Different coffees have different caffeine content. In order to qualify as a "decaffeinated" coffee, at least 97 percent of the caffeine naturally existing in the bean must be removed.

DECAFFEINATO (ITAL) Decaffeinated.

DECANT To pour wine from the bottle into a serving container so that any sediment remains in the bottle.

DECANTER A glass carafe or bottle into which old wines (usually red) are decanted, prior to service. *See* Carafe.

D

111

DECANTING The purpose of decanting a wine is twofold. First, aeration during the decanting process allows the wine to "breathe," to gain in bouquet, and to dissipate any "off" odors or gasses that may have accumulated under the cork. Second, separating the wine from its sediment allows it to be served perfectly bright and clear, thus enhancing its appearance. Decanting is recommended for full-bodied red wines and port, but unnecessary for white, rosé, and sparkling wines.

Decanting requires little preparation and is extremely simple. Before starting, prepare the following pieces of equipment: A candle holder and candle, a corkscrew, and a colorless glass decanter or carafe (33 ounce minimum). Be sure that it has been rinsed with a small amount of tepid water and is absolutely free of odor, for certain detergents, if not completely rinsed away, can ruin a wine's bouquet. Do *not* store decanters closed with their own stoppers, but instead stuff the necks gently with a bit of tissue paper.

Follow this simple step-by-step procedure:

1. Stand the bottle upright for at least 24 hours before decanting so that the sediment, which is lying along the side of the bottle, can drop gently to the bottle's bottom. If a 24-hour time period is not possible because of immediate ordering, let the bottle rest horizontally for the time being. Decanting should not be done more than one hour before the wine is to be served because the wine may lose its bouquet. Very old wines should be decanted immediately before serving, as the wine fades and oxidizes rapidly. Bottles of vintage port might have to be stood upright for longer than 24 hours to allow the crusted sediment, known as the dregs, to settle to the bottom.

2. Gently uncork the bottle to avoid disturbing any sediment. If the bottle is lying horizontal, place it into a wicker basket and begin the uncorking process.

3. Light the candle and place the holder in front of a colorless carafe (between the wine and carafe). Then carefully tilt the wine bottle toward the open mouth of the carafe and allow its contents to trickle in slowly and smoothly. While you do this, the flame of the candle should be directly underneath the neck of the wine bottle so that you can follow the movement of sediment from the bottom of the bottle to the neck, insuring the decanted wine's clarity. When the sediment reaches the point where the neck and shoulders of the bottle meet, you should be able to see some of the sediment, which is cloudy or hazy, starting to appear. When this starts to happen, you should stop the decanting process. You will find that only one ounce or so of wine will remain in the bottle, and you will have a wine that is bright and clear in the decanter.

The remaining contents of the bottle should be discarded, and the customer should be asked if he or she would prefer to have the wine served from the decanter or replaced in the cleaned bottle. *See* Aeration and Breathing.

DECAVAILLONAGE (FR)   A ploughing method used along the row of grapevine with a special plough that sidesteps at each grapevine stem. After the passage of the plough, the soil around each stem is tidied up (called *tier le cavaillon*).

DÉCHARNÉ (FR)   *See* Thin.

DÉCHAR/RECHAR   A process by which barrels are scraped down on the inside and re-charred.

DE CHAUNAC   A red French-American hybrid grape variety developed from a cross of Seibel 5163 and Seibel 793, by Albert Seibel, but named after Adhemar deChaunac (the winemaker for the Canadian firm called Brights Wines Ltd., of Ontario, Canada) at a testimonial dinner in his honor in 1972. Originally called "Cameo," the grape is one of the most popular varieties in the East, especially in the Finger Lakes district of New York.

The wines display good color and tannin; slightly tart and sometimes herbaceous, with good aging potential. Formerly known as *Seibel 9549*.

DECIGRAM   A metric unit of weight; 1/10 of a gram; 10 decigrams are equal to 1 gram.

DECIMETER   A metric unit of length; 1/10 of a meter; 10 decimeters are 39 inches.

DECKWEIN (GERM)   Imported red wine, generally high in alcohol and color content, used to improve the color of German red wines. Seldom used today.

DECLASSIFICATION   When a wine does not meet or attain the standards (yield, production, alcohol, taste test, and so on) of law established by a district, region, country, and so on, the wine is declassified, a retrogressive (sometimes voluntary) step in the hierarchy of the wine laws.

DECRECIPTO (ITAL OR SP)   Decrepit; old and faded.

DÉCUVAGE (FR)   Draining the contents of a tank or the unloading of grapes from fermentation tanks immediately after fermentation for the pressing step. *See* Draining Off and Encuvage.

DEFECTIVE PRODUCT   Products that are unmarketable because of product deterioration, leaking containers, damaged labels, or mutilated and missing strip stamps.

DÉGORGEMENT (FR)   The process of freezing the neck of the bottle that contains champagne and a small amount of riddled sediment. This ice plug of sediment and champagne is then forced out by pressure within the bottle when the temporary cap is removed, leaving the remaining champagne crystal clear. Also known as *disgorging* and *sboccatura*.

DÉGORGER (FR)   One who disgorges bottles of sparkling wines.

DEGREE DAYS   When a vintner decides on a grape variety to plant, many factors influence him: location, the soil and its composition, drainage, and the weather that will affect his crop and possibly bring it greatness. The most important criterion in the analysis, however, is *heat summation*: the geographic classification of regions in terms of heat degree days during the seven-month growing season.

In 1936, University of California (Davis) Professor Albert Winkler decided that temperature was a basis for segregating the grape-growing areas of California into five climatic regions. For classification purposes, he used 50 degrees Fahrenheit as a base temperature applied specifically to the seven-month grape-growing season from April 1 to October 31. (The baseline is set at 50 degrees because there is almost no shoot growth below this temperature.) He then developed a formula for "heat summation" above this 50 degree base. Heat summation is defined as the mean temperature or average high and low, greater than 50 degrees, from April 1 through October 31. The resulting figure is expressed as degree days.

For example, if the mean for a day is 70 degrees (50 degrees low and 90 degrees high), the summation for the 24 hour period is 20-degree days (70 - 50 = 20). If this condition occurred every day for a 30-day month, the summation would be 600 degree days (20 degree days x 30 calendar days). *See* Heat Summation.

DEGREES BALLING   *See* Brix.

DEGREES BRIX   *See* Brix.

DEGREES CELSIUS   To convert Fahrenheit into Celsius, subtract 32 from the Fahrenheit temperature, then divide by 1.8; or subtract 32 from Fahrenheit, then multiply by 0.55.

To convert Celsius into Fahrenheit, multiply the Celsius temperature by 1.8 and then add 32; or divide Celsius by 0.55, then add 32.

DEGREES FAHRENHEIT   *See* Degrees Celsius.

DEGUSTACION (SP)   Wine tasting.

DÉGUSTATION (FR)   An old word or term that described a wine tasting.

DEGUSTAZIONE (ITAL)   Wine tasting. Also known as *assaggio*.

DEHARDENING   *See* Rest.

DEI (ITAL)   Of the.

DEKUYPER (DUTCH)   The cooper or barrel maker.

DEL (ITAL)   Of the.

DELAWARE   A pink American *Vitis labrusca* grape variety that was brought from Frenchtown, New Jersey to Delaware, Ohio in 1849. Delaware produces fine quality scented table wines with characteristic flavors when fermented off-dry. Delaware is often used as a base for sparkling wines.

DELICADO (PORT OR SP)   *See* Delicate.

DÉLICAT (FR)   *See* Delicate.

DELICATE   Wines that are soft, pleasing, and light in style, with lower-intensity flavors, and never assertive. Delicate would be the opposite of a big, robust, full-bodied wine. Usually reserved for young and fresh red wines or white wines, lower in alcohol. Also known as *delicado, délicat, delicato, delikat,* and *fein.*

DELICATO (ITAL)   *See* Delicate.

DELIKAT (GERM)   *See* Delicate.

DELIMITED   A word applied to a geographic area, with specific borders, within which a particular distilled spirit or wine may be legally may.

DELIZIO (ITAL)   Delicious.

DELLA (ITAL)   Of the.

DELMONICO GLASS   A cocktail glass that holds five to seven fluid ounces of a cocktail or sour with a frothy head.

D

DEMERARA   *See* Rum.

DEMI (FR)   Half.

DEMIJOHN   A large glass (or plastic) container that usually holds five gallons of liquid and that often is used for the transportation or storage of wine or spring/mineral water. It is a corruption of the French Dame-Jeanne by the British, which meant a large glass bottle used for the transportation of wine. It held anywhere from one to ten gallons of wine and was usually wrapped with wicker or straw. Also known as a *carboy* and *damigiana.*

DEMI-MUID (FR)   A large barrel with a capacity of 171 U.S. gallons. *See* Barrel.

DEMINERALIZED WATER   Water from which the mineral salts have been removed by passing it over a bed or *ion-exchange resins.*

DEMI-QUEUE (FR)   A large barrel with a capacity of approximately 60 U.S. gallons (228 liters).

DEMISEC (FR)   Semidry or half-dry; used mostly in the Champagne region. In the United States it is applied to rather sweet sparkling wines.

DEMI-TASSE (FR)   Literally, "half cup": often used term when requesting a cup of espresso coffee.

DENOMINACAO DE ORIGEM (PORT)   The equivalent of Italy's DOC Wine Laws.

DENOMINACIÓN DE ORIGEN (SP)   The equivalent of Italy's DOC Wine Laws.

DENOMINATION OF ORIGIN   *See* Appellation of Origin.

DENOMINAZIONE DI ORIGINE CONTROLLATA (DOC) (ITAL)   Italy's Wine Laws, enacted in 1963. On July 12, 1963, the president of the Republic of Italy, Antonio Segni, signed into law at the Palazzo del Quirinale (his official residence) the Italian Wine Laws, known as the *Denominazione di Origine Controllata* (or DOC laws), under Presidential Decree No. 930. On July 15, these laws were published in the *Gazzetta Ufficiale della Republica Italiana*, the official registry of the Italian government.

The basic aim of the wine law was to protect the name of origin and the sources of *musts* (unfermented grape juice) and wines, and to provide measures to prevent fraud and unfair competition.

These very comprehensive laws cover just about every phase of grape cultivation and wine production and provide strict controls at every step of the process. The following are some of the aspects of wine production that are regulated under these laws:

Area of production.
Type of soil.
Location of vineyard.
Type of grape variety used.
Pruning and cultivation techniques.
Allowable yields per acre (tonnage).
Allowable yield of juice per ton of grapes.
Minimum sugar levels.
Minimum acid and extract levels.
Methods of vinification.
Minimum aging requirements.

There are currently more than 220 DOCs, all delimited geographical, though a zone may extend through an entire region or apply to only a few choice plots in a single community.

DENOMINAZIONE DI ORIGINE CONTROLLATA E GARANTITA (DOCG) (ITAL)
This designation is given to those wines that are considered to be of a higher quality than DOC wines and made under even stricter guidelines. There are currently eight wines (seven red and one white) that have received the DOCG status. They are Brunello di Montalcino, Chianti, Vino Nobile di Montepulciano, Carmignano Rosso, Barolo, Gattinara, Torgiano Rosso, and Albana di Romagna (white).

DENSITY   The compactness of a substance; referred as its specific gravity. Also known as *pyknós*.

DEPLETION   A case of product shipped from the distributor to the retailer.

DEPLETION ALLOWANCE   Payments made to a distributor based on a rate per case depleted. This rate cannot lower the FOB in that territory below the minimum FOB as listed in the control states. Also known as *standard depletion allowance.*

DEPOSEE (FR) Registered.

DEPOSIT *See* Sediment.

DEPOSITO (PORT AND SP) A large tank or barrel used for the storage of wines. *See* Barrel.

DEPOSITO (ITAL) *See* Sediment.

DEPÒSITO (SP) *See* Sediment.

DÉPOSITO (PORT) *See* Sediment.

DÉPÔT (FR) *See* Sediment.

DEPRESSANTS Drugs or alcohol that slow or reduce the activity of bodily systems.

DEPTH A wine with intense complex flavors that seem to fill the mouth from front to back. Subtle layers of flavor that are long-lasting. It is a characteristic that attracts one to go on exploring them. It should be expected of most premium wines.

DEPTH CHARGE Take a shot glass full of whiskey and plunge it (glass and all) into a large glass of beer, then drink the beer.

DESCARNADO (PORT) *See* Thin.

DESENGAGE (PORT) *See* Égrappage.

DESERTO VINO (YUG) Dessert wine.

DESIGNATED DRIVER PROGRAM Informal arrangement between a customer and the operator of a beverage facility. One person in a group voluntarily does not drink alcoholic beverages and serves as the driver for the group. The person acting as the "designated driver" is usually offered complimentary "mocktails" or soft drinks.

DESLIO (SP) *See* Falling Bright.

DESSERT WINE A still wine naturally having an alcoholic content in excess of 14 percent but not in excess of 24 percent by volume. It can be dry or sweet. Also, sweet table or fortified wines meant for consumption after dinner. Also known as *deserto vino.*

DESSICATED GRAPES Cracked and shriveled grapes, resembling raisins, as a result of being attacked by *Botrytis cinerea*, the "noble rot." *See Botrytis Cinerea.*

DESTEMMING A process by which the stems of grapes are removed prior to fermentation. *See* Crusher/Destemmer.

DESTINATION INSPECTION The inspection performed at the receiving point of the consignee of material to ascertain whether the shipment is in conformance with purchase specifications and contractual documents.

DETERIORATION   Any impairment of quality, value, or usefulness. Includes damage caused by corrosion and contamination.

DETOXIFICATION   The process of weaning or removing the physiological effects of alcohol from an addicted individual. A reduction of the toxic properties of a poisonous substance in the body.

DEUXIÈME TAILLE (FR)   The third pressing of the grapes in champagne making.

DEVELOPED   A wine that has reached its point of maturity in all of its characteristics.

DEXTRIN   Soluble, partly degraded carbohydrate molecules formed from starch in its decomposition by acids, heat, or diastase (enzymes). It is in the intermediate state between starch and sugar. It is produced during mashing and, although not fermentable, it contributes to the terminal body of the beer. Also spelled *dextrine*. See Diastase and Amylase.

DEXTROSE   A basic crystalline sugar, also known as *corn sugar*, produced commercially from corn starch. Sometimes used as a substitute for malt in brewing.

DGN   *See* Dirección General de Normas.

DI (ITAL)   Of.

DIAMMONIUM PHOSPHATE   Yeast food in distilling material.

DIAMOND   A greenish-yellow American *Vitis labrusca* grape variety that yields one of the best native American white wines; light-colored, and dry, with an aromatic scent and gravelly, flinty overtones to its spicy-fruity flavor.

Diamond was produced from a cross of Concord and Iona grapes, which was developed by Jacob Moore, of Brighton, New York, in 1870. It is planted mostly in eastern U.S. vineyards, where it is widely used as a base for sparkling wines. Its popularity has dwindled greatly in recent years due to superior varieties and the fact that its yields are low. Also known as *Moore's Diamond*.

DIANA   An eastern U.S. pink hybrid grape (now rarely used) that was used as a blending grape, in an attempt to improve the quality of Catawba wines. Its name originates from Mrs. Diana Crehore of Milton, Massachusetts, who in 1834 planted a seed of an open pollinated Catawba grape variety. One red-fruited seedling was unusually fine and was named in her honor by the Massachusetts Horticultural Society.

DIASTASE   When conditions of temperature and moisture favor germination, the embryo in the barley secretes diastase, an enzyme. This acts to modify and make soluble the starch in the barley, thus preparing it for conversion at a later stage to maltose. This enzyme activity is halted by drying the malt. A preparation of amylase enzymes can also be added to the mash to enhance the conversion of starch to sugar. *See* Dextrin and Amylase.

DIATOMACEOUS EARTH (DE)   A filtering agent used in the production of some alcoholic beverages. It is essentially pure silica that is mined from the floor of the sea. It comes from the silicified cell wall or the fossilized skeletons of microscopic aquatic-life called "diatoms," of which the more well-known "plankton" forms a major part. Diatoms are the primary link in the sea's chain of life; in fact all life, for it is these tiny creatures that produce approximately 80 percent of the oxygen that man breathes. Commercial deposits mined in the United States today are about 15 million years old, and collectively contain about 10,000 known species of diatoms. Their skeletons, almost pure calcium, are totally inert and therefore impart no flavor to wine. Also known as *infusorial earth*, *keissulguhr*, or *diatomite*.

DIATOMITE   *See* Diatomaceous Earth.

DICE   *See* Ice Cubes.

DICK (GERM)   A wine that generally contains too much residual sugar and appears to be cloying.

DI CORPO (ITAL)   Full-bodied, with high alcoholic degree.

DIETHYLENE GLYCOL   A chemical used in some industrial products, such as antifreeze. Its use is not approved for use in food and beverage.

DIFFUSE   Wines and beers that taste unstructured and unfocused due to being improperly served too warm or served in warm to hot weather.

DIGESTIVE   A beverage that contains moderate to high levels of bittering substances. Alcoholic products from France that have the letter "D" stamped on their labels are examples of digestives. Also known as *digestivo*. *See* Bitters.

DIGESTIVO (ITAL)   *See* Digestive.

DINNER WINE   A still table wine, generally dry with an alcoholic content from 7 to 14 percent alcohol by volume. Also known as *table wine*.

DIONYSUS   The Greek god of wine. *See* Bacchus.

DIRECCIÓN GENERAL DE NORMAS (DGN)   In an effort to control the production and quality of tequila, the Mexican government has devised a set of strict regulations. These regulations have since become somewhat more restricted and defined and are now known as *Norma Oficial Mexicana de Calidad* (NOM).

DIRECT IMPORT OR DI   When a retailer purchases directly from a supplier (winery, brewery, or distillery), bypassing the middle level, or "distributor." This practice is illegal in most states.

DIRECT ISSUES   *See* Direct Purchases.

DIRECT PRODUCER   Grape varieties that grow on their own root system, not needing to be grafted to other root stock to thrive and produce. Seldom employed today.

DIRECT PURCHASES   Alcoholic beverages that are received and put directly into the beverage area (bar). These items never go through the storeroom; therefore, there are no requisitions for them. A system of this nature opens itself up to employee pilferage. Also known as *direct issues*.

Disbudding The removal of excess buds or very young shoots on a grapevine.

Discount Purchasing *See* Bulk Buying or Quantity Purchasing.

DISCUS *See* Distilled Spirits Council of the United States.

Disgorging *See* Dégorgement.

Displayed Consumer Offer Use of a consumer offer as part of a promotional in-store display.

Disposable Income Income that households have left after the payment of taxes and household bills.

Dissolve To mix a solid into a liquid solution.

Distillate The concentrated clear liquid obtained from distillation. Also known as *distillato*.

Distillation Distillation involves the separation of alcohol from the liquid in the fermented mash. Since alcohol boils at 173.1 degrees Fahrenheit and water boils at 212 degrees Fahrenheit, it is relatively easy to separate the alcohol and flavoring components from the mash. The higher the heat, the greater the volume of distilled neutral spirits. The lower the heat, the greater the amount of flavor that is carried through distillation. The mash enters near the top of a continuous still or column still, while steam enters near the still's bottom chambers, thus vaporizing the alcohol and flavoring components. When the vapor is drawn off, it condenses into a liquid, known as *low wine*, with an alcoholic content of anywhere from 45 to 65 percent. The low wine is redistilled, or further refined, allowing the alcohol to reach an even higher concentration and further remove unwanted impurities and flavors. The resulting liquid is called *high wine*, or new whiskey; it is crystal clear and ready for maturing. Also known as *distillazione*.

Distillato (Ital) *See* Distillate.

Distillatore (Ital) Distiller.

Distillazione (Ital) *See* Distillation.

Distilled Spirits Ethyl alcohol, hydrated oxide of ethyl, spirits of wine, whiskey, rum, brandy, gin, and other distilled spirits, including all dilutions and mixtures thereof, for nonindustrial use. *See* Spirits.

Distilled Spirits Council of the United States (DISCUS) The distilled spirits industry's trade association.

Distilled Spirits Plant An establishment qualified for producing, warehousing, or processing of distilled spirits (including distilled denatured spirits), or manufacturing of articles.

Distilleria (Ital) *See* Distillery.

Distiller's Beer The alcoholic beer or low wine ready for distillation.

Distiller's Feed Grains Highly nutritious animal feed made from the processed grain residue left behind after fermentation and distillation. Although lower in bulk than unprocessed grain, because the starch is removed during mashing and fermentation, these feeds remain high in protein and are enriched beyond the food value of the unprocessed grain because of the presence of yeasts used in fermentation.

DISTILLERY   The building that houses the apparatus where distilling of alcoholic beverages is carried out. Also known as *distilleria*.

DISTILLING MATERIAL   Any fermented or other alcoholic substance capable of, or intended for use in, the original distillation or other original processing of distilled spirits.

DISTINCTIVE   Recognizable qualities that can immediately be distinguished. Having its own character.

DDISTINGUÉ (FR)   *See* Distinguished.

DISTINGUISHED   A wine of elegance, harmony, class, and exceptional character; a step above the rest. Also known as *distingué*.

DISTRIBUIDORES EXCLUSIVOS (SP)   Exclusive distributors.

DISTRIBUTOR POST-OFF   A case price discount on alcoholic beverages that a distributor sometimes is permitted to offer to a retailer. Also known as *file-offs*, *post downs*, *posts* and *file downs*.

DISTRIBUTORS   Wholesalers (the second level of the "three-tier" system) who purchase wholesale from suppliers and sell retail to retailers.

DISTRIBUZIONE (ITAL)   Distribution.

DITTA (ITAL)   Bottled at the premises of the firm or company.

DIVE   A term that refers to a dilapidated bar.

DO (SP OR PORT)   *See* Denominación de Origen or Denominacao de Origem.

DOC (ITAL)   *See* Denominazione di Origine Controllata.

DOCE (PORT)   *See* Sweet. Also known as *adamado*.

DOCG (ITAL)   *See* Denominazione di Origine Controllata e Garantita.

DOCK GLASS (PORT)   A small, short-stemmed wine glass, which is elongated with a tulip-shaped bowl that holds two to three ounces. These glasses are used by professional port tasters for evaluation purposes. Also known as *port glass*.

DOLCE (ITAL)   *See* Sweet.

DOLCETTO (ITAL)   A red grape variety grown predominantly in the Piedmont region where it is produced in the Langhe Hills just south of the town of Alba. The Dolcetto grapevine is indigenous to the area and was subject to local government regulations as early as 1593. It is Piedmont's most widely planted grapevine after Barbera. Inherently a little weak, it is not an easy grapevine to cultivate; it requires much pruning and thrives only in the calcareous soil characteristic of the Langhe area.

Dolcetto differs from the more famous wine of Piedmont, like Barolo, in that it is lighter, with an intense purple color in its youth, is intended to be drunk young usually has a high level of acidity, and is occasionally quite sharp, almost to the point of being sour.

The name *Dolcetto* could be roughly translated to mean "little sweet one." The name, however, is misleading: Dolcetto is a dry red wine with a pleasing bitter aftertaste. Also known as *Dolsin* and *Dolsin Nero*.

DÔLE (SWISS) *See* Red Wine.

DOLOMIES (FR) Limestone rock rich in magnesium used as a fertilizer.

DOLSIN (ITAL) *See* Dolcetto.

DOLSIN NERO (ITAL) *See* Dolcetto.

DOM (GERM) Cathedral.

DOMAINE (FR) Wine estate. Synonym of Château, Clos, or Cru.

DOMAINE BOTTLED (FR) (Mise en bouteilles au domaine.) Same as Château bottled, except as practiced in Burgundy.

DOMÄNE (GERM) A domain, or vineyard estate.

DOMESTIC A term often used to describe alcoholic beverages made in the United States, as opposed to imported types. However, the term domestic should be avoided, because it has the connotation of a cheap replica or imitation. Instead, the term American should be substituted.

DOM PÉRIGNON (FR) It was not until the mid-sixteenth century that Dom Pierre Pérignon (1638–1715), a blind Benedictine monk, during his tenure as chief cellar master at Hautvillers (1668–1715), discovered the wine that is now called champagne; he perfected the technique for its production by blending wines to achieve a consistent and harmonious balance, using an oil-soaked hemp rag or the bark of a tree as a temporary bottle stopper. In 1668, Dom Pérignon bottled the first bottle of champagne.

DOP BRANDY (SOUTH AFRICA) *See* Grappa.

DOPPLEBOCK (GERM) *See* Bock Beer.

DOPPLEOHM (GERM) A large barrel with the capacity of 79 U.S. gallons. *See* Barrel.

DOPPLESTÜCK (GERM) A large barrel with a capacity of 634 U.S. gallons. *See* Barrel.

DORIN (SWISS) *See* Chasselas Doré.

DORMANCY The inactive, non-vegetative resting of the grapevine that occurs in winter and during which time the canes are pruned. *See* Rest and Quiescence.

DORTMUNDER BEER (GERM) Golden-colored beers with high levels of malt and hops, traditionally brewed in Dortmund.

DOSAGE (FR) The addition of a mixture of sugar syrup, grape concentrate, and/or brandy to champagne or sparkling wines before recorking and eventual shipping, which establishes the level of sweetness in the finished product. Also known as *dosing, liqueur d'expédition,* and *süssung. See* Liqueur de Tirage.

DOSAGE ZERO *See* Extra Brut.

DOSING *See* Dosage.

DOSSER Grape-picking baskets. *See* Brenta.

DOUBLE AUM (GERM) A barrel with the capacity of approximately 60 U.S. gallons. *See* Barrel.

DOUBLE MAGNUM An oversized bottle with a capacity of four standard 750-milliliter bottles or 101.4 fluid ounces (3-liters). It is also the largest sized bottle that French champagne is fermented in. Also known as *Jeroboam.*

DOUBLE PRUNING It is the cultural practice whereby twice the number of buds dictated by the balanced pruning formula are retained after an initial pruning in early to mid-winter. A second pruning is done after bud damage can be assessed and/or the threat of spring frost injury is minimal.

DOUBLER The pot still used for *doubling.*

DOUBLING In whiskey production, it is the redistilling of a spirit to help improve its strength and flavor.

DOUCEREUX (FR) *See* Cloying.

DOUIL (FR) A grape harvesting vat where picked grapes are placed.

DOURO (PORT) Important grape-growing region of Portugal where port wine is produced. The production of port is limited to a strictly defined area of approximately 1,500 square miles along the River Douro in northern Portugal. The slopes of the Douro, which have a very slatelike soil known as schist, are cut out and terraced for planting with vineyards. These walled terraces prevent erosion of the precious soil. The Douro is the world's second legally demarcated wine region (Italy's Chianti Classico region, was demarcated in 1716 by the grand duke of Tuscany). In 1756, during the era of the Marquis of Pombal (almost 200 years before France's *appellation contrôlée* regulations became law), the Douro region was defined to protect the quality and good name of port (known as *porto,* in Portugal). In that same year, Pombal reestablished the Oporto Wine Company.

DOUX (FR) The sweetest champagne produced that is not available in the United States and that is only produced in limited quantities for Eastern Europe. According to the European Common Market, champagnes labeled "doux" must contain more than 50 grams of sugar per liter.

DOWNY MILDEW (PLASMOPARA VITICOLA) A fungal disease native to North America, that attacks most species of wild and cultivated grape. The disease (then known as *Peronospora*) was inadvertently introduced into European vineyards in 1878 where it devastated the European grapevine *Vitis vinifera,* which is generally more susceptible to the disease than native American grapes. Today, the disease can be found on grapevines in most regions of the world that are wet during the growing season. The fungus causes direct yield losses by rotting inflorescences, clusters, and shoots, and indirect losses by premature defoliating grapevines, which increases their susceptibility to winter injury and delays ripening of the fruit.

DR. PEPPER   A sweetened carbonated soft drink containing artificial black cherry flavoring.

DRAFF   The residue left from the mashing process in making beer (or whiskey), which is then strained to produce the wort.

DRAFT BEER   According to the U.S. government, draft beer may be so labeled on cans or bottles if it is unpasteurized or if it has been bottled under sterile filtration methods. It may not be labeled "draft beer" if it has been pasteurized, but it may use the terminology "draft-brewed," "old time on tap taste," or "draft beer flavor."

Draft beer is not pasteurized; it is of a delicate and perishable nature, just like milk, eggs, and other perishables. Its flavor can be changed if it is not kept under constant refrigeration. The ideal storage temperature for draft beer is 38 degrees Fahrenheit. If the temperature is allowed to rise above 45 degrees to 50 degrees Fahrenheit for an extended length of time, secondary fermentation may occur, making the beer unpalatable.

Once sold only by the keg and in bars, it is not pasteurized—the process used to stop fermentation at a given point for shipping. Now, by filtering out the active enzymes, brewers can make it available in bottles or cans. Also spelled *draught beer*. Also known as *tap beer* and *keg beer*.

DRAINED WEIGHT   Weight of contents of a package minus its liquid and container.

DRAINING OFF   After the primary fermentation (alcoholic fermentation) of red wines (which contain skins, seeds, and pulp) the juice is drained off (kept separate) and the skins, which are still heavily laden with juice, are immediately sent to a press for further juice extraction. The white wines are allowed to settle, then drained off from the fermentation tank without disturbing the sediment that is at the bottom of the tank. From there, the white wine is transferred to another container where it remains until bottling. *See* Decuvage and Encuvage.

DRAKE TUBE   A cylindrical tube, with a capacity of more than 100 milliliters, that contains a hydrometer for measuring the specific gravity of beer or wine.

DRAM   A unit of avoirdupois weight equal to 0.0625 fluid ounces.

DRAM SHOP ACTS   State acts that define liability for alcoholic beverage sales to patrons who injure or kill third parties.

DRAM SHOP LIABILITY   Liability to third parties created by the sale of alcoholic beverages to a patron.

DRAPEAU (FR)   *See* Jacketed Tank.

DRAUGHT BEER   *See* Draft Beer.

DRAW-KNIFE   A sharp, two-handled instrument, which is pulled toward the cooper, in order to shave the staves of a wooden barrel to more or less their finished shape.

DRAW ONE   A slang term meaning to pour a beer.

DREGS (PORT)   The extremely heavy sediment found in bottles of port wine. *See* Sediment.

DRIED FRUIT BRANDY   It is a brandy that conforms to the standards for fruit brandy, except that it has been derived from sound, dried fruit, or from the standard of wine of such fruit. Brandy derived from raisins or raisin wine shall be designated as "raisin brandy." Other brandies shall be designated in the same manner as fruit, brandy from the corresponding variety or varieties of fruit except that the name of the fruit shall be qualified by the word "dried."

DRIED WHOLE MILK   It is a milk product from which only the water has been removed, leaving the milk and cream content intact.

DRIMYS (GREECE)   *See* Pungent.

DRINKING WATER   Bottled water that comes from a government-approved source (municipal or state), then filtered or treated in some manner before bottling. The water can come from the tap, a well, a lake, and so on. It can also be blended with water from other sources. The water is always processed in some way (e.g. the addition of chlorine or other chemicals, the addition or deletion of mineral salts).

DRIP IRRIGATION   Drip (or trickle) irrigation is the slow, frequent, precise application of irrigation water directly to the plant through devices known as "emitters." Emitters are placed on the soil or just below the surface of the row crop soil.

Although there are usually a large number of emitters per acre, they wet only a small portion of the soil. Drip systems utilize the simple concept of supplying a plant's daily water requirements directly to the plant. These systems can be elaborate and sophisticated but are typically the most uniform, efficient, and manageable of all the types of irrigation systems. They are especially adapted to situations where water is expensive or of low quality or where crops of high value are grown.

DRIPPING ROD   A graduated rod (sometimes glass) that measures the contents of a barrel of wine.

DROSOPHILA MELANOGASTER   A strain of fruit flies that are drawn to grapes or fermenting grape juice, by the smell of small quantities of vinegar formed during fermentation. The fruit flies lay eggs in the broken skins of the grapes, seriously contaminating the grapes or must, raising the level of volatile acidity, which could cause the wine to turn to vinegar.

DRU (FR)   Thick, dense; a very young, undeveloped distilled spirit.

DRUNK   Slang for intoxicated.

Dry   A wine with little or no noticeable residual sugar, usually containing less than 0.2 percent sugar; however, the range for a dry wine can be construed to be within the range of 0.2 to 0.6 percent sugar. most wine tasters begin to perceive the presence of sugar at levels of 0.7 percent. On champagne and sparkling wines, *dry* only refers to faintly sweet—not as dry as brut. Also known as *sec, seco, secco, suho, trocken* and *xirós*.

Dry   A designation of a cordial or liqueur, if the sugar, dextrose, or levulose, or a combination thereof, are less than 10 percent by weight of the finished product.

Dry Beer   Beers made to be drier to the taste with no aftertaste. Basically, during the cooking process, brewers extract as much sugar as possible from the malted barley and mixing grains (rice, corn, etc.), then allow the fermentation to last an additional seven to ten days.

Dry Break   When a bottle is broken and left in the case untouched for several months. The cardboard will dry out, and unless the case is shaken, the break will not be detected.

Dry County   County (or similar governmental jurisdiction) whose voters have not approved the sale of alcoholic beverages. Counties permitting sale only by private clubs are considered dry. *See* Wet County.

Dry Gin   *See* London Dry Gin.

Dry Goods   Paper, and so forth, behind a bar.

Dry Sherry   *See* Amontillado and Cocktail Sherry.

Dry Storage   That portion of the bar or storeroom utilized for the storage of nonrefrigerated goods.

Dry Vermouth   *See* Vermouth.

Dry Whole Milk   Whole milk with all the moisture evaporated.

Duela (sp)   Stave. This is the arched oak-wood strip that, in greater or smaller quantities, constitutes the contour of the barrel.

Duft (germ)   Fragrance.

DUI   Driving Under the Influence of Alcohol. *See* DWI.

Dulce (sp)   *See* Sweet.

Dulce Apagado (sp)   *See* Mistelle.

Dull   A wine that displays lack of brilliance in its appearance. A wine that is uninteresting and lacks distinction or individuality because of low acidity. Also known as *terne*.

Dumb   A wine with potential, but not yet developed enough or not offering its full quality or character. Also used to describe wines with undeveloped aromas and flavors but that display full and hard levels of tannin. Often, the wine is too young or perhaps served too cold. Wines often go through certain stages of development called a "dumb stage" where, for unexplained reasons, they "just don't taste right." Several reasons might be serving a full-bodied red wine during warm weather, wines subjected to recent rough handling, freshly or newly bottled wine, and so on. Also known as *closed-in, fermé, muto, numb* and *restrained. See* Mute and Numb.

DUMPING A close-out; alcoholic products are "dumped" onto the retail market at below list prices in order to eliminate all existing merchandise inventory.

DUNCAN TAVERN MUSEUM A tavern in Kentucky where pioneer Daniel Boone used to drink.

DUNDER The residue (sugar cane juice remains) left in the still after distillation that is generally used in the production of full-bodied rums.

DUNKEL (GERM) Dark.

DÜNN (GERM) Thin-bodied.

DUPE A shortened term or abbreviation for "duplicate." Each check has two parts: A hard copy, which is presented to the guest, and a soft copy, which is turned in at the bar for service. As the server writes on this NCR check, a "dupe" or duplicate copy of the order is inscribed.

The duplicate check control system insures management that each check is accounted for and properly priced. It also verifies the quantities of a beverage that has been ordered and served.

DUR (FR) *See* Hard.

DURIF A dark-skinned red grape variety prolifically grown in California where it has mistakenly been known for decades as *Petite Sirah*. It has for decades been commonly used as a blending grape, adding inky black color, richness, body, and a somewhat spicy-peppery character to wines. It has even been utilized as a single varietal by many California vintners in past years.

Durif also flourishes in the Rhône Valley of southern France where it is disallowed for use in *appellation contrôlée* wines, but commonly used as a blending grape for *vin ordinaire* wines.

Durif was named in 1880 after Dr. Durif, a nurseryman who propagated it mostly in the Rhône Valley. Also known as *Petite Sirah* and *Serine* in California. Incorrectly spelled *Duriff*.

DURO (ITAL) *See* Hard.

DUSTY *See* Chewy.

DUTCH GIN *see* Holland Gin.

DUTCHESS A white *Vitis labrusca* grape variety, developed from a natural crossing of an unnamed seedling of possibly White Concord, which had been pollinated with a *Vitis vinifera* species. It was developed in 1868 by Andrew Jackson Caywood of Marlboro, New York (Dutchess County). It is used both as a white wine varietal as well as a base for sparkling wines.

DWI Driving While Intoxicated. *See* DUI.

E   A letter designation used on labels of Armagnac, Cognac, and some other brandies as an abbreviation for *extra*.

EARTHY   Descriptive term used to describe scents or odors reminiscent of soil or the earth in which grapes are grown. Often used to describe wines from France. Also known as *bodengeschmack, erdig, goût de terroir*, and *yeódis*.

EAU (FR)   Water.

EAU-DE-VIE   Literally meaning "water of life." A clear distillate of fruit or grape wine, first produced by the Arabs in the seventh century and the "origin" of today's brandies and Cognacs. Grape brandies, which include Armagnac and Cognac, are known as *eau-de-vie* before barrel aging. *See* Grappa and Alcools Blancs.

EBU   *See* European Bitterness Units.

EBULLIOMETER   An instrument used in the United States to measure the alcoholic content of wine. *See* Alcoholometer.

EBULLIOMETRY   It is the technique of precise determinations of boiling and condensation temperatures. The boiling (point) temperature is that temperature at which liquids or a solution boils under a certain constant pressure.

ECHT (GERM)   Genuine.

ÉCLAIRCISSAGE (FR)   Crop thinning.

ECM   European Common Market.

EDEL (GERM)   Noble; remarkable, fine, of superior quality.

EDELBEERENAUSLESE (GERM)   The term used prior to 1971 for wines of the beerenauslese category.

EDELFÄULE (GERM)   The noble mold responsible for Eiswein, Beerenauslese, and Trockenbeerenauslese wines. *See* Botrytis Cinerea.

EDELSÜSSE (GERM)   A great sweet, noble wine.

EDES (HUN) *See* Sweet.

EDIBLE PORTION (EP) The portion remaining after trimming or fabrication that is used for consumption in a beverage facility. Pouring costs are sometimes referred to as EP costs.

EDUCACION (SP) The maturing and/or blending of a new wine.

EDULCORÉ (FR) Artificially sweetened.

EEC European Economic Community.

EFFERVESCENT WINE A wine containing more than 0.392 grams of carbon dioxide per 100 milliliters.

EFKHÁRISTOS (GREECE) Pleasing or satisfying.

EGGNOG A rich, creamy nonalcoholic dairy beverage made with egg yolks, cream, and sugar. The alcoholic version consists of egg yolks, sugar, cream, and, generally, brandy or rum. Also spelled *egg nog*. *See* Advokatt.

EGG WHITES Used to clarify wine. *See* Fining and Fining Agents.

ÉGRAPPAGE (FR) The separation of the grapes from the stalks before pressing and fermentation. Also known as *égrappees* and *desengage*.

ÉGRAPPEES (FR) *See* Égrappage.

ÉGRAPPOIR (FR) *See* Crusher/Destemmer.

EGRI BIKAVER (HUN) A dry, red table wine that is deep, rich, and robust, often referred to as "bull's blood." This wine is best when drunk before it is three years old.

EHRENFELSER (GERM) A white grape variety made from a cross of Johannisberg Riesling and Sylvaner clones by Professor Birk in Geisenheim, in the Rheinpfalz. The Ehrenfelser, named for the Ehrenfels ruins near the village of Rüdesheim, was created in 1929, but did not receive a patent until 1969.

EHRWEIN (GERM) A very fine quality wine.

EIDETIC IMAGERY OR RECOLLECTION Also known as the so-called "photographic memory." A persisting mental image of a visual scene that the subject sees as "outside his head" and is able to "read off" with unusual vividness by moving his eyes, as if scanning the original scene. A sense that is of necessity with sensory evaluation.

EINZELLAGE (GERM) *See* Vineyard.

EISBOCK (GERM) An extra strong bock beer in which the alcoholic content has been raised by freezing. When the beer begins to melt, the water is drawn off, concentrating the taste as well as raising the alcoholic level.

EISENBERG (AUS) A village and wine region near the Hungarian border in southern Burgenland. Mostly fruity red wines come from this area.

EISWEIN (GERM) This name is reserved for wine made from grapes of the BA or TBA category, picked and harvested frozen. These frozen grapes produce a wine that is both sweeter and more concentrated than the average *prädikat* wine.

The practice of making wine from grapes naturally frozen on the grapevine has long been a part of the wine culture of Germany. With the Rhine and Mosel's best vineyards lying just about as far north as grapes can ripen, working with frozen grapes is not only a tradition but sometimes a necessity as well. German winemakers have built their reputations by exploiting nature, allowing the grapes to hang on the grapevine past normal harvesting time to further ripen and be affected by *Botrytis*.

The adversary that the vintner faces late in the growing season is cold weather—the chance of an early frost or hard freeze. If the grapes are spared a freezing cold and can sufficiently dry before harvest, wines of incredible lusciousness and complexity can be produced. But if nature wins the battle and a hard freeze hits the vineyards, the winemaker has but one outside chance—to pick and crush the frozen grapes, hopefully producing the rare and unique *eiswein* Although this was once a rare product (made only every second or third decade), *eiswein* is today produced somewhat more frequently because new, colder vineyard sites are allowed to yield frozen grapes.

The production of *eiswein* is governed by a simple physical law. Water, which freezes at 32 degrees Fahrenheit, constitutes the major portion of the pulp and juice of grapes. As the grapes freeze, it is the water inside them that actually freezes, and not the other elements, of which sugar is the largest component. When these grapes are crushed, the frozen water is not pressed out, only the luscious, sugary nectar of the grapes, which is only a fraction of the juice. But while the freeze steals from juice quantity, the *must* weight gains in concentration. It becomes heavily laden with sugar, sometimes doubling its usual strength; it also has a high level of acidity. The resulting wines are characteristically rich in body with a fine natural sweetness and a mature, complex bouquet and flavor. All of the flavors of the grape are intensified and magnified, making this child of considerable risk a prized success for the vintner.

In the production of *eiswein* the grapevines are wrapped in large plastic covers to protect them from birds, wind, and snow. The grapes are then allowed to hang on the grapevines in the hope that the already present *Botrytis* will spread throughout the vineyard. When 30 to 40 percent *Botrytis* infection of the vineyard has occurred, vintners hope that cold weather will strike, hard freezing the grapes on the grapevines. Sustained day/night temperatures in the high teens to low twenties (Fahrenheit) will allow the grapes to become frozen. Sometimes, the winemakers will not harvest them until November, December, or even January. However, the longer they wait, the stronger the chance for the grapes to shrivel up and fall from the grapevines.

When the grapes are sufficiently frozen, they are harvested (usually early in the morning before the sun can thaw them) and shipped to the winery. There they are pressed in small batches in a basket press, extracting a slight 50 gallons of juice per ton of grapes. The flow of the sweet juice from the press is pencil thin, the grapes yielding less than one-third the normal volume of juice. Also known as *ice wine*.

EKLEKTÓS (GREECE)   *See* Vinous.

ELABORADO POR (SP)   *See* Criado Por.

ELBLING (GERM)   *See* Burger.

ELÉGANT (FR)   *See* Elegant.

ELEGANT (GERM)   *See* Elegant.

ELEGANT   A wine characterized by a dignified richness, grace, and refinement, with good balance; not a big robust wine. Also known as *elégant, elegante* and *racé*.

ELEGANTE (ITAL)   *See* Elegant.

ÉLEVAGE (FR)   The maturing or aging of wine or distilled spirits in a barrel.

ÉLEVEUR (FR)   *See* Broker.

ELIXIR   A term used by alchemists who sought out various recipes in search of love potions, cure-alls for man's ailments, everlasting life, rejuvenation, and aphrodisiacs. Today, elixir refers to alcoholic beverages that have medicinal value.

ELLAGIC ACID   A simple tannin or polyphenol present in grape skins, seeds, and stems that causes astringency in wine. It is usually removed by the addition of gelatin as a fining agent.

ELONGATED WINE   British term for wine that is stretched by the addition of water, often used to reduce the alcohol for purposes of excise duty.

ELTINGER   *See* Knipperlé.

ELVIRA   A native American white grape variety, introduced in Missouri in 1869 by Jacob Rommel. Also known as *Missouri Riesling*.

EMBOTELLADO (SP)   Bottled.

EMBOTELLADO EN LA BODEGA (SP)   Bottled at the bodega.

EMBOTELLADO EN ORIGEN (SP)   Estate bottled.

EMBOTELLADO POR (SP)   Produced and bottled by.

EMERALD RIESLING   A white grape variety developed in 1946, from a cross of Muscadelle and Johannisberg Riesling, by Dr. Harold P. Olmo, of the University of California, Davis.

EMILIA-ROMAGNA (ITAL)   A wine region located north of Tuscany in north-central Italy, famous for Lambrusco wine; the city of Bologna (noted for its rich cuisine Reggiano-Parmigiano cheese and prosciutto ham); and the operatic tenor Luciano Pavarotti.

EMPTY BOTTLE RETURN   *See* Bottle-For-Bottle.

ENCABEZADO (SP)   *See* Fortification.

Encapsulated Yeast   Beads of a few millimeters in diameter, consisting of an alginate that encapsulates the yeasts needed for the secondary fermentation of wine to produce sparkling wines. Also known as *calcium alginate beads*. *See* Alginate and Yeast.

Encépagement (fr)   The varietal make-up of a vineyard.

Enchertos (port)   Grafts or scions for grafting onto rootstocks.

En Claro (sp)   When the state of a new wine becomes bright, but before being fortified.

Encorchador (sp)   A person who is responsible for the "hand-corking" of wine bottles.

Encorpado (port)   *See* Full-Bodied.

Encuvage (fr)   Loading of tanks with grapes prior to pressing or fermentation. *See* Decuvage and Draining Off.

Energizer   Nutrients and nitrogen in the form of phosphates added to fermentations to increase efficiency of the yeast. *See* Ammonium Phosphate.

Engarrafado Na Origem (port)   Estate bottled.

Enjambeur (fr)   A special tractor with two wheels on each side of the row of grapevines that are to be "straddled."

En masse (fr)   *See* Mise en Masse.

Enocianina (ital)   A well-known concentrated, powdered pigment extract made from the coloring of black grapes. It is used in perfumes, and in its liquid form it is used by the Department of Agriculture when stamping and labeling various cuts and grades of meat.

Enologia (ital and sp)   Enology.

Enologist   The technician of the grapevine and of wine. His or her technical and practical know-how enable him to assume entire responsibility for the vinification and breeding of wines. He or she conducts all the analyses on the grape and the resultant wine, and interprets the results. Also known as *enologo* and *enologue*. *See* Winemaker.

Enologo (ital)   *See* Enologist.

Enologue (fr)   *See* Enologist.

Enology   The science or the study of wine and winemaking; related to viticulture, which is the science of grape culture. Also spelled *oenology*.

Enophile   Anyone who loves wine and wine lore to the point of exaltation and pays tribute to it. Also spelled *oenophile*.

Enoteca (ital)   A wine library or wine bottle collection used for display and reference. A wine bar where wines may be sampled and/or purchased. Also spelled *oenoteca*.

Enotheque (fr)   A wine library or wine bottle collection used for display and reference. A wine bar were wines may be sampled and/or purchased. Also spelled *oenotheque* and *vinothéque*.

ENOTRIA TELLUS (GREECE)   The name given to Italy (Land of Wine) by ancient Greek writers. Also spelled *oenotria*.

ENOTRI VIRI (GREECE)   The name given to Italians (Men of Wineland) by ancient Greek writers. Also spelled *oenotri*.

EN PRIMEUR (FR)   The first sale of a château-bottled Bordeaux each year.

ENTERING TRADE CHANNELS   Depicts distilled spirits shipped in bottled by bottlers or importers to wholesalers, retailers, U.S. military installations, or to any other domestic market outlet. Generally, the federal excise tax is payable as the products enter trade channels. *See* Imports for Consumption and Withdrawals.

EN TIRAGE (FR)   Literally "on the yeast," when discussing the secondary fermentation of sparkling wines.

ENTRÉ-DEUX-MERS (FR)   Literally "between the seas." A large white wine–producing district in the Bordeaux region of France.

ENTREE   The main or principal item of the dish; the meat or the fish are examples.

ENVEJECIDO POR (SP)   Aged by.

ENZIAN   A spirit distilled in most Scandinavian countries, produced from the very long roots of the yellow mountain gentian plant. It is quite bitter to the taste and is usually served well-chilled after dinner.

ENZYMES   Small organic substances produced by wine yeast that serve as catalysts during fermentation.

EP   *See* Edible Portion.

EPERNAY (FR)   A city in the Champagne region, noted for its sparkling wine production and commerce.

EPIGEAL   That part of a grapevine consisting of the trunk, which has as its functions support, transport, and reserve; the arms, which are shoots of more than a year in age; the canes, which are shoots of one year of age; and the fruiting canes bearing buds opening in the current season. The latter, in turn, bear the leaves and the flowers from which the clusters develop.

ÉPLUCHAGE (FR)   A process of hand sorting or picking over, by hand of the newly harvested grapes to eliminate defective or immature bunches, berries, and material-other-than-grapes (MOG). Also known as *triage*.

EQUILIBRATO (ITAL)   *See* Balance.

EQUILIBRADO (PORT OR SP)   *See* Balance.

ÉQUILIBRÉ (FR)   *See* Balance.

EQUIPMENT   All functional items such as tap boxes, glassware, pouring racks, and similar items used in the conduct of a retailer's on-premise business.

ERBACEO (ITAL)   Tasting or smelling of herbs.

ERBEN (GERM)   Heirs.

ERDIG (GERM)   *See* Earthy.

EREDI (ITAL)   Heirs.

ERYTHRONEURA COMES   *See* Grape Leafhopper.

ERZEUGERABFÜLLUNG (GERM)   Estate bottled by a producer, not a shipper. *See* Originalabfüllung.

ESCALA (SP)   Each series or group of barrels holding a similar wine of the same solera system.

ESCANCIADOR (SP)   *See* Sommelier.

ESCANCAO (PORT)   *See* Sommelier.

ESMAGAMENTO (PORT)   Crushing of the grapes.

ESPAGNE (FR)   *See* Cinsaut.

ESPECIAL (SP)   A specially selected vintage.

ESPORTARE (ITAL)   *See* Export.

ESPORTAZIONE (ITAL)   Exportation.

135

ESPORTO MATS   Mats made of straw where whole clusters of grapes are allowed to dry in the sun, concentrating their sugar levels, for the eventual making of sweet sherries.

ESPRESSO (ITAL)   Speed.

ESPRESSO (ITAL)   A deep, dark, strong black coffee made in a machine that forces steam through finely ground, dark roasted coffee grounds.

ESPRESSO CON GHIACCIO (ITAL)   Refrigerated or fresh espresso with fresh cold milk over ice.

ESPRESSO CON PANNA (ITAL)   An espresso served with a dollop of whipped cream on top.

ESPRESSO MACCHIATO (ITAL)   A shot of espresso "market" with a scoop of foamed milk on top.

ESPUMANTE   Term used in Brazil and Portugal for a sparkling wine. Also known as *vinho espumante. See* Sparkling Wine.

ESPUMOSA (SP)   Term used in Spain for a sparkling wine. Also known as *vino espumosa. See* Sparkling Wine.

ESSENCE   A concentrated liquid usually made from herbs, spices, or flowers.

ESSENCE   An unofficial term used by some California winemakers during the 1960s and 1970s to describe "late-harvested" wines with intense varietal character and sweetness.

ESSENCES OR EXTRACTS   Preparation of natural constituents extracted from fruit, herbs, berries, and so forth. They may not be used in the production of any formula wine except agricultural wine. The essences may be produced on wine premises or elsewhere. Where an essence contains distilled spirits, use of the essence may not increase the volume of the wine more than 10 percent nor its alcohol content more than 4 percent by volume.

ESSENTIAL OILS   Volatile oils that give distinctive odor or flavor to plants, flowers, and fruits. In wines they combine with the alcohol to help determine its bouquet.

ESSENZ (HUN)   The term used to measure the level of unfermented sugar present in the *must*. *See* Brix.

ESTAGIO (PORT)   A period of time where the wine rests or ages after being put through the *estufa*.

ESTATE BOTTLED   It may be used by a bottling winery on a wine label only if the wine is labeled with a viticultural area appellation of origin and the bottling winery: (1) is located in the labeled viticultural area; (2) grew all of the grapes used to make the wine on land owned or controlled by the winery with the boundaries of the labeled viticultural area; (3) crushed the grapes, fermented the resulting must, and finished, aged, and bottled the wine in a continuous process (the wine at no time having left the premises of the bottling winery). *See* Château Bottled, Controlled By, and Domaine Bottled.

136

ESTERS   Organic, volatile compounds that contribute fruity aromas to wines and distilled spirits. Esters are formed by reactions of alcohol and organic acids in wine. Esters sometimes contribute rather solvent-like smells, such as those of vinegar or nailpolish remover.

Beers, too, are often described as having apple, banana, grapefruit, or strawberry esters.

ESTUFA (PORT)   Huge heating chambers or ovens used to make Madeira, a fortified wine.

ESTUFADO (PORT)   *See* Vinho Estufado.

ESTUFAGEM (PORT)   The process of heating or *baking* Madeira wine through heat.

ET (FR)   And.

ÉTAMPÉ (FR)   A branded or stamped cork.

ETEREO (ITAL)   Highly refined, ethereal.

ETHANOL   *See* Ethyl Alcohol.

ETHEREAL   Referring to smell; it is a scent depending on the presence of components of the "bouquet" of the ethers (high quality alcohols) developed in the course of aging.

ETHYL ACETATE   Sometimes a wine will smell vinegary, but not taste acidic, and this is the effect of ethyl acetate. In low concentrations it has a vaguely sweet, fruity odor, but in large amounts it smell like fingernail polish remover (it is an ester). Ethyl acetate exists in all wines to some degree and often complements many other odoriferous compounds. Oxidation (possibly in a barrel) or possible exposure to wild yeasts present on the grapes can cause a volatile acid or acetic acid to form. The esters of acetic acid and ethyl alcohol combine to form ethyl acetate.

ETHYL ALCOHOL The principle alcohol found in all alcoholic beverages. Also known as *alcool éthylique* and *ethanol*. *See* Alcohol.

ETHYLENE GLYCOL *See* Glycol.

ETICHETTA (ITAL) *See* Labels.

ETIQUETA (SP) *See* Labels.

ÉTIQUETTE (FR) *See* Labels.

ÉTOFFÉ (FR) A wine with well-defined characteristics and qualities.

ETTARO (ITAL) *See* Hectare.

ETTOGRADO (ITAL) *See* Hectograde.

ETTOLITRO (ITAL) *See* Hectoliter.

EUCALYPTUS The oil odor of an evergreen species occasionally found in some California Cabernet Sauvignon or Pinot Noir wines.

EUROPEAN BITTERNESS UNITS (EBU) A scale used in Europe to measure the relative quantity of bitterness contained in the beer. *See* Bitter.

EUROPEAN OAK A general term given to all types of wooden barrels emanating from various forests, mostly in France and Yugoslavia.

EVAPORATED MILK Whole milk that has approximately 50 to 55 percent of its water evaporated, but is not sweetened like *condensed milk*.

EVAPORATION When a wine or distilled spirit is aging in a wooden barrel, a slight loss in the volume of the liquid occurs due to changes in temperature, humidity, soakage, and the porosity of the wooden barrels. The amount that evaporates is approximately 3 percent of annual production. In the Cognac and Armagnac regions of France, this evaporation is known as the *angel's share* and *shrinkage*.

EVÁRMOSTOS (GREECE) *See* Harmonious.

EVÓDIS (GREECE) *See* Fragrant.

EVYENÍS (GREECE) *See* Noble.

EXCISE MAN A British tax officer since 1651. *See* Revenuers.

EXCISE TAX Indirect tax levied by the U.S. government on the alcohol content by volume of distilled spirits and on malt beverages and the various categories of wine.

License and control states and the District of Columbia also levy excise taxes, either on the volume or value base of dis tilled spirits.

EXPANSIVE Full of taste, body and flavor; often used to de scribe full-bodied wines with mouth-filling capabilities.

EXPENSE The cost of assets consumed or converted in generating income; an expired cost.

EXPORT Goods or commodities sent or carried outside of the U.S. territorial borders for eventual sale or trade. Also known as *esportare* and *exportacion.*

EXPORTACION (SP) *See* Export.

EXPORTADOR (SP) Exporter.

EXTRA (E) A designation used on labels of Armagnac, Cognac, and some other brandies to indicate an *extra* or *extremely* high quality product. It also indicates that the youngest brandy used in the blend is at least five-and-a-half years old (although larger amounts of older Armagnacs or Cognacs have been used).

EXTRA BRUT A champagne or sparkling wine that contains less than six grams of sugar per liter. Also known as *brut de brut, brut sauvage, brut zero, dosage zero* and *nature.*

EXTRACT *See* Percolation.

EXTRACTABLES Those elements that are extracted from oak barrels, which includes vanillin and other substances with desirable odors, lignin fragments, hydrolyzable tannins, and "bodying" factors that affect the flavor impression of the wine. Substances extracted from grape skins; anthocyanins (pigmentation), flavonoids, and tannins are also extractables.

138

EXTRACTS The nonvolatile, soluble solids present in a wine. It includes everything left after water and alcohol have been removed and residual sugar subtracted (acids, proteins, tannins, pigments, etc.). Also known as *extrakt.*

EXTRA DRY Term used for a champagne that is not as dry as brut, but drier than sec (dry). According to the European Common Market, extra dry champagnes contain between 12 and 20 grams of sugar per liter.

EXTRAKT (GERM) *See* Extracts.

EXTRA SEC A slightly sweetened sparkling wine or champagne.

FAA *See* Federal Alcohol Administration Act.

FABER (GERM) A white grape variety with a slight muscat bouquet that was developed in 1967, from a crossing of Pinot Blanc and Müller-Thurgau. It was developed by scientist George Scheu in 1929 in Alzey, in the Rheinhessen, and named after its first successful producer, Mr. Schmied (Faber is Latin for Schmied or Smith).

FABRICATED PRODUCT The item after trimming, boning, and so on.

FABRICATED YIELD PERCENTAGE The yield or edible portion expressed as a percentage (%) of the amount "as purchased."

FACTORIAL ANALYSIS A statistical method to identify common factors in a set of strongly correlated variables.

FACTORY HOUSE The name of a house in Oporto, Portugal, used by the British Association of port Wine Shippers as their headquarters. In addition to meetings, tastings, and luncheons, occasional festive harvest dinners also take place there.

FAD (GERM) Insipid; flat and low in acidity.

FADED A wine that has lost its bouquet, character, and definition, usually through age or excessive oxidation. When wines are left exposed to the air for prolonged periods of time, their bouquet and taste appear to fade.

FAIBLE (FR) Weak, thin, low in alcohol, and lacking in character.

FALCETTA (ITAL) *See* Grape Knife.

FALERNIAN An ancient Roman wine.

FALERNUM A colorless, slightly alcoholic, spiced, almond-lime syrup originating in the Caribbean, used as a flavoring in rum drinks.

FALKENSTEIN (AUS) A village and one of the largest wine regions in Lower Austria. Here the Grüner Veltliner, Müller-Thurgau, and Welschriesling are grown. The grapes grow in the historical surroundings of mighty fortresses and beautiful castles.

FALLING BRIGHT   A spontaneous clearing of suspended haze and cloudiness from a newly fermented wine without outside help. Also known as *bourbeux* and *deslio*. *See* Bright.

FALSE WINE   Wines made from sources other than grapes. Also known as *second wine*.

FALUNS (FR)   Chalk deposits that are rich in fossilized shells.

FARGUES (FR)   Sweet white wine made from a blend of Sauvignon Blanc, Sémillon, and Muscadelle grape varieties. It is also one of the five communes within Bordeaux's Sauternes district entitled to be called "Sauternes."

FARINE (FR)   A flour paste mixture used to seal the *croze* on a wooden barrel.

FASS (GERM)   A barrel.

FASSGESHMACK (GERM)   The smell or flavor imparted to wine by aging in wooden barrels.

140

FASSLE (GERM)   Usually during a contest, people bet to see how far away wine can be poured (without splashing one's face or spilling it) into one's mouth through a hand-held, long-spouted drinking vessel. The Spanish name is *porron*.

FAT   A term generally referring to a heavy, intense wine that has a higher than average glycerin level. It is often rich but lacking in elegance, acidity, and complexity. Also known as *fat, pâteaux, pakhys*, and *pastoso*.

FATIGUÉ (FR)   Tired, lifeless.

FATTORIA (ITAL)   Farm or estate.

FAUCET   *See* Spigot.

FAUL (GERM)   Moldy.

F AND B   *See* Food and Beverage.

FECUNDATION   A growth of grapevines in early spring that leads to the formation of the seeds in each grape.

FEDERAL ALCOHOL ADMINISTRATION (FAA) ACT   It was enacted by Congress in 1935, and is intended to promote fair competition in the marketing of alcoholic beverages by prohibiting certain trade practices that result in the exclusion of competing products in interstate commerce.

FEDERAL EXCISE TAX (FET)   A tax imposed by the federal government on all types of alcoholic beverages, which includes imports and American-produced.

FEDERWEISSER (GERM)   *See* Nouveau.

FEEBLE   Wines that are thin in color and body, and are lacking character and distinction.

FEHÉR BÓR (HUN)   *See* White Wine.

FEIN, FEINE (GERM) *See* Delicate.

FEINSTE (GERM) The finest.

FEINTS The end (tails) of a run of distillate in a still; not used in the final product. Because the feints contain a high percentage of congeners (impurities), they are set apart from the main body of the distillate, and are redistilled later. Also known as *tails*.

FELD (GERM) Field.

FEMININE A term used to describe wines that are soft and delicate. Also known as *damenwein*.

FENDANT (SWISS) *See* Chasselas Doré.

FERMÉ (FR) *See* Dumb.

FERMENTACAO (PORT) *See* Fermentation.

FERMENTACION (SP) *See* Fermentation.

FERMENTATION The conversion of sugar contained in the grapes (by the action of yeast) into *ethyl alcohol* or *ethanol*. Yeasts are introduced into tanks of must to start the process; fermentation stops when the sugars are depleted or when the alcohol level reaches about 14 percent and kills the yeast. Secondary fermentation takes place in sparkling wines to give them their distinctive carbonation.

It was in 1789 that the famed French chemist Lavoisier made one of the first studies on the natural phenomena or fermentation; he was followed in 1810 by Monsieur Gay-Lussac who correctly devised the overall equation for fermentation. In 1857, Louis Pasteur began the first scientific study of fermentation in a town called Arbois, in the Jura region of France.

Gay-Lussac's formula for fermentation is:

$$C_6 H_{12} O_6 \quad = \quad 2C_2 H_5 OH \quad + \quad 2CO_2$$

$$\text{(sugar glucose)} \qquad \text{(ethyl alcohol)} \qquad \text{(carbon dioxide)}$$

The equation describes the following process: yeast "eat" (metabolize) sugar and in the process create, in approximate equal proportions, alcohol and carbon dioxide gas (CO_2), with heat as a by-product. If yeast is added to a sugar-water mixture, fermentation would produce only alcohol and CO_2; but when grapes and yeast are put together, the end product is wine.

The natural action of yeast in converting malted barley and hops into beer. Distilled spirits are also fermented and the resulting "liquor" is then distilled in the various methods characteristic to each type of spirit. Also known as *angegoren, fermentacao, fermentacion, fermentazione,* and *gärung.*

FERMENTATION LOCK A low-pressure valve made of glass or plastic that seals a barrel or other container of fermenting wine from the outside air while permitting carbon dioxide gas given off during fermentation to escape through

F

sulfited-water. Also known as *bosador, ventilating bung, water bung, water seal,* and *water valve.*

FERMENTATION TANK   A barrel, stainless steel tank, concrete vat, or other type structure utilized for the primary fermentation of grapes and grape juice into wine. Also known as *tinas.*

FERMENTAZIONE (ITAL)   *See* Fermentation.

FERMENTAZIONE NATURALE (ITAL)   Naturally fermented, usually in reference to sparkling wines.

FERMENTED IN THE BOTTLE   *See* Transfer Method.

FERMENTED IN THIS BOTTLE   *See* Méthode Champenoise.

FERMENTER   Any container that is used to ferment grape juice into wine. Formerly made of wood or concrete, it is now made mostly of glass or stainless steel.

FERMENTI (ITAL)   *See* Yeast.

FERMENTING   The time during which the wine or beer remains in the fermentation vats.

142

FERROCYANIDE COMPOUNDS   Used to remove trace metal from wine and to remove objectionable levels of sulfide and mercaptans from wine.

FERROUS SULFATE   Used to clarify and to stabilize wine.

FEST (GERM)   *See* Firm.

FESTBIER (GERM)   Beers made for traditional festivals (e.g. Oktoberfest). The styles as well as taste and alcoholic content of these beers vary.

FET   *See* Federal Excise Tax.

FÉTE DE LA FLEUR (FR)   Flower festival. Every year the wine fraternities celebrate the flowering of the grapevine, which occurs in May or June.

FETT (GERM)   A wine that is fat, full, or big.

FEUILLETTE (FR)   A small barrel with a capacity ranging from 112 to approximately 144 liters (32 to 38 U.S. gallons), depending on the wine region in which it is used. *See* Barrel.

FEURIG (GERM)   Fiery. *See* Hot.

FIACCO (ITAL)   Weak; a wine lacking body and structure.

FIASCO (ITAL OR SP)   Name of the straw-covered, bulbous-bodied, long neck bottle that houses some Chianti and other wines. Its origin can be traced back to 1265, according to a document preserved at San Gimignano. *Also known as fiasque.*

FIASQUE (FR)   *See* Fiasco.

FIELD BLEND   Formerly a widespread practice in many parts of the world where several different red and/or white grape varieties would be growing in the same vineyard area. They would be harvested, crushed, and fermented together to produce a single wine; thus the wine was *blended in the field.*

Field Budding   Rarely used now in favor of the more modern "bench grafting." Also referred to as *chip budding*.

Field Crushing   Around the same time (1969 to 1970) that Mirassou Vineyards of San Jose, California, first used mechanical harvesting, they introduced the concept of field crushing. Grapes are crushed and sealed in a CO_2 atmosphere in tanks alongside the mechanical harvester, within minutes of picking. By conventional methods, 2 to 20 hours may elapse between picking and crushing, during which oxidation can cause the loss of fresh flavor. *See* Mortl.

Field Grafting   The native rootstock (*Vitis rupestris*) is planted in the vineyard and allowed to grow one season. It is then notched to accept a European (*Vitis vinifera*) grapevine bud. The graft is loosely covered with soil to facilitate callousing. In spring the soil is removed and if the graft has "taken," shoots will emerge from the budded vinifera portion of the grapevine, which are then protected against wind, frost, or pest damage by a milk carton. Sometimes referred to as *budding*.

Field Selection   *See* Mass Selection.

Fieriness   Brandy or other distilled spirits that leave behind the sensation of burning.

Fiery   *See* Hot.

FIFO   *See* First-In, First-Out.

Fifth   Old term (prior to 1978) denoting one-fifth of a gallon or 25.6 fluid ounces. Also referred to as four-fifths.

Figlia (Ital)   Daughter.

Figlio (Ital)   Son.

Figs   Scent often characteristic of the Sémillon, a white grape variety.

Filant (Fr)   *See* Mousy.

Filante (Ital or Sp)   *See* Mousy.

File Downs   *See* Distributor Post-Off.

File-Off   *See* Distributor Post-Off.

Fillettes (Fr)   Half-bottles (375 milliliters) used in Alsace, Loire Valley, and Bordeaux; also known as *little girls*.

Fillings   The new whiskey after it is removed from the still.

Fils (Fr)   Son.

Filter   To screen out wine or beer solids by mechanical means.

Filtering   A mechanical process by which wine or beer is forced through a porous filter medium (paper, pads, or membranes) that traps suspended particles and thus removes them. Filtering is utilized for the purpose of removing yeast and bacteria cells, making the wine or beer microbiologically stable. It is also used before fermentation to clarify press juice and to give beverages the highest possible clarity (for consumer acceptance). Also known as *filtration*. *See* Clarifying, Fining, Microfiltration, Polishing Filter, Sterile Filtration, and Ultrafiltration.

FILTRATION *See* Filtering.

FILTRE (FR) To filter.

FIN (FR) Fine, delicate, relatively light.

FINAGE (FR) A vineyard area or subdistrict of a vineyard.

FINE *See* Fining.

FINE (FR) A term that may be found on Cognac labels, but has no legally defined meaning.

FINE (ITAL) The lowest quality grape of Marsala wine; best used for cooking.

FINE (ITAL) Fine; harmoniously made.

FINE COGNAC (FR) A term that may be found on Cognac labels, but has no legally defined meaning.

FINESSE A term applied to a wine with subtlety of flavor; breed, class, and distinction.

FINGER LAKES The clear, deep waters of the Finger Lakes of New York keep this region's climate temperate, and plentiful shale beds (similar to those in Champagne, France) help drain the soil. The slow-warming lakes retard spring growth, protecting it against the danger of frost, and keep the grapevines warmer on chilly fall nights. The Finger Lakes vineyards are located approximately 350 miles northwest of New York City, along Lakes Canandaigua, Cayuga, Hemlock, Keuka, and Seneca.

FINING The process of "polishing" or clarifying a cloudy or hazy wine or beer to brilliancy by removing suspended particles. The selected fining agent is added to the wine or beer and, as it settles to the bottom (by gravity), it attracts particles in suspension. Most wineries and breweries use fining agents to help clarify wines and beers by removing precipitates of excess pectin, peptides, iron compounds, or unstable protein, which are generally positively charged. Other wineries and breweries use agents that carry a negative charge for the softening of excessive tannin levels in beers and red wines and the removal of browning agents. Also known as *affiné, collage, coller,* and *schonen*. *See* Clarifying, Colloidal Suspension, Filtering, Fining Agents, Particle Matter, and Sterile Filtration.

FINING AGENTS Substances used in the fining of wine or beer. Among them

144

are bentonite, casein, charcoal, colloidal silica, egg white, gelatin, isinglass, Spanish Earth, Sparkolloid, and (in ancient times) animal blood. *See* Fining.

FINISH   The tactile and flavor impressions left in the mouth after the wine is swallowed. Some wines finish crisp and clean with a long, rich aftertaste, while others may be harsh, hot, or tannic with short or nonexistent finish. *See* Aftertaste.

FINIT BIEN (FR)   A wine with a pleasing finish and aftertaste.

FINKEL   The name of a high-proof spirit, distilled from potatoes, that is produced in Norway.

FINO (ITAL)   Refined.

FINO (SP)   A type of sherry made entirely from Palomino grapes. It is very dry, light, and pale in color, with a distinctive mild nutty-tangy taste.

FIOLERI (ITAL)   Glassblower.

FIORE (ITAL)   *See* Flowery.

FIRE-BREWED   The brewing kettle is heated directly by fire, rather than by the more conventional high pressure, heated steam process. Contrary to some beliefs, the resulting beer does *not* taste any different.

F

145

FIRING GLASS   A glass used for drinking toasts; firing glasses were banged down hard on the dining table simulating the sound of firing muskets, hence the need for a stout base and the name.

FIRKIN   A beer barrel used in England that contains 41 liters or 10.8 gallons. *See* Barrel.

FIRM   A wine with structure and backbone; opposite of "flabby." Also known as *fest* and *nevródis*.

FIRNE (GERM)   *See* Maderized.

FIRST GROWTHS (FR)   The five red wines (four from the Médoc, one from Graves) officially classified in 1855 (Château Mouton-Rothschild in 1973) as being of the highest quality.

FIRST-IN, FIRST-OUT (FIFO)   A rotation procedure utilized mostly for those products that are perishable or semi-perishable. It consists of issuing requsitions, which insures that products received first (existing stock that is the oldest) will be utilized first. Also known as *rotate stock*.

FISH GLUE   *See* Isinglass.

FIVE GALLON CANISTER   A metal canister with a capacity of 640 fluid ounces that holds either premix beverage or postmix syrup used for soda systems.

FIXED ACIDITY   It is the total (titratable) acidity less the volatile acidity or the nonvolatile acids of the wine. The major acids of wine include tartaric, citric malic, lactic, succinic, and inorganic acids.

FIXED COPPER AND LIME   The common name for a systemic fungicide effective against a host of grapevine diseases, among them Botrytis bunch rot, black rot, powdery mildew, and downy mildew. *See* Bordeaux Mixture.

FIXED COSTS   Costs or expenses that remain constant or are generally fixed in nature, regardless of the volume of business, such as rent, property taxes, and interest. These costs cannot be controlled by an individual (such as department head) in a company. Also referred to as *noncontrollable costs.*

FIXIN (FR)   The northernmost village of the Côte de Nuits, in Burgundy.

FIZZ   A cocktail consisting of distilled spirits, citrus juices, and sugar, with carbonated water (fizz) added at the end. It is often served as a morning-after "hangover cure-all" with a multitude of other ingredients, such as egg whites or yolks, various fruit juices, syrups, wines, and even beer.

FLABBY   Term used to describe a wine lacking character, usually due to a low level of acidity.

FLACCIDO (ITAL)   Flaccid, flabby.

FLACH (GERM)   *See* Flat.

FLACO (SP)   *See* Thin.

FLAG   A toothpick holding a cherry and orange slice as a garnish.

FLAGEY-ECHÉZEAUX (FR)   A small red wine village of the Côte de Nuits, in Burgundy. In 1131, Flagey was known as *Flagiacum.*

FLAGON   An odd-shaped wine bottle of varying size and shape, although it was a common term used to describe wine bottles of ordinary shape in earlier times.

FLAKE ICE   *see* Ice Cubes.

FLAKE STAND   *See* Worm.

FLAMBÉ, FLAMING   To burn off the alcohol by igniting with a match. Usually, brandies or other distilled spirits to be flambéed are warmed first, then poured into the dish and ignited.

FLAME TOKAY   A white table grape, used principally in California for dessert wines.

FLAME UP   *See* Proof.

FLANZY   In the early 1950s, carbonic maceration was called "Flanzy," after one of the enologists who helped develop it. *See* Carbonic Maceration.

FLASCHE (GERM)   *See* Bottle.

FLASCHENREIF (GERM)   A wine that is ready for bottling.

FLASK   A flat-sided bottle with a capacity from 8 to 33.8 fluid ounces.

FLAT   A wine or beer that is dull, lacking in vigor and liveliness due to low natural acidity. Also known as *flach, matt,* and *pesante.*

FLAT   A sparkling wine or beer that has lost its effervescence.

FLAT BEER   Draft beer may become *flat* due to any of the following: greasy glasses, not enough pressure in the beer lines, the CO_2 pressure was shut off during night, the precooler or coils are too cold, leaky pressure line, loose tap or vent connections, sluggish pressure regulator, or obstruction in beer lines.

FLAT CASE The standard size case of product (i.e., 4-bottle, 3- or 4-liter case; 6-bottle 1.5- or 1.75-liter case; 12-bottle, 750-ml or 1-liter case; 24-bottle 375-ml. case, etc). Flat cases can refer to either depletions or shipments, as appropriate.

FLAT CUBES *See* Ice Cubes.

FLAVOR Those complex impressions originating on the palate when the wine is swirled in the mouth. Also known as *geschmack, sabor, sapore,* and *saveur.*

FLAVONOIDS Flavoring compounds, which are technically phenols, found in the skins of grapes, especially red.

FLAVORED BRANDY A mixture of brandy, with a minimum of 2.5 percent sugar, flavored and colored with various types of fruit and/or herbs and that may or may not contain added sugar. By federal law it cannot be bottled at less than 70 proof (35 percent alcohol by volume).

FLAVORED GIN, VODKA, OR RUM A mixture of distilled neutral spirits that are flavored and colored with various types of fruit and/or herbs and may or may not contain added sugar. By federal law it cannot be bottled at less than 70 proof (35 percent alcohol by volume).

FLAVORED WINES *See* Apéritif Wines and Wine Coolers.

FLESHY A wine of generous substance and suppleness; a mouthful.

FLEURAISON (FR) Flowering of the grapevines.

FLEURIE (FR) A cru commune in Beaujolais, probably so named because the wine it produces is known for its delicate and flowery bouquet. Fleurie is light both in color and body, with a silky flavor, lasting up to three years.

FLEX CARD A cut case card that promotes a product and can be used any time of the year. This can be personalized for local promotions.

FLEXHOSE A flexible metal hose attached to the beverage handgun used for the service of carbonated soft drinks.

FLIERS Small particles occasionally observed floating in a glass of white wine.

FLINTY Term used to describe the taste of a wine whose bouquet is reminiscent of two flints being rubbed together or struck with steel. Characteristic of some dry, hard, almost austere white wines, especially French Chablis and Pouilly Fumé.

FLIP A popular drink in the United States during the early 1700s. It was made by combining rum, beer, cream, beaten eggs, and various spices, which were then heated by plunging a hot loggerhead (a long-handled tool with a ball or bulb at the end) into the mixture. Also known as *beer flip. See* Sling.

FLOAT   Pouring a shot of distilled spirits on top of a finished drink without stirring or mixing.

FLOATING LIQUEURS   *See* Pousse-Café.

FLOCCULATION   When fermentation is complete, the dead yeast cells agglomerate— that is, clump up and form particles large enough to settle to the bottom, forming a firm deposit, rather than remaining in suspension. This makes racking easier and less wine is lost in the lees. Also known as *agglomeration* and *clumping*.

FLOGGING A CORK HOME   To drive the cork into the bottle by means of a wooden hammer—a practice no longer used today.

FLOOT   A slang term meaning a full, eight fluid ounce glass of whiskey.

FLOR (SP)   It is a yeast-like substance (*Saccharomyces cerevisiae*) that forms a whitish film on the surface of certain sherries when the temperature in the cellar is between 60 degrees and 70 degrees Fahrenheit. After a year or so, the wine under the flor develops a distinctive yeasty taste, which is technically due to a large increase in the aldehyde content of the wine. The longer the sherry "sits on" the flor, the more flavor it extracts, and the finer it becomes.

All types of sherry start out the same, but for some relatively unknown reason flor forms on the surface of some barrels of sherry and not on others. When the flor forms a very thick white blanket, the sherry becomes a *fino*. If a thinner film forms, the sherry becomes an *amontillado*. If no film forms, the sherry becomes an *oloroso*.

After a period of 18 to 24 months of aging undisturbed under the blanket of flor (if it forms), the wine is transferred to the winery's solera system. A *fino* will be sent to the *fino* solera, an *amontillado* to the *amontillado* solera, and so on.

FLORA   A white hybrid grape variety developed in 1938 (released in 1958), from a cross of Gewürztraminer and Sémillon, by Dr. Harold P. Olmo of the University of California, Davis.

FLORAISON (FR)   *See* Flowering.

FLORAL   Related to flowery; conveying an impression or aroma of flowers. Often used to describe young, white wines with delicate aromas.

FLORAL ABORTION   Absence of or defective fertilization of the blossoms of a grapevine, or a failure to develop or set at all, causing a malformation at time of flowering. This causes the blossoms or flowers to wither and fall from the grapevines, with no fruit-bearing ability. This malady, which could be caused by bad weather or too early a spring, occurs in the springtime, leading to the loss of a potential bunch of grapes. Also known as *coulure*. *See* Berry Set, Shatter, and Shot Berries.

FLOWER CLUSTER   The flowering cluster of a grapevine. Also known as *inflorescence*.

FLOWERING   An indeterminate period in the grapevine development after bud break, when the flowers are pollinated and begin to yield small berries. Also known as *floraison*.

FLOWERY   Wines that display a pleasing, floral-like fragrance akin to flowers in general. A term usually applied to young white wines. Similar to *floral*. Also known as *fiore*.

FLOWERS OF WINE   A malady of wine caused by film yeasts (Candida mycoderma). The wine, which has been exposed to prolonged air contact, develops small white patches that grow to complete surface coverage within days. It is a common but not a serious disorder that can be treated with sulfur dioxide. Also known as *Mycoderma vini* and *piqûre acétique*.

FLÜCHTIG (GERM)   A wine with little substance.

FLÜCHTIGE SÄURE (GERM)   *See* Volatile Acidity.

FLUID OUNCE   A U.S. measure of liquid volume; 128 fluid ounces being equal to one U.S. gallon.

FLURBEREINIGUNG (GERM)   The process of consolidating groups of small vineyards on uneven terrain into large, more easily workable plots by improving access roads and drainage.

FLÛTE   An elongated-shaped wine bottle used in Alsace, France and the Rhine River in Germany. A 1972 law requires all Alsatian (France) wines to be bottled in tall, elegant "flûte" bottles, and it is compulsory for wines sold under the Alsace appellation to have been bottled in Alsace, and not shipped in casks.

FLUTE-SHAPED GLASS   The proper glassware to use for champagne and sparkling wines, which is in the shape of an elongated "V," with a capacity of approximately eight to ten fluid ounces. *See* Tulip-Shaped Glass and Saucer-Shaped Glass.

FOAM   A thick, rich, creamy collar of gas bubbles that clings to the top of a glass of beer. It is important to remember that for maximum profit and a glass of beer with eye and taste appeal, it should be served with a good foam head (¾-inch), and that a perfect glass of beer shows a ring of foam after every delicious sip. Foam is approximately 25-percent liquid beer. Also known as *head*. *See* Coney Island Head.

FOB   *See* Free On Board.

FOB POST-OFF   *See* Post-Offs.

FOCH   *See* Maréchal Foch.

FOJETTA (ITAL)   The name used in Rome to indicate generally a half-liter of wine, but it once meant a special glass carafe. The glass container was substituted for those of earthenware, pewter, or the like, since the opaque recipients quite often were used to mislead clients as to the quality and the quantity of the wine they were buying.

FOLIAGE   The growing mass of leaves on a grapevine.

FOLIAGE WIRE *See* Catch Wire.

FOLD The ratio of the volume of the fruit *must* or juice to the volume of the volatile fruit-flavor concentrate produced from the fruit-*must* or juice; for example, one gallon of volatile fruit- flavor concentrate of 100-fold would be the product from 100 gallons of fruit-*must* or juice.

FOLLATURA (ITAL) The breaking up of the *cap*.

FOLLE BLANCHE A white grape variety grown predominantly in France and California. Folle Blanche was for many years the principal grape of the Cognac and Armagnac (called *Picpoul* or *Picpoule*) regions of France. Though still used, it has been largely replaced by better producers and is now mostly found in the vineyards surrounding Nantes, in the Loire Valley of France, where it is called *Gros Plant*.

A fairly vigorous grower, the Folle Blanche grapevine produces a medium-sized cluster, very compact, comprised of round juicy berries, that yield a wine with mild apple-grape aromas. It is a mid-season ripener, seldom reaches high sugars, but maintains a high acidity. It is a low to medium producer. Also known as *Avillo* in Catalonia, Spain.

FONCÊ (FR) Dark.

FOND DE TONNEAU (FR) The head of a barrel.

FOND DE VERRE (FR) A persistence of the bouquet in the glass for hours after it has been emptied.

FONDÉ (FR) Founded or established in.

FONDO (ITAL) *See* Sediment.

FONDRE (FR) To blend (colors).

FONGICIDE (FR) *See* Fungicide.

FONTANA (ITAL) Fountain.

FOOD AND BEVERAGE A food and beverage department, either in a hotel, or similar type property. It is one of the most demanding areas in a hotel and one of the principle revenue producers. The food and beverage department is responsible for food and beverage activities in the property.

FOOT *See* Base.

FOOTED PILSNER A stemmed glass in the shape of an elongated "V," with a capacity of 8 to 10 fluid ounces, used to serve beer.

FORBIDDEN FRUIT The name of a grape concentrate for home winemakers produced by the Louis M. Martini Winery of Napa Valley California, during Prohibition. Also the name of a proprietary brand name citrus liqueur, made in the United States from grapefruit and other fruits, that have been stepped in brandy. *See* Grape Brick.

FORECASTING Predicting what will happen in the future on the basis of data from the past and present.

FOREIGN WINE   Wine produced outside the United States.

FORESHOT   In whiskey production, the first crude spirit to appear from the still.

FORMULA   A recipe.

FORMULA WINE   Special natural wine, agricultural wine, and other than standard wine (except for distilling material and vinegar stock) produced on bonded wine premises under an approved formula.

FORT (FR)   Strong, with a high alcoholic content.

FORTE (ITAL)   Strong, with a high alcoholic content.

FORTE (PORT)   *See* Robust.

FORTIFICATION   The addition of distilled spirits to a wine either to arrest fermentation and leave some residual sugar, or to give better keeping properties or to make the wine stronger. Also known as *encabezado*.

FORTIFIED WINE   A table wine to which brandy or other distilled spirits have been added to raise the alcoholic content to somewhere between 16 and 22 percent alcohol by volume. Examples are madeira, marsala, port, and sherry.

FORTIFY   *See* Fortification.

FORWARD   A wine that is early-maturing and approachable in its youth.

FORZATO (ITAL)   A wine, made from very overripe grapes, that contains a high degree of alcohol.

FOUDRE (FR)   A large barrel with a capacity of 1,000 liters (264 U.S. gallons), mostly used in Alsace. *See* Barrel.

FOULAGE   Crushing or stirring the cap.

FOULOIR (FR)   *See* Crusher/Destemmer.

FOUNTAIN INN   A pub in Baltimore, Maryland, where Francis Scott Key completed the "Star Spangled Banner."

FOXÈ (FR)   *See* Foxy.

FOX GRAPE   *See Vitis Labrusca.*

FOXTON   *See* Foxy.

FOXY   The pronounced grapy aroma and flavor of many native American grapes (*Vitis labrusca*) native to the East Coast of the United States. The term *foxy* has no proved origin, although some winemakers feel that the name was given because foxes and deer enjoy eating the grapes. Technically, a flavor substance called *methyl* (or *ethyl*) *anthranilate*, which is added to synthetic grape drinks, is responsible for this grapy aroma and flavor. Also known as *foxé, foxton, fuchsgeschmack, goût de fox, goût de renard,* and *queue de renard. See Vitis Labrusca.*

FRAGOLA (ITAL)   *See* Isabella.

FRAGRANT   A term applied to a wine that has an amply scented and agreeable aroma or bouquet. Also known as *evódis* and *fragrante*.

FRAGRANTE (ITAL)   *See* Fragrant.

FRAIS (FR)   *See* Fresh.

FRAISE (FR)   Strawberry; usually made into a liqueur or clear brandy.

FRAMBOISE (FR)   Raspberry; usually made into a liqueur or clear brandy. It is known as *himbeergeist* in Germany and parts of Switzerland.

FRAMBOISE   A type of wheat beer produced in Brussels.

FRANC (FR)   A term meaning clean and sound.

FRANC DE GOÛT (FR)   Natural, vinous flavor.

FRANC DE PIED (FR)   Ungrafted grapevines.

FRANCO (ITAL)   Blunt and straightforward; sincere.

FRANCO BORD (FR)   *See* Free on Board.

FRANCOIS   In about 1836, Francois, a pharmacist of Chalons in the region of Champagne, France, discovered a method for determining the precise amount of sugar to be added to *still wines* for the secondary fermentation into a sparkling wine. His method greatly reduced bottle breakage due to uniform amounts of sugar.

FRANCONIA (GERM)   One of 11 grape-growing regions. This is the only region from which wine is exported in a *bocksbeutel* or *boxbeutel*, the distinctive, round flagon-style bottle first introduced in 1728.

The wines of Franconia, which are made under the close scrutiny of the Frankischer Weinbauverband (Franconian Wine Association), which was founded in 1836, are pleasant, combining dryness with a certain mellowness but lacking somewhat in the varied aromas and bouquets of other German wines. Most Franconian wine is made from Müller-Thurgau, Sylvaner, and Mainriesling grapes, although new varieties such as Albalonga, Bacchus, Kerner, Ortega, Perle, and Rieslaner are being planted on increasingly more acreage. Also spelled *Franken*.

FRANKEN (GERM)   *See* Franconia.

FRANKENRIESLING (GERM)   *See* Sylvaner.

FRANKEN RIESLING (CAL)   *See* Sylvaner.

FRANSDRUIF (SO. AFRICA)   *See* Palomino.

FRAPPÉ (FR)   A drink that is super-chilled by the addition of crushed or shaved ice, which cordials are then poured over.

FRAPPER (FR)   To chill or ice, as in a bottle of champagne.

FRATELLI (ITAL)   Brothers.

FRATELLO (ITAL)   Brother.

FRAUNCES TAVERN   A tavern in New York City, where George Washington said farewell to his officers after a victory in 1783. It is one of the oldest taverns in America still in existence and was founded in 1762 by Samuel Fraunces, at the corner of Pearl and Broad streets in Manhattan, New York.

FREDDO (ITAL)   Cold.

FREDONIA   A blue-black *Vitis labrusca* grape variety developed in 1927, from a cross of Champion and Lucile, at the New York State Experimental Station at Geneva. The wine, which is rather high in acidity and low in sugar, is used mostly for blending.

FREEBIE   A slang term for services or items given or received gratis by some customers.

FREE ON BOARD (FOB)   Costs agreed upon by the buyer and seller, where the seller delivers aboard a train, ship, plane, and so forth, to the point of shipment, without charge, and exclusive of freight, which must then be borne by the purchaser. Also known as *franco bord*.

FREE PORT   A port, part of a port, or zone where cargo may be unloaded, stored, and reshipped without payment of customs or duties. Also known as *free zone*.

FREE-POUR   Pouring distilled spirits from a bottle without the aid of a measuring device.

FREE-RUN JUICE   The initial juice released by the grapes by the shear weight or pressure of the mass, before the press is used. This juice is sometimes fermented separately (since it is thought to make better quality wine); other times it is combined with press juice. The people from ancient Greece called it *Prodomos* or *Protopos*. Also known as *vin de goutte*. *See* Press Juice.

FREE ZONE   *See* Free Port.

FREIGHT DROP/SHIP   Freight, parcel post, or postage on drop shipments of *point of sale* (POS) material.

FREIHERR (GERM)   Baron.

FREISA   A red grape variety grown predominantly in the Piedmont region of Italy, which produces two styles of wine: A dry version, light in body, intended to be drunk young, and characteristically having a high level of acidity; and a slightly sweet one (*amabile*). The *amabile*, which is often *frizzante*, is the better known of the two and is considered an ideal accompaniment to desserts.

Freisa d'Asti features on its neck label black grapes superimposed on a yellow tower in Asti.

FREON   A trade name for a nonflammable gas used as a refrigerant to cool stainless steel tanks in the production of some beverages.

FRENCH 75   A cocktail consisting of champagne and Cognac, which became popular with the American soldiers based in France's Champagne region during World War II. The soldiers named the powerful drink after the French 75 millimeter artillery cannon known for its impact and accuracy of aim.

FRENCH-AMERICAN HYBRIDS Grape varieties that are crosses of American species with European *Vitis vinifera*. Also known as *French Hybrids*. *See* Hybrids.

FRENCH COLOMBARD *See* Colombard.

FRENCH HYBRIDS *See* French-American Hybrids.

FRENCH OAK Refers to the wood barrels constructed from trees located inside the forests of France. Among the more popular are Allier, Bourgogne, Limousin, Nevers, Troncais, and Vosges.

FRENCH-TYPE VERMOUTH A dry white vermouth. *See* Vermouth.

FRÈRES (FR) Brothers.

FRESCO (ITAL OR PORT) *See* Fresh.

FRESCOR (SP) *See* Fresh.

FRESH A term often applied to younger white or lighter red wines, displaying a youthful, lively fruity aroma and clean, acidic taste. Also known as *frais*, *fresco*, *frescor*, and *frisch*. *See* Young.

FRESH Term often applied to younger white or lighter red wines, displaying a youthful, lively fruity aroma and clean, acidic taste.

FRESHLY BREWED COFFEE Coffee that has just been freshly made and is less than one hour old (a generally accepted standard within the food and beverage industry). After that time, coffee begins to lose its aroma and its taste begins to deteriorate, turning flat and harsh.

FRIAND (FR) Fresh, with an agreeable taste.

FRÍO (SP) Cold.

FRISCH (GERM) *See* Fresh.

FRIULI-VENEZIA GIULIA (ITAL) One of the smallest of 20 wine-producing regions, Friuli-Venezia Giulia borders on Austria and Yugoslavia in the most northeastern region of Italy. Its terrain is predominantly rocky and hilly and the climate generally quite mild. Pordenone, Gorizia, and Udine are the important wine centers of this region.

There are six delimited zones within the Friuli region; from smallest to largest, they are Latisana, Aquilea, Isonzo, Collio, Colli Orientali del Friuli, and Grave del Friuli. The four most important of these wine-producing zones are Grave del Friuli, Colli Orientali del Friuli, Collio, and Isonzo.

FRIZZANTE (ITAL) *See* Spritz.

FROG EYES The large, lazy bubbles that mercifully soon disappear, usually in a glass of bulk process sparkling wine. It is unaffectionately known as *oeil de crapaud*, meaning toad's eyes.

FROMENTIN (ITAL) *See* Furmint.

FRONTIGNAN *See* Muscat de Frontignan.

Front-of-the-Bar   The portion of the bar where the customer sits and is served drinks.

Front-of-the-House   Those areas of a hotel, restaurant, tavern, or any facility that is in "the public eye." It is considered the lobby, dining, sitting, or drinking areas where guests and customers have direct access.

Frosting   The chilling of a glass in the freezer, with or without first wetting it, for the service of beer and some cocktails usually served "straightup." Also known as a *frozen glass or mug* and *glass frosting*.

Frothee   A proprietary brand name product, consisting of egg whites and other ingredients, used in cocktails to make an airy, foamy head.

Frozen Drink Dispenser   A machine that dispenses a *frozen* drink in fairly large quantities. Usually relegated to daiquiris, piña coladas, and margaritas.

Frozen Glass or Mug   *see* Frosting.

Fruchtig (germ)   *See* Fruity.

Fructose   A simple sugar, also known as *fruit sugar*, predominantly found in fruits, that is almost twice as sweet as glucose. Same as Levulose.

Früh (germ)   Early.

Fruit Dessert Wine   It is fruit or berry wine having an alcoholic content in excess of 14 percent but not in excess of 24 percent by volume. Also known as *berry dessert wine*.

Fruité (fr)   *See* Fruity.

Fruit Juices   The natural juices of any type of fruit, often with vitamin C, sugar, sugar substances, artificial sweeteners, citric acid, or water added.

Fruit-Like   Referring to smell and taste; it is said of a young wine the taste of which is similar to ripe fruit.

Fruits   Those fruits that are utilized either as garnishes or ingredients in cocktails. Citrus fruits, such as lemons, limes, and oranges, are the principal fruits needed for many cocktails. They should be cut into three distinct shapes, depending on the kind and type of drink served: wheels, peels, and wedges.

Fruit Squeezer   A hand-held instrument used to squeeze citrus fruits, while at the same time straining away unwanted seeds and pulp.

Fruit Sugar   *See* Fructose.

Fruit Table Wine   It is fruit or berry wine having an alcoholic content not in excess of 14 percent by volume. Such wines may also be designated "light fruit wine" or "light berry wine." Also known as *Berry Table Wine*.

Fruit Wine   Wine made from the juice of sound, ripe fruit (including wine made from berries or wine made from a combination of grapes and other fruits or berries).

Fruity   An organoleptic term applied to wines that have a definite pleasant aroma and flavor of grapes or other fresh fruits. The fruitiness is never cloying;

F

155

rather, it imparts a lively, refreshing quality to the wine. Also known as *fruchtig, fruité, fruttato,* and *würzig.*

FRUTTATO (ITAL)   *See* Fruity.

FUCHSGESCHMACK (GERM)   *See* Foxy.

FUDER (GERM)   A large barrel with a capacity of 1,000 liters (264 U.S. gallons), mostly used in the Mosel region. *See* Barrel.

FUGACE (ITAL)   Fleeting; a wine whose taste, finish, and aftertaste are extremely brief.

FULGUR   Aluminum silicate and albumin, used to clarify wine.

FULL   *See* Full-Bodied.

FULL-BODIED   A term relating to the body or mouth-filling capacity of a beverage. Usually applied to beverages comparatively high in extract, glycerin, possibly sugar, or elevated alcoholic content. Pleasingly strong bouquet, flavor, and taste, often used to describe dessert wines. Opposite of *light-bodied.* Also known as *encorpado, full, fullness, körper, körperreich,* and *voll.*

FULL CUBES   *See* Ice Cubes.

FÜLLE (GERM)   A wine or beer that is full and rich in flavor.

FULLNESS   *See* Full-Bodied.

FUMARIC ACID   It is occasionally utilized to help prevent the growth of lactic acid bacteria, to stabilize wine, and to correct natural deficiencies in grape and fruit wine.

FUMÉ (FR)   Smoked.

FUMÉ BLANC   *See* Sauvignon Blanc.

FUMEUX (FR)   A wine that is heady or displays a high level of alcohol.

FUMET (FR)   A pleasant odor or taste.

FUMIGATION   It is accomplished by drilling holes deep into the soil and injecting an insecticide/fungicide. The land is then covered with plastic sheets for a period of about two months.

FUNCTION   Sales responsibility assigned to a person or group within a sales team (e.g., on-premise function, convenient store function).

FUNDADA (SP)   Founded.

FUNGICIDE   A chemical substance used to control the growth, infection, and spread of fungi on plants. Also known as *fongicide* and *fungizid.*

FUNGIZID (GERM)   *See* Fungicide.

FUNGUS   Any number of simple, lower plants, including the yeasts, molds, and mushrooms, lacking chlorophyll, which subsists on other life forms.

FURMENTIN (ITAL)   *See* Furmint.

FURMINT   A white grape variety from Hungary that produces its classic

Tokay wines. Its origins are actually Italian: it was brought to Hungary from the Friulan hills in 1632.

The Furmint grape variety is very susceptible to *Botrytis cinerea* and produces a range of Tokay wines from dry to extremely sweet in taste. Also known as *Fromentin, Furmentin, Posip,* and *Sipon.*

FÜRST (GERM)   Prince.

FUSEL (GERM)   A slang term meaning "bad liquor."

FUSEL OIL   Actually a higher-boiling alcohol, noticeable in fermented beverages, especially distilled spirits. Fusel oil contributes to the flavor and overall quality of wine and distilled spirits, although in actuality it totals less than 0.1 percent of the beverages. It combines with esters, tannins, acids, and aldehydes to form what is commonly known as *congeners.*

FUSTO (ITAL)   A barrel of any size for the aging of wines. *See* Barrel.

FÛT (FR)   *See* Barrel.

FÛT (FR)   The trunk from just above the roots to the lower branches, giving nine to ten feet of clean, straight timber, easily sawn into staves.

FUTURES MARKET   A market in which contracts are undertaken today at prices specified today for fulfillment at some specified future time.

GALACTURONIC ACID   One of the components of the chemical composition of pectin.

GALLIZATION   A winemaking process named after Dr. Gall. *See* Amelioration.

GALLON   A United States measurement of liquid volume; one gallon being equivalent to 128 fluid ounces or to the volume of 231 cubic inches. Also known as a *wine gallon* or *bulk gallon*. An Imperial or British gallon equals 160 fluid ounces or 1.2 U.S. gallons. Also known as *gallone*.

GALLONE (ITAL)   *See* Gallon.

GAMAY (GAMAY NOIR À JUS BLANC)   (Black Gamay with white juice) The traditional red grape variety of the Beaujolais district of France that has large grape clusters with large, round, tough-skinned, juicy, black berries, and that produces a wine that is extremely fruity and berry-like, resembling cherries, blackberries, and raspberries.

   In 1395, Philip the Bold, Duke of Burgundy, banished the evil and disloyal Gamay grape from his kingdom (the areas around Dijon, Beaune, and Chalon), in favor of the bigger and fruitier Pinot Noir grape, which was in demand at that time. Also known as *Bourguignon Noir, Gamay Noir à Jus Blanc, Gamay Rond,* and *Petit Gamai. See* Gamay Beaujolais, Napa Gamay, and Valdiguié.

GAMAY BEAUJOLAIS   Originally thought to be the true Gamay of the Beaujolais district, now identified as a strain of Pinot Noir. When used on U.S. wine labels, it must be shown in direct conjunction with either Napa Gamay or Pinot Noir, as the case may be. *See* Gamay.

GAMAY NOIR À JUS BLANC (FR)   *See* Gamay.

GAMAY ROND   *See* Gamay.

GARAFAO (PORT)   Wicker or straw-covered demijohns.

GARBATO (ITAL)   Graceful.

GARGANEGA (ITAL)   A local white grape variety grown predominatly in the Veneto region, where it produces a dry white wine called Soave. Known locally as *Terlano* or *Garganega Comune*.

GARGANEGA COMUNE (ITAL)   *See* Garganega.

GARLIC   Occasionally used to plug small holes in leaking wooden barrels. *See* Toothpicks.

GARNACHA (SP)   *See* Grenache.

GARNACHO (SP)   *See* Grenache.

GARNISH   The finishing touch to a cocktail, which usually consists of citrus fruit, in the shape of wheels or wedges added to a drink (generally for eye appeal) prior to serving. Other garnishes include maraschino cherries, pineapple wedges, cocktail onions and olives, as well as certain vegetables.

GARRAFA (PORT)   *See* Bottle.

GARRAFEIRA (PORT)   The wine has been specially aged; similar to *reserve* or *special reserve*.

GARTEN (GERM)   Garden.

GÄRUNG (GERM)   *See* Fermentation.

GASCOGNE (FR)   *See* Gascony.

GASCON JAR   An Armagnac bottle of 250 ml, shaped like a claret bottle.

GASCONY   The name of the French region of Bordeaux used during the Middle Ages, prior to it being called "Aquitaine." Spelled *Gascogne* in France.

GAS CHROMATOGRAPHY   It is a versatile analytical method for the efficient separation of volatile components in a wine sample.

GASIFICADO (SP)   *See* Charmat Method.

GASSY   A table wine that displays excessive amounts of carbon dioxide. It could result from malolactic fermentation occurring in the bottle.

GATORADE   A sweetened noncarbonated soft drink, rich in electrolytes, which helps to maintain the body's fluid balance. It is especially useful during extremely hot weather where large quantities of water are depleted from the body through perspiration. It was developed at the University of Florida and named after their athletic team.

GATTINARA (ITAL)   A full-bodied, red wine made primarily from the Nebbiolo grape variety in the Piedmont region.

Gattinara's DOC, which was granted on July 9, 1967, states that Gattinara must be made from 90 percent Nebbiolo (known locally as *Spanna*), with up to 10 percent Bonarda grapes, grown exclusively within the territory known as Gattinara. It must attain a minimum of 12-percent alcohol and be aged four years (two in wood). This dry, full-bodied wine is best consumed when six to ten years old.

The Gattinara *consorzio* features on its neck label towers standing among the vineyards.

GAUGER   A seldom-used term for an official or customs officer who is in charge of "gauging spirits," to determine the relative alcoholic content.

GAVI (ITAL)   *See* Cortese.

GAY-LUSSAC   A famous French chemist who, in 1810, correctly devised the overall equation for fermentation.

Gay-Lussac's formula for fermentation is:

$$C_6H_{12}O_6 \quad = \quad 2C_2H_5OH \quad + \quad 2CO_2$$

(sugar glucose)   (ethyl alcohol)   (carbon dioxide)

It is also the standard metric measurement of alcoholic strengths contained in a beverage used in France, often abbreviated "GL."

GAZÈIFIÈ (FR)   A sparkling wine that is artificially carbonated.

GEBIET (GERM)   Wine-producing region.

GEBRUDER (GERM)   Brothers.

GEFÄLLIG (GERM)   A wine that is pleasing and harmonious.

GEFÜLLT (GERM)   Full or rich in body.

GEISENHEIM   It is Germany's premier school of viticulture, founded in 1872, in the Rheingau region.

GELATIN   A long chain protein fining agent derived from beef or pork, either fresh or dried egg whites from chicken eggs, and carries a positive charge. It is produced by hydrolysis of collagen in animal cartilages and bones by boiling in water. The jelly-like substance first extracted is gelatin, whose active component is glutin, upon which its actual fining power lies. On further treatment, more gelatin is extracted and concentrated, and finally glue is produced. Also known as *gélatine*. *See* Fining and Fining Agents.

GÉLATINE (FR)   *See* Gelatin.

GEMARKUNG (GERM)   The geographic boundary of a viticultural region or district.

GEMEINDE (GERM)   A village or parish.

GEMMA (ITAL)   *See* Bud.

GEMULTICHKEIT (GERM)   A term often used to describe the joyous atmosphere in a pub or tavern.

GENERALLY RECOGNIZED AS SAFE (GRAS)   The term means that the treating material has an FDA listing in title 21, Code of Federal Regulations, part 182 or part 184, or is considered to be generally recognized as safe by the U.S. Food and Drug Administration. It has no adverse effects when used as directed.

GÉNÉREUX (FR)   *See* Generous.

GENERIC WINE   A designation of a particular class or type of wine, but such designations also may have geographic significance (e.g., the name of a district, commune, or region where the wine originates from). A simpler definition would be a "place-name"—wines that are named after European wine-producing districts, such as Burgundy, Chablis, Champagne, Chianti, Port, Rhine, Sauternes, Sherry, and so forth. Also known as *générique*.

GÉNÉRIQUE (FR)   *See* Generic Wine.

GENEROSO (ITAL, PORT, OR SP)   *See* Generous.

GENEROUS   A term used to describe wines rich in color, body, alcohol, and extract. Also known as *généreux* and *generoso*.

GENEVA GIN   *See* Holland Gin.

GENOTYPE   The gene stock of a grapevine inherited by a specimen from its parents.

GENTIL ROSÉ AROMATIQUE   *See* Gewürztraminer.

GENUINO (ITAL)   Genuine; an honestly made wine, but not necessarily great.

GENUS   The various botanical groups of grapevine species.

G

162

GERANIUM   It is a pungent, grassy aroma so called because it really does smell like crushed stems and leaves of geraniums. It is a spoilage odor occasionally found in some wines that have undergone malolactic fermentation in the presence of sorbic acid, a stabilizer often added to some wines. The bacterial decomposition of sorbic acid causes this powerful volatile ester to form, making the wines unfit for consumption.

GERBAUDE (FR)   The presentation of flowers to the lady of the house after the wine harvest.

GERBSTOFFREICH (GERM)   A wine that is high in tannin.

GERENTE (SP)   The manager of a bodega.

GERING (GERM)   Poor.

GERMINATION   To sprout or cause to sprout, as from a spore, seed, or bud.

GEROPIGA (PORT)   A mixture of brandy and a concentrate of unfermented grape juice (reduced by evaporation) used for blending to give added sweetness and body to some port wines. *See* Grape Concentrate.

GESCHEIN (GERM)   The flowering of the grapevine.

GESCHMACK (GERM)   *See* Flavor.

GESCHMEIDIG (GERM)   *See* Supple.

GESTOPPT (GERM)   A wine that has not completely finished fermenting; either due to a *stuck fermentation* or because the winemaker has intentionally stopped the fermentation in order to create a wine with residual sugar. *See* Stuck Fermentation.

GEVREY-CHAMBERTIN (FR)   A famous red wine village in the Côte de Nuits district of Burgundy. In the seventh century, A.D., the vineyard of Gevrey-Chambertin was known as *Gibriacus*.

GEWÄCHS (GERM) *See* Kreszenz.

GEWÜRZ (GERM) Spicy.

GEWÜRZTRAMINER A native of the Pfalz region of Germany; the grape now planted in most regions of the world is a clone of the original Traminer. In Germany, the name means "spicy Traminer." Gewürztraminer is a quintessentially Alsatian wine. Twenty percent of the Alsatian vineyards are planted with this grape, and very few if any countries produce a wine of equal distinction.

Its aroma is often assertive on the palate, finishing with a touch of bitterness. It is delicious, spicy, and fruity, with a pungent flavor and a highly perfumed and flowery bouquet that is strongly reminiscent of cinnamon or grapefruit. Formerly known as *Traminer*. Also known as *Gentil Rosé Aromatique, Red Traminer, Savagnin Rosé, Traminer Aromatico, Traminer Musqué,* and *Tramini Piros*.

GEZUCKERT (GERM) A wine that has been *sugared*.

GHEMME (ITAL) A medium-bodied, dry red wine produced in the Piedmont region, from a blend of Nebbiolo, Vespolina, and Bonarda Novarese grape varieties.

GHIACCIO (ITAL) *See* Ice.

GIALLO (ITAL) Yellow.

GIBBERELLIC ACID It is one of several compounds in a family of plant hormones, or plant growth regulators, called the *gibberellins*. Beginning in the late 1950s, researchers in California discovered that Gibberellic Acid can have a number of beneficial effects on grapevines.

Applications of Gibberellic Acid at bloom on seedless table grapes generally reduces berry set, increases berry size, and promotes growth of shoots.

GIBRIACUS (FR) *See* Gevrey-Chambertin.

GIFT CARTONS Decorative boxes used to contain bottles of product for resale.

GILL An ancient drinking glass that held about one-quarter pint (four fluid ounces).

GIMLET A cocktail consisting of gin and Rose's lime juice. In the 1890s, a British naval surgeon, Sir T.O. Gimlette, was concerned with the heavy drinking his men were accustomed to. So he diluted the gin with lime juice, and although it didn't dissuade them, he unintentionally created a new drink.

GIN A distilled spirit made by the additional processing of distilled neutral spirits flavored primarily with juniper berries plus other seeds, roots, and barks.

In U.S. production, most often there is a *gin head* containing trays of herbs and other flavoring botanicals such as juniper, cassia bark, coriander seed, orange peel, cardamon, angelica, and so forth. The flavoring is picked up by the alcohol vapors as they rise; these accumulated vapors are then condensed.

The distilled neutral spirits can also be mixed or soaked with juniper berries and other flavoring materials, strained and bottled, or the flavoring essences can simply be added.

Normally, gin is not aged and is bottled at not less than 80 proof.

GIN FIZZ   A cocktail consisting of gin, lemon juice, sugar, and topped with seltzer.

GINGER ALE   A carbonated soft drink made from water, sugar or corn syrup, drops of capsicum extract or essence of ginger flavor, organic acid, and caramel color. First produced in 1809.

GINGER BEER   A carbonated soft drink made from water, sugar or corn syrup, fermented ginger, organic acid, and caramel color.

Ginger beer originated in England during the nineteenth century and was consumed in great quantities in the United States during Prohibition as a substitute for real beer.

GIN HEAD   *See* Gin.

GIN LIQUEUR   A liqueur bottled at not less than 60 proof, in which the distilled spirit used is entirely gin, and that possess a predominant characteristic gin flavor derived from the distilled spirit used.

GIN MILL   Slang name given to a bar.

GIN RICKEY   A cocktail consisting of gin and lime juice. Civil War Colonel Joe Rickey had this drink named after him at the St. James Hotel in New York City in 1895. *See* Rickey.

GIOVANE (ITAL)   *See* Young.

GIRASOL (SP)   *See* Gyropalette.

GIRONDE (FR)   An important river in Bordeaux that crosses the Garonne and Dordogne Rivers in the south and Atlantic Ocean in the north. The four most important communes that make up the Médoc district are located on the west side of the Gironde River.

GIVRY (FR)   A red wine commune in the Côte Chalonnaise district of Burgundy. Givry was the favorite red wine of King Henry IV of England (1399–1413).

GL   *See* Gay-Lussac.

GLACÉ (FR)   A drink chilled by refrigeration or immersion in ice; not with ice in it.

GLANZHELL (GERM)   *See* Brilliant.

GLASS   As we know it today, glass was first produced by the Syrians in approximately 2000 b.c. The natural raw materials used to create glass—siliceous sand, sodium carbonate or Solvay soda (soda ash), and calcium carbonate $CaCO_3$ (limestone)—are placed in huge furnaces where they are heated to about 2700 degrees Fahrenheit, and become molten.

GLASS CHILLER   A refrigerated box or container utilized for the quick chilling of glasses for beer and cocktails usually served "straight up." *See* Chilling a Glass.

GLASS FROSTING   *See* Frosting.

GLASSWORKS   The first glassworks of France were established in 1723 in Bordeaux.

GLATT (GERM)   Smooth; pleasing to the smell and taste.

GLENORA   A black seedless grape variety with tender skin and good texture. It is only medium winter hardy and is susceptible to downy mildew. It was released through the N.Y.S. Experimental Station, September 1976. It is a crossing of Ontario and Russian seedless.

GLÖGG   A traditional Swedish or Scandinavian hot, spiced drink, similar to hot mulled wine, usually consumed during the cold weather. It is made from a combination of akvavit or brandy, wine, cardamon seeds, cloves, sugar, raisins, almonds, and other ingredients. Glögg is served warm in glasses containing a small cinnamon stick, raisins, currants, or almonds. *See* Mulled Wine.

GLUCO-OENOMETER (PORT)   The name of the device used to measure the unfermented sugar in the must for the production of Portuguese port wine. *See* Brix.

GLUCOSE   The simple sugar used by the body; other sugars are usually converted into glucose by enzymes in the body before they can be used as energy sources. It is a monosaccharide hexose sugar.

GLÜHWEIN (GERM)   *See* Mulled Wine.

GLYCERIN   It is a by-product of the fermentation of grapes into wine. Glycerin increases the feeling of fatness in the mouth, giving the wine a soft, almost oily tinge on the tongue and palate.

Glycerin coats the surface of mouth and obscures acidity or tartness, so sometimes acid needs to be added to the wine to compensate. Also known as *glycerol*.

GLYCEROL   *See* Glycerin.

GLYCOL   Same as *ethylene glycol*. Any of a group of alcohols of which ethylene glycol is the type.

GLYKYS (GREECE)   *See* Sweet.

GNÔLE (FR)   Brandy.

GOAL   Target case volume in a territory for a specified time period. Must specify either shipments or depletions, 9-liter or flat cases. Also known as *quota*.

GOAL DEPLETION REPORT   Monthly report from sales statistics that provides current month and year-to-date territorial brand depletion information compared to last year and to goal.

GOBELET (FR) A pruning method used in the Beaujolais district of Burgundy, that trains the grapevine in the shape of a *goblet*.

GOBLET A bowl-shaped drinking vessel, containing a stem and base, ordinarily made of glass.

GOLDEN GINS These gins are aged in wood for a short period of time and have a light golden-brown color, extracted from the barrel. Golden gin is quite difficult to find today.

GOLDRIESLING *See* Riesling Doré.

GOLDWASSER (Also known as *Danzigwasser*, named for Danzig, now Gdansk, Poland, the town where it was first produced.) An orange-based liqueur, that can also be made with the addition of anise, caraway seeds, or even fennel. Alchemists believed for many centuries that, by mixing pure gold with alcohol, they could create "liquid gold" or the elixir of passion, stamina, and good health, for use as an aphrodisiac, or even a guarantee of immortality. By the end of the sixteenth century, a beverage was made in Europe in which flakes of gold were combined with alcohol; it was called *goldwasser*. The current production uses 23-karat gold leaf, which is quite pure and harmless to ingest. In fact, it is so thin and light (technically, it is classified as of double-X thinness), that, when the bottle is shaken, the flakes appear to be suspended and float indefinitely. The gold is purchased in thin sheets resembling tissue paper; in fact, they cost more than gold in solid form. The reason is simple: the labor needed to prepare this paper-thin gold leaf is considerable. The gold is added to the liqueur and immediately blended with rapid movements. As the liquid is agitated, the gold breaks up into tiny flecks.

GÖNCI (HUN) A small 35-gallon barrel in which Tokay wine is aged. *See* Barrel.

GONDOLA A wheeled open-topped horizontal tank that is used to collect grapes after harvesting.

GO-OUT Full fiscal year forecast made during the current year for the next fiscal year.

GORDO (SP) Name given to a full-bodied wine and also when its organoleptic characteristics show a high alcoholic strength.

GORZALE WINO (POL) Scorched, or distilled, wine. Term used for vodka in Poland until the sixteenth century to distinguish the beverage from medicinal vodkas.

GORZALKA (POL) Ancient Polish term for vodka used until the sixteenth century when supplanted by wodka.

GOUDRON *See* Tarry.

GOULEYANT (FR) Easy to drink; light, pleasant. Generally applies to "early to drink" wines (e.g., Beaujolais), fruity and fresh.

GOURMET CUBES   *See* Ice Cubes.

GOÛT (FR)   Taste; used to describe the taste of a wine.

GOÛT AMÉRICAIN (FR)   A fairly sweet wine, chiefly demisec or doux champagnes generally exported to South America or Eastern Europe.

GOÛT ANGLAIS (FR)   A fairly dry wine, chiefly brut champagnes for the English market.

GOÛT DE BOIS (FR)   Woody taste, often the result of wine stored too long in a new barrel.

GOÛT DE BOUCHON (FR)   Corky taste. A deteriorated cork imparts an unpleasant quality to the taste and aromas of wine.

GOÛT DE CUIT (FR)   Wine with a cooked flavor or with a natural flavor resulting from a hot summer or very hot soil.

GOÛT D'ÉVENT (FR)   A wine that has become insipid and flat, possibly from being opened too long.

GOÛT DE FERMENT (FR)   Taste of a wine still fermenting; or in a bottle having recently undergone a secondary fermentation.

GOÛT DE FOX (FR)   *See* Foxy.

GOÛT DE GOUDRON (FR)   *See* Tarry.

GOÛT FRANCAIS (FR)   A sweet champagne.

GOÛT DE LUMIÈRE (FR)   Light rays close to the UV wavelength are responsible for the "light stroke" that is detrimental to wine and beer.

GOÛT DE PAILLE (FR)   A wine with a taste of wet straw that is quite objectionable.

GOÛT DE PIQUÉ (FR)   A wine with a taste of vinegar.

GOÛT DE POURRI (FR)   A wine with a moldy taste.

GOÛT DE RANCE (FR)   *See* Butyric Acid.

GOÛT DE RANCIO (FR)   *See* Rancio.

GOÛT DE RENARD (FR)   *See* Foxy.

GOÛT DE SAUVAGE (FR)   Taste imparted by native American grapevines and some hybrids.

GOÛT DE TERROIR (FR)   An earthy smell or taste imparted to a wine by the soil in which the grapevine is grown. *See* Earthy.

GOÛT DE VIEUX (FR)   The distinctive smell and taste of an old wine.

GOÛT MAUVAIS (FR)   Bad taste, unfit to drink.

GOVERNO (ITAL)   A process occasionally used to produce Chianti wine, meant for early consumption. It consists of inducing a secondary fermentation by the addition of 5 to 10 percent *must*, pressed from selected grapes partly dried on wicker frames. This process adds roundness and liveliness to the wine, along with a certain prickliness, noticeable on the tip of the tongue. Also known as *governo Toscano*. *See* Cannici.

GOVERNO TOSCANO (ITAL) *See* Governo.

GRAACH (GERM) A vineyard town located on the right bank of the Middle Mosel.

GRADAZIONE ALCOOLICA (ITAL) Alcoholic grade, percentage of alcohol by volume.

GRADEVOLE (ITAL) Pleasing.

GRADI ALCOOL (ITAL) Percentage or degrees of alcohol.

GRAF (GERM) Earl or count.

GRAFTING A viticultural technique that joins a bud (that part of the grapevine that produces grapes) or other part of one grapevine to a portion of another so that their tissues unite.

GRAIN Small, hard seeds of cereal grass, such as wheat, oats, rye, rice, barley, and others, necessary for the production of beer and most distilled spirits.

GRAIN ALCOHOL *See* Ethyl Alcohol.

GRAIN NEUTRAL SPIRITS *See* Neutral Spirits.

GRAIN SPIRITS Spirits distilled from a fermented mash of grain and stored in oak containers. By recognizing the qualities developed by storage, grain spirits are distinguished from grain neutral spirits.

GRAIN WHISKIES Made in a continuous distillation process from a mash of cereals, including malted barley and other unmalted cereals, yeast, and water. Grain whiskies used to make Scotch whisky are mostly made in the Lowlands of Scotland, although some come from the Highlands.

GRAINY It is a negative term often applied to some beers with an excessive use or corn or rice adjuncts.

GRAM A metric unit of weight; 28.349 grams being equal to one ounce; 1000 grams to a kilogram, which is equal to 2.2 U.S. pounds.

GRAMS PER LITER The unit of measure equivalent to the "parts per thousand" unit of measure prescribed in the Internal Revenue Code of 1986.

GRANACHA (FR) *See* Grenache.

GRANATO (ITAL) Garnet.

GRAND CRU (FR) A great growth that is a legal grade of quality. It is authorized for certain superior French wines from classified Burgundian or Alsatian vineyards.

GRAND CRU (FR) A champagne vineyard rated at 100 percent.

GRAND CRU CLASSÉ (FR) A great growth that is a legal grade of quality. It is authorized for certain superior French wines from classified (1855) Bordeaux vineyards.

GRANDE CHAMPAGNE (FR) Not a sparkling wine, but rather the premier grape-growing area of the Cognac region. Cognacs identified as Grande Champagne must be made exclusively from grapes grown in the Grande Champagne section of Cognac. Also known as *Grande Fine Champagne.*

GRANDE FINE CHAMPAGNE (FR)   *See* Grande Champagne.

GRANEL (SP)   Wine in bulk.

GRANDE MARQUE (FR)   An unofficial designation used to identify the best producers located in the Champagne region.

GRAND FORMAT   A term loosely used in France to denote large bottles of wine.

GRAND NOIR (DE LA CALMETTE)   A red grape variety, mostly planted in California where it is utilized as a blending grape due to its high juice yields.

GRAND RÉSERVE (FR)   A label designation on Armagnac or Cognac bottles that indicates that the youngest brandy used in the blend is at least 5 ½ years old (although they contain a very high percentage of brandy that has been aged for 20, 30, or 40 years or more).

GRANDS ECHÉZEAUX (FR)   A red grand cru vineyard located in the commune of Flagey-Echézeaux.

GRAND VIN (FR)   Great wine. An unofficial term utilized quite freely by many wineries.

GRAND VIN ORDINAIRE (FR)   A term with absolutely no legal meaning.

GRANITE SHOTTING   A procedure that hasn't been used in many years. It involved roughening up or "scoring" the inside of bottles by use of granite chips so that the crust formed by port wine is provided with a grip, thus rendering decanting much easier.

GRANO (SP)   The seeds of a grape.

GRAN RESERVA (SP)   Red wines that have been aged in oak barrels (225-liter) for a minimum of two years, followed by three years in the bottle, and may not leave the *bodega* until the sixth year after the vintage. Whites and rosés must be aged for four years, six months of which must be in oak barrels. In practice, many wineries age the wines far longer than the minimum. Gran Reservas are usually only laid down in exceptional years.

GRANULAR CORK   Used to treat wines stored in redwood and concrete tanks to help "smooth" them out.

GRANVAS (SP)   A sparkling wine that is not produced by the *méthode champenoise* (champagne method). *See* Charmat Method.

GRAPA (SP)   *See* Agrafe.

GRAPE   Any of various juicy, round, smooth-skinned, edible fruit, generally green or red-purple, borne in clusters on a woody vine. Also known as *rebe, traube, uva,* and *weinbeere.*

GRAPE   Grape was originally not the name of the fruit, but rather the name of the small hook with which bunches of grapes and grapefruit were cut and gathered. This tool we would refer to would be a "grapple," related to our word "grab." The original name for the grape itself, often used in Old English, was wineberry.

GRAPE BRICK   During Prohibition you could buy a package containing dehydrated grape juice that had a warning label on its wrapper that stated, "Do Not Mix This Package With Warm Water, Yeast, And Keep In A Warm Location For Two Weeks, for This Will Make Wine, And That Is Illegal!" *See* Forbidden Fruit.

GRAPE CONCENTRATE   Strained, dehydrated grape juice or extract, or grape juice that has been boiled down to a very sweet syrup. Also known as *concentrate* and *concentrato*. *See* Geropiga.

GRAPEFRUIT JUICE   The liquid constituent of a grapefruit.

GRAPEFRUITY   An odor or characteristic taste often identified with certain cold-climate grape varieties (e.g. Gewürztraminer and Johannisberg Riesling).

GRAPE JUICE   The liquid constituent of a grape that accounts for more than 85 percent of the grape. Also known as *traubensaft*.

GRAPE KNIFE   A hand-held knife used to cut bunches of grapes during harvest. Also known as corquette, falcetta, and serpette.

GRAPE LEAFHOPPER   (*Erythroneura comes*) The adult grape leafhopper is about one-eighth-inch long, pale in color, and its back and wings are marked with yellow and red. Grape leafhoppers are abundant during the summer on the undersides of grape leaves. They suck juice from the leaves and cause white blotches that later change to brown. As a result, many leaves fall from the grapevines prematurely. This damage prevents normal grapevine growth and interferes with proper ripening of the fruit.

The grape leafhopper is controlled with methoxychlor, malathion, or endosulfan insecticide sprays. Good coverage of the undersides of leaves is essential.

GRAPE POMACE BRANDY   *See* Grappa.

GRAPES   Although there are more than 8,000 grape varieties in the world, most of them are not suitable for the production of fine wine, nor are their parent grapevine species highly regarded. For the production of fine wine, the most prominent grapevine species are *Vitis vinifera*, *Vitis labrusca*, and French-American hybrids.

Each of the more than 8,000 different grape varieties of the world has its own individual color, aroma, taste, and flavor—sort of a "fingerprint" that identifies it either by minute and subtle nuances, or by a wide and marked margin.

GRAPE SUGAR   The natural sugar contained in ripe grapes, which is primarily glucose.

GRAPE VARIETY   The name of grape or grapes used in winemaking. Also known as *casta*, *rebsorte*, *variety*, and *vitigno*.

GRAPEVINE   Any of the species of woody vines that bear edible fruit. Grapevines are hermaphroditic or monoecious, which means that they are self-pollinating. Also known as *ampelos*, *vid*, *videira*, *vigne*, *vite*, and *weinreb*.

GRAPE WINE   It is wine produced by the normal alcoholic fermentation of the juice of sound, ripe grapes (including restored or unrestored pure condensed grape must) with or without the addition, after fermentation, of pure condensed grape must, and with or without added grape brandy or alcohol, but without other addition or abstraction except as may occur in cellar treatment. The product may be ameliorated before, during, or after fermentation by either the use of dry sugar and/or water. *See* Wine.

GRAPPA (ITAL)   Grappa, also known as *vinaccia*, is a distillate made from the stems, pulp, skins, and seeds (collectively known as the pomace) of grapes—the remains from the pressing of the grapes for winemaking. It is estimated that 224 pounds of residue or pomace yields approximately five liters of pure alcohol. The residue of pressed fruit such as apples, apricots, and pears can also be used.

This distillate is quite raw, rough, and coarse in its youth, and it is several years before it becomes palatable. Traditionally, it is served after dinner as a digestive; it is consumed straight, either at room temperature or well chilled.

The origin of the name grappa comes from a town called Bassano del Grappa in the Veneto region of Italy, where grappa was originally produced. Grappa is also known as *aguardiente*, *bagaceira*, *dop brandy*, *grape pomace brandy*, *marc*, *orujo*, *pomace brandy*, and *tresterschnapps*. *See* Alcools Blancs, Eau-de-Vie, and Rue.

GRAPPAIOLI (ITAL)   Distillers who make grappa.

GRAPPA CON RUTA (ITAL)   *See* Grappa and Rue.

GRAPPE (FR)   A cluster of grapes or a bunch of grapes.

GRAPY   Similar to fruity, with a characteristic smell of a young, often immature fruity wine, with fresh grape overtones. A taste almost of fresh-picked grapes. Most *Vitis labrusca* grape varieties display this characteristic.

GRAS   An acronym for "generally recognized as safe."

GRAS (FR)   A wine that is rich in body and fat, and is fleshy.

GRASIG (GERM)   *See* Green.

GRASSY   A term applied to certain white wines, especially Sauvignon Blanc, that display a vegetal, herbaceous odor, often reminiscent of freshly mowed grass. In low levels, it adds character to the wine, but in the extreme, it becomes unappealing to most consumers.

GRAVELLEUX (FR)   Gravelly.

GRAVES (FR)   An important wine district in the southern part of Bordeaux along the Garonne River, that produces both dry red and white wines. Graves and Sauternes are the only districts in Bordeaux that produce white wines. Only three grape varieties are permitted: Sauvignon Blanc, Sémillon, and Muscadelle. Graves translated means *gravel*, which is the composite makeup of the soil.

On March 4, 1937, the wines of Graves were officially granted their AOC designation. In 1953, a classification of the wines of Graves was begun by the INAO, who completed the task in 1959.

GRAY RIESLING   *See* Grey Riesling.

GRAU (GERM)   Gray.

GRAUER BURGUNDER (GERM)   *See* Pinot Gris.

GRECHETTO (ITAL)   A white grape variety grown primarily in the region of Umbria, where it produces Orvieto and Torgiano Bianco.

GRECO (ITAL)   *See* Albana.

GRECO DI ANCONA (ITAL)   *See* Albana.

GREEN   An immature, undeveloped wine that usually displays an austere, somewhat sour taste. Green wines are usually unbalanced and are characterized by a high level of malic or tartaric acid. Also known as *grasig, green wine, grün, verde, verdoso,* and *vert. See* Unripe and Young.

GREEN BEER   A term generally applied to young or immature beers that have just finished fermenting and are still cloudy.

GREEN DRAGON TAVERN   A pub located in Boston where Paul Revere and his fellow patriots held their meetings.

GREEN-GRAFTING   A viticultural practice that entails the mounting of a variety (scion) on a rootstock while the stems of the two partners are still in a herbaceous (green) rather than a ligneous (brown) state.

GREEN HUNGARIAN   A white grape variety grown in California where it is used primarily as a blending grapes, although several wineries do make a varietal wine from it.

GREEN MALT   Malt that has germinated, but has not yet been dried or kilned.

GREENNESS   A form of green.

GREEN OLIVE   A term applied to certain red wines, especially Cabernet Franc and Cabernet Sauvignon, that display a distinct aroma and taste of green olives. In low levels, it adds character to the wine, but in the extreme, it becomes unappealing to most consumers.

GREEN TEA   A nonfermented tea. Opposite of black tea.

GREEN WINE   *See* Green and Vinho Verde.

GREFFE-SOUDE (FR)   Nursery-prepared plant that is grafted onto American rootstocks.

Grêle (FR) *See* Hail.

Grenache A lightly-colored red grape variety used mostly in the U.S. rosé wines or as a blending grape. It is widely grown throughout the Mediterranean, especially in France's southern regions where it is partly responsible for Châteauneuf-du-Pape and Tavel rosés. In Spain it produces the reds from Rioja and Catalonia.

Grenache is of Spanish origin and was first introduced as a California variety wine by Almaden in 1941.

The grapevine yields small to medium-sized round, reddish-purple berries, which grow in large clusters, that produce a wine with hints of strawberry in the aroma. Also known as *Garnacha, Garnacho, Granacha,* and *Grenache Noir.*

Grenache Noir *See* Grenache.

Grenadine A red syrup (both alcoholic and nonalcoholic) with an unusual flavor derived from the pomegranate or red currants.

Grey Riesling *See* Chauché Gris. Grey Riesling is often incorrectly spelled *Gray Riesling.*

Grey Rot *see* Rot.

Grignolino (Ital) A lightly-colored red Italian grape variety grown mostly in the Piedmont region. The Grignolino grapevine is indigenous to the Asti area and its presence there can be traced back to 1252. Small and inconsistent in yield, it is a difficult grapevine to tend and thrives only in certain types of light, sandy soil.

Grillo (Ital) A white grape variety indigenous to Sicily, which is often used to make table wines or Marsala.

Grind To crush or pulverize coffee beans into fine particles by use of mechanical or hand (seldom employed) means.

Grip A seldom-used term used to describe the manner in which wine holds onto the insides of a glass; or its mouth-filling capabilities, which are firm and rich.

Gris (FR) *See* Vin Gris.

Gris (FR) Grey.

Grist Grain, necessary for the production of whiskey or malt beverages that must be ground or already has been ground.

Grits Coarsely chopped corn or other hulled grains used as an adjunct in the brewing of beer.

Grog (Austral) Term for "any alcoholic drink."

Grog A name for rum, derived from the nickname of Admiral Edward Vernon (1684–1757), the English naval officer for whom George Washington's estate was named. The admiral was known as "old grog" because he wore a shabby boat coat made out of grogram, a coarse fabric woven from silk and wool and often stiffened with gum. He ordered his men to take a daily drink of rum and water as a caution against scurvy, and until September 1, 1862, sea-going sailors from the United States were served grog. Also known as *Navy Grog*.

GROG BLOSSOM   The British, during World Wars I and II, were said to occasionally have a Grog Blossom, which was a rosy nose, presumably from years of drinking.

GROLLEAU (FR)   A red grape variety native to the Loire Valley, where it is often referred to as Groslot. It produces rather thin and ordinary wines and is often used in making the rosé wines of Anjou.

GROSLOT   *See* Grolleau.

GROS PLANT   *See* Folle Blanche.

GROSSE (GERM)   Great or big.

GROSSIER (FR)   A coarse or rough wine.

GROSSLAGE (GERM)   A composite vineyard made up of numbers of individual vineyards with subregions.

GROSS MARGIN   Revenues minus direct product costs.

GROSSOLANO (ITAL)   Coarse; heavy, rough, with high alcohol and tannin.

GROSS WEIGHT   Weight of a container plus its contents.

GROUND WATER   Water beneath the earth's surface between saturated soil and rock that supplies wells and springs; necessary for proper cultivation of grapevines.

GROWLERS   A slang, seldom-used term for "pails of beer to go."

GROWTH (FR)   A standard of quality, applied to wines of France; also known as *cru*.

GROWTH CYCLE   Used to denote the annually recurrent events that mark growth, development, and fruiting of the grapevines.

GRUMELLO (ITAL)   A full-bodied red wine produced from the Nebbiolo grape variety in the Valtellina district of Lombardy, located in the northern part of Italy.

GRÜN (GERM)   *See* Green.

GRÜNER SYLVANER (GERM)   *See* Sylvaner.

GRÜNER VELTLINER (AUS)   A white grape variety, which is grown extensively in areas of Lower Austria and Vienna. The wine is effervescent, light with a spicy-fruity taste, and very refreshing.

GUIGNARDIA BIDWELLII   *See* Black Rot.

GUINGETTE (FR)   A local tavern or roadside inn, that features live music and dancing.

GUM ARABIC   A substance obtained from various species of acacia trees or shrubs and is occasionally used to clarify and stabilize wine.

GUN FLINT A scent of flint-sparks, which is noticed in some white wines (e.g., Pouilly Fumé of France). Also known as *pierre-à-fusil*.

GUNPOWDER PROOF *See* Proof.

GUT (GERM) Good.

GUTEDEL (GERM) A white grape variety brought to Baden, from Lake Geneva in 1780. It is thought to have come from Turkey or even Egypt, where it was mentioned as early as 2,800 B.C.; later imported into France. It is correctly known as *Chasselas Doré*.

GUYOT (FR) A pruning method used in the Beaujolais district of Burgundy, which consists of training grapevines on a single vertical axis.

GYPSUM *See* Calcium Sulfate and Plastering.

GYROPALETTE An automated riddling machine used for the production of sparkling wines. There have been many variations of this automated system, and one very successful one is used in the sparkling wine house of Domaine Chandon in Yountville, California. Their machine, VLM (very large machine), is an improved version of the smaller French automatic riddling machine ("gyro-palette"), which stood 4 feet high, wasted 13 feet of airspace, and was capable of riddling 504 bottles at once. The machine at Domaine Chandon, which stands 17 feet high, once described as "cubist gyroscopes," can riddle 4,032 bottles at once! It can also be programmed to turn and/or tilt three times in 24 hours. A bottle of sparkling wine can be machine riddled in 12 days (three movements a day) as opposed to the approximately 30 days of a traditional hand-riddling cycle. Also known as *girasol*.

HA *See* Hectare.

HABILLAGE (FR) A bottle-dressing (combination of label and foil capsule).

HABZÓ (HUN) *See* Sparkling Wine.

HAIL Precipitation in the form of pellets of ice and hard snow, which is detrimental to grapevines. During heavy hailstorms, the hail damages clusters of berries, as well as breaking the delicate canes and other parts of the grapevine. Also known as Grêle.

HALBROT (SWISS) *See* Rosé Wine.

HALBFUDER (GERM) A large barrel with a capacity of 500 liters (132 U.S. gallons), mostly used in the Mosel region. *See* Barrel.

HALBSTÜCK A large barrel used in Germany with the capacity of 600 liters (158.5 U.S. gallons). *See* Barrel.

HALBTROCKEN (GERM) The designation *halbtrocken* went into effect on August 1, 1977, and was created by the wine authority of the Common Market in Brussels. The reason for this designation was the fact that some people prefer wines drier than most of the German wines on the market.

Halbtrocken wines contain a maximum of 18 grams per liter of residual sugar (which can also be expressed as 1.8 grams per 100 ml, or 1.8 percent residual sugar). The variance here can be 10 grams per liter. For example, if the wine contains 5 grams per liter of acidity, the maximum sugar level can only be 15 grams per liter.

HALB UND HALB A light-brown, citrus liqueur from Germany made from a base of alcohol and flavored with cloves and other spices.

HALF AND HALF In England, a drink consisting of equal parts stout and ale.

HALF AND HALF A commercial mixture of half 18 percent cream and half 3.5 percent milk.

Half-Barrel   *See* Keg.

Half-Bottle   A bottle with a capacity of 12.7 fluid ounces or 375 milliliters.

Half-Cube   *See* Ice Cube.

Half-Dice   *See* Ice Cubes.

Half-Keg   A container with a capacity of seven and three-quarter gallons of beer.

Hammondsport   A wine-producing district in the Finger Lakes region of New York State.

Handgun   A hand-held dispensing head with a flexible hose, connected to a postmix or premix system for an automatic soda system utilized in some bars.

Hand Shaker   A combination of a large mixing glass and a stainless steel container that fits over it. It is used for cocktails that need to be hand shaken for incorporation of ingredients. Also known as *mixing cup, mixing glass,* or *mixing steel.*

Happy Hour   A limited period of the day, usually one to two hours before dinner where patrons can enjoy alcoholic beverages whose prices have been discounted or special sized drinks. Also known as *attitude adjustment hour.*

Hard   A wine (generally red) with excessive tannin that usually dissipates with age. Not necessarily a fault in a young, immature wine because it may indicate a long maturity period. Similar to *green.* Also known as *âpreté, dur, duro, hart,* and *sklirós.*

Hard Cider   The result of fermentation of cider without the addition of sugar. It is relatively low in alcohol (about 5 to 8 percent) and has a very limited shelf life. *See* Apple Juice, Apple Wine, Cider, and Sweet Cider.

Hardening   The process by which a plant or tissue is made more resistant to any environmental extreme, such as low temperature.

Hard Liquor   A term commonly taken to mean distilled spirits; beverages that contain at least 40 percent alcohol (80 proof). Also known as *liquor.*

Hardy   Unless qualified, it means the grape variety is among those that have performed well in hardiness trials in many vineyard sites and is not subject to damage by extremes in temperature.

Harmonious   Also known as *evármostos* and *harmonisch. See* Balance.

Harmonisch (germ)   *See* Harmonious.

Haro (sp)   The primary wine-producing town of Rio Alta.

Harsh   A "green" or "hard" wine with excessive tannin, carried to an extreme. *See* Astringency.

Hart (germ)   *See* Hard.

Harvest   The annual gathering or picking of the grapes for eventual winemaking. Also known as *crop. See* Vintage.

HARVEST CYCLE   Although ice-making machines vary considerably in methods of forming and releasing ice, the operating cycles are similar in most cases. The water-contact or water-container surfaces are chilled to below the freezing point in the ice-making cycle. When the ice reaches a certain thickness, the water-contact or water-container surface is heated briefly to release the ice.

HARVEY WALLBANGER   A cocktail consisting of orange juice, vodka, and Galliano liqueur. It seems that in southern California (according to legend), Tom Harvey would arrive at his favorite pub after a day's surfing and order an "Italian Screwdriver"; then after consuming several of them, he would attempt to leave and start "banging" into walls! Hence the name.

HAT   *See* Cap.

HAUT (FR)   High. In the United States it means "sweet."

HAUTAIN (FR)   A pruning method by which the grapevines are trained, often with *espaliers* (posts larger than standard size) in an upward manner for greater sun exposure.

HAUT-MÉDOC (FR)   The southern portion of the Médoc, famous for the red wines of Saint-Estèphe, Pauillac, Saint-Julien, and Margaux.

HAUT SAUTERNE   A U.S. generic white wine of medium sweetness. Rarely produced nowadays.

HAZY   *See* Cloudy.

HEAD   The upper portion of a grapevine consisting of the top of the trunk and upper arms. Also known as the *crown*.

HEAD   The creamy collar of foam that sits on top of a glass of beer. Also known as *foam*. *See* Coney Island Head.

HEAD OR HEAD BOARDS   The ends of a barrel. Each head is made of at least three or more pieces of oak held together by wooden dowels and usually caulked with straw.

HEADING LIQUID   A liquid formula, when added to beer, increases the head retention and produces a thick, foamy head. This condition exists when there is insufficient malt used when making the beer. This practice is seldom used nowadays.

HEADS   In distillation, elements that boil at low temperatures and vaporize first. Also known as *produit de tête*.

HEADSPACE   In a barrel or tank, the space of air between the top of the wine and the top of the container. This space is the result of evaporation or leakage. *See* Ullage.

HEADSPACE   A distilled spirits bottle of a capacity of 200 milliliters or more shall be held to be so filled as to mislead the purchaser if it has a headspace in excess of 8 percent of the total capacity of the bottle after closure.

HEAD TRAINING   The oldest form of grapevine training, which has been used for centuries, can still be found in California's older vineyards. With the "head" system, the grapevine is kept rather low to the ground. In the early stages of its growth, it is allowed to develop "arms" that radiate from the main trunk, somewhat like the spokes of a wheel. The leaf and fruit-bearing canes, or grapevine branches, emanate from these arms. On each of these arms are "spurs" or year-old segments of growth that generate tiny buds that in turn produce new growth and bear next year's grapes. By controlling the number of buds left on the grapevine through pruning, the number of grape clusters produced can be controlled.

This technique, however, has some problems. The low position of the grapevine makes soil cultivation, pruning, and harvesting quite difficult due to the shape of the grapevine. Head-trained grapevines give low yields and not necessarily the best quality. Although the radial configuration of the grapevine arms does allow fairly good air circulation around the grapevine and exposure to the sun, more modern training techniques have demonstrated a clear improvement in both of these factors. *See* Training and Cordon Training.

HEADY   A term that usually refers to wines with excessive alcohol content. Roughly equivalent to "strong" wines. Also, used loosely as a term for sparkling wines that show a persistent foam on their surface.

HEARTS   In distillation, elements that vaporize between the heads and tails. Also known as *madilla* and *middle liquors*.

HEARTY   A term generally used to describe full-bodied red wines with high alcoholic and extract levels.

HEATER   *See* Brandy Heater.

HEAT INSTABILITY   Used to describe protein precipitation in a wine that causes cloudiness or haziness.

HEAT SUMMATION   The geographic classification of regions in terms of heat degree days during the seven-month growing season. The mean temperature or average high and low, greater than 50 degrees, from April 1 through October 31. The resulting figure is expressed as degree days. *See* Degrees Days.

HEAT TREATED VINES   A process in which samples from the best grapevines are taken from the vineyard. The best of these grapevines are then tested against an index plant to isolate viruses. The most virus-free grapevines are raised in a hot house where the heat causes the grapevines to grow faster than viruses. The top three inches of the grapevines are then cut off. The process is repeated and grapevines are then vineyard planted.

HEAVY   A term used to describe a wine that is high in alcohol, but hasn't the flavor or acidity to balance it. An excessively full-bodied wine of little distinction that lacks finesse and, because of this, is tiring to drink. Also known as *ponderous* and *varys*.

HEAVY BODIED BLENDING WINE   Wine made from fruit without added sugar, with or without added distilled wine spirits, and conforming to the definition of natural wine in all respects except as to maximum total solids content.

HEAVY GOBLET   A stemmed glass with a large, round bowl with a capacity of 8 to 10 fluid ounces and used to serve beer.

HEBEGESHMACK (GERM)   A yeasty smell and taste.

HECHO EN MEXICO (SP)   Made in Mexico.

HECTARE (HA)   A metric measure equal to 10,000 square meters of land or 2.471 acres. Also known as *ettaro* and *hectarea*.

HECTAREA (SP)   *See* Hectare.

HECTOGRADE (HG)   The metric system for measuring the alcoholic content of wine. Also known as *ettogrado*.

HECTOLITER (HL)   A metric measurement equal to 100 liters or 26.418 gallons or 11.111 cases of 12 750-milliliter bottles. In the ECC, wine production is referred to in hectoliters per hectare (hl/ha). Also known as *ettolitro* and *hectolitro*.

HECTOLITRO (SP)   *See* Hectoliter.

HEFE (GERM)   *See* Yeast.

HELBON (GREECE)   The name of an ancient wine.

HELENA   A white grape variety developed in 1958, by Dr. Harold P. Olmo of the University of California, Davis.

HELIX-TYPE CORKSCREW   A corkscrew with an open-core design and usually manufactured as either a wire helix or from a solid round bar of steel in which the metal is cut away to form the helix. In the latter case, the helix is generally more web-shaped than the wire helix and somewhat resembles an auger type. The only apparent disadvantage of the helix is that the point, pitch, and alignment can be damaged by heavy-handed use.

HELL (GERM)   Pale; the color of some beers.

HELLES BIER (GERM)   *See* Light Beer.

HERB (GERM)   Bitter.

HERBACEOUS   A term used to describe the odor or taste of herbs (undefined as to species), such as parsley, rosemary, sage, or thyme, occasionally found in a wine or beer. This grassy or vegetal smell may be contributed by hops (beermaking) or the varietal character of certain grape varieties, such as Cabernet Sauvignon, Cabernet Franc, Merlot, and Sauvignon Blanc. *See* Stemmy.

HERBEMONT   A red grape variety developed by Nicholas Herbemont about 1820, in Georgia. Some Herbemont is cultivated in the American Midwest, as well as in South Carolina.

HERBICIDE   Any chemical substance used to destroy plants or weeds or to check their growth. Some are selective and kill only certain plants.

HERB TEA Technically not *real* tea, but the commonality is that both tea and herb tea are made by an infusion process in boiling water. There are more than 400 different herbs that are suitable for use in herb teas and do not contain caffeine.

HERBS Aromatic plants that are utilized in the production of vermouth and other aromatized wines, certain liqueurs, and flavored wines.

HERMAPHRODITIC Grapevines are self-pollinating; therefore, they contain both the male and female reproductive sex organs. Also known as *monoecious*.

HERMITAGE (SO. AFRICA) *See* Cinsaut.

HERMITAGE (FR) The name of a village in the southern part of the Rhône Valley famous for its full-bodied red wines.

Hermitage red wine is produced from 100-percent Syrah grapes, which are grown on some 210 acres. The white Hermitage, which has a smell of hazelnuts and is produced from a blend of Roussanne and Marsanne grapes, is difficult to obtain because of small production, and ages quite elegantly. Red Hermitage wines are best when 10 to 12 years old, and white Hermitage wines when 3 to 4 years old. The wines of Crozes-Hermitage (about 1,200 acres) are lighter than those of Hermitage and should be drunk when they are younger.

HEROLDREBE (GERM) A red grape variety grown predominantly in Württemberg. It is a cross of Portugieser and Limberger, which was named for August Harold of the State Agricultural Institute of Weinsberg, where it was developed in 1956.

HERSTELLER (GERM) A manufacturer or producer of alcoholic beverages.

HERZHAFT (GERM) Hearty.

HESSISCHE BERGSTRASSE (GERM) One of 11 qualitätswein (quality) regions.

HETEROZYGOTE A grapevine not breeding true to type for its particular characteristics.

HEXENE A green taste some grapes have if picked unripe.

HEXOSE Any of the simple sugars, like fructose, galactose, glucose, or mannose, with molecules that contain six carbon atoms each.

HG *See* Hectograde.

HIGHBALL A cocktail containing blended whiskey (or any type of whiskey) and ginger ale (or other carbonated mixer). In St. Louis in the 1880s, early railroaders used a ball on a high pole as a signal for railroad trains to go ahead or speed up. This signaling device was called a "highball."

When bartenders found that ice, whiskey, and soda water could be mixed speedily into a delightful drink, they called it a "highball."

Highland Scotch A growing area for barley and a Scotch producing area noted for its *smoky* or *peaty* smell and taste.

High-Proof Concentrate A volatile fruit-flavor concentrate (essence) that has an alcohol content of more than 24 percent by volume and is unfit for beverage use (nonpotable) because of its natural constituents (i.e., without the addition of other substances).

High Wine When the vapor is drawn off during the distillation process, it condenses into a liquid known as *low wine*, which has an alcoholic content of anywhere from 45 to 65 percent. The low wine is redistilled, or further refined, which allows the alcohol to reach an even higher concentration and further remove unwanted impurities and flavors. The resulting liquid is called *high wine*, or new whiskey; it is crystal clear and ready for maturing.

Himbeergeist (germ) *See* Framboise.

Himrod A white seedless grape variety developed from a cross of Thompson Seedless and Ontario, in 1952 at the New York Experimental Station at Geneva.

183

Hippocras An ancient "highly spiced" honey wine that was made more than 2,300 years ago by Hippocrates, a Greek physician. He wrote about a certain cordial called "Hydromel," which was made of wine, honey, cinnamon, and other aromatic herbs and botanicals. Hippocras was quite popular in Europe until the time of Louis XV. *See* Mead.

HL *See* Hectoliter.

Hoch (germ) Very high quality.

Hochfarbig (germ) A wine that is "deeply colored."

Hochfeine (germ) Very fine.

Hochgewächs (germ) A superior vineyard.

Hochheim (germ) The eastern-most vineyard village of the Rheingau.

Hock For many years the wines from Hochheim, Germany (which contains five vineyards between Mainz and Wiesbaden) were referred to, mainly by the British, as *hock*; earlier, the British called them *Rhenish* wines.

Hof (germ) A court or manor house.

hogshead A barrel used in many wine-producing countries, where its capacity varies from region to region. It is occasionally also used for storing or shipping distilled spirits and beer. *See* Barrel.

Hoist a Few A slang term for drinking a glass of beer.

holandas (sp) Distilled grape wine spirits.

Holland or Dutch Gin A gin produced primarily in Holland from a low-proof, distilled malt spirit to which juniper and other botanicals are added, resulting in a more heavy body than the dry gins produced in the United

States and England. Another general characteristic of Holland gin is that it retains and imparts some of the taste and odor of the grain. also known as *Geneva* or *Schiedam*. Geneva is spelled *jenever* in Belgium.

HOLLEJO (SP)   Grape skin.

HOLLOW   A term sometimes applied to a wine that has a beginning and end, but no middle. It lacks a positive center impression or middle body.

HOLZGESCHMACK (GERM)   A wine with a woody taste.

HOME BREW   Illegal or illicit beer that was made at home in the U.S. during Prohibition.

HOMOGENIZED   A process by which milk is spun at very high speeds in order to break down the fat globules, transforming them into a stable emulsion, otherwise they would rise to the surface, requiring the milk to be shaken prior to use. Pasteurization of milk is required by law, whereas homogenization is not.

HONEST   A term occasionally used to describe a simple but well-made wine.

HONEY   The smell of honey often detected in sweet wines made from grapes that have been attacked by *Botrytis cinerea*.

HONEY WINE   *See* Mead.

HONIGARTIG (GERM)   A wine with a honeyed odor and taste.

HONOR BARS   A system by which guests are expected to keep track of the amount of alcoholic beverages they have consumed and then pay the appropriate sum of money. Also known as the *honor system*.

HONOR SYSTEM   *See* Honor Bars.

HOOCH   A home-concocted drink made of boiled ferns and flour by the Alaskan Indians of the Hutsnuwu tribe, who called it "hoochino." Soldiers who were sent from the United States to Alaska, after the territory was purchased from Russia in 1867, added molasses and distilled it, shortening the name to "hooch." Hooch was the Army's term for distilled spirits during the first and second World Wars.

HOOP DRIVER   A tool used for driving the hoops on a barrel in order to make them tighter.

HOOPS   The metal rings that surround a wooden barrel, needed to hold the wooden staves together, while giving support to the barrel.

HOPPY   An odor detected in some ales caused by a high level of hops used in the brewing process.

HOP EXTRACT   The processing of hops to extract and isolate its "bittering" oils, which are often used in brewing beer.

HOP JACKET   A stainless steel tank where the wort is filtered (removing the hops) and stored after brewing.

HOP LEAF   The flowers of the hop plant in a loose, dried form.

Hop Pellets   The dried flowers of the hop plant that are formed and pressed into pellets for later use in beermaking.

Hops   The dried flowering cones from the unfertilized female hop plant called "catkin," which is a perennial herb-like climbing vine (*Humulus lupulus*) of the cannabis family. Hops use is almost indispensable to the aroma, taste, and character of beer. The hops contain a naturally occurring amount of resin, plus various oils, which are the perfect "bittering" agents for beer. They provide the backbone of aroma and taste to most beers and ales alike. There are many varieties of hops, all of which lend variety to beer bitterness, flavor, and bouquet. The taste of hops is generally characterized by a slight bitterness in some beers, to a distinctive bitter, almost astringent taste in others.

Hops also possess antiseptic properties that inhibit the growth of bacteria. This is particularly important in the brewing of the nonpasteurized draft beers.

Horchata (sp)   An unusual alcoholic beverage made from either almonds or pumpkin seeds.

Horgazuela (sp)   *See* Palomino.

Horizontal Back Card   Large display card used to promote a product on large case stackings.

Hospices de Beaune (fr)   A charity hospital located in Burgundy that hosts an annual wine auction to raise money. The Hospices de Beaune (which was designed by Flemish architect Jacques Viscrere) was established by Nicolas Rolin and his wife, Guigone de Salins, in 1443. Rolin was a tax collector for the Grand Chancellor, Philippe le Bon, of the Duchy of Burgundy, in 1395, during the reign of King Louis XI. There were no wine auctions held at the Hospices de Beaune in 1956 and 1968, due to poor wine vintages.

Host Bar   A private party or function with unlimited drinks, where guests do not pay for individual drinks. The host or sponsoring organization pays the final tab, calculated by each bottle opened, regardless of whether the contents have been totally consumed. Some state liquor laws permit the organization to claim any opened, unempty bottles (often referred to as "stubs"), while other states prohibit such actions. Also known as *sponsored bar* or *open bar*.

Hot   Highly alcoholic wines with heady odors; fiery, burning qualities noticed in the smell and back of the throat when swallowing. It is characteristic of certain dessert wines, lacking substantial fruit. Also known as *feurig, fiery,* and *schnapsig*.

Hot Caudle   A cocktail made with spiced and sweetened hot wine or ale, bread or gruel, spices, and a beaten egg yolk.

Hotte de Vendange (fr)   A hood or backpack used to carry freshly picked grapes during harvest. Also known as *caque*. *See* Brenta.

HOT TODDY A drink of brandy, whiskey, or other distilled spirits, with hot water, sugar, lemon juice, cloves, cinnamon, and other spices. Also known as *toddy*.

HOUR GLASS A glass in the shape of an "hour glass," generally with a capacity of 8 to 10 fluid ounces, used to serve beer.

HOUSE BRANDS *See* Well Brands.

HOUSE STYLE *See* Blending.

HOUSE WHISKEY *See* Well Brands.

HOUSE WINE The wine of the "house" or restaurant that typically comes in large bottles (3 or 4 liters or larger) and is served in half- or full carafes. Also, a wine specially blended or bottled for the restaurant or bar.

HÜBSCH (GERM) Nice.

HUDSON RIVER VALLEY The oldest wine-producing district in the United States, located in New York State.

HUE Usually the separation of colors of wine seen at the edge of the glass.

HULL The outer covering or "shell" of cereal grains. Also known as *husk*.

HUNTER RIVER RIESLING (AUSTRAL) *See* Sémillon.

HUSK *See* Hull.

HÜXELREBE (GERM) A white grape variety developed in 1927 in the Rheinhessen, from a cross of Chasselas Doré and Courtillier Musqué, and named for Fritz Huxel, a vintner at Westhofen, Germany.

HYBRID The group of grape varieties referred to as hybrids, French-American hybrids, or French hybrids. They are crosses (and sometimes recrosses) of some native American grapevine species, such as *Vitis labrusca, Vitis riparia,* and *Vitis rupestris,* with *Vitis vinifera,* the European grapevine species. In France and several other wine-producing countries, the growing of hybrids in wine districts entitled to the *appellation contrôlée* are banned.

Much hybridization took place during the 1870s as a result of the Phylloxera epidemic, in order to develop grapevines resistant to its ravages. Other hybridization has taken place in order to develop grape varieties that have the ability to withstand severe cold winters, are disease resistant, and yield balanced wines in shortened growing seasons. Also known as *hybride. See* Crossbreeding.

HYBRIDE (GERM) *See* Hybrid.

HYBRIDIZATION *See* Crossbreeding.

HYDROGEN ION EXCHANGE A process that utilizes hydrochloric acid as a regenerator to eliminate sediment from wine.

HYDROGEN SULFIDE (H_2S) A smell of rotten eggs that results from a variety of causes, most commonly from the reduction of elemental sulfur during fermentation. Most yeast strains will produce some amount of it. The presence of metal ions, such as aluminum, zinc, iron, or tin, seems to promote H_2 S formation. Vineyard spraying with elemental sulfur or sulfur containing compounds close to harvest time is often a cause. Removal of this undesirable volatile component is possible with limited aeration during racking and before bottling. Also known as *böckser*.

HYDROMEL   The Roman equivalent of mead, which was weak and watered. *See* Mead.

HYDROMETER   A cylindrical glass instrument of various lengths, with a scale running along its length and a bulbous weighted end. It is used in winemaking or beermaking to measure the unfermented sugar content prior to fermentation. Usually, a small sample of grapes are crushed and the liquid is strained and immediately placed into a graduated cylindrical tube where a hydrometer is placed into the tube and allowed to bounce around freely until the weight of the displaced liquid equals the weight of the hydrometer and its movement ceases. The point where the hydrometer meets the surface of the grape juice is noted, and a reading of the hydrometer is taken.

Other hydrometers measure specific gravity and potential of alcohol. Also known as *mustimeter* and *saccharometer*.

HYDROMETER TESTING JAR   A tall glass or plastic cylinder (graduated or ungraduated) that holds liquids to be read by a hydrometer.

ICE   Water that has been frozen by submitting it to temperatures below its freezing point, 32 degrees Fahrenheit. Also known as *ghiaccio*.

ICE (ITAL)   *See* Instituto Commercio Estero.

ICE BREAKER   *See* Ice Crusher.

ICE BUCKET   A container used for temporary storage of ice cubes, made available to guests for cocktails. A metal vessel that contains ice and water for the chilling of bottles of white wine and sparkling wine. Also known as a *wine bucket*.

ICE CHEST   *See* Ice Storage Bin.

ICE CRUSHER   A motor-driven machine with spiked rollers to crush large pieces of ice or ice cubes. Also known as *ice breaker*.

ICE CUBES   Water that has been frozen and formed into the shape of a "cube" by metal or plastic trays with partitions.

Commercial ice-making machines can produce different shapes and sizes of ice cubes; some of them have been dubbed "crescent" cubes, "cubelets", "flake ice", "flat" cubes, "gourmet" cubes, "full" cubes (also called "dice"), "half-cubes" (also called "half-dice"), "ice nuggets", and "regular" and "square" cubes. Of these, the standard sizes are:

Regular (1 ⅛" x 1 ⅛" x ⅞"; 30 cubes per pound)
Full (also called "dice") (⅞" x ⅞" x ⅞"; 48 cubes per pound)
Half-cubes (also called "half-dice") (⅜" x ⅞" x ⅞" ; 96 cubes per pound)

ICED-COFFEE   Freshly brewed coffee with sugar and/or milk and has ice, either in cube or crystal form added for chilling.

ICED-TEA   Freshly brewed tea with sugar and/or lemon juice and has ice, either in cube or crystal form added for chilling.

ICED-TEA GLASS   A tall, cylindrical-shaped glass with the capacity of 12 to 14 fluid ounces. Also known as a *Tom Collins* glass.

ICED-TEA SPOON   A long-handled spoon with a shallow bowl used for stirring iced-tea.

ICE HARDNESS   A scale that measures the ratio of true ice to entrained water per pound of ice, which determines the relative "hardness" of various shaped ice cubes.

ICE-MAKING MACHINE   Modern ice-making machines can produce from 100 to 3,300 pounds of ice per hour, depending on the make and model of the machine. There are basically two types of machines: one produces cubes; the other, flakes. The capacity of an ice-making machine is generally expressed in production per 24 hours. It is important to note that most ice-making machines give varying production ratings for different temperature levels of the air-cooled or water-cooled condenser unit, as well as for different temperatures of water used.

ICE NUGGETS   *See* Ice Cubes.

ICE SCOOP   Plastic or metal scoop used to remove ice from ice-making machines.

ICE STORAGE BIN   An insulated container usually made of styrofoam, with a hinged or sliding door used for the storage of ice. *See* Ice Chest.

ICE TUB   Rectangular, shallow rubber or plastic tubs used behind the bar for ice cubes and/or bottled beer for fast chilling and service.

ICE WATER JACKET   *See* Jacketed Tank.

ICE WINE   *See* Eiswein.

IDVDM   *See* Instituto do Vinho da Madeira.

IDYS (GREECE)   Delightful.

IL (ITAL)   The masculine article for "the."

IMBOTTIGLIARE (ITAL)   To bottle.

IMBOTTIGLIATO (ITAL)   Bottled.

IMBOTTIGLIATO AL CASTELLO (ITAL)   Bottled at the castle.

IMBOTTIGLIATO ALLA CANTINA (ITAL)   Bottled at the winery.

IMBOTTIGLIATO ALLA FATTORIA (ITAL)   Bottled at the farm or estate.

IMBOTTIGLIATO ALL'ORIGINE (ITAL)   Bottled at the source, or estate bottled.

IMBOTTIGLIATO DAL PRODUTTORE ALL'ORIGINE/DAL VITICOLTORE (ITAL)   Estate-bottled.

IMBOTTIGLIATO NELLA ZONA DI PRODUZIONE (ITAL)   Bottled in the production zone, but presumably not at the estate.

IMMATURE   *See* Young. Also known as *ápsitos* and *immaturo*.

IMMATURO (ITAL)   *See* Immature.

IMPAIRED Slang for intoxicated.

IMPERIAL An oversized bottle equivalent in capacity to eight 750-milliliter sized bottles or 202.8 fluid ounces (6 liters). Although it has the same capacity of a Methuselah, it is not used for champagne or port wine.

IMPERIAL GALLON A measurement of liquid volume, one gallon being equal to 160 fluid ounces, or 1.2 U.S. gallons. Also known as *British Gallon*. *See* Gallon.

IMPERIAL STOUT A very strong dark fruity brew originally made in the Czarist Russian Empire. Nowadays it is brewed mostly in Great Britain, Denmark, and Finland. *See* Stout.

IMPORTATORE (ITAL) Importer.

IMPORTAZIONE (ITAL) Importation.

IMPORT DUTY Levy on distilled spirit products imported into the United States. Import duties are assessed on a proof gallon.

IMPORTS Goods or service, acquired or purchased from a foreign nation, necessary for continuation of business or a way of life.

IMPORTS FOR CONSUMPTION Alcohol beverages for which U.S. custom duties have been paid, regardless of whether they are stored in government-supervised warehouses before being shipped for resale. The federal excise tax is payable on entering trade channels. *See* Entering Trade Channels and Withdrawals.

INAO *See* Institut National des Appellations d'Origine.

IN BIANCO (ITAL) A white wine vinified "without the skins."

IN BOND When used with respect to wine or distilled spirits, "in bond" refers to wine or distilled spirits possessed under bond to secure the payment of the taxes imposed by 26 U.S.C. Chapter 51, and on which such taxes have not been determined. The term includes any wine or distilled spirits on the bonded wine premises or a distilled spirits plant, or in transit between bonded premises (including, in the case of wine, bonded wine premises). Additionally, the term refers to wine withdrawn without payment of tax under 26 U.S.C. 5362 and to distilled spirits withdrawn without payment of tax under 26 U.S.C. 5214 (a) (5) or (a) (13) with respect to which relief from liability has not yet occurred. Also known as *all-in-bond*. *See* Bonded Wine Premises and Bottled-in-Bond.

INDEXING Identification of viral infections in grape varieties that do not display any obvious symptoms by grafting buds or other parts of the grapevine onto other, very susceptible varieties.

INDIAN QUEEN TAVERN The name of a tavern in Philadelphia, where Thomas Jefferson penned his first draft of the Declaration of Independence.

INDIA PALE ALE A very bitter ale with a hoppy aroma and taste. It was the kegged ale that the British sent to their troops serving in India in the past century.

INE (ITAL) *See* Instituto Nazionale Esportazione.

INEBRIATED Slang for intoxicated.

INFERNO (ITAL) A full-bodied red wine produced from the Nebbiolo grape variety in the Valtellina district of Lombardy, located in the northern part of Italy.

INFERNOTTI (ITAL) The traditional name for very secret wine cellars that have often been hidden for decades. Also known as *crutin* in Piedmont, Italy.

INFESTATION To inhabit, spread in, or overrun in large numbers, so as to be harmful, unpleasant, or bothersome. A situation that sometimes occurs in vineyards that have been infested with certain insects, animals, or even disease, which is hostile and to the point of being dangerous to grapevines.

INFLORESCENCE Also known as *flower cluster*.

INFUSE To steep in boiling liquid until the liquid absorbs the flavor of the seasoning agent. A process used in making tea and coffee. Also known as *infusion*.

INFUSION *See* Infuse and Maceration.

INFUSORIAL EARTH *See* Diatomaceous Earth.

INJERTO (SP) Graft.

INKY Term used to describe intensely dark, almost black in color red wines.

INN A place of repose for travelers that usually offers both lodging and liquid refreshments. *See* Bar, Cocktail Lounge, Pub, Saloon, and Tavern.

INNKEEPER One who manages an inn.

INOCULATING The action of adding yeast or bacteria to a biological environment in order to trigger development or fermentation.

INÓDIS (GREECE) *See* Winey.

IN-ROOM BAR In-room refrigerator and storage cabinet stocked with a variety of drinks and snacks and refilled daily; all items consumed are charged to the guest's hotel bill. In some types of in-room bars, charges are instantly transferred for addition to the room charge. In such computerized systems, printouts are instantaneous, and provide a wealth of information, from restocking reports to usage tracked by room type. Also known as *mini-bar*.

INSECTICIDE Any substance used to kill insects. *See* Pesticide.

INSIPID A tasteless, thin, characterless wine, lacking firmness and structure. Also known as *insipido*.

INSIPIDO (ITAL) *See* Insipid.

INSTITUT NATIONAL DES APPELLATIONS D'ORIGINE (INAO) (FR) On July 30, 1935, a French law established the Institut National des Appellations d'Origine for wines and distilled spirits, and decrees governing each wine appellation were laid down by the minister of agriculture.

INSTITUTO COMMERCIO ESTERO (ICE) (ITAL) A governmental organization based in Rome and known in the United States as The Italian Trade Commission that is the Italian government's foreign trade promotion organization. It has offices throughout Italy and in more than 80 cities across the world.

INSTITUTO DO VINHO DA MADEIRA (IDVDM) (PORT)   The Madeira Wine Institute, an official governing body regulating all laws and matter to do with Madeira wine.

INSTITUTO NAZIONALE ESPORTAZIONE (INSTITUTE NATIONAL EXPORTATION) (INNE) (ITAL)   A round red seal with the words "Marchio Nazionale" appears on the neck of many Italian wine bottle exported to North America. It indicates compliance with governmental quality control procedures.

INSTITUTO SPUMANTE ITALIANO METODO CHAMPENOISE (ISIMC) (ITAL)   An organization of Italian wineries making spumante by utilizing the champagne method.

INTENSE   A term describing a wine with highly concentrated qualities (e.g., bouquet and displays a well-defined flavor).

INTERLAKEN   A white seedless grape variety developed from a cross of Thompson Seedless and Ontario grapes in 1947 at the New York Experimental Station at Geneva. The clusters are medium in size with small, golden berries.

193

INTERNODE   On a grapevine, the portion on the shoot or cane between two nodes (buds).

INTERPROFESSION (FR)   An interprofessional syndicate or lobby of grape growers, winemakers (vintners), or producers who combine their efforts and money in an organized manner to protect their wines and reputation, and, at the same time, form a promotional arm. Synonymous with *Comité Interprofessionnel*.

INTOXICATED   Significantly or legally under the influence of excessive alcohol consumption and being incapable of complete control of one's actions. Other synonyms are alky, bombed, drunk, inebriated, impaired, juiced, lit up, loaded, looped, lush, oiled, pickled, pissed, plastered, ripped, sloshed, smashed, soused, stewed, stoned, three-sheets-to-the-wind, under-the-table, waffled, and zonked.

INVAIATURA (ITAL)   *See* Véraison.

INVECCHIAMENTO (ITAL)   Aging.

INVECCHIATO (ITAL)   Aged.

INVENTORIES   Stocks of raw materials, intermediate products, and finished goods held by producers or marketing organizations.

INVERT SUGAR   A mixture of glucose and levulose (fructose) in approximately equal proportions found in some fruits. It is produced artificially by the hydrolysis of sucrose.

INVERT SUGAR SYRUP   A substantially colorless solution of invert sugar that has been prepared by recognized methods of inversion from pure dry sugar and contains not less than 60 percent sugar by weight (60 degrees Brix).

INVERTASE   The enzyme responsible for converting sucrose into roughly equal parts of fructose and glucose in order for fermentation to occur.

IN VINO VERITAS   The expression "In Wine There is Truth," coined by the Roman scholar Gaius Plinius (better known as Pliny the Elder) between 33–79 A.D.

IN VITRO   Multiplication of plants under controlled conditions (light, temperature, and hygrometry) inside a jar or a tube in a synthetic culture medium.

INZOLIA (ITAL)   A white grape variety native to Sicily. The cluster is large and of fine appearance and color—green-yellow, golden to amber in the part exposed to the sun's rays.

IODINE SOLUTION   A test indicator that detects the presence of starch in a wine as the possible source of a haze.

IONA   A red grape variety that is a seedling of the Diana grape (which is a seedling of Catawba) grown mostly in the eastern United States. It was named after the Iona Island located in the Hudson River, near Peekskill, New York, by Dr. C. W. Grant in 1859.

IRISH COFFEE   A drink often served to celebrate Saint Patrick's Day (March 17), consisting of cube sugar, Irish whiskey, strong black coffee (not espresso), with whipped heavy cream floated on top.

IRISH CREAM LIQUEURS   *See* Cream Liqueurs.

IRISH STOUT   *See* Stout.

IRISH WHISKEY   A distinctive product of Ireland, manufactured in compliance with the guidelines of Irish Distillers, Ltd. It is commonly thought that Irish whiskey is produced from potatoes, mainly because of the general association between the Irish and potatoes. This is not true. Irish whiskey is not a single malt or pure malt whiskey—it is a blend. It is made from a mash of cereal grains, mostly barley (malted and unmalted), wheat, oats, corn, and rye. Most Irish whiskey is produced in pot stills, which helps to give it a unique taste.

Irish whiskey must be aged a minimum of three years, but is usually aged five to eight years prior to shipping. It is light and mild to the taste, with a very complex, rich, and distinctive flavor.

IRON HAZE   Also known as *casse*. *See* Citric Acid and Cufex.

IRREGULARITY   A slight abnormality not serious enough to be classed a defect.

IRRIGATION   A "controlled system," that applies the right amount of water at the right time to the grapevines. Each variety of grape requires water in different quantities and at different periods of growth.

ISABELLA   An old, black, *Vitis labrusca*-type grape variety used mostly for sparkling wines, although its popularity in the eastern part of the United States has dwindled. Its origin is unknown, but it has been traced back to 1815 in the Prince Nurseries at Flushing, New York. The grape was named after Mrs. Isabella Gibbs of Brooklyn, in 1816. Also known as *Fragola* and *Uva Americana*.

ISIMC (ITAL) *See* Instituto Spumante Italiano Metodo Champenoise.

ISINGLASS A protein fining agent derived from dried sturgeon air bladder (viscera). It contains a large amount of gelatin and carries a positive charge. Russian isinglass is a superior grade obtained chiefly from the sturgeon. Also known as *cola de pescado* and *fish glue*. *See* Fining and Fining Agents.

ISKRIASHTO (BUL) *See* Sparkling Wine.

ISLAND BELLE *See* Campbell Early.

ISLAY SCOTCH A growing area for barley, and a Scotch-producing area noted for its robust or medicinal smell and taste.

ITALIAN-TYPE VERMOUTH A sweet white or red vermouth. *See* Vermouth.

IVES A red *Vitis labrusca* grape variety that produces a coarse wine of little distinction with a wild "foxy" taste. Ives is an accidental seedling that was first discovered by Henry Ives in Cincinnati, Ohio, in 1840.

JACKETED TANK Apparatus that circulates hot and cold water, enabling the grape *must* to be heated up when the fermentation is too slow, or cooled down if the temperature is too high. Also known as *drapeau, ice water jacket, steel jacketed tank,* and *water jacket.*

JACQUEZ *See* Lenoir.

JAHRGANG (GERM) *See* Vintage.

JAMAICAN RUM Dark, full-bodied pungent rums, distilled from molasses and used almost exclusively in cocktails.

JAMLIKE *See* Jammy.

JAMMY An odor and taste sensation often associated with fruity red wines that have concentrated flavors and a grapey, berrylike taste reminiscent of jam. Also known as *jamlike.*

JARRA (SP) A wooden or stainless steel pail with a capacity of approximately 12 liters (approximately 4 U.S. gallons) used in the blending of sherry wines.

JARZEBIAK (POL) Vodka-flavored with rowanberries.

JENEVER GIN (BEL) *See* Holland Gin.

JERK WINE A seldom-employed practice where water is added to the grape remains after pressing to extract additional "tainted" juice, which, after fermentation, is then sold at very low prices.

JEREZ DE LA FRONTERA (SP) The city in southwest Andalusia where sherry wine is produced. The Jerez area is triangular in shape and lies between the Guadalquivir and the Guadalete rivers in southwest Spain, with the Atlantic Ocean on the west. The official sherry producing zone, known as the *zone de Jerez superiore,* or "zone of superior sherry," is bounded by three major towns: Puerto de Santa Maria, Sanlúcar de Barrameda, and Jerez de la Frontera. The entire Jerez area consists of some 55,000 acres of vineyards.

JEROBOAM   An oversized bottle with a capacity of four standard 750-milli-liter bottles or 101.4 fluid ounces (3 liters). *See* double magnum.

Jeroboam was king of the newly formed Northern Kingdom of Israel, who led the 10 northern tribes in ancient Israel in revolt against King Rehoboam, the son and successor to King Solomon.

JIGGER   A U.S. term for a shot glass of alcohol, usually measuring 1.5 fluid ounces.

JIMA (SP)   The harvest of agave plants for the production of tequila.

JIMADOR (SP)   The person in charge of the harvest of agave plants for the production of tequila.

JNDV (PORT)   *See* Junta Nacional do Vinho.

JOB SPECIFICATION   A job analysis resulting from the specification of what kind of traits and experience are needed to perform the job.

JOCKEY BOX   An underbar cocktail station unit typically containing ice bins, speed rail, bottle wells, and cold plate for a postmix system.

JOHANNISBERG (GERM)   A vineyard town in the Rheingau region.

JOHANNISBERG RIESLING (ALSO KNOWN AS WHITE RIESLING AND RIESLING) Johannisberg Riesling is the predominant grape of Germany, producing the best of the distinctive wines of the Rhine and Mosel regions. Known simply as Riesling in Germany, it is also called White Riesling in California. Johannisberg Riesling was probably derived from a wild grapevine *Vitis vinifera silvestris*, still found growing naturally in woods in the upper Rhine of Germany.

The Johannisberg Riesling grapevine is only moderately vigorous, with a relatively low yield. The small cylindrical, compact, tight clusters are well filled with small, round, juicy berries, which produce wines with aromas of tropical fruits, peaches, and apricots, with floral aromas and hints of muscat grapes. The berries are characteristically greenish-yellow in color with prominent speckled russet dots. The thick, aromatic skins are susceptible to sunburn and infection by *Botrytis cinerea*. In favorable seasons this tendency can be taken advantage of to produce a late-harvest sweet wine. The fruit picks easily by hand, but juices with mechanical harvesting. Also known as *Riesling Renano, Rheinriesling, Klingelberger, Rizling,* and others.

JOURNAL   An old Burgundian (France) measurement of land equivalent to anywhere from 1/3 to 5/6 of an acre.

JOURNAL   Summary of daily transactions as they occur; book of original entry.

JUDD   Jurists Against Drunk Driving.

JUG WINE   Inexpensive wine of no particular breed or quality that is usually sold in quantity. Also known as *bulk wine*.

JUICE   The unfermented liquid (concentrated or unconcentrated) from fruit, berries, grapes, and authorized agricultural products, exclusive of pulp, skins, or seeds.

JUICED   Slang for intoxicated.

JULEP   The name of a southern American drink consisting of bourbon whiskey, sugar, water, and spearmint leaves, along with an abundance of crushed ice. The name *julep* itself can be traced back more than 600 years and stems from the Arabic *julab* or Persian *jul-ab*, meaning "rose water." The word is cited in English as early as the year 1400 and indicated "a syrup made only of water and sugar." In actuality, the mint and sugar were being blended with distilled spirits before the birth of America. The true "Southern-style" mint julep coincided with the discovery of genuine Kentucky straight bourbon whiskey around the 1880s. Also known as *mint julep*. Also spelled *julip*.

JULIÉNAS (FR)   A cru commune in Beaujolais, supposedly named after Julius Caesar. The wine produced here is sometimes harsh in its youth, but softens with one to two years of bottle aging. In a normal year, the fresh fruity wine of Juliénas is more assertive and longer-lasting than those of Saint-Amour.

JULIP   *See* Julep.

JUNG (GERM)   Young and immature.

JUNIPER BERRIES   Aromatic berries of a cypress tree whose oils are used in the making of gin and some liqueurs.

JUNTA NACIONAL DO VINHO (JNDV) (PORT)   The national official body governing all Portuguese wines, in which the Instituto do Vinho da Madeira is answerable to.

JURADE DE SAINT-EMILION (FR)   To help promote the wines of Saint-Emilion (Bordeaux), John Lackland, on July 8, 1199, established the Jurade de Saint-Emilion, a wine brotherhood still in existence today.

KABINETT (GERM) The most basic of Qualitätswein Mit Prädikat (QMP) grade of wines, which indicates the wine in question is a quality wine that must be sold under a geographic designation: the wine province, region, district, or village where it was produced. These wines are dry, must attain a minimum *must* weight of 73 degrees Öechsle, and may not be chaptalized.

KAFFEE (GERM) *See* Coffee.

KAHMIG (GERM) *See* Yeasty.

KANZLER (GERM) A white grape variety developed in 1927, from a cross of Müller-Thurgau and Sylvaner, developed by George Scheu in Alzey, located in the Rheinhessen.

KEG A container of beer with a capacity of 15.5 U.S. gallons; also known as a *half-barrel* of beer. A small barrel with a capacity of less than 10 gallons. *See* Barrel.

KEG BEER *See* Draft Beer.

KEG PARTY *See* Beer Bash.

KEG REFRIGERATOR *See* Cold Box.

KEISSULGUHR *See* Diatomaceous Earth.

KELLER (GERM) *See* Cellar.

KELLERABFÜLLUNG (GERM) Cellar bottling by the shipper.

KELLERBIER (GERM) An unfiltered lager beer with a high hop content.

KELLERGASSE (AUS) Wine cellar.

KELLERMEISTER (GERM) *See* Cellarmaster.

KELTER (GERM) A wine press.

KENNZEICHNUNG (GERM) Any statement on a bottle of alcoholic beverages; some are obligatory, others optional.

KENTUCKY COFFEE TREE A large tree (*Gymnocladus dioica*) of the legume family with brown curved pods containing seeds sometimes used as a substitute for coffee.

KERNER (GERM)　A white grape variety developed in 1969, from a cross of Trollinger (red) and Johannisberg Riesling (white), by grapevine breeder, August Herold in Weinsberg, located in Württemberg. Kerner was named after Justinus Kerner (1786–1862), a poet and senior official of the town of Weinsberg.

KERNIG (GERM)　Firm.

KHARAKTÍR (GREECE)　*See* Character.

KHONDRÓS (GREECE)　*See* Coarse.

KICK　*See* Punt.

KICKER　A chemical additive used to speed fermentation of the mash for production of beer or distilled spirits.

KICKER　A method to determine the price of a drink; for example, adding 5 to 10 cents to the base cost of the drink, instead of figuring out the cost of every ingredient.

KIEBAER　The Danish word for cherry.

KIESELSOL　(SiO_2) A generic term for aqueous suspension of silicon dioxide. Kieselsol was developed in Germany during World War II as a tannin substitute during gelatin fining. The most common use of kieselsols is as a tannin substitute in protein fining, particularly in conjunction with gelatin. Today, kieselsols are used in the juice and wine industries.

KILDERKIN　A barrel used in old England with a liquid measure of 18 imperial gallons. *See* Barrel.

KILL-DEVIL　*See* Rum.

KILN　A mesh-type flooring used to dry malt by means of a fire underneath. In the older floor malting method, the barley, after being soaked in water for two to three days, was spread on a kiln floor for germination or sprouting, which generally took 8 to 12 days. This process has been largely replaced by mechanical maltings consisting of large drums that heat the barley, but the principle of the process remains the same.

KILO　*See* Kilogram.

KILOGRAM　A metric unit of weight equivalent to 1000 grams or about 2.2046 pounds. Also known as *chilogrammo* and *kilo*.

KIR　A popular apéritif drink made with crème de cassis and dry white wine, named after the late mayor of the City of Dijon, France, Canon Félix Kir. Kir was the favorite drink of the mayor from the 1940s until his death in 1968 at age 92. Originally, Kir was made by mixing Aligoté wine (a highly acidic white wine from Burgundy) with a tablespoon or so of crème de cassis, served chilled. Today, just about any white wine is used and mixed with anywhere from several teaspoons to one-third of a glass of crème de cassis. Cassis is a black currant liqueur. To insure one is using the best cassis, only those labeled Crème de Cassis should be used. Bottles labeled Liqueur de Cassis refer to a liqueur made from black currants macerated in brandy with added sugar.

KIRCHE (GERM) Church.

KIRMISI (TURKEY) *See* Red.

KIRSCH (FR) A fruit brandy made from small, semi-wild cherries that generally come from the Black Forest (Germany), the Vosges (France), or parts of Switzerland.

KIRSCHWASSER (SWISS OR GERM) *See* Kirsch.

KISLAV (RUSS) A distilled spirit produced from watermelons.

KITCHEN WINE *See* Cooking Wines.

KIU Twenty-third century B.C. Chinese name for beer.

KLAPOTETZ A windmill with huge clappers that sounds like a carbine gun with a high-pitched whistle or shrill; used to frighten birds away.

KLEIN (GERM) Small.

KLEINBERGER (GERM) *See* Burger.

KLEVNER (SWISS) The local name for the Pinot Noir, a red grape variety.

KLINGELBERGER *See* Johannisberg Riesling.

KLIPPE (GERM) Cliff.

KLOSTER (GERM) Monastery or church.

KLOSTERNEUBURG (AUS) (KMW for Klosterneuburg Mostwaage Scale) The term used to measure the level of unfermented sugar present in the *must*; the KMW was devised by Freiherr von Babo. One degree KMW = 5 degrees Öechsle. To determine Brix, multiply KMW degrees by 1.25. To determine KMW degrees, divide Brix by 1.25. *See* Brix.

Klosterneuburg, which was established in 1860, is also the name of the Vocational School of Viniculture/Viticulture, located near Vienna.

KNIPPERLÉ (FR) A red grape variety native to Alsace, although its popularity is dwindling. Also known as *Kipperlé* and *Eltinger*.

KNOCHIG (GERM) Bone dry.

KNOCKDOWNS Gift cartons packed separately from product.

KOLA (COLA ACUMINATA) *See* Cola.

KOLSCH (GERM) A pale, golden-colored top-fermented beer traditionally brewed in Cologne.

KONSUMWEIN (GERM) An ordinary wine; not to be confused with Tafelwein.

KORKGESCHMACK (GERM) *See* Corked.

KORNBRANNTWEIN (GERM OR HOLLAND) A distilled spirit that is produced from cereal grains and considered their version of rye whiskey.

KÖRPER (GERM) *See* Full-Bodied.

KÖRPERARM (GERM)   *See* Light-bodied.

KÖRPERREICH (GERM)   Robust; full-bodied. Also known as *voll*. *See* Full-Bodied.

KOSHER SALT   *See* Coarse Salt.

KOSHER WINE   Wines made under strict rabbinical supervision and are suitable for Jewish religious practice. These wines are so labeled.

KOÚFOS (GREECE)   *See* Light-Bodied.

KOUMISS   *See* Kumiss.

KRÄFTIG (GERM)   *See* Robust.

KRÄUSENING (GERM)   A fermentation process where new, actively fermenting beer is added to lager beer as to encourage a complete fermentation and a natural carbonation. *See* Wort.

KRESZENZ (GERM)   Term used up until 1971 to designate a "growth" or vineyard, usually followed by the name of the proprietor or producer. Also known as *crescenz, gewächs,* and *wachstrum.*

KRIEK (BRUSSELS)   A *lambic-type* beer that has been further fermented by the addition of sour black cherries to produce a dry brew with an unusual cherry flavor.

KRUPNIK (POL)   A honey-flavored liqueur.

KUMISS   A drink made from sour mare's or camel's milk that has fermented and is consumed by the Tartar nomads of Asia. Also known as *arjan* and *koumiss.*

KÜMMEL   A clear liqueur made with a distilled spirit base and flavored with caraway seeds, cumin, anise, and other aromatics. It was first produced in the sixteenth century in Europe, although Holland, Poland, Germany, and the Baltic countries claim it as their own.

KUPER (GERM)   *See* Cooper.

KURZ (GERM)   Short; without a finish or aftertaste.

KVASS (RUSS)   A fermented drink made from rye and barley, and flavored with herbs or cranberries. Also spelled *kwas.*

LA (FR, ITAL, AND SP) The feminine article for "the."

LABELS A piece of paper attached to a bottle that identifies its country or place of origin, ownership, contents, its classification, identifying brand and type of product it is. In the United States, labels for wine and distilled spirits must be approved by BATF for use.

In 1903, the routine use of paper labels closely followed the invention of the fully automatic bottle-making machines by Michael J. Owen, plant manager of Libbey Glass Company, Inc. of Toledo, Ohio. Also known as *etichetta*, *etiqueta*, *étiquette*, and *rotula*.

LABOR COST The payroll cost incurred as a result of employing full-time or part-time people to prepare and provide the products and services utilized or consumed by guests. Labor costs may be fixed or variable.

LABORATORY TESTING The scientific method of determination of enological, viticultural, distillation, or brewing practices, experiments, samples, procedures, and so forth, which are necessary for production of most alcoholic beverages. Also referred to as *bench testing*.

LABRUSCA *See Vitis Labrusca.*

LACTIC ACID An organic acid that appears during the malolactic fermentation of the wine when malic acid changes into carbon dioxide and lactic acid. Eventually, this fades and becomes imperceptible in tasting. It is the principal acid of milk and from there also comes its name. Derives from the Latin for milk "lic." It is also used to stabilize wine and correct natural deficiencies in wine. *See* Malolactic Fermentation.

LACTOSE A white crystalline sugar ($C_{12}H_{22}O_{11}$) made from whey, which is found in milk.

LAGAR (SP AND PORT) Large, shallow stone tanks into which boxes of grapes are dumped prior to crushing.

LAGE (GERM) A small vineyard.

LAGER Lager was developed in Germany in about the seventh century. It was first introduced into the United States by the Germans in 1840. *Lager* comes from the German word *lagern* (to store), and is applied to bottom-fermented beer in particular because it must be stored at low temperatures for prolonged periods of time. Lagers were traditionally stored in cellars or caves for completion of fermentation. They are bright gold to yellow in color, with a light to medium body, and are usually well carbonated. Unless stated otherwise, virtually every beer made in the United States (more than 90 percent of them) is a lager. Lager is ideally served at 38 degrees to 45 degrees Fahrenheit.

LAGERING Storing beer to mellow or ripen it.

LAGERN (GERM) To store.

LAGERN BIER (GERM) A storehouse for beer.

LÁGRIMA *See* Málaga.

LAIT (FR) *See* Milk.

LAKE GARDA (ITAL) A famous lake located in the northern region of Lombardy, famous for its white Lugana wines.

LAKE KEUKA The "thumb" of the Finger Lakes region in upstate New York. Site of the largest New State wineries.

LAKEMONT A white seedless grape variety introduced in 1972, from a crossing of Ontario and Thompson Seedless, by New York State Experimental Station.

LA MANCHA (SP) A wine district in central Spain, around Madrid, famous for Valdepeñas wines.

LAMBIC A type of wheat beer generally produced in Belgium. *See* Weisse Beer.

LAMBRUSCO (ITAL) A red grape variety indigenous to the Emilia-Romagna region, it is typically *frizzante*, although a *spumante* version can be found. It can be red, white, or rosé and is best when consumed very young.

There are many strains of the Lambrusco grape variety, among them are di Sorbara (also known as *Sorbarese*), Grasparossa, Maestri, Marani, Montericcio, Reggiano, Salamino, and Viadanese.

In Italy, local growers formed what is known as a *consorzio*, to help protect and promote their wines. These *consorzios* give member wineries special labels for attachment to the bottle's neck. Each neck label depicts a different scene, insignia, or emblem. The labels on Lambrusco wines show a white cock and grapes on a red ground, or a man and woman treading grapes.

LAMPIA (ITAL) A subvariety of the Nebbiolo grape variety that is widely planted throughout the Piedmont region. It is valued for its consistent production and the consistent quality of the wine it yields. It has a three-lobed leaf and a round berry that is deep violet in color.

LANDAL A blue-black, French-American hybrid grape variety, developed from a cross of Seibel 5455 and Seibel 8216. Landal produces a fruity wine of deep color. Formerly known as *Landot 244*.

LANDOT NOIR A red, French-American hybrid grape variety that is a cross of Landal and Villard Blanc. Landot Noir is an early mid-season grape variety, which produces mostly coarse wines used for blending purposes. Formerly known as *Landot 4511*.

LANDWEIN (GERM) A category of wines defined according to the 1982 wine laws that is a step above *Tafelwein* in quality and may be *chaptalized*. Landwein is rarely exported to the United States.

LANGUEDOC (FR) A wine-producing province in the south, west of the Rhône River, which produces mostly *vin ordinaires*. *See* Midi and Roussillon.

LATE-BOTTLED VINTAGE PORTS (LBV) These are ports of a single vintage, declared by the shipper during the fourth year after the vintage. The port is bottled between July 1 of that year and December 31 of the sixth year after harvest. Generally, late-bottled vintage ports are vintages not declared as vintage ports and are usually ready to drink when released. Late-bottled vintage port replaced what was known as *crusted ports*.

LATE HARVEST A term used mainly in California to denote wines made from especially ripe grapes that have been picked or harvested later than usual. These grapes are often shriveled, resembling raisins. Also known as *récolte tardive* and *vendange tardive*.

LATERAL A branch of a shoot on a grapevine.

LATIUM (ITAL) Latium, whose regional capital is Rome, is located in the central part of Italy. It is bordered in the north by Umbria and Tuscany, in the south by Molise and Campania, in the east by Abruzzo, and in the west by the Tyrrhenian Sea.

The production of wine in Latium is approximately 90-percent white (DOC), with the remaining 10 percent mostly devoted to non-DOC reds. Some of the best wines of this region are in fact not DOC wines, and are bottled under the name of Castelli Romani. Known as *Lazio*, in Italy.

LATTE (ITAL) *See* Milk.

LATTE MACCHIATO (ITAL) A mug of steamed milk "marked" with a bit of espresso poured through the center of the foam.

LAUTER (GERM) To make clear.

LAUTER TUN A large circular copper or stainless steel vessel with perforations at the bottom that is used in brewing to separate the grain from the liquid (*wort*) by straining. Also known as *mash-tun*.

LAYER   A long cane from an adjacent grapevine that is utilized to replace a missing grapevine.

LAZIO (ITAL)   *See* Latium.

LBV   *See* Late-Bottled Vintage Port.

LCB   *See* Liquor Control Board.

LDS   *See* Liquor Dispensing System.

LE (FR)   The masculine article.

LEACHING   Filtering of raw, newly distilled whiskey through a cistern or vat filled with finely ground and tamped-down charcoal.

LEAFHOPPER   *See* Grape Leafhopper.

LEAF THINNING   *See* Thinning.

LEAFY   An odor and/or taste sensation of some wines that display a green, vegetative, or herbaceous quality analogous to the smell of leaves.

LEAKAGE   A bottle of wine that is leaking through the cork due to improper storage or a faulty cork. The correct level of humidity for a wine cellar is between 55 and 65 percent. If the humidity begins to rise, reaching 80 percent or more, corks may leak as the wine in the bottle expands.

Some wine racks are designed so that the neck of the bottle is pointed down. This leads to trouble, for it is not uncommon for wine bottles to leak at the neck or through the cork. Also known as *weeper* or *barrel leak*. *See* Ullage.

LEATHERY   An odor occasionally found in red wines rich in tannin, reminiscent of rawhide.

LEBENDIG (GERM)   A wine that is said to be racy or lively.

LECHE (SP)   *See* Milk.

LEER (GERM)   A wine that is thin, weak in character, and taste.

LEES   Dead yeast cells, pulp, skins, seeds, and other solids that settle to the bottom of a barrel or tank during and after fermentation. The lees are left behind during racking or filtering. Also known as *bottoms, lias,* and *Pé.*

LEES BRANDY   It is brandy distilled from the lees of standard grape, citrus, or other fruit wine, and shall be designated as "lees brandy," qualified by the name of the fruit from which such lees are derived.

LÉGER (FR)   *See* Light-Bodied.

LEGGERO (ITAL)   *See* Light.

LEGS   The narrow (occasionally wide) trails or streaks of a transparent liquid (primarily water) apparent on the inner walls of a wine or brandy glass that run downward after it has been swirled. Legs are not glycerin, but are rather due to a phenomena called surface-tension pump, which, due to the evaporation of ethyl alcohol at the surface, draws up a small quantity of wine. Legs are usually found in rich, full-bodied wines or brandies with high extract and alcoholic content. Also known as *arches, church windows, rivulets, ropes, sheets,* and *tears.*

LEHRE BUBE (GERM)   An apprentice brewer.

LEICHT (GERM)   *See* Light-Bodied.

LEMBERGER   *See* Limberger.

LEMONADE   A nonalcoholic drink made from lemon juice and water, usually sweetened. Also known as *limonata.*

LEMON JUICE   The liquid constituent of a freshly squeezed lemon.

LEMON AND LIME SODA   A soft drink usually made with carbonated water, sugar or sweetener, acids, and a lemon- and lime-flavored syrup.

LEMONY   A condition in a wine, especially white, where there is an excess of acidity.

LE NEZ DU VIN (FR)   The nose of wine, referring to the scent or odor of wines.

LENGTH   The continuation of flavor that lingers during tasting and after swallowing. *See* Aftertaste.

209

LENOIR   A red hybrid grape variety with unknown origin. Planted in quantity in Texas where it yields small to medium-sized berries. Formerly planted in quantity in France and Madeira, Portugal, however, its acreage worldwide is shrinking. Also known as *Black Spanish* and *Jacquez.*

LENTICEL   A tiny, round, slightly raised porelike spot found on stalks and grape berries.

LÉON MILLOT   A red, French-American hybrid grape variety with small blue-black berries in a small, loose cluster. It is a very early-ripening and very productive variety that is similar in character to Maréchal Foch. Formerly known as *Kuhlmann 194-2* and *Millot.*

LES (FR)   The plural article of "the" in French.

LESBIAN (GREECE)   An ancient sweet, red wine.

LESEGUT (GERM)   Crop.

LEVADURA (SP)   *See* Yeast.

LEVE (PORT)   *See* Light-Bodied.

LEVER   A part of a corkscrew that is attached to the lip on top of a bottle of wine, and, while the bottle is held, the handle of the corkscrew is gently lifted up in a straight motion until the cork comes completely out of the bottle.

LEVER (FR)   A viticultural procedure where the young shoots on a grapevine are passed between the trellis wires and fastened with clips or wicker.

LEVULOSE   *See* Fructose.

LEVURE (FR)   *See* Yeast.

LIAS (SP)   *See* Lees.

LIBATION A beverage, usually alcoholic.

LICENSE STATE A state in which all alcoholic beverages (retail off-premise) can be made directly from licensed "uncontrolled" retailers, rather than from state-owned liquor stores. State where private individuals can secure licenses to conduct all phases of the wholesale or retain sale of alcoholic beverages. Currently, there are 32 states and the District of Columbia where distribution is authorized by wholesalers. Also known as *open state. See* Control State.

LICENSEE Any person holding a basic permit issued under the Federal Alcohol Administration Act. Also known as *permittee.*

LICOR (SP) *See* Liqueur.

LICOR DE EXPEDICIÓN (SP) *See* Liqueur d'expédition.

LICOR DE TIRAJE (SP) *See* Liqueur de Tirage.

LICOROSO (SP) Richly sweet, almost licorice-like.

LIEBFRAUMILCH (GERM) An off-dry, white wine from the Rheinhessen region that, translated, means "milk of the blessed mother."

Liebfraumilch was at one time produced from a blend of grapes grown in Rheingau, Rheinhessen, Rheinpfalz, and Nahe. However, with changes in the German wine law (1990), vintners no longer can blend grapes from the four regions for Liebfraumilch. Only one of four regions can now be shown as a source for Liebfraumilch—Rheingau, Rheinhessen, Rheinpfalz, or Nahe—and the region must be stated on the label. No single vineyard site, district, or grape variety designations are allowed on the label. The word *Liebfraumilch* cannot be shown in type larger than that used to identify the region. The law further specifies that all Liebfraumilch must be made at least 70 percent from one of the following grape varieties: Johannisberg Riesling, Sylvaner, Müller-Thurgau, or Kerner. Additionally, the wine law (1990) restricts residual sugar to a range of 1.8 to 4.5 percent. It is estimated that 60 percent of all wines from Germany are exported under the Liebfraumilch appellation.

LIEBLICH (GERM) *See* Sapid.

LIENS (FR) The tying of the shoots and canes during the year for training the grapevine along the wires.

LIES FINE (FR) Fine Lees

LIEVITO (ITAL) Yeast, as detected in spumante.

LIGHT A pleasant, refreshing wine, lacking in body, color, or alcohol; opposite of full-bodied. Also known as *leggero. See* Little and Small.

LIGHT When referring to beer, it often means the opposite of dark-in-color.

LIGHT BEER Beer having less alcohol and fewer calories than traditional lager beers.

Light beer is usually produced by the dilution of regular beers that have been brewed with the use of high-extract grains or barley and have been allowed to ferment dry. Another method of production involves the addition of enzymes, which reduce the number of calories and the beer's alcoholic content; its flavor is also considerably lighter. The purpose of producing light beer is to make a lower-calorie beer. A regular 12-ounce beer has 135 to 170 calories; a light beer usually has under 100 calories. There are no current BATF rulings on minimum or maximum calorie levels. Light beers are ideally served at 38 degrees to 45 degrees Fahrenheit. Also known as *helles bier*.

LIGHT-BODIED Opposite of *full-bodied*. Also known as *körperarm, koúfas, léger, leicht*, and *leve*.

LIGHT RUM (also labeled *white* or *silver*) Rum that is clear in color and displays either a very light, molasses flavor or the neutrality of vodka. It must be aged a minimum of one year in either glass or stainless steel containers, but more traditionally is aged in uncharred barrels. If aged in barrels, it is further treated through carbon filtration systems, which eliminates any color that may have been picked up from the barrel.

Light-bodied rums are generally produced in Puerto Rico, Virgin Islands, Cuba, Dominican Republic, and Haiti.

LIGHT WHIPPING CREAM Cream that contains between 30- and 35- percent milkfat.

LIGHT WHISKEY Whiskey produced in the United States at more than 160 degrees proof, on or after January 26, 1968, and stored in used or uncharred new oak containers; also includes mixtures of such whiskies. If "light whiskey" is mixed with less than 20 percent of straight whiskey on a proof gallon basis, the mixture shall be designated "blended light whiskey" (light whiskey—a blend.) The first bottle was sold on July 1, 1972.

LIGHT WINE A category of table wines that was spawned in 1981 to meet the strong consumer demand for wines with a lower caloric and alcohol content that could satisfy their wine needs and simultaneously decrease their caloric intake by as much as one-third.

Light wines, according to regulations under the Federal Alcohol Administration Act (par. 3,26) Title 27 Code of Federal regulations, state that wine under 14-percent alcoholic content should be designated as table (or light) wine or that the alcohol content should be stated.

The category never really got started and, although more than a dozen wineries did market light wines, the category is now almost nonexistent.

LIGURIA (ITAL) The second-smallest wine-producing (Valle D'Aosta is the smallest) region in Italy, located on the Italian Riviera in the northwest. The region is best known for its Cinqueterre, a white wine named after the five communes in which it is produced.

LIKÖRWEIN (GERM) Dessert or sweet wine.

LIMBERGER A red *Vitis vinifera* grape variety with moderately large reddish-blue berries, thick skin, and moderate to vigorous growth. It is grown in Württemberg, Germany, Yugoslavia, Bulgaria, and Hungary, and now appears well-suited climatically to eastern Washington. Formerly spelled *Lemberger*.

LIMEADE A nonalcoholic drink made from lime juice and water, usually sweetened.

LIME JUICE The liquid constituent of a freshly squeezed lime.

LIMITED BOTTLING A wine term with no legal definition, which is used to denote a "reserve-type" wine where there is only a limited quantity produced or, actually, the entire "lot" of a single wine that the winery has to offer.

LIMON A lemon-like citrus fruit indigenous to Mexico and the Southwest United States, traditionally served with tequila drinks, instead of limes, as is the customary citrus fruit used in the United States.

LIMONATA (ITAL) *See* Lemonade.

LIMONE (ITAL) Lemon.

LIMOUSIN OAK (FR) (Technically known as *Quercus sessilis*.) Wooden barrels that are made from wood grown in the Limousin forest near Limoges, in central France. Limousin oak is soft with a loose grain, allowing rapid extraction of flavor and tannin. Limousin adds vanilla and lemony flavors, which tend to emphasize wine's acidity. Traditionally used for cognac and white French Burgundies, Limousin oak is being used extensively in California for aging Chardonnay wines.

LIMPID A term applied to wines that are perfectly clear and brilliant, with an absence of particles in suspension. Also known as *limpide* and *limpido*.

LIMPIDE (FR) *See* Limpid.

LIMPIDO (ITAL) *See* Limpid.

LINE (FR) A seldom-used measurement (equivalent to one-tenth of an inch) for the thickness of staves on a wooden barrel. Staves were measured in lines, a measure also used for corks.

LINGERING *See* Aftertaste.

LIPARÓS (GREECE) *See* Oily.

LIQUEUR Derived from the Latin word *liquefacere*, and means to dissolve or melt. The words cordial and liqueur are identical in meaning and are so indistinguishable from the point of view of nomenclature that they are always mentioned together in federal and state laws and regulations. Liqueur is generally accepted as the European name and cordial as the American.

Liqueurs are products obtained by mixing or redistilling distilled spirits with or over fruits, flowers, plants, or pure juices therefrom, or other natural flavoring materials, or with extracts derived from infusion, percolation, or maceration of such materials, and containing sugar, dextrose, or levulose, or a combination thereof, in an amount not less than 2.5 percent by weight of the finished product. This amounts to about one and one-half tablespoon of sugar (simply syrup) per liter. In practice, most liqueurs contain large percentages (up to 35 percent) of some sweetening agent. While there is no minimum alcohol level mandated by the federal government, most liqueurs are between 34 to 60 proof, while others are as high as 100 proof. Liqueurs may be designated "dry" if the sugar, dextrose, or levulose, or a combination thereof, are less than 10 percent by weight of the finished product. Also known as *licor*. *See* Cordial.

LIQUEUR DE TIRAGE (FR)   The sugar or sweetener added to still wine to induce yeast cells to begin secondary fermentation, producing a sparkling wine. Also known as *licor de tiraje*. *See* Dosage and Liqueur d'expédition.

LIQUEUR D'EXPÉDITION (FR)   The shipping dosage in Champagne that determines its relative dryness. also known as *licor de expedición* and *dosage*. *See* Liqueur de Tirage.

LIQUEUR GLASS   *See* Cordial Glass.

LIQUIDO (ITAL)   Liquid.

LIQUID SUGAR   A substantially colorless refined sugar and water solution containing not less than the equivalent of 60 percent pure dry sugar by weight (60 degrees Brix).

LIQUOR   A term commonly taken to mean distilled spirits. Also known as *hard liquor* and *liquore*.

LIQUOR DISPENSING SYSTEM (LDS)   An automatic dispensing system for distilled spirits, used for on-premise alcoholic beverage service. This type system can be preset to dispense a predetermined quantity of distilled spirit each and every time to the customer. This system provides a consistent, standardized drink and controls inventory, eliminates over- and underpouring, spillage, and free drinks. The major drawback is that it is less personal and most customers want to see the drinks being poured from the bottle at the bar rail, rather than watching the drink being dispensed from a tube.

LIQUORE (ITAL)   *See* Liquor.

LIQUOREUX (FR)   A term used to describe wines that are sweet and soft and tasting "liqueur-like," as though they had been treated with a light syrup.

LIQUOR LICENSE   A state permit to sell and/or serve alcoholic beverages.

LIQUOROSO (ITAL)   A sweet wine that has been fortified by adding grape brandy.

LIRAC (FR)   A wine commune in the Côtes du Rhône region, covering some 7,200 acres, that produces red, white, and rosé wines. The grape varieties grown here are Grenache, Mourvèdre, Cinsaut, and Syrah, for the red and rosé wines, and Clairette, Ugni Blanc, and Bourboulenc, for the white wines. Most of the wines of Lirac should be consumed fairly young.

LISTA DEI VINI (ITAL)   Wine list.

LISTAN (SP)   *See* Palomino.

L

LISTOFKA (RUSS)   A black currant-flavored liqueur.

LITER   A metric unit of capacity equal to 1,000 cubic centimeters at 20 degrees Celsius or 33.814 U.S. fluid ounces (1.0567 quarts) at 68 degrees Fahrenheit of alcoholic beverage. One U.S. gallon equals 3.78541 liters. One liter equals 0.264172 U.S. gallons. Also known as *litro.*

LITRO (ITAL AND SP)   *See* Liter.

LITTLE   A term applied to a wine with very little smell, flavor, or aftertaste; not much distinction. *See* Light and Small.

LITTLE GIRLS   *See* Fillettes.

LIT-UP   Slang for intoxicated.

LIVELY   A term usually applied to white wines that are young and fresh, with plenty of zestiness, acidity, fruit, and possibly a little carbon dioxide, making them spritzy. Also known as *nervosité, spielig,* and *vif.*

LOADED   Slang for intoxicated.

LOCALLY DISPOSABLE   Brand-identified funds designated for use for local promotional efforts, such as custom made signs.

214

LOCAL OPTION   Choice of whether or not to permit sale of distilled spirits, wine, or beer.

LODGE   The British term for a Portuguese "port" firm or producer.

LOGGERHEAD   A long-handled tool with a ball or bulb at the end, often used to heat beer or rum-based drinks. *See* Mulled Wine and Poker Beer.

LOGO   Short for logogram, a term that refers to a proprietary brand name or trademark that represents a company.

LOGROÑO (SP)   A province in the Rioja-Alta, situated in the north of the River Ebro, is the business and financial hub of the wine district. The majority of Rioja wineries or *bodegas* are to be found along the roads that run between Logroño and Haro.

LOIRE VALLEY (FR)   One of the six major wine-producing regions, located along the Loire River in north-central France.

The Loire Valley produces mostly dry white wines (75 percent of the total production), the rest being rosé and red wines. Like Alsace, France, the region lies very far north and doesn't receive sufficient sunshine to fully ripen red grapes.

Most of the wines of the Loire Valley are sold under district or village appellations, such as Anjou, Pouilly Fumé, Saumur, and Vouvray.

The river Loire has a double distinction: it is the longest river in France (625 miles) and the longest of all the world's great rivers that nurture wine grapes along their banks.

LOMBARDIA (ITAL)   *See* Lombardy.

LOMBARDY (ITAL)   One of 20 wine-producing regions located in the center of northern Italy; borders on Switzerland to the north, Veneto and Trentino-Alto Adige to the east, Emilia-Romagna to the south, and Piedmont to the west. Three of Italy's largest freshwater lakes—Maggiore, Como, and Garda—are in Lombardy. The Po, Italy's longest river, flows through this region's premier agricultural zone, the Po River Valley. Milan, Italy's industrial capital and second-largest city, next to Rome, is in Lombardy.

There are three major areas of wine production in Lombardy: Oltrepò Pavese, Valtellina, and Brescia, which includes the area south of Lake Iseo and the Lake Garda district. Two smaller areas of production also contribute to the regional output: the Colli Morenici Mantovani del Garda, located in the hills just south of Lake Garda in the province of Mantua, and the area north of Bergamo, in central Lombardy. Known as *Lombardia*, in Italy.

LONDON DRY GIN OR DRY GIN   A generic name for gin lacking sweetness. None of the grain tasted or odor is retained.

British or London dry gin.   In England, gin mash usually contains less corn and more barley, because English distillers feel that this produces a distilled spirit of extraordinary smoothness. Their gins are distilled at a high proof, then redistilled in the presence of juniper berries. English gins have a lightly balanced aromatic juniper bouquet and flavor; they are light, dry, crisp, and clean, with the delicate flavoring of the juniper berry, although this is slightly toned down. These gins are ideal for drinking straight, in martinis, or mixed in cocktails. London dry gins, although originally produced only in or near London, are now produced all over the world, and the term presently has little meaning.

LONG   A wine with a "long" finish whose taste lingers in the mouth. *See* Aftertaste.

LONG DRINK   A cocktail served in a larger-than-usual glass, which permits the addition of more mixer (carbonated beverage, fruit juice, etc.). Also known as *tall drink.*

LONGUEUR (FR)   Length; persistence of flavor in the mouth.

LONG-VATTED   A term for grapes that have been in contact with their skins for a prolonged period of time, often days after fermentation has ceased.

LOOPED   Slang for intoxicated.

LOSS LEADER   An item that an establishment offers for sale at cost or less than cost to attract customers. *See* Price Leader.

LOTE (PORT)   Newly fermented wine prior to aging or blending.

LOT   Wine of the same type. When used with reference to a "lot of wine bottled," lot means the same type of wine bottled or packed on the same date into containers.

LOUCHE (FR)   A wine that is cloudy or hazy in appearance.

LOURD (FR)   A wine that is heavy, dull, and unbalanced.

LOWLAND SCOTCH   A growing area for barley and a Scotch-producing area noted for its vanilla and *spirity* smell and taste.

LOW WINE   During distillation, when the vapor is drawn off, it condenses into a liquid, known as *low wine*, with an alcoholic content of anywhere from 45 to 65 percent. The low wine is redistilled, or further refined, allowing the alcohol to reach an even higher concentration and further remove unwanted impurities and flavors.

LOZIA (BUL)   *See* Vineyard.

LUCIDO (ITAL)   Bright, lucid.

LUFTGESCHMACK (GERM)   *See* Oxidation.

LUG BOXES   Boxes made of heavy gauge plastic, metal, or even wood, used by pickers during grape harvest. After picking the grapes, they are placed into the "lug boxes," which hold from 35 to 50 pounds. The name is derived from the task of "lugging" the heavy box around.

LUMIÈRE (FR)   Particular taste caused by the effect of direct sunlight on sparkling wines such as champagne. It often happens with bottles that have not been given anti-ultraviolet treatment. This can also sometimes happen with still wines.

LUNGO (ITAL)   Long, lengthy.

LUPULIN   A yellow resinous powder obtained from the strobiles of hops used to flavor beer.

LUSCIOUS   Soft, sweet, fat, fruity. Often used when referring to naturally sweet wines of extremely high sugar content (e.g. Sauternes, Trockenbeerenauslese). Also known as *lush*.

LUSH   Slang term for a person who is addicted to alcoholic beverages.

LUSH   *See* Luscious.

LUXURY CHAMPAGNE   An overused term with little meaning that describes the highest-quality French champagnes.

MA (FR) *See* Marque d'Acheteur.

MACABEO (SP) A white grape variety cultivated throughout the Rioja Region that produces light, fairly high acidic wines, as well as sparkling wines. Also known as *Viura.*

MACACOS (PORT) Long wooden paddles that are employed to "punch down" or "submerge" the cap in the fermentation tanks.

MACERATION A method of extracting color and flavor from fruits, seeds, flowers, herbs, spices, or grape skins by leaving them in contact with the fermenting juice and/or a neutral distilled spirit. Also, production method employed in making liqueurs and some brandies. It is also known as the *cold method,* because the flavoring materials are sensitive to heat and would be damaged by it. The cold method is a lengthy process that can take as long as one year.

Maceration is not unlike the brewing of tea. Fruit or other ingredients destined to made into liqueurs are placed directly into the distilled spirit or brandy and allowed to steep until sufficient amounts of the aroma and flavor have been extracted into the distilled spirit. Each ingredient has its own unique aroma and taste. After the steeping is complete, the distilled spirit (liqueur) is drawn off and filtered; water is added and the color adjusted, and it is finally blended with sugar syrup or occasionally honey for consistency of taste. The liqueur is then allowed to age or "marry" from several months to one year, in order to blend the flavors before bottling. Also known as *infusion.*

MACÉRATION CARBONIQUE (FR) *See* Carbonic Maceration.

MACERAZIONE CARBONICA (ITAL) *See* Carbonic Maceration.

MÂCHÉ (FR) *See* Chewy.

MACIO (PORT) *See* Soft.

MÂCON (FR) A town in the Côte Mâconnaise on the Sâone River, in southern Burgundy, just north of Beaujolais. The local red wine is fruity and very pleasant when young; but the predominant wine here (approximately 70 percent of total production) is white. The region's slopes are covered with vineyards that produce light, dry white wines, such as the world-renowned Pouilly-Fuissé.

MADD   Mothers Against Drunk Driving.

MADE AND BOTTLED (PACKED) BY   The bottler/packer must have made not less than 10 percent of the wine by fermenting the *must* and clarifying the resulting wine, and must have treated the wine in such a way as to change the type of the product.

MADEIRA (PORT)   An island off of Portugal in the Atlantic Ocean some 360 miles from the coast of Morocco, famous for its fortified wines. Madeira is a fortified wine (beginning in 1753), with an alcoholic content of 17 to 20 percent by volume, due to the addition of a high proof, 99.6 percent pure alcohol. The five styles of Madeira (driest to sweetest) are Sercial, Verdelho, Rainwater, Bual or Boal, and Malmsey.

MADELEINE ANGEVINE   A white *Vitis vinifera* grape variety grown predominantly in England where it produces light wines with a sort of *muscat* aroma.

MADERISATION (PORT)   *See* Maderized.

MADÉRISÉ (FR)   *See* Maderized.

MADERIZATION   The condition of being maderized.

MADERIZED   Term applied to a wine that is past its prime, flat, somewhat oxidized, and has acquired a brownish tinge. Directly applied to wines that have been poorly stored and subjected to excessive heat. Usually has a baked smell and flavor, reminiscent of Madeira wine. Also known as *firne, maderisation, madérisé, maderization,* and *maderizzato. See* Cooked, Cotto, and Oxidation.

MADERIZZATO (ITAL)   *See* Maderized.

MADILLA (SP)   *See* Hearts.

MADURO (PORT OR SP)   *See* Mature.

MAGER (GERM)   *See* Thin.

MAGNOLIA   A white grape variety of the Muscadine family that, along with Carlos and Dixie, is supplanting Scuppernong in the southeast vineyards of the United States.

MAGNUM   Bottle of wine equivalent in capacity to 50.8 fluid ounces or two 750-milliliter bottles. Also referred to as 1.5 liter.

MAGRO (ITAL)   *See* Thin.

MAGUEY (SP)   The agave plant used to produce tequila and mezcal.

MAGYAR ALLAMI PINCEGAZDASAG (HUN)   Hungarian State Cellars, a term that appears on labels of Tokay wine.

MAIBOCK   A bock beer of super-premium quality. *See* Bock Beer.

MAI CHIU   The Chinese term for beer.

MAIGRE (FR)   *See* Thin.

MAIN (GERM)   An important river in Franken.

MAIPO (SP)   An important wine region in Chile.

MAISCHE (GERM)   Crushed grapes prior to fermentation.

MAISON (FR)   Business or firm.

MAISON DU VIN (FR)   A wine house.

MAI TAI   A cocktail consisting of light rum, dark rum, orgeat syrup, triple sec, pineapple juice, grenadine syrup, and lime juice. This world-famous drink (created in the early 1940s) called "Mai Tai" is translated from Polynesian to mean "the best, out of this world."

MAÎTRE DE CHAIS (FR)   The employee in charge of the cellar, who is responsible for the vinification and aging of all wines. The cellar master plays a most significant role in the cellar, for the success of a wine depends on his skill and judgment. Also known as *caviste*.

MAIWEIN (GERM)   *See* May Wine.

M

219

MAJUELO (SP)   Wine made from young grapevines, generally under seven years of age.

MAKE LOVE TO A BLONDE IN A BLACK SKIRT   An expression used when drinking a pint of stout (a dark beer from Ireland). Using a stirrer, you carve the shape of a shamrock in the head of the stout. If the stout is fresh and you carve the figure correctly, you should be able to see the shamrock in the bottom of the glass in the remaining head when the stout is finished.

MAKIN'   The process of "making" or producing nontax-paid or illicit distilled spirits for use or resale.

MÁLAGA (SP)   A wine district in the south of Spain, named after the shipping port in the province of Eastern Andalucía. Málaga is also a walnut-colored wine, generally sweet or very sweet, made from Pedro Ximénez and Moscatel grapes, in the city it is named after. There is a sweeter version known as *lágrima*, made only from free-run juice. Málaga was once known as *Mountain* in old English writings.

MALATO (ITAL)   *See* Sick.

MALBEC   A minor red grape variety generally blended with Cabernet Sauvignon and Merlot in red wines of Bordeaux, France. Malbec is an abundant producer contributing color and tannin to the wine. In the Médoc of Bordeaux, it is known locally as Pressac. In southwestern France it is known locally as *Cot* or *Auxerrois*.

MALIC ACID   A fixed acid that derives from the Latin for apple "Malum." It is the principal acid of apples (hence its name) and the second important major acid found in grapes. Its tart, astringent taste makes it easily recognizable and can be found in apples, apricots, blackberries, cherries, gooseberries, nectarines, peaches, pears, and plums.

As the grapes ripen, the malic acid present at high levels in the green grapes decreases. The hotter the year, the faster it decreases during the ripening process. This is why it is more apparent when the weather has been colder. *See* Malolactic Fermentation.

MALMSEY (PORT)   A luscious, sweet, rich fortified wine, quite dark in color, similar to a cream sherry, but with more character. The grape variety (Malvasia) was transplanted by Prince Henry the Navigator from Crete to the Portuguese Island of Madeira in the 1400s. *See* Malvasia.

There is an interesting story that the Duke of Clarence, the brother of England's King Edward IV, was reputedly drowned in a barrel of Malmsey.

MALOLACTIC ORGANISM   Leuconostoc oenos strains ML-34 and PSU-1 were isolated and cultivated in the early 1960s for use in inoculating *musts* or wines for malolactic fermentation.

MALOLACTIC BACTERIA   A strain of bacteria responsible for the formulation of a malolactic fermentation. It has been recognized and studied by an impressive list of famous microbiologists, including Louis Pasteur, who in 1858 demonstrated that lactic acid in wine was caused by organisms that he called "new yeasts." In 1889, Kulisch, a German, used pasteurized cider to prove the biological nature of malolactic fermentation, though he thought the causative agent was yeast.

MALOLACTIC FERMENTATION   (Incorrectly referred to a "secondary fermentation.") It is a bacteria fermentation, converting malic acid to lactic acid while releasing carbon dioxide. This action is caused by the metabolic activity of certain strains of bacteria. The bacteria genus most often responsible for this fermentation in wine are strains of "Leoconostoc oenos." The conversion occurs mainly in wines from cooler climates where there is an excess of acidity in the grapes and wine and usually happens after or simultaneous to the alcoholic fermentation. Malolactic fermentation occurring after bottling is considered spoilage since unwanted turbidity and effervescence results from the bacterial growth.

Malolactic fermentation has three major effects on wine: 1) it reduces the fixed acidity by converting a dicarboxylic acid to a monocarboxylic acid, making the wine softer and more pleasant to drink when young; 2) it increases biological stability in the wine by assuring that a malolactic fermentation will not take place in the bottle; and 3) it increases the sensory quality and flavor complexity of the wine. Also known as *malolattica fermentazione*. *See* Lactic Acid.

MALOLATTICA FERMENTAZIONE (ITAL)   *See* Malolactic Fermentation.

MALT   Sprouted or germinated barley (unless otherwise specified) used in beer and distilled spirit-making. The three main types are pale, crystal or caramel, and black.

Barley is soaked in water and kept damp until it begins to sprout. When the sprouting has proceeded for a short time so that organic agents called enzymes are formed, the barley is dried and the process halted. Also known as *barley malt*.

MALT ADJUNCTS Various cereal grains, such as corn and rice, that are added to the mash either in substitution of or in conjunction with barley in order to provide additional sources of starch and certain desired characteristics in the beer.

MALT BEVERAGE A beverage made by the alcoholic fermentation of an infusion in potable brewing water, or malted barley with hops, or their parts, or their products, and with or without other malted cereals, and with or without the addition of unmalted or prepared cereals, other carbohydrates or products prepared there-from, and with or without the addition of carbon dioxide, and with or without other wholesome products suitable for human food consumption. Under federal regulations, the alcohol content may not be shown on the labels, except where required by state law.

MALTED MILK A highly concentrated beverage that has less than 3.5 percent moisture and a butterfat content of 7.5 to 10 percent. Also, the name of a sweetened milk beverage that combines malted cereals, milk, ice cream, and a flavoring.

MALT EXTRACTS Extracts produced by mashing malted barley together with warm water, then concentrating it, either into a syrup, or dehydrating it into powder form. Commercially-produced malt extracts (syrups or powders) are packaged in cans or plastic bags and are usually available either hopped or unhopped.

MALTING The process by which barley is germinated and kiln dried in order to develop a high level of enzyme power and desired physical characteristics for use in mashes.

MALT KILN A heated room where barley malt can be dried after its sprouting period.

MALT LIQUOR This is an American term for a lager beer with a considerably higher level of alcohol (usually above 5 percent) than most lager beers or ales. Tastes vary from brewery to brewery and brand to brand, with some even sweetened with fruit syrup. The name comes from the beer's malty flavor, which has overtones of bitterness. Its color is typically darker than that of regular beers and its taste is correspondingly heavier and fuller-bodied. Malt liquor is ideally served at 38 degrees to 45 degrees Fahrenheit.

MALTOSE A fermentable sugar (malt sugar) that can be converted to alcohol and carbon dioxide gas by the action of the yeast during fermentation.

MALT SCOTCH Often referred to as single-malt Scotch, is produced by the pot still method from a mash consisting of only malted barley. A *single-malt* whisky means a malt whisky produced by a single distillery. By way of contrast, *blended* Scotch means a blend of pot-stilled malt whiskies with whiskies produced in Scotland by the column still method from a cereal mix that may contain unmalted as well as malted barley and other grains.

Malt Scotches are generally darker in color than blended Scotches, because of increased aging in cask; they are traditionally served at room temperature. Also known as *malt whisky*.

MALTSTER   One who is in control of the malting process utilized in the making of beer and some distilled spirits.

MALT WHISKY   *See* Malt Scotch.

MALTY   Caramel taste of germinated and roasted barley.

MALVASIA   An ancient white, *Vitis vinifera* grape variety of Greek heritage, that produces wines with a "muscat flavor." Malvasia is grown extenisvely throughout Italy (as well as Spain, Portugal, France, and others) where it is used either as a blending grape (Chianti and Frascati) or is used exclusively in the production of sweet dessert wines.

Also known as *Malmsey, Malvasia Bianca del Chianti, Malvasia Bianca di Candia, Malvasia del Lazio,* and *Malvoisie.*

MALVASIA BIANCA DEL CHIANTI (ITAL)   Also known as *Malvasia Toscana* and *Malvasia Bianca Lunga. See* Malvasia

MALVASIA BIANCA DI CANDIA (ITAL)   *See* Malvasia.

MALVASIA DEL LAZIO (ITAL)   Also known as *Puntinata. See* Malvasia.

MALVOISIE (FR)   *See* Malvasia.

MALVOISIE (SWISS)   *See* Pinot Gris.

MÄLZBIER (GERM)   A dark, sweet, malty beer, that is low in alcohol.

MAMERTINE   An ancient wine of Rome.

MAMMMOLO (ITAL)   A local red *Vitis vinifera* grape variety occasionally used in the blend of certain Chianti wines from Tuscany.

MANDARINE LIQUEUR   A sweetened alcoholic beverage consisting of a base of alcohol, minimum 2.5 percent sugar, and flavored and colored with dried peels of mandarins (tangerines).

MANDARINO (ITAL)   An almond-flavored Marsala wine.

MANDELBITTE (GERM)   A bitter, almond-like flavor.

MANDILARIA (GREECE)   A local red *Vitis vinifera* grape variety occasionally used as a *mistelle* in the production of some vermouth-type wines.

MANGARA (PORT)   A local term for the mildew *Oidium tuckeri.*

MANHATTAN   A cocktail consisting of bourbon or blended whiskey, sweet red vermouth, dash of bitters, and garnished with a cherry.

The former Manhattan Club, a six-story building erected on Madison

Avenue in 1859, was originally a residence for Leonard Jerome, the father of Jennie Jerome (1854–1921), a New Yorker (one-sixteenth Iroquois Indian). In 1874, she married Lord Randolph Churchill, and two years later she bore a son, Sir Winston, who would later figure quite heavily in English politics. It was this same Lady Churchill who first persuaded a reluctant bartender there to mix bourbon "with a lesser portion of sweet vermouth and aromatic bitters" to please a guest of honor. As one of New York's leading socialites, she was giving a party in honor of Samuel J. Tilden's election as a reform governor. She named the drink a "Manhattan" after the club where the celebration was being held, and it is still one of the world's most popular cocktails.

MANNE (FR)   The part of the shoot on a grapevine that will flower.

MANSENG (FR)   A local white *Vitis vinifera* grape variety native to the Juracon region, where it produces full-bodied dessert wines.

MANTA (PORT)   *See* Cap.

MANZANILLA (SP)   The palest, lightest, and driest *fino*-type sherry made. Manzanilla sherries are produced in the town of Sanlúcar de Barrameda, near the coast, at the mouth of the Guadalquivir River, approximately 10 to 15 miles outside of Jerez. Manzanilla are also more astringent or "tonic" in taste than *fino* sherries, which is probably due to both the ocean breezes and the unique soil content of the vineyards where the grapes are grown.

M

223

MANZANITA   A type of soil consisting of moderately, well-drained gravelly silt loams that have a heavy clam loam subsoil. This soil is formed in alluvium, derived dominantly from basic igneous rock sources (volcanic rock materials) and is characterized by a rich brick-red color, caused by a high iron content.

MAP   *See* Marketing Action Plan.

MARASCHINO LIQUEUR   A sweetened alcoholic beverage consisting of a base of alcohol, minimum 2.5 percent sugar, and flavored and colored with Dalmatian marasa cherries, rose petals, and spices.

MARC (FR)   *See* Grappa.

MARCA (ITAL)   Of marked character (of grape, type, and district).

MARCHE (ITAL)   *See* Marches.

MARCHES (ITAL)   One of Italy's 20 wine-producing regions, located in north-central part of Italy, with its entire east coast on the Adriatic Sea. It is bordered to the west by Umbria, to the south by Abruzzo, and to the north by Emilia-Romagna and Tuscany. Marches' most famous wine is Verdicchio, a white dry wine. Known as *Marche*, in Italy.

MARCHIO (ITAL)   Trademark.

MARCHIO DEPOSITATO (ITAL)   A registered brand name.

MARCHIO NAZIONALE (ITAL)   *See* Instituto Nazionale Esportazione.

MARCHIO REGISTRATO (ITAL)   A registered brand name.

MARÉCHAL FOCH   A red, French-American hybrid grape variety originally developed in Alsace, France. It is a very early ripener with small-clustered, small-berried black grapes that can produce good quality table wine. The grapevines are hardy and medium in vigor and production while being quite disease resistant. Formerly known as *Foch* and *Kuhlmann 188-2*.

MARGARITA   A cocktail consisting of tequila, triple sec, and freshly squeezed lemon juice, with the rim of the glass coated with coarse salt.

It was purportedly concocted by a Virginia City bartender in memory of his girlfriend, who was accidentally shot during a barroom brawl.

MARGAUX (FR)   A commune in the Haut-Médoc district of Bordeaux that produces almost exclusively red wines, noted for their bouquet, finesse, and silky texture. Margaux also includes the townships of Arsac, Cantenac, Labarde, and Soussans, comprising some 2,800 acres of vineyards.

On August 10, 1954, the wines of Margaux were officially granted their *Appellation Contrôlée* designation.

MARGIN   The edge of a leaf blade on a grapevine.

MARIE-JEANNE (FR)   A formerly used bottle in Bordeaux, which contained approximately 84.53 fluid ounces or about three regular-sized (750-ml) bottles.

224

MARIENSTEINER (GERM)   A white grape variety that is cultivated mostly in Germany and Switzerland, where it produces wines with good body and high acidity. It is a cross of Sylvaner and Rieslaner grape varieties, developed in Würzburg.

MARKANT (GERM)   Prominent; a wine that displays "typical" of its type and character.

MARKET   A center of business within a territory.

MARKET   The potential number of guests who could frequent an establishment serving alcoholic beverages. The group that is desirous to attract.

MARKETING   It is the performance of business activities that direct the flow of goods and services from producer to consumer or user. It is also a social process by which individuals and groups obtain what they need and want through creating and exchanging products and value with others.

MARKETING ACTION PLAN (MAP)   A clear and concise communication from sales promotion to field sales regarding marketing plans for each brand.

MARKETING PLAN   A detailed set of marketing objectives and programs for achieving them for a particular product. Wider in scope than an advertising plan because it contains programs for all marketing functional areas, including personal selling, product development, and pricing.

MARKET SEGMENTS   Subgroups of consumers, each with some common characteristic that influences that group's demand for a product.

MARKET SHARE   A product's or service's piece of the total market for that product or service. Usually expressed in a percentage basis or on a point scale.

Percentage of an industry's sales accounted for by a single firm. The percentage of product category sales realized by a specified product or brand.

MARKET TEST *See* Test Market.

MARKENWEIN (GERM) A registered brand name. *See* Trademark.

MARK-UP The amount added to the raw cost to cover overhead and profit in arriving at the selling price; the cost of doing business.

MARQUE (FR) Mark; generally used when referring to "trademark." *See* Trademark.

MARQUE D'ACHETEUR (FR) Used for private-label champagne, called "buyer's own brand" in the trade. This appears on some champagne labels as the initials MA.

MARQUE DEPOSÉE (FR) A registered brand name. *See* Trademark.

MARRYING BOTTLES *See* Consolidating Bottles.

MARRYING WINES *See* Blending.

MARS A red seedless grape variety that is a cross of Island Belle and Arkansas 1339 made in 1972. The clusters are medium in size with the berries being larger than Reliance. The flavor is strong and typically *Vitis labrusca* in character, resembling somewhat that of Campbell Early.

MARSALA (ITAL) Marsala is both the name of a city in northwest Sicily and the name of a blend of grapes, most notably the Catarratto and/or Grillo grapes, with a maximum of 15-percent Inzolia allowed.

Like sherry and port, Marsala is a fortified wine; it bears some resemblance to Madeira, in that one or more of its constituents are cooked or heated during the processing.

MARSALA VERGINE (ITAL) *See* Vergine.

MARSANNE (FR) A white grape variety that produces wines with a floral fragrance and a steely backbone to the taste. It is grown extensively in the Rhône Valley, where it is used in the production of some red Hermitage wines as well as the solo grape for white Hermitage and white Saint-Joseph wines.

MARTIN METHOD A device that detects fraudulent substances used in chaptalization of wines by means of nuclear magnetic resonance.

MARTINI A cocktail consisting of gin or vodka, white dry vermouth, and garnished with a lemon peel or green cocktail olive.

"Martinez," was the original name of this popular drink, first introduced in 1860. The original recipe was considerably different from what we know today. It consisted of one jigger of gin; one wine glass of sweet vermouth; a dash of bitters, two dashes maraschino liqueur. It was then shaken well and garnished with lemon slice.

The vodka martini was really popularized by James Bond movies in which the super spy requested his "vodka martini" be served to him "shaken, not stirred."

MARZEMINO (ITAL) A red grape variety grown primarily in the Trentino-Alto Adige and Lombardy regions. Marzemino produces deep-colored wines with a "plummy" odor and taste that are meant for early consumption.

MARZENBIER (GERM) A medium-strong, amber-colored beer originally brewed in March (hence its name), laid to rest during summer's heat and generally drunk before October, with any remaining beer consumed at Oktoberfest.

MASCULINE Akin to big and full-bodied; opposite of feminine.

MASH Ground malt (sprouted barley), or any other material capable of or intended for use in the fermenting process, that is soaked and then cooked in water to convert the soluble starches into sugar. The mash is then utilized in the making of both beer and whiskey.

MASHING The preparation of base ingredients for fermenting through the addition of water and sometimes heat.

After cleaning and milling, coarse ground grain (meal) is mixed with water. This suspension is heated to bring the starch into solution (extraction), where the enzymes of the malt can break it down into grain sugar.

This may be done by infusion mashing—the heating of uncooked grain with malt to conversion temperature—or, as in the United States, by cooking and then conversion.

The grains in solution are cooked, often under pressure, to break down the cellulose walls and gelatinize and liquefy the starch for conversion to grain sugars by adding malt.

The converted mash is pumped to the fermenter, or, in the case of Scotch or malt beverages, the screened solution (wort) is drawn off for the adding of yeast in the fermentation process. The fermented mash yields the distiller's beer, the low-alcohol solution distilled for beverage spirits.

MASH RAKE A tool occasionally used in beer or whiskey making as a stirring rod or device to stir or mix the mash and break up solid matter.

MASH TUN *See* Lauter Tun.

MASSERIA (ITAL) Similar to a *fattoria*. *See* Fattoria.

MASS SELECTION Consists of visually identifying and marking healthy and productive grapevine stumps in the vineyards and removing stems to serve as reproductive material. Also known as *field selection*.

MASTER BLENDER It is the master blender's job to maintain the integrity of the company's signature taste.

In order to keep his nose and taste buds in top form, the master blender lives under the rigid routine of an athlete. His is a difficult job: he must be able to discern, by taste and smell, the year that the grapes of a certain wine were grown and from which sections of the region the grapes came—even from which section within a section. Since the same section may produce quite a different variety of wines in different years, the taster's job is as much an art as a science. He must, in effect, analyze with one sniff the life history of each sample brought to him.

MASTIC   *See* Masticha.

MASTICHA (GREECE)   It is a sweetened aniseed liqueur with a distilled spirit base and flavored with *mastic*, a sap or resin from the mastic bush or shrub (or sap from trees of the cashew family). It is made primarily on the island of Chios; however, it originated on the mainland of Greece. *See* Anise-Based Spirits and Ouzo.

MATARO   *See* Mourvèdre.

MATCHSTICK   An undesirable odor and/or taste reminiscent of burnt matches, derived from an excess of sulfur dioxide, which is added to a wine. Fairly common with newly bottled wines, with time it will usually dissipate. *See* Sulfur Dioxide.

MATHASER BIERSTADT   The world's largest beer garden, founded in 1901, in Munich, West Germany, contains 16 restaurants and has room for 5,200 people.

MATT (GERM)   *See* Flat.

MATTONE (ITAL)   Brick-red.

MATURE   The stage in the aging of wines, beers, or distilled spirits when they have developed all of their characteristic qualities to full perfection. Also known as *maduro, mature wine, maturing, maturity,* and *mûr. See* Aging, Barrel Aging, Ripe, and Ripe for Bottling.

MATURE WINE   *See* Mature.

MATURING   The process of aging a wine, beer, or distilled spirit, either in wooden barrels or stainless steel/glass until it is in peak condition and ready for consumption. *See* Mature.

MATURING CELLARS   Underground cellars in which alcoholic beverages are aged at constant temperatures, generally 52 to 55 degrees Fahrenheit year round, where they remain for a variable length of time, depending on the quality and type.

MATURITY   *See* Mature.

MATURITY   The stage of fruit development when it has reached the maximum quality point where it is ready for harvest. *See* Ripeness.

MÄUSELN (GERM)   *See* Mousy.

MAUVAIS GOÛT (FR)   Bad taste, unfit to drink.

MAUZAC BLANC (FR)   A white grape variety that produces sound wines with good balance and considerable acidity. It is widely planted in some of France's vineyards, especially in the Languedoc.

Mavro (Greece)   Black.

Mavrodaphne (Greece)   A red grape variety that is responsible for the ever-popular red sweet dessert wine of the same name, which has some similarities to port.

Mavron (Greece)   A red grape variety native to Cyprus that produces sturdy red wines with moderate tannin levels and a fairly high alcohol level.

Mavrud (Bul)   A red grape variety that produces wines that are fairly robust, but unfortunately tend to oxidize easily.

Mayoral (SP)   *See* Chef de Troupe.

May Wine   A festive German white wine punch, often sweetened, containing strawberries and perhaps other fruit, that is flavored with woodruff, an aromatic herb. Also known as *maiwein*. *See* Woodruff.

Mazer   An ancient wooden drinking vessel traditionally used for the consumption of mead. The container was frequently carved from hard wood, such as maple or oak, and contained two handles.

Mazuelo (SP)   *See* Carignan.

Mead   A clear, pale, or golden-colored wine, made from heather or clover honey, that can be dry or sweet. It cannot contain more than 14 percent alcohol, but in practice most mead is between 8 and 12 percent alcohol by volume. It may not be flavored or colored, and distilled spirits cannot be used. Mead is a very ancient, mildly intoxicating beverage that was quite popular in England and Northern Europe during the fifth and sixth centuries A.D. Also known as *honey wine*, *pyments*, and *sack mead*. *See* Hippocras, Hydromel, Metheglin, and Melomel.

Meaty   *See* Chewy.

Mechage (FR)   *See* Sulfur Stick.

Mechanical Beverage Control System   An automated distilled spirit system that is preprogrammed to record the number of drinks dispensed from a bottle, as well as to regulate the size of each drink. Also known as *metered pour*.

Mechanical Harvester   Modern technology has dictated change in the vineyards. Mechanical harvesting has evolved into the preferred method of grape picking today. Among some of the advantages mechanical harvesting offers are greater efficiency in harvesting and increased control over grape quality.

A mechanical harvester is approximately 18 feet in length, 12 feet in width, and weighs about 18,000 pounds. The driver of this machine sits on the top and expertly guides this gentle giant through the vineyards, straddling each row of grapevines as the *pivotal pulsator* removes the ripe grapes from the grapevines. As the harvester moves down the rows of grapevines, the pulsator or *trunk shaker* vigorously shakes the trunks on the grapevines, causing the grapes at the top of the grapevines to drop into the machine below. At the same time the curved tips of the four to six pivotal strikers, which consist of a double bank of flexible horizontal rods, reach up under the foliage canopy of the grapevine and strike the ends of the cordon, or cane, ejecting the fruit from the ends of the canes. The combination of the pulsator and pivotal strikers gives maximum efficiency in harvesting all of the ripe grapes on each grapevine.

As the grapes drop into the harvester they travel along a 15-inch-wide conveyor belt past suction blowers that expel any leaves that may have entered the machine along with the grapes. This minimizes possible green leaf off-flavors and bitterness, which characterized some of the earliest mechanical harvester experiments. The grapes then move up the conveyor to the top of the machine, where an extension of the conveyor carries them across the row to a gondola moving parallel to the harvester. The mechanical harvester picks an average of one acre of grapes (two to four tons) per hour. The daily tonnage of grapes picked by one machine is equal to that of 30 manual laborers.

The mechanical harvester was first developed in the early 1950s by University of California at Sacramento agricultural engineer Lloyd Lamouria while working with viticulturist Albert Winkler. However, it wasn't until 1969 or 1970 that Mirassou Vineyards of San Jose, California, became the first winery to use the harvester on a commercial scale. At that time, only a handful of California winemakers actually believed machine-harvested grapes were equal to hand-harvested grapes. During its infancy, this machine had a number of obstacles to overcome: it was quite rough with the grapes, sometimes tearing them off the grapevines; the grapevines were not trained to accommodate mechanical harvesters; the space between rows was often times not sufficient for the harvesters; occasionally, grapevines were pulled out of the ground; and, finally, some machines were unable to make a clean separation between fruit and leaves.

MECHANICAL IMPACT   Mechanical impact is contact with another object. It may be a spoon, a beer tap, or another glass. This contact can cause minute abrasions that are invisible to the eye. These abrasions weaken the glass and make it more susceptible to breakage from further impact or thermal shock. Any severely abraded glass must be removed from service.

MEDALLIONS   Tiny medallions embossed on necks of certain wine bottles or carafes. Originally, Italian winemakers used lead medallions to certify the proper volume of a bottle. The glass version serves no official function today, except perhaps to provide a better grip.

MEDIA (SP)   A barrel equal to one-half butt. *See* Barrel.

MEDICINAL   A wine, beer, or distilled spirit possessing the properties of a medicine odor or taste.

Medio Seco (SP) *See* Semidry.

Medium-Bodied A descriptor meaning average in extract, alcohol, aroma, and flavor.

Medium-Dry *See* Semidry.

Medium-Sweet *See* Semisweet.

Médoc (FR) This is the largest and most important wine district of Bordeaux, and possibly the greatest producer of red wines in the world. The word Médoc comes from an ancient Celtic Tribe that once lived there.

Bordeaux is divided into many districts, most of which are called *communes*. The four most important communes, which make up the Médoc district, are located on the west side of the Gironde River. The Médoc produces dry red wines, with only one exception: A white wine of Château Margaux. The communes from north to south are Saint-Estèphe, Pauillac, Saint-Julien, and Margaux. On the right bank of the Dordogne River are the districts Saint-Emilion and Pomerol, both of which produce only dry red wines. South of Médoc, along the Garonne River, in the capital of Bordeaux, lies the Graves district, where dry red and white wines are produced. Farther south is the district of Sauternes, noted for its extremely sweet white wines and a few dry white wines as well.

Médoc Noir (HUN) *See* Merlot.

Meiodoce (PORT) *See* Semisweet.

Melanconium Fuligineaum *See* Bitter Rot.

Mellow A "soft," ripe, and often matured wine without any rough edges. A characteristic that is normally associated with maturity and age. Also known as *myelódis*. *See* Soft.

Mellow A term with no legal meaning, often used in reference to some red "jug" table wines from California that usually display some sweetness.

Melnik (BUL) A red grape variety that produces wines high in tannin, extract, and color that age quite gracefully. The full name of this grape variety is Shiroka Melnishka Losa.

Melody A white grape variety that was produced in 1965 from a cross of Seyval and Geneva White 5 (Pinot Blanc and Ontario).

Melomel Mead that is blended with fruit juices other than apple. *See* Mead.

Melon d'Arbois (FR) It is the local name in the Jura region for the Chardonnay grape.

Melon de Bourgogne (FR) Most of the wines of the Loire are sold under district or village appellations, such as Anjou, Pouilly-Fumé, Saumur, and Vouvray. There is one notable exception and that is Muscadet, which is sold under its grape varietal name. Technically speaking, the Muscadet grape is actually the Melon de Bourgogne, which was transplanted from Burgundy, by order of King Louis XIV in 1639 and again in 1709.

MEMBRANE This surface covering the inner wall of a cell that plays an active part in exchanges between cells and their surrounding medium.

MENCIA (SP) A red grape variety that produces wines that are lightly-colored, quite delicate, and oftentimes sweet, with a fairly high alcoholic content.

MENDOCINO A wine-producing region located north of San Francisco, California near Ukiah, noted for its production of Zinfandel and other red wines.

MENISCUS The meniscus (dividing line between water and air) is the curved upper surface of a column of liquid; as a result of capillary it is convex when the walls of the container are dry, concave when they are wet. The lowest point on this curve is always read as the volume, never the upper edges.

MENTHES (FR) Mint; especially crème de menthe.

MERCAPTANS A slightly sour, particularly objectionable, onion-like, garlic-like, skunky, or even rubbery smell of ethyl and methyl alcohol reacting with hydrogen sulfide. It is also reminiscent of H_2S (hydrogen sulfide) or a "gas leak." It is due to breakdown of sulfur dioxide, originally used as a preservative.

MERCHANDISING Sales promotion as a comprehensive function including market research, development of new products, coordination of manufacture and marketing, and effective advertising and selling.

MERCHANDISING ALLOWANCE Where legal, promotional funds used to support distributor programs, such as shelf improvement, increased distribution efforts, special on-premise programs, and other programs.

MERCURIALES (FR) Opening wine prices offered by growers to négociant or other parties, particularly in the Bordeaux trade.

MERCUREY (FR) A commune in the Côte Chalonnaise district of Burgundy immediately to the south of the Côte D'Or, which yields some good wines that resemble those from farther north. Most Mercurey is red and is produced entirely from the Pinot Noir grape.

The name Mercurey originates from a grand temple dedicated to the god Mercury, the site of which is now occupied by a windmill.

MERITAGE A term originating in California, denoting those wines made entirely from a blend of the traditional Bordeaux grape varieties, which can be the winery's best wine of its type. Meritage red varietals are Cabernet Sauvignon, Merlot, Cabernet Franc, Petit Verdot, Malbec, Gros Verdot, and Carminière. White grapes are Sauvignon Blanc, Sémillon, and Muscadelle.

MERLOT It is one of the predominant grape varieties of the Bordeaux region of France. In the Médoc and Graves district, it is blended in significant amounts with Cabernet Sauvignon and Cabernet Franc; in the districts of Pomerol and Saint-Emilion it constitutes the predominant grape in the wines. Merlot is also used straight as a varietal in many parts of the world.

Merlot gives scented, soft, and fruity wines with hints of green olives, which are responsible for much of the softness and suppleness of the wines in which it appears. It is used extensively to soften and tame the more assertive bitter and tannic Cabernet Sauvignon. Merlot lacks early tannic harshness, and, by blending Cabernet Sauvignon with Merlot, the Cabernet Sauvignon develops faster, shortening aging requirements.

The grapevine has long, medium-small clusters with medium-sized, black juicy berries. Also known as *Médoc Noir*.

MERLOT BLANC   A local white grape variety generally found in Fronsac, Bourg, and especially Blaye, in Bordeaux, France.

MERSIN   An an orange-based liqueur, produced in Turkey, that is white in color.

MESEGUERA (SP)   A white grape variety native to Valencia, where it produces wines with delicacy and a fine aroma.

MESSWEIN (GERM)   *See* Sacramental Wines.

METABISULFITE   Either potassium or sodium, when mixed with water, produces sulfur dioxide gas, which is used in winemaking as a sterilant and antioxidant. *See* Sulfur Dioxide.

METABOLISM   The sum of processes by which food is manufactured and broken down for energy gain.

METALLIC   A term used to describe an acrid, tinny, unpleasant taste or sensation, detected in some beers or in low alcohol wines. The taste is sometimes acquired through contact with metal during the fermenting or aging process. Sometimes, beer will take on metallic-like flavors, even in a bottle. Also known as *metallico*.

METALLICO (ITAL)   *See* Metallic.

METAMERISM   A change in observed color of wine, depending on the nature of the illuminating light.

METER   A metric unit of length; one meter being equal to 39.37 inches.

METERED POUR   *See* Mechanical Beverage Control System.

METHANOL   *See* Methyl Alcohol.

METHEGLIN   A Welsh mead spiced with aromatic herbs. *See* Mead.

MÉTHODE CARBONIQUE (FR)   *See* Carbonic Maceration.

MÉTHODE CHAMPENOISE (FR)   Fermented wine is bottled with yeast cells and sugar added to induce a secondary fermentation. When secondary fermentation is completed, wine is aged, yeast sediment is removed by freezing the neck of the bottle, thereby removing the crown cap and allowing internal pressure to force the sediment out. Additional champagne is added with some occasional sugar. Bottle is corked, aged, labeled, and sold. It is also known as *fermented in this bottle* and *méthode traditionnelle*.

MÉTHODE TRADITIONNELLE (SP)   A synonynm for Méthode Champenoise.

METHUAN TREATY   A treaty of 1704 whereas French wines were required to pay a third more duty than Portuguese wines, regardless of the quality level.

METHUSELAH   An oversized bottle, equivalent in capacity to eight 750-milliliter sized bottles (202.8 fluid ounces) or 6 liters. It has the same capacity of an Imperial and is used exclusively for champagne.

Methuselah was an ancient patriarch of Babylonia who distinguished himself by his incredible longevity, living 969 years. In addition (according to legend), he sired many sons and daughters and was Noah's grandfather.

METHYL ALCOHOL   Colorless, volatile, flammable, poisonous liquid $CH_3 OH$, obtained by the destructive distillation of wood and synthesized chiefly from carbon monoxide and hydrogen. It is mainly used in fueld, solvents, antifreeze, and so on. Also known as *methanol* and *wood alcohol*.

METHYL ANTHRANILATE   *See* Foxy and *Vitis Labrusca*.

METHYLATED SPIRITS   Ethyl alcohol made unfit for consumption by the addition of methyl alcohol.

METHODO CHARMAT (ITAL)   *See* Charmat Method.

METODO CLASSICO (ITAL)   A formerly used term for a sparkling wine that was made by the *méthode champenoise* method. *See* Classimo.

METRIC SYSTEM   A universal system of measure; the units being multiples or divisions of 10, 100, 1000, and so on.

METRIC TON   The equivalent of 1,000 kilograms, 2,204.62 pounds, or approximately 10 quintals of wine. Also known as *tonelada*.

MEUNIER   A black *Vitis vinifera* grape variety mainly cultivated in Champagne, France, where it is blended with Chardonnay and Pinot Noir to form the basis of most champagnes. Although not widely known, it is planted in larger amounts than either its cousin, Pinot Noir or the white Chardonnay. Also known as *Müllerrebe, Pinot Meunier,* and *Schwarzriesling*.

MEUNEL OAK   Oak suitable for use in barrels coming from Poland and Lithuania.

MEURSAULT (FR)   A white wine, made from Chardonnay grapes in the heart of the Côte de Beaune in Burgundy. Meursault is the second largest wine-producing commune of the Côte de Beaune. Meursault gets its name from the Roman Legions, who dubbed it *muris saltus*, "the mouse's jump" in Latin. Time and the Gallic accent corrupted *muris saltus* to Meursault.

MEYNIEU 6   A white French-American hybrid grape variety, originally developed in Bordeaux, now planted to a small degree in the upper Midwest, where it produces mostly neutral tasting wines.

MEZCAL   *See* Tequila.

MÉZESFEHÉR (HUN)   A white grape variety that produces mostly sweet, rich dessert wines.

MEZZO SECCO (ITAL)   *See* Semidry.

MG   Abbreviation for milligram; A metric unit of weight; 1000 mgs equals one gram.

MICHET (ITAL)   A red grape variety that is a subvariety of the Nebbiolo grape and has round, violet-colored berries and a five-lobed leaf. It is grown predominantly in the Piedmont region, and, while it has a limited and less consistent production than the Nebbiolo, its quality, nevertheless, is extremely high.

MICKEY   *See* Mickey Finn.

MICKEY FINN   Whiskey or other distilled spirits to which a powerful narcotic or purgative "knock-out drops" has been added given to an unsuspecting person so that they could be robbed. Mickey Finn was a Chicago bartender famous for this concoction. Also known as a *mickey*.

MICROBREWERY   The name applied to small breweries of modest size and production. *See* Brewpub.

MICROCLIMATE   The climate of a small distinct area that has either slightly or greatly varying degrees of elevation, fog intrusion, humidity, proximity to water, susceptibility to frost, precipitation, temperature changes (heat versus cold), and wind. Individually or collectively, these elements do affect the quality of a wine to a lesser or greater degree.

234

MICROCUTTING   A fragment of a stem containing a preexistent bud; the microcutting is removed from a mini-plant grown *in vitro* and planted in an aseptic nutrient medium to produce an identical mini-plant.

MICROFILTRATION   A very low pressure (generally from 5 to 15 psi) semipermeable membrane process used in the separation of particles in the.05 to 5.0 micrometer range from aqueous solutions, such as wine. *See* Filtering.

MICRO-FLORA   Colonies of wine yeast and smaller quantities of other yeast and bacteria that collects on the skins of the grape before harvest.

MICRON   A millionth of a meter (about 0.00004 inch).

MICROPOROUS   A type of membrane or other material suitably able to filter out yeast.

MIDDLE LIQUORS   *See* Hearts.

MIDDLE RHINE (GERM)   *See* Mittelrhein.

MIDI (FR)   A major grape-growing area in southern France along the Mediterranean Sea producing mostly coarse, highly alcoholic wines. This vast area is now known as the Languedoc-Roussillon. *See* Languedoc and Roussillon.

MILCH (GERM)   *See* Milk.

MILDE (GERM)   *See* Soft.

MILDEW   A serious cryptogamic (fungal) disease that attacks grapevines in rainy or damp seasons, crippling both green tissue and the fruit. Mildew must be treated with various fungicide sprays. The two most basic types are *downy* and *powdery* mildew.

MILK   A liquid beverage coming from cows, goats, sheep, mares, camels, yaks, lamas, and even reindeer, that is meant for human consumption. Also known as *lait, latte, leche,* and *milch.*

MILK SHAKE   A drink containing milk, flavored ice-cream, and ice.

MILK STOUT   A low alcoholic, medium-sweet beer with a high lactic acid content and dark color. *See* Stout.

MILLERANDAGE (FR)   *See* Shot Berries.

MILLÉSIME (FR)   *See* Année.

MILLÉSIMÉ (FR)   A "dated" or vintage wine. *See* Année.

MILLIGRAM (MG)   A metric unit of weight; 1000 mgs equal one gram.

MILLILITERS (ML)   A metric unit of volume; 1000 mls equal one liter.

MILLING   The mechanical process by which whole grain is reduced to suitable size, with the outer cellulosic wall broken to expose more starch surface to the cooking and conversion of starch to sugars.

MILLOT   *See* Léon Millot.

MIND YOUR P'S AND Q'S   In the old alehouses before cash registers were invented, there was a chalkboard where the barkeep would put chalk marks to keep track of how many "pints" (p's) and "quarts" (q's) you consumed. When you were ready to leave the pub, the barkeep would add up the chalk marks and tell you how much you owed. To make sure that the barkeep remembered this task, the owner would often tell him to "Mind your p's and q's" before leaving.

MINERAL OIL   An oil spread on the surface of wine in storage tanks to prevent the access of air that would cause oxidation. Rarely used today.

MINERAL WATER   Natural still or sparkling water that comes from the earth. All mineral water contains some minerals, but to be classified a "natural mineral water" in Europe, the water must have at least 500 milligrams of minerals (standards set by the European Common Market in 1980—effective 1984) per liter *as it flows from the ground*—minerals that are collected in the water as it travels over great distances through geological formations. The minerals are thus dissolved and become an integral part of the water. Minerals are thought to be more readily absorbed by the body when in solution than as a component of solid food.

In most countries of Western Europe where bottled mineral waters are a common household beverage, no drinking water can be classified as a "natural mineral water" unless it contains dissolved minerals in its natural state. Italian law requires that mineral water be bottled only at its source. In Italy, if the mineral water has a mineral content under 500 milligrams per liter, it is considered to be of low mineral content and must be classified as *oligominerale.*

The U.S. federal government has not established a formal definition for mineral water. In 1979, however, California set a minimum standard of total dissolved solids for mineral water sold in that state at 500 milligrams per liter. This means that a water cannot be called a mineral water unless it has at least 500 milligrams of minerals dissolved in it.

The mineral content of bottled waters varies from state to state, country to country, and producer to producer. In addition to being basically low in sodium, and virtually calorie and carbohydrate free, mineral water contains many trace elements and minerals, which also vary in their interest to consumers. Some producers are even flavoring their mineral waters with natural citrus extracts such as mandarin orange, lemon, and lime.

Among these elements and minerals are aluminum, ammonia, bicarbonate, boron, bromide, calcium, carbonate, chloride, chromium, cobalt, copper, fluoride, iodine, iron, lithium, magnesium, manganese, nickel, nitrate, phosphorus, potassium, selenium, silica, sodium, strontium, sulfates, zinc, and others. Also known as *acqua minerale*.

MINIATURE BOTTLE   A small bottle usually containing less than two fluid ounces. Also known as *airline bottles* or *nips*.

MINI-BAR   *See* In-Room Bar.

MINT   A term suggesting the odor or taste of fresh green mint, noted especially in some Cabernet Sauvignon and Zinfandel wines. The odor/flavor of mint can range in intensity and type from eucalyptus-like to peppermint, spearmint, or wintergreen. In the case of wintergreen, the odor is *methyl salicylate* (methyl alcohol + salicylic acid).

MINT JULEP   *See* Julep.

MINTY   Suggesting the odor or taste of fresh mint. *See* Mint.

MINUIT, PETER   After purchasing "New Amsterdam," he established the first public brewery in 1622. *See* New Amsterdam.

MIRABELLE (FR)   A fruit brandy made from small, golden-yellow plums with a highly aromatic perfume, that generally come from Alsace, as well as some Central European countries.

MISE (FR)   The bottling.

MISE D'ORIGINE (FR)   Bottled by the shipper.

MISE EN BOUTEILLES AU CHÂTEAU (FR)   Estate bottled at the designated château.

MISE EN BOUTEILLES AU DOMAINE (FR)   Estate bottled at the designated château.

MISE EN BOUTEILLES DANS NOS CAVES (FR)   Means that the wine was bottled "in our cellar," however, it is not a legally defined term and has no real significance.

MISE EN BOUTEILLES DANS LA REGION DE PRODUCTION (FR)   An ambiguous term that is not legally defined and has no real significance.

Mise en Bouteilles à la Propriété (fr)   Bottled by the proprietor, shipper, or negociant.

Mise en Masse (fr)   The sparkling wine bottles arranged neck down after the riddling process for longer aging "on the yeast." Also known as *en masse.*

Mise en Place (fr)   A place for everything and everything in its place. Literally, everything set up and ready for business.

Mise Sur Pointe (fr)   *See* Sur Pointe.

Mission Grape   A white *Vitis vinifera* grape variety that was extensively grown in California during the eighteenth and nineteenth centuries, where it was used primarily to make sweet table wines, notably Angelica.

It was originally planted by the Jesuit priest Father Juan Ugarte at a mission in southern California in 1697. Although the grape is grown extensively in Argentina and other Spanish-speaking countries where it is known as the *Criolla*, it is believed that grapevine cuttings were brought to South America from Europe in the 1500s.

Missouri Riesling   *See* Elvira.

Mistela (sp)   *See* Mistelle.

Mistelle   Grape juice, from which fermentation has been arrested or prevented by the addition of brandy or other distilled spirits. The result is a wine with a natural residual sugar and alcoholic content of approximately 15 percent. The process is called *mutage.* Some mistelles are used as sweetening wines in the production of apéritifs and vermouths; others stand alone as apéritifs. Some examples of mistelles are Pineau des Charentes and Ratafia de Champagne. Also known as *dulce apagado, mistela, muté,* and *muting. See* Ratafia and Süssreserve.

Mittelrhein (germ)   One of 11 Qualitätswein grape-growing regions located along the Rhine River in the northwestern part of Germany. The region is famous for its spectacular vineyards on the steep Rhine slopes. Its wines, almost exclusively white, are hearty and stylish. Also known as *Middle Rhine.*

Mix   To put or blend together ingredients into a single mass or compound.

Mixed Drink   *See* Cocktail.

Mixer   An electric appliance utilized for mixing or blending together ingredients for certain types of cocktails instead of hand shaking them.

Mixing Cup   *See* Hand Shaker.

Mixing Glass   *See* Hand Shaker.

Mixing Steel   *See* Hand Shaker.

Mixologist   *See* Bartender.

Mixology   The art of following a recipe or formula to produce a standard and consistent drink according to specifications. An experienced mixologist can be compared to a chemist or a chef, producing perfect tasting and eye-appealing drinks every time. Unfortunately, mixology is slowly becoming a lost art, for most of the mixes are premixed and the popularity of "standard drinks" are also fading.

ML Abbreviation for milliliter; A metric unit of volume; 1000 mls equal one liter.

MOCKTAILS Any cocktail or other type of beverage that is prepared without the addition of an alcoholic beverage. Also known as *virgin drinks*.

MOELLEUX (FR) A wine that is soft, supple, and well-rounded. Mellow (possibly sweet), with a richness of body and full taste.

MOG Material other than grapes, (birds, bird nests, excessive leaves, stems, canes, etc.)

MOLASSES A thick, usually dark brown syrup produced by boiling the sugar, which evaporates the water, crystallizing the sugar. Also known as *blackstrap molasses*.

MOLDS Filamentous fungi that are found both in the vineyard and in the winery. They commonly produce large numbers of spores, which explains their wide distribution in nature. Mold growth often is observed on walls, cooperage, and other damp surfaces in the winery. Their development in wine or on wine contact surfaces may result in off-flavors. *See* Mycelia and Torula.

238

MOLDY An organoleptic term referring to undesirable odors (mustiness) or flavors, usually among wines made from grapes infected with mold, or wines that have been stored or aged in stale, unclean wooden barrels that have harbored mold. Also known as *schimmelgeschmack*. *See* Bottle Stink, Mousy, and Musty.

MOLECULE The smallest particle of a compound that can exist in a free state and still retain the characteristics of the compound.

MOLETTE (FR) A local white grape variety grown predominantly in Seyssel, where it is mainly used in the production of sparkling wines.

MOLINARA A red grape variety grown predominantly in the Veneto region of Italy where it is used (along with several other grape varieties) in the production of Bardolino and Valpolicella wines. The name Molinara is derived from the vernacular *Mulinara*, which means that when the grapes are in bloom they seem pruinose, or dusted with flour.

Molinara is also known as *Brepon*, *Rossanella*, and *Rossara*. In the Bardolino area, it also bears the name *Rossone*.

MOLISE (ITAL) The youngest of Italy's 20 wine-producing regions; originally it was part of Abruzzo, but a change in the laws of 1963 made it a separate region. Its DOC wines include Biferno Bianco, Biferno Rosso, Biferno Rosato, Pentro di Isernia Rosato, Pentro di Isernia Bianco, and Pentro di Isernia Rosso.

MONASTRELL (SP) A very prolific red grape variety that produces wines of light color and body, with a fruity, scented bouquet and lingering finish. Also known as *Morastel*.

MONBADON (FR) *See* Burger.

MONBAZILLAC (FR) A fairly sweet, golden-colored dessert wine produced in the Bergerac region in southwest France.

MONDEUSE NOIRE A red grape variety grown predominantly in Savoie, France where it produces dense, deeply-colored wines with considerable tannin, high acid, fruit, and flavor. In Veneto and Friuli-Venezia Giulia, Italy, the Mondeuse Noire is known as *Refosco*. Also known as *Crabb's Black Burgundy*, *Petite Pinot*, and *Refsko*.

MONFERRATO (ITAL) A major wine-producing district south of the Po Valley in Piedmont, noted for its production of Barbera wines.

MONICA (ITAL) A red grape variety grown in Sardinia, where it produces fairly nondescript wines destined for early consumption. Among the wine names are Monica di Sardegna and Monica di Cagliari.

MONIMPEX (HUN) It stands for The State Export Monopoly on bottles of Tokay wine.

MONOECIOUS *See* Hermaphroditic.

MONOPOLE (FR) A wine blended by a merchant-shipper and given a brand or trademark name. It is the French term for *monopoly*.

MONOPOLY STATE *See* Control State.

MONTAGNE A tavern on lower Broadway in Manhattan, New York, that was the headquarters of the Sons of Liberty, the site where The Revolutionary War was planned.

MONTAGNY (FR) A commune in the Côte Chalonnaise of Burgundy that produces very fine white wines from the Chardonnay and Pinot Blanc grapes.

MONTALCINO (ITAL) It is a picturesque and very hilly section of Tuscany situated approximately 25 miles southeast of Siena and Chianti Classico, approximately 1,600 feet above sea level. It is bordered by the Orcia River to the south and the Ombrone River to the west. The terrain is comprised of a variety of soil types, mainly a mixture of clay, with some carbonate, lime, and gravel. Montalcino is best known for its long-lived red DOCG wine, Brunello di Montalcino, made from the Sangiovese Grosso grape variety. Montalcino also grows some Moscadello di Montalcino grapes. Famous in ancient times, this was one of the most distinguished wines of Tuscany; slightly sparkling, straw-colored, with an intense aromatic bouquet and the sweet and distinctive characteristic flavor of the Moscato grape. *See* Brunello di Montalcino, Rosso di Montalcino, and Sangiovese Grosso.

MONTICELLO A dark red grape variety, introduced in 1973, from a cross of (Fredonia and Niagara) and (Fredonia and Athens), at the Virginia Polytechnic Institute.

MONTEFIASCONE (ITAL) A vineyard town on Lake Bolsena in Latium famous for its production of Est! Est!! Est!!! di Montefiascone, a dry or semidry white wine made from a blend of Trebbiano Toscano, Malvasia, and Rossetto grapes.

MONTEPULCIANO (ITAL) A red grape variety grown predominantly in Abruzzo, with some also cultivated in Marches and Apulia. The Montepulciano grape produces light–medium bodied wines meant for early consumption. Also the name of a province in Tuscany famous for its production of Vino Nobile di Montepulciano, a red wine.

MONTEREY RIESLING (CAL) *See* Sylvaner.

MONTHÉLIE (FR) Small red wine commune in the Côte de Beaune, just above Volnay.

MONTILLA (SP) A sherry-"style" wine produced from Pedro Ximénez grapes, in the villages of Montilla and Moriles in the hills of southern Spain near Córdoba.

MONTRACHET (FR) The most noted vineyard of the Côte de Beaune in Burgundy, straddling the communes of Puligny and Chassagne. Montrachet, made entirely from the Chardonnay grape, is considered by many to be the finest dry white wine in the world.

Translated, its name means "Bald Hill" because the barren hilltop is uncovered and literally bald today. Originally, one man owned the entire vineyard of Montrachet and called it Le Montrachet. Upon his death the land was divided up among his survivors. His eldest son or "chevalier," received a part renamed Chevalier-Montrachet. Another part went to his illegitimate son (whom he acknowledged as a youthful discretion), hence the name Bâtard-Montrachet, and finally the last part to his unmarried daughters (whom he believed were still virgins), Les Pucelles.

French novelist and dramatist Alexandre Dumas (1802–1870) was known to have declared that "Le Montrachet should be drunk kneeling, with one's head bared."

MOONSHINER One who produces moonshine.

MOONSHINE A homemade distilled product, made from virtually any ingredients, that is extremely high in alcohol and quite rough; originally from the southern part of the United States. Moonshine is also a group of non–tax paid distilled spirits that are sold illicitly. Also known as *shine* or *white lightning*.

MOORE'S DIAMOND *See* Diamond.

MORASTEL (SP) *See* Monastrell.

MORBIDO (ITAL) *See* Supple.

MORDANT A wine that is acrid, containing an excess of tannin and acidity, causing it to be astringent.

MOREL A seldom-used process in which the grapes are fermented unstemmed and are gradually pressed by means of a cross-peg stirrer. Named after a French born winemaker who made wines in St. Helena, California, in the late 1880s. *See* Carbonic Maceration.

MOREY-SAINT-DENIS (FR)   A small red wine commune located in the northern end of the Côte de Nuits in Burgundy, noted for its production of robust and fleshy red wines.

MORGEN (GERM)   An acre of land. *See* Acre.

MORGON (FR)   A cru commune in Beaujolais that produces a full-bodied but not coarse wine that usually requires nearly a year in the barrel and another year in the bottle before it is ready to drink. It takes three years to actually reach its prime.

MORIO-MUSKAT (GERM)   A white grape variety developed in the 1930s, from a cross of Sylvaner and Pinot Blanc with no Muscat in its parentage, by Peter Morio of the Bavarian Institute for Wine and Grape Development in Würzburg, located in the Rheinpfalz. Morio-Muskat produces wines with a fairly high acidity and a robust Muscat bouquet.

MORONEAN (GREECE)   An ancient wine.

MORTL   There are a number of different types of field crushing equipment used throughout the world. One type is the German-made Mortl system, which crushes the grapes in the field right after they are picked from the grapevines. The Mortl holds five tons of grapes and is pulled through the vineyard by a tractor. This process provides the ultimate in freshness preservation between the time the grapes are picked and the juice is processed. *See* Field Crushing.

MOSCATEL DE MALÁGA (SP)   *See* Muscat of Alexandria.

MOSCATEL DE SETÚBAL (PORT)   A very long-lived sweet, fortified wine made from the Muscat of Alexandria grape variety.

MOSCATEL GORDO BLANCO (SP)   *See* Muscat of Alexandria

MOSCATEL ROMANO (SPB)   *See* Muscat of Alexandria.

MOSCATEL ROXO (PORT)   A black strain of the Muscat of Alexandria grape variety.

MOSCATO BIANCO (ITAL)   *See* Muscat Blanc.

MOSCATO CANELLI (ITAL)   *See* Muscat Blanc.

MOSCATO D' ASTI (ITAL)   *See* Muscat Blanc.

MOSCOW MULE   A cocktail created and popularized in 1946 at Jack Morgan's Cock N' Bull Restaurant in Los Angeles, California. It consists of vodka and ginger beer, with a wedge of a fresh lime.

MOSEL (GERM)   A wine-producing region along the Mosel River and its two tributaries, the Saar and the Ruwer, producing a distinctive, pale, flowery white wine of generally low alcohol content. Also spelled *Moselle*.

MOSELBLÜMCHEN (GERM)   A white wine, light in body, with some residual sugar, theoretically from the Mosel. Its name translates to mean "little flower of the Mosel."

MOSEL-SAAR-RUWER (GERM)   *See* Mosel.

MOSELLE (GERM)   *See* Mosel.

MOSELTALER (GERM)   A generic light white wine generally produced in the Mosel region.

MOSKHÁTOS (GREECE)   *See* Musky.

MOST (GERM)   *See* Must.

MOSTO (ITAL OR SP)   *See* Must.

MÔSTO (PORT)   *See* Must.

MOSTGEWICHT (GERM)   The *must* (or sugar) weight of grape juice usually expressed in degrees Öechsle.

MOTHERS AGAINST DRUNK DRIVING (MADD)   A national coalition of concerned citizens whose aim is to increase public awareness and knowledge regarding alcohol abuse or misuse by disseminating information to the public, alcoholic beverage industry, and local and state legislators.

MOU (FR)   Flat and flabby, lacking character and acidity.

MOUILLÉ (FR)   Watered.

MOULIN-Á-VENT (FR)   A cru commune in Beaujolais (south of Chénas) produces the best-known and probably the finest of all Beaujolais wine. A nearby windmill (*Moulin-à-vent*)—still standing, minus its sails—is the source of its name. The character and taste of the wine are due to the granite-like quality of the local soil. Moulin-à-Vent is a dark-colored, full-bodied wine that takes a long time to mature; it lasts up to four or five years, but peaks in about three years.

MOUNTAIN   *See* Malàga.

MOUNTAIN   A loosely-used term with no legal meaning, often used on California jug wine labels—for example, "Mountain" Chablis, "Mountain" Burgundy, and so on. According to BATF, there is no legal requirement that grapes used in these jug wines come from vineyards located in mountainous areas. In addition, it is not necessarily so that mountain-grown grapes are superior to grapes grown in flat areas or in valleys.

MOURISCO DE SEMENTE (PORT)   A lesser strain of the Mourisco Tinto, a red grape variety.

MOURISCO TINTO (PORT)   A red grape variety that produces wines with good color, plenty of tannin, and ages fairly well.

MOURVAISON (FR)   A red grape variety cultivated in southeast near Provence, produces mostly common wines.

MOURVÈDRE   A red grape variety that produces wines that tend to be soft and velvety, with gentle plum flavors. It is used primarily as a blending grape in the Rhône Valley of France as well as in Australia, Spain, California, and Algeria. Also known as *Mataro*.

MOUSEY *See* Mousy.

MOUSINESS *See* Mousy.

MOUSSE (FR) The froth or foam on the surface of a glass of champagne or beer.

MOUSSEC (ENG) *See* Sparkling Wine.

MOUSSEUX (FR) *See* Vin Mousseux.

MOUSY A term for a disagreeable, acetic acid-like odor and taste produced by bacterial infection. It usually occurs when newly fermented wines are left too long on their lees. Also spelled *mousey*. Also known as *filant, filante, mäuseln, mousiness, oleoso, ölig,* and *ropiness*. *See* Bottle Stink, Moldy, and Musty.

MOÛT (FR) *See* Must.

MOUTERIJ A malt house in Holland.

MOUTWIJN The base distilled spirit utilized for Holland (Dutch) gin, produced by three passes (runs) through pot stills.

MOUTWIJN GENEVER A Holland (Dutch) gin that has been twice redistilled through various botanicals, primarily juniper berries.

MOUTHFILLING Wines or beers that display intense, full flavors that can be markedly fruity, and fairly high in extract and possibly alcoholic content. Also known as *vollmundig*.

MOUTON (FR) It is a linguistic corruption of *motte* (mound) and not *sheep*, as some believe.

MR. & MRS. T. It stands for Taylor, who developed the original recipes in 1962 for Bloody Mary Mix, Piña Colada Mix, Margarita Mix, Sweet N'Sour Mix, Lemon X, and Sour Mix.

MTSVANE (USSR) A white grape variety that produces wines that are fresh and aromatic, quite fruity, and destined for early consumption.

MUDDLER A hardwood instrument, hand-held, which is used for crushing ice, fruit, cube sugar, fresh mint leaves, or other herbs.

MUFFA NOBILE (ITAL) *See* Botrytis Cinerea.

MUG A heavy, flat-bottom beer glass or stein, generally with a capacity of 12 to 14 fluid ounces and contains a handle.

MUG HOUSE A slang term for a bar or tavern.

MUI QUAI LU A liqueur made in China from fermented rose petals.

MULLED WINE A sweetened and spiced red wine drink to which sugar, lemon peel, and spices such as nutmeg, cloves, and cinnamon are added. It is then heated by a *loggerhead* and served very warm to hot. Also known as *glühwein*. *See* Glögg, Loggerhead, and Poker Beer.

MÜLLERREBE (GERM) *See* Meunier.

MÜLLER-THURGAU An early ripening white grape that produces a mild wine with an effervescent flavor and distinct muscatel bouquet. Professor Hermann Müller (1850–1927), a Swiss ampelographer from Thurgau, developed the Müller-Thurgau grape variety in 1882. This was the first hybrid developed by scientists at the Geisenheim viticultural station in Germany. For many years it was thought to be a cross between the Johannisberg Riesling and Sylvaner grapes, but there is no evidence to support this theory. Müller-Thurgau is the most-planted grape variety (in acreage) in Germany. Also known as *Rivaner*.

MULTICOUNTY APPELLATIONS An appellation of origin comprising two or no more than three counties in the same state may be used if all of the grapes were grown in the counties indicated and the percentage of the wine derived from grapes grown in each county is shown on the label, with a tolerance of plus or minus 2 percent.

MULTISTATE APPELLATION An appellation of origin comprising two or no more than three states that are all contiguous may be used if 1) all of the grapes were grown in the states indicated, and the percentage of the wine derived from grapes grown in each state is shown on the label, with a tolerance of plus or minus 2 percent; 2) it has been fully finished and blended and does not result in an alteration of class or type in one of the labeled appellation states; and 3) it conforms to the laws and regulations governing the composition, method of manufacture, and designation of wines in all the states listed in the appellation.

MULTIUSE WINE BRAND A wine that is capable of being merchandised as an apéritif, to be sold by the glass, as well as fitting nicely into a standard wine list.

MÜNCHENER (GERM) Literally from Munich. This type of beer was originally produced in Bavaria; it is now brewed in many parts of the world. It is slightly darker in color than Pilsner-type beers, although milder and less bitter than other German types. It also has a more pronounced malty aroma and taste, with a sweet finish and aftertaste. Munich beer is ideally served at 38 degrees to 45 degrees Fahrenheit.

MUNSON, THOMAS VOLNEY A local hybridizer who developed many grape varieties suitable for planting in the hot and dry Texas sun. He was also instrumental in helping the French to reestablish their vineyards after the devastating effects of the phylloxera plague. Because of his work, he was awarded the Legion of Honor by the French government in 1888.

MÛR (FR) *See* Mature.

MURETO DO ALENTEJO (PORT) A red grape variety used primarily for the production of locally consumed, light-colored wines.

MUSCADELLE A white grape variety that is generally blended in small proportions with the Sémillon and Sauvignon Blanc, which gives intense fruit and a faint Muscat flavor to the wine. Muscadelle is cultivated mostly in

Graves and Sauternes in the Bordeaux region of France. Also known as *Muscadelle de Bordelais*, and in France and some parts of California, known as *Sauvignon Vert*. It is argued that the Muscadelle is the same grape variety as the Tocai of Italy. *See* Tocai.

MUSCADELLE DE BORDELAIS (FR)   *See* Muscadelle.

MUSCADET (FR)   Muscadet, which is made from the Melon de Bourgogne grape variety, is produced in the far western part of the Loire Valley and is a bone-dry, steely, clean, light white wine, usually high in acidity; it is perfect for serving with raw shellfish. The best Muscadet is Sèvre-et-Maine.

MUSCADINE   A native American grape of the grapevine species *vitis rotundifolia*. Muscadines are indigenous to the south Atlantic states and produce heavily aromatic, sweet cordial-type wines. The best known type of muscadine is Scuppernong, a white grape variety. Also known as *Muscadinia*.

MUSCARDIN (FR)   A red grape variety grown predominantly in the Rhône region, where it produces wines that are light in color, with high acidity and low fruit.

MUSCAT   A white *Vitis vinifera* grape variety that is widely planted throughout the Mediterranean area, as well as in parts of northern Europe and California. There are many varieties, subvarieties, and styles of the Muscat, which vary from region to region and country to country.

245

MUSCAT Á PETITS GRAINS   *See* Muscat Blanc.

MUSCAT BLANC   A white *Vitis vinifera* grape variety that produces wines with an intense spicy-perfumed aroma and a grapey taste that resembles a fresh fruit salad. It is prolifically grown in the Piedmont region of Italy where it forms the base of many Muscat-type wines. Among them are Asti Spumante, Moscato Bianco, and others. Although its correct name is *Muscat à Petits Grains*, it is known by a host of other names that include *Moscato Bianco, Moscato Canelli, Moscato d'Asti, Muscat de Frontignan, Muskateller*, and *Sargamuskotaly*.

MUSCAT DE FRONTIGNAN (FR)   A white grape variety grown in parts of southern France and California, where it produces mostly fortified dessert wines. *See* Muscat Blanc.

MUSCATEL   A sweetened, amber-colored, fortified wine, generally produced in California from the Muscat grape. Although quite popular during the 1940s to 1960s, its popularity has dwindled.

MUSCAT GORDO BLANCO (AUSTRAL)   *See* Muscat of Alexandria.

MUSCAT HAMBURG   A black grape variety, sparsely grown in California, that produces lightly-colored, intensely spicy wines that are often fortified or allowed to contain some residual sugar. Also known as *Black Muscat*.

MUSCAT OF ALEXANDRIA   A white *Vitis vinifera* grape variety widely planted throughout the Mediterranean area, as well as in California. It produces mostly table wines that are quite varietal in character with some underlying bitterness, and are often sweet or slightly sweet. Also known as *Moscatel de Málaga*, *Moscatel Gordo Blanco*, *Moscatel Romano*, and *Muscat Gordo Blanco*.

MUSCAT OTTONEL   A white grape variety with an exceptionally strong but pleasant muscat aroma that is planted in central and eastern Europe and displays an exceptionally strong but pleasant spicy aroma. Also known as *Muskotály*.

MUSELET (FR)   *See* Wire Hood.

MUSCULAR   A term that describes robust, full-bodied, and assertive wines, generally displaying good acidity and great texture. Also known as *nerbo*, *nervig*, and *sinewy*. *See* Brawny and Powerful.

MUSHROOM   Some very old red Bordeaux and Cabernet Sauvignon wines occasionally have an odor that reminds one of fresh-picked, dirt-laden mushrooms.

MUSIGNY (FR)   A red wine-producing vineyard located in the commune of Chambolle-Musigny, in the Côte de Nuits of Burgundy. Its wines, made from the Pinot Noir grape, can be described as fleshy and seductive.

MUSKATELLER (GERM)   *See* Muscat Blanc.

MUSKAT-SYLVANER (GERM)   *See* Sauvignon Blanc.

MUSKOTÁLY (HUN)   *See* Muscat Ottonel.

MUSKY   A peculiar characteristic odor of wines made with the Muscat grape as the base, especially during fermentation, when the odor can be detected. Also known as *moskhátos*.

MUSQUÉ (FR)   The heavily perfumed odor often associated with wines made from the Muscat grape variety.

MUST   The unfermented juice or any mixture of juice, pulp, skins, and seeds prepared from fruit, berries, or grapes. The term is derived from the Latin term *mustum*. Also known as *most*, *mosto*, *Mòsto*, and *moût*. *See* Stum Wine.

MUST WEIGHT   The quantifiably measurable amount of sugar in ripe grapes or *must*.

MUSTARD   *See* Wild Mustard.

MUSTIMETER   *See* Hydrometer.

MUSTY   An unpleasant odor or flavor in wine similar to a moldy smell, which is often due to an unclean cellar or can result from aging wine in wooden barrels that have decayed or become waterlogged. *See* Bottle Stink, Moldy, and Mousy.

MUTAGE (FR)   *See* Mistelle.

MUTÉ   Also known as *muto*. *See* Mistelle and Süssreserve.

MUTING   *See* Mistelle.

MUTO (ITAL)   *See* Muté.

MUY AÑEJO (SP)   Well aged, longer than añejo; used in reference to rum and tequila.

MYCELIA   A concentration of fungus filaments. *See* Molds.

MYCODERMA   A spoilage bacteria, mold, or yeast that consumes alcohol, impairing the odor and flavor of wine. It is taken from the Greek words *mykes*, meaning fungi, and *derma*, meaning skin.

MYCODERMA ACETI   *See* Acetobacter.

MYCODERMA VINI   *See* Flowers of Wine.

MYELÓDIS (GREECE)   *See* Mellow.

MYRTILLE (FR)   *See* Myrtle.

MYRTLE   An evergreen bush whose berries are often used to make fruit brandy or fruit-flavored brandy. Also known as *myrtille*.

MYSLIWSKA (POL)   A hunter's vodka.

NABI   National Association of Beverage Importers.

NACKENHEIM (GERM)   A wine-producing town located in the Rheinhessen, overlooking the Rhine River, just south of Mainz. Nackenheim produces fruity white wines from Johannisberg Riesling and Sylvaner grape varieties.

NACHGESCHMACK (GERM)   *See* Aftertaste.

NAGYBURGUNDI (HUN)   *See* Pinot Noir.

NAHE (GERM)   One of 11 Qualitätswein grape-growing regions, located near the Rhine River.

NAIVE   Generally used when referring to wines of little merit.

NAMA   *See* Commandaria.

NAME BRAND   *See* Call Liquor.

NAPA GAMAY   Originally thought to be the true Gamay of the Beaujolais district, now identified as Valdiguié, a very heavy producer of "ordinary" wines in the Midi Region, in southern France. However, it may continue to be called Napa Gamay in California. *See* Gamay.

NAPA VALLEY   A viticultural grape-growing region in California, located northeast of San Francisco, which many consider the most celebrated wine region in the United States.

NAPLES   A red grape variety developed in 1952, from a cross of Delaware and (Mills and Iona).

NAPOLEON (FR)   A label designation on Armagnac or Cognac bottles that indicates that the youngest brandy used in the blend is at least 5 ½ years old (although they contain a very high percentage of brandy that has been aged for 20, 30, or 40 years or more).

NARIZ (SP)   A wine taster's term that compares the relative pungency between two or more similar wines or *musts*.

NASE (GERM)   *See* Nose.

NATIONAL LIQUOR BEVERAGE ASSOCIATION (NLBA)   A trade association of the alcoholic beverage industry whose goal is the promotion of distilled spirits through consumer awareness.

NATIVE AMERICAN GRAPE VARIETIES   A term used to describe native American grapes and grapevines, mostly found east of the Mississippi River. The grapevines, properly identified as *Vitis labrusca* species, have a pronounced grapey or "foxy" odor and flavor that characterizes them, as well as wine made from these grapes.

Around 1000 A.D., explorer Leif Ericson first discovered these wild grapevines growing when he landed on the east coast of North America near Newfoundland. In fact, he found so many grapevines that he named the place "Vineland the Good." *See* Vitis Labrusca and Wild Grapevines.

NATIVE PRODUCT   A term sometimes used by state legislatures to distinguish goods produced within a state from out-of-state ("imported") goods.

NATURAL OR AU NATUREL   Designation for bone dry; used on the labels of bottles of sparkling wine. Also known as *natur, naturale,* and *ultra brut.*

NATURAL SPRING WATER   *See* Spring Water.

NATURAL WATER   A term that refers to drinking water, that comes either from an underground spring or from a well. No adulteration of the water is permitted; however, filtering, and so on, may be permissable.

NATURAL WINE   The product of the juice or must of sound, ripe grapes or other sound, ripe fruit (including berries) that contains not more than 21 percent by weight (21 degrees brix dealcoholized wine) of total solids.

NATURAL WINE   A term (without legal meaning) that refers to wines made "natural," without additives or preservatives that would effectively change the taste or alcohol content.

NATURALE (ITAL)   *See* Natural.

NATUR (GERM)   *See* Natural.

NATURE   *See* Extra Brut.

NATURE (FR)   Natural; a still or sparkling wine that has not been sweetened.

NAVY GROG   *See* Grog.

NBWA   National Beer Wholesalers Association.

NCADD   National Commission Against Drunk Driving.

NCPID   National Coalition to Prevent Impaired Driving.

NEAR BEER   A "beer-like" malt beverage made from cereals, which has been brewed either to have a low alcoholic content (less than 0.5 percent alcohol-by-volume) or to be dealcoholized. Near beer was first brewed during Prohibition as a substitute for beer. *See* Bevo, Needled Beer, and Nonalcoholic Malt Beverage.

NEAT *See* Straight.

NEBBIOLO (ITAL) A major *Vitis vinifera* red grape variety grown predominantly in the Piedmont region. The Nebbiolo produces wines that are usually rough and tannic when young, but with age evolve into wines of extraordinary power, depth, and complexity. When blended with other varieties, the Nebbiolo grape gives the resultant wine body and substance.

The Nebbiolo in fact is not one grape but a family of grapes whose variations probably arriving through mutation. There are two subvarieties—Michet and Lampia, which are widely planted throughout the area.

The Nebbiolo is a strong, vigorous grapevine that buds early and matures late, from October 15 onward. This latter characteristic, together with the fact that the grapevine is resistant to the cold and humidity of late autumn, makes the grapevine a favorite with Piedmont's producers. The Nebbiolo grape is used to produce Barolo, Barbaresco, Gattinara, Ghemme, and many other wines.

Its clusters are medium to large in elongated pyramid shapes with wings, somewhat compact, occasionally with a wing rather developed. The grapes are medium-sized, rotund, tending toward ellipsoidal.

Originally called *Vitis vinifera Pedemontana* (the grapevine of Piedmont), the grape is referred to as *Nubiola, Nebiola, Nibiol,* and *Nebiolium* in documents dating back to the Middle Ages. Its present name and spelling, officially sanctioned in 1962, is derived from the word *nebbia* (fog). Some say that it was given this name because of the persistent fog found in the area of cultivation, while others believe it alludes to the thick bloom that forms on the grape skins, making them look as if they were surrounded by tiny patches of fog.

Nebbiolo is known by several other names, including Spanna (in the provinces of Vercelli and Novara, a term that reflects the method of cultivation), Chiavennasca (in the province of Sondrio in Lombardy), and *Picotener, Picultener,* or *Pugnet* in Valle D'Aosta and around Carema.

NEBBIOLO BIANCO (ITAL) *See* Arneis.

NEBUCHADNEZZAR A large bottle with a capacity of 20 750-milliliter sized bottles (507 fluid ounces) or 15 liters (it weighs approximately 65 pounds when full). The bottle was named after Nebuchadnezzar (605–562 B.C.), a warring sixth century B.C. king of Babylon who sacked Jerusalem around 600 B.C. His exploits are described in II Kings 24 and 25, and Daniel 4.

NEEDLED BEER A slang term that referred to "near beer" as brewed during Prohibition, which often contained illegal distilled spirits. *See* Near Beer.

NEEDLING The process of inserting an electric probe (often called a "needle") into a tank of fermenting beer, which stimulates and hastens the aging process.

NÉGOCIANT (FR) Also known as *negoziante. See* Broker.

NÉGOCIANT-ELEVEUR (FR)   A shipper who buys wine in barrels from growers and then ages and bottles it in his or her own cellars. *See* Broker.

NÉGOCIANT-MANIPULANT (FR)   Champagnes produced under the complete control of the house (producer). This appears on some champagne labels as initials NM. *See* Broker.

NEGOZIANTE (ITAL)   *See* Négociant.

NEGRA MOLE (PORT)   A local red-skinned grape variety often used in a blend to produce Madeira wines.

NEGRO AMARO (ITAL)   A red grape variety cultivated in Apulia, where it produces dark-colored, full-bodied wines such as Matino Rosso and Rosato.

NEGRONI   A cocktail consisting of Campari, gin, and sweet red vermouth, with a splash of seltzer and twist of lemon.

NEMATODES   A soil-borne vineyard parasitic pest (worm) that has long, cylindrical, unsegmented bodies and a heavy cuticle. It generally lives in the soil and feeds on roots of grapevines. Nematodes are not generally found in the northwestern part of the United States due to its soil composition.

NERBO (ITAL)   *See* Muscular.

NERO (ITAL)   Very dark red to the point of almost being black.

NERELLO MASCALESE (ITAL)   A red grape variety cultivated primarily in Sicily. Also known as *Nirello Mascalese* and *Niereddu Mascalese*.

NERVEUX (FR)   Lively; a young, fresh wine that has a promise of great life, longevity, and improvement.

NERVIG (GERM)   *See* Muscular.

NERVOSITÉ (FR)   *See* Lively.

NET (FR)   *See* Clean.

NET PROFIT   Sales of products minus expenses and costs.

NET RATE   A wholesale rate to be marked up for eventual resale to the consumer.

NETT (GERM)   *See* Clean.

NETTO (ITAL)   *See* Clean.

NET WEIGHT   Weight of the contents, not including the container (gross less tare).

NEU (GERM)   New.

NEUBURGER (AUS)   A white grape variety that produces a full-bodied, mild wine with a particularly fine bouquet. It is a cross of Pinot Blanc and Sylvaner, developed in the Wachau district of Lower Austria.

NEUCHÂTEL (SWISS)   A dry, tart white wine produced on the northern shore of Lake Neuchatel from the Chasselas grape.

The vineyards of Neuchâtel are also the source of a light-colored, intriguingly fragrant red wine, and of one of Switzerland's celebrated rosés, *oeil de perdrix* (an ancient wine term meaning the pink color of a partridge's eye); both are made from the Pinot Noir grape.

NEUTRAL   A term applied to an alcoholic beverage exhibiting low intensity in olfactory, tactile, and taste sensations. Also known as *neutre* and *neutro*.

NEUTRAL BRANDY   Brandy produced at more than 170 degrees proof.

NEUTRAL SPIRITS   Distilled spirits, distilled from any material at or above 190 proof, that lack any distinctive taste, color, and odor—thus being neutral in character. These distilled spirits are used for blending with straight whiskey and for making gin, vodka, and liqueurs. Also known as *grain neutral spirits* and *pure alcohol*.

NEUTRE (FR)   *See* Neutral.

NEUTRO (ITAL, PORT, OR SP)   *See* Neutral.

NEUTRON PROBE   A moisture reading device that measures the amount of water in the soil and monitors the uptake of water by the grapevines. In a sense, this allows the viticulturist to "see" underground. The neutron probe is a tube about one foot long and one inch in diameter. The tip contains an isotope of *Americium Beryllium*, which sends out atoms that have an affinity for the hydrogen ions in water. To utilize this device, a two-inch diameter hole is drilled in the soil, usually to a depth of five feet. An aluminum tube is then placed in the hole and this becomes a monitoring station.

N

253

To check soil moisture content, the probe is inserted into the tube at various depths. As the ions are discharged into the soil, they are deflected by the hydrogen atoms and then counted by a sensor as they bounce back to the probe. A microprocessor built into the unit converts these bulk readings into a calibrated reading of inches-of-water-per-foot.

The neutron probe is effectively able to measure minute differences in the amount of soil moisture in hundreds of an inch. This means viticulturists can not only tell what part of a grapevine's root zone is utilizing the water, but also determine how much water has been used. *See* Tensiometer.

NEVERS OAK (FR)   (Technically known as *Quercus robur*.) Named after the city of Nevers, in central France. Its relatively hard wood and fine, medium grain make it suitable for aging both red and white wines without overpowering flavors. Nevers oak has a moderate tannin extraction and a rich, buttery, oak flavor that greatly softens wine's acidity. Nevers is used extensively for Cabernet and Merlot, as well as red and white wines in Burgundy.

NEVRÓDIS (GREECE)   *See* Firm.

NEW AMSTERDAM   The sight of the first American brewery. *See* Minuit, Peter.

NEW YORK MUSCAT   A red grape variety developed in 1961, from a cross of Muscat Hamburg and Hubbard, at the New York State Experimental Station at Geneva. The wine that it produces is rich, with a *muscat* flavor.

Nez (FR) *See* Nose.

Nez Fleuri (FR) A flowery nose; an odor often exhibited by some white wines.

Nez Fruité (FR) A fruity nose; an odor often exhibited by some white wines.

Nez Subtil (FR) A subtle nose; often used to describe a wine that has a fine, delicate odor.

NIAAA National Institute on Alcohol Abuse and Alcoholism.

Niagara A white *Vitis labrusca* grape variety of the "concord-type" that is used for both dry and sweet wines as well as nonalcoholic grape juice. Niagara is a cross of Concord and Cassady, introduced in the 1870s. The grapes are light yellow in color, with large bunches. Wine made from Niagara grapes displays a strong characteristic flavor, while being low in acidity.

Niche Marketing A marketing plan that creates a narrow or select market that is highly desired by a small segment of the population.

Nielluccio A red grape variety native to Corsica that produces light-bodied wines with high alcohol levels.

Niereddu Mascalese (ITAL) *See* Nerello Mascalese.

Nierstein (GERM) The foremost vineyard village of the Rheinhessen region, located on the Rhine River, noted for its production of high quality white wines, primarily from the Johannisberg Riesling grape variety.

Night Cap A slang term for a drink (alcoholic beverage) before retiring to bed.

Nineteenth Hole (19th hole) Any place, as the bar or lounge of a clubhouse, where golfers meet for drinks, light snacks, and conviviality after playing a round of golf.

Nine-Liter Case The industry standard size case. 100 flat cases of 1.75-liters contains 1,050 liters and therefore is equal to 117 9-liter cases.

Nip The British term for a quarter of a bottle; also the name of the smallest bottle that champagne is sold (usually six fluid ounces). A term often used in reference to miniature bottles.

Nirello Mascalese (ITAL) *See* Nerello Mascalese.

Nitrogen Yeast cells need nitrogen to multiply. Although fruit juices contain some nitrogen, when diluted there is usually not a sufficient amount for a satisfactory fermentation. For this reason, ammonium salts (sulfate or phosphate) are usually added, as these contain a rich source of nitrogen. The salts are conveniently sold as yeast nutrients. *See* Nutrients.

Nitrogen Gas An inert gas often used in the production of alcoholic beverages to maintain pressure during filtering and bottling of sparkling wine. It is also utilized in some "wine-by-the-glass programs" in conjunction with a "nitrogen system." In this type system, the inert nitrogen gas, injected under gentle pressure through a sealed stopper, replaces the wine as it is removed from the bottle, and preserves the wine by keeping it oxygen free. The wine may be quickly dispensed and easily stored after use.

NLSA National Liquor Stores Association.

NM (FR) *See* Négociant-Manipulant.

NOAH A white *Vitis labrusca* grape variety developed by Otto Wasserzieher of Nauvoo, Illinois, first planted in the late 1860s.

NOBILE (ITAL) *See* Noble.

NOBLE A term that describes a wine that displays the ultimate combination of elegance, breed, body, structure, and maturity. The wine also has great balance and character. Also, a wine made from noble grapes—the best varietals, such as Cabernet Sauvignon, Pinot Noir, Chardonnay, or Sauvignon Blanc. Also known as *evyenís* and *nobile*.

NOBLE A red *Muscadine* grape variety grown in Florida, North Carolina, and other parts of the southeast.

NOBLE ROT *See* Botrytis Cinerea.

NOBLESSA (GERM) A white grape variety developed in 1975 from a cross of Madeleine Angevine and Sylvaner grape varieties.

NOBLING (GERM) A white grape variety developed in 1939 from a cross of Gutedel and Sylvaner grape varieties in Freiburg, located in Baden.

NODE The enlarged or thickened part of the grapevine cane or shoot where leaves, clusters, tendrils, and buds begin to grow.

NOGGIN An English measure for beer, equaling one-quarter pint or four fluid ounces.

NOIR (FR) Black.

NOIRIEN (FR) *See* Pinot Noir.

NO-HOST BAR *See* Cash Bar.

NOM *See* Norma Oficial Mexicana de Calidad.

NOMENCLATURE Set or system of official names or titles given to items of subsistence.

NONALCOHOLIC MALT BEVERAGE A malt beverage that is *not* alcohol free, but rather it contains less than 0.5 percent alcohol by volume. Nonalcoholic malt beverages cannot be labeled or advertised as beer, lager, ale, porter, stout, or any other designation commonly associated with malt beverages. They may, however, be labeled as "malt beverage," "cereal beverage," or "near beer." *See* Bevo and Near Beer.

NONBEVERAGE WINE Wine or wine products made from wine that are rendered unfit for beverage use. Can also be labeled as *Not For Sale or Consumption As Beverage Wines*. *See* Cooking Wines.

NONCONTROLLABLE COSTS *See* Fixed Costs.

NONFAT DRIED MILK Skim milk that has been pasteurized and homogenized with the water content removed through heat and evaporation.

NONFERMENTABLE REDUCING SUGAR *See* Reducing Sugar.

NONFERMENTABLES *See* Reducing Sugar.

NONREFUNDABLE A specified condition upon the terms of purchasing a commodity whereby the item purchased may not be returned for cash, credit, or replacement.

NONPERISHABLE Distilled spirits and some other alcoholic beverages that do not spoil or deteriorate readily.

NONVINTAGE (NV) A term that applies to those sparkling wines whose *cuvées* contain wine from previous vintages. The term can also be applied to some table wines that do not display a vintage date on their label. Also known as *sans année*. *See* Blending and Reserve Wine.

NORMALWEIN (AUS) *See* Vino da Tavola.

NORMANDY (FR) A northern province famous for its production of Calvados, an apple brandy. *See* Calvados.

NORMA OFICIAL MEXICANA DE CALIDAD (NOM) A designation marked by an individualized number on the label of every bottle of classified tequila; it is the official Mexican seal of quality and authenticity. *See* Dirección General de Normas.

NORTON A red *Vitis labrusca* grape variety that produces wines dark in color with high acidity, and a "concordy" odor and flavor. The name derives from Dr. Daniel Norborne Norton of Richmond, Virginia, a grape breeder who called it Norton's Virginia Seedling in about 1815. Formerly known as *Norton Seedless*.

NOSE The combination of aroma and bouquet. *See* Aroma and Bouquet. Also known as *nase* and *nez*.

NOUAISON (FR) Fertilization of the flower and the beginning of the fruit.

NOUVEAU (FR) A term used to indicate a "new wine" (of the year) that has been fermented to capture the ultimate in lightness and freshness, in addition to its intense grapey aromas and flavors. This youthful red wine seldom has any aging potential; therefore, it is meant to be enjoyed within a short time after vinification. The term is often used in conjunction with Beaujolais. Also known as *federweisser, primeur, vin de l'année, vin de primeur, vinho claro*, and *vin nouveau*. *See* Beaujolais Nouveau, Carbonic Maceration, and Vino Novello.

NOVELLO (ITAL) *See* Vino Novello.

NSF National Sanitation Foundation.

NU (FR) Bare; the raw cost of the wine prior to bottling.

NUANCE A slight, subtle, or gentle variation of flavor or smell exhibited in some wines. *See* Subtle.

NUBE (SP) *See* Cloudy.

NUCLEUS   The central, usually spherical or oval mass of protoplasm present in most plant cells, containing most of the hereditary material and necessary to such functions as growth, reproduction, and so on.

NUITS-SAINT-GEORGES (FR)   A red and white wine town on the Côte de Nuits in the region of Burgundy. The red wines of the Côte de Nuits are velvety, round, smooth, full, and usually not high in tannin. There is only one white wine produced, called Nuits-Saint-Georges Blanc.

The name *Nuits* was derived from the tribe of *Nuithons* who were closely associated with the Burgundians and lived there at one time.

NUMB   A still wine, sparkling wine, or beer that has been overly chilled to the point that very little odor or taste can be detected. *See* Dumb and Closed-In.

NUMBER OF PORTIONS   The number of servings. *See* Cover.

NURAGUS (ITAL)   A local white grape variety grown primarily in Sardinia.

NUTRA-SWEET   *See* Aspartame.

NUTRIENTS   A yeast "food" or energizer, largely made up of vitamin B$_1$, magnesium sulfate, potassium phosphate, urea, and ammonium phosphate, which supplies the *must* with a suitable source of nitrogen and phosphorous. Its use will keep yeasts healthy throughout fermentation and will maximize alcohol content by preventing premature cessation of fermentation (often referred to as a "stuck" fermentation). Also known as *seed yeast, yeast energizers, yeast nutrients*, and *yeast starter*. *See* Nitrogen and Stuck Fermentation.

NUTTY   A term denoting the characteristic nut-like odor and flavor of Madeira, Marsala, sherry, or vin santo. Wines exposed to excess oxygen will often display a similar oxidized or *rancio* odor.

NV   *See* Nonvintage.

O   A letter designation used on labels of Armagnac, cognac, and some other brandies as an abbreviation for *old*.

OAK   Any number of large hardwood trees of the genus *quercus* that is suitable for the aging of wines. It is a ring-porous wood having relatively large "pores" or tubes in the spring portion of each annual ring. These are part of the pattern of oak lumber and are easily seen with the naked eye in the end grain. Oak is also the preferred wood for the aging and storage of wines because it adds and develops greater complexity in the taste and odor. Also known as *rovere*.

OAK CHIPS   Chopped, split, or ground pieces of oak that are often used in place of wooden barrel aging to give wine an *oaked* odor and/or flavor without the necessity of barrels.

OAKY   The odor and/or taste of wines aged in small oak barrels. Some oak barrels impart a toasty or sort of spicy, vanillin odor and taste to wine, which is desirable in moderation, but undesirable if exaggerated. Delicate use of oak aging can add subtle complexity to full-bodied wines.

OAST   A kiln that is used for the drying of hops or malt to be used in beer or distilled spirits.

OAT   A hardy, widely-grown cereal grass often used in the production of distilled spirits and some beers.

OATMEAL STOUT   A brewed beverage, rich, flavorful, and quite dark in color, in which oatmeal is added to the roasted malt. *See* Stout.

OBJECTIVE   Relating to information that is independent, factual, or real, and can often be measurable.

OBSCURA (SP)   *See* Candling.

OCCUPATIONAL TAX   A fee charged for one of the federal permits authorizing an individual to deal as manufacturer, wholesaler, or retailer in distilled spirits, wine, or beer.

OCHA (JAPAN) A green tea.

OCHOKO (JAPAN) Small porcelain cups traditionally used for serving saké. Also known as *sakazuki*.

ÖCHSLE (GERM) *See* Öechsle.

OCKFEN (GERM) One of the very best white wine–producing villages located along the Saar River.

OCTAVE (SP) A barrel with a capacity of approximately 16 U.S. gallons, used for sherry wine. *See* Barrel.

ODEUR (FR) Smell or odor in the simple direct sense; smell of a cork, wine, yeast, barrel, and so on.

ODEUR BALSAMIQUE (FR) The odor or smell of balsam or incense.

ODEUR BOISÉ (FR) A woody or oaky smell.

ODEUR D'IODE (FR) An iodine smell, which is often used to describe the odor of Scotch whisky.

ODEUR DE RÉSINE (FR) A resin smell, often characteristic of Retsina wines of Greece.

ODEUR DE SUIE (FR) A sooty or smoky smell.

ODEUR EMPYREUMATIQUE (FR) The smell or odor reminiscent of something burning.

ODEUR ÉPICÉE (FR) A spicy smell.

ODEUR FLORALE (FR) A floral scent.

ODEUR FRUITÉE (FR) A fruity smell.

ODEURS PRIMAIRES (FR) The primary smells that describe odors emanating from the grape itself, often found in young wines.

ODEURS SECONDAIRES (FR) The secondary smells that describe odors emanating from fermentation, caused by the yeasts.

ODEURS TERTIAIRES (FR) Tertiary or aging smells that develop as the wine ages either in wood or in the bottle.

ODOR The odor of a wine, beer, or distilled spirit, or, simply, the way it smells.

ODORE DE FUSTO (ITAL) A barrel smell; this odor can be positive and pleasing if moderate, or unpleasant if excessive or if the barrel is in poor condition.

ÖECHSLE (GERM OR SWISS) A term derived from Christian Ferdinand Öechsle (1774–1852), a chemist in the early nineteenth century, who lived in the town of Pforzheim in Baden, Germany. He devised the method used to measure the level of sugar present in the *must*.

Öechsle is a measurement of the specific gravity of *must* (it refers to the number of grams by which one liter of grape *must* is heavier than one liter of water). Each quality category of German wine (Spätlese, Auslese, etc.) has to have a certain minimum Öechsle level to justify its title. When you divide by eight, you get the future alcoholic content of the wine. You must remember, however, that it includes the sweetness of unfermented sugar of a Spätlese or Auslese wine. Therefore, the actual alcoholic strength is likely to be less, since part of the sugar remains in the wine as unfermented residual sugar. To determine Brix, take Öechsle, divide by four and subtract one. To determine Öechsle, take Brix, add one and multiply by four. Also spelled *Öchsle*. *See* Brix.

OEIL DE PERDRIX (FR)   A term that literally means "eye of the partridge." In the nineteenth century it was the common name for a wine that had a slight pinkish or copper tint in its color; often applied to pink or rosé-colored champagne. *See* Vin Gris.

OELIG (GERM)   Of marked viscosity.

OENOLOGY   *See* Enology.

OENOPHILE   *See* Enophile.

OENOTECA (ITAL)   *See* Enoteca.

OENOTHEQUE (FR)   *See* Enotheque.

OENOTRI (GREECE)   *See* Enotri Viri.

OENOTRIA (GREECE)   *See* Enotria Tellus.

OFC   Old Fine Canadian; used when referring to whisky.

OFF   A term referring to wines or beers that do not show their true character in smell and/or taste or display undesirable attributes. It is often due to improper storage or aging, and, in advanced cases, the seriously negative odor or taste is a result of some type of spoilage. Also referred to as *off-odors* or *off-flavors*.

OFF-DRY   *See* Semidry.

OFF-FLAVORS   *See* Off.

OFFICE INTERNATIONAL DE LA VIGNE ET DU VIN (OIV) (FR)   An organization established in 1924 that carries out studies and investigations on a worldwide scale in technical, economic, scientific, and legal areas.

OFF-ODORS   *See* Off.

OFF-PREMISE OUTLETS   (Off Sale) Retail establishments specializing in the sale of alcohol beverages, usually package stores, in which alcohol beverages are sold in bottles or cans to be consumed elsewhere.

OFIQUE (SP)   A method of refrigeration that stabilizes the wine and prevents it from becoming cloudy.

OÏDIUM   *See* Powdery Mildew.

OIL CAN   A slang term that refers to the 32-ounce beer can.

OILED   Slang for intoxicated.

OILER A slang term for a person who drinks alcoholic beverages excessively.

OILINESS *See* Oily.

OILY A tactile impression of fat, roundness, or a slightly slippery taste created by the combination of high glycerine and slightly low acidity. It is found in some wines, most noticeably Chardonnay, as well as in sweet, late-harvest wines. Also known as *liparós, oleoso, oiliness,* and *ölig.*

OINOCHOE (GREECE) A pitcher-like vessel with a three-lobed rim, for dipping wine from the crater or bowl and pouring it into the drinking cup. Also known as *olpe.*

OINOS (GREECE) *See* Wine.

OIV (FR) *See* The Office International de la Vigne et du Vin.

OJEN (SP) *See* Anise-Based Spirits.

OJO DE LIEBRE (EYE OF THE HARE) (SP) The local name in Catalonia for the Tempranillo grape variety. *See* Tempranillo.

OKTOBERFEST (GERM) A beer festival held each year in Germany that begins the end of September and lasts into the beginning of October. An estimated 1.2 million gallons of beer are consumed by 5 million visitors during this 16-day festival.

In 1810, when Prince Ludwig, the Crown Prince, married Theresia of Sachsen-Hildburghausen in Munich, his father Max Joseph, the royal Wittelsbach of Bavaria, threw him a large and massive wedding. The party was so successful that the meadow where it was held was renamed "Theresia's Meadow." That tradition or party, which actually started out as a wedding ceremony, still continues to this day, except it is known as the Oktoberfest.

OKOLEHAO (HAWAII) An 80-proof distilled spirit made from cooked *ti roots.*

OKOWITA (POL) *See* Aqua Ardens and Aqua Vitae.

ÖL The Scandinavian (Denmark, Iceland, Norway, Sweden) Word for beer.

OLASZRIESLING (HUN) *See* Welschriesling.

OLASZ RIZLING (HUN) *See* Welschriesling.

OLD (O) A designation used on labels of Armagnac, cognac, and some other brandies to indicate a well-aged product (not in a negative sense).

OLD A wine or beer that is past its prime or peak. Also known as *over-the-hill, passé, pasado, shot,* or *tot.*

OLD BOTTLED SHERRY (SP) A seldom-used term that describes an "amontillado-type" sherry that is slightly sweetened, often meant to be aged in the bottle.

OLD EAST SHERRY (SP) A seldom-used term that describes an "oloroso-type" sherry that is full-bodied and sweet.

OLD-FASHIONED A cocktail containing whiskey, bitters, a dash of soda, and garnished with fruit. The origin of the old-fashioned is traced to the bar at the Pendennis Club in Louisville, Kentucky, which first opened its doors in 1881. Many older recipes called for a sprig of mint, making it similar to the Mint Julep. Some papers in the 1800s make reference to Juleps made "the old-fashioned way." The drink was first introduced in the East at the original Waldorf bar some time in the 1890s.

OLD-FASHIONED GLASS   An ordinary short, squat bar glass without a base (foot) or stem, with a capacity of six to eight ounces. Also known as *on the rocks glass*, *rocks glass*, and *tumbler*.

OLD TOM GIN   A British dry gin usually sweetened by the addition of sugar syrup that was quite popular during the eighteenth century. It is rarely seen today.

OLD VINES   A loosely-used grape growers' term to indicate those grapevines that are more than 30 years of age. The term "old vines" is occasionally used on wine labels to indicate the use of such grapevines in the making of said wine.

OLEOSO (ITAL OR PORT)   Oily. *See* Mousy.

ÖLIG (GERM)   *See* Mousy.

OLFACTION   The sense of smell and the act of smelling. Also known as *olfacto*.

OLFACTO (PORT)   The nose or aroma/bouquet of a wine or beer.

OLFACTORY   To do with the sense of smell.

OLIGOMINERALE (ITAL)   *See* Mineral Water.

OLOROSO (SP)   One of two basic types of sherry that is dark amber to walnut in color, semisweet, and full-bodied.

OLPE (GREECE)   A small pitcher-like vessel used for serving wine. Also known as *oinochoe*.

OLTREPÒ PAVESE (ITAL)   One of three major wine-producing areas located in the northern region of Lombardy. Oltrepò Pavese was once part of Piedmont and is also referred to as "Vecchio Piemonte," or Old Piedmont. This area has for the past century been Milan's chief supplier of Barbera and Bonarda wines.

Centering around the city of Pavia, the Oltrepò Pavese has, since antiquity, been renowned for the abundance of its wines. So much wine has been produced there that by the Middle Ages area producers were already exporting their wines across the Alps to offset surplus production.

The principal grape varieties of the area cultivated exclusively in hillside vineyards are both red: Barbera and Bonarda (also known as *Croatina*). Increasing amounts of vineyard space, however, are being devoted to such white varieties as Riesling Italico, Riesling Renano, Moscato Bianco, Pinot Grigio, Chardonnay, and Müller Thurgau. Pinot Nero and Uva Rara (red grapes) are also grown.

OLUTEZA   The Finnish word for beer.

ONCTUEUX (FR)   A term generally applied to wines that are full-bodied, generally sweet, and fat and rich.

ONDENC (FR)   A white grape variety mostly cultivated near Bordeaux, although its total acreage has dwindled significantly in recent years.

ON-OFF SALES   A retail establishment licensed to not only sell and serve alcoholic beverages for "on-premise" consumption, but also is permitted by the license to offer certain types of alcoholic beverages for "off-premise" consumption elsewhere.

ON-PREMISE RETAIL DEALER   *See* On-Premise Outlets.

ON-PREMISE OUTLETS   (On Sale) Retail establishments where alcoholic beverages are consumed on the premises—generally taverns, bars and grills, restaurants, clubs, and so forth. In some states these outlets also have licenses to sell for off-premise consumption. Also known as *on-premise retail dealer*.

ONTARIO   A white grape variety developed in 1908 from a cross of Winchell and Diamond, at the Experimental Station of New York.

The clusters are large and loosely formed with above average quality berries that are light yellow in color.

264

ON-THE-ROCKS   Wine or a cocktail served over ice cubes.

ON-THE-ROCKS GLASS   *See* Old-Fashioned Glass.

ON THE YEAST   Period during secondary fermentation when yeast cells are allowed to remain in contact with the wine, thereby contributing to traditional "yeasty" nose of champagne. The process may last anywhere from three weeks to several years, depending on the producer.

OOLONG   A dark tea from China and Taiwan that is a cross between black fermented tea and green unfermented tea, which is partly fermented before being dried out. It is also a large, distinctive leaf of unique character and fragrance likened to "ripe" peaches.

OP (ITAL)   Old Particular: A type of marsala *superiore* wine.

OPAQUE   Absence of light; often used when referring to dark red wines or stout.

OPEN BAR   *See* Host Bar.

OPEN CONTAINER LAW   Ordinance in some communities that prohibits the drinking of alcoholic beverages on sidewalks and in public areas.

OPENING INVENTORY   The dollar value of the amount of goods on hand at the beginning of a given period.

OPEN STATE   *See* License State.

OPORTO (PORT)   A seaport city in northern Portugal, on the Douro River, famous for its production of *port*, a fortified wine.

OPÓS (GREECE)   Sap.

OPPENHEIM (GERM) An important vineyard village of the Rheinhessen famous for its production of white wines made primarily from the Sylvaner grape.

OPTIMA (GERM) A white grape variety developed in 1970, from a cross of (Sylvaner and Johannisberg Riesling) and Müller-Thurgau, at the Geilweilerhof Grape Research Institute, located in the Rheinpfalz.

ORANGEADE A drink made with orange juice, water, and a sweetener. Also known as *orange crush*.

ORANGE BITTERS Concentrated orange-flavored bitters, containing herbs, used in cocktails.

ORANGE BLOSSOM A cocktail that is the same as a "screwdriver," except that gin is substituted for the vodka.

ORANGE CRUSH *See* Orangeade.

ORANGE FLOWER WATER A flavoring extract from an orange zest often used in cocktails.

ORANGE JUICE The liquid constituent of an orange.

ORANGE MUSCAT A white *Vitis vinifera* grape variety mostly cultivated in California where it is utilized in the production of dessert wines.

ORANGE PEKOE A fine grade of black tea of China, Sri Lanka (Ceylon), and India, made from delicate, medium-sized leaves, slightly larger than pekoe. The term does not refer to a type or flavor of tea, but rather a leaf grade or size term.

Broken orange pekoe refers to the high-quality small leaves and tips separated from the batch through mechanical sieves. At its best, orange pekoe has a rich body and flavor. *See* Pekoe.

ORANGE SODA A soft drink usually made with carbonated water, sugar or sweetener, caramel coloring, acids, and a syrup made from oils of oranges.

ORANIENSTEINER (GERM) A white grape variety developed in Geisenheim from a cross of Johannisberg Riesling and Sylvaner.

ORDER FORM A form utilized to record items ordered from each purveyor, acting as a check for verification when items are received.

ORDINAIRE (FR) *See* Vin Ordinaire.

ORDINARY A common wine or beer without any special breed, however sound it may be. Generally applied to wines or beers meant for everyday consumption; opposite of complex. Also known as *ordinaire* and *simple*.

ORGANIC Wines made from organically-grown grapes, vinified naturally, but that have had minimum sulfite additions at bottling.

ORGANICALLY GROWN Wines made from organically-grown grapes, but traditionally vinified, that contain sulfites.

ORGANOLEPTIQUE (FR) *See* Organoleptic.

ORGANOLEPTIC   The evaluation of all types of beverages in an analytical context by utilization of the senses: sight, smell, taste, and tactile or viscous perceptions. Also known as *organoleptique* and *sensory evaluation.*

ORGEAT   A sweet-almond-flavored nonalcoholic syrup used in certain cocktails. It is a combination of almond flavoring, orange flower water, and barley water.

ORIGINALABFÜLLUNG (GERM)   Label terminology used prior to 1971 to indicate an estate-bottled wine. The term was replaced with *erzeugerabfüllung.*

ORO (ITAL)   Gold.

ORRIS ROOT   A root sometimes used in the nineteenth century by the French to restore the perfume to Bordeaux wines destroyed by blending or mixing.

ORTEGA (GERM)   A white grape variety developed in 1971 in Würzburg from a cross of Müller-Thurgau and Siegerrebe, and reportedly named after "the Spanish philosopher Jose Ortega y Gasset." Its wines tend to be full and aromatic, with balanced acidity.

ORTSTEIL (GERM)   A geographic portion of a wine-producing commune.

ORUJO (SP)   *See* Grappa.

ORVIETO (ITAL)   Orvieto is named for the city in southwestern Umbria, where its wines are produced in the Paglia and Upper Tiber valleys, as well as throughout the province of Terni. The Orvieto Classico area is in the heart of this DOC zone.

Orvieto is a crisp, straw-colored white wine best consumed very young and is made from 50 to 65 percent Procanico grapes (also known as Trebbiano Toscano) and 15 to 25 percent Verdello, with the rest a blend of Grechetto, Drupeggio, and Malvasia Toscano grapes. It is produced in both *secco* (dry) and *abboccato* (semidry) styles.

OSAP   Office of Substance Abuse Prevention.

OSMOSIS   The tendency of a solution to pass through a semipermeable membrane from areas of weaker to higher concentrations in an effort to equalize the concentrations.

OSSIDATO (ITAL)   *See* Oxidized.

OSTERREICHER (GERM)   *See* Sylvaner.

OTHELLO   A black-skinned grape variety developed in 1858 from a cross of Clinton and Black Hamburg by Charles Arnold, in Paris, Ontario, Canada. The grapes are large and black in color with a high level of *methyl anthrinilate.*

OUILLAGE (FR)   *See* Topping.

OUNCE   A U.S. liquid measurement; 16 fluid ounces being equal to one pint.

OUNCE BEVERAGE CONTROL SYSTEM   An automated system that is pre-programmed to analyze and record beverage sales by number and type of drinks dispensed, as well as calculate the actual consumption of each type of beverage through the use of figures generated by physical inventories and issues. Also known as *ounce beverage control technique* and *ounce control method*.

Ounce Beverage Control Technique *See* Ounce Beverage Control System.

Ounce Control Method *See* Ounce Beverage Control System.

Outras Castas (port) Varieties of grapevines that are not *Vitis vinifera*.

Ouvrée (fr) An old Burgundian vineyard term for a measure of 0.0428 hectares or one-tenth of an acre.

Ouzo (greece) It is a liqueur with a licorice-like flavor. It has a brandy base, and its sweet fragrant flavor comes from either cold flavoring the distilled spirit with aniseed (*Pimpinella anisum*) or by distilling pure aniseed-flavored distilled spirit with gentian root and other herbs. It is drier than anisette and is higher in alcohol—mostly in the 90 degree range. Found in all the Mediterranean countries, where it is usually taken with water or served on rocks, which turns it an opalescent, milky, yellowish-white. *See* Anise-Based Spirits and Masticha.

Oven Ready The product ready to be cooked; it may be purchased with this specification, or it may be fabricated in the restaurant.

Overaged Refers to a wine that has been aged longer than necessary, either in the barrel or glass bottle.

Overcropping The growing of more grape clusters than a grapevine can bring to maturity at normal harvest time, or can yield and have remain healthy. This can result from disease, insects, light pruning, or water stress.

Over-Fining A condition that exists when a fining agent is used in excess, which actually causes further hazing instead of clearing wine.

Overpouring The pouring of an excessive quantity of an alcoholic beverage to a customer that does not adhere to a standardized recipe. *See* Burned Drinks.

Overproduction The production of a quantity that exceeds normal needs or demands.

Overproof A distilled spirit whose alcoholic content is more than 100 proof.

Overripe A term applied to grapes left on the grapevine beyond normal maturity, causing the berries to dry out, concentrating their flavor. Generally, wines made from these grapes tend to be heavy, unbalanced, and lacking acidity. However, some grapes, notably Zinfandel, often benefit from some overripeness during harvest. Also known as *surmaturité*.

Over-The-Hill *See* Old.

Own Production When used with reference to wine in a bonded winery, the term means wine produced by fermentation in the same bonded winery, whether or not produced by a predecessor in interest at the bonded winery.

The term includes wine produced by fermentation in bonded wineries owned or controlled by the same or affiliated persons or firms when located within the same state.

OWN-ROOTED   A grapevine grown from a cutting on its own root system that develops its own root system, as opposed to grafted or budded rootstocks.

OXIDASE   Any of a group of enzymes that causes browning of fresh fruit and that is particularly abundant in damaged or moldy fruit. It is easily destroyed by heat, sulfur dioxide, or Vitamin C. Fruits high in Vitamin C do not brown easily or only after the vitamin has been destroyed during the course of the fermentation.

OXIDATION   A chemical change in alcoholic beverages due to exposure of excessive oxygen during aging in barrel, while in glass, or from a bad cork. Oxidation causes a loss of freshness in both smell and taste, while causing a browning of the color. Also known as *luftgeschmack* and *oxidation*. *See* Cooked, Cotto, and Maderized.

OXIDIZED   A condition of oxidation.

OXYDATION (FR)   Oxidation; beneficial in the glass for a wine or brandy, but detrimental to wine or brandy in a partially empty bottle, that is kept for a long time.

P   A letter designation used on labels of Armagnac, cognac, and some other brandies as an abbreviation for *pale*.

PA   *See* Promotional Allowance.

PACKAGE   The container that holds beer (either a bottle or can), wine, or distilled spirits.

PACKER   A proprietor of wine premises who fills wine into a container larger than four liters.

PAID BAR   A private room bar setup where all drinks are prepaid. Tickets for drinks are sometimes used.

PAGLIERINO (ITAL)   *See* Straw.

PAGO (SP)   The area of a vineyard or a distinctly named vine yard.

PAKHYS (GREECE)   *See* Fat.

PALATE   In organoleptic evaluation, the sense of taste in the mouth as an entity.

PALATABILITY   Agreeable to the taste.

PALATINATE (GERM)   The largest wine-producing region in Germany, located along the Rhine River to the east, France to the south and southwest, the Mosel-Saar-Ruwer to the west, and the Rheinhessen to the north. The Palatinate (also called the *Rheinpfalz*) produces almost exclusively white wines made from Sylvaner, Müller-Thurgau, and Johannisberg Riesling grape varieties.

PALE (P)   A designation used on labels of Armagnac, cognac, and some other brandies to indicate a *pale* color (not in a negative sense).

PALE   A term used to describe the lighter color of ale (or some other types of beer) in its relationship to porter or stout.

PALE   A wine that is deficient in color or intensity of color. Also known as *pallid* and *pallido*.

PALE ALE (ENG)   A copper-colored ale, usually full-bodied, highly hopped, and quite bitter.

PALE CREAM (SP)   A pale-colored cream sherry.

PALE DRY   Dry and light-colored.

PALHETE (PORT)   The term for Rainwater Madeira, a very pale, light, fortified wine. The term is derived from the word *palha*, meaning straw. Also spelled *palhetinho*. *See* Rainwater Madeira.

PALHETINHO (PORT)   *See* Palhete.

PALLET   Low-set, portable stand, generally made of wood, on which supplies can be stacked to keep them off the floor.

PALLID   *See* Pale.

PALLIDO (ITAL)   *See* Pale.

PALMA (SP)   A high-quality fino sherry.

270

PALMA (SP)   Special chalk marks placed on wooden barrels containing sherry wine, that denote a developing fino sherry.

PALMCHAM   A carbonated wine produced from the juice of the adoka tree in Ghana, South Africa.

PALO CORTADO (SP)   A true rarity among sherries. Although there is no literal translation for Palo Cortado, these sherries have been described as an intermediate classification...the lightest of the olorosos. Palo Cortado has a very fresh and clean bouquet, somewhat resembling a well-made amontillado, yet its taste is reminiscent of a full-bodied oloroso.

   Like all fine sherries, the Palo Cortados are produced from Palomino grapes, which are grown in the chalky albariza soil unique to the Sherry region. They do not develop any type of "flor" and are quite rare. Of a thousand barrels, perhaps only one will develop the distinctive color of brushed gold and the bouquet of almonds, an amontillado nose and oloroso body, characteristic of Palo Cortados. Therefore, a sherry producer cannot produce this style of sherry every year, and its production amounts to less than 1 percent of the total. The production of Palo Cortado was greatly cut by the devastation of *Phylloxera* during the 1870s.

PALOMINO (SP)   A white grape variety that is pale in color, fairly large, and grows predominantly in *albariza* soil. This grape is used in the production of 85 percent of all sherry wine. The grape is also cultivated in South Africa and California, where it is also used to produce "sherry-type" wines.

   The grape is also known locally by many different names, such as *Listan*, in Sanlúcar; *Horgazuela*, in Puerto de Santa Maria; and *Alban*, *Temprana*, and *Tempranilla* in other areas. In South Africa it is known as *Fransdruif*.

PANIER À VENDANGE (FR)   Small straw baskets used by grape pickers in Burgundy and Champagne. *See* Brenta.

PANSA BLANCA (SP)   *See* Xarel-lo.

PAPYRI   A 1300 B.C. Egyptian regulation of beer shops to prevent people from overindulging.

PAR   *See* Par Stock.

PARADIS (FR)   Warehouses utilized for the storage of the oldest of Cognacs, often up to 100 years of age.

PARAFFIN   A white, waxy, odorless, colorless, tasteless solid substance used for sealing small holes in wooden barrels. Also known as *waxing* and *wax lined*.

PARASITE   An organism that lives on or in the body of another organism and obtains food from it.

PARCELLE (FR)   A small parcel of land within a vineyard, usually belonging to one individual.

PARELLADA (SP)   A white grape variety that forms the basis for much of the still and sparkling wines produced. It produces light and fruity, flavorful white wines with apple/banana aromas.

PARFAIT AMOUR LIQUEUR   A sweetened alcoholic beverage consisting of a base of alcohol, minimum 2.5 percent sugar, with various flavorings, including anisette, citrus peels, coriander, flower petals, lemon, orange, rose petals, vanilla, violets, and other flavors. It is made in several colors, mainly bright violet. It is similar in color and taste to Crème de Violette and Crème Yvette.

PARING KNIFE   A small, sharp-pointed knife with a 2.5- to 3.5-inch blade, used for peeling and cutting lemons, limes, oranges, and other citrus fruit for garnishes.

PARROCO (ITAL)   Parish priest.

PAR STOCK   The minimum/maximum specified amount of a product on hand to satisfy customers' needs for a specific period of time. Usually refers to the amount of alcoholic beverages needed during a shift or business day at the bar. Also known as *bar pars* and *par*. *See* Safety Stock.

PAR STOCK LIST   An inventory of all items kept in supply, along with the quantity of each item that should always be available in stock.

PARFUM (FR)   *See* Perfume.

PARLOR CAR   A railroad car, often with individual swivel seats or tables, that serves alcoholic beverages as well as some food.

PARTICLE CORK   *See* Agglomerated Cork.

PARTICLE MATTER   Minute particles in a liquid that are held in suspension, such as dead yeast cells, grain fragments, grape pulp or skins fragments, protein matter, and so on. They are generally eliminated by means of fining agents. *See* Colloidal Suspension and Fining.

PARTIDISTA (PORT)   *See* Broker.

PARTS PER MILLION (PPM) A phrase used to indicate the number of units existing per a total of one million units. It is the same as milligrams per liter, and is often written as mg/liter.

PASADO (SP) *See* Old.

PASSABILE (ITAL) Passable; acceptable, inoffensive.

PASSAGEM (PORT) *See* Racking.

PASSÉ (FR) *See* Old.

PASSION FRUIT LIQUEUR A sweetened alcoholic beverage consisting of a base of alcohol, minimum 2.5 percent sugar, and flavored with a mixture of tropical juices and the fruit of a passion flower.

PASSERILLAGE (FR) *See* Passito.

PASSITO (ITAL) A sweet wine made from overripe grapes that have been allowed to dry or shrivel from the sun, causing higher sugar levels, which are then pressed. Also known as *passerillage* or *roti*.

PASS THROUGH A post-off that is passed through to the consumer. *See* Post-Off.

PASTEUR, LOUIS (FR) A chemist and bacteriologist (1822–1895) born in a town called Arbois, in the Jura region, and credited as conducting the first scientific study (1857) of fermentation.

PASTEURISÉ (FR) *See* Pasteurization.

PASTEURIZATION The process by which a liquid or substance is heated to a minimum of 160 degrees Fahrenheit and held at that temperature for a specified period of time to destroy bacteria and microorganisms while stabilizing the product. In the case of beer or wine (if needed), they are pasteurized after bottling, then cooled rapidly. Also known as *pasteurisé* and *thermolization*.

PASTIS (FR) A category of *anise-based distilled spirits* produced in France, whose leading brands are Pernod and Ricard. *See* Anise-Based Spirits.

PASTOSO (ITAL, PORT, OR SP) *See* Fat.

PÂTEAUX (FR) *See* Fat.

PATENT STILL A newer type of "continuous stills" that is able to produce purer distilled spirits at a faster rate and in greater quantity than older types. *See* Coffey Still, Column Still, Continuous Still, and Still.

PATRONS Another term for customers or "people" who frequent an establishment.

PAUILLAC (FR) A renowned wine-producing commune in the Haut-Médoc, north of the city of Bordeaux, where some of the greatest red wine–producing vineyards lie.

On November 14, 1936, the wines of Pauillac were officially granted their *Appellation Contrôlée* designation.

PAUVRE (FR) Poor, small.

PAUVRETÉ (FR)   Poverty; a thin brandy with little to recommend.

PAXERETE (SP)   A sweet wine made partly from the Pedro Ximénez grape variety, often used as a sweetener for sherry.

PÉ (PORT)   *See* Lees.

PEACH-FLAVORED BRANDY   A mixture of brandy, with a minimum of 2.5 percent sugar, flavored and colored with fresh and dried peaches. By federal law it cannot be bottled at less than 70 proof (35 percent alcohol by volume).

PEACH LIQUEUR   A sweetened alcoholic beverage consisting of a base of alcohol, minimum 2.5 percent sugar, and flavored and colored with fresh and dried peaches. It is sweeter and lower in proof than peach-flavored brandy.

PEACHES   An odor reminiscent of peaches, occasionally detected in some young white wines like Johannisberg Riesling, Muscat, Gewürztraminer, as well as some fruity, late-picked white grape varieties that have been affected by *Botrytis cinerea*.

PEAK   A wine or beer that reached its apex for drinking (i.e., neither too young nor to old). *See* Shelf-Life.

PEAR BRANDY   *See* Poire.

273

PEAR LIQUEUR   A sweetened alcoholic beverage consisting of a base of alcohol, minimum 2.5 percent sugar, and flavored and colored with pears.

PEAR WILLIAMS   *See* Poire.

PEAT   It is a soft, not fully formed coal in a primary state; it is made up of decomposed, compacted, and carbonized vegetal material, mainly sphagnum moss mixed with mud and roots, often found in swamps. During the smoking process (Scotch whisky), the barley lies above the smoking peat on screens, which allows the burning vapors to permeate the barley, swirling around and under it. This not only dries out the barley but infuses it with a unique smoky aroma and taste.

PEAT REEK   The dark, oily, almost acrid smoke emanating from the burning or smoldering dried peat, utilized to dry and impart a flavor to green malt, in the making of Scotch whisky.

PECTIC ENZYME   A group of enzymes obtained from the pith of certain fresh citrus fruits that breaks down pectin. *See* Pectinase.

PECTIN   A water-soluble carbohydrate, obtained from certain ripe fruits, that in excess, tends to cause cloudiness in wine. It can be eliminated by the use of pectic enzyme. *See* Pectic Enzyme and Pectinase.

PECTINASE   An enzyme used to clarify and stabilize wine and to facilitate separation of juice from the fruit. *See* Pectic Enzyme, Pectic Haze, and Pectin.

PECTIN HAZE   A haze occasionally encountered in wine caused by excessive levels of pectin. *See* Pectic Enzyme.

PÉ DE CUBA (PORT)   *See* Pied De Cuve.

PEDICEL   The stalk or small stem of a grapevine, that attaches the grape berry to the cluster structure.

PEDRO XIMÉNEZ (SP)   A moderate-sized, white grape variety that is used in the making of sweet wines, especially sherry.

The Pedro Ximénez grapes that grow on the lower slopes of the *albariza* and *barro* type soil are left outside in the sun, for 12 to 14 hours to dry after harvesting, which concentrates their sugar levels. They are then placed on esporto mats (made of grass) to further dry. So intense is their sweetness that fermentation usually stops at about 14 percent alcohol, resulting in a high degree of residual sugar. The color is usually rich and dark brown and liqueur-like in its concentration. It is traditionally served after meals in place of a brandy or cordial. Abbreviated *PX*.

PEDUNCLE   The botanical term for the thick stalk by which a bunch of grapes is attached to the cane on a grapevine. This stalk is a valuable source of tannin in red wine.

PEEL   A shape of citrus fruit that contains the outer layer (zest) and inner, bitter layer (pith). Also known as *skin*.

PEG   A small glass used for whiskey that holds the equivalent of about 1.5 fluid ounces. In England, it is a drink usually made with brandy or whiskey and soda water.

PEKOE   A fine grade of black tea of Ceylon and India, made from the small leaves at the tips of the stems. *See* Orange Pekoe.

PELURE D'OIGNON (FR)   A very light-colored wine, similar to that of an onion skin.

PENN, WILLIAM   The famous American statesman was probably the first to operate (in 1638) a brewery on a large commercial scale; it was located in Pennsbury, Bucks County, Pennsylvania.

PENTOSE ($C_5H_{10}O_5$)   Any of a group of monosaccharides (simple sugar) with five atoms of carbon in the molecule, including ribose, arabinose, and so on. *See* Reducing Sugar.

PEPPERMINT LIQUEUR   A sweetened alcoholic beverage consisting of a base of alcohol, minimum 2.5 percent sugar, and flavored and colored with peppermint.

PEPPERMINT SCHNAPPS   A colorless, mint-flavored liqueur, with the sugar content about half of that of white crème de menthe. It is also higher in proof.

PEPPERY   An aromatic smell or taste, evocative of black pepper, herbs, or spices, with a pungent flavor. A biting harshness, possibly due to hard tannins and high alcohol, that may dissipate or become smoother with additional age. Noticeable in young ruby and vintage ports and many young, full-bodied red wines.

PEPTONIZE   To digest, dissolve, or metabolize through fermentation.

PERCEIVED COST The customer's perception of how much money a bottle of wine or other alcoholic beverage should cost, distinct from what the producer may believe it is worth.

PERCEIVED VALUE The customer's perception of how much money a bottle of wine or other alcoholic beverage is worth, distinct from what the producer may believe it is worth.

PERCENT OR PERCENTAGE Percent by volume.

PERCENTAGE METHOD A method of calculating a figure (wholesale or selling price), using percentages rather than dollar values.

PERCEPTION The complete process of receiving information through one of the senses, comparing this information with past experiences, identifying and evaluating it, and storing it for future reference.

PERCOLATION The percolation method of producing liqueurs is similar to the percolation of coffee. Distilled spirits are put into the bottom of a tank, and the botanicals (fruits, flowers, etc.) are placed in a basket-like container, tray, or bag at the top of the tank. The distilled spirits from the bottom of the tank are then pumped to the top where they are sprayed over the botanicals, dripping back to the bottom to be repercolated over and over until the desired flavor has been extracted. The final product is called an *extract*.

PERFUME An organoleptic term referring usually to the floral or flowery olfactory sensations sometimes encountered in the aroma and bouquet of some white wines, notably Johannisberg Riesling, Gewürztraminer, and Muscat. Perfume can also be detected in some beers and distilled spirits, especially liqueurs. Also known as *parfum*.

PERISHABLE Subsistence that deteriorates readily if not properly treated or refrigerated.

PERLAGE It refers to the bubbles in a glass of sparkling wine and how long they persist. Also known as *perlaggio*.

PERLAGGIO (ITAL) *See* Perlage.

PERLANT (FR) Pearling; a slightly sparkling wine, but less so than pétillant and crémant, and much less than mousseux. In France, the wine usually contains 1.5 to 2.5 atmospheres of pressure.

PERLE (GERM) A white grape variety developed in Alzey in the Rheinhessen, from a cross of Gewürztraminer and Müller-Thurgau. The wines are mild and flowery smelling.

PERLWEIN (GERM) An artificially carbonated sparkling wine containing 2.5 atmospheres of pressure. *See* Artificially Carbonated Wine.

PERMITTEE *See* Licensee.

PERNAND-VERGELESSES (FR) A small village town just north of Aloxe-Corton and adjacent to Corton-Charlemagne in Burgundy's Côte de Beaune, which produces good quality red and white wines.

PERONOSPORA *See* Downy Mildew.

PERPETUAL INVENTORY A daily, ongoing bookkeeping system that adds to and subtracts from the inventory as bottles enter and leave the storeroom.

PERRICONE (ITAL) A red grape variety grown in Sicily. Also known as *Pignatello*.

PERRY A sparkling wine, produced in England, which is made from pears.

PERSISTANCE (FR) *See* Persistence.

PERSISTENCE A term that refers to one of the characteristics of a very good wine—the length of time that the bouquet and the flavor of a wine or beer remains after being swallowed. Also known as *persistance* and *persistenza*.

PERSISTENZA (ITAL) *See* Persistence.

PERSONAL SELLING It is the person-to-person or one-on-one personalized communication by which the attributes or benefits of a given product or service are conveyed.

PESANTE (ITAL) *See* Flat.

276

PESSAC-LÉOGNAN (FR) An *appellation contrôlée* established in 1987 that applies only to those red and white wines that are produced in the northern ten communes of Graves, located southwest of the city of Bordeaux. It was recognized that these ten communes consistently produced superior quality wines than those further south.

PESTICIDE Any chemical compound used to kill insects and other vermin. *See* Insecticide.

PETER MINUIT *See* Minuit, Peter.

PÉTILLANT (FR) *See* Spritz.

PETIOLE The stem portion of a leaf that attaches the leaf blade to the shoot on a grapevine.

PETIOLE ANALYSIS By taking a sample of the *petiole* and analyzing it, viticulturists can determine the current nutritional status of the entire grapevine.

PETIT (FR) Small; little in the sense of body, alcohol, and other constituents.

PETIT CHABLIS (FR) A lesser appellation in Chablis made from the chardonnay grape variety, which, according to AOC regulations, must attain 9.5-percent alcohol. It is the simplest of the four classifications, accounting for less than 10 percent of production, and is rarely exported to the United States.

PETIT CHÂTEAU (FR) A term with many meanings depending on where it used. In Bordeaux it denotes some of the lesser proper ties (not from the 1855 Classification); in the United States it is used when referring to *cru bourgeois* wines or other wines from Bordeaux.

PETITE CHAMPAGNE OR PETITE FINE CHAMPAGNE (FR) These terms mean that the cognac is a blend made from grapes grown in the Grande Champagne and Petite Champagne sections of Cognac; at least 50 percent of it must be from grapes grown in the Grande Champagne section.

PETITE PINOT   *See* Mondeuse Noire.

PETITE SIRAH   *See* Durif.

PETITE SYRAH (FR)   *See* Syrah.

PETIT GAMAI   *See* Gamay.

PETIT VERDOT   A red *Vitis vinifera* grape variety mostly cultivated in the Médoc, in the Bordeaux region of France where it is used in small amounts as a blending grape, along with Cabernet Sauvignon and Merlot. Small parcels of Petit Verdot are planted in California and Chile where there, too, it is utilized as a blending grape. Also known as *Verdot*.

PETTY CASH   A small cash fund used in a beverage operation for small incidental expenses that do not warrant a formal purchase order.

PEYCHAUD'S   A type of bitters produced in New Orleans, used almost exclusively in the Sazerac cocktail.

PEZSGO (HUN)   *See* Sparkling Wine.

PFLÜMLI (SWISS)   A prune brandy.

PH   The "Potential of Hydrogen." The concept of pH was introduced in 1909 by the Danish chemist Sorensen as an expedient means of expressing the hydrogen ion concentration in a solution. "P" symbolized the Danish word *potenz* (power) and "H" represented hydrogen. pH serves, therefore, as shorthand for "acid power." The definition would be the logarithm of the reciprocal of the hydrogen-ion concentration in gram equivalents per liter of solution, on a scale whose values run from 0 to 14, with 7 representing neutrality; numbers less than 7 increasing acidity and numbers greater than 7 increasing alkalinity.

PHENOLS   They are a group of more than 100 related compounds that occur naturally in wine grapes, mostly in the skins, seeds, and stems. Although winemakers often use "tannins" and "phenols" interchangeably, tannins are a subclass of phenols—admittedly, a very large and important one. About 6 percent of the total phenolic content of red and white grapes is in the juice and pulp. The rest is in the skins and seeds; therefore, the integrity of the grape skin becomes an important concept in winemaking. *See* Phenolics, Tannin, and Astringency.

PHENOLICS   They are generally categorized into two major groups: flavonoids and non-flavonoids. The flavonoid group consists of *tannin* (often expressed as gallic acid) and a number of *catechin* compounds, which are bitter and often involved with browning. Among other subgroups, the flavonoids also include the anthocyanin (red) and leucoanthocyanin (white) color pigment compounds. The non-flavonoids are a much smaller and less important group of phenolics, existing primarily as derivatives of the aromatic compound, cinnamic acid.

When complex structures are formed from primary phenols, such as in grapes during maturation and in winemaking processes, such compounds are called phenolics. *See* Phenols, Tannin, and Astringency.

PHOSPHATES *See* Nutrients.

PHOTOSYNTHESIS The process by which grapevines are able to manufacture carbohydrates by combining carbon dioxide from the air and water from the soil, utilizing light energy in the presence of chlorophyll in the leaves. This in turn nourishes both the grapevine and the fruit it bears. *See* Chlorophyll.

PHYLLOXERA VASTATRIX A native eastern and southern United States aphid-like pest, which lives on wild grapevine species that have varying levels of tolerance or resistance to it. It is a parasitic, microscopic, burrowing plant louse, yellowish in color, that eats away at the roots of grapevines. This insect, *Daktulosphaira vitifoliae* (identified by Dr. Asa Fitch in his book "The Noxious, Beneficial, and Other Insects of the State of New York" in 1856), was moved to Europe and California during the last century on cuttings from some of these grapevine species. It decimated vineyards in those areas, beginning in the 1860s, because the wine grapevine *Vitis vinifera* is highly suspectible to infestation. It is speculated that *Phylloxera* was accidentally exported to Europe on some grapevine cuttings that were actually sent to help control the spread of powdery mildew.

278

PHYSICAL INVENTORY A physical bottle-by-bottle count of stock physically on the premises at the end of an accounting period.

PHYTOTOXIC Causing injury or death of grapevines or parts of grapevines.

PICARDAN NOIR (FR) The local name for Cinsaut grape variety in the Rhône Valley.

PICHET (FR) A small, opaque carafe, decanter, or jug popular in restaurants.

PICKLED Slang for intoxicated.

PICK-UP STATION A section of the front of the bar where servers place orders for drinks, receive drinks, turn in collected monies, and return empty glasses.

PICOLIT (ITAL) A brightly golden-colored dessert wine, produced in dry, semidry, and sweet versions (without the help of *Botrytis cinerea*, known as *muffa nobile* or *noble rot*). The sweet version is made from dried grapes (called *passito*). Picolit commands extremely high prices; the dry and semidry types are best consumed when 3 to 8 years old; the sweet version is best consumed when 7 to 12 years old.

Picolit grapevines thrived in Friuli during the late 1700s, and by the mid-nineteenth century produced the most prestigious wines of Italy, bottles of which graced the tables of royalty throughout England, France, Russia, and Austria.

Unfortunately, the grapevine in later years produced very few grapes and was thought to have a genetic disease called *floral abortion*. Modern research conducted by Dr. Giovanni Cargnello at the Conegliano Institute, however, discovered that the Picolit grape variety is not self-pollinating, because it is purely female, and not, as is usual, hermaphroditic. Technically, Picolit is known as *Picolit Giallo*.

PICOTENER (ITAL)   *See* Nebbiolo.

PICPOUL   *See* Folle Blanche.

PICPOULE   *See* Folle Blanche.

PICULTENER (ITAL)   *See* Nebbiolo.

PIÈCE (FR)   A barrel with a capacity of 55 to 60 U.S. gallons, used in various parts of France for storage of wines. *See* Barrel.

PIECE   During the early 1800s, a term used to denote 250 bottles of wine.

PIED (FR)   Individual grapevines.

PIED DE CUVE (FR)   Previously fermenting wine that is rich in yeast is added to a barrel of *must* to help start a new fermentation. Also known as *pé de cuba*.

PIEDMONT (ITAL)   One of Italy's 20 wine-producing regions, located in the northwest, bordered by France to the west and Switzerland to the north. The Ligurian Apennines and the Alps surround Piedmont to the south, west, and north.

Piedmont is actually a contraction of the dialectical words "A Pie' Di Monte" (at the foot of the mountains). It has been producing good to excellent wines for well over a century and has used the most underrated wine grape in the world, the Nebbiolo.

Piedmont produces the greatest number of superb red wines in Italy. The production of both DOC and non-DOC wines is concentrated in the southern part of Piedmont in the provinces of Cuneo, Asti, and Alessandria. This area of exclusively hilly vineyards accounts for 90 percent of the total regional output. Other areas of production are the hills between the towns of Novara and Vercelli and the zone around the regional capital of Turin. Known as *Piemonte*, in Italy.

PIED TENDRE (FR)   *See* Colombard.

PIEMONTE (ITAL)   *See* Piedmont.

PIENO (ITAL)   Full; with richness and body.

PIEPRZÓWKA (POL)   A pepper-flavored vodka.

PIERCE'S DISEASE   A bacteria, transmitted by the sharpshooter, a large leaf-hopper, that destroys the grapevines. At one time it was called Anaheim Disease and California Vine Disease. The disease was first discovered by Newton B. Pierce, a U.S. Department of Agriculture plant pathologist assigned to the West Coast to study the problem, who reported in 1892 on detailed studies and observations that are the basis of our present-day understanding of this serious disease.

PIERRE-À-FUSIL (GERM) *See* Gun Flint.

PIESPORT (GERM) A famous vineyard town located in the Middle Mosel, noted for its production of light and delicate white wines.

PIGIATURA (ITAL) *See* Crushing.

PIGMENT *See* Anthocyanin.

PIGNATELLO (ITAL) *See* Perricone.

PIKANT (GERM) Intriguing or attractive in a tangy, spicy sort of sense.

PIKRÓS (GREECE) *See* Bitter.

PILFERAGE Stealing, especially in small quantities.

PILSENER *See* Pilsner.

PILSNER This is the most popular type or style of beer produced in the world. The word *Pilsner* is taken from the Czech town of Pilsen. Characteristically, these beers are light golden color, with a highly pronounced hops (referred to as *Bohemian*) flavor and a delightfully clean, crispy taste that refreshes and leaves the palate clean. Pilsner-style beers are usually dry to very dry in taste, although there are some slightly sweet pilsners produced. Pilsners are ideally served at 38 degrees to 45 degrees Fahrenheit. Also spelled *pilsener*.

PILSNER GLASS A tall, conical-shaped beer glass with a short stem and a full funnel-shaped bowl.

PIMM'S CUP A premixed bottled drink flavored with various herbs, spices, and sweeteners, invented in 1841 by James Pimm, in London. Years back, Pimm's Cup was produced in six different versions, each with a different base ingredient, and identified by a number of the label. For instance: Pimm's Cup #1,2,3,4,5,6. But because the gin version (No. 1) comprised 99 percent of total sales, the other variations were dropped in 1974.

PIN A barrel used in old England with a capacity of approximately four and one-half gallons. *See* Barrel.

PIÑA (SP) The *heart* the agave plant, used in the production of tequila and mezcal.

PIÑA COLADA A cocktail consisting of rum, pineapple juice, and coconut milk.

PINARD (FR) Slang for an ordinary red wine.

PINEAPPLE An odor occasionally encountered in some white wines, notably Johannisberg Riesling and Chenin Blanc, which is an ester, chemically formed from ethyl butyrate (ethyl alcohol + butyric acid).

PINEAPPLE JUICE The liquid constituent of a pineapple.

PINEAU DES CHARENTES (FR) *See* Mistelle and Ratafia.

PINEAU D' AUNIS (FR)   A red grape variety used to make rosé and red wines in Anjou.

PINEAU DE LA LOIRE (FR)   *See* Chenin Blanc.

PINOT   The name of a great grape wine family that includes such subdivisions as Blanc, Gris, Noir, St. George, and others.

PINOTAGE   A red grape variety developed in 1925 from a cross of Pinot Noir and Cinsaut, by Professor A.J. Perold in South Africa. The grapes yield deeply-colored red wines with an intense aroma and full flavor, approaching some of the fullest-bodied red wines of South Africa.

PINOT AUXERROIS (FR)   *See* Auxerrois Blanc.

PINOT BEUROT (FR)   *See* Pinot Gris.

PINOT BIANCO (ITAL)   *See* Pinot Blanc.

PINOT BLANC   A white *Vitis vinifera* grape variety with some similarities of chardonnay, producing wines that are crisp, fresh, and supple, with a floral bouquet. Pinot Blanc is cultivated in some parts of California, where it is used in sparkling wine production; however, it is grown prolifically in Alsace, France and the northern regions of Italy. It is known locally in Alsace, France as *Clevner*, in Italy as *Pinot Bianco*, and in Austria and Germany as *Weissburgunder*.

PINOT CHARDONNAY   *See* Chardonnay.

PINOT GRIGIO (ITAL)   *See* Pinot Gris.

PINOT GRIS   A white *Vitis vinifera* grape variety that produces wines that are well-balanced and full-bodied. They can be fruity, but that sensation on the palate is followed by a luscious, slightly smoky, absolutely dry finish. Pinot Gris, which is also called *Tokay d'Alsace*, is not to be confused with Hungarian Tokay; with that in mind, the European Economic Community (EEC) has banned the use of the name Tokay in Alsace, France. Also known as *Auxerrois Gris*, *Szürkebarat*, *Grauer Burgunder*, *Malvoisie* (it stems from pre-thirteenth century words derived from Monemvasia, a small Greek village), *Pinot Beurot*, *Pinot Grigio*, and, in Baden, Germany, *Rülander*.

PINOT MEUNIER   *See* Meunier.

PINOT NERO (ITAL)   *See* Pinot Noir.

PINOT NOIR   A red *Vitis vinifera* grape variety grown mostly in Burgundy, France, where it produces some of the finest wines in the world, and is also vinified, along with Meunier and Chardonnay, to produce Champagne. In addition, Pinot Noir is also extensively planted throughout the world, especially in Italy and California.

The Pinot Noir grapevine produces small compact clusters of small thin-skinned berries. The yield is low and difficult to pick because of the many small bunches. It is also an early ripener, so it usually avoids the rains that would be very damaging.

Pinot Noir wines are medium to deep ruby-red, with a distinctive aroma of mint or black cherry. They are soft, with a velvety texture, and rich, with a full finish.

There are many clones of Pinot Noir that differ measurably in fruitiness, cluster size, shape, and color intensity. Depending on the microclimate, clonal recognition becomes very important when planting a new vineyard.

Also known as *Blauburgunder*, *Blauer Spätburgunder*, *Borgogno Nero*, *Nagyburgundi*, *Noirien*, *Pinot Nero*, *Plant Doré*, *Spätburgunder*, and *Savagnin Noir*.

PINOT ST-GEORGE   A red *Vitis vinifera* grape variety cultivated almost exclusively in parts of France where it is mostly used for blending. Small quantities are planted in California where it produces fairly good wines, approaching Pinot Noir in style. Correctly known as *Negrétte*.

PIN-POINT BUBBLES   Tiny bubbles resembling continuous "chains of beads," emanating from a glass of sparkling wine or even beer. A finer and smaller bubble usually indicates a superior quality product. *See* Beads.

PINT   A United States liquid measurement of volume; equal to 16 fluid ounces (⅛ of a gallon or 0.568 liters).

PINTA (ITAL)   A bottle with the capacity of two liters, used in the Piedmont region.

PIPA (SP)   Pip. *See* Seeds.

PIPE   A barrel used to store or ship Madeira, Marsala, Port, and other fortified wines. It varies in proportion to the area in which it is used. Its capacity ranges from 418 to 534 liters (110 to 141 U.S. gallons). *See* Barrel.

PIPE   An English wine measure of 1497 stated that a pipe had a capacity of two hogshead or 126 gallons. *See* Barrel.

PIPELING   Part of the three-tier distribution network of alcoholic beverages, where a producer sells through to a wholesaler (distributor) of a certain product, without necessity of that wholesaler distributing said merchandise to retailers.

PIPS   An antiquated term for the *seeds* or pits contained in a grape berry. *See* Seeds.

PIQUANT   A term that describes a wine that is agreeably pungent, tart, or stimulating to the taste; pleasantly sharp or biting due to its lively acidity.

PIQUÉ (FR)   *See* Volatile Acidity.

PIQÛRE ACÉTIQUE (FR)   *See* Flowers of Wine.

PIQUERA (SP)   An open hole in the middle of the frontal side of the "lagar" (primary fermentation tank), through which the *must* flows out.

PIQUETTE (FR)   A term applied to any poor, thin, acid wine, usually produced by adding water to the pomace, then repressing. This wine is generally sold locally in large jugs.

PIRODNO (YUG)   Natural.

PIS   *See* Profit Investment Statement.

PISADOR (SP)   Men who interlock arms, then tread the grapes in the large vats, during the vintage.

PISCO   A Peruvian brandy distilled from Muscat or Mission grapes.

PISSED   Slang for intoxicated.

PITH   The bitter, white fibrous inner layer of a citrus fruit that lies directly beneath the outer skin. It is a good source of pectin.

PITS   *See* Seeds.

PIVO   The Czechoslovakian and Russian terms for beer.

PIWO (POL)   Beer.

PLANT DE GRAISSE (FR)   A white *Vitis vinifera* grape variety once quite popular in the Armagnac region, although its acreage is now fading fast. Also known as *Président*.

PLANT DORE (FR)   *See* Pinot Noir.

PLANTES NOBLES (FR)   Noble grape varieties.

PLANT GRIS (FR)   *See* Aligoté.

PLANT PROPAGATION   The reproduction of grapevines by seeds, cuttings, and so on.

PLASMOPARA VITICOLA   *See* Downy Mildew.

PLASTERED   Slang for intoxicated.

PLASTERING   A practice formerly extensively used in the sherry region of Spain, where gypsum or *yeso*, also known as *plaster of Paris* (calcium sulfate), was added to grapes or the *must* prior to fermentation, to increase the total acidity and lower the pH of the resulting wine. Also known as *plâtré*.

PLAT (FR)   Flat, dull; a term for wines that have little body, flavor, or spirit; lacking acidity and character.

PLATO   The term often used in brewing to designate the percent of fermentable solids in the mash. *See* Brix.

PLÂTRÉ (FR)   *See* Plastering.

PLEIN (FR)   Full; not just of body, but also of character.

PLEASANT   A favorable odor found in some wines.

PLIAGE (FR)   A process by which the shoots are tied to the trellis wire after pruning of the grapevine has taken place.

PLONK   A slang term for the lowest quality of wine.

PLUMP (GERM)   Clumsy; the wine is unbalanced, without character, and has high extract content.

PLUM BRANDY   *See* Mirabelle, Quetsch, Slivovitz, and Schwarzwalder.

PLUMMY   A term generally applied to red wines that are full of or tasting of plums.

PLUMS   An odor and taste occasionally detected in some late-harvested red grape varieties of higher than average sugar at harvest. A trait of some red wines, such as Zinfandel, Pinot Noir, Petite Sirah, and even some Portuguese port.

PLYMOUTH GIN   This is actually an *appellation*, and is only produced by the Coates firm of Plymouth, England, which was founded in 1798. It is an aromatic gin, sometimes pink in color from the addition of angostura bitters. Its taste lies somewhere between that of Dutch and London dry gin. Plymouth gin was originally associated with the British Royal Navy, which, as legend has it, invented this gin as a tolerable way of drinking bitters, which helped control intestinal disorders. They often mixed it with lime juice; hence the nickname "limey," which is frequently applied to the British.

Unfortunately, the production of Plymouth gin has dwindled in recent years.

PO   *See* Purchase Order.

PODERE (ITAL)   Farm, agricultural holding.

POGGIO (ITAL)   Hill.

POINTE (FR)   *See* Punt.

POINT OF PURCHASE (POP)   A display or in-house piece of advertising (e.g., a table tent, menu board) that is intended to encourage impulse on-premise sales.

POINT OF SALE (POS)   A piece of advertising posted within an establishment designed for customers' viewing and related sales.

POIO (PORT)   A terraced vineyard.

POIRE   A brandy made from pears, mostly in Switzerland, Austria, and occasionally France. The best known is Poire Williams, each bottle of which contains a fully mature Anjou pear—not an easy accomplishment. When the pear is about the size of a grape, it is placed, still on the branch, in the bottle. When the pear is mature, the branch is cut away, the pear washed, and the bottle filled with pear brandy.

Poire is a dry, high-proof brandy, usually clear or slightly amber-tinged in color. Also known as *Pear Williams* or *pear brandy*.

POKER BEER   Beer heated with a red-hot poker and often served as a winter drink. *See* Loggerhead and Mulled Wine.

POLE UNIT   Display piece supported by a cardboard pole, which can be free-standing or attached to the display.

POLISHING FILTER   The final filtering step in winemaking or brewing where the product is directed through an ultra-fine filtering medium, designed to totally clear the liquid to a shimmering brilliance. *See* Filtering.

POLLINATION   During bloom, pollen is deposited on the stigma at the top of the pistil. Each pollen grain may produce a tube that grows downward through the pistil to the embryo sac in the ovule. The male cells from the pollen tube are discharged into the embryo sac, resulting in the fertilization of the egg. This is necessary for the formation of a normal seed and eventual development of grapes.

POLSUHO (YUG)   *See* Semidry.

POLYMERIZATION   The joining together of phenolic substances.

POLYPHENOLS   There are many phenolic compounds in grapes and wine— often referred to as polyphenols. The "poly" prefix means "many" and simplifies discussion. About 65 percent of the polyphenols of the grape are contained in the seeds, while about 22 percent are in the stems, 12 percent in the skins, and only 1 percent in the pulp.

POLYSACCHARIDE   Any of a group of complex carbohydrates, such as starch, that upon hydrolysis yield more than two molecules of monosaccharides (simple sugars).

POMACE   The residual skins, stems, and seeds remaining after the grapes have been pressed until no more juice comes out when pressure is exerted, this highly compacted solid mass. The stems and skins, which are a good source of nitrogen, are loaded into trucks and dumped between the vineyard rows to decompose during the winter and be "disced" into the soil in the spring. Pomace is also known as *cake*.

POMACE BRANDY   *See* Grappa.

POMEROL (FR)   A major red wine–producing district on the right bank of the Dordogne River in Bordeaux, just northwest of Saint-Emilion. Most Pomerols are made with a predominance of the Merlot grape, which yields soft and velvety wines, with a fullness, warmth, and depth of flavor.

Although the wines of Pomerol were never officially classified, several of them would rank with the finest from Médoc. On December 8, 1936, the wines of Pomerol were officially given their *Appellation Contrôlée* designation.

POMMARD (FR)   A red wine commune in Burgundy's Côte de Beaune district, which lies between Beaune in the north and Volnay to the south. Pommard is noted for its production of fine quality red wines, which have been extremely popular in the United States, mostly because the name Pommard is easy to pronounce.

PONDEROUS   *See* Heavy.

PONIENTE (SP)   The cool, humid winds that often blow in the Sherry region.

PONY GLASS   A small, short-stemmed glass with a tubular bowl that holds approximately 1.5 fluid ounces.

POOR   A barely drinkable wine or beer with little or no merit, character, or quality. Also known as *pauvre*.

POP   *See* Soda Pop.

POP WINES The term usually refers to inexpensive, light-bodied wines that appear under proprietary labels with creative names. These wines, carbonated or slightly effervescent and low in alcohol, are made from an infusion of grape or other fruit flavors to produce a "soda pop" type of wine.

POROSITY A term that refers to the size limitation of materials that may pass through a medium. It is the ratio of the volume of a material's pores to its total volume.

PORPORA (ITAL) *See* Purple.

PORRÓN (SP) A drinking vessel with a long spout. Usually during a contest, people bet to see how far away wine can be poured (without splashing one's face, or spilling it) into one's mouth through the porrón.

PORT A heavy, full-bodied, sweet red or white fortified wine, traditionally served after dinner, is named for city of Oporto, in northern Portugal. The production of port is limited to a strictly defined area of approximately 68,000 acres along the River Douro in the Alto Douro (Upper Douro) region. The slopes of the Douro, which have a very slate-like soil known as schist, are cut out and terraced for planting with vineyards. These walled terraces prevent erosion of the precious soil.

The production and marketing of Porto are strictly controlled by the port Wine Institute. Stringent laws govern the production of all Porto, from the grapevine to the final product. An official certificate of origin is issued by the port Wine Institute after careful tasting and examination of each lot. The official guarantee seal over the neck of the bottle indicates the stamp of approval by the port Wine Institute ("Instituto do Vinho do Porto").

The name *Porto* is also specifically protected by law in the United States. Since 1968, the only wine in the United States that can be called *Porto* is the fortified wine produced in Portugal's Douro region. Therefore, if a California wine producer decided to produce a port-like wine, he may not call it *Porto*; it must simply be labeled a port.

PORTADOR (SP) A wooden container for transporting the grapes from the vineyard. *See* Brenta.

PORTAINJERTO (SP) A resistant rootstock on which the grapevine is grafted.

PORTER This is the predecessor of stout, and is characterized by its intense deep dark color and a persistent bittersweet taste and aroma. This top-fermenting beer is lower in alcohol than stout and should ideally be served at 55 degrees Fahrenheit. It was invented in 1729 by Ralph Harwood, a London brewer, who named it after the porters who enjoyed drinking it. *See* Stout.

PORTEUR (FR) A grape picker. *See* Chef de Troupe.

PORT GLASS (PORT) *See* Dock Glasses.

PORTION A standardized, measured part of a drink or quantity of drink served to one person.

PORTION CONTROL   The establishment of standards for the size, volume, and ingredients that are to be served, through procedures used to control beverage costs through the various steps of production.

PORTION CONTROL MEASUREMENT   Proper utilization of various devices such as automatic pourers, shot glasses, and so on, used to insure that each drink item will be measured out accurately, according to the standard size portion of each drink item offered.

PORTION COST   The raw, wholesale ingredient cost per drink, derived by dividing total yield by drink size to determine the number of drinks. The number of drinks is then divided into the total cost to obtain the individual drink cost. Also known as *prime ingredient cost.*

PORTION SIZE   A specified drink size to be served to a single customer. The drink size should be controlled or standardized to offer customers a consistent drink, but it also makes planning purchases and calculating profits easier.

PORTO   The shortened Portuguese name for the city of Oporto.

PORT-OF-THE-VINTAGE (PORT)   A formerly used term, now no longer permitted.

PORT OF (YEAR) (PORT)   A port of a single vintage; this is actually a tawny port, aged in wood, versus bottle-aging.

PORTS   Those places and activities normally associated with sea or aerial transportation services.

PORTUGUISER (GERM)   *See* Blauer Portugieser.

PORT WITH AN INDICATION OF AGE (PORT)   A tawny port with age (average) specified on the bottle (e.g., 10, 20, 30, and so on).

POS PLANNING FORM   A document utilized to determine the quantity and cost of national promotions for a brand in a given territory.

POSSET   A hot drink made of milk curdled with ale, wines, and so forth, usually spiced with nutmeg. The drink was popular in England from the Renaissance through the eighteenth century.

POST DOWNS   *See* Distributor Post-Off.

POSTES-GREFFES (FR)   *Phylloxera*-resistant American rootstocks on which European grapevines are grafted.

POSTMIX SODA SYSTEM   A carbonated beverage system in which water, along with tanks of carbon dioxide, and concentrated syrups are bulk purchased separately. One 5-gallon canister of postmix syrup yields approximately 3,840 fluid ounces of product at five parts carbonated water to one part syrup.

The ingredients are blended together in a beverage establishment by the use of a mechanical device (carbonator), and dispensed to customers by use of a push-button handgun.

A postmix system is normally less expensive to operate than either premix or bottles. *See* Premix.

POST-OFF   *See* Distributor Post-Off.

POSTS   *See* Distributor Post-Off.

POT (FR)   In Beaujolais, a bottle that contains approximately 16.90 fluid ounces or a two-thirds bottle of wine.

POTABLE SPIRIT   Distilled spirits fit for human consumption.

POT ALE   It is the residue left in the "wash still" after the first distillation in a "pot still" or continuous still. Also known as *burnt ale.*

POTASSIUM BENZOATE   A chemical used in carbonated soft drinks, fruit drinks, cocktail mixers, beverage syrups, cider, and wine coolers as a preservative. Its use in wine is not permitted.

POTASSIUM BITARTRATE   *See* Tartrates.

POTASSIUM METABISULPHITE   ($K_2S_2O_5$) A white crystalline powder, soluble in water, that contains approximately 57 percent by weight of sulfur dioxide SO_2. It is commonly used for sterilizing and preserving wine. *See* Campden Tablet and Sulfur Dioxide.

POTASSIUM SORBATE   Is "Generically Recognized As Safe" (GRAS) as a chemical preservative when used in accordance with good manufacturing practices. It is allowed in standard wine as a sterilizing and preservative agent and to inhibit mold growth and secondary fermentation. *See* Sorbic Acid.

POTATURA (ITAL)   *See* Pruning.

POTEEN   Illicit Irish whiskey, similar to moonshine. Also spelled *potheen.*

POTENTIAL ALCOHOL   An estimate, based on the brix readings at harvest, of the percentage of alcohol the finished wine will contain after fermentation, provided that all sugar is metabolized.

POTENTIAL BEVERAGE COST   The estimated or projected cost of a particular volume of alcoholic beverages, which will generate a given amount of sales volume. However, it must be kept in mind that the actual cost may differ.

POTENTIAL SALES VOLUME   The actual sales dollar an individual bottle of wine, beer, or distilled spirits would earn if all contents were sold.

POTHEEN   *See* Poteen.

POT STILL   The pot still resembles a large copper pot or kettle with a broad rounded base, topped by a long column. Initially, anywhere from 250 to 2,600 gallons of liquid to be distilled (depending on the still's size) are loaded into the base of the pot still. The liquid is then heated and kept simmering until the alcohol is vaporized and rises up into the column, taking with it flavors from the base liquid used; this gives the distillate its characteristic aroma and taste. When the vapor rises to a certain point in the column, it comes into contact with a cold condenser, which turns the vapor into liquid alcohol. Pot stills produce only single batches of distilled spirits. After each batch has been distilled, the pot still must be refilled again. Pot stills produce the finest quality as well as the highest priced distilled spirits, but the process is laborious and time-consuming. *See* Alambic and Still.

POUILLY-FUISSÉ (FR)   A dry, full-bodied white wine made exclusively from the Chardonnay grape in the region of Burgundy, west of Mâcon and north of Beaujolais.

POUILLY FUMÉ (FR)   A dry, full-bodied white wine made exclusively from the Sauvignon Blanc grape, in the village of Pouilly-Sur-Loire, located in the Loire Valley. Its name comes from the bloom of yeast on the grape's surface, which looks grey (fumé: smoked).

POUILLY-SUR-LOIRE (FR)   A small white wine vineyard town in the Loire Valley producing wines mostly from the Sauvignon Blanc grape, labeled *Pouilly-Fumé*.

POUILLY-VINZELLES (FR)   A white wine commune from the southern Côte Mâconnais in Burgundy, which adjoins Pouilly-Fuissé, producing white wines from the chardonnay grape variety.

POUND   U.S. measure of weight; 16 ounces equal 1 pound; 2000 pounds is called a *ton*.

POUNDS PER SQUARE INCH (PSI)   A measure of pressure.

POURER   A plastic or stainless steel device that can be fitted into the neck of a bottle (alcoholic or nonalcoholic), which permits the pouring of a "free," or predetermined, amount of liquid. *See* Free Pourer.

POURING COSTS   *See* Edible Portion.

POURRITURE (FR)   Rotting of the grapes.

POURRITURE NOBLE (FR)   *See* Botrytis Cinerea.

POULSARD (FR)   A red grape variety widely planted in Jura that produces lightly-colored wines that tend to oxidize quickly.

POUSSE-CAFÉ   A specialty after-dinner drink consisting of liqueurs floated on top of one another in layers, creating a rainbow effect. Also known as *floating liqueurs*.

POUSSE-CAFE GLASS   Straight-sided liqueur glass.

POWDERY MILDEW (UNCINULA NECATOR)   A fungal disease that was first recognized in California in 1859; however, it probably originated in Japan in the early 1800s. Powdery mildew gained notoriety when it was introduced into European vineyards (where it was called *oïdium*) in 1845 and spread rapidly throughout the continent. Uncontrolled, powdery mildew can cause reduced grapevine growth, yield, quality, and winter hardiness. The disease is characterized by a powdery film of spores that attacks and mildews the grapes and leaves.

POWERFUL   A full-bodied wine, high in alcohol (hard tannins for red wines), extracts, and generous flavor, that seems to "fill the mouth." Powerful could also apply to some big, full-bodied white wines, especially if they have been fermented and/or aged in oak barrels. Also known as *puissant*. *See* Brawny and Muscular.

PPM *See* Parts Per Million.

PRÄDIKAT (GERM) *See* Qualitätswein Mit Prädikat.

PRAMNIAN (GREECE) An ancient wine that was purportedly the favorite wine of Nestor.

PRECHECK The ringing up of a check prior to drinks being dispensed or offered.

PRECIOUS ROOM A locked or otherwise secured storage area within a locked storage area.

PRECIPITATION The separation out of solution of small, crystalline particles, usually bitartrate of potassium (cream of tartar), in a beer or wine, usually accomplished through chilling.

PRÉCOCE (FR) Precocious; a term for wines that are forward and mature quickly. Wines that reaches maturity quickly and, consequently, must be drunk early.

PRECOSTING A method by which sales projections and ingredients costs are utilized to calculate actual beverage costs for a given drink item, in advance of sales.

PREDATORY PRICING The act of pricing products below cost to drive out competition and then jacking prices up when the action succeeds.

PREDETERMINED COST Any cost calculated prior to it actually being incurred.

PREDICATO WINES (ITAL) The term means "title of relevance or merit," which indicates a particular typology and can only be exploited by estates that belong to the Authority for Protection of the Wines of the Hills of Central Tuscany.

Predicato is a classification of high-quality wines that utilize nontraditional Tuscan grapes. The wines were first introduced into Italy in 1982 and into the United States market in 1986.

Predicato regulates vineyard location, techniques of viticulture, and altitude. It forbids the inclusion of wines produced from grapes other than those grown in the zones singled out as having ideal soil and altitude for each of the four grape varieties. Predicato unites these Tuscan wines and is basically their family names. The four categories are:

Predicato del Muschio—A white wine, from 100 percent Chardonnay grapes.
Predicato di Bitùrica—A red wine, basically Sangiovese with a minimum of 30-percent Cabernet Sauvignon grapes.

Predicato di Cardisco—A red wine, from 100-percent Sangiovese grapes.

Predicato del Selvante—A white wine, from 100-percent Sauvignon Blanc grapes.

PREIGNAC (FR)   A sweet, white wine made from a blend of Sauvignon Blanc, Sémillon, and Muscadelle grape varieties. It is also one of the five communes within Bordeaux's Sauternes district entitled to be called "Sauternes."

PRÉMEAUX (FR)   A red wine–producing village located in Burgundy's Côte de Nuits district, which is entitled to the appellation Nuits-Saint-Georges.

PREMIER-CHAUFFE (FR)   The first distillation in the making of cognac.

PREMIER CRU (FR)   A first or top-growth wine that officially refers to the finest vineyards, under the 1855 classification in Bordeaux; in Burgundy it follows after Grand Cru.

PREMIÈRES CÔTES DE BORDEAUX (FR)   A wine-producing district that covers a strip of land some 35 miles long and 3 miles wide along the right bank of the Garonne, from Bordeaux to Saint-Macaire. Here both red and white wines are produced, with the red mostly from the north where the southern exposure receives long hours of sunshine. A renaissance château in Cadillac known as the Dukes of Epernon is the home of the Connetablie de Guyenne, a famous wine fraternity. Drunk young, the reds are rich, very fruity, and fresh. They age well, becoming rounded and smooth on the palate, with a more complex bouquet. These are firm, generous, full-bodied wines.

291

PREMIÈRES CÔTES DE BLAYE (FR)   A wine-producing district that extends north of Bourg along the right bank of the Gironde opposite the Médoc. The district of Blaye is the main producer of the red Côtes de Blaye.

PREMIÈRES TAILLE (FR)   The second pressing of grapes used to produce champagne wine.

PREMIUM   *See* Consumer Offer.

PREMIUM   A subjective term, not officially recognized, generally applied by winemakers, brewmasters, or marketers, to indicate a "superior quality" or their top-of-the-line wines or beers. Also known as *private reserve, proprietor's reserve, reserve,* or *réserve.*

PREMIUM BRANDS   Those brands of alcoholic beverages that are top quality, have brand recognition, are positioned well in a customer's mind, and generally command the highest prices. Also known as *premium pour, super call,* and *top shelf.*

PREMIUM POUR   *See* Premium Brands.

PREMIUM WELL   A *premium brand* of an alcoholic beverage that beverage service operators utilize as their *house brand* for all beverages ordered without a call name.

PREMIX   To mix ingredients prior to use.

PREMIX SODA SYSTEM   A carbonated beverage system in which all ingredients (water, concentrated syrups, and carbon dioxide) have already been mixed at a fixed ratio, prior to being purchased by the beverage facility. The carbonated water and syrup are mixed in pressurized canisters (usually 5 gallons, which yields 64 fluid ounces of product) and then dispensed directly out of these containers.

A premix system is normally more expensive to operate than postmix. *See* Postmix.

PRENSA (SP)   A wine press, usually hydraulic. *See* Press.

PRENZAS (SP)   Wine made from the third pressing of the grapes. *See* Prensa.

PREPARED AND BOTTLED BY   The bottler/packer may have treated the wine in any manner, but must not have altered the class or type of the wine in so doing.

PRE-PHYLLOXERA WINES   Wines made prior to the devastation by *Phylloxera* (a root louse) to most of Europe's grapevines in the 1870s. Some wine purists believe that these wines were superior to wines made post-*Phylloxera*; however, there is no scientific evidence to support their claim.

PRÉSIDENT (FR)   *See* Plant de Graisse.

PRESS   A machine by which direct pressure extracts the juice from the skins of grapes. Also known as *prensa* and *pressoir*.

PRESSAC (FR)   *See* Malbec.

PRESS JUICE   That portion of the wine that is pressed from the skins, pulp, and so forth, under pressure after draining off the "free-run juice." Press juice has more aroma and flavor, deeper color, and is usually richer in extract, tannins, and other flavoring materials, which is blended back, in varying degrees, with the free-run juice. Also known as *vin de presse*. *See* Free-Run Juice.

PRESSOIR (FR)   *See* Press.

PRESTIGE CUVÉE (FR)   Top-of-the-line champagnes are made from the pressings of grapes grown in the top-rated villages in vintage years, aged "on the yeast" longer than standard champagnes, and aged in the bottle for between eight to nine years.

PRETTO (ITAL)   Genuine, pure, unadulterated. *See* Vin Santo.

PREUVE (FR)   A small glass cup that is lowered into cognac barrels for a sample for evaluation and testing. *See* Wine Thief.

PRICE AFFIRMATION   Statutes in varying "Open States" in which the supplier guarantees without reservation that the price of the merchandise listed is the lowest price, FOB distillery, winery, or any of the suppliers' other shipping points, offered to and paid by any other customer anywhere in the United States, regardless of the size or type of customer, and that this price includes the same quantity discounts, cash rebates, and all other forms of discounts, allowances, and rebates as are offered any other customer in the United States for the same merchandise.

PRICE EXTENSIONS A process by which the selling price of one particular unit is multiplied by the number of units in an order or projected order in order to arrive at a total cost figure (number of units times unit price).

PRICE LEADER An item that an establishment offers for sale with an especially low price, often temporarily, meant to attract customers, where it is hoped they will also buy other items at the regualr price. *See* Loss Leader.

PRICE MARGINS The amount by which the selling price of a particular item exceeds the basic raw cost to the establishment of the item sold.

PRICE-OFF A temporary price reduction widely used as a basic offer in sales promotion.

PRICER A sign that is designed to put a feature price on display.

PRICE-VALUE RELATIONSHIP *See* Perceived Cost and Perceived Value.

PRICING POLICY A standardized pricing structure utilized by most beverage facilities that determines the retail sales value of their product(s).

PRICKLY *See* Spritz.

PRICKLY An unpleasant sharp quality, noticed in the odor and on the palate, that creates a sharp-edged, raw, possibly almost effervescent quality, caused by an excess of volatile acidity. A prickly wine may just be drinkable, for it might not have reached the final vinegary state.

PRIMARY The largest bud or shoot at each normal node of the cane or spur on a grapevine.

PRIMARY FERMENTATION It is the first stage of fermentation in which the added yeast begins to metabolize the sugar, converting it into carbon dioxide and alcohol. Also known as *alcohol fermentation*.

PRIMARY FERMENTER An open-topped vessel, usually made of stainless steel, wood, concrete, or fiberglass, in which the primary fermentation takes place.

PRIME COST *See* Product Cost.

PRIME COST PRICING The basing of a selling price on beverage cost and direct labor cost.

PRIME INGREDIENT COST *See* Portion Cost.

PRIMEUR (FR) *See* Nouveau.

PRIMING The addition of cane sugar, corn sugar, or other sweet solutions beers just prior to bottling to promote additional fermentation in the bottle.

PRIMITIVO DI GIOIA (ITAL) A very dark, red-skinned grape variety cultivated almost exclusively in southern Italy, where it produces dark, intensly-colored wines, often with some residual sugar and high alcoholic content. Some *ampelographers* believe that the elusive *Zinfandel* grape variety of California may be genetically linked to the *Primitivo*. *See* Zinfandel.

PRINCE, WILLIAM ROBERT (1795–1869) A nurseryman and heir to the Botanical Gardens at Flushing, Queens, New York, who, at the time, had the largest collection of *Vitis vinifera* varieties in America. He experimented extensively with many varieties of grapes and even offered *Zinfandel*, a red grape variety with "unknown" origin in his catalog, listed as "Black St. Peter." *See* Zinfandel.

PRISE DE MOUSSE (FR)   The secondary fermentation of wine into a sparkling wine.

PRIVATE LABEL   A shop's own label, usually carrying the shop's name on a particular item or line of wines, beers, or distilled spirits. Often good values, they are not always consistent, shipment to shipment.

PRIVATE RESERVE   Also known as *proprietors reserve*. *See* Premium.

PROCANICO (ITAL)   *See* Trebbiano.

PROCESSED   A loosely-used term often applied to "jug" wines or other similar types that have been pasteurized, over-filtered, or processed by other means, to "strip away" most of the odor and/or flavor, making the wine bland to the palate.

PROCESSING (FORMERLY RECTIFYING)   Distilled spirits are blended together or otherwise processed by the addition of distilled spirits or flavoring or coloring material.

For example, straight whiskeys are processed by blending them with distilled neutral spirits; distilled spirits are redistilled for flavoring as in the production of gin; distilled neutral spirits, with the aid of flavoring essences and other materials, are transformed into liqueurs or cordials.

PRODOMOS (GREECE)   The name given by the ancient Greeks to "free-run" grape juice. Also known as *protopos*.

PRODOTTO (ITAL)   *See* Product.

PRODUCED AND BOTTLED (PACKED) BY   A term permitted to be used by the bottler or packer if he or she has also made at least 75 percent of the wine by fermenting the *must* and clarifying the wine, or if such person has treated the wine so as to change its class. Also known as *producido por*.

PRODUCIDO POR (SP)   *See* Produced and Bottled (Packed) By.

PRODUCT   Distilled spirits, wine, or malt beverages, as defined in the Federal Alcohol Administration Act. Also known as *prodotto* and *produit*.

PRODUCT COST   The combined total of the beverage and labor costs for a given beverage item or set of beverage items. Also known as *prime cost*.

PRODUCT DISPLAY   Any wine rack, bin, barrel, shelving, and the like from which distilled spirits, wine, or malt beveragees are displayed and sold.

PRODUCT/SERVICE MIX   The combination of product and services offered to perspective customers in a beverage facility.

PRODUCT SHEET   A full-color page of pictures of product(s) that includes product information.

PRODUIT (FR)   *See* Product.

PRODUIT DE QUEUE (FR)   *See* Tails.

PRODUIT DE TÊTE (FR)   *See* Heads.

PRODUTTORE (ITAL)   Producer.

PRODUTTORE RIUNITI (ITAL)   United producers.

PRODUTTORI (ITAL)   Producers.

PRODUZIONE (ITAL)   Production.

PROFIT INVESTMENT STATEMENT (PIS)   A brand's basic financial planning document. This document is basically a *profit and loss* (P & L) for the brand that also includes a *return on investment* (ROI) analysis. The PIS can either be short or long term in nature.

PROFUMO (ITAL)   Aroma, scent, odor.

PROHIBITION   The Eighteenth Amendment went into effect January 16, 1920 (during the administration of President Woodrow Wilson, 1913–1921), and was repealed on Tuesday evening, December 5, 1933 (during the administration of President Franklin D. Roosevelt), by the Twenty-first Amendment, which was signed at 6:55 P.M. It lasted 13 years, 10 months, 19 days, 17 hours, and 32 and ½ minutes. It was referred to by many as "The Noble Experiment," or the "Volstead Act," named after Andrew J. Volstead, a Minnesota Representative, the author of the Eighteenth Amendment. Prohibition actually forbade the manufacture, sale, transportation, importation, and exportation of intoxicating bever ages. It did *not*, however, prohibit the consumption of alcoholic beverages. In fact, the act provided for certain exemptions of the Prohibition Act, including wine for sacramental purposes, medications, and toilet preparations.

295

Other prohibitions were as follows. From 1736 to 1742, the Gin Act, or Gin Prohibition, was put into enforcement in England. From 1735 to 1742, in the state of Georgia, a prohibition against "hard liquor" was imposed. The heaviest drinking by Americans took place between 1790 to 1830, where the per capita consumption of absolute alcohol was 7.1 gallons per year. From 1908 to 1934 (26 years), there was a prohibition against drinking in Iceland, which is considered to be the longest in modern time. From 1914 to 1924, there was a prohibition against drinking in Russia.

Also known as the *Volstead Act*.

PROMOTION   An act, technique, or method, that stimulates or helps bring about growth of sales or consumer acceptance.

PROMOTIONAL ALLOWANCE (PA)   Reference to either financial or marketing promotional allowance.

PROMOTIONAL EXPENSE   Advertising or other incurred expenses as a result of a newly-established brand or a new activity with an already established brand.

PRONTA BEVA (ITAL)   A quickly maturing young wine; ready to drink.

PROOF   An old English term that was once called "gunpowder proof." To test the strength of the distilled spirit, old-time distillers poured it on gunpowder or black powder and struck a match. If the distilled spirit blazed up, it was too strong. Distilled spirits at proper strength mixed with the powder would burn slowly in a blue flame. If it did not burn burn well, it was too high in water. Mixing 50 percent alcohol with 50 percent water gave a slow, steady flame. That strength was considered perfect and was called "100 proof." Today, the same scale is applied to the alcoholic content of distilled spirits on the following basis: Pure 100-percent alcohol (at 60 degrees Fahrenheit) is 200 proof; 1 degree of proof is equal to .5-percent alcohol. Divide the proof by two and you get the percentage of alcohol in the bottle. Also known as *gunpowder proof* and *flame up*.

PROOF GALLON   A U.S. gallon of liquid at 60 degrees Fahrenheit that contains 50 percent by volume (100 proof) of ethyl alcohol, having a specific gravity of 0.7939 at 60 degrees Fahrenheit referred to water at 60 degrees Fahrenheit as unity, or the alcoholic equivalent thereof. *See* Tax Gallon.

PROPAGATION   To cause a grapevine to reproduce itself by a natural reproduction, or as most commonly practiced by viticulturists, by rooting a cutting from the mother plant.

296

PROPIONIC ACID   A "spoiling" acid caused by micro-infection (bacteria), which causes a highly undesirable "goaty" odor and bitterness in the wine. The bacteria break down the tartaric acid to propionic acid. Fortunately, its occurrence is now rare.

PROPORTIONED   *See* Balance.

PROPRIETÀ (ITAL)   Property of.

PROPRIÉTAIRE (FR)   Proprietor; owner.

PROPRIÉTAIRE-NÉGOCIANT (FR)   A vineyard owner who supplements his wineholding by buying other people's grapes or wines.

PROPRIÉTAIRE-RÉCOLTANT (FR)   Owner or manager of a winery.

PROPRIETARIO (ITAL)   Owner.

PROPRIETARY BRAND NAME   *See* Brand Name.

PROPRIETARY NAME   *See* Brand Name.

PROPRIETARY WINE   Wines carrying a made-up name originated by a specific winery or "proprietor." *See* Brand Name.

PROPRIÉTE (FR)   Property or estate.

PROPRIETOR   The person qualified to operate a wine premises and includes the term "winemaker" when the context so requires.

PROPRIETORS RESERVE   *See* Premium.

PROSECCO (ITAL)   A white grape variety often used in the production of sparkling wines.

PROTEASE A protein-splitting enzyme used in winemaking and brewing that breaks down proteins.

PROTEIN HAZE A haze often encountered in wines and beer due not only to precipitation of heat-sensitive protein fractions, but also to complex formations between wine proteins and reactive phenolics.

PROTEINS One of a class of complex nitrogenous compounds that occur naturally in grapevines and yield amino acids when hydrolized. Proteins provide the amino acids essential for the growth and repair of tissue.

PROTOPOS (GREECE) *See* Prodomos.

PROVENCE (FR) A vineyard region in the French Riveria, near the Mediterranean Sea. *See* Côtes de Provence.

PROVIGNAGE (FR) The creation of a new stem by taking a cutting from a branch from a neighboring stem, without separating the branch from the stem.

A long cane is trained from an adjacent "mother grapevine" and buried in the soil where the dead grapevine was. Until the new grapevines come up, it is nurtured by the mother grapevine. This method is especially desirable for reestablishing an existing vineyard.

PROVINCIA (ITAL) Province.

PRUFÜNGSNUMMER (GERM) *See* Amtliche Prufüngsnummer.

PRUGNOLO (ITAL) *See* Sangiovese Grosso.

PRUGNOLO GENTILE (ITAL) *See* Sangiovese Grosso.

PRUINOSE Grapes that are covered with a white, powdery substance or bloom.

PRUNE An organoleptic property, often associated with very overripe, dried-out grapes, that give a pruney, pungent quality that is undesirable in some wines. The odor and/or taste is sometimes prevalent in old port wines. *See* Pflümli.

PRUNE JUICE The liquid constituent of a prune.

PRUNING The cutting off or removal of the excess portion of the grapevines to increase the vigor of the plant to produce finer quality grapes. It is a complex and highly judgmental operation that not only controls the amount of crop the grapevines will bear, but also controls the quality of the ultimate contribution that the particular crop will make to the wine. It is generally performed during the winter dormant period. Also known as *potatura* and *taille*. *See* Balanced Pruning, Cane Pruning, and Spur Pruning.

PSI *See* Pounds Per Square Inch.

PUB (ENG) A shortened term for "public house," a licensed bar where beer and distilled spirits are offered for sale; often a center of social activity for a community. Also known as *public house* and *publik house*. *See* Bar, Cocktail Lounge, Inn, Saloon, and Tavern.

Pub Crawl   A slang term for the visitation of many bars or other alcoholic beverage–serving establishments in one night.

Publican   A bartender in an English pub.

Public Bar   A bar that is open to the general public for the sale and service of alcoholic beverages.

Public House   *See* Pub.

Publik House   *See* Pub.

Puckery   *See* Astringency.

Puglia (Ital)   *See* Apulia.

Pugnet (Ital)   *See* Nebbiolo.

Puissant (Fr)   *See* Powerful.

Pulcianella (Ital)   An often-used bottle for the white wines of Orvieto, from the region of Umbria. Also known as *toscanello*.

Puligny-Montrachet (Fr)   A wine-producing village in the Côte de Beaune district of Burgundy, noted for its production of excellent dry white wines made entirely from chardonnay grapes.

Puligny-Montrachet extends for some 575 acres, with Chassagne-Montrachet as its neighbor, directly south. Puligny was once known as *Puliniacus*, in 1095.

Pulito (Ital)   *See* Clean.

Pull Date   A date a product should be "pulled" off the shelves, after which time it begins to deteriorate.

Pulp   The inner soft, moist, and fleshy part of a grape.

Pulpeux (Fr)   Pulpy; thick in the mouth.

Pulpito (Sp)   A type of hydraulic wine press.

Pulque (Sp)   A viscous, milky-white alcoholic beverage fermented (not distilled) from the juice of agave plants, that was enjoyed for centuries before the art of distilling came to Mexico from Spain. Because of its rather low alcoholic content and susceptibility to spoilage, it is consumed locally and rarely reaches the United States.

Pumped   Sustained high humidity causes corks to swell, and it is not uncommon to find them partially out of the bottle.

Pumping Over   In wine fermentation "on-the-skins," the skins float to the surface and harden, forming what is known as the "cap" or "hat." Several times a day this cap must be broken up to allow the carbon dioxide gas to escape. It is also important for the skins to stay in contact with the fermenting juice, to aid extraction. To accomplish this, the wine is pumped from the bottom of the tank over the cap of floating skins and seeds at the top of the tank three times a day. Also known as *remontage*.

PUNCH   Any drink of many ingredients; its name is derived from Hindustani and Sanskrit words meaning five.

PUNCHEON   A barrel used in the West Indies for the storage of rum with a capacity of approximately 115 to 136 U.S. gallons. *See* Barrel.

PUNCHING DOWN   In "on-the-skins" wine fermentation, the skins float to the surface and harden, forming what is known as the "cap" or "hat." Several times a day this cap must be broken up to allow the carbon dioxide gas to escape. To accomplish this, some wineries, with the aid of long paddles or oars, break up ("punch down") the cap and stir the skins back into the juice.

PUNGENT   A term that implies a powerful, asssertive, heavily scented odor, that is quite strong and penetrating. It usually indicates a high degree of volatile acidity in a wine. Also known as *drimys*. *See* Volatile Acidity.

PUNT   The dome-shaped indentation in the bottom of bottles that serves to strengthen the bottle, especially for carbonated wines and champagnes and helps to collect sediment in aged wines. Also, the punt will accommodate a wooden peg to hold bottles in place during shipping. Back when bottles were handmade, glass blowers would support the bottom of a bottle with an iron rod (called a "punty," from the Italian word *puntello* or point) while they formed the neck. Naturally this rod left a ragged mark in the still soft glass. In order to finish the bottle neatly, a little bit of glass was pushed into the bottom to form a rounded hollow and a smoother resting surface (the circumference of the indentation). Also known as *kick, pointe,* or *puntello*. *See* Champagne Bottle.

PUNTELLO (ITAL)   *See* Punt.

PUNTINATA (ITAL)   *See* Malvasia del Lazio.

PUPÎTRES (FR)   The name of the "A-framed wooden" racks that hold champagne and sparkling wine bottles for "riddling," the shaking and turning of each bottle to move the sediment to the neck of the bottle. The racks were invented in 1816 by the French champagne house of Veuve Clicquot. Also known as *riddling racks.*

PURCHASE ORDER (PO)   A written order form from the buyer, specifying merchandise from a purveyor, that is filled out in quadruplicate: one copy to the purveyor, one copy to the department head, one copy to the accounting department, and one copy to the receiving clerk.

PURCHASE REQUISITION   A form used to request the purchasing agent to order certain goods.

PURCHASE SPECIFICATION   A "standard," detailed specification established to insure proper quality, quantity, weight, and size of products procured from purveyors. Also known as *standard purchase specification.*

PURCHASE STANDARD   A criterion, a gauge, a yardstick; it is what goals of quality are set by management.

PURCHASING   The acquisition of goods and services through a purchase order and by the payment of money or its equivalent for them.

PURE BAR   A term that indicates a beverage facility that serves a wide range of only nonalcoholic beverages, in a sophisticated and highly social environment.

PURE ALCOHOL   *See* Neutral Spirits.

PURE CONDENSED MUST   The dehydrated juice or *must* of sound, ripe grapes, or other fruit or agricultural products, concentrated to not more than 80 degrees (Brix), the composition thereof remaining unaltered except for removal of water.

PURE DRY SUGAR   Refined sugar 95 percent or more by weight dry, having a dextrose equivalent of not less than 95 percent on a dry basis, and produced from cane, beets, or fruit, or from grain or other sources of starch.

PURPLE   A color characteristic in some very young red wines that will fade as the wine matures.

PURVEYOR   A seller or vendor that supplies a product or service to customer firms whether at the wholesale or retail level.

PUTRID   An awful odor of bacterially spoiled wine.

PUTTONYO (HUN)   During harvest, baskets or vats (with a capacity of 8 to 10 gallons) are filled with overripe grapes affected with *Botrytis cinerea*, which are used to make the sweet, Aszú style of wine. The baskets are then added to fermenting tanks of wine, usually between three (being the lightest) and five (being the sweetest), which is indicated on the label, "Tokaji Aszu 3 Puttonyos." The more *puttonyos* (baskets of overripe grapes) added to a tank will yield a sweeter, richer, and naturally more expensive wine.

PX (SP)   *See* Pedro Ximénez.

PYKNÓS (GREECE)   *See* Density.

PYMENTS   *See* Mead.

QBA (GERM) *See* Qualitätswein Bestimmter Anbaugebiete.

QMP (GERM) *See* Qualitätswein Mit Prädikat.

QUAFF To drink beer or wine in large gulps. *See* Chug.

QUAFFING WINE A wine that is without nuance, but is pleasant and refreshing when drunk alone or with food.

QUAICH (SCOTCH) A small, shallow drinking vessel with ears for use as handles. Also spelled *quaigh*.

QUAIGH (SCOTCH) *See* Quaich.

QUALITÄTSWEIN BESTIMMTER ANBAUGEBIETE (QBA) (GERM) A label classification for "quality" table wines that meet certain requirements for alcohol content, region of origin (must come from 1 of 11 specified wine regions), and grape variety, and is subject to examination by authorities. Qualitätswein wines must come from a particular region (*gebiet*) and may be *chaptalized*.

QUALITÄTSWEIN MIT PRÄDIKAT (QMP) (GERM) This designation is reserved for wines of the "highest quality" with special at tributes, and that have not been *chaptalized*.

The equivalent of France's *Appellation Contrôlée* wine laws, revised in 1971. Also known as *Prädikat*.

QUANTITY DISCOUNT A discount provided by the vendor to the seller, that allows huge volume purchases in return for a lower dollar amount assigned to said purchase. Also known as *volume discount*.

QUANTITY PURCHASING *See* Bulk Buying or Discount Purchasing.

QUART A U.S. measure of volume; 32 fluid ounces in a quart; 4 quarts equal 1 gallon.

QUART HOUSE The oldest retail liquor store in the United States (Marion County, Kentucky), where neighbors would bring quart jars to fill from the miller's barrels.

QUARTAUT (FR)   A barrel used for storage of wine that varies in its capacity from 14 to 15 U.S. gallons. *See* Barrel.

QUARTER BOTTLE   A bottle with a capacity of 6.4 fluid ounces.

QUARTIER (FR)   A section of a vineyard.

QUARTS-DE-CHAUME (FR)   A small, white wine–producing vineyard in the Coteaux du Layon district of Anjou, located in the Loire Valley. It is noted for its rich, sweet dessert wines produced from overripe grapes affected by *Botrytis cinerea.*

QUEIMAR (PORT)   To distill a wine.

QUENTE (PORT)   *See* Warmth.

QUERCUS ALBA   American white oak from Arkansas, Kentucky, Missouri, Ohio, Tennessee, and Wisconsin, utilized in the making of wooden barrels for the aging and/or storage of alcoholic beverages.

QUERCUS BICOLOR   American white oak from Arkansas, Kentucky, Missouri, Ohio, Tennessee, and Wisconsin, utilized in the making of wooden barrels for the aging and/or storage of alcoholic beverages.

QUERCUS GARRYANA   American white oak from Oregon, utilized in the making of wooden barrels for the aging and/or storage of alcoholic beverages.

QUERCUS GERIANA   American white oak from Oregon, utilized in the making of wooden barrels for the aging and/or storage of alcoholic beverages.

QUERCUS LYRATA   American white oak from Arkansas, Kentucky, Missouri, Ohio, Tennessee, and Wisconsin, utilized in the making of wooden barrels for the aging and/or storage of alcoholic beverages.

QUERCUS PRINUS   American white oak from Arkansas, Kentucky, Missouri, Ohio, Tennessee, and Wisconsin, utilized in the making of wooden barrels for the aging and/or storage of alcoholic beverages.

QUERCUS ROBUR   *See* Nevers Oak.

QUERCUS SESSILIS   *See* Limousin Oak.

QUETSCH (FR)   A fruit brandy made from small, blue plums with a highly aromatic perfume, that generally come from Alsace, as well as some Central European countries.

QUEUE (FR)   *See* Barrel.

QUEUE DE RENARD (FR)   *See* Foxy.

QUIESCENCE   A term that refers specifically to a plant that is nongrowing because of existing environmental conditions (e.g., low temperature), but that will grow when placed in conditions favorable for growth. *See* Dormancy and Rest.

QUIETO (ITAL)   Peaceful, composed.

QUILLAJA   The bark of the *Quillaja saponaria* tree from South America is occasionally utilized in certain soft drinks to make them foam.

QUINCY (FR)   A small vineyard town in the lower Loire Valley near Sancerre and Pouilly Fumé, noted for its dry, white wines, produced from the Sauvignon Blanc grape.

QUININE   A bitter, white crystalline alkaloid derived from the bark of the cinchona tree. It is the bittering flavor agent used in the production of *quinine water* or *tonic water*, and some bitter-lemon carbonated soft drinks. Quinine is often used in the production of bitter apéritifs, especially from France and Italy. Also known as *quinquina*.

QUININE WATER   *See* Tonic Water.

QUINQUINA (FR)   *See* Quinine.

QUINTA (PORT)   A wine estate, equivalent to a French château; or a single-vineyard designation.

QUINTAL   A metric measurement of weight, equivalent to 100 kilograms or 220.46 pounds. Also known as *quintale*.

QUINTALE (ITAL)   *See* Quintal.

QUOTA   *See* Goal.

Q

RABADI A thickened or reduced milk, popular in India.

RABOSO (ITAL) A red grape variety indigenous to parts of the Veneto region that produces full-bodied, darkly-colored red wines. Also known as *Raboso del Piave* and *Raboso Veronese.*

RABOSO DEL PIAVE (ITAL) *See* Raboso.

RABOSO VERONESE (ITAL) *See* Raboso.

RACÉ (FR) *See* Elegant.

RACIMO (SP) A bunch or cluster of grapes.

RACK A slang term often used in a brewery that means to fill a container with beer.

RACKING The process in which wine or beer is carefully moved from one barrel or tank to another in order to separate it from the lees or solids, mainly yeast sediment. This helps to clarify the wine or beer and also serves to aerate the wine if desired. Also known as *abstich, passagem, soutirage, svinatura, trasfega,* and *trasiego.*

RACOTER (FR) The replacement of dead stems by new grapevine plantings.

RACY A term that describes a wine that is "high in class," with a distinctive robust odor and lively taste. Also known as *rassig.*

RADLMASS *See* Shandy.

RAFLE (FR) The bunch without its grapes; actually just the stems.

RAHM (GERM) Cream.

RAIL That recessed portion of a bar closest to the bartender where drinks are poured, mixed, and served from. Also utilized for soiled glasses prior to washing.

RAIL The metal (formerly brass) pipe or "bar," which forms the front part of a bar, utilized as a footrest.

RAINES LAW In 1896 in New York, there was a Sabbath Law named after Senator John Raines, author of the bill, that forbade the sale of "liquor" and closed the saloons on Sunday.

RAINWATER (PORT) A type of Madeira, a fortified wine, that was believed to have been created by Mr. Habisham, a local Madeira shipper from Savannah, Georgia. Mr. Habisham made very special blends of Sercial and Verdelho Madeiras that were lighter and quite a bit paler (almost like rainwater) than most of the Madeiras that were consumed during that era (the early nineteenth century). *See* Palhete.

RAISINS A cluster of grapes or individual grape berries that have been dried in the sun or by artificial heat. Also known as *uva pasas*.

RAISIN BRANDY *See* Dried Fruit Brandy.

RAISIN WINE A wine made from dried grapes.

RAISINY An odor and/or flavor occasionally detected in wines made from grapes that have more or less dried (shriveled and/or raisined) on the grapevine; often encountered in hot climate wines.

RAKI *See* Arrack.

306

RAMADA (PORT) A special planting and pruning method of grapevines utilized in colder regions prone to spring frosts. The grapevines are trained and pruned on wires strung along posts, rather like a pergola system.

RAMOS GIN FIZZ A cocktail consisting of gin, lemon juice, lime juice, sugar, egg white, cream, and soda water. Supposedly named for Henry C. Ramos, who concocted it about 100 years ago at his famous Imperial Cabinet Bar and Saloon in New Orleans.

RANCID *See* Butyric Acid.

RANCIO (SP) A nutty odor or flavor in a wine, often used to describe a sherry-like taste occasionally displayed in wines that have prolonged air exposure. Also known as *goût de rancio* and *vino de rancio*.

RAPÉ (FR) Discarded or rejected clusters of grapes normally found during the harvest.

RÂPEUX (FR) *See* Rough.

RASPBERRY-FLAVORED BRANDY A mixture of brandy, with a minimum of 2.5 percent sugar, and flavored and colored with raspberries. By federal law it cannot be bottled at less than 70 proof (35 percent alcohol by volume).

RASPBERRY LIQUEUR A sweetened alcoholic beverage consisting of a base of alcohol, minimum 2.5 percent sugar, and flavored and colored with raspberries. It is sweeter and lower in proof than raspberry-flavored brandy.

RASPBERRIES A fruity or zesty nuance or aroma, reminiscent of raspberries, generally found in some light-bodied red wines, especially Beaujolais, some Zinfandel, and Bourgueil.

RASPON (SP) The stalk on a grapevine.

RASSIG (GERM) *See* Racy.

RASTEAU A sweet, fortified wine, similar in color to a white port.

RATAFIA (FR) A sweet, fruity apéritif made with *mistelles* in the Champagne region. Ratafias are generally aged for one year in wooden barrels, which gives the final product an oxidized color and taste. United States federal regulations prohibit use of the name for an American produced product; however, there is a French-made ratafia called Pineau des Charentes available in the marketplace.

The first written reference to ratafia appears in the eighteenth-century records of the French champagne house of Veuve Clicquot, although there is speculation that it was produced much earlier. *See* Mistelle.

RAUCHBIER (GERM) Dark beers made with the addition of smoked malt, mostly found in Bamberg or Hamburg.

RAUENTHAL (GERM) An important wine town, located in the Rheingau, producing white wines that display considerable fruit and spice, and are generally well balanced.

RAUH (GERM) *See* Rough.

RAVELLO BIANCO (ITAL) A local white wine produced near the Amalfi Drive in Campania, noted for its delicate fragrance and taste.

RAWHIDE A taster's term for a wine that displays a leathery texture, occasionally found in some red wines, that have been aged in oak barrels.

RAW MATERIAL COST The wholesale price of raw materials utilized in the production of alcoholic and nonalcoholic beverages.

RAVAT 6 *See* Ravat Blanc.

RAVAT 51 *See* Vignoles.

RAVAT 262 *See* Ravat Noir.

RAVAT BLANC A white French-American hybrid grape variety developed from a cross of Chardonnay and Seibel 5474, which is primarily cultivated in the east and midwest. Formerly known as *Ravat 6*.

RAVAT NOIR A red French-American hybrid grape variety developed from a cross of Seibel 8365 and Pinot Noir, which is primarily cultivated in the east and midwest. Formerly known as *Ravat 262*.

RAYA (SP) A vertical line or trace made with chalk on the head of a sherry butt (barrel) to identify and classify wines that will become finos or amontillados. The butts of the palest and finest sherry wines will be marked with one stroke / (raya), destined to be used for fino sherry; the fuller or heavier wines will be marked mraked with two strokes // (dos rayas), for oloroso-type sherries. This word is also used for a coarse Oloroso-type sherry.

RAYON D'OR A white French-American hybrid grape variety developed from a cross of Seibel 405 and Seibel 2007, which is primarily cultivated in the east and midwest. Rayon d'Or produces wines with a good sugar/acid balance. Formerly known as *Seibel 4986*.

RAZZA (ITAL) *See* Breed.

REBATE The practice of returning a portion of an amount paid, as for goods or services, serving as a reduction or discount. *See* Consumer Coupons and Refunds.

REBE (GERM) *See* Grape.

REBÈCHE (FR) The fourth pressing of the grapes, which is not used for champagne making.

REBO (ITAL) A red grape variety cultivated primarily in the Trentino-Alto Adige region in the north, from a cross of Merlot and Marzemino grape varieties. The cultivar was developed by Rebo Rigotti in 1948, while working at the Experimental Research Station and School of Enology at San Michele all'Adige.

REBSORTE (GERM) *See* Grape Variety.

REBSORTEN SEKTS (GERM) Sparkling wines produced from a particular variety of grape type.

RECEIVING The act of accepting delivery (receiving) of beverages that have been ordered, checking beverages and other merchandise from purveyors, and recording such transactions.

RECEIVING CLERK An employee who is charge of receiving beverages or other types of merchandise and who performs the receiving function.

RECEIVING SHEET A daily form (record) on which the receiving clerk lists all merchandise accepted as delivered, noting the invoice number and ascertains which department the goods should be delivered to.

RÉCEMMENT DÉGORGÉ (FR) Recently disgorged.

RECIOTO (ITAL) A word from the Veronese dialect that means a single bunch or cluster of the best and ripest grapes, which have received the most direct sunshine, called *recie* or *orecchie* (ears); hence the name Recioto della Valpolicella (*recioto* is also a word from the old Veronese dialect of the area). These grapes are then utilized in the process of making Recioto della Valpolicella.

There are other *recioto* wines. Some are labeled Recioto della Valpolicella Spumante, and Recioto della Valpolicella Liquoroso, or simply Recioto. Reciotos are *amabile* (semidry to sweet) and contain more than 1 percent residual sugar. The *liquoroso* designation is for a very sweet dessert wine (with a minimum of 16-percent alcohol). There is also *spumante*, which is also an amabile with remarkable amount of body and finesse.

To produce an *amabile* or *spumante*, the fermentation is halted before all of the sugar is metabolized, and the wine is immediately filtered to eliminate the yeast. The *spumante* is made by inducing a secondary fermentation that creates effervescence (less of it, however, than in champagne). *See* Amarone.

RECIOTO DI SOAVE (ITAL) A white wine coming from the province of Verona, made from partially dried grapes. It is sweet to the taste, with overtones of pears, apricots, and bananas.

RECIPE A formula used to produce beverage items for consumption.

RECIPE COSTING The practice of calculating the exact cost for every ingredient in a recipe in order to ascertain the total recipe cost and the portion cost.

RECIPE FORECASTING The practice of estimating, prior to sales, how many portions will be yielded from a standardized recipe.

RECIPE YIELD The count, weight, or volume that a standardized formula (recipe) will produce.

RECOLTA (RUM) *See* Vintage.

RÉCOLTE (FR) *See* Année.

RÉCOLTE TARDIVE (FR) *See* Late Harvest.

RÉCOLTE-MANIPULANT (FR) Identifies champagnes produced by one of the 15,000 growers in the area. This would include wines that are partially produced by cooperatives but finished by the growers. This appears on some champagne labels as the initials RM.

RECONDITIONING The conduct of operations, after original bottling or packing, to restore wine to a merchantable condition. The term includes relabeling or recasing operations.

RECTIFYING *See* Processing.

RECTIFIED AND BOTTLED BY The bottler/packer must have rectified the wine, pursuant to an approved BATF formula, on the bottling premises of a distilled spirits plant.

RED A term used to describe the color of some alcoholic and nonalcoholic beverages. Also known as *cherveno, crno, kirmisi, rosso, rosu, rot, rouge, tinto,* and *vörös.*

RED LAYER In a wooden barrel, beneath the charred layers of wood (pure carbon), is the "red layer" of caramelized wood sugars, which gives whiskey its rich, dark color. Also, the deep charred layers yield tannin and vanillin. At high external temperatures (above 90 degrees Fahrenheit), the whiskey in the barrel expands and penetrates the caramelized or "red layer" of wood behind the char, making the whiskey smoother and somewhat flavorful.

REDONDO (PORT OR SP) *See* Round.

RED TRAMINER *See* Gewürztraminer.

REDUCE To cook down; to evaporate some of the liquid, thus obtaining a stronger brew.

REDUCING   Lowering the alcoholic content of an alcoholic beverage by the addition of distilled water.

REDUCING SUGAR   Refers to the amount of unfermentable sugar that will not ferment and remain in a wine. The most common reducing sugars are glucose and fructose, along with pentose. Also known as *nonfermentable reducing sugar* or *nonfermentables. See* Pentose and Residual Sugar.

RED VERMOUTH   *See* Vermouth.

RED WINE   A wine made with coloration derived from contact with the skin of the grape, as opposed to a white wine, which is either made entirely from white grapes or from black grapes without prolonged skin contact. Also known as *dôle, rotwein, vinho tinto, vino rosso, vino tinto, vin rouge,* and *vörösbor.*

REEDY   A term that infers a wood or slightly herbaceous taste often displayed by some wines.

REFERENCIA (SP)   A sample of a wine blend retained by the shipper.

REFILLING   *See* Consolidating Bottles.

REFINED   A wine that is free from crudeness or coarseness, and is cultivated and elegant, with great subtlness.

REFOSCO (ITAL)   *See* Mondeuse Noire.

REFRACTOMETER   It is a hand-held optical instrument that measures the amount of light bent as it passes through the grape juice, which can be viewed through an eye piece. When the grapes reach the desired sugar/acid ratio, they are harvested.

REFRESH   The practice of refreshing a barrel of aging wine or distilled spirits by the addition of a "newer" or younger type. This is often practiced in the making of sherry wine and some distilled spirits. Also known as *rociar.*

REFRESHMENT BAR OR STAND   A commercial food and/or beverage establishment in transportation terminals, sports arenas, or other areas of high-volume, "fast-food" areas that cater to fast-paced individuals. These facilities offer patrons limited "fast-food," menus and alcoholic beverages, which are consumed either while standing or seated on stools.

REFRIGERATION   *See* Cold Stabilization.

REFSKO (YUG)   *See* Mondeuse Noire.

REFUNDS   Mail-in rebate sent to the consumer upon presentation of refund slip and proof-of-purchase and/or cash register receipt. *See* Consumer Coupons and Rebates.

REGE (FR)   Rows of grapevines.

REGIONAL   A wine that takes its name from an area where grapes are grown or wine made, rather than from a specific town or vineyard.

RÉGISSEUR (FR)   Estate manager.

REGNER (GERM)   A white grape variety developed in Alzey in the Rheinhessen, from a cross of Luglienca Bianca and Gamay Früh.

REGNIE (FR) A *cru* in Beaujolais, near the communes of Brouilly and Morgon, producing distinctive and appealing, fruity wines. Regnie officially received its AOC designation in 1988, making it the tenth cru in Beaujolais.

REGULAR CUBES *See* Ice Cubes.

REGULATOR That part of a tap beer system that maintains the carbon dioxide pressure at a constant level.

REHOBOAM A formerly-used large bottle with a capacity of six 750-milliliter bottles (152.1 fluid ounces) or 4.5 liters, used exclusively for champagne. Rehoboam, a son of King Solomon and grandson of David, was the last king of David's united monarchy and the first to reign over Judah.

REICHENSTEINER (GERM) A white grape variety developed in Geisenheim in the Rheingau, by Dr. Helmut Becker in 1978, from a cross of Müller-Thurgau and (Madeleine Angevine and Calabrese).

REIF (GERM) *See* Ripe.

REIMS (FR) A city located on the Marne River, which is the capital of the Champagne region. Formerly spelled *Rheims*.

REIN (GERM) Pure.

REINTÖNIG (GERM) *See* Clean.

R

REINHEITSGEBOT (GERM) The so-called German brewing purification law or The Bavarian Purity Order. It was enacted in 1516 by Bavaria's Duke Wilhelm IV, who decreed that beer could be brewed only from malt, hops, and water, with no other additives except for yeast.

RELIANCE A red seedless grape variety, which is a cross of Ontario and Suffolk Red, developed in Arkansas in 1983.

RELISH FORK A small, narrow fork, usually with two or three tines, utilized for spearing cocktail olives or onions, necessary for certain cocktails.

REMAILY A white seedless grape variety developed in 1965 at the New York State Agricultural Experimental Station, from a cross of Lady Patricia and New York 33979, by George Remaily, a commercial artist.

REMONTAGE (FR) *See* Pumping Over.

REMONTADO (SP) When a bottled wine loses its original fragrance after a long time in the bottle and acquires a *rancio* bouquet, becoming darker in color.

REMUAGE (FR) The process in which the sediment contained in a bottle of sparkling wine or champagne is carefully worked down to the neck by gentle turning (riddling) of the bottle on a regular basis. This is accomplished by a rotative twisting movement, while the bottle is placed in an ever-growing downward position, which aids in the eventual settling and collection of sediment in the bottle's neck. Also known as *riddling, ruetteln,* and *scuoti mento*.

REMUEUR (FR) Riddler.

RENAULT WINE TONIC During Prohibition, the Renault Winery of Egg

Harbor City, New Jersey, produced a wine containing 22-percent alcohol and legally sold it in drug stores.

RENEWAL SPUR   *See* Spur.

REORDER POINT   The point at which beverages and other supplies must be ordered (with sufficient lead time) in order to maintain minimum stock so that customers can still be satisfied with what is on hand.

REP   An individual or company duly authorized to represent a business organization (supplier) and to provide goods and/or services in return for monetary transactions.

REPEAL   *See* Prohibition.

REPISA (PORT)   The second pressing of the grapes.

REPOSADO (SP)   A designation that indicates that the tequila has been aged at least one year.

REPRODUCING APPARATUS   A stainless steel tank equipped with various devices specially designed for yeast reproduction, necessary for the production of all types of alcoholic beverages.

REQUISITION   A written order (usually on preprinted forms) requesting the beverage storeroom to withdraw items from stock and issue them or other merchandise.

RESA (ITAL)   Yield: As in either grapes or wine.

RESALE AT WHOLESALE   A sale to any trade buyer.

RESERVA (PORT)   A wine that represents an exceptional harvest that has been set aside for extra long aging to develop a depth of character and delicacy of bouquet.

RESERVA (SP)   Red wines that have been aged in oak barrels (225-liter) for a minimum of one year, followed by two years in the bottle, and may not leave the *bodega* until the fourth year after the harvest. White wines must be aged a minimum of two years, six months of which must be in oak barrels. In practice, many wineries age the wines far longer than the minimum. Reservas are usually only laid down in very fine years.

RESERVE   A term often found on wine labels of U.S.-produced wines, which has no legal or real meaning.

RESERVE   *See* Premium.

RÉSERVE (FR)   *See* Premium.

RÉSERVE (FR)   A label designation on Armagnac or cognac bottles that indicates that the youngest brandy used in the blend is at least 4 ½ years old (although they contain a very high percentage of brandy that has been aged for 12 to 20 years or more).

RESERVE WINE   Wine from previous vintages added to the *cuvée* of "nonvintage" wines to produce a wine with consistent quality and style. *See* Blending and Nonvintage.

Résidu (FR) Residue.

Residui (ITAL) *See* Residual Sugar.

Residual Sugar The measure of natural grape sugar intentionally left in the wine after fermentation. Sweetness is balanced by acidity creating a harmonious taste experience. Sweetness is a function of style, not quality. Some rare and expensive sweet wines have sugar levels as high as 20, 25, and even 30 percent. More and more U.S. wineries are listing the residual sugar on their back labels as an aid to the consumer. Also known as *residui, restsüsse,D and zuckerrest. See* Reducing Sugar.

Resin *See* Retsina.

Résine (FR) *See* Retsina.

Resinous *See* Retsina.

Resinated Wines *See* Retsina.

Resistant Rootstocks Grape varieties whose roots are less injured by the attack of root parasites than are the roots of the scion grafted upon it.

Respiration The release of stored energy and sugars in the plant for use in synthesizing enzymes, colors, aromas, flavors, tannins, glucosides, and vitamins, which is largely controlled by temperature. The loss of malic and tartaric acids as grapes begin to change color and ripen is also due to respiration and is mostly affected by temperature.

R

313

Ressaibo (PORT) *See* Aftertaste.

Rest A state of suspended growth due to internal physiological blocks. Rest is fulfilled by exposure to temperatures of 45 degrees Farenheit or less for an extended period (chilling requirement). After the rest period is satisfied, a plant may either break dormancy and begin to grow if conditions allow, or may remain dormant if conditions do not favor growth. Often known as *dehardening. See* Dormancy and Quiescence.

Rest The practice of allowing bottles of wine to "rest" or lay quietly, untouched, in one location for several days after purchase, prior to consuming.

Restored Pure Condensed Must Pure condensed *must* to which has been added an amount of water not exceeding the amount removed in the dehydration process.

Restrained *See* Dumb.

Restsüsse (GERM) *See* Residual Sugar.

Retail Package stores, supermarkets, and so forth, that purchase alcoholic and nonalcoholic beverages from wholesalers and then sell to consumers at retail price.

Retailer Any person engaged in the sale and/or service of distilled spirits, wine, or malt beverages to consumers.

Retail Establishment Any premises where distilled spirits, wine, or malt beverages are sold or offered for sale to consumers, whether for consumption on- or off-premises where sold.

RETROGUSTO (ITAL OR SP) *See* Aftertaste.

RETSINA (GREECE) A table wine that has been adulterated by the addition of between 1 to 5 percent dried and powdered pine resin, along with aromatic gums and spices, which are added either to the *must* or finished wine, contributing to Retsina's unique flavor.

The resin is actually sap (technically called *sandarac*, a type of resin used in the production of varnish), obtained from the bark of several types of trees *(Tetraclinis articulata)* from Africa and Australia. In ancient Greece, resin was used in the preparation of wine to impart flavor and act as a preservative.

Retsina, which is produced mainly in Attica from the Rhoditis, Savatiano, and Assyrtiko grape varieties, has a turpentine-like odor, which may offend the first-time, novice drinker. There is also a red "Retsina" wine called Kokkinelli. Also known as *resin, resinated wines, résine,* and *resinous.*

RETURN The transfer of distilled spirits, wine, or malt beverages from a trade buyer to the industry member from whom purchased, for cash or credit.

RETURN ON INVESTMENT (ROI) The gain or share of profit associated with the investment of capital, usually expressed as a percentage.

REUILLY (FR) A dry white wine made from the Sauvignon Blanc grape variety in the upper Loire Valley.

REVENUE Money received by an establishment from consumers for either goods sold or services rendered.

REVENUERS Alcohol Tax Unit men who enforce taxation of alcoholic beverages. *See* Excise Man.

RHEIMS (FR) *See* Reims.

RHEIN (GERM) The local name for the Rhine River.

RHEINGAU (GERM) This is one of Germany's smallest grape-growing region, and it usually produces the greatest of all German wines. It is almost all one large hillside, facing south and protected against the northern climate by the Taunus mountain chain. The wines made in this area are noble indeed, combining elegance with style and delicacy, and yet having substance and fruitiness as well. Almost every village and vineyard produces a wine whose quality is distinctive and that an expert can identify. Some of Germany's better-known winemaking estates, such as Schloss Johannisberg, Steinberg, and Schloss Vollrads, are in this area. The main Rheingau villages in which wines are made are Rüdesheim, Johannisberg, Rauenthal, Kiedrich, Erbach, Hattenheim, Oestrich, Hallgarten, Eltville, Geisenheim, and Hochheim. For many years the wines from Hochheim, which contains five vineyards between Mainz and Wiesbaden, were referred to, mainly by the British, as *Hock*; earlier, the British called them "Rhenish" wines.

RHEINHESSEN (GERM) Most of Germany's wine that is exported is made in this region; it produces even larger quantities than Mosel-Saar-Ruwer and Rheingau. Its wines, profiting from a warmer climate, are softer, rounder, and a little fuller than the aristocratic wines of the Rheingau. The main grape varieties of Rheinhessen are the Sylvaner and Müller-Thurgau, which produce very soft, sometimes fairly sweet wines with a delicate bouquet. Because this is a large area, Rheinhessen's wines vary a great deal in their characteristics. In good years, some of the finest, if not *the* finest, *Prädikat* wines of Germany are made here. Some towns with well-known vineyards are Nierstein, Oppenheim, Bodenheim, Nackenheim, Bingen, Worms, and Guntersblum. It is in Rheinhessen that most of the better Liebfraumilch wine is produced.

RHEINPFALZ (ALSO REFERRED TO AS THE PALATINATE) (GERM) This is a large wine-producing region, located along the Rhine River to the east, France to the south and southwest, the Mosel-Saar-Ruwer to the west, and the Rheinhessen to the north. The majority of the high-quality wines here are made from the Sylvaner and Müller-Thurgau grapes, with only 15 percent of the region planted with Johannisberg Riesling. Climate and soil combine here to aid in the production not only of the common wine of the German *Weinstube* or local pub, but also some outstanding wines. Wines from the villages of Forst and Deidesheim are among the finest of the Palatinate, being fuller and sweeter than Mosels, Rheingaus, and even Rheinhessens. They are also meatier and higher in alcohol (there is a saying in Germany that "when you have drunk a bottle of good Palatinate wine, you will find it hard to go home, since it has all gone to your feet"). Other major Rheinpfalz winemaking towns are Wachenheim, Ruppertsberg, Duerkheim, and Ungstein.

R

RHEINRIESLING *See* Johannisberg Riesling.

RHENISH The English name for Rhine wines of Germany, from the earliest days of their import to the eighteenth century, when the term *hock* replaced it.

RHINE WINE A generic term for any number of white wines produced in the Rhine regions of Germany.

RHINE WINE A generic wine term used in the United States for a white table wine, generally semidry to sweet, and somewhat bland tasting.

RHODITIS (GREECE) A local white grape variety that is often blended with *Savatiano* to produce ordinary table wines, along with the famous *retsina* wine. Also spelled *Roditis*. *See* Retsina.

RHÔNE VALLEY (FR) *See* Côtes du Rhône.

RHUM The French spelling of rum.

RIBEAUVILLÉ (FR) One of the most noted towns in the Alsace region, noted for its production of Johannisberg Riesling wines.

RIBOLLA GIALLA (ITAL) A white grape variety mostly cultivated in Friuli-Venezia Giulia, where it produces wines with good color and dry and crispy to the taste, with good flavor.

RICE WINE   A wine made from grain rather than rice, with an alcoholic content of 12 to 15 percent by volume. Saké, although technically a brewed product, is erroneously referred to as rice wine.

RICCO (ITAL)   *See* Rich.

RICH   A term that describes wines or even beers that display a generous bouquet and substantial body; mouthfilling fullness in taste, with fruity flavors and good acidity. Also known as *riche, ricco,* and *saftig.*

RICHE (FR)   *See* Rich.

RICK   Literally a framed, open warehouse where barrels of distilled spirits are stored for aging and maturing.

RICKEY   Comes from the Hindustani word "Rekhta," meaning poured out, scattered, or mixed.

RICKEY   A drink family name given to those cocktails (a cross between Collins and sours) made with distilled spirits and lemon or lime juice, with a sweetening agent and soda water or ginger ale added. *See* Gin Rickey.

RIDDLING   *See* Remuage.

RIDDLING RACKS   *See* Pupîtres.

RIESLANER (GERM)   A white grape variety developed in 1929 in Würzburg in Franken, from a cross of Sylvaner and Johannisberg Riesling.

RIESLING   *See* Johannisberg Riesling.

RIESLING DORÉ   A white grape variety supposedly made from a cross of Johannisberg Riesling and Courtiller Musqúe, found in Alsace, France, and the western part of the United States. Also known as *Goldriesling.*

RIESLING RENANO (ITAL)   *See* Johannisberg Riesling.

RIESLING ITALICO (ITAL)   *See* Welschriesling.

RIM   The outer edge of the bowl on a wine glass where the lips touch. Generally, the smaller and thinner the rim, the finer the quality of the glass.

RIM   The outer edge of a wine (especially red) when viewed against a white background, as the glass is tipped to a 45-degree angle, presents a good indication of the how the wine is aging. A brick-red color generally indicates maturity, whereas a brown color indicates that the wine has deteriorated or is "too old" for consuming.

RIMMING   Decorating the "rim" of a glass with either salt, celery salt, or sugar by first placing the glass upside down on the liquid tray, which usually contains lemon or lime juice, and then immediately into the salt or sugar tray, which leaves a thin layer of either on the rim of the glass. Rimming is necessary when serving such drinks as Bloody Marys, Margaritas, Salty Dogs, Gimlets, Pink Squirrels, Sours, and so on.

RIOJA (SP)   A major grape-growing region producing mostly red (although some fine quality white wines are also produced) wines in the Bordeaux style.

Rioja encompasses some 110,000 acres of vineyards in northern-central

Spain, not far from the western Pyrenees and only 200 miles south of Bordeaux, France. There are two major population centers in Rioja. The town of Haro is the traditional center of the wine district and still retains its sixteenth-century appearance, dominated by a magnificent Gothic church. The colorful and modern city of Logroño is the provincial capital and is the business and financial hub. The majority of Rioja wineries, or *bodegas*, are to be found along the roads that run between Logroño and Haro.

The average elevation of the Rioja's vineyards is well over 1,500 feet above sea level. These heights produce lighter wines than those that are made from grapes grown in lower and warmer sections of the country. Most of the vineyards are situated on either side of the Ebro River, which flows east from the Pyrenees toward the Mediterranean.

Seven tributaries cross the Rioja and one of them that lies towards the western end is called the "Rio Oja." Actually, the name Rio, which means "river," is joined with Oja. Rio Oja is the name of a mountain stream that flows into the River Ebro, some 165 miles northeast of Madrid.

Rioja is divided into three viticultural zones: Rioja Alta, Rioja Alavesa, and Rioja Baja. The first two are in the western portion of the district; the third lies east of them. Rioja Alavesa has an altitude in between that of the two other zones that, as is obvious from their names, are the high and low zones of Rioja. The two higher zones, Rioja Alta and Rioja Alavesa, produce the best wines; those from Rioja Baja are considered somewhat harsher and are higher in alcohol.

RIOJA ALAVESA (SP)   *See* Rioja.

RIOJA ALTA (SP)   *See* Rioja.

RIOJA BAJA (SP)   *See* Rioja.

RIPARIA   *See Vitis Riparia.*

RIPASSO (ITAL)   A process used in Verona for some Valpolicella and Amarone wines that is similar to the Tuscan *governo*, whereby the fermented wine is given a short, second fermentation on its lees, which enhances the wine's body and richness of taste.

RIPE   A term generally used to describe wines, beers, or distilled spirits that have reached their full term of aging or have achieved a proper state of bouquet and flavor development. They are full, soft, and mature. Also known as *reif*. *See* Aging, Barrel Aging, Bottle Aging, Mature, and Ripe for Bottling.

RIPE FOR BOTTLING   A term that means that the wine, beer, or distilled spirit has improved in the barrel to the highest point possible, after which aging usually is completed in glass or stainless steel. *See* Aging, Barrel Aging, Bottle Aging, Mature, and Ripe.

RIPENESS   It primarily means flavor and a proper balance between sugar, acid, and pH. Sugar is thus only one component of ripeness, but cannot alone define ripeness. In fact, we have no tests to measure ripeness or flavor, which is an essentially subjective, relative concept. Ripeness exists as a potential affected by individual vineyard characteristics and weather patterns. *See* Maturity.

RIPPED   Slang for intoxicated.

RIPPING   A process that tears the soil to a depth of three to five feet, to loosen it so that the grapevine can spread its roots.

RIQUEWIHR (FR)   One of the finest villages located in the Alsace region, noted for its production of Johannisberg Riesling wines.

RISERS   The name of the metal pipes often used in vineyards to support the sprinkler heads above the level of foliage, in an overhead water sprinkler system.

RISERVA (ITAL)   A DOC wine with extra barrel aging at the winery.

RISERVA SPECIALE (ITAL)   A seldom-used term denoting an extra year of aging, longer than "riserva."

RIVULETS   *See* Legs.

RIVANER (YUG)   *See* Müller-Thurgau.

RIZLING   *See* Johannisberg Riesling.

RKATSITELI (RUSS)   A white grape variety used primarily in the production of sparkling wines and for dry or semidry table wines. Some is sparsely planted since 1963 in the Livermore Valley of California, as well as New York and New Jersey, and even in China and Eastern Europe. In Bulgaria, it is known as *Sunshine Coast.*

RM (FR)   *See* Récolte-Manipulant.

ROAD HOUSE   An old slang expression for a pub or bar, located alongside a roadway.

ROASTED   A smell often found in wines made from grapes exposed to intense sunshine; slightly oxidative character reminiscent of sherry wine.

ROASTED   Grain that has been exposed to great heat, causing a browning of its sugars. Roasted grains are often used in the brewing of dark beers, especially stout and porter.

ROASTED MALT   Barley, that has been converted to malt, then roasted to a chocolate brown-black color, often used for coloring beers.

ROBE (FR)   A term that refers to the color and other visual aspects of a wine. It is generally used in relation to that of a fine red wine.

ROBE CHATOYANTE (FR)   A glistening color.

ROB ROY   A cocktail consisting of Scotch whisky, sweet vermouth, and bitters, although dry vermouth is often substituted for sweet when making a "dry" Rob Roy.

Robert MacGregor, a character immortalized in a novel by Sir Walter Scott

(1817), was said to have hidden from the from the law in an oak tree, where now only a stump remains, 400 yards along the road from the Glengoyne distillery in Scotland. The drink Rob Roy was named after MacGregor because of his "red hair."

ROBUST   A beverage (alcoholic or nonalcoholic) that is very full-bodied, mouth-filling, and full-flavored. Also known as *corsé, forte, kräftig, robusto,* and *romaléos. See* Big.

ROBUSTA   One of two types of coffee beans, the other being *arabica.*

ROBUSTO (ITAL)   *See* Robust.

ROCIAR (SP)   *See* Refresh.

ROCK AND RYE   A liqueur bottled at not less than 60 proof (in which not less than 51 percent, on a proof gallon basis, of the distilled spirits used is rye whiskey) that possesses a predominant characteristic rye flavor derived from such whiskey. It must contain rock candy or sugar syrup, with or without the addition of fruit, fruit juices, or other natural flavoring materials, and possessing a predominant characteristic rye flavor derived from the distilled spirit used. Some producers of rock and rye feature pieces of fruit, such as lemons, oranges, or even cherries floating in the bottle. Rock and rye was originally sold as a "sore throat" remedy.

ROCKS   Slang term for ice cubes; "on the rocks." Also the name of a glass— "on the rocks glass."

ROCKS GLASS   *See* Old-Fashioned Glass.

ROCKY   A term occasionally applied to the surface texture of the "head" on a glass of beer.

RODITIS (GREECE)   *See* Rhoditis.

ROEMER (GERM)   Green-tinted stemware used for wine service.

ROGNER (FR)   The cutting off of the end of young tendrils on a grapevine, with a knife to shape the foliage into a hedge.

ROI   *See* Return On Investment.

ROLHA (PORT)   *See* Cork.

ROLLING BAR   A portable service bar used in hotels, catering halls, banquets, or other locations where the bar must be mobile. Each "rolling bar" is equipped with ice bins and only the most-called-for brands of alcoholic as well as nonalcoholic beverages and mixes. Also known as *portable bar.*

ROMALÉOS (GREECE)   *See* Robust.

ROMANÉE-CONTI (FR)   A *grand cru* vineyard in the village of Vosne-Romanée, in the Côte du Nuits district of Burgundy, producing what is often regarded as the finest and most expensive of all red Burgundy wines. Romanée-Conti takes its name from Prince de Conti, who owned it from 1760 to 1795, during the rule of Louis XV.

The vineyards of Romanée-Conti are quite small, measuring about four-and-one-half acres, producing an average of 500 cases per year.

RÖMER (AUS) Special wine glasses; it is also the German word for Romans.

ROMULUS A white seedless grape variety developed in 1952, from a cross of Ontario and Thompson seedless, at the New York State Agricultural Experimental Station.

RONDE (FR) *See* Round.

RONDINELLA (ITAL) A red grape variety cultivated primarily in the Veneto region, where it is used as a blending grape to produce Bardolino and Valpolicella wines. Rondinella, which is dark violet in color, was first mentioned in documents dating back to 1882.

ROOM TEMPERATURE A synonym for the proper temperature for the service of red wines—65 to 68 degrees Fahrenheit, not 72 degrees, as practiced in the United States.

ROOSTERS The term often associated with cocktails during the seventeenth through the nineteenth centuries. *See* Cocktails.

ROOT BEER A carbonated nonalcoholic drink prepared from potable water, carbon dioxide, sugar syrup, with or without harmless organic acid, flavored with extracts from the roots and bark of certain plants, and with or without the addition of caramel color.

Root beer was initially called "birch beer," which was first introduced as a soda flavored with various roots and herbs. Later, Charles E. Hires changed the name to root beer and advertised it as "The National Temperance Drink."

ROOT ENVIRONMENT It is the nature of the soil, including root parasites, microorganisms, nutrients, and water surrounding the roots of a grapevine.

ROOTING A young grapevine produced from a cutting grown for one season, developing both roots and shoots.

ROOT PARASITES Destructive organisms living in or on roots of grapevines.

ROOTS Its first function is anchoring the grapevine to the land from which it can absorb water and the nutrients dissolved in it that will later be transported to the rest of the plant. Finally, the system stores up reserve sustenance.

ROOTSTOCK Specialized stock material to which fruiting varieties of grapes are grafted to produce a commercially acceptable grapevine. Grape rootstock varieties are used for their tolerance or resistance to root parasites, such as *phylloxera* and nematodes, or for vigor. *See* Souche.

ROPES *See* Legs.

ROPINESS *See* Mousy.

ROSADO (PORT OR SP) *See* Rosé Wine.

ROSATO (ITAL) *See* Rosé Wine.

Rosé Clair (fr)   Light rosé.

Roséfoncé (fr)   Deep rosé.

Rosette   A red French-American hybrid grape variety, mostly used in the production of rosé wines. Formerly known as *Seibel 1000*.

Rosé Wine   A wine made from red grapes that has a light pink color, acquired by only short contact with the skins; wines made from a mixture of red and white grapes; or wines made by blending red and white wines. Also known as *bleichert, clarete, halbrot, rosado, rosato, roseewein, ruzica, vinho rosado, vino rosado, vino rosato,* and *vin rosé*.

Roseewein (germ)   *See* Rosé Wine.

Rossanella (ital)   *See* Molinara.

Rossara (ital)   *See* Molinara.

Rossignola (ital)   A red grape variety cultivated primarily in the Veneto region, where it is used as a blending grape to produce Bardolino and Valpolicella wines. It is also cultivated in Liguria, where it produces fairly light-bodied red wines. Rossignola, which is dark violet in color, was first mentioned in documents dating to the beginning of the nineteenth century.

R

Rosso (ital)   *See* Red.

Rosso di Montalcino (also called Rosso di Brunello or Rosso dei vigneti Di brunello)   A red wine produced from the same vineyards that produce the world-famous Brunello di Montalcino. Rosso di Montalcino was granted its DOC status on November 25, 1983 and is made solely from Brunello grapes (also called Sangiovese Grosso). Rosso di Montalcino can be made from very young grapevines not considered suitable for Brunello di Montalcino or a Brunello wine aged for a shorter period of time than required under DOC. *See* Brunello di Montalcino, Montalcino, and Sangiovese Grosso.

Rossola (ital)   *See* Trebbiano.

Rossone (ital)   *See* Molinara.

Rosu (rum)   *See* Red.

Rot (germ)   *See* Red.

Rot   A gradual decomposition of alcoholic or nonalcoholic beverages by the action of bacteria, or fungi. Also the action of mold, parasites, or bacteria on grapevines, eventually causing their destruction.

Rotate Stock   *See* First-In, First Out.

Rotgipfler (aus))   A white grape variety that is usually blended with Zierfandler, to produce Gumpoldskirchner, a wine that is outstanding in quality. Aging brings out its full body and superior bouquet.

Roti (fr)   *See* Passito.

Rotling (germ)   A pale-colored red wine made from a blend of both red and white wines.

ROTONDO (ITAL) *See* Round.

ROTTEN EGG SMELL *See* Hydrogen Sulfide.

ROTULA (PORT) *See* Labels.

ROTWEIN (GERM) *See* Red wine.

ROTGUT A slang term for a low grade wine, beer, or distilled spirit, usually consumed by derelicts.

ROTUNDIFOLIA *See Vitis Rotundifolia.*

ROUCANEUF A red hybrid grape variety, mostly cultivated in the south and southwestern parts of the United States. Formerly known as *Seyve-Villard 12309.*

ROUGE (FR) *See* Red.

ROUGEON A deeply-colored red. French-American hybrid grape variety, developed from a cross of Seibel 880 and Seibel 4202. It is mostly used as a blending grape. Formerly known as *Seibel 5898.*

ROUGH A term that describes a coarse or hard wine (usually found in red wines with high tannin levels), generally immature, not well-balanced, with a raspy or astringent taste. This type of wine is usually of ordinary quality. Also known as *âpre, aspro, râpeux, rauh, ruvido,* and *trakhys.*

ROUND A term that describes a wine that is harmonious, full, and well-balanced with no major defects or rawness. Also known as *redondo, ronde, rotondo, rund,* and *strongylós.*

ROUNDED-OUT A term used to describe the maturing process of red wines during which they precipitate out the harsh tannins and the wines become softer.

ROUSING The vigorous stirring of a wine or beer (in a tank or barrel) after a fining agent has been added, by means of a wooden or stainless paddle.

ROUSSANNE (FR) A white grape variety, primarily cultivated in the Rhône Valley, where it used to produce Châteauneuf-du-Pape, Hermitage, Croze-Hermitage, Saint-Joseph, and other famous wines.

ROUSSILLON (FR) A wine-producing region located in the southern part of the country, mostly producing ordinary table wines of no particular regard. *See* Languedoc and Midi.

ROVERE (ITAL) *See* Oak.

ROVIFERM *See* Actiferm.

ROYAL (FR) A label designation on Armagnac or cognac bottles that indicates that the youngest brandy used in the blend is at least 5 1/2 years old (although they contain a very high percentage of brandy that has been aged for 20, 30, or 40 years or more).

ROYALTY A red grape variety developed in 1938, from a cross of Alicante Ganzin and Trousseau, by Dr. Harold P. Olmo of the University of California, Davis.

RUBBERY   An undesirable odor of *mercaptans* occasionally detected in some white wines, probably due to the breakdown of high levels of sulfur dioxide.

RUBILANDE   A white French-American hybrid grape variety developed from a cross of Seibel 2859 and Seibel 4643. Formerly known as *Seibel 11803*.

RUBINO (ITAL)   *See* Ruby.

RUBIRED   A red grape variety developed in 1938, from a cross of Alicante Ganzin and Tinto Cão, by Dr. Harold P. Olmo of the University of California, Davis. It is cultivated primarily in California, where it is used as a blending grape.

RUBIS (FR)   *See* Ruby.

RUBY   A color displayed by many young, red wines. Also known as *rubino* and *rubis*. *See* Ruby Port.

RUBY CABERNET   A red grape variety developed in 1948, from a cross of Carignan and Cabernet Sauvignon, by Dr. Harold P. Olmo of the University of California, Davis. Ruby Cabernet produces wines that are usually light, fruity, and pleasant but without much character.

RUBY PORT (PORT)   Traditionally, this is the very youngest port, which takes its name from its ruby color. Ruby port, by law, must be aged in wood a minimum of three years or so and bottled while it still retains its deep red color and vigorous taste. It is usually rich and fruity and is best consumed when young. No cellaring is necessary.

RÜCKGRAT (GERM)   *See* Backbone.

RUDE (FR)   *See* Astringency.

RÜDESHEIM (GERM)   An important wine-producing village located in the Rheingau region, famous for its full-bodied and fruity wines.

RUE   A strong scented herb from the *Ruta graveolens* family, with yellow flowers and bitter-tasting leaves, formerly used for medicinal purposes, but now used occasionally as a flavoring for *grappa*.

RUETTELN (GERM)   *See* Remuage.

RUH   The storage of beer after fermentation, prior to bottling or shipping.

RÜLANDER (GERM)   The German name for the Pinot Gris, a white grape variety. Pinot Gris was first cultivated in 1711 by a merchant named Johann Seger Rüland from Speyer, who discovered the grapevine in 1689 in the dilapidated garden of an official of the Speyer law courts named Seuffert.

RULLY (FR)   A commune in the Côte Chalonnaise of Burgundy, noted for its very fine white wines from the Chardonnay and Pinot Blanc grapes.

RUM   An alcoholic distillate from the fermented juice of sugar cane, sugar cane syrup, sugar cane molasses, or other sugar cane by-products, produced at less than 190 proof in such manner that the distillate possesses the taste, aroma, and characteristics generally attributed to rum, and bottled at not less than 80 proof. It also includes mixtures solely of such distillates. In ancient times, Rum was originally called Barbados Brandy, Barbados Water, or Kill-Devil.

There are three main types: 1) light-bodied, dry rums, characterized by those of Puerto Rico; 2) full-bodied, rich rums, exemplified by Jamaica rum; 3) the pungently aromatic Batavia Arak from Java.

RUM LIQUEUR   A liqueur bottled at not less than 60 proof, in which the distilled spirit used is entirely rum, and that possesses a predominant characteristic rum flavor derived from the distilled spirit used.

RUMBULLION   A popular seventeenth century term for rum, that originated either from the English or in the West Indies. A popular Colonial drink, called *rumfustian*, was produced from rum, eggs, spices, and hot cider. Also known as *rumbustion*.

RUMBUSTION   *See* Rumbullion.

RUMMER   A glass or other type vessel used for drinking toasts in praise of someone or something.

RUMMY   An old slang term used to describe a person that drinks too much alcohol.

RUN   The completed distillation of one batch of "low wine."

RUND (GERM)   *See* Round.

RUNNING TAB   A guest check system of dispensing and serving drinks, but not collecting any monies until the guest is ready to leave the premises.

RUPESTRIS   *See Vitis Rupestris*.

RUSSIAN ISINGLASS   *See* Fining.

RUSSIAN TEA   Tea traditionally served with lemon juice or slices, rather than cream or milk.

RUVIDO (ITAL)   *See* Rough.

RUWER (GERM)   *See* Mosel-Saar-Ruwer.

RUZICA (YUG)   *See* Rosé Wine.

RYE   A small, dark cereal grain often utilized in the production of certain distilled spirits, especially *rye whiskey*.

RYE LIQUEUR   A liqueur bottled at not less than 60 proof, in which not less than 51 percent, on a proof gallon basis, of the distilled spirits used is rye whiskey, that possesses a predominant characteristic rye flavor derived from such whiskey.

RYE MALT WHISKEY   *See* Rye Whiskey.

RYE WHISKEY   A distilled spirit, distilled at not more than 160 proof from a fermented mash of grain containing at least 51 percent rye grain, and stored at not more than 125 proof in charred new oak barrels. Straight rye whiskey is seldom sold today, although very often American Blended Whiskey or Canadian whisky is incorrectly referred to as "rye." Also known as *Rye Malt Whiskey*.

RYUMOCHKI (RUSS)   Small shot glasses used for drinking vodka straight.

R

SAAR (GERM) *See* Mosel-Saar-Ruwer.

SABOR (PORT OR SP) *See* Flavor.

SABOROSO (PORT) *See* Sapid.

SABROSO (SP) *See* Sapid.

SACA (SP) The action of drawing out a specific quantity of wine from the "solera" for consumption.

SACCHARIFY A term that means to convert starch or dextrin into sugar, as by chemical means. In whiskey distilling it refers to the process that takes place during the malting and mash-tun stages by which the enzyme diastase turns the starch in the cereals into sugar that is ready for the fermenting action of the yeast.

SACCHARIMETER An instrument used to quantifiably measure the amount of sugar in a solution.

SACCHARIN $C_7 H_5 NO_3 S$ A sweet, white, powdery synthetic product derived from crystalline coal tar, 300 to 500 times as sweet as sugar. It was discovered accidentally by Ira Remsen and C. Fahlberg in 1879, and introduced as a substitute for sugar, and has been primarily utilized since as an artificial sweetener in some nonalcoholic carbonated beverages.

SACCHAROMETER *See* Hydrometer.

SACCHAROMYCES A genus of fungi, reproducing by budding, necessary for the production of certain types of alcoholic beverages.

SACCHAROMYCES CARLSBERGENSIS The name of the first pure beer yeast culture, which was isolated in 1883, by Professor Emil Hansen of the Carlsberg Brewery in Denmark.

SACCHAROMYCES CEREVISIAE The name of the principal yeast strain used in the fermentation grapes into wine.

SACCHARUM OFFICINARUM (SP) The type of cane sugar from which rum is derived.

SACK An obsolete English term originating in Elizabethan England (1558–1603) that means a sweet fortified wine, mostly sherry, from Spain. It is reported that *sack* was the favorite drink of the English dramatist William Shakespeare (1564–1616). Also known as *canary sack*.

SACK MEAD *See* Mead.

SACRAMENTAL WINES Wines used during religious ceremonies of the mass and produced under the strictest regulations and requirements of a particular faith. These were permitted to be made during Prohibition. Also known as *altar wine*, *messwein*, *vin de messe*, and *vinos de misa*.

SACRAMENTO A wine-producing district in California, north of San Francisco.

SACY (FR) A white grape variety cultivated primarily in the Yonne district of Chablis. Also known as *Tresallier*.

SADD Students Against Drunk Driving.

SADON (FR) A measurement unit typical of the Saint-Estèphe commune in Bordeaux, which corresponds to 10 rows of 100 grapevines.

SAFETY STOCK The minimum stock needed to function for a shift or day. *See* Par Stock.

SAFTIG (GERM) *See* Rich.

SAGGIAVINO (ITAL) *See* Wine Thief.

SAINT-AMOUR (FR) A cru commune in Beaujolais whose grapes produce a rich red wine that is tinged with violet and has a spicy aroma, with hints of kirsch. In parts of Saint-Amour, the soil contains some limestone, which produces the delightful Beaujolais Blanc—a drier and more delicate wine than Mâcon Blanc, and with slightly less body.

SAINT-AUBIN (FR) One of the lesser known red and white wine–producing villages, situated behind Chassagne-Montrachet, in the Côte de Beaune district of Burgundy.

SAINT BERNARD Those dogs that are usually identified with the carrying of a small keg of brandy or other distilled spirits around their necks to give "relief and warmth" to stranded skiiers in Scandinavian countries.

SAINT-EMILION (FR) A major red wine–producing district located on the right bank of the Dordogne River, in Bordeaux. The wines produced are predominantly from the Merlot grape, with some Cabernet Sauvignon in the blend.

On November 14, 1936, the wines of Saint-Emilion were officially given their *Appellation Contrôlée* designation.

In 1954, the INAO laid down a classification for Saint-Emilion that divided the 76 great vineyards into two classes: *premier grand cru* and *grand cru classé*.

To help promote the wines of Saint-Emilion, John Lackland, on July 8, 1199, established the Jurade de Saint-Emilion, a wine brotherhood still in existence today.

SAINT-ESTÈPHE (FR)   A notable red wine commune located in the northern part of the Médoc, in the Bordeaux region, noted for its robust, full-bodied red wines, made predominantly from the Cabernet Sauvignon grape, with some Merlot, Malbec, Cabernet Franc, and Petit Verdot in the blend.

On November 14, 1936, the wines of Saint-Estèphe were officially given their *Appellation Contrôlée* designation.

SAINT-JOSEPH (FR)   A wine-producing district located in the northern part of the Côte du Rhône, noted for its production of red, white, and rosé wines. The red wine is made solely from the Syrah grape, which yields a somewhat full-bodied wine. The white wines, also full-bodied, are produced from the Roussanne and Marsanne grapes. Red Saint-Joseph is best when it is four to six years old, and the white and rosé wines when they are two to four years old.

SAINT-JULIEN (FR)   A famous red wine commune located between Pauillac and Margaux, in the Médoc district of Bordeaux, noted for its refined, high-quality red wines made predominantly from the Cabernet Sauvignon grape, with some Merlot, Malbec, Cabernet Franc, and Petit Verdot in the blend.

On November 14, 1936, the wines of Saint-Julien were officially given their *Appellation Contrôlée* designation.

SAINT MARTIN   The patron saint of the wines of Portugal, whose birthday is celebrated around the middle of November each year.

SAINT-PÉRAY (FR)   A wine-producing village in the northern Côtes du Rhône, known mostly for its white wine, which is one of the lightest of all Rhône whites. Since 1929, some of its production also goes into the making of *brut* and *demisec méthode champenoise* sparkling wines.

SAINT-VÉRAN (FR)   A white wine village located in southern Mâcon, in the Burgundy region, producing wines similar to those of Pouilly-Fuissé.

SAINT VINCENT   The patron saint of Champagne, whose birthday is celebrated on January 22 of each year; used to be the patron saint of Burgundy, France.

SAISON (BEL)   A sharply refreshing, amber-colored ale, that displays a faintly sour taste.

SAKAZUKI (JAPAN)   *See* Ochoko.

SAKÉ   A colorless brewed alcoholic beverage made from rice that is legally defined as a rice beer. Saké is an ancient fermented beverage known to have been made since approximately 3000 B.C. in China. But it was not until about 600 years ago that saké as we know it today was produced. *Saké* means "the essence of the spirit of rice," and, although it is native to China and Japan, it is produced in other parts of the world, including California.

SALATO (ITAL)   Salty.

SALE   A transaction involving the delivery of goods or services for an agreed sum of money or other valuable consideration.

SALES BROCHURE   A brochure featuring current or upcoming promotions for specific brands of alcoholic beverages.

SALES INCOME   The amount of money received from customers for goods and services rendered.

SALES JOURNAL   A business record used for posting all sales transactions by type.

SALES MIX   The total number of each drink item on the menu, considered in relation to one another, that is sold during a specified period of time.

SALES VALUE   The value of the item at a certain selling price.

SALMANAZAR   An oversized bottle with the capacity of 9 liters or 12 750-milliliter bottles, primarily used in the Champagne region of France. Salmanazar was also the name of an eighth century B.C. Assyrian king who ruled over the Judean kingdom from 732 to 734 B.C.

SALOON   An old western term for a bar. *See* Bar, Cocktail Lounge, Inn, Pub, and Tavern.

SALT   Used for rimming glasses, necessary for certain cocktails. *See* Rimming.

SALTED WINE   It is a wine or wine product, not for beverage use, that contains not less than 1.5 grams of salt per 100 milliliters of wine.

SALTY   A salty taste comes from the salts of certain acids found in wine. It can be detected on the middle front top of the tongue.

SAMBUCA   A generic anise-licorice–flavored liqueur, that is obtained from the white flowers of the *Sambucus nigra*, a kind of elderberry bush of the honeysuckle family. Sambuca is clear in color and similar to anisette, with more flavor, higher in alcoholic content, and much drier. Sambuca is predominantly produced in Italy.

SAMOGON (RUSS)   Bootlegged vodka.

SAMPANJAC (YUG)   *See* Sparkling Wine.

SAMTIG (GERM)   *See* Velvety.

SANCERRE (FR)   A small village town located in the Loire Valley that produces a dry white wine made exclusively from the Sauvignon Blanc grape; however, it lacks the richness and full-bodied quality of Pouilly Fumé.

SANCOCHO (SP) *See* Cotto.

SANDARAC *See* Retsina.

SANGAREE A tall drink served in the southwestern United States. It is the corruption of the Spanish word "Sangria"—a similar drink in Spain and Spanish America.

SANGIOVESE DI ROMAGNA (ITAL) A medium-bodied, dry, red wine made from 100-percent Sangiovese grapes, in the Emilia-Romagna region. *See* Sangiovese Piccolo.

SANGIOVESE GROSSO (ITAL) A red grape variety, cultivated predominantly in the region of Tuscany, where it used to produce Chianti, Brunello di Montalcino, and Vino Nobile di Montepulciano wines. The grape is also cultivated in many other regions, including Abruzzo, Campania, Emilia-Romagna, Lombardy, Marches, Sicily, Veneto, and Umbria.

The Sangiovese grape is one of Italy's most noble varieties, believed to have originated from Tuscany, where it is widely cultivated. Its name comes from "Sanguis Jovis," Latin for Jupiter's Blood. Also known as *Sangiovese Grosso (Brunello)*, *Prugnolo*, and *Prugnolo Gentile*. *See* Brunello di Montalcino, Montalcino, Rosso di Montalcino, and Sangiovese Piccolo.

SANGIOVESE PICCOLO (ITAL) The lesser clonal selection of the famous *Sangiovese Grosso*, a red grape variety, noted for its production of extremely full-bodied, dry red wines. Also known as *Sangioveto, San Gioveto*, and *Sangiovese di Romagna*. *See* Sangiovese Grosso.

SANGIAVETTOE (SP) The local name in Argentina for the Sangiovese Piccolo grape variety. *See* Sangiovese Piccolo.

SAN GIOVETO (ITAL) *See* Sangiovese Piccolo.

SANGIOVETO (ITAL) *See* Sangiovese Piccolo.

SANGRIA (SP) A refreshing sort of "wine punch" made from a mixture of wine (red or white), slices of citrus fruits (lemon and orange), sugar, and sometimes soda water.

SAN JOAQUIN A grape-growing district located in the Central Valley of California.

SANS ANNÉE (FR) *See* Nonvintage.

SANTA CLARA A grape-growing district in California south of San Francisco.

SANTCHOO *See* Alaai.

SANTÉ (FR) Health.

SANTENAY (FR) The southernmost village of the Côte de Beaune, located below Chassagne-Montrachet in Burgundy, producing good quality red and white wines.

Santenay was known as *Sentennacum* during the Gallo-Roman occupation.

S

331

SAÔNE (FR)   A river located in southeast France, flowing south into the Rhône River at Lyon.

SAPERAVI (RUSS)   A red grape variety sparsely planted in New York State that is used for table and dessert wines.

SAPID   A term used to describe wines that are savory and luscious tasting, as opposed to insipid. Also known as *lieblich, sapido, saboroso, sabroso,* and *savoureux.*

SAP IS DOWN   The dormant period when the "sap" is down and the trees can be cut for use as wine or whiskey barrels.

SAPIDO (ITAL)   *See* Sapid.

SAPORE (ITAL)   *See* Flavor.

SAPPY   Juicy; lively, straightforward taste; often intensely grapey flavor.

SARAP (TURKEY)   *See* Wine.

SARDEGNA (ITAL)   *See* Sardinia.

SARDINIA (ITAL)   The second largest island in the Mediterranean; has, for centuries, been a little-known wine-producing region, unknown even to most Italians from the mainland and Sicily. It is located across the Tyrrhenian Sea, south of Corsica, about 125 miles west of Rome.

332

Sardinia produces dry white, dry red, and sweet dessert wines, although very little reaches the United States.

In ancient times, Sardinia was referred to as "Ichnusa" from the Greek word "Ichnos," which, translated, meant "footprint." Known as *Sardegna* in Italy.

SARGAMUSKOTALY (HUN)   *See* Muscat.

SARMENTER (FR)   Raking and burning of the grapevine shoots cut during pruning.

SARSAPARILLA   Any of a number of tropical American, spiny, woody vines (genus *Smilax aristolochiaefolia*) of the lily family with large, fragrant roots and toothed, heart-shaped leaves. The name comes from the Spanish (*zarsaparrilla*) word for a bramble (*zarza*) and a small vine (*parrilla*). The dried roots of any of these plants and birch oil or sassafras is used to make a carbonated, flavored drink. Sarsaparilla first appeared in the United States in the 1840s, and, although it is still found today, it is not popular as it was years ago. Incorrectly spelled *sasparilla* or *sarsaprilla.*

SASELLA (ITAL)   A full-bodied red wine produced from the Nebbiolo grape variety in the Valtellina district of Lombardy, located in the northern part of Italy.

SATURATION   The degree of intensity of a color detected in wine or beer.

SAUBER (GERM)   *See* Clean.

SAUCER-SHAPED GLASS   A flat, *saucer-shaped* stemmed glass with a large surface area, often used for the service of sparkling wines and champagne.

Because of this glass's large surface area, sparkling wines served in it will go prematurely flat. The proper glassware to use is either a *flute-shaped* or *tulip-shaped* glass. Also known as *bird-bath glass*.

During the time of Helen of Troy, milk was served from glasses in the shape of a woman's breast, and today's popular flat saucer-shaped champagne glass derives its shape from a mold of Marie Antoinette's left breast.

SAUERKRAUT   An undesirable odor of bacterially spoiled wines, due to high levels of lactic acid. The odor may be encountered in wines that have undergone an excessive malolactic fermentation.

SÄUERLICH (GERM)   *See* Acidulous.

SAUMUR (FR)   A wine town along the south bank of the Loire Valley in the Anjou province, producing delightfully dry white wines from the Chenin Blanc grape, which is sometimes made into a sparkling wine via the *méthode champenoise.*

SÄURE (GERM)   *See* Acidity.

SAUTERNE   A white generic table wine produced in the United States, that can range from dry to semisweet tasting. There are no federal regulations that stipulate the grape varieties that American-produced "sauterne" wine may contain.

SAUTERNES (FR)   A district in the southern part of Bordeaux, noted for its extremely sweet white wines and a few dry white wines as well.

Sauternes, along with German *Trockenbeerenauslese,* is among the sweetest wines in the world and among the most expensive. It is produced from three white grape varieties: Sauvignon Blanc, Sémillon, and Muscadelle.

Sauternes are made by utilizing a mold called the "noble rot" (technically *Botrytis cinerea*). This mold is present as spores at all times in most vineyards. Depending on the grape variety, the time of year, and climatic conditions, it can greatly enhance or severely damage the grapes in a vineyard.

The five communes entitled to be called Sauternes are Sauternes, Barsac, Preignac, Fargues, and Bommes. (Only wines from the commune of Barsac are entitled to the Barsac *appellation contrôlée;* however, a decree of 1936 gave this commune the right to the illustrious Sauternes appellation as well.) On September 30, 1936, the wines of Sauternes were officially given their *Appellation Contrôlée* designation. The Sauternes appellation requires a minimum alcoholic content of 13 percent, and chaptalization is permitted. The sweet wines of Sauternes and Barsac were among those ranked by the 1855 classification of Bordeaux wines.

To help promote the sweet wines of Sauternes, a wine brotherhood, the Commanderie du Bontemps de Sauternes et Barsac, was established and is active today. *See* Botrytis Cinerea.

SAUVIGNON BLANC   A white grape variety cultivated in many parts of the world, including France, Italy, Spain, the United States, Austria, Australia, South Africa, Germany, South America, and eastern Europe, producing mostly dry wines, although semidry and even sweet wines are produced.

Sauvignon Blanc produces dry wines, anywhere from light- to full-bodied, that display a fresh aroma of green olives, hay, lemon, melon, vanilla, and new-mown grass that can sometimes be quite herbaceous.

In Bordeaux, France, Sauvignon Blanc is blended with Sémillon and Muscadelle to produce either the dry white wines of Graves, or the luscious sweet dessert wines of Sauternes. In the Loire Valley of France, Sauvignon Blanc is used the production of Pouilly Fumé, Sancerre, and Quincy, which are often described as being "flinty."

In California, it is speculated that Sauvignon Blanc was first planted around the 1850s, although it made its first appearance in 1878 in the Livermore Valley and wasn't bottled as a separate varietal until Wente Bros. 1935 vintage. The wines produced in California are generally made in the dry or semidry style, which display wondrous varietal fruit and character, with plenty of acidity.

In California, Sauvignon Blanc is also known as and can legally be labeled as *Fumé Blanc*. Also known in other parts of the world as *Blanc Fumé, Muskat-Sylvaner, Sauvignon Jaune, Savagnin Musqué,* and *Surin*.

SAUVIGNON JAUNE (FR) *See* Sauvignon Blanc.

SAUVIGNON VERT *See* Muscadelle and Tocai.

SAVAGNIN MUSQUÉ A name occasionally used in California to denote the Sauvignon Blanc grape variety. *See* Sauvignon Blanc.

SAVAGNIN NOIR (FR) The local name in the Jura region for the Pinot Noir grape variety. *See* Pinot Noir.

SAVAGNIN ROSÉ *See* Gewürztraminer.

SAVATIANO (GREECE) A white grape variety that is often blended with *Rhoditis* and *Assyrtiko* in the production of *Retsina*. *See* Retsina.

SAVIGNY-LES-BEAUNE (FR) A red wine–producing village in the Côte de Beaune, producing light-bodied wines with good fruit and flavor.

SAVEUR (FR) *See* Flavor.

SAVOUREUX (FR) *See* Sapid.

SAXON A type of old English beer, named after the section of England where it originated.

SAZERAC A cocktail made from bourbon whiskey, Peychaud's bitters, Pernod, and sugar.

SBOCCATURA (ITAL) *See* Dégorgement.

SCANT A term used to indicate "just barely" (for example, "one scant teaspoon").

SCANTLING   Wooden beams, timber, scaffles, or metal supports used to hold wooden barrels in a winery or distillery. Also known as *wedges*.

SCANTLING PIPE (PORT)   A barrel with a capacity of approximately 138 U.S. gallons, or 627 liters.

SCARNO (ITAL)   *See* Thin.

SCENT   An agreeable odor or smell of a wine, beer, or even some distilled spirits, evocative of perfume. Also known as *senteur*.

SCHAL (GERM)   *See* Stale.

SCHARZHOFBERG (GERM)   A white wine–producing vineyard located on a very steep hillside in Wiltingen on the Saar, famous its superb wines made from the Johannisberg Riesling grape.

SCHAUMWEIN (GERM)   A sparkling wine containing a minimum of 3.5 atmospheres of pressure and 8.5 percent alcohol by volume. This designation is for the lowest quality (usually bulk-produced) sparkling wines. *See* Charmat Method.

SCHEUREBE (GERM)   A white grape variety developed in 1916 at Alzey, in the Rheinhessen by botanist George Scheu, genetically cross-pollinating Johannisberg Riesling with Sylvaner in an effort to combine the elegance and fine flavor of the former with the early ripening characteristics of the latter. In 1956 the variety was officially named Scheu-Rebe in honor of its breeder and released commercially in 1959.

SCHIAVA GENTILE (ITAL)   *See* Schiava Grossa.

SCHIAVA GRIGIO (ITAL)   *See* Schiava Grossa.

SCHIAVA GROSSA (ITAL)   A red grape variety cultivated primarily in the northern region of Trentino-Alto Adige, where it produces mostly fresh and fragrant, light-colored wines, low in tannin, with good fruit, that should be consumed rather young. Its subvarieties include *Schiava Gentile, Schiava Grigio, Schiava Meranese,* and *Schiavone*. Also known as *Trollinger* in Württemberg, Germany, and *Black Hamburg*, in England.

SCHIAVA MERANESE (ITAL)   *See* Schiava Grossa.

SCHIAVONE (ITAL)   *See* Schiava Grossa.

SCHIEDAM GIN   A type of gin named after one of the Dutch towns where it is distilled. *See* Holland Gin.

SCHIETTO (ITAL)   A simple yet acceptable wine.

SCHIMMELGESCHMACK (GERM)   *See* Moldy.

SCHIUMA (ITAL)   The froth or smoke that emanates from the neck of a sparkling wine when opened and poured. *See* Spuma.

SCHLEGELFLASCHEN (GERM)   The slender, swan-necked bottles in which most German wines are bottled.

SCHLOSS (GERM)   Castle; equivalent of the French word château.

SCHLOSS BÖCKELHEIM (GERM)   An important white wine–producing village located on the Nahe River, mostly planted in Johannisberg Riesling grapes.

SCHNAPPS   A northern European generic term for alcoholic beverages, especially the clear, unaged distilled spirits such as vodka, gin, and akvavit. A clear, white distilled spirit whose distinctive aroma or taste (similar to vodka), made from grain or potatoes, is popular in northern Europe. Usually consumed neat. Often flavored with fruit essences. Also spelled *snaps*.

SCHNAPPS   When used in conjunction with the term "flavored," indicates a liqueur, which contains a minimum of 2.5 percent sugar.

SCHNAPSIG (GERM)   *See* Hot.

SCHÖNUNGSREIF (GERM)   A wine that is ready for fining.

SCHÖN (GERM)   Lovely.

SCHÖNBURGER (GERM)   A white grape variety developed in Geisenheim, from a cross of Spätburgunder and (Gutedel and Muscat Hamburg).

SCHÖNEN (GERM)   *See* Fining.

SCHOONER   A tall drinking glass that holds about 16 fluid ounces of beer.

SCHUYLER   A red grape variety, developed in 1947 from a cross of Zinfandel and Ontario, at the New York State Experimental Station at Geneva.

SCHWANZ (GERM)   *See* Aftertaste.

SCHWARZRIESLING (GERM)   *See* Meunier.

SCHWARZWALDER (GERM)   A fruit brandy made from small plums with a highly aromatic perfume that generally come from Germany, as well as some central European countries.

SCHWEFEL (GERM)   Sulfur smell.

SCHWEIF (GERM)   *See* Aftertaste.

SCHWER (GERM)   Heavy or full-bodied.

SCION   It is the shoot or bud that will be grafted onto the stock of a grapevine, which contains the leaf and fruit-bearing parts of the variety the grower desires.

SCOBICIA DECLIVIS   Commonly known as the "lead cable borer." This tiny beetle tunnels a hole about the size of a pencil lead in wooden barrels.

SCOOPER   A tall, long-handled grain shovel often used to turn or flip over barley during the kilning process.

SCOTCH ALE   A medium-dark, full-bodied ale, with a rich malty taste, generally produced in Scotland.

SCOTCH WHISKY   A distinctive product of Scotland, made in compliance with the laws of Great Britain. Scotch's unique flavor and character come from the water used in its production, and the type and amount of malt whisky used. Its distinctive smoky taste comes from the peat fires over which the barley malt is dried. Its primary base grain is barley (distilled by pot stills for heavy-bodied whisky) or corn (distilled by continuous or Coffey stills for lighter-bodied whisky). Most Scotch whisky is blended—a blend of malt and grain whiskies.

After distillation is completed, Scotch is put into uncharred oak barrels, used sherry barrels or used American oak bourbon whiskey or wine barrels, where it ages for a minimum (by law) of three years. However, in practice most whiskies mature for much longer, often five to ten years or more, depending on the distiller. Scotch sold in the United States is generally aged a minimum of four years; if it's less than four years old, the bottle must carry an age label. In practice, however, Scotch is generally allowed to remain in wood for five years or more before bottling. When there is an age stated on the label of a blended Scotch whisky, it identifies the youngest whisky in the blend.

Scotch can be distilled in Scotland, yet be bottled in the United States, which saves large sums of money, with little or no sacrifice to the product's quality.

SCREW *See* Worm.

SCREWDRIVER A cocktail consisting of vodka (or gin) and orange juice. This very popular drink was supposedly created by oilmen or oil riggers, who would use their tools to stir it.

SCUD A slang term used to describe mold that may develop on wines that are low in alcohol content.

SCUOLA DI OENOLOGIA DI CONEGLIANO (ITAL) Italy's premier enological and viticultural school, established in 1876, is located in the northeast region of Veneto.

SCUOTIMENTO (ITAL) *See* Remuage.

SCUPPERNONG A grape variety of the *Vitis rotundifolia* (Muscadine) family, native to the southeastern United States. Scuppernong was named after a stream of this name in North Carolina, where it was first found growing as early as 1524, by Giovanni da Verrazanno (the Florentine explorer).

SEC (FR) Dry, but when used on champagne or sparkling wine labels, indicates a semidry sparkling wine.

SECAILLER (FR) Replacing of the acacia stakes in a vineyard that are in poor condition.

SECATEUR (FR) Shears or snippers used for pruning and for cutting grapes from grapevines.

SÉCHÉ (FR) Dried out; excessive oxidation.

SECCO (ITAL) *See* Dry.

SECO (PORT OR SP) *See* Dry.

SECONDARY The basal and the second largest bud or shoot at each node of the cane or spur on a grapevine.

Secondary Fermentation   An induced fermentation in a stoppered bottle, utilized in the production of sparkling wines. It is accomplished by adding sugar and yeast to a base wine already present in "champagne bottles." The secondary fermentation generally lasts about six weeks, but the wines are usually aged a minimum of one year before the bottles are opened.

Second Wine   *See* False Wine.

Sediment   The slow reaction and eventual precipitation of fruits, tannins, tartrates, pigments, and other compounds, as the wine matures in the bottle. A brown deposit, known as sediment, settles on the side or bottom of the bottle. Sediment is quite harmless, although aesthetically unpleasant, and tastes like sand. Generally found in red wines. Also known as *beeswing, chemise, crust, culattone, deposit, deposito, depòsito, déposito, dépôt, dregs,* and *fondo.*

Seedling   A grapevine grown from a seed, rather than a cutting. Also known as *semis.*

Seeds   The pits contained in a grape berry. They comprise about 5 percent of the grape, usually being two to four per berry depending upon the variety of grape. The seeds are very high in tannins and astringent oils, containing roughly 72 percent of all phenolics found in wine. Also known as *pipa, pips,* and *pits.*

Seed Yeast   *See* Nutrients.

Sehr Fein (germ)   Very fine.

Sekt (aus or germ)   *See* Sparkling Wine. From the Latin word *siccus,* meaning dry.

Select   A term that implies that the alcoholic beverage contains certain qualities or attributes that set it apart from the rest. The term, however, carries no legal definition or application.

Selected Late Harvest   A term generally used in the United States to imply that the individual cluster or berries within a cluster were hand selected because of certain attributes. The term, however, carries no legal definition or application.

Select Harvest   A term that implies that the harvest was "picked out" from the rest or other such connotation. In reality, it has no legal definition or application.

Sélection de Grains Nobles (fr)   A designation of wines from Alsace, recognized as a classification in the wine laws of 1984 and that are subject to the same restrictions as the *vendanges tardives,* with even higher minimum levels of natural sugar and alcohol. Only produced in truly great years from individually selected grapes affected by the "noble rot" (*Botrytis cinerea*), *sélection de grains nobles* wines are pure nectar, highly concentrated, with a lingering flavor. Produced in very small quantities, these wines are very difficult to obtain in the United States.

338

Self Whiskies   A term used in Scotland to denote either a "straight" or unblended Scotch malt whisky.

Selo de Garantia (port)   The official seal of guaranteed origin and authenticity for wines used on bottles from demarcated regions, such as Bairrada, the Dão, the Douro, or Vinho Verde.

Seltzer   Tap water that has been filtered and then artificially carbonated. It contains no added minerals or salts. In most cases, it is salt free.

Seltzer is named after *Niederselters*, a village near Wiesbaden, Germany. *See* Club Soda.

Selvatico (ital)   *See* Coarse.

Semidry Wine   A wine that contains between 0.6-percent and 2.2- percent sugar. Also known as *abocado, abboccato, amabile, demisec, medio seco, mezzo secco, off-dry, polsuho, semisecco,* and *vino abocado. See* Sugar In Wine.

Semifreddo (ital)   Chilled.

Sémillon   A white *Vitis vinifera* grape variety, cultivated in many parts of the world, including France, California, Washington state, Australia, New Zealand, Chile, Argentina, and South Africa. Sémillon produces wines that smell like fresh figs or like freshly laundered bed sheets drying in the sun; a steely, spicy aroma, and crisp herbaceous flavor, with underlying hints of citrus.

In the Sauternes district of France, it is blended along with Sauvignon Blanc and Muscadelle to produce luscious, sweet dessert wines, while in the Graves district, it produces dry, crisp wines. In California, it is occasionally stands as a single varietal, but more often is blended along with Sauvignon Blanc, or even used in "jug wine" blends. Also known as *Blanc Doux, Chevrier, Colombier,* and *Hunter River Riesling.*

Semiperishable   Subsistence that is canned, dried, dehydrated, or otherwise processed to the extent that such items may, under normal conditions, be stored in nonrefrigerated spaces. Semiperishable subsistence is not to be confused with nonperishable subsistence, which do not require care or protection in storage.

Semis (fr)   *See* Seedling.

Semisecco (ital)   *See* Semidry Wine.

Semisweet   An often-used term that translates to mean half dry...or half sweet. Also known as *medium-sweet* and *meiodoce.*

Semplice (ital)   *See* Simple.

Seneca   A white grape variety developed in 1930, from a cross of Lignan Blanc and Ontario, at the New York State Experimental Station.

Sensoriel (fr)   *See* Sensory Evaluation.

Sensory Evaluation   Also known as *sensoriel. See* Organoleptic.

SENSUOUS   The rich, alluring odor and/or taste of a silky, soft, and elegant wine; generally reserved for full-bodied red wines.

SENTEUR (FR)   *See* Scent.

SEPARATOR   A machine used in dairies for the separation of cream from milk.

SEPTIMER (GERM)   A white grape variety developed in Alzey in the Rheinhessen, from a cross of Müller-Thurgau and Gewürztraminer.

SEQUOIA SEMPERVIRENS   California redwood, utilized in the making of wooden barrels for the aging and/or storage of alcoholic beverages.

SERBESA   The term used in the Philippines for beer.

SERCIAL (PORT)   A fortified wine from the island of Madeira, Sercial is the driest Madeira; it is similar to a *fino* sherry, although slightly sweeter.

The sercial grape variety is viticulturally similar to the German Johannisberg Riesling, and was in fact brought to Madeira from Germany. In reality, it bears absolutely no resemblance to the Johannisberg Riesling in taste.

SERIOUSNESS OF COLD INJURY   It is indicated by the amount of decrease in fruit production and/or quality resulting from cold injury, noticed on a grapevine.

SERINE (FR)   *See* Durif and Syrah.

SERPENTIN   The "serpentine-shaped" condenser coil found on a still.

SERPETTE (FR)   *See* Grape Knife.

SERVER   A waiter or waitress in a beverage facility who takes orders and serves drinks to customers.

SERVICE   The act or manner of serving beverages that are requested to customers.

SERVICE BAR   A bar that provides alcoholic beverages exclusively to service personnel for patrons seated elsewhere.

SERVING TEMPERATURE   The optimum temperature for the service of wines and beers are as follows:

Serving temperatures (Fahrenheit) for wines and beers

Dry, full-bodied red wines	65–68 degrees
Dry, light-bodied red wines	60–65 degrees
Dry white wines	50–55 degrees
Sparkling wines and champagne	42–46 degrees
Sweet red and sweet white wines	42–46 degrees
Dry, light-bodied beers	38–45 degrees
Dry, full-bodied beers	55–60 degrees

SERVIR (FR) To serve.

SET *See* Berry Set.

SETINE An ancient Roman wine.

SETÚBAL (PORT) *See* Moscatel de Setúbal.

SETUP Bottles of nonalcoholic mixes, ice, and glasses, usually provided free to customers who either bring in or purchase separately bottles of distilled spirits.

SÈVE (FR) Sap; a well-balanced or "knit" wine with a promise of a good future.

SEVERE *See* Austere.

SEYVAL A white French-American hybrid grape variety, introduced into the Finger Lakes district in 1949. In the Midi region of France in 1921, Seyve-Villard developed this grape variety by crossing Seibel 5656 and Rayon d'Or. The grape is cultivated primarily in the eastern part of the United States, where it produces sound wines with good flavor and acidity. Formerly known as *Seyve-Villard 5276* and called *Seyval Blanc*.

SEYVAL BLANC *See* Seyval.

SFORZATO (ITAL) *See* Sfurzat.

SFUGGENTE (ITAL) Fleeting; describes a wine whose bouquet and taste are quite short.

SFURZAT (ITAL) A red wine produced in the region of Lombardy in the north, from a blend of Rossola, Brugnola, Pignola Valtellinese, Merlot, and Pinot Nero grapes. The wine, which is made from partly dried grapes that have been allowed to dry on racks from the harvest until December, is slightly reminiscent of port. Also spelled *Sfurzato*.

SFUSO (ITAL) Wine that is sold in bulk, usually quite inexpensive.

SG *See* Specific Gravity.

SGRADEVOLE (ITAL) A wine or beer that is not pleasing to drink.

SHAFT AND GLOBE The name used by bottle collectors for long-necked wine bottles that were in existence in the early seventeenth century.

SHAKER The combination of a 12- to 14-ounce mixing glass and a stainless steel container that fits over the glass.

SHAKING One of the three methods utilized for making cocktails; the other two being stirring and blending.

SHALLOW A term that describes wines lacking depth or character. Also known as *superficial*.

SHAM PILSNER GLASS A tall, conical-shaped beer glass with a narrow bottom.

SHANDY A drink in which beer is mixed with either lemonade or ginger beer. It is quite popular in England and Germany, where it is often consumed by cyclists. Also known as *alsterwasser* and *radlmass*.

SHARP A wine that displays an unpleasant, excessive amount of acidity (or acetic acid), which becomes almost piercing and biting to the taste.

SHATTER Essentially, shatter is caused by extreme heat early in the growing season when the grape berries are quite small or, worse yet, still in the period of "bloom" when the grapevine's flowers are in the process of transforming themselves into grape berries. If temperature extremes are experienced during this critical time, we have shatter, which is the drying up and falling off of many of the grapevine's flowers, or the falling off of the tiny berries, depending, of course, on the stage of development. *See* Berry Set and Shot Berries.

SHEETS *See* Legs.

SHEKAR A Hebrew word that means strong drink, from which our word *cider* is derived. *See* Cider.

SHELF LIFE The length of time a beverage can be stored, maintaining optimum flavor and drinkability, before losing quality. *See* Peak.

SHELF TALKER A small display that attaches to a shelf and promotes the product and/or price. It can also include a refund or product information pad.

SHELL A type of drinking glass, generally for the service of beer or cocktails, that is shaped like a tall, tapered plain cylinder.

SHERIDAN A red grape variety developed in 1921, from a cross of Herbert and Worden, at the New York State Experimental Station.

SHERMAT A winemaker's name for "sherry material," that is given to the base wine or cuvée prior to being fortified, as in the making of sherry wine.

SHERRY (SP) A fortified and blended nonvintage wine, made via the *solera system*; it contains 17- to 22-percent alcohol. It is traditionally produced in Spain, although certain other countries produce a similar product that they also call sherry.

Sherry originated in southwest Andalusía in the region of Jerez. The town of Jerez was founded by the Phoenicians in 1100 B.C., who brought their sailing ships to an inland city near the Bay of Cádiz off the Atlantic coast, and named it *Xera*. After the Roman conquest, Xera was Latinized to *Ceret*, which the Moors pronounced as *Scheris*. This was subsequently Hispanicized to *Jerez* and Anglicized, in reference to the beverage, into *sherry*.

The Jerez area is triangular in shape and lies between the Guadalquivir and the Guadalete rivers in southwest Spain, with the Atlantic Ocean on the west. The official sherry-producing zone, known as the *zone de Jerez superiore*, or "zone of superior sherry," is bounded by three major towns: Puerto de Santa Maria, Sanlúcar de Barrameda, and Jerez de la Frontera. The entire Jerez area consists of some 46,000 acres of vineyards.

Sherry Glass   *See* Copa or Copita.

Shine   *See* Moonshine.

Shipment   A case of product shipped from the producer/importer to the distributor.

Shiraz (austral and so. africa)   *See* Syrah.

Shirley Temple   A nonalcoholic cocktail consisting of gingerale and grenadine syrup, named after the child actress, Shirley Temple.

Shochu (japan)   *See* Sochu.

Shoe Pegs   *See* Garlic and Toothpicks.

Shoot   A green growth from a bud of a spur, arm, or trunk on a grapevine. A shoot always bears leaves and tendrils, and it may have fruit clusters. Its name is changed to "cane" in the fall when the leaves drop and the wood hardens. *See* Canes.

Shooter   A slang term for a shot of "liquor."

Short   A term applied to a wine that is lacking a good finish and a long, lingering aftertaste. Opposite of *long*.

Shortage   The amount by which quantity supplied is less than quantity demanded at the existing price; the opposite of a surplus.

Short Drink   A cocktail often served in a smaller than normal sized glass. *See* Burned Drinks.

Shot   *See* Old.

Shot   *See* Straight.

Shot Berries   If a temperature extreme is encountered midway in the flower-to-berry transformation, successful pollination, called "berry set" usually does not take place, which prevents the berry from maturing and developing. Instead, small grapes of good quality, which unfortunately contain very little juice, are formed. These are then called shot berries, due to their size relationship to BB's or "buck shot." Also known as *millerandage*. *See* Berry Set and Shatter.

Shot Glass   A small glass of varying capacity (although incorrectly believed to contain 1.5 ounces), used for pouring a specific amount of a distilled spirit.

Shout (austral)   A term that means "to buy a round of drinks."

Shrinkage   *See* Evaporation.

Shrub   A fruit drink made from citrus juice, rum, and sugar, which was quite popular in eighteenth century England.

Sicera (latin)   *See* Cider.

Sicilia (ital)   *See* Sicily.

Sicily (ital)   The largest island in the Mediterranean, off Italy's southern coast, is also one of top wine-producing regions of Italy.

Sicily not only produces Marsala, a fortified wine from its southern shores, but also a host of red, white, and rosé wines. Some Sicilian wines tend to be of a higher alcoholic nature due to the fact that they receive a great deal of sunshine throughout the year. This heat, which oftentimes actually bakes the grapes or causes them to become "sunburnt," is noticeable in white wines. Because of the higher concentration of coloring matter in the skins, a slightly deeper color is attained. Wines produced from grapes with very high sugar levels also tend to be "flat," lacking a sufficient acid backbone supporting the high sugar and alcohol levels.

Credit must be given to the skills of the modern Sicilian winemakers, who in spite of difficult working conditions have produced wines that display lightness of body, freshness of taste, and a good balance between fruit and acidity. Known as *Sicilia*, in Italy.

SICK   An unsound wine or beer displaying cloudiness, murkiness, or off-taste. Also known as *malato*. *See* Bacterial Spoilage and Spoiled.

SIDE CAR   A cocktail consisting of brandy, triple sec, and lemon juice.

SIDRA (SP)   *See* Cider.

SIDRE (FR)   *See* Cider.

SIEGER (GERM)   A white grape variety developed in the Rheinhessen, from a cross of Madeleine Angevine and Gewürztraminer.

SIEGERREBE (GERM)   A white grape variety that was developed in 1929, from a cross of Madeleine Angevine and Gewürztraminer, by George Scheu, at the Alzey experiment station, in the Rheinhessen.

SIEGFRIED (GERM)   A white hybrid grape variety, developed from a cross of Johannisberg Riesling and a *See* dling of Oberlin 595. The Siegfried grape produces wines with considerable Johannisberg Riesling characteristics.

SIFON (SP)   *See* Siphon.

SIGNATURE DRINK   A drink specialty of the house, which is designed and/or prepared in some novel manner so as to make it almost a "designer drink." Signature drinks are unique to the establishment and is what they are often known for.

SIKES SCALE   The English method of measuring the alcoholic strength of alcoholic beverages by use of a hydrometer. The method was named after Bartholomew Sikes, a British inventor. Also incorrectly spelled *Sykes*.

SIKERA (GREECE)   *See* Cider.

SILKY   A term that describes a wine that is significantly velvety smooth, soft, and finely textured on the palate. Also known as *soyeux*. *See* Velvety.

SILLERY (FR)   The name given to the region of Champagne during the Middle Ages, many years before a sparkling wine was made.

SILVANER   *See* Sylvaner.

SILVER BULLET   A name given to an extremely ice-cold, dry vodka martini during the 1950s and 1960s.

SILVER RUM   *See* Light Rum.

SIMPLE   Also known as *semplice*. *See* Ordinary.

SIMPLE SUGAR OR SYRUP   A syrup made by mixing equal parts of sugar and water, then boiling until all the sugar dissolves.

SIN CRIANZA (SP)   A regional wine that has not been aged in wood.

SINEWY   *See* Muscular.

SINGAPORE GIN SLING   A cocktail consisting of gin, cherry-flavored brandy, lemon and orange juice, and seltzer. This drink, originally called a "Straits Sling," was created in 1915 by Ngiam Tong Boon, a bartender of the Long Bar at the Raffles Hotel in Singapore.

SINGLE MALT SCOTCH WHISKY   A single malt Scotch whisky is the product of one particular distillery. *See* Malt Scotch.

SINGLES BAR   An establishment licensed to serve alcoholic beverages, that caters specifically to both single men and women, by promotions, interaction, and so on.

SINGLE-VINEYARD   A vineyard designation for a specially delimited growing area within a selected vineyard site, where the grapes possess more intense characteristics than those grown in adjoining parts of the vineyard. This is often due to optimum soil and ideal climatic conditions that result in a wine with more varietal character and concentrated flavors. A limited release wine produced from grapes grown in these selected vineyards will be designated "single-vineyard" on the label. Also known as *vigna, vigneti,* or *vigneto.*

SINGLE WHISKEY   A whiskey that is the product of one particular distillery.

SINGLINGS   Brandy after the first distillation and prior to the second distillation.

SINKER   A heavy, perforated, stainless steel, or wooden plate utilized for keeping the *cap* of grape skins below the surface during fermentation.

SINK WORKBOARD   *See* Bar Workboard.

SIPHON   An apparatus consisting of a bent tube used for carrying liquids out over the top edge of a container through the force of gravity and atmospheric pressure exerted upon the surface of the liquid. Also known as *sifon.*

SIPON (YUG)   *See* Furmint.

SITE   Point of origin; shipping point.

SITE SELECTION   The selected area for planting and propagation of grapevines. It is as important as grape variety selection. It is a complex of above-ground environment, root environment, and management characteristics. The above-ground environment of a grapevine can be restrictive by its low temperature. The root environment is critical with respect to root pests and to availability of water. Management characteristics are relatively minor; they include the site's size, slope, and nearness to both market and to other vineyards. The selection must be made rationally and scientifically.

SIZZANO (ITAL) A dry, red wine produced in the northwest region of Piedmont, from a blend of Nebbiolo, Bonarda, and Vespolina grape varieties.

SKADARSKA (YUG) *See* Kadarka.

SKIM MILK It is fresh fluid milk that has been almost entirely defatted by means of centrifugal force, leaving approximately 0.5-percent butterfat.

SKIN The outer covering or surface of a grape, which accounts for 5 to 12 percent of the grape. Approximately 23 percent of all phenolics are contained in the skins. From the skin and the layers of cells immediately beneath the skin come the color of wine (particularly red wine) and much of the flavor characteristics. As the grape size increases, these flavor constituents decrease in their relationship to the rest of the grape; therefore, the best wine grapes are small. They have a higher ratio of flavor-rich components that contribute to varietal character in a wine.

SKIN *See* Peel.

SKIN CONTACT A winemaking technique, whereby the grape skins (usually red) remain in contact with the fermenting juice, for color and flavor extraction. Many flavor components are found in grape skins rather than the juice. To get these components into the wine, many wineries crush the grapes and leave the skins, juice, and *Seeds* (collectively called *must*) together in a tank for a number of hours or days before fermentation and/or pressing.

SKLIRÓS (GREECE) *See* Hard.

SKUNKY A particularly unpleasant odor occasionally detected in beers left for prolonged periods of time in direct sunlight, or unpasteurized keg beer that has been left unrefrigerated.

SLA State Liquor Authority.

SLADKO (BUL) *See* Sweet.

SLATKO (YUG) *See* Sweet.

SLING A cocktail for which a mug is filled with two-thirds strong beer and sweetened with sugar, molasses, or dried pumpkin. Rum is then added to this mixture and stirred with a loggerhead. It also is the name of a family of cocktails, often with gin as its base. *See* Flip.

SLIPSKIN A term applied to those grape varieties that possess a rather tough skin that separates readily from the pulpy flesh...hence *slipskin*.

SLIVOVITZ A fruit brandy made from small, blue plums with a highly aromatic perfume, usually produced in central Europe and Hungary.

SLOE GIN It is not actually a gin, but rather a red liqueur made from sloe berries (blackthorn berry), which give it a rather tart, plum flavor.

SLOE GIN FIZZ A cocktail consisting of sloe gin, lemon juice, sugar, and soda water.

SLOP The spent grains and fluids that are drawn off from the bottom of the continuous still after distillation and are dried and used as high-protein feed supplements for both livestock and poultry.

SLOUSHED Slang for intoxicated.

SLURRY Mashed apples; used in the making of apple brandy.

SMALL A wine or beer that features no particular characteristics or qualities, and has a light smell, body, and taste. *See* Light and Little.

SMALL BEER An old English term, dating back to about 1568, for a weak beer (low alcohol); in Colonial times, a thin ale was dubbed "small beer."

SMASH A short drink made from brandy, bourbon, or other distilled spirits, mixed with sugar and mint. Another name for a small mint julep.

SMASHED Slang for intoxicated.

SMELL Olfactory sensation noticed directly by the nose; to be distinguished from aroma.

SMOKY An elusive, tactile impression, noticed either in the bouquet or on the palate, that some wines leave, evoking this compound. Often found in wines made from the Sauvignon Blanc grape variety in the Loire Valley of France (e.g. Pouilly-Fumé). Also, the odor given off by wines or beers that have been fermented or aged in charred oak barrels.

SMOOTH Wines that display on the palate a soft, silky, and well-rounded texture, absent of roughness or harshness. Opposite of astringent.

SNAKE-HEAD WHISKEY A slang "cowboy" term denoting a cheap whiskey.

SNAPS The Scandinavian spelling of *schnapps*, referring to akvavit.

SNERVATO (ITAL) A poorly made wine or one that is over-aged and characterless.

SNIFTER The "traditional" balloon-shaped, wide-brimmed brandy glass. The main consideration is to select a glass that will enhance the beverage's bouquet. The glass should be large enough (10 to 12 ounces) to enable the liquid to move around with ease, spreading the bouquet over a wide surface area. Ideally, the neck should be slightly indented to help the spirit retain its bouquet. Also known as *brandy glass* and *brandy snifter*.

SNOWBALLS A distillers' term to indicate the bubbles appearing inside vats of fermenting mash, due to fermentation.

SOAPY A term applied to those wines and beers that are low in acidity, making them flat and uninteresting.

SOAVE (ITAL) A famous dry white wine produced northeast of Verona in the region of Veneto, from a blend of Garganega and Trebbiano Toscano grapes.

SOCHU (JAPAN) A 70-proof clear grain spirit distilled from a combination of barley, corn, wheat, sugar cane, or sweet potatoes, although occasionally rice will also be used. It is triple distilled and aged in white oak barrels. This manufacturing process creates its slightly sweet, smooth, distinctive taste and aroma. Also known as *shochu*.

SODA A carbonated soft drink of water, flavored with syrup and fruit. Also known as *soude*.

SODA OUT A cocktail that is finished by topping with soda.

SODA POP Any carbonated, nonalcoholic beverage consisting basically of sugar syrup or other type sweeteners, natural or synthetic acids, flavoring agents, carbonated water, and natural and artificial colors.

In 1812, English author Robert Southey wrote that the name "pop" is derived from the sound produced when the cork or cap is removed from the bottle, which contains carbon dioxide. Also known as *pop* and *soft drink*.

SODA SYSTEM *See* Post-Mix Soda System and Premix Soda System.

SODA WATER Water charged under pressure with carbon dioxide.

SODIUM CARBONATE A chemical used to reduce excess natural acidity in wine.

SODIUM CASEINATE A chemical used to clarify wine.

SODIUM METABISULPHITE A chemical used for sterilizing wine.

SODIUM SALT OF SORBIC ACID As a sterilizing and preserving agent and to inhibit mold growth and secondary fermentations.

SOFT An organoleptic term that refers to the way a wine feels in the mouth; pleasant and smooth without any harsh edges. Also known as *macio* and *milde*. *See* Mellow.

SOFT DRINK A nonalcoholic, carbonated beverage. *See* Soda.

SOIL There are countless types of soil throughout the world, suitable for the growing of grapes. Winemakers and grape growers constantly strive for the "best" soil for their grapevines, but, unfortunately, the "best" type of soil is often disputed by both sides. What is accepted by all sides is that grapevines do best on well-drained soils that are able to supply adequate amounts of nutrients and water. Some elements that must be considered are drainage, soil structure, access to water, nourishment or lack of it, microclimate of the grapevine, soil acidity, presence of minerals, depth, slope, and exposure to sunlight.

SOLEAR (SP) The actual "sunning" or drying of grapes in the sun, for later use in sweetening some sherry types.

SOLERA (SP) A system of "fractional" blending, which produces a consistent style of fortified wine. According to some sherry producers, *solera* comes from the word *suelo*, meaning ground or land, and it refers to the butts (barrels) nearest to the ground. Others say it comes from the Spanish word *solar*, which refers to the tradition that holds a family together.

The solera system involves a series of white American oak barrels arranged in rows or tiers, often eight to ten barrels high. The arranging of barrels in tiers is not a requirement of the system or of law. The original or bottom row of barrels is called the *solera*, while the upper, or younger, rows, which are on the top, are called the *criaderas* (cradles). Each row is known as a scale, and moving the wine from tier to tier is often referred to as "playing the scales."

The wine first sold is that on the bottom row, which is then replaced with wine from the second tier, and so on up, through as many as ten tiers. The wine from the most recent vintage is poured into the barrels on the top tier, which were not completely filled; thus, the youngest wine is blended with a slightly older wine of the same type, which has in turn been blended with a still older wine, and so on down, through the tiers. Wines of a superior quality are created in this way.

Wine is not siphoned from tier to tier, but is rather transferred into containers so that wine from various casks on the same level can be blended for even further standardization. By law, the maximum amount that can be drawn out of a barrel of fully mature sherry is 33 percent.

One of the reasons for the blending is to "tame" the young, rough wine. The key to the solera system is that aged sherries in the bottom "educate" the younger ones by giving them character and taste. The wine is also aerated as it passes from tier to tier, and, in addition, picks up subtle nuances from the oak barrels.

During this entire process, approximately 10 percent of the wine is lost through evaporation, whereas in an aging cellar, where the barrels are tightly bunged, the amount would be only 1.5 to 2 percent.

SOLERA DATE (SP) The date that appears on the label of some sherries identifies the year the solera "was established" and has nothing to do with when the grapes were harvested or when the sherry was bottled. If, for example, a sherry from a producer states on the label, Solera 1908, this means that the solera was established in 1908. The chances of having any of the wine remaining in the current system is quite remote.

SOLID A term applied to a wine that has a firm and sound foundation and backbone, which allows the wine to improve with age. Also known as *solide*.

SOLIDE (FR) *See* Solid.

SOM (ITAL) Superior Old Marsala.

SOMATIC EMBRYOGENESIS *In vitro* culture technique for production of plantlets that are normally produced by seeds. The method allows scientists to modify existing plants—only one or two agronomic characteristics—without using sexual crossing.

SOMMELIER (FR) One who is in charge of the service of wine and the wine cellar in a restaurant. Their traditional uniform is a black and gray striped apron with a cellar key and wine-tasting cup on a silver chain, dangling from their neck. Also known as *escancao, escanciador, kellner, wine butler, wine captain, wine steward,* and *wine waiter. See* Tastevin.

Sonoma Riesling (cal) *See* Sylvaner.

Sonne (germ) Sun.

Sonoma Valley An important viticultural area north of San Francisco and west of Napa Valley, noted for its many fine vineyards.

Soplica (pol) A dry and very fine golden-colored vodka.

Sor (hun) Beer.

Sorbates *See* Potassium Sorbate and Sorbic Acid.

Sorbic Acid It is a short chain fatty acid that, together with its salt, potassium sorbate, exhibits antimicrobial properties. During malolactic fermentation, if the growth of lactic acid bacteria is in the presence of sorbic acid, heat, bacteria, a high pH, and low alcohol, a powerful odorous compound (2-ethoxyhexa-3 5 diene) will form, which is responsible for the so-called geranium smell. *See* Potassium Sorbate and Stabilizing.

Sorbitol A white, sweet, odorless, crystalline alcohol, present in some berries and fruits. It has no relation to sorbates or sorbic acid.

Sorrentine An ancient Roman wine.

Sortenbukett(germ) A wine that displays a fine varietal aroma.

Sottile (ital) *See* Subtle.

Souche (fr) *See* Rootstock.

Soude (fr) *See* Soda.

Sound A descriptive term that refers to a healthy, good-smelling, clean-tasting, well-made wine or beer, with no major flaws or defects.

Souple (fr) *See* Supple.

Sour *See* Acetic and Volatile Acidity.

Sour The name of the largest drink family, which consists of a distilled spirit (generally whiskey), lemon juice, and sugar, garnished with a cherry or orange slice. Also known as *whiskey sour*.

Sour Beer *See* Spoiled.

Sour Glass A medium-sized, short-stemmed glass with a tubular bowl that holds approximately six fluid ounces.

Souring *See* Spoiled.

Sour Mash A type of whiskey produced by using spent distiller's beer (residue from a previous distillation) to aid in fermenting a new batch of mash. The lactic acid present permits pH adjustment and suppresses the reproduction of undesired bacteria. Sour mash got its name because the spent distiller's mash has a slightly acid taste, although the resulting distilled spirits are anything but sour. Most bourbon and Tennessee whiskey is *sour mash* whiskey.

Sour Milk Milk that has gone sour due to bacterial contamination.

Sour Mix A premixed, nonalcoholic beverage mixer, consisting of sugar syrup, lemon and/or lime juice, egg whites, and oftentimes a preservative. Sour mix is generally utilized in beverage facilities as a bar substitute for sugar and lemon or lime juice in cocktails. Also known as *sweet and sour mix*.

SOURNESS   *See* Sour.

SOUSED   Slang for intoxicated.

SOUTIRAGE (FR)   *See* Racking.

SOYEUX (FR)   *See* Silky.

SPA (ITAL)   Società Per Azioni. Joint-stock company.

SPA   *See* Standard Price Allowance.

SPACER   A term used in an English pub for a nonalcoholic beer.

SPALLIERA (ITAL)   A pruning method for grapevines, used in Sicily. *See* Cordon.

SPANISH EARTH (SP)   A complex silicate (used as a fining agent for wine and beer), known as *silicaceous*, was originally found only in certain types of soil in Spain, although some has been discovered in certain parts of the United States. Also known as *tierra de vino. See* Fining Agents.

SPANNA (ITAL)   The local name used for the Nebbiolo grape variety in the provinces of Vercelli and Novara in the region of Piedmont. *See* Nebbiolo.

SPARGING   The spraying and distribution of hot water over the spent grains and hops in the mash-tun to recover all the sugars and other extracts that might be remaining.

SPARKLETS   Small capsules containing carbon dioxide that dissolve upon contact with a liquid; used to carbonate certain nonalcoholic beverages.

SPARKLING BURGUNDY   A sweetish, red sparkling wine generally produced in New York State.

SPARKLING WINE OR CHAMPAGNE   An effervescent wine containing more than 0.392 grams of carbon dioxide per 100 milliliters of wine, resulting solely from the secondary fermentation of the wine within a closed container. Most champagne and sparkling wines contain 70 to 100 pounds per square inch when finished. Also known as *biser, cava, champanski, espumante, espumosa, habzú, iskriashto, moussec, mousseux, pezsgo, sampanjac, sekt, spumante, vinho do rodo, vinho espumante, vin mousseux, vino espumosa, vino spumante, vonkelwyn,* and *Xampan*.

SPARKOLLOID   It is a proprietary fining agent made up of a mixture of refined polysaccharides (a carbohydrate sugar type compound) and diatomaceous earth. It forms a coagulum due to the normal inorganic ions present in wine. It has little absorption capacity and acts mainly by entrapping haze particles and finds its principle usage in cases of particularly difficult haze problems. *See* Fining and Fining Agents.

SPÄT (GERM)   Late.

SPÄTBURGUNDER (GERM)   *See* Pinot Noir.

SPÄTLESE (GERM) A term that means "late-picking" or "late-harvesting" of the grapes. The date of the harvest is not as important as the degree of ripeness of the grapes.

SPÄTROT (AUS) *See* Zierfandler.

SPEAKEASY A term applied to illicit saloons in New York City in 1899 (which predated Prohibition). Speakeasies served alcoholic beverages only to persons who would appear at the door and softly speak the password in order to enter. Also, an old Irish term for a place where illicit whiskey was sold.

SPECIAL INVENTORY A physical counting of stock on hand at irregular periods of time, due to extraordinary circumstances.

SPECIAL NATURAL WINE A product produced from a base of natural wine (including heavy-bodied blending wine) to which natural flavorings are added.

SPECIALLY SWEETENED NATURAL WINE A wine product made with a base of natural wine and having a total solids content in excess of 17 percent by weight (17 degrees Brix dealcoholized wine) and an alcohol content of not more than 14 percent by volume.

SPECIES A member of a botanical genus family.

SPECIFICATION An exact, detailed, accurate description of the quality and type of beverage to be supplied to an establishment. Specifications are used to insure consistent quality.

SPECIFIC GRAVITY (SG) The ratio of the weight or density of a given volume of liquid as compared to the weight or density of an equal volume of water at the same temperature. Water having a density of 1.00; substance less dense than water will register less than 1.00; substance more dense than water will register over 1.00. *See* Density.

SPEED POUR A pouring device inserted into the neck of a bottle of distilled spirits that aids in its dispensing.

SPEED RACK A stainless steel trough, either suspended or attached to the underbar directly in front of a bartender, usually at the cocktail station, that contains bottles of distilled spirits or mixes that have the greatest consumer demand. Also known as *bottle trough* and *speed rail*.

SPEED RAIL *See* Speed Rack.

SPENT BEER The stillage or residue material remaining after distillation, for the production of distilled spirits.

SPENT LEES The stillage or residue in the distilled spirits still, after the distillation of the *foreshots*, potable distilled spirits, and feints.

SPERONE (ITAL) The spur of a grapevine.

SPICY An organoleptic term that evokes an impression of spices, either through odor, taste, or both, which can be reminiscent of various spices (e.g. cinnamon, black pepper, and mint), as well as an attractive herb-like character.

Spicy can also be used to describe the odor and/or taste of certain types of wine, such as Muscat, Gewürztraminer, and even some Zinfandels.

SPIEL (GERM)   Flexible; balanced.

SPIELIG (GERM)   *See* Lively.

SPIGOT   A metal faucet or wooden tap utilized for drawing liquids from a barrel or tank, or to draw off the contents of a barrel. Also known as *faucet* and *tap*. *See* Zwickel.

SPILE   A barrel stopper or bung. Also known as *bonde*.

SPILLAGE ALLOWANCE   A discretionary portion of a distilled spirits bottle (e.g. one or two ounces) that management may assume will be lost accidentally. This *spillage allowance* is not factored into the calculation of the number of drinks per bottle.

SPINNER   The term applied to a *capsule* on the neck of a wine bottle that is not set properly and therefore is able "to rotate."

SPIRITS   That substance known as ethyl alcohol, ethanol, or spirits of wine in any form (including all dilutions or mixtures thereof, from whatever source or by whatever process produced), but not denatured spirits unless specifically stated. *See* Distilled Spirits.

SPIRITS STILL   The third still used for the final run in the production of distilled spirits.

SPIRITUEUX (FR)   High in alcohol; applied to distilled spirits or wines.

SPIRIT WHISKEY   A mixture of neutral spirits and not less than 5 percent on a proof gallon basis of whiskey, or straight whiskey, or straight whiskey and whiskey, if the straight whiskey component is less than 20 percent on a proof gallon basis.

SPITZEN (GERM)   Peak; indicates top quality.

SPITZENJAHR (GERM)   An excellent vintage.

SPITZENWEIN (GERM)   An excellent wine.

SPLASH   A measurement containing a small amount of an ingredient added to a drink.

SPLICE THE MAIN BRACE   An old Navy term meaning to drink whiskey. The term often appears in Herman Melville's writings.

SPLIT   A small wine or champagne bottle containing a single serving of approximately 6.4 fluid ounces.

SPLIT CASE   Same as a Broken Case.

SPOGLIA (ITAL)   *See* Spoiled.

SPOILED   A decayed wine or beer that is caused by poor vinification, bacterial contamination, improper storage, or poor beverage handling. Also known as *spoglia*, *sour beer*, and *souring*. *See* Bacterial Spoilage and Sick.

SPONSORED BAR   *See* Host Bar.

SPORTS BAR   An establishment licensed to sell and serve alcoholic beverages in an environment permeated by sports paraphernalia, which often includes a large screen television and satellite television reception, capable of picking up various local and national sporting events.

SPOUDÉOS (GREECE)   Excellent.

SPRAYING   The care of treatment of grapevines by the application of liquid fungicides and insecticides as needed.

SPRIGHTLY   A term used to describe a wine or beer that is lively and full of flavor.

SPRING WATER   A term used to indicate water from a deep underground source that flows naturally to the surface. If that water remains unprocessed and unchanged—nothing added or taken away—the term "natural" may be added and the product is called "Natural Spring Water.

SPRINKLER IRRIGATION   The irrigation of vineyards by means of surface pipes and sprinkler heads. Also utilized in some instances as frost protection.

SPRITIG (GERM)   *See* Alkohelreich.

SPRITZ   Slight effervescence or prickle on the tongue in a wine that may be caused by leaving some dissolved carbon dioxide in the wine, but is more often the result of the addition of carbon dioxide gas to certain table wines. Also known as *crackling, frizzante, pétillant, prickly, spritzig, spritzy, vino de aguja,* and *vino frizzante.*

SPRITZER   A tall drink made with a base of wine (white, red, or rosé) and filled with a carbonated mixer.

SPRITZIG (GERM)   *See* Spritz.

SPRITZY   *See* Spritz.

SPRUCE BEER   Beer or nonalcoholic malt beverages, famous during the Revolutionary War, produced by the addition of tops of spruce trees or spruce boughs to the fermenting liquid.

SPUMA (ITAL)   Foam, froth, effervescence. *See* Schiuma.

SPUMANTE (ITAL)   *See* Sparkling Wine.

SPUR   A short fruiting unit of one-years' growth on a grapevine, usually consisting of one or two nodes that are retained at pruning. *See* Renewal Spur.

SPUR PRUNING   A practice that is very common in very old vineyards where there is no trellising of stakes and wires. It is a method whereby the spurs are retained as fruiting units with the canes tied to the support wires. *See* Pruning and Cane Pruning.

SQUARE CUBES   *See* Ice Cubes.

SQUEEZIN'S   A slang term for the end product or *tails* of a distillation. *See* Tails.

STAATSWEINGÜT (GERM)   State wine estate or domain.

STABILIMENTO (ITAL)   A bottling plant.

STABILIZER   Any additive used in winemaking and brewing to keep them stable and retard deterioration. *See* Sorbic Acid.

STABILIZING   Various treatments, including additives, used in the production of alcoholic and nonalcoholic beverages that keeps them stable, thereby retarding deterioration. Among them are ascorbic acid, cold stabilization, filtering, fining, pasteurization, refrigeration, sorbic acid, and sulfur dioxide.

STABLE   A wine or beer is said to be stable if there is no chance of refermentation taking place.

STAGIONATO (ITAL)   A wine that is correctly aged or matured.

STAHLIG (GERM)   *See* Steely.

STAINLESS STEEL   A type of metal used exclusively in winemaking due to the fact that it is neutral (does not impart odor, taste, or add metal ions to the wine), is inert to acids and alcohols, is durable, cleans easily, can withstand severe temperature changes, is basically corrosion proof, and is unaffected by chemical cleaners. Also known as *acciaio inossidabile*.

STAKE   A post, made of wood, metal, or even cement, utilized as a support for the grapevines and/or wires utilized for training of the grapevine.

STALE   A term used to describe a wine or beer that has lost its lively, fresh, youthful character, and has become dull and tasteless, with a musty, cardboard taste. Often the result of the beverage being kept too long. Also known as *schal*.

STALKY   *See* Stemmy.

STAMPING   The process of marking a wine (on its capsule, cork, barrel, or cardboard box) to identify it.

STANDARD   An approved criterion, measure, or basis for comparison, against a yardstick, that is used to evaluate quantity, quality, and volume.

STANDARD BEVERAGE COST   *See* Beverage Cost.

STANDARD COST   *See* Beverage Cost.

STANDARD COST PERCENTAGE   *See* Cost Percentage.

STANDARD DEPLETION ALLOWANCE   *See* Depletion Allowance.

STANDARD DISTILLED SPIRITS BOTTLE   A standard distilled spirits bottle that is so made and formed, and so filled, as not to mislead the purchaser. An individual carton or other container of a bottle shall not be so designed as to mislead purchasers as to the size of the bottles.

STANDARD DRINK LIST   A list of the alcoholic beverages or cocktails offered for sale in a retail, on-premise establishment.

STANDARD DRINK RECIPE   *See* Standard Recipe.

STANDARD DRINK SIZE   *See* Standard Portion.

STANDARD GLASSWARE   Glassware of a specific quality, quantity, type, and size for a given drink.

STANDING PLAN   An established routine, formula, or set of procedures used in a recurring situation.

STANDARDIZED DRINK   *See* Standard Recipe.

STANDARDIZED RECIPE   *See* Standard Recipe.

STANDARD OF PERFORMANCE   In a performance-based objective, that part of the objective stating, in terms of measurable or observable performance, the standard for carrying out a given unit of work.

STANDARD PORTION   A carefully regulated measurement of each individual serving of a beverage, made in accordance with a standardized drink recipe. Also known as *standard drink size.*

STANDARD PRICE ALLOWANCE (SPA)   A general term used to describe any number of discounting or promotional activities.

STANDARD PURCHASE SPECIFICATIONS   *See* Purchase Specification.

STANDARD RECIPE   A written, regulated formula established by management that has been systematically tested for preparing any particular type of alcoholic drink and that yields a consistent, known quality and quantity of product each and every time it is requested. A standard recipe includes a listing of ingredients, quantity, procedures, and equipment needed. Also known as *standard drink recipe, standardized drink,* and *standardized recipe.*

STANDARD-SIZED BOTTLE   A bottle with a capacity of 750 milliliters, or 25.4 ounces.

STANDARD WINE   Natural wine, specially sweetened natural wine, special natural wine, and standard agricultural wine.

STANDARDS OF FILL   Set standards according to the BATF as to the exact quantity of alcoholic beverage that an accepted size bottle must contain.

STANDARDS OF IDENTITY   The federal government's definition of the various classes and types of distilled spirits, wines, and malt beverages.

STANDARD YIELD   The total number of portions that will be produced by a standard recipe.

STAR BRIGHT   *See* Falling Bright.

STARCH   A white, tasteless, odorless food substance of the polysaccharide group found in plants, such as the various grains utilized in the production of distilled spirits and malt beverages.

STARKA   A vodka flavored with brandy, port, honey, and vanilla, plus the leaves of several different types of Crimean Apple and pear trees, that is produced in the Slavic countries.

STARKBIER (GERM)   A beer that has the highest alcohol level (up to 7 percent) of any beer in Germany. It was first brewed in the early seventeenth century by the Franciscan Monks of the Paulaner Abbey, for the sole reason

356

that it helped them through the long 40-day fast of Easter. However, it was not until the middle of the eighteenth century that its reputation spread to Duke Wilhelm V, who ordered the building of beer halls, namely "Hofbrauhaus," in 1589.

STARTER   A highly concentrated and already fermenting yeast culture, that is used to "start" fermentations in larger volume *musts*.

STATE STORES   Those retail premises operated by some states, from which alcoholic beverages are purchased.

STATION   A work area in a bar that is set up with all the essentials for the service of alcoholic beverages. Also known as *cocktail station* and *pouring station*.

STATIONARY BAR   *See* Cocktail Mix Station.

STAVES   The curved lengths of wood, generally one inch in thickness and made of oak, that form the side of a wooden barrel. The individual staves vary in width from two to four inches.

STEAM BEER   A highly carbonated, deep brown-gold-colored beer, with an aromatic odor of cloves, orange peels, and peaches, and a tangy-bitter taste with a dry finish. The name *steam* originates from the final *krausening* stage of fermentation, during which a partially fermented wort is added to speed the fermentation; at this point the active head produced by this process releases a *steam*. Steam beer is a bottom-fermented beer, like lager, yet with a taste of ale. Steam beer originated in San Francisco, California, during the Gold Rush.

STEEN   The local name in South Africa for the Chenin Blanc grape variety. *See* Chenin Blanc.

STEEP   To soak or infuse in liquid; a process by which grain is soaked in water in huge cisterns to begin the germination process. This is a necessary step in the production of distilled spirits and malt beverages.

STEEL JACKETED TANK   *See* Jacketed Tank.

STEELY   A term used to describe the taste of stony, gravelly, rocky, acidic, or mineral flavors or nuances found in some white wines, such as French Chablis or Puligny-Montrachet. Also known as *stahlig*.

STEIN (GERM)   Stone.

STEIN   An earthenware beer mug, or similar mug of pewter or glass, generally large and ornate. *See* Tankard.

ST. EMILION (FR)   *See* Saint-Emilion.

ST-EMILION (FR)   The local name for the Trebbiano grape variety in the Cognac region. *See* Trebbiano.

STEMMY   A greenwood effect, or the smell and taste of damp twigs, often displayed in wines fermented in contact with the stems for prolonged periods of time. The taste sensation is similar to chewing on dried grape stems. Also known as *stalky*, *stemminess*, *twiggy*, and *weedy*. *See* Herbaceous.

Stemminess *See* Stemmy.

Stemmer *See* Crusher/Destemmer.

Stemmed Cherry A cherry (generally maraschino) with a stem.

Stemmed Glass One of the three parts of a glass, the other two being the bowl and base (foot).

Stems The thick stalk by which a bunch of grapes is attached to the cane on a grapevine. This stalk is a valuable source of tannin in red wine. Approximately 5 percent of all phenolics present in wine are contained in the stems, which have a pH of more over 4.0.

Stenospermocarpy The technical term for grapes that are seedless, either by natural reproduction or through hybridization.

Sterilants A sterilizing agent, as heat, steam, sulfur dioxide, ascorbic acid, and other chemicals, that inhibits wild yeasts and spoilage bacteria in *musts* or on bottles and equipment.

Sterile Bottling The main function of sterile bottling is the removal of yeast cells from a wine, usually at 0.45 microns or smaller. *See* Sterile Filtration.

Sterile Filtration For certain wines that have a small amount of residual sugar and that, if any yeast were present, might begin a fermentation in the bottle. The wine is passed through a special filter (0.45 microns) that is so fine that even microscopic yeast cells are removed. *See* Clarifying, Filtering, Fining, and Sterile Bottling.

Sternewirt (germ) A taproom located inside a brewery.

St. Estèphe (fr) *See* Saint-Estèphe.

Steuben A red grape variety developed in 1947, from a cross of Wayne and Sheridan, at the New York State Experimental Station

Steward A person who is charge of the storeroom where alcoholic beverages are stored.

Stewed Slang for intoxicated.

Stiff Similar to dumb.

Still Apparatus used to concentrate and produce distilled spirits. Stills may be classified by the method of introducing fermented mixture. *See* Alambic, Coffey Still, Column Still, Continuous Still, Patent Still, and Pot Still.

Still The opposite of sparkling; table wines that contain noticeable or perceptible amounts of carbon dioxide. Also known as *tranquillo*.

Stillage The residue in the still after the distillation of the alcohol. It is drawn off for making distillers feed.

Still House A building where the actual process of distilling takes place and that houses the various pieces of equipment necessary for distilling.

Still Wine   Wine containing not more than 0.392 grams of carbon dioxide per 100 milliliters. The opposite of a sparkling wine.

Stimulants   Any agent temporarily increasing functional activity, such as drugs, caffeine, and alcohol.

Stimulus   An agent or factor capable of inciting or provoking a sensory response.

Stinger   A cocktail consisting of brandy and white crème de menthe.

Stir   One of three methods of mixing a drink, incorporating the ingredients, the other two being shaking and blending.

Stirrer   *See* Swizzle Stick.

Stirrup Cup   A cup used for serving the "parting drink," or last drink, served to a welcome guest. The name comes from an old custom of having a last drink with a guest after he had mounted his horse, and had his feet firmly in the "stirrups."

Also, the name of a drink consisting of whiskey and boiling water, to which a dollop of butter was added, that was drunk immediately. Although the drink is obsolete and its origin lost in antiquity, it was at one time served in Louisville, Kentucky.

St. Julien (FR)   *See* Saint-Julien.

St-Laurent   A red grape variety cultivated primarily in Austria, although at one time it flourished in Alsace, France. It produces wines light in color, with good fruit and fairly high acid levels.

Stock   It is the underground portion, the root system of a grapevine, onto which the scion is grafted.

Stockless Purchase   When the buyer purchases a large quantity of product, but arranges for the supplier to store and deliver it a little at a time, as needed. This procedure is illegal in certain states.

Stoffa (ITAL)   *See* Stuffing.

Stoffig (GERM)   *See* Stuffing.

Stolno Vino (YUG)   *See* Vino da Tavola.

Stoned   Slang for intoxicated.

Stopfen (GERM)   *See* Cork.

Stop Fermentation   The term that describes how, in winemaking, a little pure grape brandy is added to a sweet dessert wine to check the fermentation. This prevents complete conversion of the natural grape sugar into wine alcohol and carbon dioxide so that the wine is sweeter than if fermentation had run its course.

Storing   The process of aging or "laying away" barrels, bottles of wine, or other items for future use.

Stout   A top-fermenting beer that obtains its dark (almost black) color from roasted barley, with a very high extract level. It contains mostly this roasted barley, which is rendered sterile before germination, and a small amount of malt for added flavor. It is quite thick and malty, with an intense bitterness and underlying sweet taste. Stout is relatively low in carbonation and should be served at 55 degrees Fahrenheit. Specific types of stout are Bitter Stout, Imperial Stout, Irish Stout, Milk Stout, Oatmeal Stout, and Porter.

STOVER   A white hybrid grape variety, introduced in 1956 (named in 1968), from a cross of Mantey and Roucaneuf, by Floridian Professor Loren Stover.

STRAIGHT   Distilled spirits poured straight from the bottle without ice, soda, water, and so forth. Also known as *neat* and *shot*.

STRAIGHTFORWARD   A term that describes a wine that is simple, honest, and direct, without any pretense or subtlety.

STRAIGHT UP   A cocktail that is strained and served "up-off-the-ice" in a stemware glass. Some examples are martini, Manhattan, and sours. Also known as *up*.

STRAIGHT WHISKEY   Alcohol distillate from a fermented mash of grain, distilled at 160 proof or less and stored during aging at between 80 to 125 proof. Straight whiskey must be aged for not less than 24 calendar months in new charred white oak barrels. Its proof is reduced to a level of not less than 80 by the addition of distilled water.

Straight whiskies must be made with a minimum of 51 percent of the grain that identifies that particular whiskey. Bourbon, for example, is made with at least 51 percent corn. Other straight whiskies are rye, bottled-in-bond whiskey, straight corn whiskey, and straight whiskey without an identifying grain tag, which simply means it was produced from a mash that contained less than 51 percent of any one grain type (e.g., corn).

A blend of straight rye whiskeys or a blend of straight bourbon whiskeys is a mixture of only straight rye whiskeys or straight bourbon whiskeys, respectively.

STRAINER   *See* Cocktail Strainer.

STRATEGIC PLANNING   Long-range planning to set organizational goals, objectives, and policies and to determine strategies, tactics, and programs for achieving them.

STRAVECCHIO (ITAL)   A very old wine or brandy. This term has no legal meaning.

STRAW   A term often used to describe the color of young, white wines that range in color from pale yellow to greenish gold. Also known as *paglierino*.

STRAWBERRY-FLAVORED BRANDY   A mixture of brandy, with a minimum of 2.5 percent sugar, and flavored and colored with strawberries. By federal law it cannot be bottled at less than 70 proof (35 percent alcohol by volume).

STRAWBERRY LIQUEUR   A sweetened alcoholic beverage consisting of a base of alcohol and minimum 2.5-percent sugar, and is flavored and colored with raspberries. It is sweeter and lower in proof than strawberry-flavored brandy.

STRENCHERB (GERM)   *See* Brut.

STRIPPER   A hand held tool used to obtain "twists" or "peels" from certain citrus fruits.

STRIP STAMP   Tax stamp of the U.S. Internal Revenue Service, affixed over the closure of bottles of distilled spirits. Green stamps are used for bottled-in-bond distilled spirits, and red stamps are used for most other distilled spirits. The strip stamps are required only in a handful of states.

STRONG   A term that refers to wines, beers, or distilled spirits that display a high level of alcohol. The alcohol can be detected in the odor as well as in the taste, which often is harsh, hot, or has burning qualities.

STRONG   A term generally applied to those wines that are full in flavor, with good acidity, extract, body, and level of alcohol.

STRONGYLÓS (GREECE)   *See* Round.

STRUCTURE   A term that describes a wine's "framework," which is determined by the interaction of essential components that create tactile impressions in the mouth (e.g. acid, tannin, and alcohol).

STRYFNÓS (GREECE)   *See* Astringent.

STUBS   *See* Hosted Bar.

STUCCHEVOLE (ITAL)   *See* Cloying.

STÜCK (GERM)   A barrel of varying size, usually containing approximately 300 U.S. gallons. *See* Barrel.

STUCK FERMENTATION   The gradual and premature cessation of fermentation, prior to all the sugar being metabolized by the yeast, into alcohol and carbon dioxide. This can be caused by many factors: 1) excessive heat, cold, or death of yeast cells; 2) low rate of heat dissipation during fermentation "pasteurizes" the yeasts; 3) low levels of yeast "food"; nutrients, largely made up of vitamin B_1, magnesium sulfate, potassium phosphate, urea, and ammonium phosphate, which supplies the *must* with a suitable source of nitrogen and phosphorous. *See* Gestoppt and Nutrients.

STUFFING   A term that refers to the body, character, and extract of certain red wines. Also known as *stoffa* and *stoffig*.

STUM WINE   *See* Must.

STURDY   A term that describes a solid, substantial, and full-bodied wine, with good structure that can stand considerable aging.

STYLE   Originates in the winemaker's vision of the grape's potential expression. Wine styles vary because of the diversity and intensity of aromas and flavors, the wine emphasis (fruit or wood predominating in the aroma or flavor), and balance (toward tannin, acidity, or sweetness). Winemakers affect style by their selection of grapes, vineyard management techniques, and winemaking methods and equipment.

SUAVE (SP) *See* Supple.

SUBIRAT PARENT (SP) A white grape variety used for sparkling wines.

SUBJECTIVE A state of mind where personal reaction, opinion, and judgment are usually the result.

SUBTLE Gentle or delicate nuances and flavors, not easily detected, that are displayed in some wines. Also known as *sottile. See* Nuance.

SUCARYL A trademark name for a compound used as low calorie sweetener.

SUCCINIC ACID One of the more prominent by-products of fermentation. It is one of the principal acids utilized in the formation of esters that helps to promote vinous character (winy aroma and flavor of wine).

SUCKERING Removing water sprouts and tendrils from grapevines that originate either below the ground surface or on the trunk of the grapevine and are not fruitbearing. These suckers siphon off nutritive material, which should be directed to the production of grapes.

SUCKERS Shoots that spring from a bud at the base of a grapevine.

SUCRÉ (FR) *See* Sweet.

SUCROSE The form of sugar that occurs in sugar cane and sugar beets and is commonly known as table sugar. Each molecule contains one molecule each of glucose and fructose.

SUCROSITY The impression of sweetness on the palate, with or without the actual presence of sugar.

SUDS In the late 1800s and early 1900s it was customary to carry home a bucket (pail) of beer from a local tavern. To prevent the beer from foaming over, lard or other fats were rubbed on the inner surface, which assured the purchaser of a full bucket of what humorously called "suds." Also referred to as a "bucket of suds."

SÜFFIG (GERM) Palatable, simple wines, generally consumed locally in taverns.

SUFFOLK RED A red seedless grape variety introduced in 1972, from a cross of Fredonia and Russian *Seedless*, by the New York State Experimental Station at Geneva.

SUGAR Pure dry sugar, liquid sugar, and invert sugar syrup, used in the making of some alcoholic and nonalcoholic beverages.

SUGARING OF WINE *See* Chaptalization.

SUGAR IN WINE Wines are often placed in three categories of sweetness: dry, semidry, and sweet. A wine below 0.6 percent is considered dry (truly dry wines contain less than 0.2 percent sugar); between 0.6 percent and 2.2 percent, semidry; while wine with greater than 2.2 percent sugar is generally considered sweet.

SUHO (YUG)   *See* Dry.

SULFITE EXEMPT   Wines made from organically-grown grapes, vinified naturally, made without added sulfites, and exempt from sulfite notice label requirements.

SULFUR DIOXIDE   SO$_2$ A naturally-appearing substance used worldwide for its antimicrobial and antioxidative activity.

It serves winemakers as a yeast/bacterial sterilant and an anti-browning agent. Normally a gas, it exists in solution through a complex set of equilibrium reactions that result in the transformation of the gas into dissolved-free and bound forms.

Sulfur dioxide is effective as a sterilant/anti-browning agent only when present in the solution form ("free"). The total sulfur dioxide is the sum of the free, bound, and chemical transforms. Since sulfur dioxide is not usually destroyed in wine, the total represents the sum of all sulfur dioxide in the wine at all stages of processing.

Excessive levels of free sulfur dioxide are sensory disadvantages (creating a disagreeable irritant to the nose), and the total sulfur dioxide content is subject to federal and state regulations. Also known as *anidride solforso* and *zolfo*. *See* Campden Tablet, Matchstick, Metabisulfite, Sodium Metabisulfite, and Sulfur Stick.

SULFURIC ACID   A measurement of the total acidity in wine used in France and other European countries.

SULFUR STICK   A flat, yellow stick or wick made of sulfur, used in cleaning or *disinfecting* the inside of a wooden barrel by the burning of a sulfur stick. Also known as *mechage*. *See* Sulfur Dioxide.

SULTANA   *See* Thompson Seedless.

SULTANINA   *See* Thompson Seedless.

SUNBURNED   A condition that grapes take on when grown in extremely hot climates; the condition carries on into the taste.

SUN IN SACKS   *See* Chaptalization.

SUNSHINE COAST   *See* Rkatsiteli.

SUPER CALL   *See* Premium Brands.

SUPERFICIAL   *See* Shallow.

SUPÉRIEUR (FR)   Superior.

SUPERIORE (ITAL)   A wine that contains a higher percentage (generally one-half of one degree or more) of alcohol than the minimum regulation required under DOC or DOCG law. Under some laws, additional bottle aging is also a requirement of use of the term.

SUPPLE   A term that describes a wine or beer that has smoothness and softness on the palate and is easy to drink; acidity and alcohol are balanced. Also known as *geschmeidig, morbido, souple,* and *suave.*

SUPPLIER Firms that bottle domestic or foreign-produced alcoholic beverages or that import bottled alcoholic beverages for resale. Frequently, "vendor" and "supplier" are used interchangeably.

SURFACE TENSION *See* Legs.

SURIN (FR) *See* Sauvignon Blanc.

SUR LATTES (FR) Champagne bottles stacked on wooden battens, similar to plaster lath, which are placed between each row, making the stacks quite firm during the secondary fermentation.

SUR LIE (FR) A wine that is fermented and aged on the lees, which adds an extra dimension of aroma and flavor to the wine. *See* Autolysis.

SURMATURITÉ (FR) *See* Overripe.

SURPLUS The amount by which quantity supplied exceeds quantity demanded at the existing price. Any excess or amount left over.

SUR POINTE (FR) Bottles of champagne neck down so as to collect the deposits in one place; this operation follows the "riddling" stage. Also known as *mise sur pointe.*

SÜSS (GERM) *See* Sweet.

SÜSSRESERVE (GERM) Prior to fermentation, some of the unfermented juice, which is high in natural sugar, is filtered and held under refrigeration until after the fermentation is complete. At this point, a small amount of this sugar-rich juice, called *muté* (in California) is then added back to the wine to add a sweet flavor. *See* Mistelle.

SÜSSUNG (GERM) *See* Dosage.

SVINATURA (ITAL) *See* Racking.

SWAMPY Extremely unpleasant odor, occasionally found in some beers or even wines, that are reminiscent of the odors of rotting vegetation frequently encountered in a swamp.

SWEET The presence of noticeable sugar in a beverage. Also known as *adamado, doce, dolce, dulce, edes, glykys, sladko, slatko, sucré,* and *süss.*

SWEET A basic taste sensation dependent upon the level of natural residual sugars in a wine. A sweet (as opposed to dry) wine is one that usually retains some sugar after fermentation has ceased. Sweetness is also derived, to a lesser degree, from alcohol and glycerin, both present in wine.

SWEET AND SOUR MIX *See* Sour Mix.

SWEET CIDER Freshly squeezed apple juice that may not be fermented. *See* Apple Juice, Apple Wine, Cider, and Hard Cider.

SWEETENING The addition of juice, concentrated juice, or sugar to wine after the completion of fermentation and before tax payment.

SWEET LIGHTNIN'   Moonshine that has honey, maple syrup, or other sugary substances added to help make it palatable.

SWEET MASH   Sweet mash is similar to sour mash except that neither a lactic acid culture nor a stillage has been added.

SWEET VERMOUTH   *See* Vermouth.

SWEET WINE   A wine that contains more than 2.2 percent sugar. *See* Sugar In Wine.

SWIZZLE STICK   Another name for a drink stirrer.

SYKES   *See* Sikes Scale.

SYLLABUB   A drink made of hot, but not curdled, sweetened milk or cream mixed with brandy, wine (table or fortified), beer, or hard cider, and sugar, and beaten to a froth. Whipped cream is then floated on top. The drink was popular from the Renaissance through the eighteenth century.

SYLVANER   A white grape variety grown predominantly in Germany and Alsace, France, although it is said to have originated in Austria, but its actual origin cannot be reliably ascertained.

Sylvaner produces a light, fragrant (somewhat neutral), fresh, and tart (high in acidity) white wine of steelish color.

Sylvaner is also spelled *Silvaner*, and is also known as *Frankenriesling, Franken Riesling, Grüner Sylvaner, Monterey Riesling, Oesterreicher, Sonoma Riesling,* and *Zöldsilváni.*

SYLVOZ   A grapevine training and pruning method utilized in Europe, especially Italy and France.

SYMPHONY   A white grape variety developed from a cross of Grenache and Muscat of Alexandria, by Dr. Harold P. Olmo at the University of California at Davis. It produces a muscat-flavored wine with a rich, full muscat character, while avoiding the bitterness associated with many muscat wines.

SYMPOSIUM   In ancient Greece (around 400 B.C), a social-drinking gathering during which individuals expressed judgment and compared wines of similar origin, while simultaneously creating a glossary for the less knowledgeable.

SYNDICAT DES VIGNERONS (FR)   A grape grower's union.

SYNTHETOS (GREECE)   *See* Complex.

SYRAH   A black-skinned grape variety with small to medium-sized, oval berries in rather loose, long, and cylindrical bunches. It is grown chiefly in the Rhône Valley of France, where it produces dark, full-bodied, and long-lived wines, with fruit flavors of wild blackberries, plums, and cassis. It is the major grape in the blend of such great wines as Hermitage, Cornas, and Côte Rotie, to name just a few. It also grown prolifically in Australia, where it is known as *Shiraz*, while some is also planted in California, where, for years, the Durif grape variety was mistakenly identified as *Syrah* and often called *Petite Sirah* or *Petite Syrah.*

Syrah is known locally in the Rhône Valley as *Serine*; in Australia, it is often incorrectly referred to as *Hermitage*, which in actuality is the name of a great red wine–producing village in the Rhône Valley, as well as the local name for the Cinsaut grape variety in South Africa.

SYRUPY The tactile sensation of a very sweet wine that is low in total acidity.

SYSTEMIC FUNGICIDES OR PESTICIDES Any of a group of fungicides or pesticides that are absorbed into the tissues of the plants, which in consequence becomes poisonous to funguses and insects that feed on them.

SZARAZ (HUN) *See* Dry.

SZEMELT (HUN) *See* Auslese.

SZÜRKEBARAT (HUN) *See* Pinot Gris.

TA *See* Total Acidity.

TABLESPOON (T) A U.S. measure of volume equal to three teaspoons or one-half ounce. Sixteen tablespoons being equal to one cup (eight fluid ounces).

TABLE TENT A small tabletop, folded paper flyer (often tent-shaped) that promotes alcoholic or nonalcoholic beverages at a restaurant table.

TABLE WINE A still white, red, or rosé wine having an alcoholic content between 7 and 14 percent by volume. Such wine may also be designated as "light." Also known as *dinner wine. See* Vino da Tavola.

TAFELWEIN (GERM) A term that literally means "table wine." According to the 1971 German Wine Law, "tafelwein" is a separate category of wines, one step below Qualitätswein. Tafelweins, which may be *chaptalized,* represent a small portion of German wines, and very few are exported to the United States. *See* Table Wine and Vino da Tavola.

TAFT, WILLIAM, PRESIDENT OF THE UNITED STATES (1909–1913) In 1909, President Taft signed the Food and Drug Act, which required certain standards of identification for whiskey and imposed greater federal control on the production of distilled spirits.

TAGLIO (ITAL) *See* Blending.

TAILLE (FR) *See* Pruning.

TAILLES (FR) The second and third pressing of the grapes used to make champagne.

TAILS During the last run in distilling, those elements that have the highest boiling points and then vaporize last, thus dropping the alcoholic content to a very low proof. Also known as *backings, feints, produit de queue,* and *squeezin's.*

TALL BOY A slang term that describes a 16-ounce can of beer.

TALL DRINK *See* Long Drink.

TAM   *See* Territorial Allocation Model.

TANK   A large container used for the fermentation or storage of wine, beer, and distilled spirits. *See* Barrel.

TANKARD   A tall, one-handled drinking vessel with a lid, used for serving beer; usually made of pewter or silver. *See* Stein.

TANNAT (FR)   A red grape variety cultivated predominantly in the Jura Region. Also known as *Harriague*.

TANNIC   Also known as *tannico*. *See* Tannin.

TANNIC ACID   An astringent acid usually added to *must* or wine, to increase the wine's longevity by slowing down the aging process. Not to be confused with tannin.

TANNICO (ITAL)   *See* Tannic.

TANNIN   A group of organic bitter compounds, better known as phenolics. They are "large" phenols with astringent, leather-forming, protein-precipitating properties. Tannins are considered phenolic polymers (giant molecules formed when thousands of the same initial molecule are linked together), which have the gustatory effect of astringency and/or bitterness. Tannin content is popularly referred to as a group of phenolic compounds—primarily anthocyanin pigments, flavonoids, and flavonols, among others. The pigments impart density and richness to wine, while flavonoids and flavonols are responsible for bitterness, astringency, and antioxidative properties.

Tannin is found in seeds, stems, and skins of grapes, and is extracted from wooden barrels. It is quite astringent and causes a puckering sensation in the front of the mouth. Tannin, which is more concentrated in red wines than in white, contributes to the aging capacity of wine. One of the five elements that gives wine longevity; the others being sugar, alcohol, acidity, and carbonation. Also known as *tannic*. *See* Phenols, Phenolics, and Astringency.

TAP   *See* Spigot.

TAP BEER   *See* Draft Beer.

TAP BOX   *See* Beer Box.

TAPHOUSE   *See* Tavern

TAPMAN   *See* Bartender.

TAPPING CABINET   *See* Beer Standard.

TAPON (SP)   *See* Cork.

TAPPO (ITAL)   *See* Cork.

TAPROOM   Same as Barroom.

TAP ROOTS   (Sometimes called the "heart root.") The deepest penetrating roots, from whence emanate feeder roots and from these very fine roots, called "hair" roots (like the feeder roots, that grow somewhat laterally), extend the absorption area for water, minerals, and other nutrients from the soil. The greatest concentration of roots is within a radius of six feet of the trunk of a grapevine to a depth of eight feet.

TAPPIT-HEN An old Scottish bottle size, originally with a capacity of 76.84 fluid ounces or the equivalent of three bottles of Portuguese port wine; no longer used. Also known as *tregnum*.

TAREFA DE BARRO (SP) A large earthenware container or small barrel utilized for fermenting small batches of wine.

TARE WEIGHT The weight of a container or package, less contents.

TARRY A wine taster's term applied to certain Cabernet Sauvignon, Zinfandel, Barolo, and other full-bodied wines, which are said to have the odor and/or taste of melting road tar on a hot summer day. It is most palatable, much more than one could expect. Also known as *goudron* and *goût de goudron*.

TART The sharp, astringent taste of fruit acid that, when present in a moderate amount, lends a pleasant freshness to a wine.

TARTAR More precisely named "cream of tartar"; tartar is a crystalline material that settles to the bottom of wine containers after a wine has been stored cold for several days. *See* Cold Stabilization, Cream of Tartar, Crystalline Deposits, Tartaric Acid, and Tartrates.

TARTARIC ACID (KHT) The principle natural fixed acid found in grapes and wine. Tartaric acid often occurs in such high levels in wine grapes that it crystallizes out as cream of tartar when the wine is chilled. Also known as *acide tartrique*. *See* Cold Stabilization, Cream of Tartar, Crystalline Deposits, Tartar, and Tartrates.

TARTRATES As alcohol is formed during fermentation, potassium and tartaric acid, which come from the grape, combine to form white crystals. These crystals are called *bitartrates, potassium bitartrate*, or, more simply, tartrates. Cream of tartar is just ground tartrate crystals.

As fermentation progresses, a considerable quantity of yeast is grown and the tartrates, in the form of cream of tartar, begin to crystallize out of solution. This separation of tartrates takes place because tartar is less soluble in alcohol than it is in water or grape juice so that, as the percentage of alcohol increases during fermentation, more and more tartrates are precipitated out. Incidentally, newly fermented wine is cloudy and has a pronounced "yeasty" aroma. Upon standing, the yeast gradually settles down to the bottom of the barrel or tank. Suspended particles of skin and pulp and the tartrates also settle to the bottom. All this forms a sediment known as *lees*. *See* Cold Stabilization, Cream of Tartar, Crystalline Deposits, Tartar, and Tartaric Acid.

TASSE (FR) Cup.

TASTE The overall flavor impression of an alcoholic or nonalcoholic beverage.

TASTE BUDS Any of the small papilla (nipple-like projections) embedded principally in the epithelium of the tongue that contain *taste receptors*, which function as the sense organs of taste. Each person has approximately 10,000 of these papilla cells.

TASTEVIN (FR)   A shallow, saucer-like silver cup, about three-quarter of an inch in depth by three inches across, with a handle, and a surface that is indented with dimples, both on the bottom and sides, in order to refract the light when tasting young wines. It is often used by a sommelier to examine wine prior to its being served. It has given its name to the celebrated Burgundian confraternity of wine, the Confrérie du Tastevin. *See* Sommelier.

TAURASI (ITAL)   A red wine produced in the southern region of Campania from a blend of Aglianico, Piedirosso (red feet), and Sangiovese and/or Barbera grapes.

TAVEL (FR)   A village certainly best known for its rosé wines; located on the right bank of the Rhône River in the Côtes du Rhône region. These rosés are soft and plump, with just the right amount of taste and fullness. They are quite dry, and have a light, bright crimson color. They are produced from a blend of Grenache, Cinsaut, Clairette, Picpoul, and Bourboulenc grapes.

TAVERN   It derives from *taberna*, Greek for hut, and from the old French *taverne*, meaning a place where alcoholic beverages are sold for consumption on the premises. Also known as *taphouse* and *taverna*. *See* Bar, Cocktail Lounge, Inn, Pub, and Saloon.

TAVERNA (ITAL)   *See* Tavern.

TAWNY   Brownish-colored. A term applied to ports and other red wines that have a brownish or golden tinge, instead of the customary ruby, which results from the loss of pigment by oxidation and during long aging, filtering, or fining, or from the use of grapes not heavy in color.

TAWNY PORT (PORT)   A port wine whose name is derived from the tawny color of the wine; this comes from long maturing in barrels, which causes the wine to lose some of its redness. Much smoother than ruby port, tawny port usually spends a minimum of six to eight years in the barrel (which helps round out the fieriness of the alcohol), resulting in a wine with a smooth texture and a touch of sweetness. Some tawny ports are described as having a nutty smell and taste. Tawny ports do not improve significantly in the bottle, for they have already matured in the barrel and are ready to consume.

TAX DETERMINATION   Fixing the amount of federal excise tax as the distilled spirits leave the distilled spirits plant. Actual payment is made within 30 days of the end of the half month tax period, not calendar shipping date. *See* Tax Liability and Tax Period.

TAX GALLON   Unit of distilled spirits subject to the federal excise tax. Since the federal excise tax is based on a proof gallon, a tax gallon is synonymous with a proof gallon. *See* Proof Gallon.

TAX LIABILITY   On production of distilled spirits, producers incur liability for the federal excise tax. The distilled spirits and tax liability are transferable under government supervision. *See* Tax Determination and Tax Period.

TAXPAID WINE Wine on which the tax imposed by law has been determined, regardless of whether the tax has actually been paid or the payment of tax has been deferred.

TAX PERIOD Each month consists of two tax periods of about one-half month; the first to the fifteenth, and the sixteenth to the end of the month. *See* Tax Determination and Tax Liability.

TAXPAID WINE BOTTLING HOUSE Premises established primarily for bottling or packing tax paid wine.

TAXPAID WINE PREMISES Premises on which tax paid wine operations other than bottling are authorized to be conducted.

TAZA (SP) Cup.

TAZZA (ITAL) Cup.

T-BUDDING A grafting procedure that involves cutting off the upper portion of a mature grapevine. A *T-shaped* incision is knifed into the remaining trunk, and the outer layer is peeled back to make a pocket for a dormant bud of the desired new grape variety. A white bandage is wrapped tightly around the graft and, if all goes well, the bud draws nourishment from the parent plant. Utilizing this procedure almost insures full production of the new grape variety by the second harvest after conversion, instead of the normal five-to seven-year period.

TÉ (ITAL AND SP) Tea.

TEARS *See* Legs.

TEASPOON (TSP) A U.S. measure of volume equal to one-third of a tablespoon, or one-sixth fluid ounce.

TEE (GERM) Tea.

TEEDUM BARREL A barrel or other type storage vessel where moonshiners kept their private drinking "liquor."

TEETOTALER The term is found in the records of the Laingsburg, Michigan Temperance Society of the 1830s. Two forms of pledges had been offered members; the first one called for moderate drinking, and a later type advocated total abstinence from "ardent spirits."

Members were identified on the rosters as "O.P.—Old Pledge" and "T—Total." The latter were soon known as "teetotalers," and in time the term became applicable to those who abstained from all beverages containing alcohol.

TEINTURIER (FR) A generic name for those grape varieties with color in the flesh as well as the skin of the berry (as opposed to most varieties whose juice is colorless).

TEMPRANA (SP) *See* Palomino.

TEMPRANILLA (SP)   *See* Palomino.

TEMPRANILLO   The premier red grape variety of Rioja, which may be regarded in the same context as the Cabernet Sauvignon in Bordeaux of California, although it is not related to that particular variety. It is the Tempranillo that imparts a deep color and fine acid balance to the wine. Also known as *Cencibel, Ojo de Liebre (eye of the hare), Tinta Roriz,* and *Ull de Llebre.*

TENDER   A term that is applied to young, light-bodied, not especially long-lived wines that are easy to drink. Also known as *tendre.*

TENDONE (ITAL)   A modern pruning method employed in Sicily that is a more economic and rapid method than others traditionally employed, because it lends itself to mechanical harvesting. There is also an increase in the per-plant yield, approaching three times that formerly harvested from the same varieties of grapes. With grapevines supported on tensioned wires held high by intermittent stakes, the sun is better able to bathe the grape and leaf in its golden endowments. The result is invariably a better wine.

TENDRE (FR)   *See* Tender.

372

TENDRIL   A long, slender, curled structure borne at some of the nodes of a shoot on a grapevine. This "coil-like" appendage can firmly attach itself to any object to help support the grapevine.

TENIMENTO (ITAL)   Farm, agricultural estate.

TENNESSEE WHISKEY   Proprietary whiskey from the state of Tennessee that has gone through the leaching process before aging in new, charred oak barrels. It is distilled at not exceeding 160 proof from a fermented mash of not less than 51 percent corn.

TENSIOMETER   *See* Neutron Probe.

TENTH   A half-bottle, equivalent in size to 375 milliliters, or 12.8 fluid ounces.

TENUTA (ITAL)   Estate or farm.

TENUTA VINICOLA (ITAL)   A wine estate, similar to a château.

TEQUILA   An alcohol distillate from a fermented mash (juice and/or sap) derived primarily from a blue variety of the genus Agave (*Agave tequilana weber*), with or without additional fermented substances. It is bottled at not less than 80 proof. The Agave species, often confused with cacti, are distinguished by the succulence of the leaves rather than the stems. The Agave is known in the United States as the American aloe or century plant, because it was mistakenly believed to bloom only once every 100 years. The Agave plant takes between 8 and 12 years to mature before it can be used, and only the heart of the plant, often called the *piña,* or "head," is used.

Tequila, by government decree, can only come from a specific geographic area of Mexico known as tequila, which is within the state of Jalisco, about 40 miles from Guadalajara. If produced outside these geographical limits, it is called mezcal.

Tequilero (sp) One who produces tequila.

Tercero (sp) A barrel with a capacity of one-third of a pipe. *See* Barrel.

Terlano (ital) *See* Garganega.

Terlano (ital) A light-bodied, dry white wine produced in the Italian region of Trentino-Alto Adige, principally from the Chardonnay and Pinot Blanc grape varieties.

Terne (fr) *See* Dull.

Teroldego (ital) A red grape variety cultivated primarily in the northern region of Trentino-Alto Adige, producing wines of light color, considerable fruit, and a short life.

Territorial Allocation Model (tam) A standard model for territorial allocations, based on quantification of brand strategy, against which to measure plans before they are implemented.

Territory A specified area, usually but not always a state, in which wholesalers conduct business. Goals and promotional spending are established within this area.

Terroir (fr) A wine that is earthy tasting or that has a taste of the earth.

Terzo (ital) A barrel with a capacity of one-third of a pipe. *See* Barrel.

Testa and Coda (ital) The *heads* and *tails*, as used in the distillation process.

Test Market A field experiment that introduces new products or programs into a limited number of representative markets; used to evaluate products or program elements or to evaluate the interac tions in a total plan. Also known as *market test*.

Tête de Cuvée (fr) Top or outstanding growth; generally used in Burgundy. Also known as *vin de tête*.

Texture The "feel" of a wine as it enters the mouth, which is sensed on the palate. The relative smoothness and taste of a sound, well-made, and round wine. *See* Body.

Thasian (greece) An ancient wine.

Thé (fr) Tea.

The Indian Queen Tavern The name of the tavern in Philadelphia where Thomas Jefferson framed his first draft of the Declaration of Independence.

The Noble Experiment A slang term for Prohibition.

The Old Talbott Tavern A tavern located in Bardstown, Kentucky, which is the oldest tavern in continuous use west of the Alleghenies, since 1779.

The Real Mccoy An expression that derives its name from Captain Bill McCoy, who was a smuggler during Prohibition 1920–1933). He was a man of integrity who shipped to the United States nothing but "genuine." The reputation of his scotch whisky was so high that it came to be known as "The Real McCoy," a byword for quality.

THERMAL SHOCK   It is the result of temperature change. Glass holds temperature, and quick temperature changes can cause enough stress in the glass to cause breakage. For example, glass with ice in it cannot be emptied and put directly into the dishwasher. Similarly, glass coming out of the dishwasher cannot be put directly into service. In both cases the glass must be given time to reach room temperature. Never put cold water or ice into a warm or hot glass. Cracks that result from thermal shock usually form around abrasions caused by mechanical impact. The thicker the glass, the more time it needs to reach room temperature.

THERMOLIZATION   *See* Pasteurization.

THERMOREGULATION   The process of controlling the temperature of stainless steel tanks during fermentation.

THIEF   *See* Wine Thief.

THIN   A term that describes a wine or beer that is lacking body; watery, weak, light, neutral tasting, and possibly low in alcohol. Also known as *debole, décharné, descarnado, flaco, maigre, mager, magro, scarno, watery, weak, weich,* and *welch.*

THINNING   A method employed in the vineyards to regulate the balance between leaf surface exposed to the sun and the amount of fruit that can be brought to maturity. It consists of the removal of clusters of grapes so as to insure that the remaining grape clusters would be low and have the best chance for optimum maturity. Also known as *cluster thinning, crop thinning,* and *leaf thinning.*

THOMPSON SEEDLESS   A small, white, seedless grape variety, named after William Thompson, an Englishman who first planted the grape variety in Sacramento Valley, California, in 1872. It is used predominantly in "jug wine blends" because it is considered a "juice grape." Thompson Seedless is also the predominant grape variety used in raisin production. Also known as *Sultana* and *Sultanina.*

THREE-SHEETS-TO-THE-WIND   Slang for intoxicated.

THREE STAR (FR)   A label designation on Armagnac or cognac bottles that indicates that the youngest brandy used in the blend is under 4 ½ years old (although they contain a blend of brandies five to nine years old).

THREE-TIER SYSTEM   A system for the distribution of alcoholic beverages that involves separate and distinct manufacturers, wholesales, and retailers, with alcoholic beverages passing from one level to the next and ultimately to the consumer. This system has historical significance and is supported by most state laws.

THRESHOLD LEVELS   The minimum detectable amount of a substance, whether by smell or taste.

TIED-HOUSE   The FAA Act (1934), which prohibits a supplier (that is, a manufacturer, importer, or wholesaler) from having "any interest, direct or indirect" in a retail operation, and vice versa. Tied-House is a violation of many state laws.

TIERCE (FR)   A barrel with a capacity of one-third of a pipe. *See* Barrel.

TIER LE CAVAILLON (FR)   *See* Decavaillonage.

TIERRA DE VINO (SP)   *See* Spanish Earth.

TIGHT   *See* Closed-In.

TILTS   A wooden wedge used for finely adjusting barrels to a desired position.

TIMORASSO (ITAL)   A white grape variety from the Alessandria district of Piedmont. Also known as *Timuassa, Timorosso, Timorazza,* and *Morasso.*

TINA (SP)   *See* Barrel.

TINAJA (SP)   A large earthenware container or type vessel, utilized for the fermentation and aging of wine.

TINAS (SP)   *See* Fermentation Tank.

TINETA (SP)   *See* Brenta.

TINNY   A metallic taste occasionally found in "canned" beer, as if from the "tin," or can. Contrary to popular belief, there is absolutely no difference in taste between canned and bottled beer. The cans used today do not give off a metallic taste, as they once did when they were made of tin or steel. The "tinny" off-taste is attributable to the flavor of "old" beer.

TINO (SP)   *See* Barrel.

TINTA RORIZ (PORT)   *See* Tempranillo.

TINTO (PORT OR SP)   *See* Red.

TINTO BASTO (SP)   *See* Tinta de Madrid.

TINTO DE MADRID (SP)   A red grape variety. Also known as *Tinto Basto.*

TINTOMETER   An instrument utilized for measuring the color of wine.

TIPO VINTAGE (PORT)   *See* Vintage-Character Port.

TIQUIRA   A distilled product made from tapioca roots, produced in Brazil.

TIRAGE (FR)   The laying of bottles on their sides in large stacks for the secondary fermentation, which will change the still wine into a sparkling wine.

TIRE-BOUCHON (FR)   *See* Corkscrew.

TIRED   A wine that is showing signs of age; lacking freshness. A tired wine can be slightly oxidized or beginning to dry out, that is, losing its fruit.

TISCHWEIN (GERM)   A common or ordinary wine.

TITRATABLE ACIDITY   *See* Total Acidity.

TOASTED BARRELS   *See* Charring.

TOASTING   The custom of honoring an individual or drinking to someone's health, wealth, or good fortune.

TOASTY   The agreeable odor of grilled or burned "toasted bread," detected in some wines, which is derived from: 1) the charred wood inside of a wooden barrel; 2) autolysis (prolonged contact with the yeast); 3) barrel fermentation of some wines, most notably Chardonnay; or 4) an oxidized odor detected in some old wines, especially whites.

TOBACCO   The scent of fresh, burning tobacco, detected in some red wines, especially Graves, from France.

TOCAI (ITAL)   A white grape variety cultivated almost exclusively in the Friuli-Venezia Giulia region, in the northeast, where it has been cultivated for centuries, producing dry, white wines with an underlying bitterness.

In the 1950s, the Hungarian government attempted to stop Italian usage of the name Tocai, arguing that their "Tokay" was the original. In 1954, after extensive studies by a panel of experts, an International Court in Trieste decided that Hungary did not have exclusive rights to the name Tocai and that the Hungarian grape Furmint (used to make Tokay) is a different grape variety entirely. According to the panel's findings, both these grapevines actually originated in Italy. It is believed that the Italian missionaries to the court of King Steven the Saint brought them to Hungary in the eleventh century. Also known as *Sauvignon Vert, Tocai Friulano,* and *Tokai.* It is argued that the Tocai is the same grape variety as the Muscadelle of France. *See* Muscadelle.

TOCAI FRIULANO (ITAL)   *See* Tocai.

TO DROWN A SHAMROCK   An old Irish term, meaning to have a drink in every bar or pub in town.

TODDY   *See* Hot Toddy.

TODDY   An intoxicating alcoholic beverage made from the sweet sap of various East Indian palm trees.

TOKAI (ITAL)   *See* Tocai.

TOKAJI EDES (HUN)   A sweet Tokay wine.

TOKAJI PECSENYEBOR (HUN)   Tokay wine of the lowest quality.

TOKAJI SZARAZ (HUN)   A dry Tokay wine.

TOKAY   A generic U.S.-produced wine, that remotely resembles the famed dessert wine of Hungary.

TOKAY (HUN)   A sweet dessert wine produced in the village of Tokaj-Hegyalja in northeastern Hungary. Tokay is predominantly made from the Furmint (white grape variety), which can be harvested at various degrees of ripeness. Tokay wines are bone dry to exquisitely sweet white wines.

When a sweet Tokay wine is to be produced, the grapes are left to hang on the grapevines until they start to shrivel and resemble raisins. It is at this point that a beneficial *Botrytis* mold attacks the grapes, adding a rich scent of honey and increasing the viscosity of their juice. After harvest these grapes (called *aszús*, meaning dried-out grapes) are placed into wooden tubs called *puttonyos*, which hold about seven gallons of wine. The grapes are crushed, and the juice is added to the one-year-old wine that has been stored in *gönci*, small 35-gallon barrels. The number of *puttonyos* (generally up to five), which is indicated on the label, is proportionate to the degree of sweetness of the harvested grapes.

TOKAY D'ALSACE *See* Pinot Gris.

TOKKURI (JAPAN) The name of the decanter that is traditionally used for the heating of saké.

TOLERANCE The lawful limit of toxic residue allowable by law in or on edible substances.

TOM AND JERRY A cocktail consisting of an egg yolk, an egg white, sugar, allspice, white rum, and milk. The "Tom and Jerry" was created from Edan's *Life in London,* also known as *Days and Nights of Jerry Hawthorne and his Elegant Friend, Corinthian Tom,* in 1928.

TOM COLLINS A cocktail consisting of gin or vodka, lemon juice, sugar, and soda water.

TOM COLLINS GLASS *See* Iced Tea Glass.

TOMATO JUICE The liquid constituent of a tomato.

TONEL (PORT OR SP) *See* Barrel.

TONELADA (SP) *See* Metric Ton.

TONELERO (SP) *See* Cooper.

TONIC WATER A carbonated water flavored with quinine, an alkaloid of the cinchona bark. Originally introduced to bring down tropical fevers, it is now a widely used mixer, usually with gin or vodka. Also known as *quinine water.*

TONNE An English wine measure of 1497 that stated that a tonne had a capacity of two pipes, or 252 gallons. *See* Barrel.

TONNEAU (FR) A large Bordeaux barrel equivalent in capacity to four barrels, or 900 liters (237 U.S. gallons). *See* Barrel.

TONNELERIE (FR) Factory where barrels are made.

TONNELIER (FR) *See* Cooper.

TONSIL PAINT In the old western movies, the name given to whiskey by cowboys.

TOOTHPICKS Tiny wooden pins used for plugging small holes in leaking wooden barrels. Also known as *shoe pegs. See* Garlic.

TOP FERMENTATION A term that refers to the use of a type of yeast that generally will convert sugars to alcohol and CO_2 at temperatures between 60 degrees and 70 degrees Fahrenheit. Some top-fermented beers include ale, cream ale, porter, stout, and weisse beer.

Top Hat A slang term or phrase denoting a container of beer (usually made of white cardboard with a waxed inner lining), much like a take-out container, which is taken out of a bar for future drinking.

Topping A winery practice of adding wine to wooden barrels (to fill them "to the top") to replace what was lost through evapora tion and soakage. Topping minimizes contact with air and, thus, oxidation. Also known as *colmatura, ouillage, topping off,* and *topping up.*

Topping d Off *See* Topping.

Topping Up *See* Topping.

Top Shelf *See* Premium Brands.

Torbido (Ital) *See* Turbid.

Torchia (Ital) A wine press.

Torpid Yeast that has lost motion, vigor, and ability to "bud," due to low fermentation temperatures.

Torre (Ital) Tower.

Torula Any of a group of yeast-like fungi that reproduce by budding. In some wine and distilled spirits aging cellars, the walls and ceilings are covered with this microscopic gray mold, which feeds on the alcohol vapors. *See* Molds.

Toscanello (Ital) *See* Pulcianella.

Toscano (Ital) *See* Tuscany.

Tostatura (Ital) *See* Charring.

Tot (Germ) *See* Old.

Total Acidity (TA) A measurement of the potential acidity in must or a wine, usually expressed in terms of tartaric acid (United States) or sulfuric acid (France). Also known as *acidità totale* and *titratable acidity.*

Total Cost The sum of fixed and variable costs.

Total Revenue Total receipts from the sale of a product. When there is a single price, total revenue is the price times the quantity sold.

Total Solids The degrees Brix of unfermented juice or dealcoholized wine.

Toublé (Fr) A term that describes a wine or beer that is cloudy or hazy.

Touraine (Fr) One of the major wine-producing provinces of the Loire Valley, best noted for red and white wines from several of its villages, notably, Vouvray, Bourgueil, and Chinon.

Trade Buyer Any wholesaler or retailer of distilled spirits, wine, or malt beverages.

Trademark Includes "any word, name, symbol, or device or any combination thereof adopted and used by a manufacturer or merchant to identify and distinguish his goods…from those manufactured and sold by others and to indicate the source of the goods." Also known as *marchio, markenwein,* and *marque déposée.*

TRADE SHOWS   Events held in major cities, often in conjunction with industry conventions, where business firms can display, demonstrate, and sell their products.

TRADITIONELLE FLASCHENGAERUNG (GERM)   Traditional fermentation in the bottle; also the current term for sparkling wines made in the traditional champagne method.

TRAINING   The systematic arrangement of the necessary parts of the grapevine on a trellis so as to position the leaves for best exposure to light and the fruit for ease of harvest. The grapevine shape in turn will influence the extent to which the grapevine will grow, fruit will develop, and harvesting will take place. *See* Cordon Training and Head Training.

TRAKHYS (GREECE)   *See* Rough.

TRALCIO (ITAL)   A grapevine shoot.

TRAMINER   The former name of the Gewürztraminer grape variety, now seldom used. *See* Gewürztraminer.

TRAMINER AROMATICO (ITAL)   *See* Gewürztraminer.

TRAMINER MUSQUÉ (FR)   *See* Gewürztraminer.

TRAMINI PIROS (HUN)   *See* Gewürztraminer.

TRANQUILLO (ITAL)   *See* Still.

TRANSFER METHOD   A method developed in Germany in the 1930s that is a modification of the *méthode champenoise.* In fact, the two methods are identical, except that the transfer method does not employ the riddling technique. Instead, when the wine has been sufficiently aged, the bottles are moved to a large tank in which pressure is used to remove the corks, suck the wine out of the bottles, and then chill it to below 32 degrees Fahrenheit. After being filtered, the wine is transferred to clean bottles, and the final dosage is added. This does appear to be an easier and certainly cheaper way of making high-quality sparkling wines. However, during the filtering process it has been found that the filtration can strip the subtlety that the winemaker has worked so diligently to create. The reverse is also true—if the winemaker starts off with a mediocre wine, the filtering can improve the wine by clearing it of "off" flavors. Sparkling wines made in this manner are labeled *fermented in the bottle.* Also known as *transvasage.*

TRANSFER TO BAR   Foods requisitioned from the kitchen by the bar staff, for use in the preparation and service of drinks. Examples are citrus fruits, dairy products, eggs, and so on.

TRANSPIRATION   The water loss from the leaves is affected by light intensity, temperature, humidity, and wind. Warm days and cool nights increase pigmentation in grapes. The color and taste of grapes is also influenced by pH, the level of which is affected by temperature during ripening.

TRANSVASAGE (GERM) *See* Transfer Method.

TRAPPIST Strong beers brewed by Trappist monks in either Belgium or the Netherlands. The name Trappist is authorized by law for those beers brewed exclusively by the monks. Most of the beers are deeply-colored, with high levels of alcohol.

TRASFEGA (PORT) *See* Racking.

TRASIEGO (SP) *See* Racking.

TRAUBE (GERM) *See* Grape.

TRAUBENKELTER (GERM) A hydraulic wine press.

TRAUBENSAFT (GERM) *See* Grape Juice.

TREADING A technique formerly used in many parts of Europe, especially Portugal and Spain, that consisted of teams of male workers, who would interlock arms and commence to tread the grapes for several hours at a time in shallow stone tanks.

380

TREBBIANO (ITAL) A white grape variety grown predominantly in Italy, although it is also cultivated in lesser quantities in France and California. Trebbiano produces wines that have a neutral flavor and good acidity, with little body.

The grape is believed to have originated from Tuscany in the thirteenth century, and exported to France around the times of the Pope's transfer to Avignon from Rome. There was even once a black Trebbiano grape (doesn't' exist now) around the mid-1300s. In the Cognac region of France the grape is known as *St-Emilion*, and in France and California as *Ugni Blanc*.

Also known as *Albano, Procanico, Rossola, Trebbiano d'Abruzzo, Trebbiano di Lugana, Trebbiano di Romagna, Trebbiano di Soave, Trebbiano Giallo, Trebbiano Nostrano,* and *Trebbiano Toscano*.

TREBBIANO D'ABRUZZO (ITAL) A dry, white DOC wine produced in the southern region of Abruzzo, from 100-percent Trebbiano grapes.

TREBBIANO DI LUGANA (ITAL) *See* Trebbiano.

TREBBIANO DI ROMAGNA (ITAL) *See* Trebbiano.

TREBBIANO DI SOAVE (ITAL) *See* Trebbiano.

TREBBIANO GIALLO (ITAL) *See* Trebbiano.

TREBBIANO NOSTRANO (ITAL) *See* Trebbiano.

TREBBIANO TOSCANO (ITAL) *See* Trebbiano.

TREGNUM *See* Tappit-Hen.

TREIXADURA (SP) *See* Loureiro.

TREN (SP) A bottling line, used in preparation for shipping.

TRENTINO-ALTO ADIGE (ITAL) The northernmost wine-producing region in Italy, making some of Italy's finest red and white wines, many of which are of DOC quality. Such diverse grape varieties as Chardonnay, Gewürztraminer, Pinot Bianco, Pinot Grigio, and Sauvignon Blanc constitute the whites, and Cabernet Sauvignon, Merlot, Pinot Noir, and Schiava make up the reds.

TRESALLIER (FR) *See* Sacy.

TRESTERSCHNAPPS (GERM) *See* Grappa.

TREVISO (ITAL) One of the seven provinces that make up the region of Veneto; also known as the Marca Trevigiana, it borders on the Dolomite Mountains to the north , the region of Friuli-Venezia Giulia to the east, the province of Venice, 25 miles to the south, and Padova to the west. The Piave River, one of Italy's most important waterways, flows south through the province to the Adriatic.

A wide range of both native and imported grape varieties are grown in the area. Of the total wine production, 60 percent is red and 40 percent is white. Most of the wine produced in the province of Treviso comes from six grape varieties. Three are white: Prosecco, Verduzzo, and Tocai Italico; and three are red: Merlot, Cabernet, and Raboso. Other varieties grown are Verdiso, Pinot Bianco, Pinot Grigio, Pinot Nero, Riesling Italico, and Sauvignon Blanc.

TRIAGE (FR) *See* épluchage.

TRIM That part of a product removed to prepare the item for consumption.

TRIOSE A monosaccharide, $C_3 H_6 O_3$, having three carbon atoms in its molecule, which is often used for sweetening some alcoholic and nonalcoholic beverages.

TRIPLE SEC A clear, sweet, orange-flavored liqueur.

TROCKEN (GERM) *See* Dry.

TROCKEN (GERM) A designation of wine that went into effect on August 1, 1977, that was created by the wine authority of the Common Market in Brussels. The reason for this designation was the fact that some people prefer wines drier than most of the German wines on the market.

Trocken wines contain a maximum of nine grams per liter of residual sugar (which can also be expressed as 0.9 grams per 100 ml, or 0.9-percent residual sugar). The sugar level cannot exceed the acidity level by more than two grams. For example, if a wine has five grams of acidity, its maximum sugar level can only be seven grams per liter.

TROCKENBEERENAUSLESE (GERM) Sometimes abbreviated as TBA. A wine made entirely from late-picked, individually selected grapes (resembling raisins), that have been allowed to dry and shrivel on the grapevine after they've been attacked by *edelfäule*. These grapes, which are extremely high in sugar, produce one of the sweetest and rarest wines in the world, extremely rich and luscious tasting. *See* Botrytis Cinerea.

TROLLINGER (GERM) *See* Schiava Grossa.

TRONCAIS OAK (FR) A single, small, state-owned forest in the Allier region, just south of Nevers, noted for its production of extremely hard wood. Troncais has a medium-tight grain and moderate flavor and tannin extraction. Its flavors are similar to Allier, though slightly richer, with an intense, undefined, spicy component. Troncais is used with Nevers and Allier in Burgundy, as well as in Bordeaux, for Chardonnay and Cabernet Sauvignon.

TROUSSEAU GRIS *See* Chauché Gris.

TRUNK The relatively permanent above-ground, main stem or body of the grapevine. There may be one or more trunks per grapevine.

TRYFERÓS (GREECE) Mild.

TUILÉ (FR) A term that refers to the brick-red or tile-red color often displayed by red wines when they are becoming old and tired.

TULE REEDS A thin strip of a flexible grass, that grows in marshes, especially in the southwest United States, and that is utilized in barrel-making. These thin strips are often placed in between wooden staves on a wine or whiskey barrel, forming a tight joint, thus preventing leakage.

382

TULIP-SHAPED GLASS The proper glassware to use for champagne and sparkling wines, which is in the shape of a tulip, with a capacity of approximately eight to ten ounces. *See* Flute-Shaped Glass and Saucer-Shaped Glass.

TUMBLER *See* Old-Fashioned Glass.

TUMULTUOSA (ITAL) *See* Tumultuous.

TUMULTUOUS The noisy and sometimes violent bubbling observed during the primary fermentation of wine, beer, or distilled spirits. Also known as tumultuosa.

TUN *See* Barrel.

TUN TAVERN The first recruiting of marines is reported to have been done at this tavern. The proprietor of the inn, one Robert Mullan, was commissioned a captain of the marines and served as one of the chief marine recruiters during the Revolutionary War. Lures of the recruits included offers of prize money, bounties, promises of pensions, and prospects of ample grog and other rations. Traditionally, Tun Tavern, located in Philadelphia, is regarded as the birthplace of the Marine Corps.

TURBID A cloudy or muddy appearing beer or wine, resulting from having its sediment stirred or shaken up. Also known as *torbido* and *turbio*.

TURBIO (SP) *See* Turbid.

TURN-THE-TABLES-OVER *See* Turnover.

TURNOVER The frequency and number of times a stock of beverages is sold and replenished in a given operating period of time; an activity ratio. Also known as *turn-the-tables-over*.

TURNSOLE A purple vegetable dye obtained from the *Croton tinctoria* plant, sometimes used in the nineteenth century by the French to "darken" the wines of Bordeaux.

TUSCANY (ITAL)   One of Italy's 20 wine-producing regions, located in central Italy, north of Latium, famous for its production of Chianti, Carmignano, Brunello di Montalcino, and Vino Nobile di Montepulciano (red wines), and Vernaccia di San Gimignano, Galestro, and Vin Santo (white wines). Known as *Toscano*, in Italy.

TWADELL   A seldom-used measuring system in the United States, utilizing a hydrometer for determining degrees sugar in the must.

TWIGGY   *See* Stemmy.

TWIST   A strip of citrus fruit peel used as a garnish in some cocktails.

TYLOSES   The internal grain patterns of wood (used in barrel-making) with its maze of interwoven crossmembers.

TYPE   Further division of the classes of alcoholic beverages. Thus, whiskey types, brandy types, and so on, used in the Universal Numeric Code (UNI-MERC). *See* Class.

TYPHA LATIFLOIA OR LATIFOGLIA   A plant whose flat leaves (after drying) are occasionally used to patch leaks in wooden barrels, almost like gasket material. In Italy, it is used as a wrapping for the "fiasco-shaped" wine bottles.

ÜBERSCHWEFELT (GERM) Wines that are overly sulfured, which can be detected by their pungent odor.

UBHIYA The term for beer in the Zulu nation of Africa.

UBRIACO (ITAL) Inebriate.

UGNI BLANC (CAL AND FR) *See* Trebbiano.

UISGEBEATHA Gaelic, meaning "water of life." *See* Aqua Vitae.

ULLAGE The air space in a bottle between the top of the wine and bottom of the cork. Also known as *coulage* and *headspace. See* Leakage.

ULL DE LLEBRE (SP) The local name in Catalonia for the Tempranillo grape variety. *See* Tempranillo.

ULTRA BRUT *See* Natural.

ULTRAFILTRATION It is a tangential-flow filtration system that utilizes a higher pressure range (usually from 10 to 150 psi) membrane system in order to separate high molecular weight dissolved materials from aqueous solutions on the basis of size. Lower weight molecules (such as salts, sugars, color pigments, flavor constituents) can pass through membranes designed for wine filtrations, while solids, colloids, and larger molecules cannot pass through. *See* Filtering.

UMBRIA (ITAL) One of 20 wine-producing regions that is surrounded by Tuscany, Latium, and the Marches. It is known as the "green heart of Italy" because it lies in the center of the peninsula and is rich in woods and pastures. The hillsides and gentle inclines of the Umbrian landscape are carpeted with olive trees and grapevines; the region's major freshwater lake—Trasimeno, which gives its name to one of the area's three DOC wines—is surrounded by vineyards. The Tiber River flows from north to south through the eastern part of the region, creating the Upper Tiber Valley, a major viticultural zone of Umbria. Perugia, the region's capital city, stands on a hilltop just east of

Lake Trasimeno. The smaller towns of Orvieto and Torgiano have lent their names to the two DOC wines of the region.

Umbria's major wine-producing areas include the Colli Altotiberini to the north, the Colli del Trasimeno to the west, Torgiano (near Assisi), and the well-known Orvieto zone in the southwest.

UNBALANCED   A wine whose various components have not cohesively come together. (for instance, alcohol, tannin, fruit, and acidity). The opposite of balanced. Also known as *unharmonisch*.

UNCINULA NECATOR   *See* Powdery Mildew.

UNCTUOUS   A term that describes a wine that is rich and lush tasting, with an almost oily texture to it, found in some full-bodied, very sweet wines.

UNDERBACK   The receiving tank for the wort, necessary in the brewing process of beer.

UNDERBAR   That location of the bar that houses equipment (blenders, etc.), ice bins, bottle wells, speed racks, and other supplies necessary for the production of cocktails.

UNDERPROOF   A distilled spirit containing less than 100 proof.

UNDER-THE-TABLE   Slang for intoxicated.

UNDEVELOPED   Wines that need further aging, either in wooden barrels or in glass bottles. Also known as *unenwickelt*.

UNENWICKELT (GERM)   *See* Underdeveloped.

UNFILTERED   A term that refers to a wine that has been bottled without being clarified or stabilized by filtration. However, the wine could have received other cellar treatments (e.g., fining).

UNFINED   A term that refers to a wine that has been bottled without being fined by using one of many fining agents. However, the wine could have received other cellar treatments (e.g., filtering).

UNGEZUCKERT (GERM)   Unsugared; pure.

UNHARMONISCH (GERM)   *See* Unbalanced.

UNIMERC   *See* Class and Type.

UNION   It is where the stock and scion (parts of grapevines) are joined together.

UNIT   A specified quantity, usually refering to the number or amount in a pack; may be expressed as weight in pounds or ounces; volume in quarts, liters, or gallons; or count in each dozen, case, gross, and so on.

UNIT COST   The price paid to acquire a specific unit.

UNITED STATES WINE   Wine produced on bonded wine premises in the United States.

UNIT PRICE   A supplementary system of pricing commodities, especially beverages, by showing the prices in terms of standard units (ounces or milliliters); it facilitates a comparison of prices of competing items.

UNIVERSITY OF BORDEAUX, ENOLOGY INSTITUTE (FR) The name of Bordeaux, France's premier enological and viticultural school, which was founded in February 1948.

UNIVERSITY OF CALIFORNIA, DAVIS The name of California's premier enological and viticultural school, located in Sacramento. The University purchased the Davis Farm in 1906.

UNMERCHANTABLE WINE Wine that has been tax paid, removed from bonded wine premises, and subsequently returned to a bonded wine premises for the purpose of reconditioning, reformulation, or destruction.

UNRIPE Wines made from grapes that have not yet reached physiologic maturity. These wines lack aroma, taste, and other tactile impressions displayed in mature grapes. They also tend to be thin and watery tasting with relatively high levels of acidity. *See* Green and Young.

UNSOUND The opposite of sound.

UNTERSCHWEFELT (GERM) Lacking sulfur; those wines with insufficient levels of sulfur dioxide will oxidize quickly and be subject to bacterial infestation.

UP Any drink that is served without ice or *straight* up. Also known as *straight up*.

UPCHARGE Premium charged on a gift product to either fully or partially capture the additional cost of the gift wrap, carton, and so forth.

URALT (GERM) Brandy that has been aged at least one year.

URBANA A grape variety developed from a cross of Governor Ross and Mills at the New York State Experimental Station in 1912.

URSPRUNGSBEZEICHNUNG (GERM) A statement of origin.

URZIGER (GERM) A small village in the northern part of the Mosel, that produces dry white wines with a "spicy" character that are slow-maturing.

USABLE PORTION The portion of a product that has a value; the amount being used in a recipe, that has a resale value.

USÉ (FR) Worn out; a wine that has been kept too long.

USQUEBAUGH *See* Aqua Vitae.

UVA (ITAL AND SP) *See* Grape.

UVA AMERICANA (ITAL) *See* Isabella.

UVA DE MESA (SP) A dessert grape.

UVAGGIO (ITAL) *See* Cuvée.

UVA PASAS (SP) *See* Raisins.

VA *See* Volatile Acidity.

VALAIS (SWISS) One of the most famous wine districts in Switzerland is Valais, a deep, sheltered valley at the headwaters of the Rhône, where carefully cultivated, terraced vineyards step up the mountainsides, reaching very high altitudes (the Visperterminen vineyard, the highest in Europe, is at 4,000 feet). The high Alps shield Valais from winds and storms, giving it one of Switzerland's most temperate climates in summer, although the winters are bitterly cold. Since Valais is the most arid section of Switzerland, the grapevines are irrigated with water taken from mountainside canals fed by the melting glaciers. The rich lowlands of Valais are famous for their lush fruits, especially the pears that are used to make Switzerland's celebrated pear brandy. Winemakers of the Valais district produce delicate white wines and Dole, a full-bodied red wine.

VALDEPEÑAS (SP) A grape-growing district located within the La Mancha area, south of Madrid. Valdepeñas produces a large quantity of light-bodied red wines, referred to as *vino manchego.*

VALDIGUIÉ (FR) A red grape variety, a very heavy producer of "ordinary" wines in the Midi Region, in southern France. Also known as *Napa Gamay.* *See* Gamay.

VALGELLA (ITAL) A full-bodied red wine produced from the Nebbiolo grape variety in the Valtellina district of Lombardy, located in the northern part of Italy.

VALLE D'AOSTA (ITAL) Smallest of Italy's 20 wine-producing regions, located in the northwest corner, producing some well-made white and red wines.

VALMUR (FR) One of seven *grand cru* vineyards of Chablis.

VALPOLICELLA (ITAL) A dry, light-bodied red wine from the region of

Veneto, produced from a blend of Corvina, Rondinella, Molinara, and other grape varieties; best consumed young.

The consorzio of Valpolicella features a Roman arena at Verona on its neck label.

VALTELLINA (ITAL)   A grape-growing district situated in the Adda River Valley in the northern province of Sondrio, near Switzerland, is one of the few places where the Nebbiolo grape thrives. This grape, a well-known Piedmont variety, is called *Chiavennasca* in Lombardy and has been grown there since the fifth century A.D. It is the principal variety of the area and is cultivated in the terraced vineyards that scale the steep, rugged north bank of the valley. Here the grapes receive optimum exposure to the sun, as well as all the other microclimatic conditions needed to flourish. Among the varieties cultivated are Rossola, Brugnola, Pignola Valtellinese, Merlot, and Pinot Nero (Noir).

The area's two DOC wines, Valtellina and Valtellina Superiore, are produced from the Nebbiolo grape. The bottle label of a Valtellina Superiore will usually carry the name of the designated area where the wine was produced. DOC law recognizes only four such geographic subdistricts for Valtellina Superiore: Sassella, Grumello, Valgella, and Inferno.

VANILLA   The smell of vanilla bean extract that is evident in certain wines, especially Chardonnay and Cabernet Sauvignon that have been aged in certain types of new oak barrels.

VAN BUREN   A red grape variety developed in 1935, from a cross of Fredonia and Worden, at the New York State Experimental Station.

VANESSA   A white seedless grape variety developed in 1965, from a cross of Bath and Interlaken, at the New York State Experimental Station.

VAPID   A mildly oxidized odor.

VAPPA (ITAL)   *See* Aigre.

VARIABLE COSTS   Costs that increase or decrease in direct relationship with the volume of business. A cost that is controlled by an individual (such as department head) in a company. In this case, the manager can exert some influence and act to lower the expense. Also referred to as *controllable costs*.

VARIETAL   A wine made wholly or predominantly from a single grape variety, named on the label (for example, Cabernet Sauvignon, Chardonnay, Pinot Noir, Zinfandel).

VARIETAL CHARACTER   The specific and unique combination of odor, taste, and sometimes tactile impression of a wine, which is directly attributed to the source grape variety.

VARIETAL DESIGNATION   Varietal designations are the names of the dominant grapes used in the wine. Cabernet Sauvignon, Seyval, Johannisberg Riesling, Cayuga White, Pinot Noir, Baco Noir, Chancellor, and Chenin Blanc are examples of grape varieties. A varietal designation on the label requires an appellation of origin and means that at least 75 percent of that grape variety is used in the wine. Wines made from *Vitis labrusca* grapes, such as Concord, are an exception because of the grape's intense flavor. These wines must contain a minimum of 51 percent of that grape variety, and it will be so stated on the label. If the label carries no percentage statement, the wine must contain at least 75 percent of the *labrusca* variety.

Wine labels are not required to bear a varietal designation. Other designations (red wine, white wine, table wine) are used to identify the wine without label information on the type of grape used or where it was grown. On California wine labels, designations such as "Chablis" or "Burgundy" indicate wines that are similar in name only to the wines originally made in geographic regions indicated by those names. Other notable examples of U.S.–produced "generic" wines are Sauterne, Rhine, Chianti, champagne, Tokay, Madeira, sherry, and port. There are no federal regulations that stipulate the grape varieties that American-produced "generic" wines may contain.

Some wines, such as Pommard (France) and Rüdesheimer (Germany), are designated with distinctive names that are permissible only on specific wines from a particular site or region within the country of origin.

VARIETY *See* Grape Variety.

VARYS (GREECE) *See* Heavy.

VASO VINARIO (ITAL) Any type of vessel that contains wine, including the modern tanks in stainless steel.

VAT An English word for a tub or barrel. A large container used for the fermentation or storage of wine, beer, and distilled spirits. *See* Barrel.

VAT-ROOM The building where all the vinification processes are carried out and the barrels filled with wine are stored. Also known as cuverie.

VATTING Before bottling, the flavoring whiskeys are mixed with a proportion of grain whiskey and left to marry for several weeks.

VATTING A process used during fermentation, whereas the skins are left in contact with the must for a longer period of time, to extract additional tannins, color, and flavonoids.

VAUD (SWISS) A wine-producing canton that is made up of three grape-growing areas: Chablais, which is upstream from where the Rhône enters Lake Geneva; Lavaux, bordering the lakefront east of Lausanne; and La Côte, located between Lausanne and Geneva. Nearly all of Vaud's wines are white, called Dorins (many also use the name of the commune or village from which they come on their labels). Charming, fragrant reds, labeled Salvagnins, are also produced throughout Vaud from a blend of Pinot Noir and Gamay grapes.

VAUDÉSIR (FR) One of seven *grand cru* vineyards of Chablis.

VDQS (FR) *See* Vins Délimités de Qualité Supérieure.

VECCHIO (ITAL) Old.

VEEBLANC   A white grape variety developed from a cross of Cascade and Seyve-Villard 14287, at the Horticultural Research Institute, Vineland, Ontario, Canada.

VEEPORT   A red grape variety developed in 1961, from a cross of Wilder and Winchell, at the Horticultural Research Institute, Vineland, Ontario, Canada.

VEGETAL   An odor and/or taste of a wine characterized by a grassy, herbaceous component, often reminiscent of freshly mowed grass, or of vegetable soup.

VELDT (FR)   A now extinct unit of measurement that was used in the Cognac region and contained approximately two gallons (27 veldts equaled a cognac barrel of 205 liters; 35 veldts equaled 72 U.S. gallons). Also spelled *veltes*.

VELHO (PORT)   Old.

VELHISSIMO (PORT)   Very old; not an indication of quality.

VELINCH   *See* Wine Thief.

VELLUTATO (ITAL)   *See* Velvety.

VELO (SP)   A surface film, made primarily of *flor*.

VELOUTÉ (FR)   *See* Velvety.

VELTES (FR)   *See* Veldt.

VELVETY   A soft, silky, and smooth-tasting wine, that is opulent and textured on the palate. This term could also be applied to some beers and distilled spirits. Also known as *samtig, vellutato,* and *velouté*. *See* Silky.

VENDANGE (FR)   *See* Année and Vintage.

VENDANGE TARDIVE (FR)   *See* Late Harvest.

VENDANGEUR (FR)   A grape picker.

VENDEMMIA (ITAL)   *See* Vintage. Also known as *annata*.

VENDIMIA (SP)   *See* Vintage. Also known as *añada, año* and *cosecha*.

VENDOR   *See* Supplier.

VENENCIA (SP)   The name of the special elongated silver receptacle that has a flexible whalebone handle with a silver cup at one end and a decorative hook, also of solid silver, at the other end. This cup is plunged into the barrel and immediately filled with sherry wine. It is then removed and poured into several glasses from a height of perhaps 12 to 18 inches.

VENENCIADOR   The user of a *venencia*.

VENETO (ITAL)   One of Italy's 20 wine-producing regions, located in the northeast. Veneto takes its name from its capital, Venezia (Venice), once one of the most powerful sea nations in all history. It was also home to Marco Polo, who brought exotic spices back to Europe from the Far East.

   There are three distinct wine zones: the Verona area, famous for Soave, Valpolicella, Amarone, and Bardolino; Euganean hills between Vicenza and Padova, where table wines are made; and the areas of Treviso and Conegliano, which lie about 40 miles due north of Venice. The latter are best known for excellent varietal wines, especially Tocai, Merlot, and Cabernet.

VENTILATING BUNG *See* Fermentation Lock.

VENTURA A red grape variety developed from a cross of Chelois and Elvira, at the Horticultural Research Institute, Vineland, Ontario, Canada.

VENUS A red seedless grape variety developed in 1964, from a cross of Alden and New York 46000, by Dr. J. N. Moore, at the Arkansas Agricultural Experiment Station.

VÉRAISON (FR) A term that refers to the commencement of maturation of grapes, which is distinguished by a change of color; the original green gives way to the true color (usually red) of the grape, prior to it reaching its final maturity. Also known as *invaiatura*.

VERBAND DEUTSCHER SEKTKELLEREIEN (GERM) The Association of German Sekt Wineries.

VERBESSERN (GERM) A formerly-used term to denote *chaptalization*. Replaced by *anreichern*. *See* Chaptalization.

VERBRAUCHER (GERM) A consumer.

VERDE (ITAL) *See* Green.

VERDELET A white French-American hybrid grape variety, developed in the late 1880s, from a cross of Seibel 5455 and Seibel 4938, by Louis Seibel in the late 1880s in France. It produces wines with a clean vinous taste, low in acidity and slightly aromatic, like Gewürztraminer. Formerly known as *Seibel 9110* and called *Verdelet Blanc*.

VERDELET BLANC *See* Verdelet.

VERDELHO (PORT) A semidry type of Madeira wine, with a clean taste and a gentle, smooth flavor. The Verdelho grape is a cross between the Spanish Pedro Ximénez and the Italian Verdea grape varieties.

VERDELLO (ITAL) A white grape variety used in the blend for the production of Orvieto wine, from Umbria.

VERDICCHIO (ITAL) A dry, white wine from the region of Umbria, made from a blend of Verdicchio, with the possible addition of Trebbiano Toscano and Malvasia Toscano; best consumed young.

Verdicchio is occasionally bottled in the traditional "amphora-shaped" bottles that were used to bring wine from Greece to the Italian peninsula in ancient times. It is one of the oldest wine bottle shapes in the world, predating the Bordeaux bottle.

The *consorzio's* neck label on bottles of Verdicchio depicts a heraldic lion.

VERDOGNOLO (ITAL) Greenish reflections, as detected in some freshly made white wines.

VERDOLINO (ITAL) Light green.

VERDOSO (SP)   *See* Green.

VERDOT (FR)   *See* Petit Verdot.

VERGINE (ITAL)   Considered to be the finest Marsala; made by the solera system. By law, it cannot contain less than 18-percent alcohol. What makes Marsala *vergine* so special is that it is made from the best wines of the vintage and must be aged for at least five years in barrels before it can be sold by the producer; it is therefore extremely dry. When properly stored, Marsala *vergine* can be aged for 10 to 15 years. Also known as *Marsala vergine*.

VERKAEUFER (GERM)   A vendor.

VERMENTINO (FR)   A white grape variety cultivated primarily on the island of Corsica.

VERMOUTH   According to the Bureau of Alcohol, Tobacco, and Firearms (BATF regulation 1976-C), vermouth is a type of apéritif wine that is made from grape juice and has the taste, aroma, and characteristics generally attributed to vermouth. The BATF regulations also state that apéritif wines fulfilling the characteristics of vermouth shall be so designated. Vermouth, although fortified (containing between 15 to 21 percent alcohol), is often referred to as an "aromatic" or "aromatized" wine, meaning a wine that has been altered by the infusion of *Artemisia absinthium* (any number of related aromatic plants) or bitter herbs. Some of the ingredients used (there are more than 100) are allspice, angelica, angostura, anise, benzoin, bitter almond, bitter orange, celery, chamomile, cinchona, cinnamon, clove, coca, coriander, elder, fennel, gentian, ginger, hop, marjoram, mace, myrtle, nutmeg, peach, quinine, rhubarb, rosemary, saffron, sage, sandalwood, savory (summer), thyme, vanilla, woodruff (May Wine).

The red vermouths, most notably those from Italy and France, are always sweet and contain approximately 130 to 160 grams of sugar per liter (13 to 16 percent residual sugar per 100 ml). The white vermouths, also mainly from Italy and France, can be dry, semidry, or sweet, and contain less than 40 grams of sugar per liter (4 percent or less residual sugar per 100 ml).

VERNACCIA DI ORISTANO (ITAL)   A white grape variety cultivated primarily in Sardinia.

VERNACCIA DI SAN GIMIGNANO (ITAL)   A white grape variety native to Tuscany, although small parcels are also cultivated on the island of Sardinia. It produces dry white wines with considerable body and acidity, with an aromatic odor and slightly bitter taste.

VERRE (FR)   Glass. The traditional Bordeaux tasting glass is tulip-shaped, and preferably crystal to capture the brilliant reflections of the *robe*. It must be large enough to allow the swirling motion that releases all the subtleties of the bouquet.

VERSCHLOSSEN (GERM)   *See* Closed-In.

VERSCHNEIDEN (GERM)   The blending or mixing of various grape varieties or wines according to the German Wine Laws. *See* Blending.

VESOU (SP)   In the production of rum, the sugarcane, minus its leaves, are cut and shredded by heavy rollers, and the juice is (called *vesou*) collected, strained, decanted, and filtered.

VERT (FR)   *See* Green.

VEUVE (FR)   Widow.

VID (SP)   *See* Grapevine.

VIDAL BLANC   A white grape variety developed in 1929, from a cross of Ugni Blanc and Rayon d'Or, by J.L. Vidal, director of the Fougerat Research Station at Bois-Charente (in the Cognac region). Formerly known as *Vidal 256*.

VIDEIRA (PORT)   *See* Grapevine.

VIDURE (FR)   *See* Cabernet Sauvignon.

VIEILLE RÉSERVE (FR)   A label designation on Armagnac or cognac bottles that indicates that the youngest brandy used in the blend is at least 5 ½ years old (although they contain a very high percentage of brandy that has been aged for 20, 30, or 40 years or more).

VIEILLES VIGNES (FR)   Ungrafted grapevines.

VIEILLISSEMENT (FR)   The maturing of wines by laying them down in a cellar, with proper storage conditions (e.g. light, heat, humidity, and so on).

VIEJISIMO (SP)   Very old.

VIEJO (SP)   Old.

VIENNA BEER   Amber-colored beers, medium-bodied with pronounced malty flavors. Although this was once a style of beer emanating from Vienna, it is now produced all over the world, with the name carrying little meaning.

VIERTELSTÜCK (GERM)   A barrel used in the Rhine region with a capacity of approximately 79 U.S. gallons. *See* Barrel.

VIEUX (FR)   A label designation on Armagnac or cognac bottles that indicates that the youngest brandy used in the blend is at least 5 ½ years old (although they contain a very high percentage of brandy that has been aged for 20, 30, or 40 years or more).

VIF (FR)   *See* Lively.

VIGNA (ITAL)   *See* Single-Vineyard.

VIGNAIOLA (ITAL)   *See* Vigneron.

VIGNE (FR)   *See* Grapevine.

VIGNERON (FR)   A vineyardist; those who nurture grapevines; a grape grower; also a combination winemaker and grape grower. Also known as *vignaiola*.

VIGNETI (ITAL)   *See* Single-Vineyard.

VIGNETO (ITAL) *See* Single-Vineyard.

VIGNOBLE (FR) *See* Vineyard.

VIGNOLES A white French-hybrid grape variety, developed from a cross of Pinot Noir and Seibel 6905, that produces good quality wines, well-suited for either table or sparkling wine production. Formerly known as *Ravat 51.*

VIGOR The rate of growth of a grapevine.

VIGOROUS A term that describes a young and lively wine, with good balance and acidity.

VIGOROUS GRAPEVINES Grapevines with shoots that grow rapidly and produce considerable growth.

VIILE (RUM) *See* Vineyard.

VILLA (ITAL) A country manor house.

VILLARD BLANC A white French-American hybrid grape variety, developed from a cross of Seibel 6468 and Seibel 6905, that produces wines with a good balance of acid and fruit. Formerly known as *Seyve-Villard 12375.*

VILLARD NOIR A red French-American hybrid grape variety, developed from a cross of Chancellor and Seibel 6905, which produces wines that are heavy and full-bodied. Formerly known as *Seyve-Villard 18315.*

396

VIN (FR) *See* Wine.

VIÑA (SP) *See* Vineyard.

VINACCIA (ITAL) *See* Grappa.

VINAI (ITAL) Winemakers.

VINAIGRE (FR) *See* Vinegar.

VINAIGRIER (FR) The small wooden barrels in which vinegar is made.

VIN BLANC (FR) *See* White Wine.

VINCENT NOIR A red grape variety developed at the Horticultural Research Institute, Vineland, Ontario, Canada. It produces wines that are useful in blending.

VIN CLAIR (FR) A clear wine.

VIN CUIT (FR) *See* Cotto. Also known as *cuit.*

VIN DE CARAFE (FR) A term for good, plain wine, usually sold in bulk to restaurants and served in a carafe.

VIN DE CUVÉE (FR) Wine made from the pressing of the grapes in Champagne.

VIN DE GARDE (FR) Wine for keeping or laying down. Due to the richness of its components (color, tannin, and bouquet), it develops slowly and preserves all its qualities while reaching a grand old age.

VIN DE GOUTTE (FR) *See* Free-Run Juice.

VIN DE L'ANNÉE (FR) *See* Nouveau.

Vin de Messe (FR)   *See* Sacramental Wines.

Vin de Pays (FR)   A classification of wines established in 1973, which are one step above *vin ordinaire* in quality.

Vin de Presse (FR)   *See* Press Juice.

Vin de Primeur (FR)   *See* Nouveau.

Vin de Sable (FR)   Wines made from grapes grown predominantly in sandy soil.

Vin de Table (FR)   *See* Vino da Tavola.

Vin de Taille (FR)   Wine made from the harder and less desirable pressings of the grapes, for the production of champagne.

Vin de Tête (FR)   *See* Tête de Cuvée.

Vindima (PORT)   *See* Vintage. Also known as *ano* and *ano de colheita*.

Vin Doux Naturel (FR)   A category of sweet, fortified dessert wines (red or white), with an alcoholic content in excess of 14 percent by volume.

Vin du Pays (FR)   Country wine; used to describe small wines of each region that are consumed locally.

Vine   Any plant with long, thin stems that grows above the ground or climbs a wall or other supports by means of tendrils.

Vine Capacity   The capability for the total growth of the grapevine. It is measured by determining the weight of annual cane prunings produced. *See* Cane Weight.

Viñedo (SP)   *See* Vineyard.

Vinegar   A wine or wine product not for beverage use, which contains not less than 4.0 grams (4.0 percent) of volatile acidity (calculated as acetic acid and exclusive of sulfur dioxide) per 100 milliliters of wine. Also known as *aceto*, *vinaigre*, and *wine vinegar*. *See* Volatile Acidity.

Viner (FR)   The practice of adding alcohol to a wine, in order to fortify it.

Vinered   A grape variety developed in 1964, from a cross of Brocton and Self at the New York State Experimental Station.

Vine Size   *See* Cane Weight.

Vine Stock   The name given to the different varieties of grapevines from which wines are generally made.

Vineux (FR)   *See* Vinosity.

Vine Vigor   It is the seasonal rate of growth of the shoots of a grapevine.

Vineyard   Land devoted to cultivating grapevines. Also known as *einzellage*, *lozia*, *vignoble*, *viile*, *viña*, *viñedo*, *vinha*, *vinhedo*, and *weinberg*.

Vin Gris (FR)   A term used to describe the color of a pale, almost rosé color of certain wines, made either with limited skin contact, or grapes grown in those geographical areas of the world far from the equator, where the red grapes do not fully ripen, therefore, the color is not deeper or darker. Occasionally referred to as *oeil de perdrix*—literally, eye of the partridge. Also known as *gris*.

VINHA (PORT)   *See* Vineyard.

VINHEDO (PORT)   Small vineyard. *See* Vineyard.

VINHO (PORT)   *See* Wine.

VINHO ABAFADO (PORT)   Fortified wine. Also known as *abafado, alcolisado, vinho alcolisado,* and *vinho generoso.*

VINHO ALCOLISADO (PORT)   Also known as *alcolisado. See* Vinho Abafado.

VINHO APERITIVE (PORT)   *See* Apéritif Wine.

VINHO BRANCO (PORT)   *See* White Wine.

VINHO CANTEIRO (PORT)   Wine that has been made and matured without being placed through *estufagem.*

VINHO CLARETE (PORT)   Light red wine.

VINHO CLARO (PORT)   *See* Nouveau.

VINHO CONSUMO (PORT)   *See* Vin Ordinaire.

VINHO DE MESA (PORT)   *See* Vino da Tavola.

VINHO DO RODO (PORT)   *See* Vinho Espumante.

VINHO ENGARRAFADO (PORT)   Bottled wine.

VINHO ESPUMANTE (PORT)   *See* Sparkling Wine. Also known as *espumante* and *vinho do rodo.*

VINHO ESTUFADO (PORT)   Wine that has already been through the estufa. Also known as *estufado.*

VINHO GENEROSO (PORT)   *See* Vinho Abafado.

VINHO LIQUOROSO (PORT)   A sweetened dessert wine with a higher than normal alcoholic content.

VINHO MADURO (PORT)   Mature wine.

VINHO ROSADO (PORT)   *See* Rosé wine.

VINHO SECO (PORT)   Dry wine. *See* Dry.

VINHO TINTO (PORT)   *See* Red wine.

VINHO VERDE (PORT)   A Portuguese term for "green wine", it is produced in the northern part of Portugal, in a hilly region known as Minho. These wines are often quite young, most of them bottled only four months after harvest, and are not meant to be stored away for prolonged aging. Their charm lies in their youthfulness, "spritzy" character, and absolutely clean, crisp, and refreshing taste.

VINI (ITAL)   Wines.

VINI BIANCHI (ITAL)   White wines.

VINICULTURA (SP)   *See* Viniculture.

VINICULTURE   The theory, art, and science of winemaking. Also known as *vinicultura*.

VINIFERA   *See Vitis Vinifera.*

VINIFICATION   The entire process of converting grapes or other ripe fruits into wine, which includes crushing/destemming, fermenting, pressing, aging, bottling, and so on. Also known as *vinificato, vinificazione, vinify*, and *weinbereitung*.

VINIFICATO (ITAL)   Vinified. *See* Vinification.

VINIFICAZIONE (ITAL)   *See* Vinification.

VINIFY   *See* Vinification.

VINI PREGIATI (ITAL)   Valued wines.

VINI ROSATI (ITAL)   Rosé wines.

VINI ROSSI (ITAL)   Red wines.

VINI TIPICI (ITAL)   A category for wines typical of certain defined grographical areas.

VIN MOUSSEUX (FR)   *See* Sparkling Wine. Also known as *mousseux*.

VIN NATURE (FR)   A natural, unsweetened wine.

VINO (ITAL AND SP)   *See* Wine.

VINO ABOCADO (SP)   *See* Semidry Wine.

VINO BIANCO (ITAL)   *See* White Wine.

VINO BLANCO (SP)   *See* White Wine.

VINO CLARETE (SP)   A light, red-colored wine.

VINO COMUN (SP)   *See* Vin Ordinaire.

VINO CORRIENTE (SP)   *See* Vin Ordinaire.

VINO COTTO (ITAL)   *See* Cotto.

VINO CRUDO (SP)   *See* Young.

VINO DA ARROSTO (ITAL)   A robust, aged red wine.

VINO DA PASTO (ITAL)   *See* Vin Ordinaire.

VINO DA TAGLIO (ITAL)   *See* Blending.

VINO DA TAVOLA (ITAL)   Table wine; a defined wine classification according to the laws of 1963, equivalent to *normalwein* (Austria); *stolno vino* (Yugolsavia); *vin de table* (France); *tafelwein* (Germany), *vinho de mesa* (Portugal), and *vino de mesa* (Spain). *See* Table Wine.

VINO DE AGUJA (SP)   *See* Spritz.

VINO DE CALIDAD (SP)   Quality wine. Must be a Denominación de Origen wine made from the free-run or lightly pressed juice of ripe, healthy grapes, that has undergone a controlled fermentation.

VINO DE COSECHA (SP)   Wines of a particular vintage year. In special cases, if the purpose is to maximize the quality of the wine, a maximum of 15 percent of wine of a previous year may be added. Also known as *vino de vendimia*.

VINO DE COSECHA PROPIA (SP)   Estate bottled.

VINO DE CRIANZA (SP)   *See* Crianza.

VINO DE MESA (SP)   *See* Vino da Tavola.

VINO DE PASTO (SP)   *See* Vin Ordinaire.

VINO DE RANCIO (SP)   *See* Rancio.

VINO DE VENDIMIA (SP)   *See* Vino de Cosecha.

VINO DE XÉRÈS (SP)   Sherry wine.

VINO ESPUMOSA (SP)   *See* Sparkling Wine. Also known as *espumosa*.

VINO FRIZZANTE (ITAL)   *See* Spritz.

VINO GENEROSO (SP)   Fortified wine.

VINO LIQUOROSO (ITAL)   A very sweet wine.

VIN NOUVEAU (FR)   *See* Nouveau.

VINOMETER   An instrument utilized to measure the approximate alcohol content of dry wines. It consists of a capillary tube, with a scale on one end and an opened-out other end where wine is poured for measuring. The device is not very accurate and is used mostly for home winemakers.

VINO NOBILE DI MONTEPULCIANO (ITAL)   A dry, full-bodied red wine, produced in a small area surrounding the town of Montepulciano, in the province of Siena, in Tuscany.

This wine was famous in the fourteenth and fifteenth centuries and was a favorite of Pope Paul III. Its name, "vino nobile," is derived from the fact that is was produced exclusively for the titled families who lived in the area.

Vino Nobile de Montepulciano was granted DOC status on July 12, 1966, and was raised to a DOCG wine on February 17, 1981. It must be aged a minimum of two years(if aged three years it is entitled to be labeled *riserva*), and must have a minimum of 12.5-percent alcohol. It is a blend of Prugnolo Gentile (Sangiovese Grosso), Canaiolo Nero, Malvasia del Chianti, and several other grape varieties. The Vino Nobile di Montepulciano *consorzio* features on its neck label a griffin rampant on a white background within a red circle.

VINO NOVELLO (ITAL)   A new or freshly fermented wine similar to Beaujolais Nouveau of France. Italian law of 1989 stipulates that the appellation *vino novello* can be applied only to table wines with geographic origin or table wines possessing characteristics typical of the growing zone of the grape. They must be made with grapes of the current vintage and bottled before December 31, but may not be released before November 6. The maximum limit on residual-reducing sugars cannot exceed 10 grams a liter, which means that the wine can also be moderately sweetish. The minimum alcohol level is set at 11 degrees. And at least 30 percent of the wine must be obtained through the carbonic maceration system in which the entire grape is used. The wine is also required to bear a vintage date. Also known as *novello*. *See* Nouveau.

VIN ORDINAIRE (FR) Inexpensive, common, ordinary, everyday wines below the VDQS level of quality, without any special breed, however sound they may be. The term includes almost 70 percent of all French wines; these are not controlled by the government and are simple wines made locally for everyday consumption. Also known as *ordinaire, vinho consumo, vino comun, vino corriente, vino da pasto,* and *vino de pasto.*

VINO PRETTO (ITAL) A wine that is pure, genuine, and unadulterated. *See* Vin Santo.

VINO ROSADO (SP) *See* Rosé wine.

VINO ROSATO (ITAL) *See* Rosé wine.

VINO ROSSO (ITAL) *See* Red wine.

401

VIN SANTO (ITAL) This unfortified dessert wine is produced in several regions of Italy, each claiming that theirs is the true area of origin. Vin Santo Toscano is made from the ripest Trebbiano and/or Malvasia grapes, which are tied together and either hung from the beams of a well-ventilated room or dried on wicker trays. This process results in the evaporation of a high percentage of the grapes' water content, at the same time increasing the percentage of sugar. The higher the sugar content of the grape, the higher the resulting alcoholic content and the richer the final product. For a sweet Vin Santo, the bunches are left to raisin for about two-and-one-half months; for a Vin Santo that is semidry to dry, they are left about two months.

The grapes are crushed during the winter and the must placed into oak barrels with a capacity of 225 liters (59.4 U.S. gallons) for a period of about two years, followed by three years in smaller oak barrels called *caratello*, which have a capacity of approximately 50 liters (13 U.S. gallons). The same barrels are used over and over again, and a small amount of the previous Vin Santo in the barrel is always left inside to blend with the new must (this is similar to Sherry solera production). The barrels are filled to three-quarters capacity, closed with a cork bung, and placed in the winery's attic or a room exposed to heat, where the wine is left to ferment slowly for three years. Each winter, fermentation is interrupted by the cold, but starts again in the spring. During fermentation, carbon dioxide accumulates and creates high pressure that slows down the process. For this reason the barrels are stored directly under the roof of the winery, where the summer heat causes the wood of the top part of the barrel not in contact with the wine to contract, allowing air to enter and oxidation to occur. This gives Vin Santo its characteristic amber-brown color and contributes to the complexity of its aroma. Another characteristic of this special aging process is the development of a sort of "cooked" or *maderized* taste in the wine.

Vin Santo has an unmistakable nutty bouquet and a somewhat nutty-creamy, tangy taste, reminiscent of dried apricots, which is similar to that of an amontillado sherry, bual Madeira, or dry Marsala. Its alcoholic content is usually somewhere between 15 to 18 percent. It is an excellent apéritif, served chilled from the refrigerator, or enjoyed at room temperature after dinner. Vin Santo is best consumed when 6 to 10 years old and often has a life of more than 20 years.

Before the wine was known as Vino Santo, this famous Tuscan Italian dessert wine was called *Vino Pretto* until 1349, when the name was changed. Vin Santo is occasionally spelled *vino santo*.

The origin of the unusual name of this dry or sweet dessert wine has not been firmly established. Some sources claim the wine is called "saintly" because it is used during Holy Mass or because the grapes are crushed during Holy Week. Others claim that during the Council of Florence called by Pope Eugenius VI in 1340, Cardinal Bessarione, primate of the Greek Orthodox church, upon being served a glass of Vin Santo (then called *Vino Pretto*), exclaimed, "This is the Wine of Xantos," referring to a wine from his homeland. His colleagues understood him to be calling the wine "Santo" and the name stuck. Whichever story one believes, one thing is for sure: the name Vin Santo literally translated means "holy wine" or "wine of the Saints."

VINOS DE MISA (SP)   *See* Sacramental Wines.

VINO SECCO (ITAL)   Dry wine. *See* Dry.

VINO SECO (SP)   Dry wine. *See* Dry.

VINOSITY   A term pertaining to the "wine-like" aroma or flavor of wine, due to its alcohol content. Also known as *vineux, vinoso, vinous flavor, weinig,* and *winey.*

VINOSO (ITAL)   *See* Vinosity.

VINO SPUMANTE (ITAL)   *See* Sparkling Wine.

VINO TIPICO (ITAL)   A category of wines that are one step below the DOC level.

VINOUS   A term applied to a wine without a specific, distinguishable odor, however well it is made. Also known as *eklektós.*

VINOTHÈQUE (FR)   *See* Wine Library.

VINO TINTO (SP)   *See* Red wine.

VIN ROSÉ (FR)   *See* Rosé wine.

VIN ROUGE (FR)   *See* Red wine.

VINS AROMATIQUES (FR)   Wines that display very pronounced aromas or scents.

Vins Délimités de Qualité Supérieure (VDQS) (FR) A classification of wines that are just slightly below the AOC designation in quality. First authorized for use on December 18, 1949.

Vin Sec (FR) Dry wine. *See* Dry.

Vintage The year in which the grapes (crop) were picked or harvested, and wine was made from them, with the date of that year shown on the label. A season of unusually favorable growing conditions is called a "vintage year" and is said to produce "vintage wines," connotating a very good year. Also known as *jahrgang, recolta, vendange, vendemmia, vendima, vendimia,* and *weinlese.*

Vintage Character (Port) A port that is made from a blend of two or more vintages, which is similar in style and character to a "late-bottled vintage port." Also known as *tipo vintage* and *vintage style.*

Vintage Chart A report, chart, or guide, developed to give retailers, restaurateurs, and consumers an indication as to how a particular vintage or growing season progressed, and what the final outcome was, relative to the quantity and quality of the grapes harvested.

Vintage Date A vintage date on the label indicates that 95 percent or more of the wine is produced from grapes grown in that year. If a vintage date is shown on the label, an appellation of origin, other than a country, will also be shown.

Vintage Ports (Port) Vintage ports are produced only in years that are declared by the shippers to be the very best (usually only three or four vintages in a decade). They are aged for two years in wooden barrels, then bottled somewhere between July 1 of the second year and June 30 of the third year after the harvest. Vintage port is very difficult to drink in its youth because of its tannin, high alcohol, and concentration of fruit and sugar. However, those who are patient enough to wait 15 to 20 years will be rewarded with one of the world's greatest fortified wines. Surprisingly, it was not until 1775 that the first vintage port was produced.

Vintage Style *See* Vintage-Character Port.

Vintage Wine Wine from a single year stated on the label, rather than a blend from several years.

Vinted and Bottled By According to the BATF, this term carries no legal meaning.

Vintner One who sells wine. The term is used broadly to designate grape growers, wine blenders, and wholesaler wine merchants. Another correct term for a grape grower is "wine producer." An individual who conducts the crushing and fermentation in the winery is called a winemaker.

Vinum Latin for wine. *See* Yayin.

Viognier (FR) A white grape variety grown predominantly in the Côtes du Rhône region, where it produces wines that are full-bodied, rich, and heady, with a fine floral fragrance. Some Viognier is planted in small parcels in California.

VIOLACEO (ITAL) Violet or purple color detected in some red wines.

VIOLETS An intriguing scent occasionally detected in some red wines, mostly from northern Italy, as well as Bordeaux and the Rhône Valley of France.

VIRGINIA In Jamestown in 1608, the first wine bottles in the United States were produced.

VIRGIN BRANDY *See* Alcools Blanc.

VIRGIN DRINKS *See* Mocktails.

VIRGIN MARY A Bloody Mary minus the vodka.

VIRIL (FR) Virile; powerful, masculine.

VISCOSITY *See* Viscous.

VISCOUS A term generally applied to full-bodied red or white wines that taste concentrated and fat, almost thick and syrupy, with a high extract level and usually considerable alcohol. This term also can be applied to intensely sweet dessert wines, which have that syrupy character. Also known as *viscosity*.

404

VITAMIN C (ASCORBIC ACID) *See* Antioxidant and Campden Tablets.

VITE (ITAL) *See* Grapevine.

VITICOLE (FR) A viticultural region.

VITICOLTURA (ITAL) *See* Viticulture.

VITICULTEUR (FR) *See* Viticulture.

VITICULTURA (SP) *See* Viticulture.

VITICULTURAL AREA A U.S. viticultural area is a well-defined grape-growing region with soil, climate, history, and geographic features that set it apart from the surrounding areas and make it ideal for grape growing. A viticultural area appellation on the label indicates that 85 percent or more of the wine is produced from grapes grown in the particular area.

VITICULTURE Cultivation of the grapevine, or the theory, science, or study of the production of grapes. Also called viniculture, when applied to the growing of grapes for wine. Also known as *viticoltura, viticulteur, viticultura,* and *weinbau.*

VITIGNO (ITAL) *See* Grape Variety.

VITIS Grapevine; derives from the Latin *vitaceae,* which refers to woody, climbing plants, and *vinifera,* which refers to the berries or grapes that the plant produces.

VITIS AESTIVALIS A species of grapevines native to eastern North America.

VITIS LABRUSCA A species of grapevines native to eastern North America that display a sort of "foxy" aroma and flavor. The grapevines were first identified in the early part of seventeenth century. Also known as *fox grape* and *labrusca*. *See* Foxy, Native American Grape Varieties, and Wild Grapevines.

VITIS RIPARIA   A species of grapevines native to North America. Also known as *riparia*.

VITIS ROTUNDIFOLIA   A species of grapevines native to North America and grown predominately in the south Atlantic states, where they are generally identified as *Muscadine* grapes. Also known as *rotundifolia*.

VITIS RUPESTRIS   A species of grapevines native to North America. Also known as *rupestris*.

VITIS VINIFERA   European grapevine species considered by many to be the premium grapes in winemaking, (e.g., Chardonnay, Cabernet Sauvignon, Johannisberg Riesling, Pinot Noir).

VIURA (SP)   The local name in the Rioja region for the *Macabeo* grape variety.

VIVACE (FR)   A term applied to a wine that is fresh, lively, and vivacious.

VIVANT   A white grape variety developed at the Horticultural Research Institute, Vineland, Ontario, Canada.

VIVO (ITAL)   Lively, brilliant, harmonious; a wine that can take more aging.

VO (FR)   (Very Old) A label designation on Armagnac or cognac bottles that indicates that the youngest brandy used in the blend is at least 4 ½ years old (although they contain a very high percentage of brandy that has been aged for 12 to 20 years or more).

VODKA   An alcoholic distillate from a fermented mash of primarily grain, that is distilled at or above 190 proof, bottled with aging at not less than 80 proof, and processed further to extract all congeners with the use of activated charcoal. According to the United States federal standards of identity, the final product must be "without *distinctive* character, aroma, taste or color." However, no federal law requires vodka to be *entirely* without aroma or taste; therefore, some vodkas display distinctive characteristics in aroma *and* taste. Federal law governs the production of vodkas in the United States.

Vodka seems to have first appeared in either Russia or Poland around the twelfth century, when it was first known as *zhizenennia voda* (water of life) in the Russian monastery-fort of Viatka. The word *vodka* is a diminutive of the Russian word for water, voda (although it has been proved that the Russians took this word from the Poles). By the fourteenth century, vodka began to be used as a beverage; formerly, it was mainly used in perfumes and cosmetics. However, it was primarily employed as the base ingredient of many "wonder drugs" or "cure-all" elixirs. During the fifteenth century, Poland produced many types of vodka as well as several "grades" that varied according to the number of times the vodka was distilled and refined.

Vodka was originally made from the most plentiful and least expensive ingredients available, which in most cases was the potato. Today, grain rules as the main base ingredient for vodka throughout the world, not potatoes as is often believed. The early vodkas, even if made from grains, were strongly flavored, and therefore it became a common practice to add certain spices to mask the sometimes harsh, raw taste of the grain. It was not discovered until the early 1800s that charcoal could be used to absorb most or all of the aromas and flavors of congeners in the vodka—thus, the relatively tasteless, colorless vodka that is produced today.

VOLATILE ACIDITY (VA)   A term that refers to the "vinegar" overtones in wine from a relatively high level of volatile acidity. Volatile acidity covers most of the "spoilage" acids in wine, including acetic, butyric, formic, and propionic, formed during fermentation. These can be detected in the aroma and taste. Also known as *acetic, acetic acid, acidità volatile, flüchtige säure, piqué, pungent, sour,* and *vinegar. See* Acescence, Acetaldehyde, Acetobacter, and Vinegar.

VOLATILE FRUIT-FLAVOR CONCENTRATE   Any concentrate produced by any process that includes evaporations from any fruit mash or juice.

VOLATILE OIL   An oil that readily evaporates or vaporizes. Volatile oils give their distinctive odors and flavors to grapevines and other fruit-bearing plants.

VOLL (GERM)   *See* Körperreich and Full-Bodied.

VOLLMUNDIG (GERM)   *See* Mouthfilling.

VOLNAY (FR)   A red wine–producing village located in the Côte de Beaune, between Pommard and Meursault, that produces outstanding, light-bodied red wines that are delicate and quite fruity.

The vineyards were originally named after Volen or Velen, the Gaulish Goddess of spring. Volnay was also the favorite wine of King Louis XI of France, who reigned from 1461–1483.

VOLSTEAD ACT   *See* Prohibition.

VOLUME   The measure of a cube, expressed as "cubic"; it is the length multiplied by the width multiplied by the height.

VOLUME DISCOUNT   *See* Quantity Discount.

VONKELWYN (SO. AFRICA)   *See* Sparkling Wine.

VORNEHM (GERM)   Aristocratic and distinguished.

VÖRÖS (HUNG)   *See* Red.

VÖRÖSBOR (HUN)   *See* Red wine.

VOSGES OAK (FR)   An isolated forest located in the evergreen Vosges mountains behind Alsace. Vosges has a tight grain due to modest rainfall, with a relatively neutral oak flavor and medium tannin extraction, which remains in the background, focusing attention on the wine's fruit. Vosges is traditionally used for large wine barrels.

VOSNE-ROMANÉE (FR)   A red wine–producing village in the Côte de Nuits district of Burgundy, making exceptional wines with good bouquet, balance, and flavor.

VOUGEOT (FR)   A small, world-famous wine-producing village located in the Côte de Nuits district of Burgundy, famous for its production of fine red and white wines.

VOUVRAY (FR)   A white wine made exclusively from Chenin Blanc grapes, known locally in the district of Anjou in the Loire Valley as Pineau de la Loire or Blanc d'Anjou. The taste of Vouvray can range from bone dry to semidry and even sweet. There is also a delightful sparkling version produced in limited quantities.

VS (FR)   (Very Superior) A label designation on Armagnac or cognac bottles that indicates that the youngest brandy used in the blend is under 4 ½ years old (although they contain a blend of five to nine years old).

VSOP (FR)   (Very Superior Old Pale) A label designation on Armagnac or cognac bottles that indicates that the youngest brandy used in the blend is at least 4 ½ years old (although they contain a very high percentage of brandy that has been aged for 12 to 20 years or more).

VUOTO (ITAL)   Empty, superficial, short-flavored, lacking character in taste and bouquet.

VVSOP (FR)   (Very, Very Superior Old Pale) A label designation on Armagnac or Cognac bottles that indicates that the youngest brandy used in the blend is at least 5 ½ years old (although they contain a very high percentage of brandy that has been aged for 20, 30, or 40 years or more).

WACHAU (AUS)   A wine-producing district in the Kamp Valley, which is considered the wine paradise of Lower Austria. It is noted for its production of Rhine Rieslings and Schluck, a dry white wine made from the Sylvaner grape.

WACHENHEIM (GERM)   A wine-producing town in the Rheinpfalz, noted for its production of medium-bodied, dry white wines, made predominantly from the Sylvaner and Johannisberg Riesling grapes.

WACHSTRUM (GERM)   *See* Kreszenz.

WAFFLED   Slang for intoxicated.

WALDMEISTER (GERM)   *See* Woodruff.

WALK-IN REFRIGERATOR   *See* Cold Box.

WÄLSCHRIESLING (GERM)   *See* Welschriesling.

WARMTH   The sensation felt when consuming brandy or similar types of distillates, noticeable flavor characteristics in wines is made from grapes from hot climates. Also known as *caldo, chaud* and *quente.*

WASH   A term applied to the liquid obtained by fermenting wort with yeast. It is the wash that forms the raw material of the first distillation in the *pot still* process and of the only distillation in the *patent still* process.

WASH STILL   The still utilized for the primary distillation of alcoholic wash.

WASSAIL   The ancient name for toasting, derived from the old English *waes* and *whal*, which meant "be whole or be well." Also a large bowl of spiced ale or wine, roasted sliced apples, sugar, and spices. The exact ingredients may vary according to locality.

WASTE   That portion of the product that is not usable or edible.

WATER BUNG   *See* Fermentation Lock.

WATERING HOLE   A slang expression for a bar. *See* Bar.

WATER JACKET *See* Jacketed Tank.

WATER OF LIFE *See* Aqua Ardens and Aqua Vitae.

WATER-SEAL *See* Fermentation Lock.

WATER SPROUT A shoot that originates along the trunk or arms on a grape-vine, from wood older than previous season's wood. Water sprouts seldom bear fruit, but, the next season, shoots growing from them are fruitful.

WATER TABLE The top of a permeable body of rock of a zone saturated with water.

WATER TREATMENT The addition of various chemicals or other substances to water in order to adjust the hardness, pH, and acidity.

WATER VALVE *See* Fermentation Lock.

WATERY *See* Thin.

WAX LINED *See* Paraffin.

WAXING *See* Paraffin.

WEAK *See* Thin.

WEDGE *See* Scantling.

410

WEED CONTROL Necessary to prevent the weeds from robbing vital nutri-ents from the soil, to maximize air circulation around the grapevines, and also as a means of insect control, since weeds harbor certain insects that can carry grapevine diseases.

WEEDY *See* Stemmy.

WEEPER *See* Leakage.

WEEPING The secretion of lymph from the "incisions" made in pruning of grapevines.

WEHLEN (GERM) A famous vineyard village in the middle Mosel whose wines are characterized by a flowery bouquet, excellent balance, and a little natural sparkle.

WEICH (GERM) *See* Thin.

WEIGHT The measure of "mass": the heaviness of a substance; expressed as ounces, pounds, tons, grams, and kilos.

WEIN (GERM) *See* Wine.

WEINBAU (GERM) *See* Viticulture.

WEINBAUGEBIET (GERM) A viticultural region.

WEINBAUGEBIETE (AUS) A viticultural region.

WEINBEERE (GERM) *See* Grape.

WEINBERG (GERM) *See* Vineyard.

WEINBEREITUNG *See* Vinification.

WEINGESETZ (GERM) Wine law; with reference to the current laws adopted on July 14, 1971.

WEINGUT (GERM) Wine estate.

WEINGÜTESIEGEL OSTERREICH (AUS) The seal of quality that appears on labels of Austrian wines.

WEINIG (GERM) *See* Vinosity.

WEINKELLEREI (GERM) *See* Wine Cellar.

WEINLESE (GERM) *See* Vintage.

WEINMOND (AUS) Wine month.

WEINPROBE (GERM) Wine tasting.

WEINREB (GERM) *See* Grapevine.

WEINSBERG SCHOOL (GERM) Germany's oldest experimental facility for viticulture, founded in 1868 by King Karl of Württemberg. Among its many contributions to the industry was the development of the Kerner grape variety.

WEINTRAUBE (GERM) Bunch of grapes.

WEISSE (GERM) *See* White.

WEISSBIER (GERM) *See* Weisse Beer.

411

WEISSBURGUNDER (AUS AND GERM) *See* Pinot Blanc.

WEISSE BEER (GERM) A beer made either entirely or predominantly from wheat. It is usually unfiltered and contains some yeast residue, and therefore is cloudy in appearance. It is highly acidic, crisp, and acrid tasting, often being served with raspberry syrup or essence of woodruff. Weisse beer is ideally served at 38 degrees to 45 degrees Fahrenheit. Also known as *weissbier* and *weizenbier*. *See* Berliner Weisse, Lambic, and Wheat.

WEISSHERBST (GERM) A rosé wine of a minimum QbA quality, popular in Baden.

WEISSWEIN (GERM) *See* Blanc de Blancs.

WEIZEN (GERM) Wheat.

WEIZENBIER (GERM) *See* Weisse Beer.

WELCH (GERM) *See* Thin.

WELL-BALANCED A term used to describe wines or beers, whose many odors, flavors, tastes, and other components are cohesive and are in perfect harmony with each other. Also known as *ampleur* and *bien equilibré*.

WELL BRANDS House brands with little name recognition, that are generally lower in quality and price. They are used when customers ask for generic drinks. Also known as *bar brands, bar whiskey, house brands, house whiskey,* and *well-stock*.

WELL-STOCK *See* Well Brands.

WELSCHRIESLING A white grape variety cultivated predominantly in Austria, Germany, Hungary, Italy, Rumania, and Yugoslavia that produces a spicy wine that varies in color from pale yellow to gold. Also known as *Olaszriesling, Olasz Rizling, Riesling Italico,* and *Wälschriesling.*

WET BAR   A small drink preparation area with sewer and water lines permanently hooked up to the front bar, which is separate from other facilities.

WET COUNTY   Counties permitting the sale of alcoholic beverages "by-the-drink" (on-premise) and "by-package" (off-premise) or by package only.

Under this definition, counties could have private clubs or unlicensed outlets selling distilled spirits and still be considered legally dry for distilled spirits, or a wet county could be without a distilled spirit outlet. *See* Dry County.

WETTABLE POWDER (WP)   A chemical powder that can be added to water for spray applications on grapevines.

WHEAT   An annual cereal grain used in the production of some distilled spirits and, occasionally, beers. *See* Weisse Beer.

WHEEL   A citrus fruit sliced in the shape of a wheel and used as a garnish on some beverages.

WHISKEY   An alcoholic distillate made from a fermented mash of grain, distilled at less than 190 proof, in such a manner that the distillate possesses the taste, aroma, and characteristics generally associated with whiskey. Whiskeys are distinguished by the grain used, the proof at which the mash is distilled, and the age. The minimum proof that a whiskey can be bottled at is 80; there are no maximum proof standards.

Whiskey obtains its characteristic brown color from four sources: Coloring matter from the barrel, oxidation, charred barrels, and the addition of caramel for color adjustment. *See* American-Made Whiskey.

WHISKEY SOUR   *See* Sour.

WHISKY   This spelling identifies the distilled spirits of Scotland and Canada.

WHISTLE-BELLY VENGEANCE   A drink made from sour beer, molasses, and crusts of brown bread. It was popular in the United States during the late 1600s and early 1700s.

WHITE   A term that implies a clear, colorless, or lightly tainted color, usually straw, gold, and yellow. Used to describe certain types of alcoholic and non-alcoholic beverages. Also known as *beloe, beyaz, bianco, bijelo, bjalo, blanc, blanco, branco,* and *weisse.*

WHITE GOODS   A term often used to describe those distilled spirits that are clear in color. Examples are gin, rum, tequila, and vodka. *See* Brown Goods.

WHITE LIGHTNING   *See* Moonshine.

WHITE PORT (PORT)   Port wines, made exclusively from white grapes that tend to run from dry and slightly tangy to those of a medium sweet character.

Generally, the *must* is allowed to ferment longer (or closer to dryness) than wines destined to become red port.

WHITE RIESLING   *See* Johannisberg Riesling.

WHITE RUM   *See* Light Rum.

WHITE VERMOUTH   *See* Vermouth.

WHITE WINE   A wine made without any trace of red coloring matter, usually derived from contact with the skin of the red grape. White wines may run in color from a pale, almost watery appearance to a deep gold and even amber, yet all are considered white wines. Also known as *fehér bór, vin blanc, vinho branco, vino bianco,* and *vino blanco.*

WHITE ZINFANDEL   An extremely popular and quaffable *varietal* wine produced primarily in California, from the red Zinfandel grape variety. White Zinfandel is basically a white wine made by limited skin contact (several hours) or no-skin contact with Zinfandel grapes, extracting a hint of color. White Zinfandel is generally quite fruity smelling, with some residual sugar, which adds to the sensory impression of the wine.

WHOLE BERRY FERMENTATION   *See* Carbonic Maceration.

WHOLESALE   Engaging in the sale of beverages (alcoholic and nonalcoholic) in quantity for resale to consumers.

413

WHOLESALER   A merchant middleman who sells chiefly to retailers.

WHORTLEBERRY   A species of European blueberry occasionally used in the production of fruit-flavored liqueurs or brandies.

WICKER BASKET   *See* Wine Cradle.

WILD BEER   Draft beer that froths uncontrollably when dispensed due to excessively warm temperatures, which is a temporary condition.

WILD GRAPEVINES   *See* Native American Grape Varieties and Vitis Labrusca.

WILD MUSTARD   The green *Brassica* plants (planted in the fall) whose blossoms paint the vineyard with a golden color, are rich in nitrogen, and are usually plowed into or disced into the ground for needed nutrients in the springtime. Also known as *mustard. See* Cover Crops.

WILD YEAST   Yeasts indigenous to certain vineyards (which collect on the grape's waxy outer layer during the growing season) to make wine, rather than on pure cultured strains. *See* Yeast.

WILTINGEN (GERM)   An important vineyard village of the Saar River near Trier, famous for its production of dry white wines made from the Johannisberg Riesling.

WINE   A living alcoholic beverage produced by fermenting grape juice. This includes any alcoholic beverage made in the manner of wine, including sparkling and carbonated wine, wine made from condensed grape *must*, wine made from agricultural products other than the juice of sound, ripe grapes, imitation wine, compounds sold as wine, vermouth, cider, and perry. In each instance, it is considered wine only if containing not less than 7 percent and not more than 24 percent of alcohol by volume, and if for nonindustrial use. *See* Grape Wine. Also known as *bor, oinos, sarap, vin, vinho, vino, wein,* and *wino.*

WINE BAR   A bar that features a selection of wines and that provides customers with the opportunity of ordering wine, by-the- taste, by-the-glass, or by-the-bottle.

WINE BASKET   *See* Wine Cradle.

WINE BROKER   *See* Broker.

WINE BROTHERHOODS OR FRATERNITIES (FR)   There are membership organizations within an appellation or region composed of grape growers, shippers, or brokers, whose main concern is to maintain traditions of quality. The Bordeaux wine fraternities are:

> la Jurade de Saint-Emilion
> la Commanderie du Bontemps de Médoc et des Graves
> la Commanderie du Bontemps de Sauternes et Barsac
> la Commanderie du Bontemps de Saint-Croix-du-Mont
> la Compagnons de Bordeaux
> la Hospitaliers de Pomerol
> la Gentilshommes du Duché de Fronsac
> la Compagnons de Loupiac
> la Vignerons de Montagne-Saint-Emilion
> les Baillis de Lalande-de-Pomerol
> les Echevins de Lussac-Saint-Emilion-Puisseguin-Saint-Emilion
> la Connetablie des Prémieres Côtes de Bordeaux & des Graves
> la Connetablie des Côtes de Blaye
> la Connetablie des Côtes de Bourg
> la Connetablie de l'Entre-Deux-Mers

These 15 wine fraternities are also members of the Grand Conseil du Vin de Bordeaux.

WINE BUCKET   *See* Ice Bucket.

WINE BUTLER   *See* Sommelier.

WINE-BUY-THE-GLASS   The merchandising of special wines by the individual glass rather than only by the bottle.

WINE CAPTAIN   *See* Sommelier.

WINE CELLAR   A location (generally subterranean), where wine is stored under optimum conditions of temperature, light, humidity, and security. Also known as *adega* and *weinkellerei.*

WINE COOLERS   They are a blend of wine, fruit juices, carbonated water, and sugar, typically containing 6-percent alcohol or less. Some producers also bottle flavored wine-, spirit-, and malt-based coolers. Also known as *coolers*. *See* Flavored Wines.

WINE CRADLE   A wicker or straw basket designed to hold a bottle of mature wine (mostly red) that contains sediment, in nearly the same horizontal position it occupied in the cellar. The basket permits the removal of the bottle from storage, without disturbing its sediment, for the eventual opening and decanting. Also known as *basket, cradle, wicker basket, wine basket,* and *wire basket.*

WINE GALLON   *See* Gallon.

WINEGLASS   A stemmed glass with the capacity of eight to ten ounces, in which wine is served.

WINE GROWING   Because wine is a farm product, produced usually by the grower who cultivates the vineyard and ferments the grapes into wine on the farm, the entire production is referred to as *wine growing* and the producer is called a *wine grower*. It is preferred to *wine manufacturer,* as is the word *manufacture* in connection with wine. One of the highest recommendations for wine and one of the reasons for its purity, its dietary and health values, and the regard in which it is held by the medical profession is the fact that it is a product of nature—a beverage grown, not manufactured.

WINEMAKER   A term used to describe the person in charge of producing wine in a winery. Also known as *bodeguero. See* Enologist.

WINE MERCHANT   *See* Vintner.

WINE PREMISES   Premises on which wine operations or other operations are authorized to be conducted.

WINE RACK   A fixed rack (generally made of wood or metal), with alternating stacked compartments and individual openings for the storage and display of wine bottles, while in a horizontal position.

WINERY   The accurate description of the building in which the juice of grapes is fermented into wine. The term is not properly applied in the United States to any except bonded winery premises. It is preferred to *plant* or *wine factory,* which creates the incorrect impression of manufacturing.

WINE SPIRITS   Brandy or wine spirits authorized for use in wine products.

WINE STEWARD   *See* Sommelier.

WINE TASTER   A person with a trained palate, who specializes in the organoleptic evaluation of alcoholic beverages, especially wine.

WINE THIEF   Glass, stainless steel, or plastic tube or cylinder used to extract samples of wine, *must,* or distilled spirits from a barrel for analytical purposes. Also known as *baster, barrel thief, canuto, chantepleure, preuve, saggiavino, thief,* and *velinch.*

WINE VINEGAR   *See* Vinegar.

Wine Waiter   *See* Sommelier.

Winey   Also known as inódis. *See* Vinosity.

Winkel (germ)   A famous vineyard town located in the Rheingau that produces fine quality, dry white wines.

Wino (pol)   *See* Wine.

Wino   A slang term for a person who is addicted to cheap wine.

Winter Hardiness   The ability of a grapevine to survive the freezing cold of winter; refers to timing and dormancy, age, size, and vigor of the grapevine.

Winzerfest (germ)   Wine festival.

Winzer (germ)   A grape grower.

Winzergenossenschaft (germ)   Grape growers' cooperative association.

Winzerverein (germ)   Grape growers' cooperative.

Winzersekt (germ)   A sparkling wine created by an individual winery with its own special taste. It is produced by the traditional champagne method.

Wire Basket   *See* Wine Cradle.

Wire Hood   A wire that holds sparkling wine and champagne corks in place and that must be twisted counterclockwise to remove from the bottle. Also known as *cage* and *muselet*.

Wísniówka (pol)   A cherry-flavored vodka.

Withered   A term applied to a wine that has lost its freshness, bouquet, fruit, and flavor, due to prolonged storage in a barrel or a bottle, or after being opened too long.

Withdrawals   Tax paid withdrawals are the quantity of distilled spirits removed from government-supervised premises and on which federal excise taxes are determined. Tax-free withdrawals are withdrawals of distilled spirits free, or without payment, of the federal excise tax. Examples of such withdrawals are denatured alcohol (treated to make it unfit for consumption), shipments destined for export in bond, tax-free alcohol for use at hospitals, and so forth, and distilled spirits for use by the United States government.
    See Entering Trade Channels and Imports for Consumption.

Wode (pol)   Water.

Wódka (pol)   Vodka.

Wood   *See* Barrel.

Wood Aging   *See* Aging and Barrel Aging.

Wood Alcohol   *See* Methyl Alcohol.

Wood Port   A formerly-used term to denote port wines that were aged in wooden barrels and consumed soon after bottling.

Woody   Characteristic odor and/or flavor of certain wines aged in wooden cooperage for an extended period. Smells somewhat like wet wood.

WOODRUFF Any of a genus (*Asperula odorata*) of wild plants of the madder family, a perennial, grown in moist rich soil in the woods, that also makes an excellent ground cover. Woodruff has small, white, pink, or blue lily-shaped flowers, and is used to flavor wine. Also known as *waldmeister*. *See* May Wine.

WORM On a corkscrew, the piece that is inserted into the cork. Also known as *bore* and *screw*.

WORM The worm and its surrounding bath of cold running water, or worm-tub, form together the condenser unit of the *potstill* process of manufacture. The worm itself is a coiled copper tube of decreasing diameter attached by the lyne arm to the head of the *pot still* and kept continuously cold by running water. In it, the vapors from the still condense. Fed by the still, it in turns feeds the receiving vessel with the condensed distillate. Also known as *worm box* and *flake stand*.

The worm is being replaced gradually by the more modern tubular condenser.

WORM BOX *See* Worm.

WORMS (GERM) A vineyard town located on the Rhine River, near the southern edge of the Rheinhessen. Worms produces dry, white wines that are mostly used in the production of Liebfraumilch.

WORT Wort is the liquid drawn off the mash-tun in which the malted and unmalted cereals have been mashed with warm water. Wort contains all the sugars of the malt and certain secondary constituents. After cooling, it is passed to the fermenting vats.

In *malt* distilleries the cereals are all malted; in *grain* distilleries only a proportion is malted, the remainder being unmalted.

WP *See* Wettable Powder.

WSWA Wine and Spirits Wholesalers of America.

WUCHTIG (GERM) *See* Fat.

WÜRTTEMBERG (GERM) One of the 11 qualitätswein wine-producing regions, that is noted for its production of red wines.

WÜRZBURG (GERM) A city in Franconia, noted for its production of dry and austere white wines with a fullness of body.

WÜRZER (GERM) A white grape variety developed in the Rheinhessen, from a cross of Gewürztraminer and Müller-Thurgau.

WÜRZIG (GERM) *See* Fruity.

XAMPAN (SP)   The Catalonian term for a sparkling wine. *See* Sparkling Wine.

XAMPANERIA (SP)   A Catalan term for a "champagne bar."

XAREL-LO (SP)   A white grape variety, used primarily in the production of sparkling wines. Also known as *Pansa Blanca* and *Xarello*.

XARELLO (SP)   *See* Xarel-lo.

XÉRÈS (FR)   Sherry.

XIRÓS (GREECE)   *See* Dry.

XITHUM   Egyptian beer made from barley.

XO (FR)   (Extremely Old) A label designation on Armagnac or cognac bottles that indicates that the youngest brandy used in the blend is at least 5 1/2 years old (although they contain a very high percentage of brandy that has been aged for 20, 30, or 40 years or more).

XXX   An ancient Egyptian symbol denoting purity. Originally, distillers used the symbol "X" to indicate the number of times the product was distilled, "XXX" signifying a triple-distilled product. More than a century ago, brewmasters adopted the triple "XXX" designation for use on certain beer bottles. The "X" symbol, however, has no legal meaning.

YARD OF ALE   An elongated drinking glass, measuring approximately 36 inches in length and containing 42 ounces of ale. It was used primarily in England during the seventeenth and eighteenth centuries in roadside taverns or pubs, where keepers kept them close to the door so that small "pint-sized" waitresses could easily pass up a cold ale to stagecoach drivers who were required to stay aboard to contain the horses.

YARD OF FLANNEL   A recipe that is a reputed remedy for colds. It is made by mixing ale with eggs, brown sugar, and nutmeg. It is then served at a rather warm temperature.

YATES   A red grape variety developed in 1937, from a cross of Mills and Ontario, at the New York State Experimental Station.

YAYIN   The Biblical term related to "vinum," meaning wine.

YEAST   Microorganisms of the family *Saccharomyces cerevisiae*, in which the unicellular form is conspicuous and belongs to the fungi. The size and shape of yeast cells can vary in length and width, as well as from spheroidal to ellipsoidal to cylindrical. Yeast brings about fermentation in the making of alcoholic beverages by converting the sugar to roughly equal parts of ethyl alcohol and carbon dioxide. Also known as *fermenti, hefe, levadura,* and *levure.* *See* Calcium Alginate Beads, Encapsulated Yeasts, and Wild Yeast.

YEAST ENERGIZERS   *See* Nutrients.

YEAST NUTRIENTS   *See* Nitrogen and Nutrients.

YEAST STARTER   *See* Nutrients.

YEASTY   The fresh, unoxidized odor of freshly-made bread, often detected in newly made wines, or the odor of fermentation or its lees, which are comprised primarily of dead yeast cells. It is a positive odor often associated with some young white or sparkling wines. If detected in red or other types of wines, it is a negative sign. It can also be applied to the smell of fresh-made bread. Also known as *kahmig.*

YEÓDIS (GREECE)   *See* Earthy.

YESO (SP)   *See* Plastering.

YIELD   The amount of usable or edible parts of a product.

YIELD OF EXTRACT   The number of pounds of extract obtained from 100 pounds of brewing material, generally expressed in a percent.

YIELD PERCENTAGE   The ratio (%) of the usable (edible) amount to the amount "as purchased."

YIELD   A term that refers to the production of a given acre of vineyard land, expressed as "tons per acre" in the United States and as "hectoliters per hectare" in Europe. It also refers to the yield of "juice" extracted from each ton of grapes pressed.

YIELD PER ACRE   *See* Yield.

YIELD PER TON   *See* Yield.

YOUNG   A fresh, undeveloped wine that has not yet reached its peak and needs barrel and/or bottle aging to improve. Also known as *giovane, immature,* and *vino crudo. See* Fresh, Green, and Unripe.

YONNE (FR)   A small, inconsequential wine-producing town in the northern part of Burgundy, producing fair-quality wines.

YVORNE (SWISS)   One of the better-known white wines, produced in the Chablais district from the Chasselas grape variety, southeast of Lake Geneva.

ZANTE CURRANT *See* Black Corinth.

ZART (GERM) Tender; a light wine that can be described as delicate.

ZECHFENTHAL *See* Zinfandel.

ZELL (GERM) A vineyard town located in the lower Mosel, famous for its production of large quantities of QbA wines under the name of Zeller Schwarze Katz.

ZELTINGEN (GERM) The largest wine-producing town in the middle Mosel, producing a large quantity of dry white wine, from the Johannisberg Riesling grape.

ZENFENTHAL *See* Zinfandel.

ZEST A lively, crispy wine.

ZEST The outer layer or "peel" of a citrus fruit, which contains the coloring and essence of oils. Used in cooking and certain alcoholic drink recipes.

ZESTER A small, hand-held tool that is used to obtain zest from citrus fruit, necessary for decortive purposes, as well as garnishes for certain alcoholic drink recipes.

ZHIZENNIA VODA The twelveth century name for vodka that meant "water of life," used in Russia and Poland. Also spelled *zhiznennia*.

ZHIZNENNIA VODA *See* Zhizennia Voda.

ZIERFANDLER (AUS) A white grape variety that is usually blended with Rotgipfler to produce Gumpoldskirchner, a wine that is outstanding in quality. Aging brings out its full body and superior bouquet. Also known as *Spätrot*.

ZIN *See* Zinfandel.

ZINFANDEL A very popular red grape variety that has been planted throughout California for more than a century. Although now thought by some

Ampelographers to be the same grape as the Italian Primitivo, its European origin is still somewhat uncertain.

In California, the Zinfandel grape produces pleasant, good, and often complex and excellent dry red wines, with a distinctly spicy, berrylike flavor reminiscent of raspberries. Considerable quantities of a semidry white Zinfandel or "blush" are also produced.

Also known as *Black St. Peter, Black Zinfandel, Zinfenthal, Zechfenthal, Zenfenthal,* and *Zin. See* Primitivo di Gioia and Prince, William Robert.

ZINFANDEL CLUB An informal wine club located in London, England, founded in October 1976.

ZING An exciting, refreshing beer or wine that usually displays good acidity.

ZOLFO (ITAL) *See* Sulfur Dioxide.

ZOMBIE A cocktail consisting of light rum, dark rum, gold rum, pineapple juice, papaya juice, lime juice, falernum or simple sugar, apricot-flavored brandy, orange curacao or passion fruit syrup, and 151-proof Demeraran rum. Another Don-the-Beachcomber drink that featured perhaps every type of rum he had on hand at his bar. This drink boasted a challenge that many simply could not pass up—"only one to a customer."

ZONA (ITAL) Zone.

ZONKED Slang for intoxicated.

ZUBRÓWKA This is a flavored vodka produced in Slavic countries; it has a yellow-green tinge and a distinctive smell and taste that is derived from various botanicals that have been added. Bottles of it at one time contained a single blade of grass, but these are no longer available in the United States, because U.S. scientists believed that the grass contained *coumarin*, a toxic compound found in some plants, that was said to cause liver cancer. The vodka, minus the grass, is now available in the United States and is free from anything harmful. Also known as *Bison Vodka* or *Buffalo Vodka.*

ZUCCHERAGGIO (ITAL) *See* Chaptalization.

ZUCKERREST (GERM) *See* Residual Sugar.

ZUKUNFT (GERM) A wine that has a good aging potential.

ZUSAMMENSCHLUSS (GERM) An association, organization, or cooperative that is involved in the production or sale of wine or other alcoholic beverages.

ZUSETZEN (GERM) The addition of "legal" additives in the production of alcoholic beverages.

ZWICKEL A device, similar to a spigot on a wine barrel (test petcock), that enables the brewmaster to sample the aging beer for evaluation purposes. *See* Spigot.

ZWICKLE A bung tap used to loosen or tighten bungs on a barrel. *See* Bungstarter.

ZYMASE An enzyme, present in yeast, that promotes fermentation by breaking down glucose and some other carbohydrates into alcohol and carbon dioxide.

ZYMURGY That branch of applied chemistry that deals with the fermentation process, especially beer and wine.

ZYTHOS (GREECE) Beer.

ZYTNIA (POL) A type of vodka.